The Realm of the Extra-Human

World Anthropology

General Editor

SOL TAX

Patrons

CLAUDE LÉVI-STRAUSS

MARGARET MEAD

LAILA SHUKRY EL HAMAMSY

M. N. SRINIVAS

MOUTON PUBLISHERS · THE HAGUE · PARIS

DISTRIBUTED IN THE USA AND CANADA BY ALDINE, CHICAGO

The Realm of the Extra-Human

Ideas and Actions

Editor

AGEHANANDA BHARATI

MOUTON PUBLISHERS · THE HAGUE · PARIS
DISTRIBUTED IN THE USA AND CANADA BY ALDINE, CHICAGO

General Editor's Preface

Religion, ritual, sacred belief — the subject matter of this and its companion volume, *The realm of the extra-human: agents and audiences* — are controversial in every sense. Where these elements or the concepts behind them lie in the human psyche; when, how, and why they came into the human experience; how we discover, describe, study, interpret them; what theorizing is valid; whether these are good questions: all these problems (and others) are dealt with differently by different scholars. Not only are the scholars influenced by differing private beliefs and scholarly traditions, but also by the differing cultures in which they are reared. The editor, who has his own views, describes the spectrum in his entertaining introduction to the two rich volumes by scholars with and without religion and from many of the changing world's cultural traditions, which show off contemporary work in all its variety.

Like most contemporary sciences, anthropology is a product of the European tradition. Some argue that it is a product of colonialism, with one small and self-interested part of the species dominating the study of the whole. If we are to understand the species, our science needs substantial input from scholars who represent a variety of the world's cultures. It was a deliberate purpose of the IXth International Congress of Anthropological and Ethnological Sciences to provide impetus in this direction. The *World Anthropology* volumes, therefore, offer a first glimpse of a human science in which members from all societies have played an active role. Each of the books is designed to be self-contained; each is an attempt to update its particular sector of scientific knowledge and is written by specialists from all parts of the world.

Each volume should be read and reviewed individually as a separate volume on its own given subject. The set as a whole will indicate what changes are in store for anthropology as scholars from the developing countries join in studying the species of which we are all a part.

The IXth Congress was planned from the beginning not only to include as many of the scholars from every part of the world as possible, but also with a view toward the eventual publication of the papers in high-quality volumes. At previous Congresses scholars were invited to bring papers which were then read out loud. They were necessarily limited in length; many were only summarized; there was little time for discussion; and the sparse discussion could only be in one language. The IXth Congress was an experiment aimed at changing this. Papers were written with the intention of exchanging them before the Congress, particularly in extensive pre-Congress sessions; they were not intended to be read aloud at the Congress, that time being devoted to discussions — discussions which were simultaneously and professionally translated into five languages. The method for eliciting the papers was structured to make as representative a sample as was allowable when scholarly creativity — hence self-selection — was critically important. Scholars were asked both to propose papers of their own and to suggest topics for sessions of the Congress which they might edit into volumes. All were then informed of the suggestions and encouraged to re-think their own papers and the topics. The process, therefore, was a continuous one of feedback and exchange and it has continued to be so even after the Congress. The some two thousand papers comprising *World Anthropology* certainly then offer a substantial sample of world anthropology. It has been said that anthropology is at a turning point; if this is so, these volumes will be the historical direction-markers.

As might have been foreseen in the first post-colonial generation, the large majority of the Congress papers (82 percent) are the work of scholars identified with the industrialized world which fathered our traditional discipline and the institution of the Congress itself: Eastern Europe (15 percent); Western Europe (16 percent); North America (47 percent); Japan, South Africa, Australia, and New Zealand (4 percent). Only 18 percent of the papers are from developing areas: Africa (4 percent); Asia-Oceania (9 percent); Latin America (5 percent). Aside from the substantial representation from the U.S.S.R. and the nations of Eastern Europe, a significant difference between this corpus of written material and that of other Congresses is the addition of the large proportion of contributions from Africa, Asia, and Latin America. "Only 18 percent" is two to four times as great a proportion as that of other Congresses;

moreover, 18 percent of 2,000 papers is 360 papers, 10 times the number of "Third World" papers presented at previous Congresses. In fact, these 360 papers are more than the total of ALL papers published after the last International Congress of Anthropological and Ethnological Sciences which was held in the United States (Philadelphia, 1956).

The significance of the increase is not simply quantitative. The input of scholars from areas which have until recently been no more than subject matter for anthropology represents both feedback and also long-awaited theoretical contributions from the perspectives of very different cultural, social, and historical traditions. Many who attended the IXth Congress were convinced that anthropology would not be the same in the future. The fact that the next Congress (India, 1978) will be our first in the "Third World" may be symbolic of the change. Meanwhile, sober consideration of the present set of books will show how much, and just where and how, our discipline is being revolutionized.

The present volume joins others in the *World Anthropology* series which deal with related cultural and psychological phenomena and well-being, and with related phenomena as they appear in various parts of the world through time.

Chicago, Illinois   SOL TAX
March 15, 1976

Table of Contents

SECTION THREE

SECTION FOUR

Introduction

AGEHANANDA BHARATI

Many years ago, Alfred Kroebér (1952: 115) mused that Lewis Henry Morgan had "left room for David Bidney to have God and prayer in his interpretation of culture." Kroeber is dead, David Bidney is alive, and God, though dead to some theologians, may well be alive to some anthropologists apart from Bidney. But He may be too alive for anthropologists who would like to take some divine command for their methodology, coated as the case may be in a kind of guiding or goading inspiration, implying the need for some privileged information inaccessible to the more worldly anthropologists. In the subsession generated by the main body of the IXth ICAES Congress section on cults, rituals, and shamanism, historians among the anthropologists who study religion got together; they captioned the subsession "History, Ecology, and Evolution in the Anthropological Study of Religion." The ecology part, though, seemed to relate to the order of the day rather than to the content of the subsession. The other two terms, on the other hand, permeated the subevent with passion if not always with decorum.

Long before the Congress I had read a piece by A. Gallus of the Australian Institute of Aboriginal Studies, "A biofunctional theory of religion" (1972: 343 ff.). Spiked with perfectly respectable-looking diagrams, the main thrust of this opusculum was that the mythic and religious way of thinking is a mode of understanding the universe. Taken as any emic statement in any specific culture, this is, of course, quite true and very old hat. But Gallus projected much more than this: to him, the anthropologist studying religion must also use mythical, religious, magical, etc., tools and attitudes. In one of the comments, Stephen P. Dunn of Berkeley remarked: "Gallus's essay seems to me marked by a fundamental, consistent, and pervasive wrong-headedness, and this indicates that he and I [i.e. Dunn] inhabit a radically different intellectual universe" (1973: 559). Let me add that most of today's anthropologists, myself included, coinhabit Dunn's universe and very few inhabit Gallus's. But those few remaining denizens were present, in body or in spirit, at the subsession "History, Ecology, and Evolution." Few of them had submitted a paper to this section, which makes it a bit easier to be acerbic about them, because standards of basic politeness should prevail between editors and their symposiasts.

The whole subsession centered upon the paper by Alois Closs, a veteran Austrian scholar, who could not come due to ill health. His lineal and lateral disciples, however, were there, and it is they who had promoted the meeting: Paul W. Leser (Hartford Seminary Foundation, Jack A. Lukas (Central Connecticut State College), and A. Gallus from Australia, the presence of the latter fulfilling a secret wish of mine: his *Current Anthropology* article had so infuriated me that I initiated a spell, as it were, to bring him here for a good clash of minds. But there was no clash because, in his presentation, Gallus created a wall of soft, nostalgic impenetrability that changed my polemic verve into the kind of instant melancholy which immobilizes academic discussants. Just as one cannot argue shamanism with a shaman, or evangelism with Graham, except to agree murmuring "aye aye," one cannot argue the anthropology of religion with a religious anthropologist (i.e. with a scholar who thinks religiously as he talks anthropology).

As chairman of the whole section, I stated my premises at the beginning of the submeeting. Briefly, I said that the origin of religion cannot be studied, not because some theories may be false, but because all theories may be correct, a facetious way of putting the radical Popperian position, i.e. that a statement to be scientific (as opposed to poetical, metaphysical, etc.) has to be FALSIFIABLE IN THEORY. Because no theories of the origin of religion, or shamanism, or any of the many fundamental themes of religious behavior are falsifiable in theory, they are not scientific, whatever else they may be, although some of them are certainly interesting and erudite (Max Mueller, Paul Deussen, Rudolf Otto, Mircea Eliade, C. G. Jung, and others). This, of course, does not mean to say that the origin of any specific, localized theme of religious behavior cannot be studied — it can and should, if valid evidence, falsifiable in theory and in practice, can be adduced (archaeological, linguistic, and other empirical evidence supplying the data for verification-falsification).

Gallus's melodious response contained precisely the assumptions anthropologists inhabiting Dunn's and own my intellectual universe exclude. He made these methodological recommendations and criticisms: one must not try to understand religion through logical thinking, because logical categories are alien to religious thought. One cannot understand the functioning of religion unless one knows its origin. Just as one must understand the wheel and the steam engine to understand the jet engine, one must first understand the primitive origin of religion to understand its later development. (My interjection at this point, that one does not have to understand ancient Rome to understand Sophia Loren and Carlo Ponti went unheeded.) Religion is existentialistic, it is an experience; he (Gallus) cannot understand all this antihistoricism [sic] of some anthropologists. The main task of the anthropologist studying religion is to study its origin.

Neither Gallus nor Lukas mentioned *Kulturkreis*, but this ancestry was abundantly evident. Leser, however, did mention Graebner and he gave me the impression of being a *Kulturkreis* advocate rather than a descendant, and if this is true, he is probably the only active and teaching *Kulturkreis* anthropologist in America (though he was born in Germany). He regretted that Hultkrantz from Sweden was absent, since Hultkranz was, in Leser's opinion, perhaps the most knowledgeable anthropologist specializing in shamanism. In Hultkrantz's own paper in this section, however, shamanism does not figure importantly; in it, Hultkrantz tries to establish a kind of ecological determinism, claiming that rituals and belief patterns reflect the ecological conditions of Great Basin Indians' practices. Leser, in defending the quest for origins and the speculative-historical approach to this quest, explained that Spencer and even Darwin had already said many things anthropologists claimed as their own discoveries in later days: the rejection of the polygenist doctrine on account of cross-cultural similarities in "numerous, small, unimportant points." It did not become quite clear whether or not Leser wanted to have the audience infer an analogous situation in the area of religious behavior, i.e. a monogenous rather than a multilineal or multiconvergent cluster of origins. Father Schmidt, so Leser quoted, had said that "he was not opposed to evolution, but only to evolutionism." Less pompously and archaically put, this means that evolution is a fact; theories of evolution are not facts, because theories are not meant to be facts — a not very exciting point that I give to freshman classes. Finally, Leser said that *Kulturkreis* was a method, not a theory, a method for historical reconstruction, that is.

As we pointed out a bit earlier, all these oral contributions were in support of Closs' paper, or to be more precise, they were meant to rouse anthropological conscience to shame for having ignored, or for not having paid sufficient attention to Closs. Gallus complained bitterly that British and American anthropologists do not read anything published in German, and he suggested bad faith on the part of English-speaking anthropologists for that shortcoming. Yet, as I read and reread Closs' paper, unable to consult the author who did not come to the Congress, a certain armchair complacency seems to me to underlie the erudition displayed by Closs. He doubts or rejects the dogmatisms of his teachers and colleagues — of primitive monotheism, of the evolutionary schemes suggested by the earliest writers, and of the early comparativists — and he seems to suggest an eclectic approach as an alternative to any single-thrust study of religious types. The fact is, I would rejoin, that latter-day anthropologists in this area of specialization have long been doing this; all reductionism, psychological or any other sort, has been shelved, at least in North American and most British studies. The new ethnography, componential analysis, and other rigorous techniques which resulted from the nonreductivist eclecticism of the anthropological study of religion during the sixties are not mentioned by Closs, nor were they as much as admitted into discussion by his votaries in this subsession.

It was clear at the time when papers and abstracts kept coming into the editorial offices of the Congress, that the Soviet-bloc scholars would present a strongly historical bent, and discussions during the session bore this out. However, the pleasantly hardnosed historicism of our Soviet and Hungarian colleagues (especially Bassilov, Guryevitch and Dömötör) lacked the sort of Rousseauian nostalgic overtone characteristic of the work and the recommendations of Central European historical reconstructionists.

One got the paradoxical feeling that scholars from the socialist countries, by and large, were much less dogmatic about historicist theories than many of their continental European colleagues. A certain rugged, serious, earthbound, unromantic empiricism seemed to inform much of what Russian and Eastern European scientists presented, and represented at the meeting. They reflected a much less formalistic, and a more substantivist approach to such paradigmatic themes as shamanism, spirit belief, and spirit manipulation. Quite independently, of course, this attitude is shared by Western anthropologists who work with shamanistic systems in different parts of the world. William Stablein pointed out that John Hitchcock, a discussant who had brought with him some excellent recent material gathered in Nepal, defined "shamanism" much more widely than traditional anthropologists tended to: a shaman, so Hitchcock said, does not have to enter on a spirit flight, nor does he have to climb down a spirit ladder, nor does he have to do or even know about any of the feats commonly listed among the shaman's deeds. This was echoed by a Latin American colleague (he also has no paper in this volume) who expressed amazement at what he thinks is still the majority view (i.e. that shamanism and spiritism should be sought in distant lands) when these phenomena are amply present among Puerto Rican and Brazilian immigrants in New York and California and among their steadily increasing Anglo-American clientele; he refers to this syndrome as "urban shamanism." Here too, just as in Hitchcock's antidefinitional charting of the shaman's offices, we have a healthy eclecticism which is bound to bear fruit unless it bogs down in subsequent exclusive definitions.

Nishimura, a discussant from Tokyo, suggested that the essence of religion is revelation and that both an ontological and an epistemological venture are needed to trace religious behavior to some revelational scheme. Although Nishimura did not use any of the terminology of the "new ethnography," it stands to reason that his division between the ontological and the epistemological might parallel or, with some amount of disciplinary cross-fertilization, be equated with the emic and the etic schemes — the ontological approximating the latter, the epistemological the former. Nishimura's stress on the clear distinction between the two seemed a pointer in this direction. In a private discussion with him, we learned that the "new ethnography" was either not known or not used by Japanese anthropologists; he also agreed that his terminology (ontological, epistemological, eternal, perennial: terms he used frequently in his presentation to the subsession) tends to obfuscate possible methodological convergence to a "new ethnography." At this time, his terminology was hypertrophic in the direction of philosophical, or rather, of philosophically archaic presuppositions.

Lee from Korea, whose paper is included in this volume, made a very revealing remark during his more general discussion at the subsession: research in shamanism and funerary ritual is looked at askance by the Korean government, because these things are marked as "superstitions." Hence support for this sort of seminal research is not forthcoming for the Korean scholar. We have here a cross-cultural problem, freshly emerged: all Third World governments regard, actively or covertly, shamanism, curing by extra-human agencies or references, and in fact everything the anthropologist studies under "religious behavior," as SUPERSTITION; and neither funds nor visas should be granted for the study of superstitions. This knowledge, pinpointed in a footnote, as it were, by Lee, should give rise to a controlled study of governmental decisions toward anthropological research projects. Indianists and Africanists in the profession will underwrite the need for such research.

Hassan es-Shamy from the United Arab Republic did not submit a paper to this section, but his energetic and sometimes brilliant suggestions were felt as a fine leaven to the meetings. Proceeding from the axiom of the psychic unity of mankind, he rejects the official Islamic notion that folk religion not encompassed in the Quran and the *haditha* is of another order than official Islam. The extra-human personalities, forces, and agencies perceived by the Muslim peasant or nomad in the Near East are of one piece, as it were, with Allah, the solely postulated divinity of Islam. Es-Shamy suggests that folk religion must answer all questions of the cognitive and the affective realms and that the actual Muslim (not the doctor of the *ulama*) cathects figures from a much wider, older, probably all-Semitic pantheon containing Egyptian and other pre-"Book" divinities. The kind of knowledge that sought for survival at different times in the history of these peoples warrants a selective approach, and a choice, from the multiplicity of available extra-human choices, by these audiences. Because traditional religion does not, or does not always, have answers to these queries, and because no sources other than the wider folk traditions are available, it is from the total of these wider traditions that answers are sought and agents manipulated. Es-Shamy stresses the importance of the actor's perception of congruence and of cognitive incongruence; if he does not experience incongruence, there is none, anthropologically speaking. More grist to the emic-etic mills (not mentioned by es-Shamy).

Gurvitch, from the Soviet Academy of Sciences, made an eloquent plea for the establishment of a caucus on shamanistic studies; he designated them as urgent anthropology, and he drew attention to conventions held and to be held as clearing-house warmings, as it were, for information on shamans and other practitioners so far bracketed as "shamans" by field anthropologists and theoreticians. There was a sigh of exhilaration among the Western-world anthropologists in the hall, for this proclamation by one of our leading Soviet colleagues in the field might well bode a genuine, and a genuinely feasible period of cooperation unheard of so far. Gurvitch's suggestion was echoed and repeated independently during another meeting by Hungarian colleagues. I have taken due note; correspondence and other means of planning will be activated with these ends in mind, once *World Anthropology* and the Herculean labor that is going into its production come to a conclusion.

Fotis Litsas from Greece spoke during the subsession on "History, Ecology, and Evolution"; Gurvitch addressed the full main session; es-Shamy spoke on both occasions. The papers to be perused in the remaining sections of this preface to the second volume of the *Realm of the extra-human* were available to the scholars assembled during the main session; some of them were discussed by their authors during the brief three hours at the disposal of that session, the others will be seen in print only now, in this present volume. As in the case of the other volume, the choice of papers mentioned here (and that of papers not mentioned), rests squarely on my thematic predilections, not on the quality of the papers. All of them are important contributions, though one may not like all that is important in one's own field. The days of the encyclopedists are gone with the days of Renaissance men. There simply is too much knowledge for encyclopedists and for Renaissance men, and short of the somewhat stupid and certainly stale popular wisdom dictum that modern science knows more and more about less and less (and more power to this, if it is true), no one can even hope to know and no one can hope to LIKE all that is done in her or his field. It needs no apology.

Mathur, a discussant from the University of Lucknow, India, talked about rites of the right and the left, advising colleagues not familiar with the South Asian situation that there is no correlation whatever to the occidental political connotations for these terms — a matter which I elaborated in *The Tantric tradition* (1969). Also, Mathur, like many Indian colleagues, OVERESTIMATES the importance of and, hence, the scholarly familiarity with Indian religious terminology. It may well be the case that antiintellectual, anthropologically literate, Eastern wisdom seekers in the urban West know more about these terminologies today than do solid anthropologists not interested in the field of South Asian religions. I think this suggestion could be tested right away: ask a paying member of "Transcendental Meditation" in Amsterdam, Holland or in Halifax, Nova Scotia, the meanings of terms like *kundalinī*, *vāmācāra*, *śakti*, etc., and he will astound you with his exegetical skills; then ask a senior anthropologist interested in any other region of the world, or even interested in Indian villages like most American anthropologists working in the South Asian area, and they will be mute and defensive. They shouldn't be, simply because, short of this terminology being cultist, it is not relevant to any anthropologist except those few who study Hindu and Buddhist esotericism; while this is a legitimate pursuit, from the anthropologist's vantage point, there could not have been more than half a dozen people in the large hall at the time who could possibly have known these Sanskrit terms. Onetime outlandish, esoteric vocabulary did find its way into the anthropological workshop many decades ago, but it did so precisely because it had some paradigmatic cross-cultural relevance (*kula*-ring, potlatch, totem, to mention but a few of the oldest war-horses). *Vāmamārga, dakṣiṇamārga,* and *śakti* are idiosyncratic terms, connoting such a highly unique syndrome that they cannot be incorporated in a general anthropological dictionary. Other than that, Mathur did communicate some very interesting theories he derived from his study of esoteric forms of practice: when a person of low caste, i.e. of low social status, renounces mundane attachments in the line of religious endeavor specified in all Indian traditions, he becomes a puritan, a vegetarian, a *bhagat*, a ritualist, a shaman; but when a high-caste person renounces his worldly status through entry into esoteric ritual, he tends to become a sensualist or even a lecher (the semantic demarcation is hard to draw with Indian speakers), albeit supported by readings and interpretations permissible within the esoteric tradition. This MAY be the sociological etiology of much Indian esotericism; the other alternatives, of course, would be to read them in terms of Gluckman's rites of rebellion or discussant Norbeck's rites of reversal. Perhaps, and this did not strike us at the time of Norbeck's own presentation from the panel, his suggestions about the role of play in religious behavior might provide a heuristic instrument for tracing esoteric behavior in Hinduism and northern Buddhism.

Mir Erenow, from Tel Aviv, who had not submitted a paper to this section, presented a very interesting statement about the secular ritual of the Israeli labor party. He tied his research typologically to the Gluckmanian type of rebellion ritual, where leaders can be criticized under specific, ritualized conditions when no such criticism is otherwise feasible.

Deshen, from the University of Tel Aviv, has done signal fieldwork on Moroccan immigrants in Israel and on religious and symbol change in this community. His work has great potential for cross-cultural analysis. So far, migration caused by political contingency has not been incorporated into any large-scale cross-cultural apparatus like the

Human Relations Area File or the *Ethnographic atlas*. These immigrants do not distinguish secular from religious leadership, because democratic notions are a superimposition of an alien terminology on a native corpus. We have here a pattern in which the study of religion provides a feeder to applied anthropology in new states. Religious leaders retain their status at first, and political leaders use religious symbols for secular parties. The subjects do not conceive clearly of a political party, hence they "change the signs to symbols." Political change, on the other hand, provides leverage to the anthropological study of religion and neopolitical structure. "In the process of social change," Deshen avers, "political parties and their leaders must represent themselves in religious terms."

Lanternari, veteran anthropologist from Rome, spoke about the charismatic significance of dreams experienced by the founders and by their followers in a new millennial type movement in Ghana. He linked innovative behavior to stereotyped dream experiences. He inferred that social mobility within the wide framework of Pentecostal movements may show some linkage to such stereotyped dreams.

My fellow chairman of the meeting, Samarendra Saraf of Saugar University, India, made some incisive remarks about ritualistic idiom in Hinduism from the panel; because his paper is included in this volume, and because he is also writing the epilogues to this and its companion volume, mention of his contribution at this point would be redundant.

Patai, doyen of the mother cult in the Judaic tradition, agreed with es-Shamy, of the United Arab Republic, that there should be thorough research into the diffusional elements of ancient all-Semitic mother cults in the practice and behavior of southern and eastern Mediterranean peoples today — Muslims, Jews, and Christians. We are reminded (though this was not brought up during the discussion) of discussant I. A. B. van Buitenen's terminological suggestion of polarized terms, e.g. ORTHODOXY and ORTHOPRAXIS; this dual terminology might help us to bridge conceptually, as anthropologists, what has been suggested by van Buitenen, who is a Sanskritist. Robert Fornaro, a discussant whose paper appears in the companion volume, used this binary terminology in his studies. With the strong, felicitous symbiosis between anthropologists and Asian area philologists at the University of Chicago such interdisciplinary fertilization comes naturally.

The question of access loomed large in the minds of all American and many European anthropologists assembled in Chicago: there was a poignant awareness, supported by the increasing number of visa refusals, of the entire tradition of fieldwork being in jeopardy, we hope temporarily, yet with ominous overtones. Quite clearly, the unconsciously condescending ways of earlier anthropologists who went out to study "primitives" had to be abandoned when Third World countries became independent: no visa officer or consul would or should give a visa to a person who wants to study his primitives, because the implication is that he himself is a primitive, or that his people are lesser people. This impasse has long gone — but during the interstice between the last international Congress and this present one, anthropologists belonging to Third World countries have, rightfully, begun to resist the irrefragably wealthier and better-funded American or Western European anthropologist, who can hire informants, assistants, and other personnel which the native anthropologist cannot. Also, there is a feeling of intellectual colonialization. Asian and African anthropologists complained that some of their colleagues write books and papers, not to teach their countrymen, but to impress their erstwhile European and American mentors in the hope of being invited back to the West. At a conference specially convened to air these grievances, Asian sociologists and anthropologists met in Simla in the Himalayan foothills to declare the need for an Asian sociology and an Asian anthropology. During many discussions of various degrees of informality, this topic was brought up again and again and discussed with acumen and emotion: is there such a thing as an Asian versus a Western anthropology? If there is, what would it have as its themes, different from those studied in Western anthropology and sociology? Or does Asian and African anthropology in this academically politicized sense simply mean a moratorium against the hitherto unchecked ingress of foreign scholars and an emphasis on native scholars and their support?

While these subjects were probably aired in many Congress sections and their subsequent subsections, they were particularly prominent in the section on ritual, cults, and shamanism. This was to be expected, for it is in these delicate, self-conscious researches that people, scholars and layman alike, feel touched to the core, more perhaps than in any other subfield of the discipline. Câmara from Mexico insisted that the regional academicians should be able to decide what topics guest anthropologists should not study. Colleagues from other countries seemed to share this view, though few pronounced it so candidly. Certainly, none of the assembled scholars would have claimed that only a Christian anthropologist could and should study Christian ritual and belief systems, or that only a Hindu anthropologist should and could study Hindu forms. But when the question was of a national order, a shift in attitude was quite evident: the scholar who is native to the region and whose ritual and belief complex is to be investigated should have primary access to his subjects, and his research should be given primary consideration in the international academic setting; so far, the papal edicts, so to speak, of Western savants pronouncing about non-Western cults have been quoted, commented upon, and dissertationed about, both by Western AND by scholars native to the cults in question. I must agree, of course, with the statement made by a young Buddhist anthropologist from a Southeast Asian country, who does not want to be quoted by name, that there is something grotesque and a considerable amount of *hubris* in a Buddhist-born anthropologist's quoting Melford E. Spiro on Buddhism when talking about village Buddhism to fellow Buddhists. Yet, from a logistic viewpoint, this is, as yet, unavoidable for reasons implied in these discussions: wealth and research support, previous access, and greater international academic power being some of these reasons. There are others.

For the remainder of this preface, let me briefly survey a selection of those papers whose authors did not or could not present their views at the Congress for reasons of schedule, space, and other organizational logistics.

Boglár from Hungary shows by the example of Piaroa Indians in Venezuela that their full human and aesthetic potential cannot come to fruition except in the ritualistic context and the process of ritual-centered creativity.

Bourguignon fills a long-felt lacuna in the Human Relations Area File complex and in the *Ethnographic atlas* in her cross-cultural analysis of spirit possession; she suggests a contrastive typology between those societies which generate or perpetuate institutionalized trance as the trigger to spirit possession and those who don't.

Canfield investigates the perceived corpus of suffering and its religious amelioration in the Islamic tradition of rural Afghanistan. He goes well beyond older psychological speculations of religious practice and adherence as means to relieve stress.

In a fine, abstract, theoretically fertile paper, Grace Harris distinguishes "displaying" and "marking" sets in symbolic systems. Inward-and outward-looking symbols are two crucial varieties of the "marking" set, and they are instantiated, as well as categorically emended, by the Star of David and by the sacred candelabra as items in the symbolic inventory of Israeli nationalism.

A fine ethnological report, including ethnomedical data, was contributed by Ionescu-Milcu about the Iron Gates region on the lower Danube; it is pleasant to find in this paper how well colleagues from the socialist countries master field-methodological material created in the Western hemisphere, together with culture-historical models of European vintage.

An instructive survey of problems of American religion, ethos, and culture is presented in a critical synopsis by Jennings, and though the scientist seems to remain the cynosure of American contemporary folklore, Jennings shows that science is not likely to provide any ultimate utopia.

Kadetotad from India investigates a religious sect in a southern Indian village, presenting a clear matrix of extra-humans reflecting the social structure of the region; unlike some of his colleagues, he does not presuppose non-Indian anthropologists' familiarity with Hindu technical terms, he uses *mantra*, *yantra*, etc., as regional sememes rather than as terms of pananthropological importance.

To my mind and taste, Alice Kehoe contributed the most elegant formal analysis of ritual systems in general. There are psychologistic and Durkheimian elements in her presentation, but these serve as propellants to her argument rather than as points for analytic reduction.

Laura Makarius uses orthodox psychological matrices for her study of conscious violation of taboos, but because the whole taboo complex is genetically linked with psychology, in the phylogenesis of anthropology, it is hard to see with what other tools it could be probed — and this is a case where the "new ethnography" might be less than helpful. In very few societies does violation of a taboo elicit a critique of the taboos violated in that society; rather, the "deliberate" violation Makarius speaks about could be seen as part of a total system in which violation is as endogenous to the scheme as the taboo itself.

Jacques Maquet gives us a fine, rigorous, yet humanistic, analysis of the world/nonworld dichotomy as relevant not only to the anthropologist interested in religious behavior, but to a much wider range of disciplines.

Becher's Yanomamö study stands squarely in the "interesting-story" category, which I regard a private, unencroachable domain. However, its cross-cultural potential is immediately obvious: genital mutilation of an initiatory and a more general visualistic order does concern all anthropologists working with religious behavior.

Olga Penavin's piece is probably the most unambiguous example of what I called the "interesting-story tellers"; her research is honest, precise, and fascinating to her and to those few anthropologists today who have retained some of the enthusiasm of the mythological reductionists of the last century.

In Stablein we find that there is enormous excitement and potential for the orientalist-philologist turning anthropologist: his analysis of ritualistic and therapeutic facets of Nepalese sacerdotism is informed by his concurrent interest in primary textual materials in Tibetan and Sanskrit.

Harvard's Evon Z. Vogt sees rituals of reversal as "rewiring" broken circuits within the social system of the much, but never exhaustively, researched Zinacantecos. There should be great potential in comparing H. Fabrege's just-published (1973) findings, on the ethnomedical and ethnopsychiatric spheres of these people, with Vogt's analyses — the obvious advantage of an intensively studied society being precisely his sort of high-power interdisciplinary fertilization.

REFERENCES

BHARATI, AGEHANANDA
  1969   *The Tantric tradition.* London: Rider.
DUNN, STEPHEN
  1973   Article in *Current Anthropology* 13(5):559.
FABREGE, H.
  1973   *Illness and shamanistic curing in Zinacantan.* Stanford: Stanford University Press.
GALLUS, A.
  1972   A biofunctional theory of religion. *Current Anthropology* (December):343 ff.
KROEBER, ALFRED
  1952   *The nature of culture.* Chicago: University of Chicago Press.

SECTION ONE

Spirit Possession Belief and Social Structure

ERIKA BOURGUIGNON

The American anthropologist David French noted not long ago in a discussion of psychological anthropology that, although anthropologists have accumulated a great deal of information, they "do not know what they know, they do not know the questions for which they have accumulated the answers" (French 1963:417). Here we attempt to assess what we know with respect to a limited area of anthropological data and to formulate some of the questions to which we appear to have found answers. To phrase it somewhat differently, it is our aim to bring together some widely scattered bits of information and to try to make some sense of them.

The area of investigation is a well-known, widespread type of sacred belief, known as belief in possession by spirits. The method is that of cross-cultural statistical research. A sample of 488 societies drawn from the *Ethnographic atlas* (Murdock 1967) is considered, and data on spirit possession belief culled from the literature on these societies is related to data coded in the *Ethnographic atlas*. I am aware that the cross-cultural statistical method is not universally accepted by anthropologists, and I share many of the reservations that have been offered. For example, I am aware of the unevenness of the ethnographic sources which we used, the varying amounts of detail provided by them on the subject matter that interests us, the possible errors of coders, etc. I am aware that a whole series of rather basic problems have been discussed but, in the

The data on which this report is based were assembled as part of a larger study supported by a grant from the U.S. Public Health Service, MH–07463. The calculations for the present paper were carried out by Mr. August Brunsman III to whom I am indebted for his assistance.

nature of the case, have not found fully satisfactory solutions. I have in mind such problems as the definition of the universe with which we deal, the units of which this universe is composed, the issue of sampling, to mention only three (for detailed discussion of these and related matters see Bourguignon and Greenbaum 1973). On the other hand, some working procedures have been widely accepted in this field and, without claiming to brush the problems aside, it seems to me a worthwhile experimental enterprise to seek to put some order into our data in a systematic way such as is required by statistical analysis. A number of things have generally become clear as statistical studies have grown in volume in recent years. For example, we have discovered on what groups and on what types of subject matter we have ample information and where the information is thinnest. The need for systematic and uniform methods of reporting data has been made abundantly clear to anyone attempting any comparisons and applications of standard methods of coding to any sample of the ethnographic literature, however drawn. Nonetheless, Naroll (1970) has been able to show that we have in fact learned a good deal so far from cross-cultural studies. It is in this spirit of wary optimism that I wish to proceed with our discussion of spirit possession beliefs.[1]

As any reader of ethnographies knows, such beliefs are very widespread indeed. They do not appear terribly "exotic" to the Western anthropologist because they are part of his own cultural heritage, both that deriving from Biblical sources and that coming down to us from classical antiquity. The Hebrews and the Greeks both believed in forms of spirit possession, and the traces of their beliefs (and practices) are still very much with us. On the current cultural scene, spirit possession is a favorite subject of novels, films, plays, television drama, etc. And some of these are based on historical events, to mention only the most famous and most widely utilized account, that of the "diabolical possessions" of Loudun.

Tylor spoke of "the savage theory of daemonical possession and obsession, which has been for ages, and still remains, the dominant theory of disease and inspiration among the lower races" (1958: II, 210). He saw it as an obvious derivative of the theory of animism and as rational in its "proper place in man's intellectual history." He cites a scattering of examples ranging from Tasmania to West Africa and then, in accordance with his evolutionary scheme, moves on to examples from "barbaric and civilized nations," where these beliefs are, however, gradually replaced

---

[1]   Our sampling method has been discussed in some detail elsewhere (Bourguignon 1968, Bourguignon, ed. 1973). Our sample is representative of the universe of the *Ethnographic atlas*, although it is not a random sample.

by expanding medical knowledge. The impression we are left with is one of virtual universality of such beliefs. Oesterreich (1922), in his monumental volume on possession, cites hundreds of examples and introduces an ordering principle, which distinguishes between "voluntary" and "involuntary" possession. Beyond that, all of us can cite examples from the ethnographic literature. Yet so far we have only shown that we "know" about the widespread existence of possession beliefs, but just what is it that we know? What can we summarize, beyond citing examples? What conclusions can we draw?

In our study we drew a sample of 488 societies, representing all of the six major ethnographic regions into which the *Ethnographic atlas* divides the world.[2] In doing so, we found that beliefs in spirit possession were present in 74 percent of our sample of societies, that is, in 360 of our 488 societies. This is, indeed, a striking finding. However, even more striking and important is the observation that such beliefs do not appear with equal frequency in all parts of the world. They have their highest incidence, 88 percent, in the Insular Pacific and the lowest, 52 percent, in aboriginal North America. The second lowest figure, 64 percent, refers to South America, whereas the rest of the world ranges from the 77 percent for the Circum-Mediterranean region to the previously mentioned 88 percent for the Insular Pacific. The Americas are distinctly different, then, from the Old World.

We have found it useful to distinguish between beliefs in possession by spirits which find their expression in altered states of consciousness and those which do not. We have termed the former "possession trance" and the latter "possession." Possession beliefs of the second type find their expression in alterations of well-being or capacity. The criterion, then, which distinguishes between the two forms of belief is the presence of an altered state of consciousness in possession trance and its absence in possession. Both are explanatory systems, and as such they not only explain behavior or experience but also serve to structure it and to integrate it into the behavioral environment in which a given cultural group lives. As explanatory elements they are part of the cognitive system by which a society lives; as molders of behavior and experience they are part of the normative system; and since ritual actions are predicated on these cognitive and normative elements, they serve to structure the rituals surrounding those kinds of behavior to which the concepts of possession trance or possession are applied.

[2] The coded data on societal dimensions utilized here are taken from the *Ethnographic atlas*, although coding categories were modified and simplified somewhat (see Bourguignon and Greenbaum 1973; Bourguignon 1968).

A few examples of each type will serve to clarify the distinctions which have guided our coding of the data. In Haiti, where possession trance is a key element in the Afro-Catholic folk religion known as *vodû*, the individual in an altered state of consciousness, in a ritual context, acts out the behavior, the role of the spirit he (or she) impersonates. Each spirit is known to have his musical rhythms and his songs, his preferred foods and drinks, special interests and competencies, his likes and dislikes, his manner of speaking, preferred colors, emblems, etc. In fact since there is no formal mythology, the snatches of songs, the behavior of possessed persons, the things done and said, serve to delineate the character of the particular spirit. To make sure his identity is recognized, furthermore, the spirit generally announces his name. As part of ritual initiation the spirit is permanently lodged in the head of his devotees, and must be removed at death. We may call this passive or latent possession and distinguish it from the active phases of possession trance, when the spirit "mounts" his worshiper. A similar situation, where both possession and possession trance appear as distinguishable elements of a single complex, exists in many African and Afro-American religions. In the *zar* cults of East Africa (Messing 1959; Lewis 1971), however, the initial phase of this latent possession is expressed as illness, and only when the spirit is called does an active possession trance occur. At this point, the spirit is generally not caused to leave the patient but is transformed into a guardian. Possession is permanent; possession trance, impersonating a particular spirit entity, occurs on ritual occasions only. Obeyesekere (i.p.) has described a situation for Ceylon which also involves a combination of long-term possession, and periodic possession trance. In this case, the possession trance occurs spontaneously and is considered an illness, a persecution of the patient by spirits of the dead and by demons. To free the patient from the permanent possession as well as the periodic possession trance, the spirits must be exorcised.

In these last two examples, possession as a form of illness or disturbance is a prelude to possession trance or a state between periods of possession trance. In other situations, possession illness may be unrelated to possession trance. This is the case in Haiti where possession by the dead is caused by sorcery and brings about illness but not possession trance. It also occurs in societies where possession trance does not exist at all. For example Boyer (1962) tells us that the Mescalero Apaches believed that the hostile powers of carnivores could penetrate a person's body through the skin or the mucosa and could thus cause illness or death. Among the Aymara of Bolivia (La Barre 1948: 223–225) evil spirits of various types may cause illnesses, such as tertian fever, by possessing the patient. Cure is by shamanistic exorcism. Indeed, a belief in the existence of possession illness, in the absence of possession trance, is rather widespread in South America.

However, possession is not always either illness or potential possession trance. Thus, Harner (1962) tells us that among the Jívaro, men acquire certain types of souls as a result of a vision quest and then also as a result of killing another person. The acquisition of such a soul is felt as a "sudden surge of power" and self-confidence, increasing intelligence as well as physical strength. Such a soul also protects a man from being killed in warfare or through sorcery. Possession here is an acquisition of new powers and capacities, to some extent thus a modification of personality. This acquired soul remains with its host until he reveals its identity prior to a killing expedition. It does not involve occasional episodes of altered states of consciousness, impersonation of another entity, etc. The life of the Jívaro warrior involves a series of such soul acquisitions and varying increases of power for shorter or longer periods of time. The whole pattern is one of considerable complexity, but for our purposes it suffices to note that it involves possession and alteration of capacities but not alteration of state of consciousness.

Quite a different relationship between a possessing spirit and its host, which we code as possession and not possession trance, appears in certain African forms of witchcraft belief. For example, the Fang (Fernandez 1961) believe in the existence of witchcraft beings *(evus)*. Such a being resides inside some men and physical evidence of its presence may be found upon autopsy. A man having an active *evus* acquires power through it, but it has its own character. A man's ambition "heats up" his *evus* and causes it to harm others. This is a form of possession in which the power of an individual is modified through the entity inhabiting him, the possession is permanent, but no possession trance, or temporary altered state of consciousness, results.

If we sort out our 360 societies with possession belief in this way, we find that some have only possession trance (16 percent), some have possession belief of other types (22 percent) and some have both (35 percent). Indeed, for the world as a whole and for the Old World areas, the largest group of societies are those which have both types of manifestations. In the Americas, however, possession trance is relatively rare (5 percent for North America and 12 percent for South America). The largest number of societies is that having possession only (27 percent and 34 percent respectively). Again, it should be remembered that almost half the societies of our North American sample have no belief in possession of any kind.

The differences between the major regions of the world suggest that diffusion may well have been at work here. But we may also ask whether possible functional relationships might exist between these types of beliefs and various societal attributes, particularly those related to societal complexity.

To test for possible functional relationships between types of possession beliefs and other societal characteristics, we grouped societies having possession beliefs into two categories: (a) those having possession and (b) those having possession trance regardless of whether they also had another possession belief. The reason for this grouping is, first, a test of the importance of the presence or absence of the phenomenon of possession trance in a society and, second, the observation, noted above, that possession may often be linked to possession trance as a stage or a phase of a single cognitive and behavioral complex. It should be noted that our concern here is not with the INCIDENCE of certain types of behaviors and beliefs or their specific form beyond the broad contours outlined and exemplified above. The question we asked was this: what kinds of societies, societies having what sorts of attributes, are more likely to have possession only, and how are they different from societies having possession trance?

We did, indeed, discover a series of statistically significant differences between societies that have possession belief only and those that have possession trance, whether or not they also have a separate possession belief. The following differences were found to be significant below the .001 level of probability: the societies having possession belief only are more likely than the possession trance societies (1) to depend on a combination of hunting, gathering and fishing for 46 percent or more of their subsistence; (2) to have no class stratification and no slavery; (3) to be nomadic or seminomadic in settlement patterns rather than sedentary; (4) to have no jurisdictional hierarchy above the local level; (5) to have an estimated total population size of less than 100,000; and (6) to have a mean size of local population of less than 1,000. Also, they are less likely to have male genital mutilation (significant at p below .01) and they tend toward the practice of segregating adolescent boys (significant at p below .09). These general characteristics listed were also consistent with the first one: they all correlate with a hunting, gathering and fishing economy. Rather consistently, then, we find possession trance societies "more complex" than possession belief only societies.

If we are to account for these differences, we need to take a closer look at the differences between possession belief and possession trance, to show what they have in common and how they differ so that we may be able to understand why the types of societies with which they are associated differ so importantly.

What do they have in common?

To begin with, all forms of possession belief are contingent on a belief in spirits. They further suppose a relationship between human individuals and other entities such that a take-over of some aspects of the individual's functioning is possible. This involves the distinction between certain aspects of the "self" and other aspects. The body remains constant as a vehicle for one's own "soul" or "souls" and perhaps for other spiritual principles or powers. Yet one or more of these principles may be supplemented or supplanted by an alien principle, temporarily or permanently.

Beattie and Middleton (1969) have suggested that a belief in spirits, by attributing problems of everyday living to spirits, makes it possible to deal with these problems by extending to the spirits the methods used in dealing with people, that is, extending the field of social relations beyond the human community. In a rephrasing of psychoanalytic formulations, Spiro (1967), among others, has suggested that spirits represent projections and displacements of affective elements that grow out of the parent-child relationship. This, too, is a matter of enlarging the field of social relations. The differences between the approach of the British social anthropologists, however, and that of the American psychoanalytically informed cultural anthropologists, it seems to me, are that the former operate by hypothesizing an isomorphism between two sets of relationships, whereas the latter suggest the psychological mechanisms by which such an isomorphism is to be explained.

Although these hypotheses refer to belief in spirits in general, they are relevant to belief in spirit possession specifically. Possession by spirits suggests the possibility of communication between spirits and humans. Prayer, sacrifices and other types of ritual are forms of communication addressed by human beings to spirits. Divination, omens, dreams, etc. involve, in many cultural contexts, communication from spirits to humans. Yet it is in the specifics of this communication, which is essential to any validation of belief, that possession trance and nontrance possession belief differ importantly. These differences may also be expected to give us a clue to the reasons why we may expect to find them associated with different kinds of societies.

How do they differ?

In possession trance, the individual temporarily loses his (or often, her) identity and impersonates that of another. Some aspects of the self are displaced or suppressed. In nontrance possession, by contrast, there may be added powers that supplement those of the self, but do not replace or displace them. There is no impersonation and no loss of consciousness or alteration of consciousness, no substitution of another sense of identity. Instead, there may be an enhanced sense of power and identity, a sense of self is not lost but enhanced or diminished. And where illness is not involved, the relationship may be of long duration or permanent.

In psychological terms, the difference with respect to selfhood seems to be of crucial importance here. And this suggests the relevance of the concepts of self-reliance, achievement and independence — and their opposites, obedience and dependence — to the differences between possession trance and nontrance possession belief. The possession trancer can achieve his ends, can become strong and influential, only by becoming another, by dependence on, and obedience to another. It is not he as the vehicle who is respected but his spirit. To be a worthy vehicle, he must be obedient to the rules the spirit imposes. The Jívaro warrior, the Havasupai shaman, the Fang witch and others who acquire powers as supplements to their own do not impersonate the possessing entities. Rather, their own selves are enhanced by the powers they acquire.

Now it will be recalled that possession is significantly more likely to be found in societies which depend on hunting, gathering and fishing combined for 46 percent or more of their subsistence (significant below .001 level). In this connection it is interesting to note that Barry et al. (1959) in their study of the relationship between economy and socialization found that, "responsibility and obedience are positively correlated with accumulation of food resources; achievement, self-reliance and independence are negatively correlated with accumulation." Extremes in low accumulation are hunting and fishing, and the extreme in high accumulation is animal husbandry, intermediately high in accumulation is agriculture only and intermediately low in accumulation is a combination of agriculture, hunting and fishing. It appears reasonable to expect that religious beliefs and practices will on the one hand reflect the universe in which a society lives and on the other will extend the patterns of personal interactions, which are developed by socialization practices, from human interactions to interactions with spirits. The beliefs and practices are thus determined by at least two strands of causal relations: they represent a reflection both of the individual's personality and his typical relations to self and others, and they represent a projection of the society's interaction with its behavioral universe including the use made of its environment for purposes of subsistence.

Essentially, our findings then are consistent with the model of the relationship between maintenance systems, child-training practices, and adult behavior and cultural products posited by Harrington and Whiting (1972) and the findings of the large literature which they review. Possession beliefs of all types incorporate an affirmation of the interdependence of man and spirits, but each type of society makes this assertion in a manner appropriate to it. High accumulation societies visualize a universe in which man is dependent on and obedient to spirits who dominate him. Yet at times this domination can be put to human use, for through spirit possession trance direct communication may be established between man and spirit; through the self-effacing of human vehicles the power of spirits may be harnessed for the good of the society and even for that of the spirit's vehicle. In low accumulation societies, an alteration of capacities is perceived as due to an interaction of self-reliant humans with spirits whose powers may be harnessed or who may be defeated in the battle against disease represented by exorcism. Man, in each case, seeks to enhance his power, to increase his control over the uncontrollable, and he does so in ways consistent with his patterns of interactions with other humans and his perception of his own self: through submission and obedience in high accumulation societies, through the harnessing of whatever spiritual forms will enhance his self-reliance in low accumulation societies.

The bits of scattered knowledge about hundreds of societies around the world do fall into place with the application of rather simple techniques of ordering and we discover that we do "know" something after all as a result of knowing detail after detail of what sometimes appear to be ethnographic esoterica and items in a collection of museum specimens.

REFERENCES

BARRY, H., I. CHILD, M. BACON
    1959   Relation of childtraining to subsistence economy. *American Anthropologist* 61:51–63.
BEATTIE, J., J. MIDDLETON
    1969   *Spirit mediumship and society in Africa.* New York: Africana Press.
BOURGUIGNON, ERIKA
    1968   *A cross-cultural study of dissociational states, final report.* Columbus, Ohio: The Ohio State University Research Foundation.
BOURGUIGNON, ERIKA, *editor*
    1973   *Religion, altered states of consciousness and social change.* Columbus, Ohio: Ohio State University Press.

BOURGUIGNON, ERIKA, LENORA GREENBAUM
1973   *Homogeneity and diversity.* New Haven: HRAF Press.
BOYER, L. B.
1962   Remarks on the personality of shamans. *The Psychoanalytic Study of Society* 2:233–254.
FERNANDEZ, J. W.
1961   Christian acculturation and Fang witchcraft. *Cahiers d'Études Africaines* 2:244–270.
FRENCH, DAVID
1963   "The relationship of anthropology to studies in perception and cognition," in *Psychology: a study of a science.* Edited by S. Koch. New York: McGraw-Hill.
HARNER, MICHAL
1962   Jívaro souls. *American Anthropologist* 64:258–272.
HARRINGTON, CHARLES, J. W. M. WHITING
1972   "Socialization and personality," in *Psychological anthropology.* Edited by F. L. K. Hsu. Cambridge, Mass.: Schenkman.
LA BARRE, WESTON
1948   The Aymara Indians of Lake Titicaca Plateau, Bolivia. *American Anthropological Association, Memoir* 68.
LEWIS, I. M.
1971   *Ecstatic religion.* Baltimore: Penguin Books.
MESSING, S. D.
1959   "Group therapy and social status in the Zar cult of Ethiopia," in *Culture and mental health.* Edited by M. K. Opler. New York: Macmillan.
MURDOCK, G. P.
1967   *Ethnographic atlas.* Pittsburgh: University of Pittsburgh Press.
NAROLL, RAOUL
1970   What have we learned from cross-cultural surveys? *American Anthropologist* 72:1227–1288.
OBEYESEKERE, G.
i.p.   "Psycho-cultural exegesis of a case of spirit possession from Ceylon," in a special volume of *Contributions to Asian Studies.* Edited by Steven Piker.
OESTERREICH, T. K.
1922   *Die Bessessenheit.* Langensalzach: Wendt und Klauswell.
SPIER, LESLIE
1928   Havasupai ethnography. *American Museum of Natural History Anthropological Papers* 29:81–392.
SPIRO, M. E.
1967   *Burmese supernaturalism.* Englewood Cliffs: Prentice-Hall.
TYLOR, E. B.
1958   *Religion in primitive culture* (originally published 1871). New York: Harper Torchbooks.

Pastoral Images and Values in Southwest Donegal

EUGENIA S. CRAMER

My interest in Ireland and in southwest Donegal sprang originally from an interest in pastoralism as a system of environmental exploitation. The subject is both fascinating and pertinent — fascinating because when one looks at it cross-culturally, regularities emerge in such things as social organization and food taboos (or, as I shall be discussing here, belief systems), and pertinent because protein intake and modern problems of sufficient protein production are involved. For several years now I have been collecting information on the social organization of people who live by their herds, and the people of Donegal interested me because their system can be seen as the "end product" of a longstanding pastoral adaptation.

Pastoralism is practiced all over the world, nowadays in mostly marginal environments. As a system of environmental exploitation it takes several forms, some of which can make a fairly productive environment into a marginal one through degradation of natural resources. A modern form, one that is still practiced in parts of Western Europe and one that is "good" from the conservation point of view, is transhumant pastoralism, in which seasonal residence shifts are regular events and people move to accommodate their herds. The Irish have been pastoralists for 2,500 years and the people of southwest Donegal practiced transhumant pastoralism up until the beginning of the twentieth century, when economic development first became an issue. Although economic development is still very much an issue, transhumant pastoralism has disappeared, so one of the questions I had in mind when I began my study was whether or not the beneficial effects of transhumance, i.e. resource conservation, had been eradicated when the system disappeared.

I shall discuss some preliminary formulations from my dissertation, the title of which is "Sacred and profane livestock in southwest Donegal." The study was funded as an ecological project of which the major emphasis was the material aspects of a population's adaptation to a very harsh environment, but here I am more concerned with the normative aspects of adaptation and the feedback between cultural norms and material imperatives. After I had gathered the material facts, I wanted to know how and why those practices which make sense ecologically came to be part of a cultural tradition or, in Parsons' terms, part of a logically congruent symbolic system, as well as part of the action system involving imperatives resulting from scarcity (Parsons and Shils 1962: 173).

My conclusions are tentative ones, and my evidence is drawn from several sources — first, from my own fieldwork, a year's stay in southwest Donegal. I focused on the decision points in livestock-production strategies and collected economic and ecological data. My information was drawn from a sample of thirty farmers who kept livestock; after the preliminary survey work had been done, these people were interviewed at length about production decision, marketing, husbandry practices, etc. Second, an extensive resource survey carried out in the area in 1965 was very useful in providing exact descriptions of soils and their potential uses. This document is one on which most of the government's subsequent policy has been based (*An Foras Taluntais* 1967). A third source of information was historical documents concerning the area; the written history of Ireland dates from about A.D. 500 and the census records are reliable from about 1841 on, so production statistics, population figures, etc., were available. A fourth source was interviews with all those officials who were involved in any way with economic development, especially as this applied to livestock-improvement schemes.

In additon to standard survey and interview work, I also used other methods, including participant observation and detailed photographic recording with videotape. In this case, participant observation meant attending any and all events that took place — political, religious, social, and recreational gatherings, as well as those having to do with community affairs and problems. I attended all the livestock fairs and as many other activities having to do with livestock as I could — I helped drive cattle and dose them, I went to sheep-dippings and shearings, I helped buy and sell sheep, and toward the very end of my fieldwork, I was accorded the very high honor of being asked to help judge cattle at a local show. It was as a result of data gathered in this way, through informal conversations, that I began to question the facts that

I had obtained in the more formal procedures, and eventually I came to conclusions which extend somewhat beyond the strictly material considerations involved in livestock production.

There were a number of incongruities which could not be resolved simply by reference to economics. One of the most striking of these was the distinction drawn between cattle and sheep, differentiations in the manner of handling and evaluating these animals (as well as their owners) which carried through many aspects of life — ritual, legal, social, political — and which were not explicable simply in terms of the economic worth of the animals. These distinctions seemed to proceed from an intrinsic estimation, a set of unstated assumptions about the values attached to each category of animal. When I asked, I discovered that these assumptions were not simply unstated, they were almost completely unverbalized except as rationalizations, in one form or another, for traditional practices. For example, there was absolute unanimity in answer to my question about livestock preferences: everyone agreed that it was better and easier to keep cattle, that there was less work involved and that the work was more pleasant. It happens that there is MORE work involved in the care of cattle (according to my preliminary calculations), and it is harder work in terms of energy expenditure. Although some people admitted to a strong liking for sheep, no one felt that keeping sheep was a desirable occupation.

Before citing other examples of differentiations, I might stop to describe the area I was in. Southwest Donegal comprises about 275 square miles of the northwestern corner of Ireland. Donegal is part of the geographical entity of northern Ireland, but not of the political entity of Northern Ireland. It is one of the twenty-six counties of the Irish Republic, though most of its border faces Northern Ireland. Historically, Donegal was part of the province of Ulster, the northernmost province of Ireland but, in 1922, Donegal and two other counties of Ulster were separated from what had been their traditional market and trade region and made part of the Irish Republic, while the rest of Ulster became Northern Ireland. The effect of this separation has been to isolate Donegal from its natural trade region, the interior of Ulster province. Although livestock is still sold into the north, the people have been forced to rely on the south for most of their manufactured goods as well as for markets for their agricultural produce. The political division has thus enhanced an isolation which had in the past resulted from Donegal's geographical remoteness and its scarce natural resources.

The resources of the area are almost completely in the form of grazing land, mostly unimproved bog; this constitutes some 63 percent of all the land available, and no more than 2–3 percent of all land is classified as good agricultural soil. Some 10 percent is "improved," that is, it has been reclaimed for agricultural purposes, mostly for potatoes, oats, or hay. Although land reclamation involves a great deal of work, the improvement often shows spectacular results, e.g., boglands which in a virgin state carry one sheep per four acres can be drained, fenced, and fertilized so that four sheep per acre can be stocked. There are new techniques available for reclaiming bog land but these are effective only for sheep, since the treatment of the bog surface renders it even more spongy than it would be in its virgin state and cattle tend to be too heavy to negotiate these fields well during all but the driest seasons of the year. There is another fact which the government publications on the benefits of reclamation do not mention: if cattle are grazed on reclaimed lands during the dry season, the milk takes on an "off-taste" which is unpalatable to humans.

The climate is almost as wretched as the soil: gale-force winds; a growing season bounded more by rainfall than by temperature variations, with the heaviest rains coming during the harvest season; and extreme variation from year to year in both rainfall and in the duration of the frost-free season.

One advantage of all these natural disadvantages is that southwest Donegal has not been subject to governmental interference on the same scale as have other parts of Ireland. In 1607, when the British decided to colonize most of the north, the colonists who arrived to take over in Donegal went home almost as quickly as they had come, presumably because they found the land and the climate beyond agricultural redemption. The problems which the area faces today result from all these factors — the area's remoteness, its poor natural resources, its intractable climate, its isolation from markets for agricultural produce. In combination, the effect of these factors on the population has been a reduced standard of living in comparison with other parts of Ireland.

After many years of subsidizing the area rather than making much effort toward genuine development, government policy has changed and the attempt now is to make the people economically self-sufficient, primarily by means of increased livestock production. The government believes that the only way to accomplish this — given the area's limitations — is to develop what they call a fully "rationalized" economy. This means full use of all resources with the aim of a higher income for the people on the land. It would involve full-scale land reclamation and a shift in emphasis from cattle production to sheep production, for the reasons I have mentioned.

The traditional economy is a mixed one based on cattle and sheep, with strong emphasis on cattle production. Government subsidies for beef cattle have met with very favorable responses in the area but a similar subsidy for sheep and numerous grants available for land reclamation have failed. The number of sheep has held constant or decreased slightly in some areas even while the subsidy rate has gone steadily up. Government officials explain this by pointing to the farmers' "prehistoric mental outlook" and their refusal to adopt modern production methods. These charges are not justified by the facts; cattle are produced in the area at gross margins which exceed the average in other parts of Ireland and the mortality rate (or more broadly, the risk factor) for cattle is lower in Donegal than in any other part of the country. It is the refusal to increase SHEEP production that the government officials find offensive. The economic explanation is that cattle are more valuable than sheep, i.e., a cow is worth from $100 to $150, whereas the equivalent in sheep, five or six ewes, would be worth only about $65 to $85.[1] But this does not suffice to explain either the reluctance to increase sheep production or the other distinctions that are made between these animals.

The differential treatment of animals is especially apparent at livestock fairs. Each town of any size has a fair day once a month, when cattle and sheep are brought in from surrounding farms and offered for sale, mostly to buyers who come from Northern Ireland, but also to the local farmers.

Sheep can be sold anywhere in the town and are usually tied up in front of houses, shops, or anywhere convenient. Cattle, however, are always sold on what is generally referred to as the "Cattle Hill." This is invariably the highest spot in the town, and is usually a grassy area set aside for this purpose only.

Both cattle and sheep are driven into town early in the morning, but cattle must be sold by noon at the latest. Those cattle which are not sold by noon are either taken home or removed to a different (fenced) place after noon and the area is cleared. While on the hill, cattle are never hobbled or tied — they are allowed to graze and are watched over by their owner or by someone he asks to do this for him. Sheep are always tied and they are left standing until they are sold or until their owner emerges from the pub — whichever comes first. They are usually

[1]   The concept of equivalence referred to here is that of livestock equivalent units (L.S.E.), an ecological term in which cows are the measure of all things, i.e., one cow = five to six ewes, or one and a half horses. The measurement is based on grazing pressure, or the amount of energy consumed.

cleared away before sunset, though it is not uncommon to see sheep standing about until the pubs close.

When I asked informants to explain to me why cattle had to be sold on a hill, or why they had to be away by noon, or why they were not tied up, the answers were usually of the order. "We've always done it that way." When I asked why sheep could not be sold on the Cattle Hill and were never allowed to graze there, the answer was, "It wouldn't be right."

Both cattle and sheep are sold by bargaining but the emotional pitch of these bargaining sessions varies considerably. A deal is struck between buyer and seller by means of an intermediary, who suggests to both parties a more reasonable attitude, and the whole performance is concluded with a ritual handshake. I videotaped many of these performances and several curious things emerge from an analysis of the tapes: bargaining for cattle is a much longer procedure, which can take the better part of an hour; the sale of cattle involves a much greater display of emotion; selling cattle carries with it far more responsibility on the part of the people who gather to watch. When a buyer approaches a cattle owner, he discusses general topics for a while before venturing to ask a price. The seller often refuses even to name his price and must be persuaded by a third party to do so. When a lower bid is made, the seller appears to be deeply offended by the suggestion that his animals might be worth so little. The intermediary often has to soothe his feelings before the bargaining can proceed. A new offer is made, and the seller will reject this also. So it goes on, with the seller displaying less vehemence and more uncertainty each time he refuses. Eventually he may be persuaded by the onlookers and the go-between to part with the animals but the performance is always carried out with a good show of reluctance on the seller's part. Cattle are never criticized nor are comparative prices mentioned.

Buying sheep is quite different. It involves fewer offers and counteroffers, for one thing, and it is carried out with an (assumed) air of indifference. A buyer asks the selling price and the seller responds readily with some outrageous price. The buyer prods a few of the sheep and observes that several of them probably won't make it through the winter. He then suggests a price that is much too low. The seller will ignore this commentary and the ridiculous price that is offered, even to the extent of pretending to be deeply engrossed in conversation with some bystander. (I was often this bystander and initially was amazed when informants began an intricate political discussion or a long interpretation of some insignificant Gaelic proverb.) An intermediary appears and the buyer will then make another offer, after observing that Sean down the street is selling better sheep for 10/- ($1.50) a head less. The intermediary may have to interrupt the conversation of the seller to point out that another offer has been made, and again the seller will appear to be uninterested but will pause in the conversation long enough to suggest, offhandedly, another price. Here the intermediary will suggest that the difference be split and the offer is then considered by both parties. If one or the other disagrees, the matter is dropped and there is no sale though the buyer may return later in the day to see if the price has been reduced. The performances in both these situations are quite stereotyped and are carried out regardless of the amount of money involved; a bullock selling for $75 commands the entire performance outlined earlier, while sheep at $150 will still receive the seemingly careless treatment just described.

It should be emphasized that as the cattle owner is not truly offended, neither is the sheep seller indifferent. These performances are games for which everyone knows the rules. Styles differ, of course, as does aptitude for the performance.

Both cattle and sheep sales are concluded with a ritual handshake, the major function of which seems to be to draw a crowd. Payment for cattle is then made in the pub, and all the onlookers join the principals there for free drinks. Payment for sheep in the pub is optional; they can be paid for in the street if the seller likes. Part of the selling price must be returned to the buyer, generally a small percentage of the price which is called the luckpenny. This is supposed to remove the bad luck which it is believed may arise as a result of the transfer of animals, although some sheep farmers have a reputation for selling "unlucky" animals and the local farmers would not buy an animal from these men.

Violation of any of the parts of these rituals can and does occur, though some apparently are more important than others. Members of the younger generation may refuse to participate in the special handshake on the grounds that it is painful and unnecessary, but they will stoutly deny that it is possible to sell animals without the help of an intermediary. Although it is not necessary to buy drinks in the pub when sheep are sold, it is mandatory to buy drinks when a cow is sold, and a man who has sold cattle is expected to be generous on these occasions.

There are legal distinctions between cattle and sheep. If a motorist hits a cow on the road, the motorist is always responsible for damages, even though the law says that an owner must exercise due caution with his animals. The verdict always goes against the motorist, although the question of negligence on the cow's part may be hotly debated. Sheep, on the other hand, are responsible for their own welfare and if one is struck on the road, it is nobody's concern but the sheep's.

During my stay, charges were brought by the County against a man who had been left in charge of a relative's cattle over the winter. The man was charged with cruelty to animals because he had allowed the cattle in his charge to roam freely until the neighbors complained, whereupon he confined the herd to a field without adequate provision for feed. (Cattle are normally kept in barns through the winter and fed on hay and grain supplements.) Several of the animals died and went unburied; the rest were found in an emaciated state by a County official, some so far debilitated that they had to be done away with. The punishment for this offense was quite severe, involving a suspended prison sentence and a heavy fine. The judge expressed indignation at this man's conduct and noted with some relief that abuses of this sort seldom took place in the County and that such a case had never come before him. It struck no one as odd that what was defined as cruel and unusual treatment for cattle is exactly that accorded to sheep every winter. They are left to fend for themselves and are turned into pastures which their owners know to be insufficient for this purpose. There is no thought of supplemental feeding, and in a severe winter, the mortality rate may be as high as 50 percent.

These are ritual and judicial differentiations. There are social distinctions as well. As I have said, the universal response is that it is better to keep cattle than to keep sheep. Cattle farmers are said to be more intelligent, more reasonable, more modern, more interested in community problems and affairs, more apt to be a good example to the rest of the people. Sheepmen are supposed to be lazy, backward, unwilling to contribute to the welfare of the community, uninterested in anything except government handouts. I think these charges can be recognized as social distinctions which are accorded on different grounds. I am going to bypass most of them and consider only two aspects of these "reputations," the political and the economic overtones.

It is a fact that sheep farmers do not participate in local politics; even the wealthy sheep farmers who have large herds do not do so. I should note here that there are no local elective offices in southwest Donegal, and being a committee member or an official in charge of special events are the major ways in which authority is exercised. All the members of the local committees and all those men who hold positions of authority on special occasions are primarily cattle farmers (some of whom keep sheep as well).

Recruitment for either of these offices is on two traditional bases:

wealth and education. The most important of these is wealth, which generally coincides with "inherited" position. In the past, this has always meant extensive cattle holdings, and seemingly this still holds true. The second basis for recruitment is education; certain posts automatically assume leadership, e.g. that of priest or headmaster of the local school. Beyond this, some people who are neither wealthy nor well educated do participate, especially the shopkeepers whose interests are very much affected by such things as local development committees or the annual agricultural show. Most of these men still have one foot in the country; they may keep small herds of cattle, which are likely to be pedigreed animals. The main point is that there are crosscutting variables that can influence political participation, so that a shopkeeper who lacks the benefit of inherited social position may still become a local "leader," but even wealthy sheep farmers do not participate in politics or in the local authority structure.

The fact that it is sheep farmers who have the reputation of being noncontributors to the economy is also of interest because the outward circumstances in support of this charge in some cases apply to cattle farmers as well. Since the sheepmen occupy some of the very poorest lands in the area, they are almost invariably eligible for unemployment but the unemployment rolls are by no means composed simply of sheep farmers.

In certain instances the classification of noncontributor is extended to cattle farmers, too, most particularly in the matter of willingness to buy drinks in the pub. Generosity is expected on these occasions and any cattle farmer who does not extend it is apt to be thoroughly damned, even by the teetotallers in the group. For sheep farmers, as I have said, participation in this redistributive ceremony is optional — but the definition of a man's social worth seems to depend very largely on this factor and the responsibility for spending part of one's earnings in the place where they are earned is taken very seriously.

Another instance of the differentiation between cattle and sheep is in animal health practices and specifically in willingness to consult a veterinarian. I asked the question, "Under what circumstances would you call the vet?" When cattle were involved, the response was, under any and all circumstances which were the least bit doubtful — that is when the owner could not immediately identify the problem and solve it. Sheep farmers almost never called the vet and the reasons given for this were as numerous as my informants: they weren't sure what the animals might have died of, they tried treating them with home remedies, or, very commonly, they said that whatever the precipitating cause, the real cause was starvation and the vet wouldn't be any help for that. Again, there is an underlying economic variable here which does not explain as much as it should. A cow is worth twice as much as the equivalent number in sheep, so a visit from the vet would cost about one-fifth the value of one sheep, or 1/50th of the value of a full-grown cow. On this basis, the economic explanation seems quite reasonable. But during the thirties, there was a government regulation in effect prohibiting the sale of livestock outside the country. Since the market for livestock is in Northern Ireland and that is now defined as another country, cattle dropped in value until they were almost worthless. Calves were sold for 10/- ($1.50) and good cows went for a few pounds, maybe $10 or 15. Sheep did not lose their value to the same extent because there was quite a lively trade in smuggling wool across the border. The veterinarians report that their business in treating cattle was not affected. They were called just as frequently then as now (although they did not get paid as often) and no one neglected a sick animal, even though cattle had very little monetary value for almost a decade.

There are various superstitions associated with animals, apart from those involved in selling them. There is a covert belief in the evil eye prevalent in the area but it affects only livestock and accounts for accidents that befall animals, e.g. cows that fall into drains or run wild for some unknown reason.

The Irish share with pastoralists all over the world the belief that milk won't turn to butter unless all is ritually "well," and they add various things to the milk or recite appropriate formulae while churning. I got conflicting reports about the effect of the presence of strangers in the house during churning but I always took my turn, either because it was an honor for a stranger to do so or because strangers HAD to.

There are only a few examples in which Christianity enters much into matters to do with livestock. One of these is the treatment of ringworm, a disease common in cattle and one that is easily transmitted to humans. Most people in southwest Donegal believe that doctors have no effective cure for this disease and they consult various folk "specialists" whose cure consists mostly of reading certain pages from the Bible in a prescribed order, odd prayers, and the like. Also in this vein, I am told that the priest used to be called on to cure the evil eye, but the clergy nowadays does not go out on errands of this sort — or if they do, they are not likely to be aware of it. I was also told that cows bought from Protestants are sprinkled with holy water when their new owner takes them home, but this activity was always reported as something that the *amadan* [half-wit] did.

The other thing I want to mention is the calendrical system, not because it is associated with differentiating livestock but because it is an important regulating mechanism in production strategies. Certain days of the year are through long tradition associated with livestock. St. Patrick's Day is "celebrated" by bringing the sheep down from the mountains where they have grazed over the winter; what we call Halloween is a traditional market day for cattle; St. Bridgid's Day is the first day of spring and therefore the time when spring planting is begun. Many of these dates are sanctified simply by tradition, and no one thinks to question them. Other production decisions are matters for community decision; for instance hay cutting will be begun by all the members of a townland on the same day or within the same week. A great many production decisions, therefore, are not a matter of conscious individual choice but rather have their referents in tradition or in joint decision making.

Now, having described some of the distinctions between cattle and sheep and some of the premises on which the production system operates, I want to offer several sorts of explanation for what I have been describing. First, I believe that the distinctions "sacred and profane" are applicable here because most of the ritual, social, legal and economic discriminations between these animals and their owners are made not on the basis of a set of empirically testable beliefs but rather on the basis of a set of assumptions that are nonempirical and unquestioned, even unquestionable — beliefs about the appropriateness of this differential treatment (Alland 1970). It is considered morally wrong to allow cattle to be exposed to winter weather or to fail to provide them with supplementary feed; it is considered foolish to do anything else with sheep. Cattle are sold in a special place, kept apart for that purpose; sheep can be sold anywhere. The sale of a cow demands its own form of redistribution; the sale of sheep demands nothing but leaves the option of participating in redistribution. Sheep herding is not seen as a desirable profession, even by those who practice it almost exclusively. The legal system supports the privileged position of cattle and ignores sheep altogether. The ritual involved in selling animals maintains and reinforces the importance of cattle owners in the society and offers them at the same time an opportunity to display their prowess. (Selling cattle is, by the way, an exclusively male ritual and stories are told about the ridiculing of widows and spinsters when they attempt to sell their cattle. Selling sheep is open to all and sundry.) Informants say that buying and selling at the fair is more fun than a poker game and that being able to out-bluff the other fellow is the greatest satisfaction of all.

You will remember that Durkheim says that religious phenomena are always characterized by a bipartite division of the cognized universe, a division which puts everything that exists into two classes which radically exclude each other. "Sacred" things are those which the interdictions protect and isolate; "profane" things are those to which these interdictions are applied and which must remain at a distance from the first (Durkheim 1961: 56). He goes on to say that when a number of sacred things sustain relations with each other so as to form a system having a certain unity, the totality of these beliefs and their corresponding rites may be seen as a religion. Each religion recognizes a plurality of sacred things but there can also be groups of religious phenomena which do not belong to any special religion. These last, Durkheim suggests, may be left over from a previous religious system. I believe it is in this sense that cattle and sheep and the corresponding rites are part of a belief system and that they form their own "group" of religious phenomena. This group of religious phenomena, beliefs pertaining to cattle and sheep, may well be left over from a previous religion; the Irish were pastoralists a thousand years before they became Christians; and the Church, I think wisely, defines virtue on grounds other than production.

I don't want to get too deeply involved with Durkheim: my point is simply that the collectivity — that is, the majority of farmers in southwest Donegal, no matter what church they belong to — accept certain beliefs and rites as "sacred," attach values to certain animals and not to others in ways that are fully in accord with Durkheim's definitions. I am suggesting that the system of livestock production that has traditionally operated in the area is one that has come to have exactly that quality of subjective validity, of conviction based on faith in "tradition" which anthropologists are accustomed to categorizing in more primitive societies as "religion." What the Irish government official sees (or, for that matter, what I, as an American, saw) as something which should be a pragmatic action system governed by imperatives resulting from scarcity (Parsons and Shils 1962) has, for these people, entered into the realm of "sacred" knowledge.

Before I speculate on the reasons for this, I will offer another example, one drawn from a more clearly defined group of pastoralists. The *aBrog Pa*, high-altitude nomadic pastoralists of Tibet, are Mahayana Buddhists, a religion which among other things forbids the taking of life and this creed is one which pastoralists find difficult to live by. For such sanctions as they apply in many situations having to do with livestock, these people refer not to Buddhism but to a pantheon of mountain and soil gods. This religion is one which was practiced before Buddhism and it is quite clear from the monograph on this group (Ekvall 1968) that most of the beliefs which are associated with these numerous gods have the effect of conserving resources. Since Buddhism involves no such policies, it is not in conflict with this system.

The soil gods prohibit the cutting of peat for fuel; I suspect that at certain times of the year, these same peat bogs provide good grazing for the herds. Yaks are the mainstay of the people and they have considerable totemic and symbolic significance. Every year each tent must allow a male yak to go free as a sacrifice to the gods, and these animals then serve two purposes: they are auxiliary stud animals and when meat is scarce they can be hunted. Wild yaks — which are not subject to the privations of the domestic beasts — are often the major item in the diet through the winter. The mountain gods deplore digging in the soil, but some edible wild tubers are acceptable in religious offerings (Ekvall 1968: 55), that is, as occasional supplementary food which would make extra resources available in times of great scarcity.

I believe much of the production system in southwest Donegal, whether or not it goes by the name of religion, has a similar effect — that of the conservation of resources. From this I will offer a second explanation, one that is tied to the first. A belief in cattle as "sacred" animals and sheep as "profane" ones not only makes good logical sense, given the premises on which the society operates, but it makes good ecological sense. Cattle are the major source of energy production in this environment, while sheep are the scavengers. Sheep may also serve as buffers between the environment and the cattle-dependent population. In a good year, the sheep will do well and provide extra income; in an ecological sense, they are almost "unearned" resources. But in a bad year, they will die off, and in times of severe shortage the lack of attention which is accorded them prevents the environment from being overgrazed. I also think that the belief system I have described is evidence of a population's adaptation to its environment and that a good many of these practices make more sense in an ecological framework than they may make in a social one.

Two examples will illustrate this point: the ecological value of keeping cattle and the advantages of celebrating St. Patrick's Day by bringing the sheep down from the hill.

The best statement on the advantages of keeping a cow comes from Irish literature. The speaker is an eldery man whose "dairy herd" consists of one cow:

... the cow is the hub of the household. You first have to get a wife, and then a cow. And the first thing you would have to look for in the wife would be if she was a good milker. You might get the cow as dowry with the wife, and you could not do better, unless there was a bit of money as well. If you had the cow, you could live without the wife, but if you had not the cow, you would not be able to live at all (Cross 1943:121–123).

This is about the best summation I know: the advantage of keeping cattle in this very harsh environment is that their manure provides what is often the only fertilizer applied to the land. This circumstance is most likely the primary reason why they are kept indoors during the winter and, on some farms, at night. There are no predators in the area, nor are they in need of shelter over the winter. Tests done on the predominant breeds — the Aberdeen Angus and the Shorthorn — indicate that they are well adapted to cold conditions. Keeping cattle indoors conserves manure, though the reason given for this practice is that they might come to some harm, or "it wouldn't be right" to leave them out. In parts of Africa similar practices exist. Schneider, for example, reports that among the Turu, cattle are kept penned most of the time and allowed to graze for only seven or eight hours a day. The Turu are dependent on the manure for fertilizing their millet crops and for fuel (Schneider 1970: 16). Cattle in southwest Donegal not only recycle the energy which they take from the grass, they make it possible for the human population to convert this energy into utilizable form, that is into potatoes and vegetables. And, of course, milk and milk products provide the necessary protein.

My other example is St. Patrick's Day, the traditional day for bringing home the sheep. Sheep graze the lowlands until shortly after lambing time, which is late in April or early in May. The government would like the farmers to produce more early lambs, which would involve bringing the sheep down earlier and feeding them grain supplements. This last is a tricky business since all supplements are expensive and must be imported from the south of Ireland. Very few people are willing to and the reason most often given is that grazing land is let over the winter on a contract which extends to St. Patrick's Day, not beyond, and there is no discount for taking them off the hill earlier. Although this is the stated reason, there are better ecological reasons, including a practice called "flushing," that is getting extra grass to the ewe just before the lamb is born so that she will have more milk. Another reason is that soil temperatures in the lowlands are more constant than those of the hills, so the grass comes in earlier in the lowlands. In some years it comes before the spring equinox, in other years later, but the advantage of St. Patrick's Day is that it presents an excellent minimax solution — it minimizes losses to the sheep and still maximizes pasture. Bringing the sheep down earlier would induce overgrazing; bringing them down later would raise the mortality rates in lambs. If the fields are overgrazed, then the amount of hay available for cattle will be seriously reduced. As it is, the sheep are left just long enough for them to take advantage of the early grass and not long enough to damage the later crop of hay. As a minimax solution, this is quite satisfactory — it aims at reducing the risk of serious losses.

This is one of the areas in which the government argues for change. Experts say that it would be better to bring the sheep down earlier or later, depending on the weather each year, and that every man should decide for himself what course of action to follow. It seems almost unnecessary to point out here that in the absence of a minimax solution, the alternate choices carry with them a much greater risk of error. The more difficult and treacherous the environment, of course, the greater the risk, and if a farmer makes the wrong decision, he will not only lose money on his sheep, he will damage his capacity to keep cattle over the winter. As the farmers see it, change would constitute a threat to the cattle; as I see it, change in the direction of an effort to keep all the sheep alive during the worst times would ultimately constitute a serious threat of the resources available. The difference is merely a matter of the level of abstraction at which systemic connections are viewed.

In conclusion, I am suggesting that the system of beliefs attached to livestock and to the production system represents a conservative adaptation, which has had the effect of conserving resources. The system of production which now exists is outmoded by modern standards because it does not involve full utilization of all natural resources and because it does not provide the highest possible income. What it does and what it has done in the past is to provide a secure income for large numbers of people and allow a population to persist in its environment without degradation of the existing resources. The belief system as it pertains to livestock mirrors the vital role of cattle as recycling agents and the auxiliary role of sheep as scavengers. Sheep bear the brunt of environmental caprices and the natural reduction of their numbers in bad years has probably contributed to the maintenance of good grazing and prevented the encroachment of undesirable species (which accompany overgrazing). The belief system also supports a system of social relations which pertained in the past when, for example, an individual's actions were predicated on his need for extra labor from neighbors and kinsmen at harvest time. Nowadays the availability of tractors has eliminated this dependence, at least in part, and will do so increasingly in the future.

I am not suggesting that the system of livestock production practiced in southwest Donegal is the best of all possible systems, but rather that both the production system and its concomitant belief system have evolved as response to very specific and very difficult climatic conditions. The difficulties with changing the system, as I see them, are not so much in changing the belief system as in the ecological consequences of a shift in production emphasis, which will undoubtedly cause environmental degradation if maximum stocking rates are achieved. In the good years all would be well, but in the bad years the area would be seriously overstocked with sheep and this in turn would cause pressure on the system of cattle production, which, as I have said, is already operating at what even the government experts admit is maximum efficiency. The choice may be between higher incomes for fewer people and potential degradation of the environment, or some kind of compromise based on a more traditional economy and a better distribution of labor. Whatever the solution, I believe it will have to come from the people of southwest Donegal themselves, not from the government. One can only hope that it will be based on as shrewd an assessment of the long-term odds as the previous system has proved to be.

REFERENCES

ALLAND, ALEXANDER, JR.
   1970   "That's the way our grandfathers did it." Mimeographed paper presented at American Anthropological Association Meeting.
An Foras Taluntais
   1967   *West Donegal resource survey report.* Dublin: Foras Taluntais (The Agricultural Institute, Irish Republic).
CROSS, ERIC
   1943   *The tailor and Ansty.* Cork: Mercier Press.
DURKHEIM, EMILE
   1961   *The elementary forms of the religious life.* New York: Collier Books.
EKVALL, ROBERT B.
   1968   *Fields on the hoof.* New York: Holt, Rinehart and Winston.
PARSONS, TALCOTT, EDWARD A. SHILS, editors
   1962   [1951] *Toward a general theory of action.* New York: Harper and Row.
SCHNEIDER, HAROLD K.
   1970   *The Wahi Wanyaturu.* Chicago: Aldine.

Ritual and Religions: An Ethologically Oriented Formal Analysis

ALICE B. KEHOE

Homo sapiens is a mammal. From this premise I derive the postulate that ethological principles ought to be applicable in the analysis of human behavior. Working from an ethological orientation, I present here an etic categorization of religious behaviors emphasizing functional bases for human rituals. A derivable corollary views religions as concatenations of concepts and behaviors, amenable to several analytic perspectives; this study is one.

ETHOLOGICAL THEORY

Generalizations based upon ethological observations have formed the substance of recent symposia and books, such as the popular works of Lorenz, Morris, and Tiger. The methods of ethology have been consciously employed in a few studies of human behavior, notably by Blurton Jones and his colleagues observing young children. Blurton Jones (1972: 4) argues the validity of the position from which he has operated by discussing insights gained using principles

...peculiar to ethology... (1) emphasis on the use of a large variety of simple observable features of behaviour as the raw data; (2) emphasis on description and a hypothesis-generating, natural history phase as the starting point of a study; (3) distrust of major categories of behaviour whose meaning and reality have not been made clear; (4) belief in the usefulness of an evolutionary framework for determining which kinds of questions need to be asked about behaviour.

Applying the evolutionary framework to observations of human rituals yields a multitude of similarities between formalized behavior in *Homo* and in other animals. The propriety of utilizing ethological formulations for analyzing human actions is clear from Julian Huxley's definition of ritual (1966: 250):

Ritualization may be defined ethologically as the adaptive formalization or canalization of emotionally motivated behaviour, under the teleonomic pressure of natural selection so as: (a) to promote better and more unambiguous signal function, both intra- and inter-specifically; (b) to serve as more efficient stimulators or releasers of more efficient patterns of action in other individuals; (c) to reduce intra-specific damage; and (d) to serve as sexual or social bonding mechanisms. Ritualized behaviour-patterns can all be broadly characterized as DISPLAY. They are based on motivated intention-movements, either singly or in combination, frequently with the addition of displacement and redirected activities.

Lorenz adds (1966: 276–277):

The first and probably most important characteristic of ritualization [is that]... a phylogenetically adapted motor pattern which originally served the species in dealing with some environmental necessities... acquires a new function, that of communication.... The second characteristic of ritualized motor patterns is a change of form...all those elements which, even in the unritualized primary movement, produce visual or auditory stimulation, are strongly exaggerated, while those serving the original, mechanical function are greatly reduced or disappear altogether. This "mimic exaggeration" results in a ceremony which is, indeed, closely akin to a symbol and which produces that theatrical effect.... In the interest of great unambiguity of the communication, the speed and amplitude of ritualized movements are strictly regulated, a phenomenon termed "typical intensity" by Desmond Morris.... The same aim is served by frequent, rhythmical repetition which very often is in itself sufficient to recognize a behaviour pattern as ritualized.

Higher mammals display both a greater number of ritualized patterns and subtler shadings of communicated signals than do animals with more primitive brains. *Homo* unequivocally fits into this evolutionary trend. Not only has man been prolific in the invention of rituals, but his

...ritualization resembles that seen in animals in showing the same pair of divergent trends — towards simplification and communication and immediate almost automatic action on the one hand, as in the mechanization of prayer...; and to the complexification, delayed action, long continuances, and bonding function on the other, as in the Mass (Huxley 1966:266).
During vertebrate phylogeny ritualization has tended increasingly towards more efficient bonding, with more elaborate ceremonies, in which individual learning plays an increasing role, notably in the primates (Huxley 1966:257).

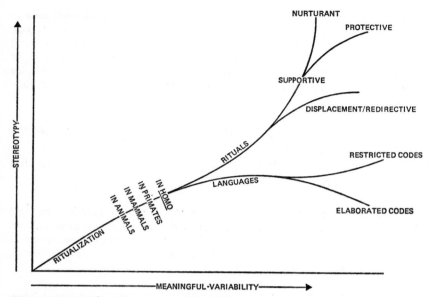

Figure 1.   Evolutionary trend of ritualization culminating in *Homo sapiens* rituals and languages

LANGUAGE AND RITUALS

Figure 1 diagrams the two divergent trends in human ritualization. One direction has led to the thousands of human languages; as Huxley (1966: 258) notes, language itself is "ritualized [adaptively formalized] behaviour." The other direction has led to rituals, in the colloquial sense of the term. The trends represent only a tendency for ritualized human behavior to be dominated by one or the other mode.

Languages place *Homo* at the end of the evolutionary development of formalized communicative actions in which fine calibrations of meaning are conveyed by small shifts in the basic motor pattern. Although species-specific, human languages exhibit tremendous variability in surface structures, enabling them to serve as group identity symbols (as for French Canadians, Bretons, Catalans) as well as the means to coordinate group behavior. The vital role played by languages in bonding human communities is unquestioned.

Within languages, further divergence has appeared in the development of what Basil Bernstein terms "restricted" and "elaborated" codes. Elaborated codes may constitute the presently final product of the vertebrate phylogeny trend noted by Huxley. Bernstein's discussion (1965: 153) claims that elaborated codes required the speaker to select from a relatively extensive range of alternatives.... Meanings will have to be expanded and raised to the level of verbal explicitness.... An elaborated code facilitates the VERBAL construction and exchange of individualized or personal symbols...[and] induces in its speakers a sensitivity to the implications of separateness and difference and points to the possibilities inherent in a complex conceptual hierarchy for the organization of experience (Bernstein 1965:156–157).

In Figure 1, elaborated codes represent language progressing along the vector of meaningful variability.

Stereotypy is the vector along which restricted codes are found. Restricted codes are

...based upon a common, extensive set of closely-shared identifications and expectations.... The speech is here refracted through a common cultural identity which reduces the need to verbalize intent...with the consequence that the structure of the speech is simplified, and the lexicon will be drawn from a narrow range (Bernstein 1965:155).

These restricted codes are not simply the speech of the uneducated. They are used in all social classes as a bonding mechanism that communicates a sense of brotherhood. In contrast, elaborated codes connote a receptivity to hierarchical structures. Hence the inarticulate manner of so many youth today can be interpreted as a ritualized restricted code asserting an egalitarian ideology, the common humanity of all young people in our global village.

Rituals may be a major offshoot of the evolutionary trend leading to elaborated linguistic codes. Even in *Homo* there is a tendency "for ritualized behaviour to evolve in the direction of an ethological reflex, by producing signals which release appropriate action with the minimum of delay" (Huxley 1966: 257). In rituals, more than in the homologous restricted codes, extra verbal or nonverbal communication is a dominant component. It is possible that, as Reynolds (1968) and Holloway (1966) imply, the phylogenetically older nonverbal communicative mode may involve the brain's limbic system, which is more primitive than the brain areas concerned in human verbal language, and through this more readily induce emotional responses. Kinetic rituals are analogous to phylogenetically ancient animal ritualizations and, for this reason alone, may be more suitable for the evocation of reflex-type reactions. Natural selection may have guided rituals, especially those of a "social charter" nature, along the stereotypy vector to implant more powerfully the values that articulate societies.

Two principal classes may be distinguished within the category "ritual." SUPPORTIVE[1] RITUALS reduce anxiety by communicating the acceptance and integration of an individual into a group with whose values he wishes to identify. DISPLACEMENT/REDIRECTIVE RITUALS function primarily to reduce physiological tension in the group as a whole, although their secondary effect is to bond the participants by explicating their common goals. It is important to realize that both classes of ritual are likely to produce and manage measurable biochemical changes in the persons taking part (cf. discussion in Chapple 1970, especially 316–317). Rituals do more than communicate: they MOVE. Their motive force is often recognized, as in the phrase *rites de passage*. Etymology illuminates the domain of experience canalized by ritual: emotions. The physiological and limbic system aspects of ritual demand an ethological explanation.

Discussing the ontogeny of emotional behavior, Candland (1971: 128) states:

Emotion, especially that of the "coarser" [to use James's descriptive phrase], fixed kind, is mainly an unlearned response, unlearned in the sense that irritability to stimulation may be considered unlearned. Emotions, especially those of the finer kind, develop by reinforced discrimination and generalization from the original diffuse irritability. Response patterns that are adaptive are reinforced and persist; those which are nonadaptive are extinguished.... Emotion is both general [reflecting changes in physiological functioning] and specific.

From this foundation stem both the universality of ritual in human societies and the variety of ritualized behaviors. Ritual in *Homo* is a mode of interaction phylogenetically more primitive than human languages, reinforced experientially rather than intellectually.

Supportive Rituals

Supportive rituals generally focus upon an individual, or a group of individuals, suffering anxiety, whatever its stimulus: grief, loneliness, illness, frustration, or conflict. Because anxiety can be literally crippling, producing psychosomatic complaints or conversion hysteria, natural selection would favor rituals that restore the anxious to full personal and social capability. For the sufferer, the supportive ritual soothes, stimulating hormonal changes toward normal homeostasis. The ritual also communicates behavioral guidelines that act as an obstacle to the future arousal of anxiety by obviating crises of decision. The tendency to enhance communication by formalization of behavior canalizes therapeutic actions

[1] The term "supportive ritual" is based upon the concept "supportive behavior" developed by Raphael (1971).

into supportive rituals, which can be recognized by their stress upon the sanatory power of their codes.

Parental behaviors seem to form the underlying models for supportive rituals. Thus, the ritual may be nurturant (maternal model) or protective (paternal model). Nurturant rituals range from the almost totally ritualized and regulated life of cloistered religious orders to the short occasional secular rituals allaying a specific conscious anxiety — for example, the four evening meetings in which La Leche League members imbue new mothers with the confidence integral to successful breastfeeding. Protective rituals similarly range widely, from the mesmeric powers exercised by life-demanding charismatic prophets to the very mild leadership perfunctorily displayed by a meeting chairman insisting upon Roberts' *Rules of order*. Nurturant rituals communicate the cooperative support of an undifferentiated group coordinated by one who is only *primus inter pares*, while protective rituals emphasize the derivation of support from a hierarchical structure.

Comparison of nurturant and protective rituals suggests a relationship similar to that between restricted and elaborated codes in language. The nurturant ritual tends to be relatively egalitarian and emotional. The protective ritual tends to be hierarchical and more intellectual; whether one looks at The Handsome Lake's Good Message, or Mahatma Gandhi's Satyagraha doctrine, one sees a graded, conceptually complex code. The two poles of supportive ritual (for, of course, the two varieties are not mutually exclusive) may exemplify a tendency in human ritualization toward divergence into restricted and elaborated codes.

Displacement/Redirective Rituals

Displacement/redirective rituals incorporate behavior that seems irrelevant to the stated or apparent purpose of the rite. Unlike supportive rituals, these stress the efficacy of the ritual act rather than a code. Actions such as dancing, drumming, shaking rattles, elaborate posturing, and repetitive movements cannot bring rain, or fertility, or herds of game, or the removal of evil. This category of ritual is closely analogous to displacement and redirective activities performed by animals, for which a standard ethological explanation is as follows:

In many interactions between individuals there is simultaneous arousal of tendencies both to advance and to hold back or withdraw, so that there is some sort of conflict within the central nervous system between the mechanisms governing the various possible courses of action. A conflict situation may also arise if there is but a single motivation, but its expression is in some manner frustrated [this may be the more common human situation]; maybe by the inaccessibility of the objective. In such circumstances animals commonly do one of two things. They may make as though to act and then stop; in fact, they may thus make alternating intention movements towards the various courses of action which might be appropriate to the situation. But they may...suddenly perform some action whose normal context is quite foreign to the situation — a displacement activity.... These two types of behavior — intention movements and displacement behavior — so commonly seen in conflict situations — provide an ample source of raw material upon which selection can then operate and from which a more complex ritualized signal may be evolved (Ewer 1968:26–27).

On a more sophisticated level, Eibl-Eibesfeldt argues (1970: 179–180):

Two drives, each independently inhibiting a third one, mutually inhibit each other in a conflict situation, [and] lose their inhibiting capacity on the third, which is then free to be discharged.... In principle all displacement activities can be explained by the disinhibition hypothesis. Tinbergen's overflow hypothesis [that "an energy surplus that cannot be discharged into its normal channel will then flow over into another channel and discharge itself into an irrelevant activity"] as a basis for displacement activities has not been proved or disproved to date.... When a releasing stimulus simultaneously activates and inhibits a behavior pattern, the result need not always be a conflict movement.... An animal that is attacked or threatened by a higher-ranking one does not necessarily challenge the dominant animal but redirects his aggression against a still lower-ranking one...REDIRECTION ACTIVITIES.

Of particular interest are the redirection activities in which animals vent their excitement upon an inanimate object, as when herring gulls disputing a territory pull grass with their beaks rather than attack each other. The canons of ethology prohibit labeling the grass a symbol of the enemy, but the anthropologist can observe the parallel to human sorcerers torturing a hair filched from an enemy.

Displacement/redirective rituals, like supportive rituals, have a tangible physical component of physiological change. Unlike supportive rituals, the displacement/redirective type itself induces the rise in tension, the reduction of which produces the participants' feeling of well-being at the rite's close. Rhythm is frequently effectively employed toward heightening the tension in a ritual, a quickening rhythm simulating the quickened heartbeat and breathing of excitation. Many rituals strengthen the effect of rhythm by placing the participants in relative sensory deprivation, either by simple deprivation, such as a darkened arena, or by bombarding one sense to the exclusion of normal perceptions. Sensory deprivation may lead to dissociated states, perhaps the ultimate in tension. The rituals thus build upon biological processes to achieve the effect of a crisis reached and resolved. Natural selection may have perpetuated these rituals when the feeling of participants, that together they had achieved something good, functioned as a social bonding mechanism.

RITUAL AND RELIGIONS

The source of both supportive and displacement/redirective rituals would be chance actions, as chance mutation is a source of morphological traits in animals. As with mutations, only a few actions prove adaptive, but these would be reinforced and persist. The ritual acts themselves may be irrational or highly esoteric, but if the action proves effective in reducing anxiety, managing conflict, or promoting social bonding, the ritual must be considered adaptive. There is a feedback element, in that each successful reenactment of the rite reinforces its efficacy in the eyes of its audience: they learn to respond to it. Maturana's elegant description of the nature of organisms applies equally to societies:

Living systems are units of interactions...organized in a closed causal circular process that allows for evolutionary changes in the way the circularity is maintained.... Each internal state requires that certain conditions [interactions with the environment] be satisfied to proceed to the next one.... If this does not happen, the system disintegrates; if the predicted interaction takes place, the system maintains its identity [integrity].... For every living system, its niche is represented in its organization as the domain of its possible interactions, and this domain constitutes its entire cognitive reality (Maturana 1970:5-6).

Most human beings predicate reality to be ordered in a cosmos, the conceptualization of a domain of possible interactions. The cosmos may be endowed with transcendent being or force; such a cosmology is usually labeled a religion. Religions seem to be, like languages, a class of phenomena uniquely developed in *Homo sapiens*. Frequently, rituals are associated with religions, but ritualization *per se* can be a basic animal response in *Homo*, with no necessary connection to any beliefs. The communicative effectiveness of formalized behavior leads to rituals, religious or secular, to be distinguished on the basis of semantic and contextual features. When concepts of transcendence are invoked, we consider a ritual to be religious; when only mundane business is conducted via the ritual, we consider it secular. The deliberative repetitive movements and strict adherence to prescribed order in the Mass are religious because they pertain to symbols of God and spirit; the same characteristics in a meeting run according to parliamentary procedure are secular because beliefs in transcendence are excluded from the communications of the meeting. There is no formal difference between religious and secular rituals.

The Ghost Dance religion (Mooney 1896; Kehoe 1964, 1968) can be analyzed to illustrate some of the formulations advanced here. The religion arose as an adjustment movement (Berndt 1962: 25) conceived by a Paiute Indian, Jack Wilson or Wovoka, in 1889. Wovoka believed himself to have been given a code to preach to his fellow Indians. He developed what I would term a protective supportive ritual, with nurturant overtones, religious because it was claimed to have come from a transcendent God. The rite, a circle dance in which participants clasped hands (the nurturant aspect), was based upon traditional Paiute rituals, indicating the form had adaptive value. Displacement activity appeared in the movement and singing of the dance, sometimes culminating in trances. Eventually the celebrants became physically tired and ended the dance with a feast, inducing a feeling of well-being. The dominant protective style of the rite came through the words of the songs and the short sermons punctuating the dancing, describing the intended beneficence of God the Father. Wovoka's code resolved the crisis of indecision besetting the Plains Indians at this initial reservation period, for he stated plainly: "Do not refuse to work for white man or do not make any trouble with them until you leave them" (Mooney 1896 [1965: 23]).

Half a century after Wovoka's visions, the Ghost Dance religion survived among some older Sioux Indians. By 1962, the middle-aged and elderly Dakota Ghost Dance believers in Saskatchewan, Canada, had come to stress the supportive aspects of the ritual; the displacement activities were felt to be too strenuous for the aged worshipers. These Indians were satisfied to celebrate only a "prayer meeting" in which a circle of seated believers employed the redirected activities of inhaling a sweetgrass smudge and smoking a holy pipe, then ritually communicated their common values and aspirations in prayer and exhortations. The ceremony ended with a feast. Wovoka's dream of a return to the traditional Indian hunting life never materialized, but the Dakota community remained bonded by the ritual and was able to reduce tensions from anxiety (quite realistically grounded) to tolerable levels. In the pioneer settlement milieu in which it arose, the Ghost Dance religion was adaptive.

The Ghost Dance religion is nearly extinct because its code does not address itself to the problems of Indians today. Whereas in 1889 the prime anxiety of thousands of Plains Indians centered on the threat to their personal cultural identity posed by the end of the nomadic hunting pattern, the anxiety today centers on the perception that as Indians they are relegated to a lower-class ghetto-bound status. Wovoka's promise of reunion with the traditional past in an afterlife is no answer to today's anxieties. The ritual forms and their functions remain, however, in numerous ceremonies, such as the give-away which now bonds many Indian communities. These phylogenetically ancient mechanisms of formalized behavior persist, changing semantic content and behavioral details. Ethology predicts that rituals will last as long as the race.

REFERENCES

BERNDT, R. M.
 1962   An adjustment movement in Arnhem Land. *Cahiers de l'Homme* 2:1–112.
BERNSTEIN, B.
 1965   "A socio-linguistic approach to social learning," in *Penguin survey of the social sciences 1965.* Edited by J. Gould, 144–168. Baltimore: Penguin.
BLURTON JONES, N.
 1972   "Characteristics of ethological studies of human behaviour," in *Ethological studies of child behaviour.* Edited by N. Blurton Jones, 3–33. Cambridge: Cambridge University Press.
CANDLAND, D. K.
 1971   "The ontogeny of emotional behavior," in *The ontogeny of vertebrate behavior.* Edited by H. Moltz, 95–169. New York: Academic Press.
CHAPPLE, E.
 1970   *Culture and biological man.* New York: Holt, Rinehart and Winston.
EIBL-EIBESFELDT, I.
 1970   *Ethology: the biology of behavior.* New York: Holt, Rinehart and Winston.
EWER, R. F.
 1968   *Ethology of mammals.* New York: Plenum Press.
HOLLOWAY, R. L., JR.
 1966   Cranial capacity, neural reorganization, and hominid evolution: a search for more suitable parameters. *American Anthropologist* 68: 103–121.
HUXLEY, J.
 1966   "A discussion on ritualization of behaviour in animals and man," in *Philosophical transactions of the Royal Society of London,* series B. Edited by J. Huxley, 251:249–271.
KEHOE, A. B.
 1964   "The Ghost Dance religion in Saskatchewan: a functional analysis." Unpublished doctoral dissertation, Harvard University.
 1968   The Ghost Dance religion in Saskatchewan, Canada. *Plains Anthropologist* 13:296–304.
LORENZ, K.
 1966   "Evolution of ritualization in the biological and cultural spheres," in *Philosophical transactions of the Royal Society of London,* series B. Edited by J. Huxley, 251:273–284.

MATURANA, H.
1970 "Neurophysiology of cognition," in *Cognition: a multiple view.* Edited by P. Garvin, 3–23. New York: Spartan Books.
MOONEY, J.
1896 *The Ghost-Dance religion and the Sioux outbreak of 1890* (reprinted 1965). Chicago: University of Chicago Press.
RAPHAEL, D.
1971 "Symposium on supportive behavior," in *Abstract of the 70th Annual Meeting, American Anthropological Association.* Washington: American Anthropological Association.
REYNOLDS, P. C.
1968 Evolution of primate vocal-auditory communication systems. *American Anthropologist* 70:300–308.

The World/Nonworld Dichotomy

JACQUES MAQUET

In different religious literatures, as distant in time and space as the *Vinaya Piṭaka* (in the Buddhist Pāli Canon, probably committed to writing in the first century B.C. but representing a much earlier tradition), John Cassian's *Institutes* and *Conferences* recording in the fifth century A.D. the sayings of the anchorites living in Egypt's deserts, Benedict's *Rule* (sixth century A.D.), the talks of the thirteenth century Japanese Zen Master Dōgen recorded and compiled in *Shōbōgenzō Zuimonki,* and Peter Rideman's *Account* of the Hutterite doctrine (sixteenth century), a central theme recurs insistently: there is a radical opposition between the way of life advocated in these writings and the world (see Chadwick 1958, 1968; Masunaga 1971; Rideman 1950). In other spiritual texts concerned with asceticism and mysticism, disciples are urged to leave the world; and if they cannot help living in it, they are told to avoid, at least, "being of the world."

The term "world" is commonly used with the above denotation in texts originally written in English; when it translates a term from another language, the consensus of so many translators, widely distributed across centuries and continents, seems to warrant the existence of equivalent terms in the original writings.

The duality world/nonworld is an overt verbal dichotomy; it expresses two cross-culturally meaningful categories. Not many highly abstract categories have the distinction of being used with the same fundamental sense in several literate and independent traditions encompassing a time-depth of about twenty centuries.

The behaviors to which the opposite words refer are also clearly and explicitly contrasted. Those who leave the world become hermits (from the Greek *erēmia* [desert]), monks (from the Greek *monos* [alone]), anchorites (from the Greek *anakhōrein* [to withdraw]), or cenobites (from the Greek *koinos* [common] and *bios* [life]). They go to the forest or the desert, or they wander homelessly, as "lonely as the rhinoceros." They live in austerity and in celibacy. Their communal practices include discipline, silence, meditation, or prayer. Their lifestyles are in obvious contrast with those of the majority population in any society. The dichotomy is not only conceptual, it is behavioral and institutional.

1.   On the basis of the evidence provided by the texts and the patterned behaviors, it seems possible to delineate a minimal semantic content of the two categories, which has a cross-cultural validity.

The world from which one withdraws is, first of all, one's family. The different eremitic and monastic traditions make it clear that hermits and monks have to break up their previously existing family ties (with father and mother, brothers and sisters, and sometimes with wife and children — as in the exemplary case of Gautama), and they have to refrain from initiating new involvements such as marriage. Celibacy is usually seen as a consequence of the renunciation of the pleasure of sex; however it is primarily the rejection of family responsibilities.

The world is also made of economic involvements. The Pāli word *bhikkhu*, generally translated as "monk" means literally "beggar." The wanderer-mendicant, characteristic of early Buddhism as well as of Jainism and the Hindu tradition (where it appears in the fourth *āshram* of life following the stages of celibate student, householder, and hermit), represents the maximal disengagement from the processes of production and exchange of commodities. The same may be said of the Christian anchorites of Egypt. Even when Buddhist and Christian monasteries became wealthy landowners, the economic noninvolvement of the monks was supposed to be preserved. The aim of the noninvolvement is certainly to destroy the striving for wealth, but it serves also to eliminate the care and worry of possessing even a modest property.

The world also stands for the ties of power and pressure embodied in government, stratification, and social dependence. To leave the world is to withdraw from these institutions. Monks should be neither rulers nor subjects. Indeed they usually claim the right to be exempted from the subjects' obligations, such as paying taxes and tributes, or being drafted into the army.

The social inequality of castes and classes is another component of the mental construct "world." Those who leave it are no longer nobles or commoners, members of the privileged minority or of the crowd, *kshatriyas* or *vaishyas*. Even in traditional India, land of the *Homo hierarchicus,* monks, hermits, and wanderers were supposed to be beyond the pale of the caste system.

Feudal and clientage dependencies, where they exist, are also worldly institutions. In the European Middle Ages, the individual monk was neither lord, nor vassal, regardless of his feudal status before entering the monastery.

In the literature and practice of some of the great spiritual traditions, world thus refers to the main social networks along which life in society is organized. It refers also to a set of values. To anthropologists particularly sensitized to cultural variation, it may be surprising to discover that the worldly values are, in fact, the same under different cultural garbs: pleasure and wealth, prestige and power. The reason for the generality, if not the universality of the worldly values lies in their necessary association with the basic societal networks. Worldly values are the expected rewards for the proper fulfillment of the societal roles defined by kinship, exchange, government, and other networks. For those who do not value prestige and power, there is little stimulation in the political competition.

The pursuit of worldly values is a necessary assumption of the social order. As long as a man has a family and a lucrative occupation, he cannot be detached from worldly values, even "in spirit." And when somebody has broken up his social involvements, it would be absurd to seek worldly values. He has deprived himself of the usual means of obtaining such values and he would suffer from an internal inconsistency.

This fact clarifies somewhat the debate on whether one can "be in the world, but not of the world," that is, perform worldly roles while being detached from worldly values. It is a feat unlikely to occur frequently. One can hardly imagine what nonworldly values could motivate somebody to be active in mundane matters.

2. This sketchy approximation of a minimal content of "world" as a conceptual construct common to several civilizations suggests a textual and historical investigation of that question to be worthwhile. Can we reach similar conclusions about the other concept of the dichotomy, "nonworld"?

It should be noted first that whereas the term "world" — and its equivalents in other languages — appears in the religious and spiritual literatures, the term "nonworld" does not. Such words as desert, forest, monastery, cloister, hermitage, and community are used. Besides denoting the new physical locations of those who have left the world, they connote figuratively the antithesis of the world.

This antithesis is not simply negative: not to have social involvements, not to pursue some values. It is positive: individual freedom.

Social roles curtail individual freedom. The repressive character of the state has been recognized for a long time and coercion is indeed the characteristic political sanction. As for the productive and economic systems, the restrictions they impose upon individual activities are immense. Work is the result of a divine curse, according to the Bible. Earning one's living, either by direct productive activity or by providing services, is the major occupation of nearly everybody "in the world." The amount of time devoted to work is considerable and does not permit one to pursue many other activities.

Family and marriage are not usually viewed as oppressive institutions. Yet the constraints they generate are probably the most pervasive and the least escapable. The role demands of wife or husband, mother or father — to mention the most onerous — conflict continually with an individual's independence. Everyday interaction is, by itself, a constantly alienating experience.

Nonworld is liberation from societal constraints. It is also liberation from the pursuit of worldly values. It is not a search for the logical antitheses of the latter: weakness for power, poverty for wealth, meekness for prestige, and deprivation for pleasure. These antitheses are worldly also. In fact they can be seen as the failure to achieve the goals and rewards of social life. Certain formulations suggest that inverted values should be sought for themselves; the vow of poverty, obedience, and chastity is one of these ambiguous formulations. But the Christian practice shows clearly that monks do not join the ranks of the underprivileged in their societies: paupers, unemployed, and others who are weak, humiliated, and deprived. In contemporary Burma, a peasant who becomes a monk usually sees his material life improved — he eats better and does not work — and his status changed — the respect shown to him "amounts to veneration" (Spiro 1970: 396). Paradoxical as these situations are, they do not reveal any inner inconsistency. The worldly pursuits, whether successful or not, are outside the scope of the fundamental nonworldly value: individual freedom.

3. Freedom for what? It could be for itself, but it is not. The need for freedom certainly motivates some persons who withdraw from ordinary social life, but it is not the ultimate value of the eremitic or monastic institutions. Individual liberation is a means necessary to reach the final goal. This goal is also the reason why one leaves the world.

In the historic nonworldly traditions, the ultimate value is expressed in religious or philosophic terms congruent with the dominant ideational system. In the Christian tradition there is the personal vocation to follow Christ. In the year 271, "Antony, son of well-to-do Egyptian peasants, heard the words of Jesus read by a priest: 'If you would be perfect, go, sell what you possess and give to the poor. . . .; and come, follow me' " (Knowles 1969: 10). This story of the event that started desert anchoritism is also the paradigm for all Christian departures from the world: one enters the secluded life in fidelity to one's personal vocation. God calls me to the estate of perfection; I shall comply.

In the Buddhist tradition, the paradigmatic story is that of Buddha himself. Gautama, having realized the transitory nature of life that entails sickness, age, and death, leaves the world, is enlightened, and so escapes the wheel of endlessly recurring lives.

In the mystic traditions, the ultimate goal is a unitive state of consciousness in which the self becomes one with a personal deity or with the whole being. To express the ultimate meaning of a nonworldly life one can also atone for one's and mankind's sins, and thereby obtain salvation for oneself and others; or accumulate merit, and thus influence spiritually the destiny of a few, or many, persons; or honor and glorify God by the ritual *opus Dei* of chanting and praying.

Under these different expressions of the ultimate goal of the nonworldly life lies a common core. The "charters" of the orders and communities, their internal organization, and their practices disclose more similarities than are to be found in their ideational systems. The practices best reveal the basic goal of those who leave the world: to achieve inner self-realization. The wording is contemporary, yet it seems to describe adequately what we know of these phenomena of the distant past as well as of today.

Realization denotes the actualization of potentiality. It implies that there should be change and progress; it excludes immobility and stability. The metaphors include "the way," "the ascent," "the growth," "the quest," "going to the other shore." The potentialities referred to do not come into existence easily: sustained and strenuous effort is required. Silence, solitude, and quiet are not associated with rest and relaxation. On the contrary, they set the scene for struggle, tension, anguish, and doubt. Something difficult is to be achieved, and it requires total commitment.

"Self" indicates what is to be realized and changed. It is not the natural environment, or the society, or the techniques of production. The main thrust of the effort is toward changing the self. We understand this term in the usual and precritical meaning of our everyday speech. When we say "I," we refer to the empirical ego, and particularly that "deeper" part of it, the "real" self. In ordinary language, the real self is viewed as more "genuine" than physical appearance or social roles. Even if the self is philosophically deemed to be an illusion, as in Buddhism, and if an essential part of self-realization is to reject the idea of the permanent self, it may be maintained that the nonworldly Buddhists attempt to change what is referred to as "me" in any language.

"Inner" indicates how self-realization is pursued: directly, not through the mediation of aesthetic creation, charitable action, teaching, leadership, or any other activity expressive of the self. Realization is sought in direct relation to the self.

The traditional Christian distinction between active and contemplative life is pertinent to our discussion. Historically it concerns two categories of religious societies, the active and the contemplative. The members of either order are called religious (as opposed to secular): they have taken the vows of poverty, obedience, and chastity. They are all concerned with the "kingdom of God," but they differ in the means they use for promoting it. The active communities run schools and hospitals, preach and proselytize, publish books and perform sacerdotal duties; the contemplative orders organize a secluded life of individual and collective prayer. In Catholic theology, the adjudication of the respective values of "good works" versus prayer is founded on the story of Martha and Mary, concluded by Jesus' saying that "Mary has chosen the good portion, which shall not be taken away from her" (Luke X: 42). On that basis, the superiority of contemplative life — represented by Mary — is asserted. We are not concerned here with assessing the comparative value of action and contemplation. The Martha and Mary episode clarifies what is meant by INNER self-realization: it is definitely on the contemplative side.

4.   The world/nonworld dichotomy, commonly used in different textual and behavioral traditions, has been analyzed here as a pair of constructs, similar to Weber's ideal types. In the Weberian sense, the latter are unified analytical constructs based on concrete individual phenomena seen from a specific point of view. That is to say, they are presented more systematically and in greater unity than in the empirical data (Shils and Finch 1949: 90). These accentuated abstractions are useful tools: actual phenomena may be categorized by reference to the constructs; cross-cultural similarities are revealed by them. But they should not be confused with facts. They are ways to get at the facts.

To sum up: the world is societal organization and its values; the non-world is individual freedom from the oppressive social networks, seen as the necessary condition for inner self-realization.

5. The world/nonworld dichotomy belongs to the discourse of religion and spirituality. The concept "world," as it has been constructed here, is very close to the anthropological notion of "a culture." A culture, (as distinct from "the culture," a more abstract use of the same concept) has been the privileged unit of anthropological study since the functionalist heyday. Always associated with a particular society identifiable as such by its members, a culture is made of interrelated societal networks, of congruent ideational configurations, and of a technico-environmental system of production. In nonliterate tribes and traditional kingdoms, anthropologists have viewed cultures as entire, and usually well-integrated "blueprints for living," covering the whole gamut of what is necessary for the individual life from birth to death, and for the group survival across succeeding generations. In order to stress that all-encompassing character of a culture, it has been said to be global or total.

As we have seen, the world consists of the matrimonial, familial, economic, and political institutions, and their associate ideational sets of values. A total culture is a particular societal order (e.g. monogamous, capitalist, and republican) and its associate values (e.g. matrimonial fidelity, free enterprise, and democracy). A total culture is the world as it exists at a certain time and a certain place. This partial identity of "the world" and "a culture" suggests that the world/nonworld duality can be related to the conceptual toolkit of anthropologists. The latter should include not only our traditional terms — such as the time-honored CULTURE and SOCIETY — but also terms derived from them to analyze the dissent phenomena of the sixties, such as counterculture, mainstream, alternative, utopia, and intentional community.

The concept of culture remains the most original and significant contribution of anthropology to the knowledge of man as pursued by the social sciences. Furthermore, as Kroeber and Kluckhohn pointed out in the early fifties: "the idea of culture, in the technical anthropological sense, is one of the key notions of contemporary American thought" (Kroeber and Kluckhohn 1952: 3).

Counterculture does not yet belong to the anthropological vocabulary. It emerged in the North American intelligentsia of the late sixties, in the same milieu that had adopted culture in its anthropological meaning, a few decades earlier. Counterculture has been used repeatedly in the comments of the media on student unrest, the hippie communes, and the psychedelic scene. Anthropology should claim the offspring of its focal concept.

Counterculture, if it has to have an operational value in anthropological analysis, is not to be used as a synonym for any marginal or nonconformist lifestyle that may be found in large-scale urban societies. The artistic and literary bohemias of Paris, London, and New York are subcultures: behavioral patterns different from those of the majority but restricted to certain domains (such as avant-garde aesthetic tastes, unconventional clothing, and an allegedly more candid sex life), and particular to an occupational subgroup among the inhabitants of Paris, London, or New York. Bohemians are doing certain things in their own way, but so are clergymen, truck drivers, and college professors. The bohemian subcultures, like the others, are restricted to certain activities and do not encompass a total way of life. They are variations on the common cultural themes, not alternatives to them.

Countercultures are more ambitious. They are, or tend to be, as complete as the collective heritages of the mainstream societies. They are not only alternative world views and value systems; they are also alternative ways to organize interpersonal relationships, and alternative ecological adaptations of man to his natural environment. The "blueprint for living" is complete, and its realization is attempted in a real society, a community.

This point is crucial. As long as an alternative lifeway remains in books and talk — and even in a few expressive details such as long hair and no-bra, sandals and beads — it is not counterculture. This construct, to be anthropologically useful, has to denote a total way of life practiced by a group of people. The terms "intentional community" and "utopian community" have been used for designating such groups.[1] They are most appropriate, but not synonymous as they connote two different types of communities.

Since Ferdinand Tönnies' famous opposition between *Gemeinschaft* and *Gesellschaft*, "community" belongs to the specialized vocabulary of sociology. The communes and similar groups of the present retain an important characteristic of Tönnies' *Gemeinschaft:* the face-to-face relationship of the members based on friendship or neighborhood. In that sense, they are communities. But neither of the two qualifications, intentional or utopian, fits the Tönnies community (Tönnies 1957).

Intentionality refers to the way one becomes a member: by an individ-

[1] The terms "intentional community" and "utopian community" are currently used in the abundant literature on the subject. See extended bibliographies in Zablocki (1971: 335–339); Fairfield (1972: 386–389); Kanter (1972: 270–286).

ual voluntary decision to join, rather than by birth. This has important consequences: intentionality stresses the adult individual's commitment, and excludes the possible negative reaction of children born into the community (as exemplified by the first generation born in the Oneida Community in nineteenth-century New England, and by the *sabras* in Israeli *kibbutzim*. Stressing the voluntary decision suggests that the individual development of the member remains a focal concern, whereas collective continuity seems more important in societies where membership is mainly by birth. Intentionality makes a community very close to an association, the "voluntary fraternity [gathering] together those who pursue in common certain limited objectives" (Maquet 1971: 220). But it differs in that it offers its members a complete alternative way of life instead of the pursuit of specific targets.

A utopian community is a workable model of a total society. The model could — and should, in the view of its members — be realized for the whole society. Utopian, in this sense, does not imply that the project is impractical. As the utopian community claims the ability to replace the mainstream society with a model that would better fulfill society's functions, it has to include in its program patterns of procreation, enculturation, and education. If the community survives, its membership will be eventually based mainly on birth.

Today's alternative communities are either intentional or utopian. The two qualities are not logically exclusive, of course, but they do not fit well together. Intentional communities want to provide a complete alternative for those adults who have similar views on what life should be, and who attempt to realize their views. Their interests, tastes, and perspectives may be shared by only a few individuals — for example to follow the Sufi way in contemporary America, or to live communally as independent women or as former drug addicts. Utopian communities want to be functioning models of another social order designed for everybody.

Is it a realistic ambition? On the production level, building a completely self-sufficient community on a technical and economic base outside of the larger society is probably impossible in an industrially advanced age. Yet it is the ideal goal of most contemporary utopian communities.

On the societal level, they suceed better in creating other networks of interaction between their members, and in defining new roles. In the sixties, some communities have realized, or at least experimented with, new models of societal organization in marriage (e.g. multilateral marriage instead of monogamy) and family (e.g. extension of the educational responsibilities beyond the parents to several adults) as well as in decision-making processes, labor-remuneration systems, and patterns of sharing goods and services.

On the ideational level, countercultures are particularly rich and articulate. Their philosophical views, basic values, conceptions of "the good life," and ethical concerns are overtly and clearly expressed.

Countercultures embodied in intentional or utopian communities are alternatives to the mainstream and challenges to it. Advocates as well as adversaries of the countercultures perceive of them as so radically different from the mainstream as to be incompatible. To live in the mainstream and to adopt positions of the counterculture is judged intellectually and experienced existentially as contradictory.

From this brief survey of some anthropologically oriented concepts used in regard to the dissent manifestations of the sixties, a new dichotomy emerges: mainstream/alternative.

5.   Starting from a preresearch overview of two extremely distant sets of phenomena — eremitism and monasticism and their textual expression, the recent American countercultures and the sociological and parasociological literature about them — two dichotomies have been formulated: world/nonworld (W/NW) and mainstream/alternative (MS /ALT). It is obvious that they are not unrelated. Let us attempt to clarify their relationships, and see what the latter reveal.

The terms of the dichotomies have been used indifferently thus far as nouns (world, cultural mainstream, social alternative) and as adjectives (worldly society, mainstream culture, alternative society, nonworldly community). In either case, they are signifiers referring to the same category: sociocultural units (such as a society, a culture, a community, a monastery). In the following comparisons, this convention is observed (for example, "world" means "a worldly sociocultural unit"). The context will clarify what type of unit is referred to (total society, community, etc.).

In each dichotomy, the relationship between the terms is one of incompatibility between a larger unit (W, MS) and a smaller (NW, ALT). The smaller unit is materially a part of the larger, but asserts itself as opposed. The opposition is at the ideational and societal levels. The two oppositions are isomorphic:

$$W : NW : : MS : ALT$$

There is a partial identity of the concept "mainstream" and "world." MS's intention connotes more attributes than W's intention. Consequently W's extension denotes more objects (here: sociocultural units) than MS's extension:

MS $\rightarrow$ W and W $\leftrightarrow$ MS

Any mainstream unit is worldly, but worldly units are not restricted to the mainstream. These other worldly units are the alternative units, as opposed to the mainstream units in the dichotomy MS/ALT. Thus:

W $\rightarrow$ MS $\vee$ ALT.

If a unit is worldly, it is either mainstream or alternative. We know that "if MS, then W": a mainstream unit is necessarily worldly. What about the alternatives? The utopian alternatives are worldly. They offer another social order which provides for the collective survival of the community and of the larger society. Some intentional alternatives (intentional communities are those which offer another complete lifestyle but are not self-perpetuating) are certainly worldly (a commune of artists, for example) whereas others seem to be nonworldly (a monastery, for example). Thus:

ALT $\rightarrow$ W $\vee$ NW

This is perfectly consistent with the convention stated above, that the terms of the two dichotomies refer exclusively to sociocultural units. Yet it should be understood that three of these terms (MS, ALT, and W) refer directly and properly to such units, whereas the fourth one (NW) has for a direct and appropriate referent the human individual. Nonworld provides the freedom necessary for those who pursue inner self-realization; as an attribute, it is to be ascribed primarily to an individual. If it is predicated of a community, the meaning is the following: the community gathers nonworldly individuals, or is organized to facilitate the quest for individual growth. In that sense it has been stated: "If a unit is alternative, then it is either worldly or nonworldly."

As mainstream is necessarily worldly, it cannot be nonworldly, and a nonworldly unit is necessarily an alternative:

NW $\rightarrow$ ALT

6.   The type of formulation used in the preceding section indicates with some precision the relationships between the two dichotomies. They are not only isomorphic; they are interconnected so as to constitute a single system of conceptual constructs. The social phenomena from which they have been induced are widely distributed in time and space. This broad basis warrants their cross-cultural validity.

For the contemporaries of Gautama, the social order was that of the kingdoms of northern India in the sixth century B.C.; for the Alexandria Christians of the fourth century A.D., it was the urban culture of the late Roman Empire; for the disciples of Dōgen, it was the social structure and the way of life of the Kamakura period; for us, it is the industrially advanced society of urban America. Each of these total cultures is different from the others, but for those who were, or are, living in the corresponding societies, they were, or are, the world or the mainstream. It is mainstream because, for each generation, institutions and norms of conduct are there as a given whole that cannot be easily changed, and because the majority of individuals in each generation are willing to conform their lives to the patterned expectations of their collective heritage. It may be that they are well adapted to the particular social order of their time and place, or that they cannot imagine another one, or that they repress any idea of change as dangerous, or that they are resigned to an unsatisfactory life.

There is also a frustrated minority of people who do not want to take the social order for granted. The activist option — to work to change "the system" directly through reform or revolution — may seem the most rational course of action, but is chosen rarely, and succeeds still more rarely in changing society within the lifespan of a generation. Rather than confronting the social order supported by the establishment's power, the unsatisfied men, in the few historical instances mentioned above, and in many others, prefer to set up alternative communities in which they can escape "here and now" the alienations of the world.

Ambitious utopians, besides building the framework of a better life for themselves, hope that their New Jerusalems will become the social order of the mainstream for the following generations.

Other alternative communities, the intentional ones, are refuges where like-minded persons pursue their chosen values in an environment facilitating their quest. Their values were, and are, the attainment of enlightenment and wisdom, or the eternal life for one's individual soul, or the return to the fundamental oneness, or the warmth of brotherly love away from the loneliness of the anonymous cities, or a pace of life gentler than the mainstream competition, or a sexual and emotional development fuller than what the matrimonial institution permits, or any other value not favored by the mainstream. In the historical instances mentioned in this paper, intentional communities were in most cases monasteries providing the secluded freedom of the cloister for those seeking inner self-realization.

Alternative communities — utopian or intentional, worldly or nonworldly — may be considered embodiments of a general societal type that is neither particular to a single tradition, nor universal (it does not seem to have been reported in nonliterate societies). Anthropological research's focus on the mainstream — under the name of "a culture" —

has led us to overlook this important category of social phenomena.

For some individuals, the pursuit of one's inner self-realization requires a still more complete freedom from the social constraints than the monastic one. They want to be liberated from any societal organization: from the alternative community as well as from the mainstram social order. They go beyond the borders of the social life into the asocial condition of the hermit or the wanderer. The solitude of the homeless man reaches the ultimate in individual freedom and in nonworldliness.

It is difficult to assess how frequently the eremitic solution has been adopted, since its discreet nature does not make it very visible. But it happens that the solitary life is chosen by an appreciable number of nonworldly individuals at certain times and in certain traditions. According to the *Lives of the fathers*, the deserts of Thebes and Mount Sinai were blossoming with hermits in the fourth and fifth centuries A.D. In India, the spiritual wanderers have been many and very noticeable for more than twenty-five centuries. According to the Hindu tradition, the ideal life pattern for ALL the men of the three superior *varna* includes, as the last two stages, the hermit's life of study and meditation in the forest, and the nomadic existence of the completely unattached spiritual wanderer.

The general conceptual system presented here reveals the fundamental similarity and the vigorous persistence of mental categories, human values, and lifeways across distant and diverse civilizations. These common elements are usually hidden under the ideational differences of religious idioms. These interconnected constructs make it possible to perceive these common elements in a solidly grounded comparative perspective.

REFERENCES

BHARATI, AGEHANANDA
    1970   *The ochre robe*. New York: Anchor-Doubleday.
    1974   "Monasticism," in *Encyclopaedia Britannica III*, volume twelve. Chicago.
CHADWICK, OWEN
    1958   *Western asceticism*. London: SCM Press.
    1968   *John Cassian*. Cambridge: Cambridge University Press.
FAIRFIELD, RICHARD
    1972   *Communes USA*. Baltimore: Penguin.
KANTER, ROSABETH MOSS
    1972   *Commitment and community*. Cambridge: Harvard University Press.

KNOWLES, DAVID
1969   *Christian monasticism*. New York: McGraw-Hill.
KROEBER, A. L., CLYDE KLUCKHOHN
1952   *Culture*. Cambridge: Peabody Museum.
MAQUET, JACQUES
1971   *Power and society in Africa*. New York: McGraw-Hill.
MASUNAGA, REIHŌ, *translator and editor*
1971   *A primer of Sōtō Zen: Dōgen's Shōbōgenzō Zuimonki*. Honolulu: East-West Center Press.
RIDEMAN, PETER
1950   *Account of our religion, doctrine, and faith*. Bungay, England: Hodder and Stoughton. (Original German edition in 1565.)
SHILS, EDWARD A., HENRY A. FINCH, *translator and editor*
1949   *Max Weber on the methodology of the social sciences*. Glencoe, Illinois: Free Press. (Original German edition in 1904.)
SPIRO, MELFORD E.
1970   *Buddhism and society*. New York: Harper and Row.
TÖNNIES, FERDINAND
1957   *Community and society*. East Lansing: Michigan State University Press (Original German edition in 1887.)
ZABLOCKI, BENJAMIN
1971   *The joyful community*. Baltimore: Penguin.

Rituals of Community in an American Religious Youth Group Meeting

E. M. SCIOG

"The Seekers" is the young adult group of the High Street Congregational Church, Old Town, East Coast, United States. Members of the group are students drawn from a number of colleges, junior colleges, and universities in the metropolitan area as well as young professionals and academicians residing and working in the area.

As one of the older urban areas of the East, Old Town is noted as one of the more gracious and pleasant environments, although it, too, has its share of urban blights, pollution, slums, and social conflict. Its proximity to the major urban centers of the East and its high prestige as a residential location have attracted young professionals from diverse backgrounds, and the quality of the academic institutions surrounding it draws a highly mixed student body.

Within this environment the High Street Church, like many other traditional religious bodies, has long sponsored youth groups, such as the Seekers, in an attempt to bring this population into its orbit.

Membership figures for the Seekers at present are approximately 400, with an average weekly meeting attendance of 350. In comparison with other church-sponsored youth organizations in the Protestant community, the group is extraordinarily large. The usual membership of such an organization is between fifteen and thirty.

The members and sponsors of the Seekers are themselves aware of the great discrepancy in numbers between themselves and other comparable organizations. This discrepancy, which has developed within the past three or four years, is a phenomenon inexplicable to the group other than in terms of the power of God. This interpretation of their growth is founded on one of the basic beliefs of the group and one common in

American Protestantism, millenarianism. This belief centers around what is known as the "second coming of Christ." "The second coming" is the key symbol of the process in which Christ will return to earth, rule a thousand years, and then end the world, rewarding the faithful with eternal life. This thumbnail sketch of millenarianism outlines the goal of all adherents to this belief. The Seekers are specifically postmillennialists, who believe in the active role of man in bringing about a Christian world prior to the advent of Christ, as opposed to premillennialists, who deny that man can do anything and that Christ will Himself put the world to rights after His coming.

The Seekers consider themselves to be actively involved in this process of regenerating the world, in anticipation and preparation for the pre-destined rule of Christ. Their interpretation of millenarianism demands that the world be made "good" before Christ will enter it. This "making good" (their own term) consists of both a theological and a social component. First, the world must be converted to Christianity or, as they put it, everyone must find Jesus. Second, the social world must be articulated with Christ's teachings on interpersonal relations, i.e., love thy neighbor as thyself. This social relationship is known as the Fellowship.

The Seekers are, in their own way, intensely mission oriented. Their ultimate goal is the Christianization of the world, but their immediate concern is with the community around them, particularly their friends and acquaintances. The prime method of conversion is for an individual to capitalize on crisis situations, in which family, friends, and acquaintances might find themselves at some time or another, and attempt to convince the sufferer to accept a religious solution. Divine intervention is also called upon by a believer on behalf of a certain individual. This request is carried out during the meetings of the group, and petitions of this type occupy a substantial portion of the meetings.

In recent years, however, the rate of conversion and the sudden climb in membership have far exceeded the amount of effort which the Seekers have contributed to God's work. It is therefore obvious to them that many of their new members have been directly converted, not through any human agency, but through the power of God Himself.

An interesting belief associated with this type of millenarianism, which the group's growth has reinforced, is that which states that men alone are not sufficiently capable of remaking the world and that God Himself will take an active hand in the work to be done. Further, these conversions through the act of God have had the effect of confirming their belief in the ultimate disposition of the world, as well as spurring many members on to greater efforts at converting their friends and relatives.

Several years ago "the Seekers" was no larger than any other similar organization in the city. Because membership records have been and, in fact, still are rather carelessly kept, awareness of any growth in membership came very slowly. Even in retrospect, several informants, the clergyman included, could not determine the rate of growth prior to 1971. All agreed, hazily, that around 1968 the group began to get larger. Membership at that time was approximately fifty persons. Although no one had ever been concerned about keeping a record of membership, by the summer of 1972 the story of how the group had grown was beginning to evolve. In the summer of 1972 the membership was nearly 200. That previous autumn, only ten months earlier, the group had numbered barely 150. In the autumn of 1970 it had been only 100. Between 1968 and 1970 agreement on figures for any particular months or seasons is impossible to obtain. The membership, or rather more properly, the attendance figures for the autumn of 1972 literally staggered the group, being double their previous number, and the preceding chronology has become fixed in the oral history of the Seekers.

There is no way to substantiate objectively this chronology of group growth, which was obtained from four of the most senior members of the group as well as the clergyman. The version of these members is the one that has formed the basis of the group story. In reality, the growth curve of the group most likely approximates the chronology; but from the point of view of the membership, this story actually represents their historical growth.

The great crowd of newcomers in the autumn of 1972 necessitated the removal of the meetings from the basement classroom of the church to the sanctuary on the floor above, which was the only place within the church large enough to hold the meeting. At first, the incredulity of the minister and older members was expressed both privately and publicly. No one could believe that such an unprecedented jump in membership could be permanent. Most people expected attendance to drop drastically within a few weeks. To the astonishment of all concerned, membership continued to increase throughout the autumn, until in December the estimated attendance was 400.

A very interesting observation I made was the fact that the actual number of people was never counted. Informants always spoke in approximations. Authoritative pronouncements on attendance figures were never made by anyone in my presence or during the course of any meeting I attended. Neither, as far as I was able to ascertain, was such an announcement made at meetings I did not or could not attend. On three occasions I made head counts, one each in September, November and December.

From the figures I obtained attendance varied between 360 and 390.

The Seekers' membership is socially homogeneous. The age of members ranges from eighteen to late twenties. White middle-class (or aspiring middle-class) college students and young professionals are the rule. White blue-collar workers are rare as are middle-class blacks. Ghetto-dwelling lower-class blacks are never seen. The ratio of men to women is about equal, only slightly favoring men. Most members are unmarried.[1]

In other aspects their heterogeneity is outstanding. Members are drawn from a wide variety of regional backgrounds, coming from every major geographical area of the country and from rural and urban areas alike. Religious backgrounds are also highly varied. A high percentage is Catholic (approximately 40 percent). Methodists, Lutherans, Episcopalians, and Baptists are also represented. Some continue to practice their original religions, attending their own churches for regular Sunday service and coming to the Seekers meetings as well. As a group, the Seekers are well aware of their religious heterogeneity and appear to be proud of it. They believe that at least half of their present membership is composed of former Catholics, although, as in the case of accurate membership figures, no one has ever kept count.

As an official part of the church organization, the group is under the leadership of one of the resident clergy, Reverend Hanson, the appointed "minister of youth." He is in charge of leading major portions of the meetings and also is responsible for the administrative matters which confront the group, such as deciding on dates for religious retreats, organizing travel arrangements for such retreats, and choosing scriptural passages to be studied by the group. He considers himself, and is so regarded by the rest of the clergy at the church, as a kind of spiritual guide to the group. Group members refer to him as "a good guy," "a very nice man," and "someone you can talk to." While Reverend Hanson may indeed function as a spiritual guide in intimate encounters with individuals or small groups, his role in the specific ritual gathering with which this paper is concerned, the Sunday Evening Meeting, is strictly that of a master of ceremonies. He engages in the minimal participation necessary for maintaining order and the smooth flow of the meeting.

During this meeting, the minister is assisted by a self-selected group of subordinates known as "lay ministers." Members of the lay ministry are

---

[1] The information presented here was acquired by a number of informal surveys of members. In this way I accumulated background information on more than a third of the membership. No official records are kept. I was further aided in this assessment of the social characteristics of members by the practice of publicly introducing newcomers. Newcomers would be obliged to stand and tell their names and occupations as well as places of origin.

drawn directly from the general membership of the Seekers. Anyone fulfilling one basic criterion is eligible. This criterion is sufficient commitment to the group to engage in a large amount of voluntary labor, mostly
organizational in nature. This work consists of assisting the minister in
administrative affairs, such as handling paperwork. The lay ministers also
host the infrequent social affairs of the group and assist in the conduct of
the main meeting.

A new member of the group is confronted with a hierarchy of leadership, although the only clear demarcation is between the minister, an
ordained member of the clergy, and the rest of the group. Opportunity for
an ordinary member to become a lay minister is limited only by the individual's commitment to the group.

The Sunday Evening Meeting of the Seekers is conducted within the
framework of the High Street Church's organization of Sunday affairs.
At the morning service, 10 A.M., the time schedule of the various church
group meetings is available for the congregation, together with the week's
order of worship. On this schedule the Seekers meeting is always listed.
This meeting is the main weekly event for the group. It is the only time
when all members of the group come together. During the course of an
ordinary week, several small group meetings, led by one or more of the
lay ministers to discuss Scripture and to pray, may or may not be held.
At most, one or two of these meetings will be held in any given week, and
attendance averages about fifteen persons.

Outside the context of purely group activity, i.e. the meetings and
infrequent social gatherings noted above, members form small friendship
cliques. Members of the Seekers who are college students may room
together. Groups of friends visit and entertain each other, go to restau-
rants and movies. Other members of the group date, go steady, or are
engaged. Belonging to the Seekers has certain social advantages for many
members.

Sunday at the High Street Church is an exceedingly busy day. Besides
morning and evening services, the church sponsors many special groups,
including the Seekers. Classes are held on the Bible, and lectures on
topics relating to the teachings of Christ are given at least twice a month.
Besides these general types of meetings, the church sponsors numerous
age-graded groups, one of which is the Seekers. There are groups for
children, high school students, young marrieds, and businessmen. None
of them, however, approaches the size of the Seekers or can match its
heterogeneity of regional backgrounds or religious faiths.

These other groups have little relevance to the Seekers. Aside from
having a clergyman as the official leader of the group, most members of

the group (those who are not members of the congregation) have almost no contact outside of it. The existence of other church-sponsored groups is known, but is irrelevant to participation in the Seekers. No group actions, i.e. socials or lectures, are prepared in concert with other groups; nor does the recognition of any group other than their own within the structure of the church or even the recognition of the church itself ever become a necessity for members.

The Seekers meeting is actually split into two parts. The first part consists of a lecture on some Biblical topic; this begins at 5:30 in the afternoon and ends at 7:00. Less than a third of the full membership ever show up for this lecture. The average attendance over a period of ten weeks was 125 persons. Many of the lay ministers attend this part of the meeting. Following the lecture a supper of sandwiches and punch is served and members stand about the lecture room, located in the basement of the church, and engage in informal conversation for half an hour. At 7:30 the evening service is conducted; those members of the group who attend the lecture also attend this service, which lasts an hour.

The church service which some members of the Seekers attend has a typical Congregationalist format, consisting of hymn — prayers — sermon — hymn — prayers — closing hymn; the central element is the sermon. (This pattern is meant to be schematic and the category of prayers encompasses such elements as benedictions, etc.) This general pattern of the service varies little from church to church in the Congregationalist denomination within the Old Town area, nor is it different from Congregationalist services in other areas of the country. Minor variations are found particularly within the prayer category. At the conclusion of the service, the congregation is asked to clear the sanctuary quickly so that the Seekers' meeting can begin.

The part of the congregation that does not belong to "the Seekers" leaves and Seekers members who did not attend the evening service arrive for the Evening Meeting. Most of the group attend only this one weekly meeting and see their "brothers" and "sisters" only at this time. The group spends a good deal of time becoming settled. Greetings are exchanged and informal conversation is carried on. People inquire into events of the past week and comment on absent friends. During this time small, more acquainted groups stand about together waiting for the meeting to start. In actuality, however, the tendency to sit with friends is counterbalanced by an explicit injunction to sit with strangers and others with whom one is only minimally acquainted. I have often been in such a position. In several instances I had been conversing with four friends prior to the start of the meeting, and I had expected to sit with them when we were called to order. (It is customary to stand and converse before the meeting is called to order, so most people do not choose their seats until they are required to sit down.) In all such cases, however, I never sat with more than two of the persons with whom I had been conversing. When the time comes to be seated, groups of four or five tend to break up into couples and trios that sit quite a distance from each other. With such a large number of people attending meetings, especially within the last eighteen months, many people do not know even a substantial fraction of the members. In order to meet this situation (or perhaps this pattern has always been typical of the group), the dispersal of cliques for meeting seating arrangements is actively encouraged; individual members are also quite enthusiastic about meeting new "brothers" and "sisters."

About fifteen minutes after the regular evening service has ended, one of the lay ministers steps up to the microphone, which he and several assistants have set up in the front of the sanctuary, and calls the meeting to order. At his word, the groups of friends disperse for the remainder of the meeting. As the crowd settles down in the pews, the lay minister, Jack, welcomes members and visitors to the meeting.

All meetings are opened by one of the lay ministers. In the case of the particular meeting, which I shall describe below, Jack officiated. Other lay ministers, whom I observed assisting the minister in this capacity, were Paul, Jim, and Mike. I never observed a woman undertake this task, although there are a number of women lay ministers. One of these persons always shares the burden of conducting the meeting with the minister.

As Jack called the meeting to order, several instrumentalists milled about in the front, tuning their guitars, and someone was fussing with the overhead projector. Tim, Don, and Peggy, on guitars and piano respectively, provided the accompaniment. After a slight period of confusion, everyone was finally ready to begin and Jack put the verses of the first hymn on the projector, raised his hands to gather the full attention of the assembly, and shouted into the microphone, "And a one, two, three!"

In an excellent imitation of a symphonic maestro, Jack (who actually is a legitimate music major at a nearby college) conducted the several verses with great gusto. His light-hearted and joyous approach to the whole business communicated itself to the group, and they responded to his goading to sing louder for the Lord with enthusiasm. He put up the verses for the next hymn amid a scattering of applause and shouts for some special favorite tune.

In general, Jack prefaced his introduction of each hymn with comments such as, "You remember this one," and "We haven't done this in a while." Every few meetings a new hymn or hymns are taught to the group as a whole, and they have built up quite a repertoire. Because most members of the group know the repertoire of hymns available, people hazard guesses as to the identity of the next hymn and comment in satisfaction if one of their favorites is chosen.

The hymns that are sung are joyful and rendered in a semi folk style to the accompaniment of the guitars and piano. The verses and tunes are sometimes composed by talented members of the group or taken from hymnbooks and jazzed up a bit. The central themes of the texts are praise at the salvation of man by Christ and affirmation of a service commitment to Jesus. A sample verse of one of the most popular hymns runs as follows:

Jesus came down to be our Savior.
Jesus came down to be our Savior.
Jesus came down to be our Savior.
He is the Way. He is the Truth. He is the Light!

Occasionally the *Pilgrim hymnal* will be taken out and something will be sung to a more traditional rhythm and accompaniment, such as the well-known verses of "Stand up, stand up for Jesus."

After three or four hymns have been sung, each more boisterous than the preceding one (because Jack encouraged foot stamping, hand clapping, and loud singing), Jack announced that it was time to get on to the next item on the agenda. Visitors, in the persons of interested members of the congregation and curious parents, but particularly prospective group members, abound at each Sunday meeting. It is the second order of business to effect their introduction to the group at large. Jack asked the visitors to stand, and tell their names, occupations, and home towns. It generally takes quite a bit of time before these introductions are completed, but the entire group always listens with full attention, and several people in any pew, including all the lay ministers and a large number of ordinary members, as far as I have been able to ascertain, take notes.

After all the strangers had been identified and welcomed, Jack surrendered the microphone to Reverend Hanson, who proceeded to the third part of the meeting.

Following a short welcoming speech of his own, Reverend Hanson opened his New Testament to the biblical passage of the week. Each week a certain passage of scripture is designated for meditation and discussion. Members are advised to read the passage during the week and come prepared to say something about it at the following meeting.

Although officially designated as a discussion, and referred to as such by members when they describe the elements in the Sunday evening meeting, that which ensues is not precisely a discussion in the common sense of the term.[2]

The minister began by citing the source and the page number of the scriptural passage for the benefit of those not in possession of that knowledge. He then addressed the group with the question, "Who has something to share?" A scattering of people raised their hands and the minister selected volunteers at random; each of them, in turn, stood and addressed the group as a whole.

The nature of this "sharing" or, as the minister sometimes phrases it, "contribution" is couched in terms of the relationship of the passage to (preferably) recent personal experiences of the contributor.

In the passage Paul talks about being steadfast and unyielding in faith no matter what trials you are undergoing. And I guess if he can say that and really mean it in his predicament, being in prison and all that, I can stick out the troubles, the little everyday troubles that I've been having. After all, he had a rougher time than I've ever had yet. It kind of bucked me up to have somebody give advice like that to someone like me, when he's in a really bad situation like that. So I decided to stick out the troubles I'd been having on the job, and not let them get me down the way they had been, and trust in God that everything will turn out all right in the end if I stick to my faith and pray. But since I read that passage things have been a lot easier.

These comments, of which the above is typical, consist of the application of the passage to individually unique and often rather vaguely or generally stated experiences. Most often the passage is interpreted as a remedy to a currently stressful situation or mental state. The association of the passage may also refer to an individual's total life orientation, as below:

I realized that he was saying in the passage just what I've been trying to do in my life, but he sort of put it in a clearer perspective — like a revelation.

"Revelations on reading a Bible passage" would certainly be a more appropriate description of this part of the meeting than "discussion," and, indeed, members do occasionally speak of this part of the meeting as "sharing what God has revealed to you in the scriptures."

The "discussion," then, consists of a static series of revealed statements — testimony. There is never any critical discussion of the merits of

[2]   The manner in which I am describing the organization of the Sunday Evening Meeting, as a division into four parts: hymns, introduction of strangers, Bible discussion, and sharing, is not my own construct, but is the way in which my informants perceive the structure of the meeting.

any particular interpretation. Each is accepted, solemnly and without comment, as worthy in itself as a revealed truth.

After six or seven people commented on the Bible passage to the group as a whole, the minister instructed the members to break up into small groups and discuss the passage among themselves. The members did this by including eight or so individuals seated nearest them in a circle. As stated above, large cliques are not encouraged to sit together; the largest number of close friends or acquaintances, who had been conversing together at the start of the meeting, in any one of these groups is usually less than three. In ten consecutive weeks I was never in a small group with the same people. The group members are very gregarious and each week a different friend would say: "Let's sit over there, I haven't seen so-and-so for weeks." In this way, individuals would tend to sit with one or two different friends each week. Because any given individual makes the rounds of all his or her friends and acquaintances in this manner, the structure of small groups in the course of the meetings is never the same from week to week. The friendship cliques never form an identifiable group during the meeting.

Ideally, each small group is led by one of the lay ministers who takes it upon him- or herself to initiate the discussion, prompt each member of the group who has read the passage to make a comment, and fill up the silences with relevant talk. Visitors, whose position has been marked by members of the group, are distributed among a number of small groups. Outsiders are never allowed to remain outside spectators, but are incorporated into a small group.

The explicit purpose of these small groups is to give everyone a chance to say something. The minister, on occasion, makes this function absolutely clear. Upon closing the discussion and ordering the formation of small groups, he will sometimes say: "I'm sorry we haven't time to hear everybody who has something to say, but although you can't tell it to the whole group, you can share your observation within the small group." Informants say they feel obliged to say something if they have read the passage, and feel that the only persons who have a valid excuse for not having something to contribute are visitors and those who were not able to find out what passage was assigned.

If everyone in the group has made his contribution before the minister signals for attention, the lay minister, either alone or with some talkative members, assumes the responsibility for making further interpretations of the passage. Often individuals are asked by the lay minister to elaborate on the circumstances of the situation to which they are applying the passage.

At this point, Jack sometimes takes the microphone, and initiates a short interlude of singing. There seems to be no set rule about singing at this point in the meeting. Weeks may go by without any singing and then for two or three weeks in a row Jack (Paul, Jim, or Mike) will get up and say, "Let's sing a hymn." Usually only one hymn is sung, in the same folk style as the opening ones and with the same kind of text, stressing joy in salvation.

When the hymn ended, the minister rose and initiated the final segment of the meeting by asking, "Does anybody have anything he or she would like to share with the rest of the group?" This part of the meeting is called "sharing" by group members, and all consider it to be the most important event of the meeting.

The structure of this final phase of the meeting is the same as that of the Bible discussion. After Reverend Hanson asked his question, several people raised their hands and individuals were chosen at random. In general, things that are "shared" with the group as a whole are those that have been classified by members as having great importance. Because almost all "sharing" is articulated in terms of personal experience, comments made to the entire group are expected to be of great personal importance, even catastrophic to the teller.

Those things considered to be worthy of "sharing" with the entire membership are such events as a confession of personal acceptance of Christ, the conversion of someone not present, the discovery of other "Christian groups" or "fellowships in Jesus" in other places, and the announcement of a very great personal experience or tragedy.

After six or seven individuals spoke, the minister declared that the time had come to form small groups, but first asked if there was anyone left with an important message to share. After the last of these most urgent "sharings" was aired to the group at large, people formed their small groups again.

An interesting feature of this part of the meeting is that immediately after something was shared, the group as a whole offered a silent prayer for what was "shared," whether it be the death of a member or a close relative of a member or the discovery of another group like themselves. During the moment of prayer, the minister invited members to say a prayer aloud. At this, several people in succession composed a spontaneous prayer about the particular "sharing." If the thing "shared" was of great joy a prayer of praise was composed; if tragic, one of consolation. In general, the graver the thing "shared," the longer the time spent in prayer. Occasionally, the minister will be one of the contributors of a prayer.

The particular function that members perceive these prayers to have varied with the nature of the thing "shared." They believe that all happy things that happen to them are the result not only of their own efforts but of divine dispensation as well. They believe that one must work for personal goals, material gain or praise, or the conversion of a non-Christian, but the ultimate attainment of these is the result of the influence of Christ. When something particularly happy or unexpected happens, this event is attributed to the intervention of Christ, and appropriately He must be thanked through prayer. Conversely, suffering is also attributed to God or Christ, either as being some sort of test of faith or the fulfillment of the unknowable will of God. In these cases one prays for courage and a steadfast and unwavering belief in the fact that this is the will of God and ultimately good.

When the meeting again broke up into small groups, the explicit intent, as before, was to provide everyone with the opportunity, or perhaps obligation, to participate. The lay minister again took charge and initiated "sharing" by being the first to say something. Then each member of the small group was gently prodded in turn to contribute. Although visitors and newer members are not highly pressured to "share," the group is gratified if such persons do say something. After the second meeting I attended, several people in my small group told me how nice it had been that I, a new member, had felt moved to "share" something with them.

In this setting, it is very difficult to avoid "sharing." Once the lay minister has said his or her piece, he will indicate with a nod or a glance the direction about the circle in which the comments should flow. If the person whose turn it is to "share" says nothing, a very long, anticipatory silence ensues. Either the individual is very firmly determined not to speak and so endures the silence, or he becomes increasingly uneasy and ultimately capitulates. Sometimes one member of the group will ask, with great concern, "Haven't you anything you'd like to tell us?" Having been, in a later meeting, the focus of such a silence, I can say without reservation that it operates as a very powerful sanction and can elicit the cooperation of all but the most determined individual.

People that do not have anything to say, or cannot think of anything, feel that they somehow let the group down. This self-judgment is reinforced by the disappointment that others in the small group display when someone refuses to participate in the sharing. In addition to feeling that one has not lived up to the "norms" of the group and, in turn, is being considered deficient as a member of the Seekers by the group, this circle of "sharing" generates a very powerful emotional atmosphere. This emotional tension is not physically expressed by such phenomena as speaking in tongues or movements. It is highly internalized, but members are aware of it just the same, and the tension increases as the round of the circle is made. Members are loath to break this circle by silence and dislike it if anyone, other than recognized outsiders and newcomers, remains silent.

During the second month of attending the group meetings, I once deliberately refrained from "sharing," a course which very much annoyed the group and destroyed the atmosphere. I might indeed have been regarded as a kind of spoiler of the "magic."

The things "shared" in this smaller group are much more mundane and even petty compared to those "shared" with the membership as a whole. An illustration of "sharing" is presented below — an abridged sequence of small group "sharing" from the meeting of August 27, 1972.

Ann (lay minister): My husband has had the flu and is still in a bad way. I'd like you to pray that his convalescence will be quick. Also we're trying to form a Christian discussion group in the high school where we teach and we're hoping that it will be successful.

Dave: Lately, you know, I've been talking to my roommate Steve about Jesus, and he's beginning to seem more interested. Now he's asking questions. I want you to pray that he'll find Jesus soon because he's been leading a really unhappy, empty spiritual life and he needs Him.

Paul: I've just been realizing how much my life has changed since I met Jesus, and I've been happier than ever before. I've been a Christian for almost a year now, and I just wanted to share my joy in Jesus with all of you.

Mary: I've found a new job working with really nice people and I love it. Jesus answered my prayer with this work and I really feel that He's showed me my proper place in the world where I'll do His work best.

Tom: Well, I've decided that I really want to go on to college and I've applied to City College. I feel that this is what Jesus wants me to do, so the last few weeks I've been praying awfully hard that I'll be accepted and sure would appreciate your help.

Ellen: My dad's been terribly ill since last week. He had a heart attack and really needs your prayers to give him spiritual support.

Neil: In the last few days I've been faced with the choice of what to do with my life for the next few years and I'm not sure what the right thing to do is. I've been praying, but Jesus hasn't shown me the way yet, or maybe I just can't hear Him. Maybe if you put in a prayer or two for me I'll be able to see the way Jesus wants me to take.

Only after everyone had had his or her say were the prayers concerning these "sharings" offered. The group was silent and, at random, individuals in the group composed a short prayer about one or several of the "sharings." The prayers fell into three general groups: petition, praise, and consolation.

Dear Lord, we thank You that Ann's husband is recovering his strength and pray that he will soon recover completely in order to carry out Your work.

Jesus, thank You for what Paul told us tonight. When he told us of the change in his life found through You we see that You are surely the Truth and the Light.

Dear Jesus, may Ellen's strong faith in You sustain her and her family through this terrible time in their lives, and we pray, if it be Your will, for her father's speedy recovery.

Each "sharing" was mentioned in prayer at least once, and often more. When the creativity of the group had become exhausted and a prolonged silence signalled a tacit agreement that enough had been said, the lay minister took over and voiced one last conclusive prayer for the group. Everyone then subsided into a grave, meditative silence to await other groups which were engaged in an identical procedure.

This exact same pattern was followed by all the other small groups. In a membership amounting to nearly 400, there are many small groups consisting of eight to ten people. Eventually the sanctuary became quieter. When the room was nearly still (or, in some cases, after it had been silent for a few minutes) one of the lay ministers, or the minister himself, began to sing the closing hymn, either an "Alleluia" or "Old One Hundredth."

The meeting that began with boisterous singing, laughter, and clapping was concluded with a softly sung old hymn. At times the minister will say a closing prayer, thanking God for the opportunity to have had the joy to be a part of the meeting and wishing the group good night. At other times the meeting just breaks up after the hymn is sung. The silence is then broken by people wishing each other good night, speaking with friends and acquaintances whom they had not seen before the meeting. Soon they go home.

Some members leave immediately. However, for about twenty minutes following the close of the meeting many members remain about and converse. Some get together with the groups they had been with at the start of the meeting and resume their interrupted conversations. Others wander about looking for certain friends. One is commonly asked, "Have you seen so-and-so?" Members seem to have a large circle of acquaintances within the group. Individuals are continually introducing themselves to strange new members and are always in the process of expanding their number of acquaintances.

In the end, after individuals have seen the persons they wanted, they find their rides home. People with cars give fellow members rides home and most people leave in groups of four, five, or six.

From the foregoing description, it can be seen that the Sunday Evening Meeting of the Seekers consists of an elaborate series of rituals. These rituals — hymn singing, testimony through the discussion of a Bible passage, and sharing — have for the most part been drawn from a pre-existent corpus of ritual acts. The general outline of the meeting roughly follows that of the typical Congregational church service described above. Furthermore, this meeting very closely resembles a historical and con-temporary form of Protestant worship known as the prayer meeting, although no member has ever, within my hearing, referred to the Seekers' meeting as a prayer meeting. Most members are not even aware of the historical background of the group. Their interest and knowledge extends back as far as their joining the Seekers. The only topic of historical inter-est is the growth of the group from the late 1960's and their data on that are none too secure.

The rituals themselves are easily identifiable. In the context of the meet-ing they are deliberately marked off from each other by the minister and lay minister, who are acting in a manner which an observer would be inclined to define as the role of a master of ceremonies. They keep the performance moving and intervene to conclude one ritual and initiate the next. The members themselves also refer to these rituals as discrete and separable units.

The lay minister initiates the first ritual, that of hymn singing, and continues through the second ritual, the identification of strangers to the group. The third and fourth rituals are led by the minister. These two rituals form structurally parallel units. In each, individuals first address the group as a whole and secondly address a segment of the group, which the members perceive to be an inferior kind of substitute for the group as a whole. This relative valuation of the small group *vis-à-vis* the whole is explicitly stated by the minister every so often. He expresses regret that the group is too large for everyone to have face-to-face communication, that for each individual to confront the group as a whole is impossible. In one sense the small groups are negatively valued; they split up the whole group into dozens of tiny independent ones. However, the small groups are also perceived as having a positive aspect. The minister often expresses this positive aspect by saying that those who are too shy and reticent to ever stand up in front of four hundred people, will feel more at home and less uneasy in a group of ten or less.

Whether this division into small groups is a function of the large size of the Seekers and is a technique that has been resorted to in order to insure the participation of the maximum number of individuals or whether this technique has been used historically in similar kinds of meetings such as the prayer meeting is unclear. There is little existing literature on prayer meetings, and what there is seems to presuppose a group of thirty or less (Luccock and Cook 1916; Wells 1896). Descriptions of Young Men's Christian Association prayer meetings also presuppose a small number of participants and make no mention of the use of small groups during the course of a meeting (Hopkins 1953; Connant 1858). The present minister, Reverend Hanson, told me he was merely continuing the format of Seekers meetings that existed at the time of his appointment. The pattern of organization, it has been remarked by persons outside the group who have read versions of the present paper, closely resembles that of T-Group dynamics. Within the group, however, the relationship between their meetings and T-Groups is not explicitly drawn. At this time I would hesitate to make any interpretation of the relationships the group meeting may have to outside, secular sources.

Hymn singing, the opening ritual, is the typical opening ritual of American Protestant meetings. All denominational churches, to my knowledge, open and close Sunday services with hymns, which are known, respectively, as the processional and recessional. Singing an appropriate anthem or hymn appears to be an accepted way of opening many affairs in America — note the singing of the national anthem before football and baseball games.

For the Seekers, hymn singing is legitimated by past religious tradition. But hymns are not sung in an unthinking, unfeeling manner by the members, as if they were merely preparatory opening exercises. The hymns express their basic beliefs in salvation through Christ and commitment to the service of Christ as individuals and AS A GROUP.

Being part of the group or the fellowship of Christ, as they call it, is an extremely important part of being a Seeker. In my prefatory remarks concerning the Seekers' system of belief, I commented that they perceive the salvation of the world and the second coming of Christ as consisting of two interrelated components. First there is the salvation of each individual through belief in Christ as the Savior. The second component that I referred to is a social one. To the Seekers, it is not only the individual soul that must be saved, but the social world of men as well. When Jesus comes, He will rule not just individual souls for the millennium, but a society of souls. This social relationship is what is known to them as the fellowship, and participation in that fellowship is of equal importance to them as individual salvation.

This explicit emphasis which the Seekers put on the social ideal of the fellowship may be a clue to an explanation of the intensity with which they attempt to involve and include all persons in the actions of the group.

Strangers are introduced one by one to the group as a whole. They become known and incorporated into the structure of the meeting. There are no outsiders. The strangers, who have no knowledge of the expectations of the group and who are not really expected to perform, are drawn into groups of members and are encouraged to participate, at least marginally in the "sharing." Strangers are not allowed to collect along the sidelines. Seekers do not explicitly phrase their actions toward strangers in this manner. They term their behavior as being "friendly," "kind to strangers," and "Christian."

The structure of the Bible discussion and "sharing" rituals also serves to implement this ideal of social interaction. The main implicit demand in these two rituals seems not so much to say something significant, but just to say something. The injunction to participate can override content.

The "discussion" tends to be past-oriented. The individual states that with the aid of the revelation granted him through reading the Bible passage he or she was able to resolve a crisis. The use of the Bible passage may be a structure employed to break through embarrassment in talking about personal things.

In the "sharing" ritual people are expected to discuss their current problems. The explicit purpose of this is to gain the spiritual aid of the rest of the community for the resolution of problems, comfort in sorrow, and the sharing of good tidings. If one rejects this means of problem solving by refusing to say something, one lets down the whole group. Not to "share" something is tantamount to rejecting fellowship. The kind of fellowship the Seekers perceive is not one of real political and economic interaction as a kind of commune, but a fellowship on a spiritual plane which is demonstrated through "sharing." When an established member has nothing to say, people are upset. They are disturbed that he or she will not "share" with them. It makes no difference to say that "I have nothing to share." Nobody has nothing to "share." One should always be sharing one's faith and joy at being part of the perfect spiritual fellowship. As some fellow member said to me after the meeting at which I refused to say anything. "You should say something. Everyone has something to share."

Predictably, members are overjoyed when a newcomer starts participating in the "sharing." When I first began to participate in the group, people were overjoyed that I "felt moved to say something." I was "becoming a member of the group."

The Seekers are a highly organized, unusually large youth group of an urban Protestant church. Unlike the popular conception of people involved in the Jesus movement, these people are very sober, middle-class-oriented students and young professionals who are working for the salvation of the world and the millennium. Their concept of salvation, which is just as much social as it is individual, leads them to demand a high degree of individual participation in the rituals of the group.

REFERENCES

CONNANT, WILLIAM
  1858   *Narratives of remarkable conversions and revival incidents.* New York.
HOPKINS, C. H.
  1953   *History of the Y.M.C.A. in North America.* New York: Association Press.
LUCCOCK, H. E., W. F. COOK
  1916   *The midweek service.* New York: Methodist Book Concern.
WELLS, A. R.
  1896   *Prayer meeting methods.* Boston: United Society of Christian Endeavor.

SECTION TWO

Techniques of Control in the Esoteric Traditions of India and Tibet

AGEHANANDA BHARATI

The subtitle of this communication might be "a survey of methods for the achievement of enstasis in Indian and Tibetan esoteric lore." I use the term "enstasis" following Professor Mircea Eliade, and I think it is his own neologism. Oriental scholars so far have used the common term "ecstasy" to denote the various experiences described in the contemplative traditions of India or of the countries that were under Indian esoteric tutelage. Ecstasy was used as a generic term, purporting to subsume about a dozen Indian terms and their Tibetan equivalents — such as — *samādhi, kaivalya, mukti, apavarga, sāmarasa, mahāsukha, nirvāna* and others — each of which generates more specific experiences. There is no technical Indian term which could be called an exact equivalent of "ecstasy," the closest in esoteric literature being *unmāda*. This term, however, has a derogatory meaning. Words using the root *mad*, have a pathological connotation in Sanskrit and in the vernaculars. "Enstasis" would correspond to Indian terms such as *bhāvanā* or *āntarbhāvanā*, and these have no pejorative flavor about them.

Enstasis is the ultimate target of all codified meditative disciplines in Asia. The term might apply to some types of Christian mysticism and to sufism. Indian authors of hagiographical literature use Indian terms meaning "enstasis" when speaking about Muslim or Christian saints. From *sadhu* and *pandit* platforms in India, one often hears such statements as "when Jesus had achieved *samādhi*...." or "when Muhammad entered *kaivalya*...." Enstasis, in all these traditions, is a nondiscursive, euphoric, quasi-permanent condition of the individual agent. In Indian theological parlance (and this covers Hindu, Buddhist, and Jaina), it is tantamount to supreme insight or wisdom. All other knowledge attained by cognitive processes is vastly inferior to it — and by implication essentially opposed to enstasis, marring its guided repetition and intensification.

At this time, there can be no doubt that lysergic acid diethelymide (LSD–25) and certain other alkaloid drugs occasionally generate genuine enstatic experiences. Indian mystics have been using natural alkaloid drugs of several varieties since Vedic days. We do not know what exactly the *soma* of Vedic literature was, but as I studied the elaborate description contained in the *soma* hymns of the manner in which this potion was prepared and of its effects, it became perfectly clear to me that the state of mind described comes much closer to alkaloid drug experience than to alcoholic intoxication. I have told elsewhere in detail how the tantric adept uses hemp each time he undergoes his discipline (see entries under *vijayā* in Bharati 1970). The term for the drug, variously prepared, is *bhāng* in modern northern India, *siddhi* in Bengali (the same word as for "occult power"). The classical word used in the tantric manuals and in scholastic references is *vijayā* [victory or victory giver]. Since *Cannabis sativa*, which has the same active ingredient as marijuana, creates a strongly euphoric mood, the term *vijayā* might have been coined to connote it. I found the first mention of *vijayā* as meaning *Cannabis sativa* in the *Manjusrīmūlakalpa*, one of the oldest Buddhist tantric texts (about 300 A.D.). Siva, as the tutelary deity of ascetics and mendicants, is often iconographically depicted with an herb bowl in his hands; one of his Nepalese epithets is *ausadhīsvara*, lord of drugs and herbs (as in the *Sivasahasranāma* and in the Kashmiri *Tantrāloka*). The difference between drug-induced experience and yogic enstasis is, however, that the latter yields enstatic information beyond its actual duration, which the former does not.

All indigenous Indian traditions teach asceticism as a prerequisite to contemplation leading to enstasis. Asceticism and orthodoxy are coextensive in the yogic traditions. When an ascetic life cannot be led, asceticism is a pervasive ideal postulate.

However, there has always been a strong undercurrent, or countercurrent if you will, of non- and antiascetical teachings. I call these the esoteric traditions of India, for lack of a better term. Presumably, they are older than the Vedic tradition, on the grass-roots level, and they are certainly older than either Brahmin or Buddhist orthodoxy. There is general agreement that the ascetic trend is part of the Indo-Aryan background, although probably not an import, for the Vedas themselves, i.e. their *samhitā* portion, do not display much ascetic predilection. This comes in at a later stage, in the Upaniṣadic era, and we do not know which current of indigenous speculation carried asceticism into the Vedic tradition. Eliade thinks that the nonascetical, magical, occult, and what I would call psychoexperimental packet stems from some pre-Aryan strata of the Indian population, and that yoga in its earliest, nonsystematized forms was a conglomerate of Vedic and pre-Vedic, that is, Indian autochthonous elements.

In the course of time the Vedic elements came to represent the esoteric, institutionalized, sacerdotal, that is, the "square" aspects of Indian religion; and the non-Vedic, autonomous, psychoexperimental elements came to be regarded as dangerous and heretical. Orthodox Brahmins in the South often refer to theVeda as *trayī* [the collection of three] (Bharati 1961). They exclude the *atharvāngirasa*, the fourth Veda, because it is full of magic and of hints of autonomous experimentation. The orthodox view, both in Hinduism and Buddhism, was that enstasis could be reached through a long process of conformity to canonical instruction and discipline; and on the Hindu side, through rigid observance of the *nitya* and *naimittika* ritual, and through the performance of the meditations laid down in the canonical texts. Brahmanism is particularly suspicious of any supererogatory observance and tacitly denies that there can be any fruitful meditation outside the daily performance imposed on the *dvija* [the caste Hindu].

Yoga, in the sense given to it by Patānjali, but especially in accordance with the instructions of such tantricizing teachers as Matsyendranāth and Gorakhnāth, is felt to be harmful and basically fraudulent. Professor V. Baghavan has told me that yoga and tantra are quite redundant, and that any person who fulfilled his *svadharma* along with the prescribed daily ritual finds redemption and freedom from rebirth at the end of his life, and that all talk of shortcuts is nonsense, and against the *śāstras*.

There is, of course, an additional point to be considered as fundamental to this critique made from above, where the Brahmanical hierarchy is accepted: the pandit feels very strongly that, *śāstri*cally speaking, nothing that is not written and commented upon in elegant Sanskrit can be worthwhile. I recall the anger and dismay generated on both sides, when the late F. Edgerton taught his course on Buddhist hybrid Sanskrit at Benares Hindu University, where he was the Holkar Visiting Professor in 1953. The reaction of his students, all of whom were Sanskrit scholars from the Varanasi area, was summarized by Professor Telang, then Reader in Sanskrit at the university: "Sir, there is no such thing as Buddhist hybrid Sanskrit. There is only good Sanskrit and bad Sanskrit. Important things were written in the former, wrong things in the latter." The implication was clear: Buddhism, especially the *Mahāyāna* and *Vajrayāna* texts written in Buddhist hybrid Sanskrit, were bad philosophy, bad Buddhism, unimportant productions; and, even worse, Professor Edgerton's life work was a chimera. In the long view, Professor Edgerton won and Professor Telang lost, as, in general, Indian Sanskrit scholars now accept Buddhist hybrid Sanskrit as a special idiom, not an inferior one.

Yoga, reduced to the least common denominator, means concentration on a nondiscursive internal object of a numinous kind, or the introjection of a conceptualized object usually of some mythological sort. Patānjali's classical definition, which introduces the Sūtras, is *cittavrtti norodhah* [the blockage of the object-directed tendency of the mind]. It is not a blank, but it is ideally devoid of discursive ideas and concepts.

Classical yoga fell in line with the Upaniṣadic tradition in the sense that it also stipulated the eradication of the sensuous personality. The opposing trend is what we must subsume under the tantric tradition. It defies orthodox Hinduism and Theravāda Buddhism and has a bad name in Hindu India and in Theravāda Buddhist Asia. The tantras — Hindu, Buddhist, and Jaina — add up to an enormous mass of didactic literature, regarded as canonical by their followers, and as dangerous or downright heretical by the orthodox. The Indian tantras have little literary merit, their Sanskrit is crude — most of the extant Buddhist tantras are not in Buddhist hybrid Sanskrit, but in poor Sanskrit. There are passages in both Hindu and Buddhist tantric literature which are not Sanskrit at all, but some *Apabhramśa* or early vernacular. Again, the Brahmin's dislike for the tantras is in part due to their poor language.

In all tantras there is much pious admonition about ascetical practices and a restrained way of life, in line with the orthodox style. This, I feel, is meant to make the tantra teachings seem more in line with the orthodox. The core of the tantric method, however, contrasts sharply with the orthodox. The teaching of the tantras is not to subdue the senses, but to increase their potencies and then to harness them toward the realization of lasting enstasis — the goal of these methods is identical with that of the orthodox. To set the tenor of Tantrism, I shall quote a passage from the *Advayavajrasangraha*, an important Buddhist tantric work (1927[3]:4). It says: "...by the very acts by which an ordinary person suffers spiritual perdition, the initiate yogi obtains permanent emancipation from the fetters of birth and death."

The tantric teachers were exceedingly discreet about their teachings, and kept them secret for a long time. They developed a code language, *sandhābhāṣā* [intentional language], which was understood only by the tantric group (Bharati 1961). This terminology consisted largely of erotic similes and vocabulary, to be interpreted either literally or metaphorically by the adepts, according to their state of advancement. The tantric commentators and some of their modern students aver that *sandhābhāṣā* intends to throw the minds of the aspirants into that peculiar frame of suspended contradiction which has been deemed essential for enstatic success.

The affective-cognitive situation thus generated will seem pathological to orthodox psychiatrists. But tantric preceptors such as Jnānānanda and Sarāha deny that there is such a thing as mental disease en route to enstasis (*mana roga samahio nasi jehi, patthujano bhaso so ano ehi*). If an adept seems to "act mad," it is just because people around him, lacking the adept's frame of reference, do not understand what it is all about. The adept's behavior cannot be explained to them, much as — in the words of a tantric Bengali teacher of the last century — sexual pleasure cannot be explained to a child, or narcotic experience cannot be explained to a person who has not taken the drug. Also, the ordinarily valid socio-ethical set of values is suspended for the adept, providing another reason why Tantrism has had a bad name in exceedingly conservative India ever since its inception about 1,500 years ago.

I shall quote another passage which shows clearly what is involved in the *sandhābhāṣā*, the code language of the Tantrists. It is a *sloka* from Tarkalamkara's commentary on the *Mahānirvāna*, the most important Hindu tantra. The passage is frequently quoted by orthodox opponents of Tantrism with a view to disparaging it, and is equally quoted by Tantrists to show the implications of *sandhābhāṣā*. It is: "*...matriyonau lingam kṣiptvā bhaginīstanamardanam, gururmūrdhni pādam dattvā punarjanma na vidyate.*" Literally translated it means: "*...*inserting his organ into his mother's vagina, clasping his sister's breasts, placing his foot upon the head of his preceptor, he will not be reborn," that is, he will attain the target of all religious life. All terms in this *sloka* are loaded with code meaning. Instead of interpreting the symbolism of individual words, I shall read the derived meaning of the passage as intended for the initiate: "Having first meditated on the *śakti* located in the coccygeal center, then on the female energy represented in the heart region, he penetrates with his meditation into the uppermost center located in the cranium and experiences enstasis." This code language serves an additional purpose: it keeps the noninitiate out as it keeps the initiate holy. Tactfulness is no primary consideration of the tantric teacher — he always seems to enjoy shocking the establishment.

All yoga discipline postulates in theory the existence of a secondary somatic system consisting of *mandala* [centers], *cakra* [circles], or *kendra* [lotuses], located along an imagined spinal column in that secondary body. It is important to realize — a thing which Occidental critics and Occidental phoney esotericists alike have misunderstood — that this yogic body is not supposed to have any ontological status in the sense the physical body has. It is a heuristic device aiding meditation, not an objective system. Benevolent psychologists under the inspiration of the late C. G. Jung have attempted to allocate the various nervous plexuses and ganglia to the centers of this yoga body. They may be right, but Tantrists take some pain to explain that this body and its organs have no actual existence.

It is in the degree of emphasis that different schools within Tantrism vary greatly when they describe the yogic body with regard to its ontological or merely heuristic status. There is nothing in these differences that requires an apology, as the varying notions are said to fit varying types of aspirants. The term *adhikārabheda* [difference of training and of meditational procedure] implies different approaches. It is quite clear that the tantric teachers realized that different people are attracted by different heuristic models. In two of the most important Hindu tantric texts, the *Mahānirvāna* and the *Sat-cakra-nirūpana*, this yogic body model is taught to have six centers or lotuses counting from the base of the spine; other texts speak of twelve centers; and the Buddhist tantric tradition usually assumes four. Common to all tantric and yogic traditions, however, is the notion of three ducts passing through the spinal column, the central one being closed in animals and noninitiate human beings, namely, in all yogically untrained people. Meditation ideally opens the central duct, and lets a mystical force ascend in it. This force is called the "coiled one" (*kundalini*) by the Hindus and "female ascetic" or "the purified one" (*avadhūti*; Tibetan: *kun dar ma* or *dbus ma*). It starts from its home base, the lowest center, which is thought to be located between the anal and the genital region, and, piercing the centers one by one, is finally absorbed into the uppermost center located in the cerebral area. The other two ducts, *lalanā* and *rasanā*, called *īdā* and *pingalā* by the Hindus (Tibetan: *brkyang ma* and *ro ma*), function in all living creatures. The yogi attempts to purify them at first, by breath control (*prānāyāma*), an elaborate training which activates the motion of these two peripheral ducts.

The force that moves from the base to the top of the yogic body in the process of successful meditation is always visualized as female: the microcosmic representation of the *magna mater*, whom the Hindus conceive as *śakti*, and the Buddhist *Vajrayāna* as quiescent wisdom (*prajñā*; Tibetan: *ses rab*). The brain center is homologous with the supreme cosmic principle — the *Brahman* of the Hindus, and the great void, *mahāśūnya* (Tibetan: *stong pa nyid*) of the tantric Buddhists. The merger or absorption of the dormant power, conceived as female, with the supreme principle is of course the esoteric pivot of all the erotic symbolism which pervades tantric thought and practice. The Buddhist tantras refer to *nirvāna* as *mahāsukha* [great bliss], and this is the term they use for enstasis, achieved by the threefold control which is the core subject here. All the code language of the tantras, let us remember, refers to this process of enstasis ONLY. And because emancipation from the circle of birth and death is the eschatological sequel or concomitant of enstasis, the tantras belong to *mokṣa śāstra* as much as the orthodox, canonical scriptures. Hindu and Buddhist critics of tantric practices and teachings have constantly suggested that the Tantrist uses religion as a mantle for sexual license and debauchery. The Tantrist's perennial reply was that the complicated, expensive, and exceedingly difficult ritual procedure in tantric *sādhana* would be too high a price for sexual gratification, which is so much easier to obtain without any yogic trappings.

Orthodox yoga, namely the system of Patānjali and his protagonists, teaches the ascent of the dormant, coiled-up force as a process induced in the individual adept, after due instruction by his guru, as a procedure in which the adept practices in solitude. By contrast, the Tantrist's practice is undertaken in conjunction with a partner of the other sex. The Hindus consider her the embodiment of *śakti*, the active principle conceived as female; and the Buddhist Tantrists regard her as *mudrā* (Tibetan: *phyag rgya*) or the passive principle of intuitive wisdom, also conceived as female. The method is diametrically opposed to that of the orthodox, and enstasis is reached by activating precisely those mechanisms which the orthodox yogi seeks to suppress or eschew. Absolute, primitive celibacy is a *sine qua non* in the orthodox tradition, whereas in Tantrism the injunction of celibacy has a very specific meaning. Tantrists read the term *brahmacaryam* rather more closely in line with its ancient, literal meaning of "moving in the *brahman*," that is, keeping one's mind directed toward the absolute. In orthodox Hinduism *brahmacaryam* is synonymous with sexual abstinence.

The practical axiom of the Tantrists, formulated much more precisely in Buddhist *Vajrayāna* than in Hindu Tantrism, is briefly this: enstasis is reached when we learn to stop the *tridhāra* [threefold flow], namely, when we learn to immobilize the mind, the breath, and the seminal fluid. Tantric *sandhābhāṣā* [code language] refers to these variously as the "three jewels" (*triratna*; Tibetan: *nor bu gsum*), the "three nectars" (*amrtatraya*; Tibetan: *bdud rtsi gsum*) and by similar terms. Separately, *sandhābhāṣā* refers to the mind as "the ape" (*kapi*) because of its unsteady nature which is hard to control; to breath as "the crocodile" (*makara*) because of its slow and tenacious motion; and to the sperm by a great number of symbolic terms, such as "the sun" (*surya, aditi*) or "nectar" (*amrta*). The most frequent *Vajrayāna sandhā* term is *bodhicitta* [the *bodhi*-mind] or "the mind of awakening or illumination" (Tibstan: *chub k yi sems*), which is a doctrinarily loaded term. Anthropomorphically, the *bodhicitta* is the mind of each living Buddha, or of each enlightened person.

"Breath control" (*prānāyāma*) is common to all yogic disciplines. classical and later, and rudimentarily, it was part of the Vedic *sandhyā* ritual. The idea seems to be that by acquiring control of this relatively conscious somatic or vegetative function the adept begins to be able to control other, less conscious, somatic chains, such as the heartbeat, which he aims to arrest at will in pursuit of more intensive enstatic states. I am informed by Professor T. Szasz that arrest of respiration itself can cause hallucinatory states under certain circumstances, and that a concentration of carbon dioxide is being used in psychiatry for the therapy of certain depressive disorders.

Control of the seminal fluid is thought to entail control of all passions and the achievement of desirelessness. Of course this notion stems from the common Indian ascetic tradition, which postulates that passions mar the advance toward enstasis.

Finally, control of the mind is almost tantamount to the supreme achievement of the yogi, in all its expressions: intuitive wisdom and freedom from rebirth. Control of the mind, in the technical sense of the yogic and tantric traditions, means precisely what Patānjali said in the opening verse of the *yogasūtra, cittavrtti nirodhah*: withholding the mind from all discursive objects, or a total resorption of the cognitive, conative, and volitional functions of the mind.

This triple control is hierarchically conceived: control of breath is the first and simplest step; control of seminal ejaculation during sexual union is the next; and preventing the mind from apperceiving any external objects is the final and highest step. These controls must be practiced simultaneously, and the whole process of esoteric meditation converges toward the skill of arresting breath, seminal emission, and object apperception simultaneously. The successful retention of the three is called *yuganaddha* (Tibetan: *sku'grub* or *zung'jug*), the binding together of the opposed poles: *Siva* and *Sakti* in Hindu tantra; *prajnā* and *upāya* in *Vajrayāna*; male and female adept, as the human replica of the cosmic process of enstasis.

All the texts stress that these controls can be learned only under the guidance of a personal teacher who must be an adept himself, a *siddha* who has succeeded in stabilizing these controls in himself or herself, and who must also be able to gauge and classify his prospective disciple in regard to the latter's potential capacity for mastering these controls. This takes us back to one of the oldest insights of Indian tradition, the pervasive notion of *adhikārabheda*, meaning "difference in the individual's qualification for a specific meditation". The prospective guru must study his disciple for a considerable time, in a close symbiosis with him. The *gurukula* of the Vedic period, and the coenobit set-up of the Indian monastic tradition, are conducive to this study, and the process is by no means unilateral. Both teacher and disciple have to test each other in order to effect a complete transference. The Tantrists refer to this set-up simply as the *kula* [the family or clan, the interacting group]. Then the guru judges which *mantra* [auditory instrument] he will give to the disciple, by use of which the latter will learn the threefold control leading to en-stasis. The *Mantramahārnava* and the *Mantramahodadhi* are the most comprehensive manuals of the mantras that are given to tantric neophytes, according to their various constitutions. The number of mantras available for selection is about 2,000; many of them are shared by the Tibetan *rdo rje theg pa* (*Vajrayāna*) contemplative lore.

Breath control, as I indicated earlier, is relatively easy to achieve. The process is roughly this: using the mantra as a time unit, the adept practices retention of breath for gradually increasing periods. This brings about a certain euphoric effect, accompanied by mild hallucinations, chiefly of a photic variety, quite similar to the incipient effect of alkaloid drugs. Then he practices breath control together with his *śakti* or *mudrā*, his con-secrated female partner. With her he enters into sexual union, the pro-cedure itself being described quite casually in the tantric texts, but taught orally by the guru in great detail and related to the different somatic and psychological dispositions of the disciple and his *śakti* or *mudrā*. Most frequently, the female adept sits astride the male yogi's lap, while he takes one of the traditional yogic postures, which are slightly modified in the tantric tradition. Buddhist iconography, especially Tibetan, shows a great variety of enstatic procedures at this stage, now well known through many excellent originals and reproductions of Tibetan religious paintings (*tanka*), the *yab yum* [honorable father and honorable mother] representing the core of a large proportion of Tibetan icons.

The model is purely Indian and I do not believe, as Professor H. Hoff-mann of Indiana University seems to do, that the *yab yum* icon has indigenous *Bon* sources in Tibet. Siva, that most sophisticated and complex deity of the Hindu pantheon, is represented and worshiped in the iconic form of the *linga* or phallus; in fact, anthropomorphic representations of any kind, which are becoming more and more frequent in modern puritan India, are not admissible in formal Sivite worship. Siva is the tutelary deity of all monks and of all ascetic orders. He stands for complete control of the senses, and for supreme renunciation. His phallic representation would seem to be an inane paradox unless we took into account the tantric foundation of this complex. This is important. It is not known even to learned Hindus except those of a scholastic tantric background: the ithyphallic condition is not priapic, but it represents precisely what the Tantrist aims to master, namely the seminal retention in the laboratory setting of tantric sacral copulation. The *Jnānasiddhi*, an important *Vajrayāna* text, teaches: *nispīdya kamale vajram bodhicittam notsrjet* [having brought down the thunderbolt into the lotus, he should not let go the *bodhi*-mind]. This is *sandhābhāṣā* for the central instruction of the second *Vajrayāna* control, referring to the retention of semen in the arcane act.

Now the pervasive use of *bodhi*-mind, the mind of intuitive wisdom, as the *sandhābhāṣā* key term for the semen, and the stress on retaining it, show how closely retention and mind control are connected to the Tantrist. The moment of suspense, effected by simultaneous breath and seminal control in conjunction with the *śakti* or *mudrā* is thought to usher in suspension of all distracting cognitive functions. The Hindu Tantrists, therefore, represent these three functions of the mind as an equilateral triangle, the basic *mandala* or mystotechnical diagram; its apex points downward symbolizing the female principle, its three sides represent *jnàna* [cognition], *icchā* [volition], and *kriyā* [conation]. Enstasis is reached when the adept succeeds in eliminating temporarily in the beginning, but in ever-increasing spans of time, all thought constructs from his mind, and in concentrating on the nondiscursive, interiorized object of his meditation. This object is variously described in anthropomorphical terms as the "chosen deity" (*istam*; Tibetan: *yid dam*), or in absolutistic, speculative terms, as the case may be.

The paradoxical situation, then, is that to the orthodox Hindu and Buddhist the Tantrist appears as a libertine, whereas in reality he preserves a state of complete celibacy. The famous fifth Dalai Lama had his problems *vis-à-vis* the orthodox reformed clergy, who apparently failed to recognize the tantric disciplinary element in his poetry. He obviously practiced the controls described above, at a time when the majority of the people around him either did not remember or ignored the tantric heritage, which is so strong in the Tibetan tradition.

Of course, there have been and there are many instances of abuse. Meditational subterfuge and ritualistic procedure may have been used now and then as a pretext for sexual indulgence of a somewhat more interesting sort than is either permissible or available in a progressively puritan Indian society, which has come to regard asceticism as the only road to religious consummation. Theoretically, many orthodox Hindus grant the possibility of these controls, but they are not ready to admit that the Tantrists have achieved it in numbers which justify condoning tantric ritual and risking social disruption.

REFERENCES

Advayavajrasangraha
    1927   Gaekwad Oriental Series 50. Edited by H. P. Shastri. Baroda.
BHARATI, A.
    1961   Sandhābhāṣā. *Journal of the American Oriental Society.* New Haven.
    1970   *The Tantric tradition.* New York: Anchor-Doubleday.
Jnānasiddhi of indrabhuti
    1929   Gaekwad Oriental Series 44. Edited by B. Bhattacharya. Baroda.

Suffering as a Religious Imperative in Afghanistan

ROBERT L. CANFIELD

An Old Man at a Shrine

In front of a famous shrine in central Afghanistan I encountered an old man, a Hazara (an underprivileged ethnic group), slumped against the trunk of a large tree, weeping. I discovered that he had come to this shrine from a great distance to obtain the healing of his only surviving son. In the city where he lived a doctor had told him that the child had an advanced case of tuberculosis and gave him no hope of recovery. So the man had brought the boy to this shrine, hoping that somehow God would work a miracle of healing. Instead, the boy had died.

Moreover, now that the boy was dead, the bereaved father was trapped here because of a bureaucratic technicality. His son's death had to be recorded, lest in a few years the government require him to produce his son for service in the army, but he had no money to pay a government clerk the customary tip to ensure registration of the death. Because he was obviously very poor none of the officials would take an interest in him. He was surviving for some days by staying with some relatives, and begging. The relatives were even poorer than he, he said, and anyway they were only distant relatives. Of his close kinsmen all were dead. He was alone.

The sufferings of this man were multiple. He was brokenhearted at the loss of his only surviving son. He was deprived of raising his progeny, something highly prized in this society, and consequently of any security in old age. Moreover, he was alone, without a close kinsman, no one permanently to live with, scarcely anyone on whom to rely for succor and comfort, even less for social and economic security. And upon all this was compounded the insult of governmental insensitivity and petty corruption. He suffered the emotional shock of a loved one's death, the social loss of his future security and — unable even to pay the fees for registering his son's death — the grinding humiliation of poverty.

This is a study of suffering in Afghanistan. It has been customary for anthropologists to study religion as essentially a cultural or ideological phenomenon. Anthropologists commonly have tried to show how a people's culturally conditioned interpretations of suffering direct them to certain forms of religious ritual and magical curing. For such an approach the variables that critically "explain" the diversity of religious forms are cultural. Spiro, for example, subtitled his book (1967) "a study in the explanation and reduction of suffering," but scarcely mentions the actual conditions of suffering in Burma. Similarly, Turner (1968) was not so concerned with the concrete circumstances of suffering among the Ndembu as with their cultural orientation toward their suffering.

This paper has a rather different focus. It points out the real conditions of suffering in order to suggest that suffering materially influences social relations. Cultural resources, i.e. systems of belief and ritual, provide the toolkit for dealing with suffering, but suffering itself, by its imperious presence in real life, makes these resources desperately important. To the peasants of Afghanistan suffering is a material condition strongly inducing them to seek efficacy through the religious and magical services provided by religious specialists; suffering, therefore, is one factor in maintaining a set of social relations.

This of course is not a novel argument,[1] but it is presented as a reminder that to explain religious belief and practice we must not only look at cultural orientations but also at the actual conditions of distress inducing people to look for religious answers and to pay for religious services. Where we find people carrying on religious activities in earnest we are well advised to take note of stressful circumstances that may be incentives for religious observance. But suffering in other cultures must be looked for. If the forms through which suf-

---

[1]   An inspiration for this view of suffering has been Max Weber (see Gerth and Mills 1958: 270–725). Belshaw (1967) presents a thorough and sympathetic description of economic hardships among the peasants of Fiji. I am grateful to Mary Farvar for pointing out to me that while in Egypt, Elizabeth Fernea (1970), despite her educated disinclination, felt impelled by the urgent sickness of her child to accept and use an amulet.

fering is expressed among another people are unfamiliar, certain aspects of their suffering can evade us. It is easy to grasp that in our own society people in many walks of life have problems; ethnocentric notions may obscure our sensitivity to the kinds of burdens that people in other cultures bear. We are apt to suppose that if they do not complain as we do, they must not suffer as we do.

Another reason for this study of suffering as an impingement on social relations is that I want eventually to explain why religious leaders in Afghanistan, "mullahs," are so important. They are indeed very important. Many of them are relatively well off by Afghan standards and a few, the great "saints," are wealthy by anyone's standards. They are also influential. Religious leaders are everywhere highly esteemed, the most powerful of them being carefully respected by the Afghan government. This respect is not without reason: the power of mullahs was dramatically evinced in 1929 when an eminent saint in the country, eventually with the support of many other religious leaders, instigated a popular insurrenction that overturned the ruling monarch.

Their influence has continued to be felt since then, though contained by police control. In 1958 when King Zaher Shah took measures to allow the veil to be removed from Afghan women, the secret police quietly rounded up key religious figures and imprisoned them for a time. Even so, despite four decades of growing government control of religious leaders and two decades of Western secular influence in Afghanistan, mullah influence has not declined. In fact, recently there has been a resurgence of religious fanaticism and a corresponding rise in the power of mullahs.

There have been large demonstrations of mullahs in Kabul, the most notable being against the use of a term of religious veneration for Lenin in a government newspaper. Also, there have been a number of xenophobic acts of violence, probably induced by religious fervor (cf. Dupree 1971a). And in the last national election persons associated with eminent mullahs and conservative religious interests seem to have gained in numbers at the expense of modernist-secularistic candidates (cf. Dupree 1971b). So a student of Afghanistan life and affairs has good reason to ask what the factors are that make religious personages important, why wealth flows to them, and why their opinions exert so much influence.

There are a number of factors involved, of course, but the one I can describe here is the suffering common to the populace. If there were space I would demonstrate that the sufferings of many people in Afghanistan are so severe, so real, so inescapable that they are happy to pay dearly for the spiritual and emotional support provided by religious leaders. Here I can only present the data on their physical sufferings and economic distresses and affirm that they induce this effect.

PHYSICAL DISTRESS AND ITS PSYCHOLOGICAL IMPLICATIONS

Physical Infirmities

Until very recently descriptions of health conditions in Afghanistan were based on only impressionistic information. The most common serious diseases formerly were reported to be malaria and tuberculosis (Simmons 1954:173) but the World Health Organization has announced the eradication of malarial mosquitoes (Smith, et al. 1969: 104). Tuberculosis remains highly frequent. A tuberculine survey conducted in 1949 yielded a reaction rate of 85 percent in persons of twenty-three years or older, indicating a high incidence of tuberculosis exposure (Simmons 1954:173).

Simmons indicates that smallpox (of which there were 1,290 reported cases in 1951), measles, and whooping cough are endemic and occasionally reach epidemic proportions. He also indicated that "syphilis and gonorrhea are prevalent. . . . The highest rates of infection are encountered in Kabul and in the border towns, particularly in Herat and Jelalabad; the lowest in the central highlands" (1954: 174a). Cholera, typhoid, rabies, and typhus *(exanthematici)* also occur in high frequencies (Berke 1946). An immunological survey in 1967 revealed the incidence of positive poliovirus antibodies in children over five years of age to be more than 90 percent (Sery, et al. 1970). Moreover,

... undernutrition and avitaminosis are prevalent. Rickets is common among children of the poorer families in the cities and towns. Osteomalacia is frequently observed among the women . . . . Vitamin A deficiencies are prominent, especially in remote districts in the country and southern provinces. Minor manifestations of vitamin C deficiency are widely distributed . . . . Goiter is endemic in foci in the Amu Dariya river valley in the northeast (Simmons 1954:176).

While medical services have been improving, a growing body of solid statistics indicates that health conditions continue to be generally

Table 1. Most frequent conditions diagnosed in clinics of the Ministry of Health in selected areas of central Afghanistan (from MAP 1967)*

Conditions diagnosed:	In Obey (Herat Prov.)	In Rukha-Panjsher (Kapisa Prov.)	In Dehrahood (Urozgan Prov.)	In Urozgan (Urozgan Prov.)
Total number patients seen	1,146	1,408	1,155	1,225
Gastrointestinal				
Number of patients	496	721	559	922
Percent of clinic	40.6	51	48.4	74
Ophthalmological				
Number of patients	236	272	158	140
Percent of clinic	20.6	18.4	13.8	11.2
Pulmonary				
Number of patients	165	103	131	88
Percent of clinic	14.4	6.9	11.4	7.2
Pulmonary and extrapulmonary TB				
Number of patients	86	29	53	56
Percent of clinic	7.5	1.9	4.6	4.6
Orthopedic				
Number of patients	147	205	144	155
Percent of clinic	12.8	14	12.5	14.4
Dermatological				
Number of patients	93	156	100	122
Percent of clinic	8.1	11.2	8.7	10

* Only the most frequent disease categories are reproduced here. The percentage figures indicate the percentage of persons having a disease in each category. Because a number of patients had more than one infirmity, there were more cases reported than patients examined, so the percentages never total 100 percent.

poor. Statistics from the 1967 and 1969 reports of the Medical Assistance Program (MAP), are indicated in Table 1. These are mainly based on persoral histories and physical examinations done in field-clinic situations. (Worms, for example, were only diagnosed on the basis of their having been seen in stools; laboratory examinations would certainly have revealed a higher incidence of both intestinal parasites and tuberculosis.)

A high number of the diseases encountered were seriously debilitating: out of the five most prevalent diseases — i.e. intestinal parasites, trachoma, chronic pulmonary disease, bacillary and amoebic dysentery, and tuberculosis — all but the first seriously impair health (MAP 1969:7). Among the less frequent diseases not indicated in

Table 1 were the following serious infirmities: acute and chronic otitis media (3.8 percent), tapeworm (3.1 percent), leprosy (2.1 percent), and osteomyelitis (1.9 percent) (MAP 1969:9). A leprosy survey in the schools of Hazarajat during the summer of 1969 yielded the number of leprosy cases in the districts indicated as shown in Table 2 (MAP 1969:16).

Table 2. Number of positive tests for leprosy among students in three districts

	Students	Positive tests
Yak Awalang	983	9
Panjaw	992	10
Lal-o-Sarjangal	716	2

A report on the sorts of ophthalmic diseases found in four areas of Afghanistan is summarized in Table 3.

Incidence of child mortality is high (see Table 4). In 1969 MAP published a four-year summary of the mortality and survival rates of children under five. Out of 18,854 children born to the 3,564 mothers interviewed, 9,565 were still living, indicating a mortality rate of 49.5 percent. In Hazarajat the mortality rate was 50.4 percent.

The Mystery of Infirmity

The above disease categories are of course our own, not those of the local populations. The persons suffering from these ailments have scarcely any sense of what is wrong with them. They typically describe their ailments only in general terms — as aches here and there, in the head, back, leg, side, etc. Also, they have little recollection of the history of their discomfort.

I met a man, for example, whose arm had been broken and remained unset; the broken part now flops loosely from his elbow. He said it had been very painful for a long time but eventually it began to feel better. He didn't know why he could no longer use it. A man blind in one eye told me he had no idea why it had become blind; he simply woke up one morning and noticed that he couldn't see out of it. (Being a farmer and illiterate, he probably did not strain his eyes sufficiently to notice that one eye was failing until it was almost gone.)

A man told me he had once washed his newborn child in the river — an icy mountain stream. For some reason, he said, it died soon afterwards; he supposed he shouldn't have washed it there. Thus,

Table 3.   Incidence of ophthalmic diseases encountered in selected areas, in percent (from Barclay 1969)*

	Baghlan	Bost	Kandahar	Jalalabad
Trachoma	33	17	23	18
Leuconia	32	24	15	21
Cataract	14	14	11	19
Conjunctivitis (non specific)	7.5	11	9	11
Glaucoma	6.5	6	5	3
Absolute glaucoma	–	–	2.5	1.5
Trichiasis	5.5	5.5	9	0.7
Paunus	7.7	2.5	6.5	2.5

*   For the same reasons as noted on Table 1, these percentages do not necessarily total 100.

Table 4.   The mortality rates of children to five years of age in selected areas of Afghanistan (from MAP 1969)

Place and province	Number of women questioned	Total live births	Total now living	Percent of Mortality
Mohamand-Dara (Nangarhar)	54	278	143	48.6
Kaja-Khogiana (Nangarhar)	42	216	122	45.6
Obey (Herat)	183	1,071	453	57.7
Rukha-Panjsher (Kapisa)	29	175	73	58.4
Dehrahood (Urozgan)	76	475	264	44.5
Urozgan (Urozgan)	105	556	293	47.3
Chowki (Kunar)	147	684	416	39.4
Sharan (Kunar)	136	641	352	45.2
Total	772	4,096	2,116	48.4

lacking an understanding of anatomy and of the most elementary processes of physiology and disease, they seem not to know or perceive the natural causes for diseases and physical discomfort.

A lamentable consequence of this ignorance is the neglect of certain injuries that normally would be minor, but owing to improper care become serious. This is noticeably true of skin abrasions which are seldom washed clean, for soap is rarely used except to wash clothing, as it dries out the skin. A boy's leg, for example, which had been only slightly cut in a fall against a rock had become septic. A blister on a man's hand became badly infected and then was further infected by an unsanitary cowhide glove that was fitted on his hand to inhibit the swelling. By the time he received medical attention the swelling had crept up his whole arm. Had he not received massive injections of antibiotics, he would have faced the prospect of tetanus.

Ignorance of what is happening to their health often results in people feeling a pervasive anxiety. Fear of the unknown, a common experience, of course, is intensified by their insufficient medical understanding. The narrowness of their technological insights leaves relatively more room for disquietude. Owing to the greater extent of what is unknown, serious harm or illness seems to strike capriciously, with unaccountable severity and irregularity. The tendency therefore is to worry overmuch, to be on edge about relatively harmless misadventures of routine life.

A child in a Hazara family, an only surviving son, had fallen while running and apparently had injured his arm. The boy cried for several hours. A medical examination that evening, however, revealed that nothing was wrong with his arm. Evidently the boy's crying had resulted from his mother's emotional response to his fall: frightened by his fall, she had also cried, and this upset the boy. Having been told that there was nothing wrong, both the boy and the mother felt better, and both were quite well the next day.

Not only illness and injury but also death seems to strike wantonly and without warning. This has been especially so during epidemics. Twice in the living memory of these populations there have been epidemics which struck down persons by the scores. About twenty years ago an epidemic of scarlet fever[2] killed a number of persons. But while many were sick in most households, some families were struck more severely than others. In one household, for example, all but the mother were sick, but they all survived; in a neighboring family six persons died.

In 1915 cholera swept through the entire country with devastating effect; that year is now known as *saal-i-taawan* [the year of judgment].[3] But there was an unevenness in the distribution of the disease. For example, while many communities suffered badly, the Tajik community of Tolwaara, blessed with a pure spring, was scarcely affected.

[2] This is judged only by their descriptions of the symptoms. They called the disease *surkhakaan* which is usually translated "measles," but probably refers to any rash-producing disease.

[3] Jewett records the date precisely for us with the disease reaching Kabul in October 1915 (Bell 1948: 263), though informants could only estimate the date.

Nevertheless the value of the spring in protecting the community from the spread of the disease seems to have been overlooked; people feel that Tolwaara was protected supernaturally because it is surrounded by several shrines, two of which are famous for supernatural power. The apparent wantonness of death may be further illustrated by a

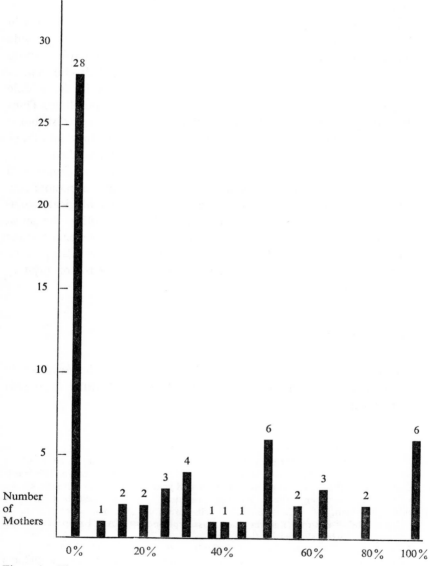

Figure 1. The percent mortality of children born to sixty-two mothers

close look at infant mortality rates in a community of 120 households.[4] In this community I collected data on the birth and mortality of offspring from sixty-two women. These mothers bore 264 live children, an average of just over three per mother. Of the children born, eighty-eight had died before puberty,[5] most of them before reaching five years of age, a mortality rate by the age of puberty of 33 percent.

Figure 1 indicates the relative success of the sixty-two mothers in bringing their children to puberty. Observe that there is a wide variation in child-rearing success, a number of mothers having lost no children and a number of others having lost all of their children. A third mode in the distribution of child mortality is in the middle range of roughly 50 percent child mortality in each household. Thus, the overall average of 33 percent child mortality is not distributed evenly, some mothers obviously being far more successful than others. It would clearly seem that some are more blessed than others.

That some people are blessed and some are not is an impression pervading not only matters of health but of social and economic success as well. Life is as inscrutable as death. Technological explanations being absent, supernatural considerations offer the most plausible means of understanding the irregularities of personal fortune (cf. Geertz 1965). In the strange caprice of supernatural powers, some people are fortunate, some are not. So a sense of mystery pervades all of life.

ECONOMIC DISTRESS

Visitors often observe that economic deprivation is less evident in Afghanistan than in many countries of Asia. Griffiths (1967:74) comments:

---

[4]   These data have a number of deficiencies. The census was complicated by the fact that most of my informants were men who do not remember these details as well as the women. Moreover, some were clearly not willing to give me this information and either reported no deaths, or denied some infant deaths already known to me through other sources. For these reasons, I have omitted data on some mothers, which, for various reasons, I felt were not trustworthy. As my data on child mortality are rather lower than those reported by MAP, I suspect the data are still somewhat skewed by these factors.

[5]   Informants sometimes found it difficult to recall ages of children. They preferred to use the terms *reeza* [small, infantile] for infants, *xord* [little] for children under puberty, and *jawaan* [young, youthful] for those over puberty.

The great contrasts between wealth and poverty common to most under-developed countries are scarcely evident in Afghanistan. . . . The signs of disease are plentiful, but the emaciated limbs and swollen stomachs of severe malnutrition are rare. There is some begging, but not the persistent buzzing swarm of importunate human flies common to other Eastern countries.

This kind of observation, though true, should not obscure our perception of the hardships that do exist. We should not surmise that economic distress is not extensive. It is found wherever one looks closely; since Griffiths wrote the above, it has become much more evident. In the marginal agricultural areas, especially in the isolated valleys of the central highlands, poverty is found among peasant land-owners; in the great agricultural centers it is found among tenant farmers; and in the cities it is found among day laborers.

Most of the poorest people in the country are Hazaras, an ethnic group distinguishable by Mongoloid features and, usually, Shiite faith (cf. Canfield 1973). The central highland region, from whence they come, is known as the Hazarajat. To illustrate the patterns of economic hardship the following paragraphs primarily describe problems of Hazaras and the Hazarajat, but this is not to imply that only they are poor. In fact, I want to use the Hazaras to argue that the greatest poverty is not in the rural districts — where admittedly it may be severe — but in the lowland plains where populations are more dense and more economically stratified. This generalization applies as much to the lowland territories of Farah, Herat, and Faizabad where few of the poor are Hazaras, as to Kabul, Ghazni, and Mazar-i-Sharif where most of them are. The phenomenon, of course, is not peculiar to Afghanistan.

Highland Peasants

In Afghanistan's diverse terrain there is a relationship between wealth and landownership in the central plains. Normally collecting heavy snows in winter, the mountains of central Afghanistan are the source of the country's great rivers — the Helmand, Hari, Morghab, Qunduz-Oxus, and Kabul rivers. In their flexuous pursuit of low ground these waters sometimes cascade through precipitous gorges, sometimes pause to wash tracts of alluvial plain. High on the mountain plateaus these plains are no more than narrow glens, but further down they become progressively wider and longer, and some, those at the confluence of the larger streams, serve as major centers of population and wealth. On the fringe of the central highlands the important centers of agricultural abundance are Besud, Uruzgan, Panjaw, Yak Awland, Bamian, and Doshi.

Further down, the waters debouch upon the broad, rich plains which are the great food baskets of the country: Kandahar, Girishk-Bost, Farah, Herat, Mazar-i-Sharif, Qunduz, Koh-Daman, Laghman-Nagarhar. Here in these expansive plains the economically successful, the socially well placed, ad the politically strong have their lands. For, as the Afghan state rose to power, those in close relation to the rulership laid claim to the most lucrative territories and they enlarged and increased their lands and profits by investing in expensive irrigation works such as canals and *karezes* (see Humlum 1959).

Thus, the most expansive and rich plains are owned largely by the wealthiest and strongest families. Most of these families are Afghans (Pushtuns), but in the north many are Uzbeks; almost invariably, except for wealthy Shiites who have recently bought into these territories, they are Sunni Muslims. In the smaller agricultural plains of the central highlands, ownership of land also entails relative abundance. Often they are owned by Sunnis, but in some areas by well-to-do Shiites. In the highest valleys and glens, however, where the tracts of irrigable plain are narrow and ownership does not necessarily entail wealth, many of these landowners are poor; most are Shiites.

There is a general tendency for the fortunes of highland peasant cultivators to decline. One reason has been the pressure of Afghan nomads in the Hazarajat. As a reward for service in the defeat of the Hazaras at the end of the last century, Afghan nomads were invited by the Amir of Kabul, Abdul Rahman, to graze their flocks in the Hazarajat. This provided them opportunity also to sell at highly inflated prices goods obtained in the Indus valley, such as cloth, tea, sugar, and salt. These were sold on credit in the spring when the nomads migrated into the highlands, and were paid for in grain after the autumn harvest. When the nomads moved to the Indus lowlands to winter their flocks they replenished their stocks of goods by selling the grain.

Nomad power over the Hazaras for a time grew to oppressive proportions so that sometimes the peasants were forced to buy goods they did not want (Ferdinand 1962). Peasants told me that sometimes the cloth would be thrown into the house through the ventilation hole in the roof, with the demand that it must be paid for (with interest) the next fall. Fortunately, the government has recently taken a more favorable stance toward the peasant cause and such repressive practices seem no longer to continue. Peasant indebtedness, however, does; around 1960 as many as 60 to 80 percent of the Hazaras in some areas were in debt (Ferdinand 1962).

The fortunes of a highland peasant can also decline because of fortuitous events that upset the delicate balance of resources and labor that enables a peasant to subsist and prosper. An example is the case of Hosain Mamad. Hosain Mamad was at one time quite wealthy, for he was the son of a strong Mir. His land produced, it is said, as much as twenty *xarwars*[6] of wheat, so he was one of the richest persons in his area. He had lots of animals, which helped to fertilize his land. Able to entertain many notables, he once fed several hundred guests when the saint of that area came to visit, an occasion that imparted to him much prestige. He spent his time supervising work on his land and in reading. Unfortunately he had no surviving sons who might have joined in the development and supervision of his economic resources, and only one daughter — a circumstance that eventually caused his good fortune to decline.

He adopted a son from a family having twelve children, but the boy turned out to be deaf and could not do much work. Also, he lost two wives and now has a third. Now in his old age, he has much less land because he had to sell some to purchase his wives. He has fewer animals, and because they provide much less manure for his fields, his land now produces only four or five *xarwars*. Too old to work it himself, he divides the yield half and half with a tenant worker, who, it is said, cheats him because he cannot supervise the work as he once did.

Another factor in the general decline of the highland peasants is the system of partible inheritance common to the Muslim world, whose dynamics are only now roughly understood (Wolf 1966:73-77). According to the requirements of Islamic law, land is divided among plural heirs, twice as much to a son as a daughter, so that no heir receives the entire estate on which the deceased subsisted. As the offspring multiply, after a few generations an heir may not receive a plot large enough for his own subsistence. In Afghanistan, land is so highly valued among the poor that the heirs try to hold the land in common, leaving it to one while the others emigrate. Even then it may not be sufficient.

For example, Khan Ali was a joint heir, with his brother and two

---

[6] Estimates of land size are commonly expressed in terms of the amount of seed that can be profitably sown on it. A *xarwar* is 80 *ser* (Samin and Nielsen 1967). See also Note 7.

male cousins, to a piece of land inherited from his grandfather that was too small to support even one person. In 1967 all of the other co-owners had left the land in Khan Ali's care and found work in Kabul; the brother as a shopkeeper, one cousin as a hired hand, and the other as a driver. Their land consisted of four *sers*[7] of irrigated land, and a quarter *ser* of cultivable dry land; altogether it was worth about 10,000 afghanis (about $250). Khan Ali had one bull, one donkey, and no sheep or goats. In spring 1967 he planted two *sers* of wheat, two *sers* of barley, and the rest in alfalfa. This, I judge from the yield of neighboring plots, would produce at least 1200 *paw*[8] of grain.

As the residents calculate their monthly consumption needs to be a minimum of ninety *paw* of grain per person, his land would in a moderate year produce enough to last Khan Ali, if he consumed it all himself, over thirteen months. This assumes that none of the grain was sold for taxes, paid as debts, or claimed by any of the other three owners. Actually, however, all three of these liens on his yield existed, so that in order to remain viable his yield had to be considerably higher than the average in his area. Obviously he was close to the margin of viable subsistence.

Khan Ali lived alone. The high price of brides had denied him the privilege of a wife, though he was about forty years old. In summer 1967 he ran short of food and money and borrowed a little from neighbors to hold him until harvest. I asked him how he would repay the debt; he didn't know. The following spring he leased the land to a man from outside his valley to pay back his debts.

As the lessee had hired someone else to work the land, Khan Ali took a bus to Kabul. He planned to work as a coolie until he could get enough cash ahead to do something more profitable. Several factors contributed to Khan Ali's economic decline but the critical one was the size of the land left him by his father. The partible inheritance rule eventually carved the land into too small a fragment for it to support even one person.

The same rule, however, while impartially applied to all classes, has relatively little detrimental effect on the wealthy, for they have benefited more directly from the burgeoning economy in the cities. The growing numbers of heirs in the great families has enhanced, rather than weakened, their strength because as their offspring have increased, their involvement in national institutions has increased. They have dispersed into the many new positions in government, in-

---

[7]   A *ser* is 16 *paw*, which in English weight is 15 pounds.
[8]   See Notes 6 and 7.

dustry, and commerce that have become available as the nation modernized. These are the families that have gained most from foreign development.

The correct generalization seems to be that to remain viable a rural family must profitably articulate with the national cash economy. Some highland families have been able to do this — but only the rich ones. During the economic surge of the past twenty years these Hazaras have invested in small business activities and have profited greatly. Mir Ramzan Khan is an example.

Mir Ramzan Khan is the oldest surviving son of a formerly powerful Hazara Mir. Like his father, he attempts to mediate disputes among his neighbors and poorer friends, and when necessary he represents them to the government. For these services he receives many benefits, usually informal and unofficial. He is often paid in cash or grain by his clients and they also help his paid servants during plowing and harvest seasons, so he does little of his own work.

He and his younger brother have not yet divided the property they received from their father. It consists of forty *sers* of land (i.e. ten times that of Khan Ali and his three co-owners), on which, in addition to the grain needed for their own consumption, they have planted a number of trees that in a few years will bring several thousand afghanis when sold in Kabul. In about 1965 they purchased a bus which carries both passengers and freight between Hazarajat and Kabul. They have also acquired a *saray*[9] in Kabul which serves as a depot for the bus and its freight.

Mir Ramzan Khan lives on his natal land and in addition to his political activities oversees the cultivation of his land, while his younger brother supervises the bus business and the *saray* in Kabul. Unlike Khan Ali, Mir Ramzan Khan was able to stabilize his already strong position by investing in the national economic network. He and his brother are growing more wealthy.

While only the well-to-do can make such profitable investments, it seems likely that many of the rank-and-file highland peasants will become poorer. This is due to a fourth and more basic factor in the decline of the highland peasant, i.e. the general insufficiency of cultivable land. The scarcity of land in the Hazarajat is indicated in the rough data available on nutritional density.

The average amount of cultivated land per Hazarajat resident is 1.78 *jeribs* (about half an acre). The national average is 2.08 *jeribs*. Average amounts

[9] An enclosed compound in the city, a caravansary.

of cultivated land per operator disclose an even greater discrepancy of
12.07 *jeribs* for the nation at large (Jung 1970:9).

Because of the land scarcity, for more than a century highland
peasants have been coming down to the lowlands and the cities during
the winter to supplement their incomes (Burnes 1842: 230). Usually
they have returned in the spring, but those who obtained steady work
have stayed, entrusting their land to relatives, some of them returning
home briefly to help with the spring plowing and the autumn harvest.
As a result, the summer population of the highlands has been greater
than the winter population.

According to a research team that visited Hazarajat in 1968, perhaps as many as 30 to 50 percent of the highland labor force have
been seasonally absent. Still, population pressure has not decreased:
"Permanent migration does not offset the natural population growth
with the result that the summertime population of the [central] region
is increasing. Consequently landholdings are becoming smaller and
the number of landless families is increasing" (Allen 1963: 2).

Rural Sharecroppers and Urban Day Laborers

The decline of the economic fortunes of the poor landowners eventually forces them, like Khan Ali in the case described earlier, to
leave their land permanently. Even so, they are unlikely to sell it;
commonly they rent it to a neighbor or mortgage it. Once pried off
their land, they seek employment elsewhere. Most go to the cities, but
some stay closer to home, moving to the nearer lowlands to work as
tenant farmers for richer landowners. We shall examine this latter
strategy first, using the Bamian valley as an example.

Bamian is a basin-shaped valley in Hazarajat at an altitude of
about 6,000 feet surrounded by mountain ridges that reach 16,000
feet. The contracts of tenant sharecroppers in Bamian's lowlands suggest that their incomes are less than those of many peasant cultivators
in the highlands, for there is a rough gradation from lowland to highland in the shares paid to tenants and hired workers. In 1968, with the
landlord providing the seed, oxen, and other equipment,[10] share-

---

[10]   Most published reports on tenancy contracts indicate that the tenant receives
"one-fifth of the crop if he provides nothing but labor. If he also supplies implements, his share is one-fourth, and if he has draft animals, he gets one-third"
(Smith et al. 1969: 250). This apparently is the case in some major agricultural
regions, but even there, the arrangements are probably more flexible.

croppers working in the most valuable lowlands received one-seventh or one-sixth of the crop; those who worked somewhat away from the central plain received one-fifth, those further out and higher up on the slopes of the mountain one-fourth, others somewhat higher one-third, and those in the highest glens of the basin one-half. The one-half contracts were different in that the worker provided his own oxen and equipment. Also, other considerations besides geographic location affected the arrangements, such as the amount of land worked by the hired hand, the kind of crop, whether other provisions are made for him (such as a strip of land whose yield is entirely his), and the like. Still, the gradation suggests the relative severity of the sharecropping contracts in different places: the lower the lands, the less the share of the tenant.

These data suggest that the peasants who still viably subsist in the highlands are better off than those who have left and acquired work as sharecroppers elsewhere. The matter needs additional research, but however accurate for lowland sharecroppers, the argument seems incontestably true for migrants who have moved to the cities.

They have come because there were more jobs than in their natal valleys, but recently they have been finding that there is a surfeit of workers like themselves to fill those jobs. The vast majority of them are impoverished. This, except for the boom years of the fifties and sixties, has been the common pattern: most Hazaras coming to the cities have been miserably poor. In general, the poverty of the Hazaras has been most severe, not in the distant highlands, but in the cities. The poorest Hazara landowners are found in the highest lands, but the poorest Hazara workers are found in the urban centers.

In competition for work in the cities, they contract to work for relatively little. That the competition of these migrant laborers for work reduces their wages is indicated by the fluctuation of wages in the cities according to their seasonal influx from the central highlands. Daily wages in Baghlan fall from 30 afghanis in summer to 20 in winter; in Mazar-i-Sharif from 50 afghanis in summer to 25-30 in winter; in Bost from 25 afghanis in summer to 18 in winter (Smith et al. 1969: 303). At these rates, assuming 300 paid days per year (which for most is much too high), a year-round day laborer would annually receive around 8,000 afghanis (about ($110) in Baghlan, 12,000 afghanis (about $165) in Mazar-i-Sharif, and 6,000 afghanis (about $80) in Bost.

Formerly, when they migrated to the cities, people used to find good jobs. During the fifties and early sixties, when the cities were prospering from massive injections of foreign aid, many Hazara peasants in quest of opportunity rented out their lands to neighbors and moved to the cities. Thus, an important factor in the large Hazara out-migration during that period was the "pull" of outside economic opportunity. More recently, however, fewer of them have been willing to leave; as already noted, those who do so are compelled by straitened circumstances. So, in more recent years it has been due to the "push" of economic difficulties at home. Jung (1970: 11) argues from census data on migrants to Kabul from all regions that "push" factors predominate:

When asked the reason for their migration to the city, 20 percent stated insufficient land; 23 percent meager income; 8 percent unemployment; and 12 percent insufficient employment.

The efflux from the Hazarajat has been accelerating. When Khan Ali left his land and journeyed to Kabul he was not alone. The bus was jammed with dozens of other men like himself, some of them so poor that upon arrival they lacked even the half afghani (half cent) necessary to ride a city bus across town to reach a relative's home. On the basis of Russian estimates and the Greater Kabul Census, Jung (1970) estimates that from 1954 to 1961 an average of 7,600 people per year immigrated to Kabul from all provinces, with the number rising abruptly since then — to 12,000 in 1962, for example, and to nearly 20,000 in 1965. Of these, 31 percent came from the central provinces. By 1969 about 40,000 persons had recently emigrated from the central provinces. Of these 48 percent had been in Kabul for more than five years, 36 percent for one to four years, and 12 percent for less than one year — that is, almost half had been in Kabul for less than five years (Jung 1970: 7). One Hazara clan lived until about fifteen years ago entirely in the central highlands, but today 70 (i.e. 60 percent) of its 114 households live in Kabul.

Most of the Hazara migrants are permanently residing in Kabul, but many of them work only as day laborers and are often without employment. A recent phenomenon in Kabul has been the groups of unemployed Hazara men in the early mornings at central locations where people needing laborers may find them. These are Kabul's poor. In 1968 their services were available at 30 to 50 afghanis per day; few worked every day.

The pull of the cities was strong when the national economy was flourishing but since 1967 it has been faltering, bringing down even further the fortunes of the poor. The main reason for the decline of the national economy, of course, has been the reduction of foreign aid. From 1960 to 1967 annual amounts of foreign aid to the country approached 100,000,000 dollars, but since 1967, despite increased aid from the People's Republic of China, this figure has dropped sharply — to 69,050,000 in 1967–68, to 50,200,000 in 1968–69, and to 44,210,000 in 1969–70 (Newell 1972: 144). The drop in foreign aid has especially affected the Hazaras who were favored by the foreign populations as domestic help. Hundreds of these are now without jobs. Moreover, inflation has continued; the price of wheat per *ser* (a common measure of the economy) rose from 20-25 afghanis in 1960 to 60 afghanis in 1968.

Since 1967 a natural calamity has greatly intensified the suffering. The snow on which Afghan agriculture depends for irrigation water in summer was for three successive years unseasonably light, resulting in one of the severest famines in Afghan history. In the summer of 1972, though a heavier snowfall augured for a better crop, the famine was so severe that in the north riots broke out as farmers demanded food for their families. According to the *New York Times*, November 14, 1972, estimates of the number of deaths reached 80,000.[11]

Meanwhile, uncounted numbers have fled the famine areas to the cities, forming new shanty districts. An informal survey of these people in Kabul revealed that perhaps as many as one-third of their families had perished that year (personal communication). The famine crisis is of course a major calamity, hopefully only temporary, but it is merely an intensified form of hardship already familiar to the poor. For many, economic hardship is today an endemic condition.

The trajectory of the highland peasant, if he is not rich, seems to be downhill. Now the whole economy sags and his prospects seem even worse. Perhaps this is the reason for the concomitant rise in religious fervor in Afghanistan. Even after twenty years of Western secular influence, in Afghanistan the ancient bond between hardship and religion remains vigorous.

CONCLUSION

For the physically afflicted and poor, suffering and hardship belong to the world of real things. Suffering is a material condition with

---

[11] Some observers feared that during the winter of 1973 as many as 200,000 would die (*U.S. News and World Report*, November 6, 1972). According to personal sources, this figure was much too high. (See also Afghanistan Council 1973.)

which the infirm and the hungry must deal. They must deal with it as they must cope with aridity or heavy snowfalls, government officers or local landlords, the price of wheat or the cost of hired labor. Like each of these circumstances, suffering raises issues — i.e. poses problems and perhaps offers opportunities — which must be coped with or exploited as part of the on-going process of maintaining survival and a degree of comfort and security.

Thus, for the afflicted and poor, religion is not simply a matter of beliefs, customs, and rituals, but it is also essentially one of material efficacy. The services of religious specialists are valued not just because the common people are socialized to value them, as mere cherished traditions of their ancestors, but primarily because their problems constrain them to demand these services. Amid their dilemmas they are willing to pay dearly to obtain a measure of relief — perhaps even deliverance — through the services of their religious leaders. Their sufferings convert their desire for a meaningful existence — a universal concern — into a social force, the pursuit of immediate and substantive efficacy. The need for power to exert influence on social and material exigencies is the mainspring of religious practice and one of the bases for the influence and wealth of Afghan religious leadership. This is what brought an aging man and his dying only son, at the price of their last farthing, to the door of a notable shrine. For the shrine was reputed to have efficacious power, power as specific to the infirmity as streptomycin.

The shrine's failure to deliver shattered an old man's world. Unfortunately I know nothing of what became of him, for he was soon gone — chased away by onlookers who were embarrassed that a foreigner had discovered his plight. One can only imagine how he might have picked up the pieces of his life. But to do this one would need to examine the cultural heritage that both "explained" to him his suffering and offered him a fresh hope, and that will have to be another study.

REFERENCES

AFGHANISTAN COUNCIL OF THE ASIA SOCIETY
  1973   *Newsletter,* January 1973. New York.
ALLEN, P. H.
  1963   "Report on Hazarajat trip." Mimeograph. Kabul, Afghanistan: Agency for International Development.

BARCLAY, A.
1969   Developing ophthalmic treatment in Afghanistan. *Transactions of the Ophthalmological Society, United Kingdom* 89:591–600.

BELL, M. J.
1948   *An American engineer in Afghanistan.* Minneapolis: The University of Minnesota Press.

BELSHAW, C.
1967   *Under the ivy tree.* Berkeley: University of California Press.

BERKE, Z.
1946   Public health and hygiene in Afghanistan. *Afghanistan* 1:1–18.

BURNES, A.
1842   *Cabool: a personal narrative of a journey to, and residence in that city in the years 1836, 1837, and 1838.* London: John Murray.

CANFIELD, R. L.
1973   *Faction and conversion: religious alignments in the Hindu Kush.* Anthropological Papers of the Museum of Anthropology 50. Ann Arbor: University of Michigan Press.

DUPREE, L.
1971a *A note on Afghanistan: 1971.* American Universities Field Staff Reports, South Asia Series 15(2). Hanover, New Hampshire.
1971b *Comparative profiles of recent parliaments in Afghanistan.* American Universities Field Staff Reports, South Asia Series 15(4). Hanover, New Hampshire.

FERDINAND, K.
1962   Nomadic expansion and commerce in central Afghanistan. sketch of some modern trends. *Folk* 4:123–159.

FERNEA, E.
1970   *A view of the Nile: story of an American family in Egypt.* Garden City: Doubleday.

GEERTZ, C.
1965   "Religion as a cultural system," in *Anthropological approaches to the study of religion.* Edited by Michael Banton. London: Tavistock.

GERTH, H. H., C. R. MILLS
1958   *From Max Weber: essays in sociology.* New York: Oxford University Press.

GRIFFITHS, M.
1967   *Afghanistan.* London: Praeger.

HUMLUM, J.
1959   *La géographie de l'Afghanistan.* Copenhagen: Gyldendal.

JUNG, C. L.
1970   *Some observations on the patterns and processes of rural-urban migrations in Kabul.* The Afghanistan Council of the Asia Society, Occasional Paper 2. New York.

MEDICAL ASSISTANCE PROGRAM
1967   *Annual Report.* Kabul: Ministry of Health of the Royal Government of Afghanistan.

1969   *Annual Report.* Kabul: Ministry of Health of the Royal Government of Afghanistan.

NEWELL, R. S.
1972   *The politics of Afghanistan.* Ithaca: Cornell University Press.

SAMIN, A. Q., G. A. NIELSEN
1967   *Conversion factors for agriculturalists of Afghanistan.* Faculty of Agriculture Research Note 2. Kabul, Afghanistan: University of Kabul.

SERY, V., O. THRAENHART, K. ZACCK, S. BROGGER, A. OMAR, A. SABOR
1970   Basis for poliomyelitis surveillance in Kabul city. *Zentralblatt für Bakteriologie, Parasitenkunde, Infektionskrankheiten und Hygiene. Abteilung originale medizinisch-hygienische Bakteriologie, Virusforschung und Parasitenkunde* 221:311–318.

SIMMONS, J. S.
1954   *Global epidemiology, a geography of disease and sanitation,* volume three. Philadelphia: Lippincott.

SMITH, H. H., D. W. BERNIER, F. M. BUNGE, F. C. TINTZ, R. SHINN, S. TELEKI
1969   *Area handbook for Afghanistan.* Washington: U. S. Government Printing Office.

SPIRO, M. E.
1967   *Burmese supernaturalism: a study in the explanation and reduction of suffering.* Englewood Cliffs: Prentice-Hall.

TURNER, V. W.
1968   *The drums of affliction: a study of religious processes among the Ndembu of Zambia.* Oxford: Clarendon.

WOLF, E.
1966   *Peasants.* Englewood Cliffs: Prentice-Hall.

New Approaches to Religious Ethnology, Especially in Austria: Main Theses

ALOIS CLOSS

Animated discussions have arisen between F. Bornemann (1938a, 1938b), P. Schebesta (1960), J. Haekel (1956a, 1964), W. Hirschberg 1966, 1972), Alois Closs (1966, 1973), R. Boccassino (1958) and E. Stiglmayr (1970) — all of them pupils of the founding fathers of the *Anthropos* group, whose original views were most clearly expressed at the *Religionsethnologische Wochen* in Louvain, Tilburg, and Milan (*Semaine* 1911–1925). The most radical departure from P. W. Schmidt's views (*Semaine* 3, 1923: 229–243) was voiced by R. Mohr (1957: 153–158) with regard to sacrifice, when he reviewed A. Vorbichler's pertinent book (1956), which already differed from Schmidt's views. It was, above all, the so-called *Kulturkreismethode* (culture history by culture circles), that was repudiated by the Austrian ethnologists at the two symposia held in Wartenstein (*Wartenstein* I and II, 1958 and 1959), without resulting, however, in any kind of agreement on the future approaches. The present differences of opinion concern, among others, the problem of how it is possible to subsume the religious phenomena of nonliterate peoples in a general history of religions, without falling back upon an even less justifiable ethnological evolutionism; for any kind of historical categorizing along the lines of the *Kulturkreislehre* (culture history by culture circles) has now been rejected in their own ranks.

1. M. Eliade's view (1969), that it is possible to launch a universal history of religions by disclosing the levels of manifestations of the phenomena concerned, without having recourse to chronological per-

Translated into English by Helmut Stumfohl.

spectives, does not obviate investigating the exact methods by which the religions of the nonliterate peoples may be included. The author, therefore, thinks that recourse must be had to: (a) history proper, by analyzing historical accounts of different times (Hirschberg 1972) and (b) by integrating the ethnoarchaeological findings (Closs 1956a). He called this a "special historical ethnology" (Closs 1956a), but beyond this a universal historical ethnology has to be developed, without the antiquated method of the culture circles.

Now it is necessary to analyze the question of how the principle of culture history can be reactivated, because the religions of nonliterate peoples can only be understood historically in the framework of their cultural relations. Beyond that, it is necessary to do research into relationships — by interconnected motives in different peoples (as done by R. Heine-Geldern), or by acculturation phenomena (U. R. Ehrenfels 1959), or by the gradient of integration between different peoples, especially related ones, e.g. Mangbetu and Azande (Closs 1960). Only as a transition and heuristically — not as a thesis — has the problem been pointed out by Closs (1964) of whether it is possible to establish cultures transcending single peoples and so relating them by Gestalt-analytical methods, e.g. megalithic culture. R. Heine-Geldern's statement (*Wartenstein* I, 1958: 166), that one can only talk of a megalithic complex, not of a megalithic culture circle, does not exclude trans-ethnic cultures, Gestaltanalytically verified; for the theory of culture circles has just been criticized because of the lack of inner coherence within those elements or motives (Closs 1960). But to deny any totality at all to the phenomenon of culture, as Stiglmayr does (1970: 53) — does he dispute any determination by main ideas too? — is certainly going too far, especially if one ascribes some development according to the "biogenetic principle" to it at the same time (1970: 173)! Above all, any paper on ethnological theory needs an exact concept of culture that fits into universal relationships.

Both the methodically improved research into relationships and into types — the latter as evidence for cultural strata (Rudolph 1971), i.e. not according to the method of culture circles — may be subsumed in the concept of a theory of interethnical systems, the development of which is stated to be the main task of ethnology as sociology, if one follows K. Jettmar (1953, 1973), who elucidated the ethnoarchaeology of Central Asia. With regard to the fact that any kind of anthropogenic phenomena, even those relating to form, develop according to natural laws, everything anthropological must be seen historically too; this does not mean, of course, that ethnology in its totality is to be treated as history. The author of a Leiden paper (for *Historia Religionum* II, 1971: 573–592) has attempted to evaluate a group of nonliterate peoples through their historical aspects, given in themselves.

2. W. Hirschberg (1972) has fallen back upon the most narrow concept of a specialized historical ethnology, investigating religious phenomena of some West African tribes. He admits only of the quintessence of such a method, i.e. the analysis of written accounts of different times as "ethnohistory," whilst the periodical *Ethnohistory* (first published in Bloomington, afterwards in Buffalo) enlarged the concept, especially with regard to linguistics, and at least one of its papers, in 1957, has even included ethnoarchaeological findings. Although the majority of the papers of this periodical deal with America (Africa is treated only once on the basis of an ancient travelog), a fundamental discussion of the concept of ethnohistory should not be neglected. According to Hirschberg's concept of culture history (1966) the Bushmen are to be treated within the framework of prehistory and following P. W. Schmidt and his friend K. Dittmer he even wrote a "Kulturgeschichte Afrikas" (1974).

3. The existence and scope of a historical ethnology — in its widest meaning, besides a special one in which there is no room for typological dating (as opposed to chronological), emergence (Stiglmayr 1970), and phaseology (Hirschberg 1972, following Mühlmann) — must be made perfectly clear, especially in religious ethnology, because it was just this very concept, which was the focus of a speculative evolutionism and against which one rose in arms, following Graebner's watchword of culture-historical ethnology. Be it as it may that evolutionism is dead (according to Mühlmann, who takes it in its classical sense), it should be mentioned that W. Koppers has established a definite line of progress in material culture — investigating economic phenomena — and this by nonspeculative methods. But when he and his late scientific friends asserted a continuous regression or deterioriation in personal culture, especially in religion, it was premature, because obvious emergences — the term has been used in a cultural context by Stiglmayr (1970: 140) for the first time — in some fields of religion have been neglected, e.g. the expansion of religious offices, the growth of ecstatic behavior, the elaboration of the image of the deity at least with the Polynesians and the first indications of a special stress on the ruling function of the sky gods of the horse-breeding pastoralists. Because of this lack, Closs (1956c) advocated a nonspeculative (i.e. based on

field findings) research into evolutionism in religious ethnology as desirable and possible. G. Schott (1961: 83–86) has declared this to be only possible when carried out in small, strictly limited areas of investigation. Such a beginning cannot be smothered by declaring the nonliterate marginal peoples of the world and their cultures to be the "youngest," as Mühlmann does.

4.   For initiating research into religious ethnological evolution, nothing is more necessary and fruitful than analyzing the so-called ethnological religious categories — according to the most modern standards of research — which have been taken by the evolutionists to be preceding stages of a belief in a deity. It is now getting clearer and clearer that any belief in a deity in itself is extensively linked with just those categories, which is to say that the belief in a deity in itself is just such a category. But there are different concepts of god (anthropomorphic, theriomorphic, and animistic ones, e.g. the Spirit of the Sky), whose typological and genetical relationships must be investigated before any solution is declared to be possible or impossible. It is asserted that the priority of a theriomorphic concept of god has been definitely established as a ruler of animals, but just this type is often thought of as anthropomorphic.

5.   "Pluriform monotheism," stated to be found with nonliterate tribes as the Nuer and Oglala (according to Th. van Baaren), is just not found in food-gathering cultures, of which there are different types which cannot be chronologically related. At least pluriform monotheism has no definite status there, and their concepts of a supreme being do not admit of any indication of an original monotheism. The ruler of animals belongs much more to hunting than to food-gathering cultures.

   This concept of god, also, does not go back to totemism, a concept which is only used now for the system of relationships between small groups and certain aspects of animals, and beyond that of some religious phenomena, e.g. the belief in an alter ego (Closs 1966). Sociological totemism has not produced any concepts of a higher being, as correctly stated by C. Lévi-Strauss. The basic concept for theriomorphic deities is better called "animalistic," according to Haekel (1956b: 52ff). Frazer has already observed that sociological totemism is in no way religious. C. Lévi-Strauss has noticed that there is no relationship at all between the sociological system and the theriomorphic system of protecting spirits of the Ojibwá. It does not seem impossible that certain types of concepts of god — like the Spirit of the Sky — may be traced back to animism; the origination of a whole group of deities from animism cannot be wholly excluded, even less so from manism; but this should be proved in every single case and the dependence of a belief in god on animism *in toto* has been disproved by facts.

Outside this it is impossible to equate all the various forms of a belief in souls with the philosophical concept of the soul and to conceive of it as a genetic unity, which has already been seen by van der Leeuw and stressed by A. E. Jensen (1951: 287). This indeed negates the concept of evolutionism in this respect too. But there is no doubt, that the roots of the ecstatic concepts of the ethnological religious categories, e.g. shamanism, are to be found in animism. The essence of shamanism is not due to any kind of influence from Iranic dualism, it is only institutionalized and altruistic spirit-induced ecstasy, which often favored the appearance of prophetic revivalism or nativism, stimulated by colonialism.

No argument can be brought to bear against calling the totality of the religious phenomena of nonliterate peoples "magic religion" (as opposed to revealed religion), introduced by M. Hermanns (1970; see also Closs 1972). The term magic does not denote anything primitive; and the element of "overpowering," prevailing in the cult of the nonliterate peoples, has to be seen not as something impious, but as a means to come to grips with the numinous. It is to van Baaren's credit to have seen that with perfect clarity (1964). Neglected presentation of the myths of nonliterate peoples from the point of view of a culture-historical ethnology is felt with particular regard to M. Eliade's treatment of the myth of eternal return (which, though certainly proved correct, is nevertheless overemphasized in relation to the whole field of facts).

6.   All this would especially emerge in a completely integrated ethnology, such as religious ethnological categories. The core of it might well comprise — just in the way Stiglmayr understands it (1970) — ethnohistory and phaseological genetics; though it could not be totally integrated, in accordance with an integrated investigation of culture, without including ethnopsychology and ethnosociology (E. Unger-Dreiling 1966). For the latter, J. Stagl (1971) is the specialist in the Vienna circle. Both are first to be investigated for their potentialities for further research into religious ethnological evolutionism. As regards religious ethnology, it should be taken into consideration that the religious function of the *pater familias* has obviously preceded that of the tribal chief, who does not direct, or at least not always, the main rituals,

especially initiation ceremonies of the most primitive tribes.

7.   In the perspective of culture history even the higher (literate) cultures (R. Heine-Geldern 1956; J. Haekel 1956a) are to be included among the subjects of ethnology, without regard to the validity of the late culture-historical method. R. Heine-Geldern in his practical expositions of the problem has treated, since 1928, the megalithic complex in its ethnological diffusion in a purely historical context but he restricted his subject in comparison with D. J. Wölfel (1951). In consequence, Wölfel's scientific friends have elaborated on the subject with regard to Eurafrica. Some quite successfully used the ethnological criteria in their analysis of Near Eastern cultural and religious problems. It was to their advantage that prehistory and literary traditions furnished a working basis. (*Almogaren* 1970–1972; J. Henninger 1968; and W. Dostal 1957).

In contrast to that, Koppers and his friends, struggling with the Indo-European problem, could not secure the support of the linguists because of the lack of a definite prehistoric localization of the Indo-Europeans. Not the least of their disadvantages was the fact that the prehistory of the horse, whose importance for the Indo-European question was stressed by Koppers (1955), could only be cleared up later by Hančar (1955). In spite of that, it has been definitely shown that Koppers' approaches and results were not altogether wrong. To have proved the dependence of Indo-European horse breeding and its religious traits on cattle breeding — as opposed to its dependence on reindeer breeding as stated by Flor (1939: 300) — is a lasting result.

The ethnological interpretation of the sociological elements of Germanic religion, the secret societies, and the sacred chieftainships — started by O. Höfler and to which the Japanologist A. Slawik (1972) positively responded (in an ethnological context) — was put into a new light by Alois Closs (1936: 549–673), who treated the religion of a Germanic tribe ethnologically by referring to prehistory and historical documentation; afterwards he treated the whole Germanic world in this way (Closs 1951: 273–366, 1956b; *Wartenstein* II, 1959: 165–193). This was again done through archaeological evidence and by constantly referring to literary sources and with a view to the possible application of ethnological criteria; but then the necessary critical caution in the employment of these categories was not even practiced in the ranks of the ethnologists themselves. The most recent of these categories — shamanism, according to Lubbok — has been analyzed by the Nordist P. Buchholz (1968) in numerous perspectives, using the sagas of Icelandic literature, whilst Alois Closs (1968) has given a survey of all the publications about Indo-European peoples, dealing with the problem in question and published up to that time. Using religious relations to animals, Closs (1966) tried to substantiate the Germanic concept of the holy, as analyzed by Baetke on the one hand, and an ethnological concept of totemism, already critically evaluated, on the other hand. A closer analysis of the concept of shamanism was given by Alois Closs (1971) by analyzing ecstatic rituals of the Balkan regions, to which prehistory and folklore have given valuable points of reference. Already in 1956 and 1959, A. Closs put his ethnological perspectives on Germanic culture and religion into a wider context. The materials contained in these papers will appear more convincing as they are critically analyzed on the basis of what has been said above about some ethnological religious categories. In this field of research, it appears clear that the above-mentioned problem is the most urgent task of religious ethnology, using new approaches, especially in Austria.

8. The science of animal behavior "looks down" as it were, speaking in an evolutionary context, on animal psychology and animal sociology. It has been declared by Hirschberg to be the special task of the Vienna Institut für Völkerkunde, beside ethnohistory. P. Weidkuhn (1965) was the first to use it ethnologically in connection with the level of culture: he compared aboriginal Australian RITUALS of encounter with animal behavior. Ethnology, however, must not be put to shame by the biologist A. Portmann, when making its excursions into the realm of animals, for Portmann has demanded that man's unique status — i.e. the differences between man and animal too — must be considered. Ethnology would especially be required to do so, even in the field of aggression. Whether there is already some kind of magic contained in animal rituals can only be decided by animal psychology, though not without referring to the ethnological concept of magic.

9. To conclude, in all these respects a new situation has arisen in the circle of the friends or pupils of the founders of *Anthropos* with regard to the state of affairs, treated sympathetically by ethnologists such as Lowie, Kluckhohn or even Kroeber, with respect to the concept of diffusion. Even W. Schmidt's (1930) point of view, already considerably different from the views ventilated at the time of the above-mentioned *Religionsethnologische Wochen*, is largely antiquated. K. Narr has, on the other hand, shown in his lectures that the radical separation

of ethnology and history, practiced in the Vienna Institute (taken over from Mühlmann), is quite erroneous. Narr is just now preparing a pertinent paper for *Saeculum*. W. Keilbach (1962), in agreement with Pettazoni, has rightly taken his stand against the close amalgamation of phenomenology and psychology in the science of religion, which is detrimental to even the most justified kind of historicism.

If any religious ethnology with culture-historical perspectives lies within those extremes — especially concerned with the ethnological ages of the different nonliterate peoples, with their religious phenomena in ceremonies and conceptions, with research into relationships critically restricted and with establishing connections between nonliterate and higher cultures (as demanded in this paper) — an overall view of nonliterate religions and, connected with it, of religion in general will still not be feasible (Rudolph 1967: 30), though it will be possible to connect these religions with a *Historia religionum*, by disclosing the levels of manifestations of their complexes and elements to the highest possible degree. Widengren's (1945), Bidney's (1954) and Rudolph's discussions of evolution and evolutionism certainly furnish valuable data for it.

REFERENCES

Almogaren
1970–1972   *Zeitschrift des Institutum Canarium Hallein*, volumes one to three. Graz: Druck u. Verlagsanstalt.
BIANCHI, U.
1964   *Probleme der Religionsgeschichte*. Göttingen.
BIDNEY, D.
1954   The ethnology of religion and the problem of human evolution. *American Anthropologist* 56:1-18.
BOCCASSINO, R.
1958   *Etnologia religiosa*. Torino: Società Editrice Internazionale. (Cf. A. Closs. *Anthropos* 53:1033–1036.)
BORNEMANN, F.
1938a Zum Form- und Quantitätskriterium. *Anthropos* 33–34:614–650.
1938b *Die Urkultur in der kulturhistorischen Ethnologie*. Mödling bei Wien: St. Gabrieler Studien.
BUCHHOLZ, P.
1968   *Schamanistische Züge in der altisländischen Überlieferung*. Münster/W.
CLOSS, ALOIS
1936   *Indogermanen- und Germanenfrage. Neue Wege zu ihrer Lösung.*

Wiener Beiträge zur Kulturgeschichte und Linguistik 4. Salzburg-Leipzig. (Cf. J. de Vries, in *Mensch en Maatschappij* 14 Jg. 2 o.J.: 1–5. Amsterdam; C. C. Uhlenbeck, *Anthropos* 32:674–677. 1937.)

1951 "Die Religion der Germanen in ethnologischer Sicht," in *Christus und die Religionen der Erde*, volume one. Edited by F. König, 273–366. Wien.

1956a Abgrenzung und Aufriß einer speziellen historischen Ethnologie. *Zeitschrift für Ethnologie* 81:161–179. Braunschweig, Limbach.

1956b Historische Ethnologie und Germanistik. *Anthropos* 52:832–897.

1956c Kulturhistorie und Evolution. *Mitteilungen der Anthropologischen Gesellschaft* Bd. 86:1–47.

1957 Religionsphänomenologie und Kulturhistorie. *Anthropos* 52:937–943.

1959 "Ethnologische Bestimmung des Altgermanentums," in *Wartenstein* II:165–193.

1960 "Gestaltkriterium und das historische Prinzip in der Völkerkunde," in *Gestalthaftes Sehen. Zum 100. Geburtstag von Ch. Ehrenfels*, 92–104. Darmstadt: Wissenschaftl. Buchgesellschaft.

1964 Ganzheit als Gesichtspunkt in der kulturhistorischen Ethnologie. *Zeitschrift für Ganzheitsforschung* 8:137–149. Wien.

1965 Die "Unwirklichkeit" des Totemismus. *Anthropos* 60:816–822.

1966 "Das Heilige und die Frage nach dem germanischen Totemismus," in *Festschrift W. Baetke*, 79–84. Weimar: Böhlau.

1967 "Integration als Gestaltungsbegriff (Vom Standpunkt der kulturhistorischen Völkerkunde)," in *Gestalt und Wirklichkeit*. Festschrift for F. Weinhandl. Edited by R. Mühler and J. Fischl, 277–284. Berlin: Duncker und Humblot.

1968 "Schamanismus bei den Indoeuropäern," in *Gedächtnisschrift für W. Brandenstein*. Studien zur Sprachwissenschaft und Kulturkunde 14:289–392. Innsbruck.

1971 Südosteuropa als ethnohistorisches Untersuchungsfeld über ekstatisches Brauchtum. *Wiener Ethnologische Blätter* 3:3–23.

1972 Prophetismus und Schamanismus aus religionsethnologischer Perspektive. *Kairos N.F.* 14:200–214. Salzburg: Otto Müller.

1973 "Altkanarier und Indogermanentum. Religions- und kulturvergleichend," in *Almogaren* III:35–53, 85 f.

DOSTAL, W.

1957 Ein Beitrag zur Frage des religiösen Weltbildes des frühen Bodenbaues Vorderasiens. *Archiv für Völkerkunde* 12:34–40. Wien.

1968a Die Beduinen in Südarabien. *Wiener Beiträge zur Kulturgeschichte und Linguistik* 16. (Cf. J. Henninger. *Anthropos* 62:298 f.)

1968b "Zur Megalithfrage Südarabiens," in *W. Caskel Festschrift*. Edited by W. Graf. Leiden: Brill.

EHRENFELS, U. R.

1959 Gestalt und Akkulturation. *Zeitschrift für Ganzheitsforschung* N.F. 3:18–22. Wien.

ELIADE, M.

1969 *Traité d'histoire des religions*. Preface by G. Dumézil. Paris.

FLOR
1939   Article in *Anthropos* 33.

FUCHS, ST.
1965   *Rebellious prophets (in India)*. Bombay: Asia Publishing House.

HAEKEL, J., editor
1956a   *Die Wiener Schule der Völkerkunde. Festschrift.* 80–91. Wien, Horn: J. Berger.
1956b   *Religionswissenschaftliches Wörterbuch.* Edited by F. König, 52 ff. Freiburg.
1958   "Zur gegenwärtigen Forschungssituation der Wiener Schule der Ethnologie," in *Wartenstein* I:127–147.
1964   Origin and development of high culture. *Davidson Journal of Anthropology* 2. Seattle.

HANČAR, F.
1955   Das Pferd in prähistorischer und historischer Zeit. *Wiener Beiträge zur Kulturgeschichte und Linguistik* 11:355–398.

HEINE-GELDERN, R.
1955   Herkunft und Ausbreitung der Hochkulturen. *Almanach der Akad. Wissensch.* 105:252–257. Wien.
1956   Der Ursprung der alten Hochkulturen und die Theorien Toynbees. *Diogenes* 13:96–117. Köln.
1958   "Das Megalithproblem," in *Wartenstein* I:162–182.

HENNINGER, J.
1967   Periodisierung der Geschichte. Kritik der These von I. Sellnow. *Anthropos* 62:210–232.
1968   "Über Lebensarten und Lebensnormen der frühesten semitischen Kultur." Symposion. Köln, Opladen.

HERMANNS, M.
1970   *Schamanen-Pseudoschamanen-Erlöser und Heilbringer,* three volumes. Wiesbaden: F. Steiner.

HERRMANN, F.
1961   *Symbolik in den Religionen der Naturvölker.* Stuttgart: Hiersemann.

HIRSCHBERG, W.
1966   Kulturhistorie und Ethnohistorie. *Mitteilungen zur Kulturkunde* 1:61–70. Frankfurt a.M.
1972   Religionsethnologie und ethnohistorische Religionsforschung. Eine Gegenüberstellung. *Wiener Ethnohistorische Blätter* Beiheft 1.
1974   *Die Kulturen Afrikas.* Frankfurt a. M.: Athenäum-Verlagsgesellschaft.

Historia religionum
1971   Article in *Historia religionum* 2:573–592.

HOHENWART-GERLACHSTEIN, A.
1954   Some problems of megalithic culture in ancient Egypt. *Wiener Völkerkundliche Mitteilungen* 2:126–131.
1956   "Hochkultur und Ethnologie," in *Die Wiener Schule der Völkerkunde. Festschrift,* 101–110. Wien.

JENSEN, A. E.
1951   Mythos und Kult bei Naturvölkern, 302–305. Wiesbaden. (Cf. A. Closs. Mitteil. Anthropol. Gesellschaft Wien 22:195–197. 1953.)

JETTMAR K.
1953   Neue Beiträge zur Entwicklungsgeschichte der Viehzucht. Wiener Völkerkundliche Mitteilungen 1:1–14.
1973   "Die anthropologische Aussage der Ethnologie," in Kulturanthropologie. Die neue Anthropologie. Edited G. Gadamer et al., 4. Stuttgart.

KEILBACH, W.
1962   Die empirische Religionspsychologie als Zweig der Religionswissenschaft. Archiv für Religionspsychologie 7:13–30.

KOPPERS, W.
1954   Der historische Grundcharakter der Völkerkunde. Studium Generale 7:135–143. Berlin.
1955   Ethnologie und Geschichte. Bemerkungen zu einem unter dem gleichen Titel erschienenen Artikel von W. E. Mühlmann. Anthropos 50:943–948.
1957   Zum Problem der Universalgeschichte im Lichte der Ethnologie und Prähistorie. Anthropos 52–53:369–389.
1959   "Grundsätzliches und Geschichtliches zur ethnologischen Kulturkreislehre, " in Wartenstein I:110–126. Horn: J. Berger.

MAIS, A.
1954   Aufgabe der volkskundlichen Archäologie. Wiener Völkerkundliche Mitteilungen 2:184–192.

MANNDORFF, H.
1956   "Angewandte Völkerkunde im Dienste der Bevölkerung unterentwickelter Gebiete," in Die Wiener Schule der Völkerkunde. Festschrift, 125–143. Wien.

MOHR, R.
1957   Article in Theologische Revue 53. Münster.

NARR, K. J.
1955   Interpretation altsteinzeitlicher Kunstwerke durch völkerkundliche Parallelen. Anthropos 50:513–554.

RAHMANN, R.
1959   Shamanistic and related phenomena in northern and middle India. Anthropos 54:681–760.

Religionsethnologie
1964   Texte. Edited by C. A. Schmitz. Frankfurt a.M.: Akad. Verlagsgesellschaft.

RUDOLPH, K.
1967   Die Problematik der Religionswissenschaft als akademisches Lehrfach. Kairos, 22–42. Salzburg: O. Müller.
1971   Das Problem einer Entwicklung in der Religionsgeschichte. Kairos, 95–118.

SCHEBESTA, P.
1960   Ursprung der Religion. Berlin: Morus.

SCHMIDT, L.
1958   "Das Verhältnis der Volkskunde zur Urgeschichte und zur Völkerkunde," in *Wartenstein* I:94–109.

SCHMIDT, W.
1930   *Ursprung und Werden der Religion (Handbuch der vergleichenden Religionsgeschichte).* Münster/W.

SCHOTT, G.
1961   Article in *Saeculum* 12.

SEMAINE D'ETHNOLOGIE RELIGIEUSE
1911–1925   Compte Rendu: (1) Session Louvain 1911 (Published 1912. Paris: M. G. Beauchesne.), (2) Session Louvain 1912 (Published 1914. Paris: E. Charpentier.), (3) Session Tilburg 1923 (Published 1923. Mödling bei Wien: St. Gabriel.), (4) Session Milano 1925 (Published 1926. Paris: Geutner.).

SIEBER, S. A.
1939   *The cultural historical method of ethnology.* Translated by W. Schmidt. Preface by C. Kluckhohn. Harvard University, Fortuny's Publishers.

SLAWIK, A.
1951   Ostasiatische Parallelen zweier nordischer Sagen. *Ethnos.* Stockholm.
1972   Japanologie in Wien und ihre Bedeutung für ethnologische Forschungen. *Wiener Völkerkundliche Mitteilungen* 19, N.F. 14: 37–40.

STAGL, J.
1971   *Zum Geschlechtsantagonismus in Melanesien.* Acta Ethnologica et Linguistica 22. Series Oceania 4. Wien.

STIGLMAYR, E.
1970   *Ganzheitliche Ethnologie. Ethnologie als integrale Kulturwissenschaft.* Acta Ethnologica et Linguistica 18. Wien: Selbstverlag des Autors.

UNGER-DREILING, E.
1966   *Die Psychologie der Naturvölker als historische Grundlagenforschung.* Wien: Herder. (Cf. A. Closs. Religionswissenschaftlich. *Kairos,* 79–80. 1967. Ethnologisch. *Wiener Völkerkundliche Mitteilungen* N.F. 14-15:146–149. 1967–1968).

VAN BAAREN, T. P.
1964   *Menschen wie wir. Religion und Kult der schriftlosen Völker.* Gütersloh: Mohn.

VORBICHLER, A.
1956   *Das Opfer auf den heute noch erreichbaren ältesten Stufen der Menschheitsgeschichte.* Mödling bei Wien: St. Gabriel-Verlag.

Wartenstein
1958   Volume one: *Beiträge Österreichs zur Erforschung der Vergangenheit und Kulturgeschichte der Menschheit.* Wenner-Gren Symposion Österreichischer Anthropologen. (Horn: J. Berger, 1959.)
1959   Volume two: *Theorie und Praxis der Zusammenarbeit zwischen den anthropologischen Disziplinen.* Wenner-Gren Symposion Österreichischer Anthropologen. (Horn: J. Berger, 1961.)

WEIDKUHN, P.
1965 *Aggressivität. Ritus — Ritualisierung. Biologische Grundformen religiöser Prozesse.* Basel. (Cf. A. Closs. *Anthropos* 63–65: 279 f. 1968.)
1966 Wo steht die religionsethnologische Verhaltensforschung? *Zeitschrift für Ethnologie* 91.
1970 Confer. über I. Eibl-Eibesfeldt. Grundriß der vergleichenden Verhaltensforschung. Ethologie. München. *Anthropos* 65:650–656.
WIDENGREN, G.
1945 Evolutionism and the problem of the origins of religion. *Ethnos.* Stockholm.
WÖLFEL, D. J.
1951 "Die Religionen des vorindogermanischen Europa," in *Christus und die Religionen der Erde,* volume one. Edited by F. König, 167–537. Wien.
1961 "Megalithikum und archaische Hochkulturen," in *Handbuch der Weltgeschichte.* Edited by A. Randa. Olten.
ZWICKER, H.
1970 *Das höchste Wesen. Der Hochgottglaube bei urtümlichen Völkern.* Bern.
ZWIEAUER, TH.
1938 *Ethnologie und Gruppierung der Grenzvölker im Norden Chinas auf Grund chinesischer Berichte.* Wien.

Religion and Ecology among the Great Basin Indians

ÅKE HULTKRANTZ

The object here will be to interpret the religion of a major aboriginal North American cultural province, the Great Basin, in terms of religious ecology. Until now, the religions of primitive or preliterate societies have usually been investigated along historical, sociological, or phenomenological lines. In addition to the traditional methodological devices, there is now also the religio-ecological approach which may be considered a particular application of both the phenomenology of culture (cf. Kroeber 1953: 362) and the phenomenology of religion (Hultkrantz 1966: 132–134, 1970: 88), but certainly also has historical and sociological implications. As applied by the author, the ecology of religion demonstrates how religion interrelates with nature. There is, thus, no presupposition of simple economic determination, no thought that ecological conditions produce religion. Ecology of religion only accounts for the forms taken by religion and for such religious content as may be derived from these religious forms.

The reason the Great Basin Indians have been selected for a religio-ecological analysis is that their culture as a totality has been viewed from ecological points of departure by the late Julian H. Steward, the Grand Old Man of Basin research, whose experiences from the Basin area inspired him to formulate a theory of cultural ecology that the present author has found valid and important. My own fieldwork as ethnologist and student of religion has taken place partly in the Great Basin area.

METHODOLOGICAL CONSIDERATIONS

The religio-ecological theory whose main features I have presented elsewhere (Hultkrantz 1966), is built upon Steward's cultural ecology (Steward 1955) but differs from the latter in several aspects. For one thing, Steward's theory is concerned with evolutionary developments produced by ecological adaptations of salient culture traits, a perspective that only secondarily enters the ecology of religion approach that I am suggesting. Furthermore, Steward's ecology concentrates upon the cultural aspects most exposed to ecological impact, that is, economic and technological culture. Finally, Steward defines "cultural types" by reference to their socio-ecological integration, whereas my "types of religion" refer to subsistence activities which, in my opinion, have a more basic formative stimulus upon religion. Still, in spite of the progressive work on culture and ecology since Steward's theory first appeared, there is in my opinion no better foundation for the elaboration of a program on ecology of religion.

Briefly, Steward suggests that environment has indirectly not only a negative, restrictive but also a positive, creative influence on culture. The more primitive the culture is in material and technological respects, the more it is exposed to the forces of environment. Steward focuses his attention on the processes by which cultures adapt to their environments and, eschewing the formulation of universal cultural laws, he observes certain regularities of ecological process. In assessing the influence of environment it is necessary to reckon with both the biotope, the material and technological level, and the traditional factors that may guide the latter — cultural values, behavior patterns and so on. In other words, ecological pressure resulting from cultural adaptation works through a filter of technological possibilities and cultural traditions. The material and technological aspects of culture form, together with those social, political, and religious patterns that are dependent on them, the "cultural core" that is most likely to be changed by environment. When one and the same cultural core appears cross-culturally as a consequence of similar ecological adaptation, Steward talks of a "cultural type." In contradistinction to the culture area, the cultural type may thus be found to be represented in quite different categories of time and place.

Space prevents me from presenting this culture-ecological theory in more detail; the interested reader is referred to the book by Steward (1955). In criticism of Steward it may be said that he too lightheartedly dismisses the possibility of historical interpretation (cf. Fock 1964). The great difficulty with the culture-ecological method is, in my opinion, the difficulty in distinguishing between historical and ecological motivation. More investigation has to be carried out on this particular point.

Now, the general framework of Steward's theory is well suited to providing the basis on which a theory of the ecology of religion may be founded. We should then remember that religion in many aspects, and particularly in mythology and dogma, has been formed by traditional rather than ecological factors. Only selected religious items may be referred to Steward's cultural core. For instance, agrarian fertility rituals are definitely dependent upon an agricultural economy made possible through the existence of a suitable ecological niche — arable lands — and, not to be forgotten is a TRADITION of agriculture. On the other hand, beliefs about the soul are not part of the ecological adaptation unless the forms of the soul are conceived in apparitions taken from the environment — animals, birds, plants, etc.

It is possible to reconstruct the following "ladder" of religio-ecological integration, illustrating the indirect, step-by-step progression of this process:

1.   Primary integration: environmental adaptation of cultural core features (technology, economics, etc.) and associated social and religious traits. Among the latter, beliefs and rituals coupled with subsistence activities.

2.   Secondary integration: religious beliefs and rituals reflecting the social structure which, in its turn, reflects economic and technological adaptation to environment.

3.   Morphological integration: religious concepts are traditional but borrow their forms from phenomena within the biotope. The example of beliefs about the soul just referred to belongs here.

This scheme should not be mistaken for an evolutionary scale. The implications are solely functional, and the problem of the real essence and origin of religion is not involved. The ecology of religion helps us to a better understanding of the presuppositions of religious forms and patterns in the local context. Moreover, we find similarities and regularities transcending time and space that were not observed before (unless they were explained by such far-fetched historical models as Father Schmidt's culture-historical theory). The religious traits of our primary integration, and Steward's cultural core, reappear in relatively fixed constellations cross-culturally as products of similar ecological adaptation and may then be said to constitute "types of religion." Arctic hunting religion represents such a type of religion (Hultkrantz 1965), desert nomadic religion another (Hultkrantz 1966: 147). A third type of religion, semidesert gathering religion, is our concern in the following.

GREAT BASIN ECOLOGY AND CULTURAL ADAPTATION

The Great Basin is here understood to be the large intermontane area between the main range of the Rocky Mountains in the east and the Sierra Nevada Range in the west, and between the Blue Mountains and Salmon River in the north and the plateaus north of the Colorado in the south. This is a vast area of interior drainage, characterized by steppes and semideserts covered with sagebrush *(Artemisia tridentata)* and, in alkali-lands, by greasewood *(Sarcobatus vermiculatus)*. The low mountain ranges that dissect the area in a north-southerly direction, particularly in Nevada, have a vegetation cover of piñon and juniper trees above 6,000 feet. The piñon belt, with *Pinus edulis* in the south and *Pinus monophylla* in the north, stretches as far north as the Humboldt River. At these altitudes there are also many roots. In places, particularly along the few small streams, many sorts of plants are growing. On the whole, however, the vegetation is xerophytic and thus little suited for nutritional purposes.

In aboriginal days the animal world was also sparsely represented. The rodents were fairly common, and so were snakes and lizards. Antelope (pronghorn) could be found in limited numbers, and there were buffalo in the eastern-most part — the Snake River plains — before 1840. In the higher mountain regions, such as the Wasatch and the Absarokas, mountain sheep, blacktailed deer, grizzly, and puma could be found. However, these big-game refuges belonged to the periphery of the Basin area. So did the Snake River plains with their salmon runs.

The Great Basin has not always been as inhospitable as it is today and was during the last millennium. Ten thousand years ago it was an attractive lacustrine area, with many small lakes and streams and fertile valleys between the mountains. Two big waters, Lake Lahontan in Nevada and Lake Bonneville in Utah — of which the Great Salt Lake is a remnant — dominated much of the area. However, the subsequent drying-up process, particularly after the altithermal 5,000 years ago, made this part of the world into an area difficult for people with limited technical resources to live in. And yet, precisely such a population made it their home before the coming of the whites.

These people belonged chiefly to the Numic linguistic family, formerly called Plateau Shoshonean (of the Uto-Aztecan stock). The main groups were the Ute of Utah and western Colorado, the Southern Paiute of southern Utah and Nevada, the Northern Paiute and Paviotso of northwestern Nevada and eastern Oregon, the Western Shoshoni (including the White Knife Shoshoni) of northeastern Nevada, the Bannock and Northern Shoshoni of southern Idaho, the Sheepeaters of the northeastern mountain ranges, the Gosiute of northern Utah, and the Eastern Shoshoni of southwestern Wyoming. A non-Numic tribe, the Washo, occupied the area around Lake Tahoe.

Ethnographic handbooks usually count these people among the most primitive groups on the earth. They do so rightly, if by "primitive" we mean technical and material poverty. For a hunting and gathering population there was not much to gain in this desolated area. Their life had to be a consequence of bare ecological necessity. This is why it is so rewarding for scholars to apply a culture-ecological approach to their way of life.

Steward has accomplished such an operation with great skill and insight (Steward 1938, 1940, 1955: 101–121). He has pointed out two main factors of environmental causation: the inhabitants of the area were of necessity gatherers of vegetable foods and lower forms of animal life rather than hunters; and the wide dispersal of this food, and its unpredictable occurrence and location, had a socially fragmenting effect. First of all, up until the conquest of the area by the whites, the population remained most limited (the average density was one person to 15.6 square miles). Furthermore, they were forced to scatter into small units consisting of the nuclear or biological family, or possibly a cluster of two or three related families, which moved from place to place. Their homes were simple wickiups of grass, brush, or reeds. During the spring and summer they gathered seeds and roots and hunted smaller animals (grasshoppers, small rodents, ants, snakes, etc.). In the autumn they harvested the piñon nuts of the mountainsides, their most important food. Occasional gatherings of many family clusters took place at this time or in connection with the collective rabbit drives and antelope hunts. The latter could, of course, be held only when there was sufficient game. On such occasions a supreme leader was chosen, either a man of great hunting experience (the "rabbit boss") or, at antelope hunts, an "antelope shaman" known for his power to charm the animals.

During the winter the Shoshoni settled in winter encampments at the foot of the piñon mountains where they had their earth caches of pine nuts. Each settlement was a local area of scattered winter houses for some twenty or thirty families and had a temporary headman, chosen because he knew where foods could be found. In a society on the continual verge of starvation this was a most important function.

Marriages were mostly, but not always, contracted between families in contact with one another. The preferred arrangement was several marriages between the children of two families, so that a husband's sister married his wife's brother. Polygamy took the form of a man married to two sisters, and polyandry that of a woman married to two brothers.

This simple sociopolitical organization was changed when, with the introduction of horses and the Plains Indian value systems from across the Rockies, mounted bands and a cohesive tribal organization took form. The Bannock, the Northern and Eastern Shoshoni, and the Ute became the most typical carriers of this equestrian culture. For matters of convenience we leave it out in the present connection because it did not represent the level of cultural integration that is of interest to us.

THE PROBLEM OF RELIGIO-ECOLOGICAL INTEGRATION IN THE GREAT BASIN

This information on environment and on material and economic culture enables us to understand the ecological integration of Great Basin religion. We shall select just those features of the religion that lend themselves to such an interpretation.

Steward has tried to delineate these features in his general study of Shoshoni ecological adaptation. He measures Shoshoni religion as an insignificant integrative factor in their society (Steward 1955: 113–114). Since the Shoshoni lacked collective activities and common interests there was, in his view, no functional need for religious ceremonialism. He grants that the collective circle dance could promote general fertility, but considers that "the religious aspect was secondary and incidental to the recreational purpose." The Ute bear dance is judged similarly. Steward also emphasizes that the relationship between human beings and supernatural powers was a matter of individual concern — he is here referring to the guardian-spirit beliefs, so typical for North America — and that the medicine man in spite of his prestige as a doctor carried no specific authority.

To Steward, then, Great Basin Indian religion has no relevance for the ecological adaptation in the area. On this point, however, I think he is very much mistaken. He has devoted only slight interest to this problem, and his concept of religion is not adequate: various notes on the vision quest and shamanism do not exhaust the religious complex, the belief systems, and associated behavior that make up Great Basin religion. As we shall see, this religion is thoroughly integrated with

Basin environment although, of course, in many respects it transmits traditional ideas of little environmental impact.

Our investigation will be focused on the following:

1. Basin ecology provides material for the morphology of religious conceptions, rites, and myths.

2. The social structure is adjusted to ecological preconditions and serves as a model for the religious structure. Thus, indirectly, ecology forms religious institutions.

3. The religious pattern, or the religious value system, is adjusted to conditions in an arid environment with collecting activity predominating. Cults and ideas reflect the ecological premises.

GREAT BASIN RELIGION IN ECOLOGICAL PERSPECTIVE

The basic pattern of the Great Basin religion was adjusted to the demands of climate, natural resources, and physiographic environment on a sparse hunting and collecting population (Hultkrantz i.p.). Traditional religious elements were transformed to fit the general ecological pattern; indeed, even religious goals were partly changed to conform with subsistence activities. It is here, however, necessary to underline the word "partly." The innermost religious values, the individual's dependence on and trust in supernatural beings, could not, as such, be altered.

Traditional Basin religion was structured on four main levels, to which may be added mythology that virtually played an independent role, with its own world scene and mythic beings. All of these levels had an ecological integration of shifting intensity.

Cosmology and Beliefs about Major Supernatural Beings

Cosmological beliefs were patterned on physiographic features in the surrounding landscape. According to Southern Paiute Indians, the Kaibab Plateau was the middle of the world. The earth was surrounded by a line of towering cliffs, resembling those that guard the Plateau periphery. The edge of the sky rested on these cliffs (Fowler and Fowler 1971: 38, 73–75).

The main deities of the Numic and Washo peoples were the Supreme Being, the Thunderbird, and the Four Winds, just as was the case among other Indian groups. These lofty conceptions were not perceptibly adapted to ecology, unless we judge the name of the Supreme Being, "Our Father," as a projection of the headman of the family (or family group). The Thunder could, besides in bird form, also appear as a snake, mouse, or badger, all well-known animals of the Basin area. Of more importance is the integration of the Great Basin landscape with the belief in supernatural beings. Many conspicuous localities had their supernatural masters. Thus, the mountains were the haunting place of *dzoavits* [evil giants], and some mountain tops were themselves conceived as spirits. Water babies, in some places part fish, like the European mermaid, lived in lakes, wells, and hot springs. The geyser areas of the Yellowstone Park were held in particular awe (Hultkrantz 1954). The Ute made offerings to the hot springs in their area (Stewart 1942: 318). Bushes, caves, and foothills were the habitations of the dangerous, dwarflike *ninimbi,* the most spoken-of spirits of the Numic peoples (Olden 1923: 33–34; Clark 1966: 180–183).

Many of these local spirits appeared in the hunters' visions as their guardian spirits. However, the host of these spirits represented another religious configuration, and had in principle nothing to do with other supernatural beings. They were mostly conceived of as zoomorphic beings, and the animals they portrayed all belong to species known to the Basin inhabitants.

Looking back at all these supernatural beings we perceive that they were more or less molded by social and ecological factors. They looked like the animals of the area (a natural condition in a hunting and gathering milieu), they were associated with striking features in the landscape, and their indefinite relations pictured the loose and fluid organization of the human social group.

Major Rituals

There were two great ecological obstacles to the development of Basin ceremonialism: the social units were small, nomadic, and widely dispersed; and there was rarely sufficient food at hand for people to assemble in larger numbers. Hence, cultic activity was restricted by ecological pressure, and that meant few ceremonial occasions and, perhaps, less ceremonial elaboration. The poverty of group rituals is one of the characteristics of the Basin in comparison with other North American culture areas.

All over the area some kind of ceremony took place in connection with the major seasonal economic activities when larger groups were assembled: at the communal rabbit hunts, at the salmon runs, at the piñon harvest. Steward thought that these ceremonies were primarily profane and recreational in purpose (Steward 1939: 265). However, the evidence collected by Park (1941: 198), Harris (1940: 53–54), and others makes it quite clear that the so-called round dance had a religious as well as a recreational aim. It was a thanksgiving ceremony with changing ecological motivations: we hear of the seed dance, the pine nut dance, the grass dance, etc., and everybody prayed for a good year and an increase of food supply. The general emphasis on rain and vegetation mirrors the needs in a semidesert region.

In addition to the rituals surrounding the gathering activities, there were hunting rituals, although hunting was relatively unimportant in the Great Basin. The most spectacular hunting ritual was attached to antelope hunting. A medicine man with antelope power charmed the curious animals into a corral (Lowie 1924: 302–305). There are also vestiges of "animal ceremonialism," i.e. the ritual treatment of the slain game in order to ensure the willingness of the animals to let themselves be killed in the future.

These were the major collective rituals of the Basin peoples. As emerges from this short survey, the goals of religious activity were closely integrated with the needs and patterns of subsistence.

Vision Quest and Shamanism

As in other places in North America, the vision quest in the wilderness leading to the acquisition of a guardian spirit, was supposed to guarantee to a man that he was provided with those supernatural powers that were needed in the society and environment he lived in. Records show that only the man who was blessed by the spirits could become a successful hunter and a good member of his society (Steward 1934). The desired powers were longevity, gambling luck, running and hunting powers and, after the influx of Plains Indian cultural values, war power.

Much desired were also doctoring powers whose possession characterized the medicine man or shaman (Park 1938). Some shamans had specialized powers. For instance, there were rattlesnake shamans who had the power to suck out the poison from persons bitten by rattlesnakes; weather specialists who could make rain; and so on. These capacities were evidently directly related to needs caused by the fauna and the climate.

Some evil-disposed or less successful shamans were accused of sorcery. Beatrice Whiting (1950) has demonstrated how sorcery among the Paiute supplied means for social control, an important function in a society that lacked superior authority.

To a certain extent, then, visions and shamanistic powers were also adjusted to the ecological pattern.

Rites of Passage and Associated Beliefs

The life crises were accompanied by ritual observances which, in comparison with similar ritual measures in others parts of western North America, had an attenuated profile. It need not be pointed out that they were all integrated with ecological presuppositions. In the girls' menstruation observances, for instance, the construction of the menstrual hut as well as the imposed taboos — not carrying wood, fetching water, or gathering seeds, etc. — had an ecological setting. The mode of burial reflected largely practical considerations (Steward 1940: 491), thus the bodies were mostly placed under rocks or in crevices and caves.

The ideas about ghosts and the afterworld were also adapted to the environment. Besides appearing as human beings and animals of the biotope, ghosts often took the form of whirlwinds — a common natural phenomenon in the area. Southern Paiute Indians appeased whirlwinds by smoke offerings (Steward 1941: 309, 348). The land of the dead that was sometimes supposed to be situated in the far west or south was a happy place with features taken from the world of the living: there was green grass for the Washo, pine nuts for the Owens Valley Paiute, and buffalo for the Northern and Eastern Shoshoni. Socially unacceptable persons were excluded from these paradisial places.

Mythology

While the great supernatural powers of religion dwell high over the terrestrial world, the mythological beings roam around in an environment that is clearly that of the Great Basin, although the events are supposed to have occurred in an imagined prehuman era. Today, features of the landscape are associated with incidents of the mythological tales. For instance, the cave where the mythic game was enclosed, and the mountain that protruded over the waters of the Great Flood are pointed out by present-day Basin Indians. The social and cultural milieu of the mythic beings is identical with precontact Basin society and culture. The actors of the mythic plots are all, or almost all, zoomorphic, their forms taken from the Basin animal world: Wolf,

Coyote, Porcupine, Skunk, Rabbit, Weasel. The characters of these animals color the personalities of their mythic replicas: Coyote is a greedy coward; Skunk is painfully stinking; and so on. The myths of the Eastern Shoshoni are divided according to the main animal actors.

Although the mythological tales are part of widely diffused migratory tales, they are unmistakably integrated with Great Basin environment. For instance, the myth about the game that was impounded in a cave and released by the trickster (Coyote) carries a heavy Basin stamp. Another myth, the theft of the pine nuts, belongs to a pattern that is widely diffused in the West, the culture-hero's theft of useful things for the benefit of the human beings (thefts of sun, light, fire, water); but the association of this idea with the pine nuts is typically Basin. Here, then, we have an excellent example of the ecological integration of a traditional mythic pattern. Another tale, the almost universally known story of the rolling head, has a Basin counterpart in the story of the rolling rock — perhaps an ecological reinterpretation?

Some of the mythic animals, we are told, have turned into stars and constellations, as also emerges from the names of the latter: the Mountain Sheep, the Jackrabbit, etc.

Myth telling was no doubt a recreational occupation, but it supplied some origin myths of serious intent, and during the winter nights it was supposed to hasten the spring and bring about fertility. Most important, mythological tales pictured Basin ecology and reflected its aboriginal society.

CHANGING ASPECTS OF BASIN RELIGIO-ECOLOGICAL INTEGRATION

This survey of Great Basin religion and mythology ought to have demonstrated the close connections between them and the environment. In contrast to Steward, I would say that the religio-ecological adaptation in the Basin area was striking and important for the whole culture pattern. In particular, I challenge his view that ritual had practically no connection with economic pursuits (Steward 1938: 45). Steward misunderstood the motives of the round dance and thereby misjudged the whole religious configuration in the Great Basin.

This balanced religio-ecological integration is certainly a result of a long-continued process. The ten thousand years of Desert culture have been decisive. Still, there have been disturbing factors. The equestrian Plains culture, going back almost 200 years among the Ute and Eastern

Shoshoni-Comanche in the eastern periphery of the Basin, has already
been mentioned. On the western periphery, the Owens Valley Paiute
were exponents of a village culture with primitive irrigation and collective mourning-anniversary ceremonies. In the south, and progressing
toward the north and west, the agricultural Fremont culture (with roots
in Pueblo or Anasazi culture) dominated Southern Paiute territory for
some centuries (950–1200 A.D.). More important, however, are the
traces of a previously extensive hunting culture.

The wetter climate and grass vegetation before the altithermal (7,000
years ago) provided support for large numbers of big game and thus
facilitated hunting on a greater scale (Butler 1972). Long afterward,
grasslands covered the areas around the shrinking lakes (Ranere 1970).
Rock drawings close to the Owens Valley show that mountain sheep
were hunted only 1,000 years ago in areas that are now deserts; indeed,
there seems to have existed a mountain sheep cult (Grant 1968). Until
the end of the last century a mountain sheep hunting culture was found
among the mountains in the northeastern periphery of the Basin (Hultkrantz 1966–1967). Religious data seem to support the hypothesis of
an earlier hunting and collecting culture, later turned mainly into
collecting. Thus, the hunting rituals are faint echoes of widely dis-
seminated rites, and are sometimes only known in mythology, not religion. The boys' puberty customs are centered around the slaying of
the first game, a remarkable feature in a largely gathering culture.
There are, here and there, traces of one of the most basic hunting beliefs, the idea of the master of animals; but this concept is never conspicuous. The poverty of mythology may possibly be seen as a de-
generation phenomenon concomitant with the deterioration of the hunting complex. In any case, data of a different kind seem to support, at
least partly, Malouf's conclusion that Basin hunting rites were related
to the corresponding rites of the more complex societies surrounding
the Great Basin. He raises the question of whether the Basin environment once was more favorable to hunting, but answers it in the negative
(Malouf 1966: 4–5). As we have seen, recent investigations support,
instead, a positive answer, and thus bear out Malouf's own observations.

All these considerations suggest that Great Basin religion lends itself
to an ecological interpretation, whether we catch it in an earlier phase,
characterized by more hunting, or a more recent phase, characterized
by more gathering. Only the gathering phase can, however, be definitely
proved to have existed, and the correlation between religion and
ecology is very neat here. Certainly, we must not exaggerate the ecological perspective; after all, religion is first of all faith and tradition.

However, the ecological perspective teaches us that ultimately it is not society, but the integration with environment which decides the development of religious forms and functions. We perceive the sticks and stones out of which the media of religious expression are created.

REFERENCES

BUTLER, B. R.
1972   The Holocene or postglacial ecological crisis on the Eastern Snake River Plain. *Tebiwa, Journal of the Idaho State University Museum* 15(1):49–63.

CLARK, E. E.
1966   *Indian legends from the Northern Rockies.* Norman: University of Oklahoma Press.

FOCK, N.
1964   Man as a mediating agent between nature and culture. *Folk, Dansk Etnografisk Tidsskrift* 6(1):47–52.

FOWLER, D. D., C. S. FOWLER, editors
1971   *Anthropology of the Numa: John Wesley Powell's manuscripts on the Numic peoples of western North America, 1868–1880.* Smithsonian Contributions to Anthropology 14. Washington, D.C.: Smithsonian Institute.

GRANT, C.
1968   *Rock drawings of the Coso Range.* China Lake, California: Maturango Museum Publication 4.

HARRIS, J. S.
1940   "The White Knife Shoshoni of Nevada," in *Acculturation in seven American Indian tribes.* Edited by R. Linton, 39–116. New York: D. Appleton-Century.

HULTKRANTZ, Å.
1954   The Indians and the wonders of Yellowstone: a study of the interrelations of religion, nature and culture. *Ethnos* 19:34–68.
1965   "Type of religion in the arctic hunting cultures: a religio-ecological approach," in *Hunting and fishing, Nordic symposium on life in a traditional hunting and fishing milieu.* Edited by H. Hvarfner, 265–318. Luleà.
1966   An ecological approach to religion. *Ethnos* 31:131–150.
1966–1967   The ethnological position of the sheepeater Indians in Wyoming. *Folk, Dansk Etnografisk Tidsskrift* 8-9:155–163.
1970   The phenomenology of religion: aims and methods. *Temenos* 6:68-88.
i.p.   "Great Basin Indian mythology and religious concepts," in *Handbook of North American Indians 10.* Edited by W. C. Sturtevant. Great Basin.

KROEBER, A. L.
1953   "Concluding review," in *An appraisal of anthropology today.*

Edited by S. Tax, et al., 357–376. Chicago: University of Chicago Press.

LOWIE, R. H.
1924   Notes on Shoshonean ethnography. *Anthropological Papers* 20(3): 185–314. New York: American Museum of Natural History.

MALOUF, C.
1966   "Ethnohistory in the Great Basin," in *The current status of anthropological research in the Great Basin: 1964.* Edited by W. L. d'Azevedo, et al., 1–38. Social Sciences and Humanities Publications 1. Reno: Desert Research Institute.

OLDEN, S. E.
1923   *Shoshone folklore.* Milwaukee: Morehouse Publishing.

PARK, W. Z.
1938   *Shamanism in western North America: a study in cultural relationships.* Studies in the Social Sciences 2. Evanston and Chicago: Northwestern University Press.

1941   "Culture succession in the Great Basin," in *Language, culture, and personality: essays in memory of Edward Sapir,* 180–203. Menasha, Wisconsin.

RANERE, A. J.
1970   Prehistoric environments and cultural continuity in the western Great Basin. *Tebiwa, Journal of the Idaho State University Museum* 13(2):52–72.

STEWARD, J. H.
1934   Two Paiute autobiographies. *University of California Publications in American Archaeology and Ethnology* 33(5):423–38. Berkeley, California.

1938   *Basin-plateau aboriginal sociopolitical groups.* Bureau of American Ethnology Bulletin 120. Washington, D.C.

1939   Some observations on Shoshonean distributions. *American Anthropologist* 41(2):261–265.

1940   Native cultures of the intermontane (Great Basin) area. *Miscellaneous Collections* 100:445–502. Washington: Smithsonian Institute.

1941   Culture element distributions: 13, Nevada Shoshone. *Anthropological Records* 4(2):209–359. Berkeley and Los Angeles.

1955   *Theory of culture change: the methodology of multilinear evolution.* Urbana: University of Illinois Press.

STEWART, O. C.
1942   Culture element distributions: 18, Ute-Southern Paiute. *Anthropological Records* 6(4):231–356. Berkeley and Los Angeles.

WHITING, B. B.
1950   *Paiute sorcery.* New York: Viking Fund Publications in Anthropology 15.

Hindu Ritual Idiom: Cosmic Perspective and Basic Orientations

SAMARENDRA SARAF

In his discursive treatise on religion, Durkheim regards all religious phenomena as "naturally arranged in two fundamental categories: beliefs and rites. The first are states of opinion, and consist in representations; the second are determined modes of action. Between these two classes of facts there is all the difference which separates thought from action" (1964:36). Lévi-Strauss echoes a similar view: "Regardless of whether the myth or the ritual is the original, they replicate each other; the myth exists on the conceptual level and the ritual on the level of action" (1963:232). Religion, thus, stands for a unified system of myths or beliefs on the one hand, and rites or rituals on the other.

As an esoteric means, a ritual is the formalized mode of behavior ordained by the code of religious values. As Firth would have it, it is "a kind of activity oriented towards control of human affairs, primarily symbolic in character with non-empirical referent ..." (1951:175). To Langer, a ritual presents "a symbolic transformation of experience that no other medium can adequately express, ... a constant reiteration of sentiments, ... a disciplined rehearsal of right attitudes" (1948:44, 124). Benedict regards it as "a form of prescribed and elaborated behaviour

To my father I owe my informal initiation into the classical language and scriptural literature. I recall with pride many sessions of fruitful discussion with him, especially those devoted to the present paper. I am also grateful to Pandita Dattātreya Bhālchandra Nawātthye, a Hindu priest, well versed in the Vedic lore and liturgy, who helped me locate the relevant data. Two of my friends from the University of Saugar, Shri Dinesh Kumar Dixit, Controller of Examinations, and Shri Narayan Shanker Dhagat, Hostel Administrator, deserve special mention; both have proved "friend, philosopher, and guide" to me, questioning me with the inquisitiveness of a disciple and challenging my statements with a philosopher's vehemence.

[that] occurs both as the compulsion neurotic, and as a cultural trait. ...
[It is] prescribed formal behaviour for occasions not given over to
technological routine" (1949:396). All above definitions hint at a common core of ritual: an activity directed towards the nonempirical,
supernatural realm.

No ritual exists as an isolated and independent phenomenon; it is
always part of a larger complex. When many ritual acts group together
to form a configuration which lends specific color, complexion, and
contour to the entire ritual complex, a ritual idiom emerges. Such a
ritual idiom invariably has both perspective and orientations: the former
rooted in the cognitive mapping of the people, the latter in their affective
and conative mapping.

Working within the above conceptual frame of reference, an attempt
will be made in the following pages to spell out and delineate the perspective and the basic orientations of the Hindu ritual idiom by examining
the Hindu complex of worship as a ritual process. The Hindu mode of
worship forms a complex from a series of minor rites that follow the
rhythm of a fixed, rather irreversible, sequence. The occasion, the
considerations regarding the auspiciousness of time of performance, and
the ritual purification or consecration of the triad (the worshiper, the
site of worship, and the entire paraphernalia of objects) lend further
qualifications to the ritual complex. There are three kinds of rituals:
those performed daily (*nitya*), those performed on specific occasions
(*naimittika*), and those performed with a desired end in view (*kāmya*)
(Kāne 1953:373). Moghe (1911:23, 25, 28) lists the Hindu calendrical
dates, days, and constellations, etc., which are regarded as auspicious
occasions for the performance of all rituals. The various objects in everyday worship are *acamani* [spoon], *pañcapātra* [mug], *kamaṇḍalu* [tumbler
with spout], *kalaśa* [metal jar], *nīrājanā* [lighted lamp which is waved
before the idol], *naivedyapātra* [pot for food offerings], *candana* [piece of
sandalwood] and *dṛṣad-upala* [flat stone for grinding condiments].

A Hindu proceeds to perform the ritual of worship only after taking a
bath (*snāna*) (Kāne 1941a:658–668). The daily bath elevates one to a
ritually pure state and qualifies one for rites toward both the gods and
the *manes*.[1] After donning fresh clothes, the *nivi* [lower garment] and
the *uttarīya* [upper garment], the worshiper is ready for the ritual (Kāne
1941a:669–672). His ritual purity and the purity of the site and the
objects of worship are equally imperative. Smearing the place of worship
with cow dung (*gomaya upalepana*) renders the site ritually pure, and

---

[1] "Snāto'dhikārī bhavati daive pitrye ca karmani ..." (Viṣṇu Sāṁhitā LXIV:40).

sprinkling palmfuls of water accompanied by the chanting of a hymn three times (*abhyukṣaṇa*) further consecrates it (Kāne 1953:316–317). The utensils for worship are cleansed by scrubbing them with ash or earth and washing them with water. A pot filled with fresh water is placed by the side of the worshiper's seat, into which some fresh blades of *kuśa* [holy grass] are dipped to consecrate the water as *praṇīta* or *prokṣaṇī*.[2] The worshiper's seat is generally a square mat woven out of the holy *kuśa* grass.

Spreading his mat before the idol, the worshiper sits on it in one of the yogic *āsanas* [sitting postures]. Three times he sips palmfuls of water with his right hand (*ācamana*), chanting a hymn[3] each time to evoke both external and internal purity. He then pours some water over his palm and washes it clean. Holding some *kuśa* blades in his right hand, he sprinkles water on and under his mat, chanting the hymn to the earth (*pṛthivī mantra*) and naming its seer (*ṛṣi*), presiding deity (*devatā*), and meter (*chanda*). He eulogizes the earth goddess and beseeches her to render his seat pure.[4]

The ritual of obeisance which commences with the naming of Lord Gaṇeśa (Ācārya 1958:1), includes nearly all principal gods and goddesses, the worshiper's parents, the patron deity (*iṣṭadevatā*), the familial deity (*kuladevatā*), the parochial deity (*grāmadevatā*), and so forth. As an expression of his intention to perform the ritual of worship, he recites a long ritual passage (*saṁkalpa*) wherein he states his place in time[5] and space.[6] He prays for the promotion of well-being, stability, fearlessness, longevity, health, prosperity, auspiciousness, and affluence[7] for himself as well as for his extended lineage, family, and all bipeds and quadrupeds.[8]

With the conclusion of the consecration of the worshiper's seat the ritual of *bhūtotsāraṇa* begins. The worshiper holds in his right hand some

[2] "Kuśodakena japasthānaṁ prokṣaṇaṁ ..." (Śarmā 1925:8).
[3] "Om apavitraḥ pavitro vā sarvāvasthāṁ gato'pi vā
yaḥ smaretpuṇḍarīkākṣaṁ sa bāhyābhyantaraḥ śuciḥ" (Śarmā 1925:8).
[4] "Om asya śrī āsanamantrasya meruprṣṭharṣiḥ kūrmodevatā
sutalaṁchandaḥ āsanaparigrahe viniyogaḥ.
Om pṛthivī tvayā dhṛtā lokā devi tvaṁ viṣṇunā dhṛtā
tvaṁ ca dhāraya māṁ nityaṁ pavitraṁ kuru cāsanaṁ" (Śarmā 1968:1043).
[5] "... Brahmaṇo dvitīyeparārdhe viṣṇupade śrīśvetavārāhakalpe vaivasvatamanvantare aṣṭaviṁśeyugacatuṣke kaliyuge prathamacaraṇe ..." (Ācārya 1958:2).
[6] "... Jambudvīpe bharatavarṣe bhratakhaṇḍe ... amukasthite vartamānecandre ... devagurau śeṣeṣugraheṣu ..." (Ācārya 1958:2).
[7] "Kṣemasthairyābhayāyurārogyaiśvaryābhivṛddhyarthaṁ samasta mangalavāptyarthaṁ samastābhyudayārthaṁ ca ..." (Ācārya 1958:2).
[8] "... Mama ātmanaḥ purāṇokta phalaprāptyarthaṁ asmākaṁ sakuṭumbānāṁ saparivārāṇāṁ dvipadacatuṣpadasahitānāṁ ..." (Ācārya 1958:2)

rice grains smeared with red sandal wood paste, some *dūrvā* [holy grass], and *kuśa* blades; he chants a hymn,[9] and, after circling his head three times with his hand, scatters the grass and rice in all directions as a measure of protection against all evil and sin that surround him and seek to frustrate his worship. This is followed by practice of *prāṇāyāma* [control of breath] for a short time. While engaged in breath control, the worshiper meditates on each of the four *padas* [steps] of the *gāyatrī* hymn, which are preceded by the three *mahāvyāhṛtis*[10] [mystic syllables] in such a manner that a step of the hymn coincides with one of the four steps of the *prāṇāyāma*. The four consecutive steps in the *prāṇāyāma* are: (a) the *pūraka* [inhaling of breath], (b) the internal *kuṁbhaka* [holding of breath after inhaling], (c) the *recaka* [exhaling of breath], and (d) the external *kuṁbhaka* [holding of breath before next inhaling] (Śarmā 1968:1044). The *prāṇāyāma* is intended for the purification of the nerves (*nāḍīs*) (Shastri 1969:30).

Performance of *prāṇāyāma* is followed by the *bhūtaśuddhi* [purification from sin inherent in the body]. This symbolizes the destruction of the *pāpa-puruṣa* [sin anthropomorphized] (Śarmā 1968:1044) so that the worshiper may qualify as a receptacle of the merits accruing from the worship. The next ritual follows immediately: *tattvaśuddhi* [elemental purification], in which the five vital airs (*pañcaprāṇas*),[11] the five sense organs (*pañcajñānendriyas*),[12] the five subtle constituents (*pañcatan-mātras*),[13] the five motor organs (*pañcakarmendriyas*),[14] as well as the primeval principle (*prakṛti*), the mind (*manas*), the intellect (*buddhi*), and the ego (*ahaṁkāra*)[15] are named to invoke their mystic and symbolic purification. This is a process whereby the purification of the three

---

9   "Om apakrāmantu te bhūtā ye bhūtā bhutale sthitāḥ
ye bhūtā vighnakartāraste naśyantu śivājñayā.
Apakrāmantu bhūtāni piśācāḥ sarvatodiśaṁ
sarveṣāmavirodhena pūjākarma samārabhe.
Raktacandana siddhārthā bhasmadūrvākuśākṣatāḥ
vikarākṛti sandiṣṭāḥ sarvavighnaughanāśakāḥ" (Śarmā 1968:1043)
10   "Om bhūrbhuvaḥ svaḥ
tatsaviturvareṇyaṁ
bhargo devasya dhīmahi
dhiyo yo naḥ pracodayāt" (Śarmā 1968:1044).
11   "Oṁ prāṇāpānavyānodānasamana me śudhyantāṁ jyotirahaṁ virajā vipāpmā bhūyāsaṁ svāhā" (Śarmā 1968:1290).
12   "Oṁ tvakcakṣurjihvāghrāṇavacāmsi me śudhyantāṁ ... svāhā" (Śarmā 1968:1290).
13   "Oṁ sparśarūparasagandhākāśāni ... svāhā" (Śarmā 1968:1290).
14   "Oṁ pāṇipādapāyupasthaśabda me śudhyantāṁ ... svāhā" (Śarmā 1968:1290).
15   "Aṁ prakṛtyahaṁkārabuddhimanaḥ ... śodhayāmi svāhā" (Śarmā 1968:1291).

bodies (*śarīratraya*),[16] as well as the immanent microcosm (*Jīvātman*),[17] is attempted. The "three bodies" refers to the gross body (*sthūlaśarīra*), which is purified by the *ātmatattva*; the subtle body (*sūkṣmaśarīra*), purified by the *vidyātattva*; and the casual body (*kāraṇaśarīra* or *para-deha*), purified by the *śivatattva* (Śarmā 1968:1291).

Invocation of the deity calls for many minor preparatory rituals. One of these is the *nyāsa* which, etymologically speaking, means to establish mystic powers in various parts of the worshiper's body — head, mouth, heart, anus, feet, all digits of both hands, palms and backs of the hands, the three eyes (*netratraya*), the whole body as armor (*kavaca*) and weapon (*astra*) (Anonymous 1968:666–670). A metal pot filled with water (*kalaśasthāpana*) is used in this ritual in the belief that the mouth, neck, and base of the pot are occupied by Lords Viṣṇu, Rudra, and Brahmā respectively,[18] and that all the holy waters of the seven rivers are represented by the water in the pot.[19] Three rituals, dedicated to the worship of the conch-shell (*śaṁkha*),[20] the bell (*ghaṇṭā*),[21] and the kindling of the lamp (*dīpa*),[22] follow.

When the worshiper is physically, psychically, and spiritually prepared for reception, he invokes the deity to preside over the occasion,[23] and the *ṣoḍaśopacāra pūjā* [sixteen modes of service] begins. The invocation eulogizes the deity as the lord of the universe, with the Smārtas and the Śāktas each reciting a hymn from the Puruṣa-Sūkta (Ṛgveda X:90:1–16) and the Śrī-Sūkta (Ṛgveda I:165:1–16) respectively and offering each of the sixteen modes of service.

---

[16] "Ātmatattvena sthūladehaṁ śodhayāmi svāhā.
Vidyātattvana sūkṣmadehaṁ śodhayāmi svāhā.
Śivatattvena paradehaṁ śodhayāmi svāhā.
Sarvattattvena tattvātītaṁ jīvaṁ śodhayāmi svāhā" (Śarmā 1968:1291).

[17] "Ātmavidyāśivatattvasthaikalasūkṣmaparākhya dehatrayābimāninaṁ jīvātmānaṁ śodhayāmi svāhā" (Śarmā 1968:1291).

[18] "Kalaśasya mukhe viṣṇuḥ kaṇṭhe rudra samāśritāḥ
mūle tatra sthito brahmā ..." (Ācārya 1958:2).

[19] "Gaṅge ca yamune caiva godāvari sarasvati
narmade sindhu kāveri jale'sminsannidhiṁ kuru" (Ācārya 1958:3).

[20] "Śaṁkhādau candradaivatyaṁ kukṣau varuṇadevatā
pṛṣṭhe prajāpatiścaiva agre gaṅgāsarasvatī.
Tvaṁ purāsāgarotpanno viṣṇunā vidhṛtaḥ kare
nirmitaḥ sarvadevaistu pañcajanya namo'stu te" (Ācārya 1958:3).

[21] "Āgamārthaṁ tu devānāṁ gamanārthaṁ tu rakṣasāṁ
kurve ghaṇṭāravaṁ hyatra devatāhvānalakṣaṇaṁ" (Ācārya 1958:3).

[22] "Bho dīpa mūlādhārastvaṁ jyotiṣāṁ patiravyayaḥ
yāvatpūjāsamāptiḥ syāt tāvattvaṁ susthiro bhava" (Ācārya 1958:3).

[23] "Āgaccha devadeveśa tejorāśe jagatpate
kriyamāṇāṁ mayā pūjāṁ gṛhāṇa surasattama" (Ācārya 1958:3).

Soon after the invocation follow the offerings of the seat (*āsana*)[24] and water, for ritual washing of feet (*pādya*)[25] and hands (*arghya*)[26] as well as for sipping (*ācamana*).[27] Then the ritual bath (*snāna*),[28] simple or elaborate, is offered to the deity. (The elaborate bath, although not a part of everyday worship, figures prominently in the occasional voluntary rituals, where it is known as the *pañcāmṛta snāna* [bath with five ambrosial liquids].) Clothes (*vastra*) are offered to maintain earthly norms pertaining to etiquette and modesty,[29] and a fresh sacred thread (*yajñopavīta*)[30] is the insigne of participation in the ritual. The latter is regarded as very sacrosanct,[31] which even the gods are believed to wear, since they also performed the primeval sacrifice (*yajña*) from which all of creation, sentient and insentient, proceeded (Saraf 1970a:9–19; Rgveda X:90:1–16; X:129:1–7). The five-mode service (*pañcopacāra pūja*) employs incense, flowers, incense powder, a lamp, and food offerings; the *pañcopacāra pūjā* is a brief form of worship generally used in everyday ritual performance (Kāne 1941:726–740). It starts with the offering of incense for anointment (*vilepana*),[32] proceeds to the next steps: offerings of a rich variety of flowers (*puṣpa*),[33] incense powders collected from various herbal sources (*dhūpa*),[34] a kindled lamp (*dīpa*),[35] and finally the food offerings (*naivedya*).[36] The worshiper then offers the eight-limbed obeisance

24   "Nānāratna samāyuktaṁ kārtasvara vibhūṣitaṁ
      āsanaṁ devadeveśa prītyarthaṁ pratigṛhyatām" (Ācārya 1958:3).
25   "Pādyaṁ gṛhāṇa deveśa sarvakṣemasamarthabhoḥ
      bhaktyā samarpitaṁ deva lokanātha namo'stu te" (Ācārya 1958:3).
26   "Gandhapuṣpākṣatairyuktaṁ phaladravyasamanvitaṁ
      gṛhāṇa toyamarghyārthaṁ paramaeśvaravatsala" (Ācārya 1958:3).
27   "Karpūravāsitaṁ toyaṁ mandākinyāḥ samāhṛtaṁ
      ācamya tāṁ jagannātha mayā dattaṁ hi bhaktitaḥ" (Ācārya 1958:3).
28   "Gaṅgāsarasvatīrevāpayoṣṇīnarmadājalaiḥ
      snāpito'si mayā deva tathā śāntiṁ kuruṣva me" (Ācārya 1958:3).
29   "Sarvabhūṣādhike saumye lokalajjā nivāraṇe
      mayopapādite tubhyaṁ vāsasī pratigṛhyatāṁ" (Ācārya 1958:5).
30   "Devadeva namaste'stu trāhi māṁ bhavasāgarāt
      brahmasūtraṁ sottarīyaṁ gṛhāṇa puruṣottama" (Ācārya 1958:5).
31   "Oṁ yajñopavītaṁ paramaṁ pavitraṁ prajāpateryatsahajaṁpurastāt
      āyuṣyamagryaṁ pratimuñca śubhraṁ yajñopavītaṁ balamastutejaḥ" (Bhalerao
      1968:681).
32   "Śrikhaṇḍaṁ candanaṁ divyaṁ gandhādhyaṁ sumanoharaṁ
      vilepanaṁ suraśreṣṭha candanaṁ pratigṛhyatāṁ" (Ācārya 1958:6).
33   "Mālyādīni sugandhīni mālatyādīni vai prabho
      mayā hṛtāni pūjārthaṁ puṣpāṇi pratigṛhyatāṁ" (Ācārya 1958:6).
34   "Vanaspatirasodbhūto gandhādhyo gandhauttamaḥ
      āghreyaḥ sarvadevānāṁ dhūpo'yam pratigṛhyatāṁ" (Ācārya 1958:8).
35   "Sājyaṁ ca vartisaṁyuktaṁ vahnināyojitaṁ mayā
      dīpaṁ gṛhāṇa deveśa trailokya timirāpaha" (Ācārya 1958:8).
36   "Naivedyaṁ gṛhyatāṁ deva bhaktiṁ me hyacalāṁ kuru
      īpsitaṁ me varaṁ dehi paratra ca paraṁ gatiṁ" (Ācārya 1958:8).

(*sāṣṭāṅga namaskāra*), the form of prostration which involves touching the ground with one's heart, head, eyes, mind, speech, feet, hands, and thighs, signifying absolute surrender,[37] before the deity and proceeds on a clockwise circumambulation (*pradakṣiṇā*), thereby invoking the destruction of all sins committed in all his former incarnations.[38] The concluding rite of bidding farewell to the deity (*visarjana*) marks the climax of devotion and dedication, surrender and dependence, when the worshiper articulates a confession of his ignorance regarding the procedure of worship and his failures in conducting it, imploring the compassion and forgiveness of the deity.[39] He also dedicates the worship and the rewards accruing from it to the deity he has invoked.[40] Bidding farewell, the worshiper dispatches the departing deity with all honors, entreating the latter to return whenever invoked for the sake of protection of earthly worship and its success.[41]

This exposition of the Hindu ritual complex of worship suggests how rituals occupy a place of prominence in the triad of the Hindu view, way, and aim of life. The Hindu VIEW of life is a conception, a cognitive product as an idealized blueprint. The Hindu WAY of life is the actual translation of the conception into action, or, as Langer has put it, "a constant reiteration of sentiments, ... a disciplined rehearsal of right attitudes" through rituals (1948:1). The Hindu AIM of life relates to the attainment of mundane and/or celestial goals (*trivarga*, i.e. *dharma*, *artha*, and *kāma*), or of unearthly goals (*apavarga*, i.e. *mokṣa*). The first relates to perspective, the second to ritualism, and the third to orientations.

---

[37] "Urasā śirasā dṛṣṭyā manasā vacasā tathā
padbhyāṁ karābhyāṁ jānubhyāṁ praṇāmo'ṣṭāṅga ucyate" (Ācārya 1958:9).

[38] "Yānikāni ca pāpāni janmāntara kṛtāni ca
tānitāni vināśyanti pradakṣiṇa pade pade" (Ācārya 1958:9).

[39] "Āvāhanaṁ na jānāmi na jānāmi visarjanaṁ
pūjāṁ caivana jānāmi kṣamasva parameśvara.
Gataṁ pāpaṁ gataṁ duḥkhaṁ gataṁ dāridryameva ca
āgatā sukhasampattiḥ puṇyācca tava darśanāt.
Mantrahīnaṁ kriyāhīnaṁ bhaktihīnaṁ sureśvara
yatpūjitaṁ mayā deva paripūrṇaṁ tadastu te.
Anyathā śaraṇaṁ nāsti tvameva śaraṇaṁ mama
tasmātkāruṇya bhāvena rakṣasva parameśvara.
Aparādha sahastrāṇi kriyante'harniśaṁ mayā
dāso'yamiti māma matvā kṣamasva parameśvara.
Rūpaṁ dehi jayaṁ dehi yaśo dehi dviṣojahi
saubhāgyaṁ dehi putrāṅśca sarvakāmāṅśca dehi me" (Ācārya 1958:9).

[40] "Gaccha gaccha suraśreṣṭha svasthāne parameśvara
pūja saṁrakṣaṇārthāya punarāgamanāya ca.
Yāntu devagaṇāḥ sarve pūjāmādāya pārthivīṁ
iṣṭakāmaprasiddhyarthaṁ punarāgamanāya ca" (Ācārya 1958:11).

[41] "... Ārādhyadevatārpaṇamastu" (Ācārya 1958:10).

To the Vedic seers, the entire cosmos appeared to be upheld, reinforced, and governed by an eternal cosmic order — the *ṛta* which pervaded everything, the earth, the sky, and the heaven — and which bound all sentient and insentient creation (Keith 1925a:83–85). The *ṛta* signifies both natural law and moral force. The Vedic conception of the *ṛta* appears to have been taken over and replaced by a more earthly conception of the *dharma* by post-Vedic times, just as the complex Vedic ritualism appears to have dwindled into the five great sacrifices (*pañcamahāyajñas*)[42] and the sixteen domestic rituals (*ṣoḍaśa saṁskāras*) (Pandey 1957; Apte 1954), besides the many cults which developed later.

The Brahmanic literature as well as the Kalpa Sūtras, which Max Muller characterized as "a kind of grammar of the Vedic ceremonial" when compared and contrasted with the Smṛtis and the Purāṇas, bears out this statement (Hiriyanna 1951:37, 130). Whatever the historical reasons for such a substitution and shift in emphasis, a marked continuity and similarity of thought prevails throughout this long passage of time in that the fundamental conception relating to the cosmos and man's place in it remains unchanged.

The *ṛta* or *dharma* apart, the three other dimensions of the Hindu cosmic conception which have hardly undergone any change are the threefold subtle constituents (*guṇas*)[43] as the substratum of the universe, the soul-body (*dehī-deha* or *kṣetrajña-kṣetra*) dualism (Tilak 1917:123–148),[44] and the doctrine of *karma* (Śrīmadbhagavadgītā III:1–35).

Besides its cosmogony and cosmology the Upaniṣadic ontology and metaphysics reiterate a triadic conception: the *Para Brahman*, the *Apara Brahman*, and the *Jīvātman* (Saraf 1970f:37–43). The *Para Brahman* is undifferentiated, indifferent, and uninvolved; he is "pure existence (*sat*), pure consciousness (*cit*), and pure bliss (*ānanda*)" (Dandekar 1953:121). The *Apara Brahman* is related to the spatio-temporal world as God (*Īśvara*), characterized by omnipresence, omnipotence, and omniscience. He is creator, preserver, and destroyer of the world; "he is sinless (*apāpaviddha*), pure (*śuddha*), moral (*dhārmya*), holy (*pūta*) and perfect (*pūrṇa*)" (Sinha 1955:16). The *Jīvātman*, "the most distinctive characteristic of which is his assumption of a body, [is] the empirical self which has experience in this changing world of the senses [and which] comes into

---

[42] "Adhyāpanaṁ brahmayajñaḥ pitṛyajñastu tarpaṇaṁ
homo daivo balirbhauto nṛyajño'tithi pūjanaṁ" (Manu Smriti III:70).
[43] "Sattvaṁ najastama iti guṇāḥ prakṛtisaṁbhavaḥ ..." (Śrīmadbhagavadgītā XIV:5).
[44] "Idaṁ śarīraṁ kaunteya kṣetramityabhidhīyate
etad yo vetti taṁ prāhuḥ kṣetrajña iti tadvidaḥ" (Śrīmadbhagavadgītā III:1).

being ... through the operation of ignorance (*avidyā*) ..." (Dandekar 1953:123).

By treating each immanent microcosm (*Jīvātman* or *vyaṣṭi*) as a replica of the transcendent macrocosm (*Para Brahman* or *samaṣṭi*), Hindu liturgy and philosophies have laid singular and central emphasis on how to lend precision and perfection to the medium (*sādhaka*) (Saraf 1970f:120–158, 185ff). As such, the entire procedural corpus of ritual worship has as its objective the following influence on the worshiper. The entire course of the worship ritual aims at the threefold preparation of the practitioner: the practices of abstinence (*yamas*), observance (*niyamas*), and bodily postures (*āsanas*) are primarily directed towards physical cultivation, contributing to the worshiper's biophysical plane of existence. The practice of control of vital body forces (*prāṇāyāma*) and the introversion of consciousness (*pratyāhāra*) are mainly aimed at mental and moral cultivation, preparing him for the psychic plane of existence. Finally, the practice of mental concentration (*dhāraṇā*) and meditation (*dhyāna*), basically seeking the spiritual development of the practitioner, sharpens the medium for the state of sublime equanimity (*samādhi*). Such a popular dictum as the "body is the only means to the attainment of all *dharma*,"[45] and the involvement of various steps of the eight-limbed Yoga (*aṣṭāṅga yoga*) (Shastri 1969), in the Hindu worship complex suggests an affinity between worship and Yoga, as well as the threefold preparation of the practitioner as a means to an end.

The Hindu worshiper visualizes his position in the larger perspective of time (*kāla*) and space (*deśa*). He seeks to establish his concordance with them. His mention of details pertaining to the country of his domicile and to the heavenly bodies, his reference to the various linear subdivisions of time, and his invocations of the celestial beings while he is engaged in chanting his mental resolve (*saṁkalpa*) to perform the worship, give ample evidence of this. To him the universe appears as one "vast whispering gallery," peopled by earthly creatures, aerial or etherial beings, and spiritual personages. He invokes divine intervention against the malevolent ones by performing the ritual arresting of all directions (*digbandha*) for his assistance and to aid the mystic assumption of the power potential in his person through *myāsa* or through recitation of the *kavaca*.

Considerations regarding the auspiciousness (Saraf 1969; 1970b; 1970c; 1970e) of time and space call for a knowledge of astrology, whereas those regarding ritual purity call for scrupulous definitions of situations with a view to ensuring a state of piety in the performer and

---

[45] "Śarīramādyam khalu dharma sādhanaṁ" (Anonymous 1968).

the ritual. The worshiper is eager to attain an external purity of place and objects through their consecration, to attain purity for himself through the bath and his donning fresh clothes, and to invoke an internal purity by sipping the water, chanting the hymns, symbolically destroying anthropomorphized sin, and performing the *prāṇāyāma*, etc.; all these rituals suggest the scrupulous care that is taken about ritual purity. The *Para Brahman* and the *Īśvara* are pure existence; the *Jīvātman* is not, bound as it is by the inexorable law of *karma* and by the fetters of ignorance. Thus the body is impure. In order to qualify both the *Jīvātman* and the body as receptive mediums, their purification is imperative.

Functionally, rituals have been both fundamental to and instrumental in the regulation of socioreligious life and the conditioning of cognitive, affective, and conative activities of the average Hindu. The worshiper's dominant psychic disposition channels all his ritual activity — everyday, occasional, or volitional worship. Whatever the form of worship, the basic orientation of ritual performance aims at one or more of the three goals: terrestrial (*laukika*), celestial (*pāralaukika*), and cosmic (*samaṣṭigata*). The psychic dispositions bind or liberate the worshiper. Those that lead to engrossment (*pravṛtti*) in this world (*laukika*) and the other (*pāralaukika*) relate to the attainment of mundane rewards (*preyas*) and the accumulation of spiritual merit (*śreyas*) respectively, whereas realization of self and release flows from a psychic disposition that is renunciative (*nivṛtti*) in nature, leading to the attainment of salvation (*niḥśreyas*).

Hindu thought and ritualism have received, at various periods, vastly different emphases on one or the other of these threefold basic orientations. For instance, Vedic ritualism places a high premium on the attainment of mundane rewards and the accrual of spiritual merit at the expense of realization of the self and release, within which, however, Purva-Mimamsa stresses celestial orientation as the *summum bonum* of Vedic ritualism (Tarkabhushan 1953; Tirtha 1967:21). The Śrīmadbhagavadgītā lays particular emphasis on a cosmic orientation when it eulogizes action without desire for reward (*niṣkāma karma*), based upon the conception that only such action frees one from the inexorable law of *karma* and leads to liberation.

When viewed in the light of the above framework of basic orientations, the Hindu worship complex appears to be oriented largely toward attainment of mundane rewards, occasionally tempered by the philosophy of *niṣkāma karmayoga* in which the worshiper seeks all sorts of favors from the deity but dedicates the worship and its fruits to the deity by saying "*ārādhyadevatārpaṇamastu.*"

From the foregoing discussion regarding perspective and orientations flows a paradigm of levels of reality, orientations, nature of existence, planes of consciousness, and goals, diagramed in Table 1.

Table 1. Perspectives and basic orientations in Hindu rituals

Level of Reality	Orientation	Nature of existence	Plane of consciousness	Goal
Para Brahman or *samaṣṭi*	Cosmic or *brahmāṇḍa*	Eternal or *sat*	Spiritual	*niḥśreyas*
Apara Brahman or *Īśvara*	Celestial or *svarga* or *pāralaukika*	Immortality or *amaratva*	Psychic	*śreyas*
Jīvātman or *vyaṣṭi*	Terrestrial or *jagata* or *laukika*	Mortality or *mṛtyu-janma*	Biophysical	*preyas*

Table 1 reveals the increasing upward and inward movement of the performer who aims at proceeding, step by step, from the gross to the subtle, from the material to the nonmaterial, from the factual to the symbolic; basically, he attempts to move from the finite to the infinite.

The Hindu ritual idiom, thus, signifies that *magnum opus* which has metaphysical and speculative bases, sustained by cardinal moral and spiritual values and reinforced by complex liturgical expression. It derives its content from a whole body of beliefs, rooted in mysticism, abstract thinking, and reasoning; its form combines solemnization and dramatization. Firmly grounded in and reiterated by such branches of Hindu thought as astrology, cosmogony, cosmology, ontology, theology, and yoga, to name a few, the whole grand scheme underlying all Hindu ritual complexes finds its expression as a way of life where singular emphasis has been on defining the code of normative patterns, value orientations, and procedural sequence.

REFERENCES

ĀCĀRYA, NĀRĀYANA RĀMA
1958 *Atha sarvapūjāprārambhaḥ*. Bombay: Nirṇayasāgara Press.
AIYANGAR, K. V. RANGASWAMI
1952 *Some aspects of the Hindu view of life according to Dharmaśāstra*. Baroda: Oriental Institute.
ANONYMOUS
1968 Nyāsa-tattva. *Kalyāṇa: Upāsanā-Aṁka* 42:666–70.

APTE, V. M.
1954   *Social and religious life in the Gṛhya Sutras.* Bombay: The Popular Book Depot.

BENEDICT, RUTH
1949   "Ritual," in *Encyclopaedia of the social sciences,* volume thirteen. Edited by Edwin R. A. Seligman, 396–98. New York: Macmillan.

BHALERAO, PRITHVIRAJ
1968   Upāsanā men śuci veṣa kā mahatva. *Kalyāṇa: Upāsanā-Aṁka* 42: 681–84.

CHATTERJEE, SATISHCHANDRA, DHIRENDRAMOHAN DATTA
1950   *An introduction to Indian philosophy.* Calcutta: University of Calcutta Press.

COOMARSWAMY, ANANDA K.
1971   *Hinduism and Buddhism.* New York: Philosophical Library.

DANDEKAR, R. N.
1953   "The role of man in Hinduism," in *The religion of the Hindus.* Edited by Kenneth W. Morgan. New York: Ronald Press.

DURKHEIM, EMILE
1964   *The elementary forms of religious life.* London: George Allen and Unwin.

FIRTH, RAYMOND
1951   *Elements of social organization.* London: Watts.

HIRIYANNA, M.
1951   *The essentials of Indian philosophy.* London: George Allen and Unwin.

KĀNE, P. V.
1941a   *History of Dharmaśāstra* 2(1). Poona: Bhandarkar Oriental Research Institute.
1941b   *History of Dharmaśāstra* 2(2). Poona: Bhandarkar Oriental Research Institute.
1953   *History of Dharmaśāstra* 4. Poona: Bhandarkar Oriental Research Institute.

KEITH, ARTHUR B.
1925a   *The religion and philosophy of the Veda and Upanisads,* volume one. Cambridge, Mass.: Harvard University Press.
1925b   *The religion and philosophy of the Veda and Upanisads,* volume two. Cambridge, Mass.: Harvard University Press.

LANGER, SUSANNE K.
1948   *Philosophy in a new key.* London: Penguin Books.

LÉVI-STRAUSS, C.
1963   *Structural anthropology.* New York: Basic Books.

MAJUMDAR, R. C., *editor*
1957   *Vedic age.* London: George Allen and Unwin.

MOGHE, GOVINDA RĀMACHANDRA
1911   *Jyotirmayūkha.* Bombay: Tukaram Pundalik Setthye.

PANDEY, R. B.
1957   *Hindū Saṁskāra: sāmājika tathā dhārmika adhyayana,* volume two. Vārānasī: Chowkhambā Vidyābhawan.

RADHAKRISHNAN, S.
1948   *The Hindu view of life.* London: George Allen and Unwin.
1956   *Indian philosophy,* volume two. New York: Macmillan.
RAGOZIN, ZENAIDE A.
1961   *Vedic India.* Delhi: Munshiram Manoharlal.
RENOU, LOUIS
1961   *Hinduism.* London: Prentice-Hall.
SARAF, SAMARENDRA
1969   The Hindu ritual purity-pollution complex. *The Eastern Anthropologist* 22(2):161–175.
1970a   The Vedic view of Yajña: its symbolism and significance. *Madhya Bhāratī* 18(18):9–19.
1970b   The trichotomous theme: a ritual category in Hindu culture. *Anthropos* 65:948–972.
1970c   Structural significance of and status evaluation among three Brāhmana groups. *The Indian Journal of Sociology* 1(1):82–94.
1970d   In search of a philosophy for fuller life. *The Call Divine* 18(5):181–189, 320.
1970e   Ritual purity-pollution theme: an analytical study. *Journal of Social Research* 14(2):14–22.
1970f   "Hindu caste system and the ritual idiom." Unpublished doctoral thesis, University of Saugar.
ŚARMĀ, VĀSUDEVU PANAŚĪKARA, *editor*
1925   *Ṛgvedīya Brahmakarmasamuccaya.* Bombay: Ṅirṇayasāgara Press.
n.d.   *Āhnikacandrikā.* Bombay: Nirṇayasāgara Press.
ŚARMĀ, YAJÑADATTA [BRAHMACĀRĪ ŚRĪ PĀGALĀNANDA]
1968   Śrī Bagalāmukhī Devī kī upāsanā. *Kalyāna: Upāsana-Aṁka,* 42:504–510, 1042–1046, 1290–1294.
SHASTRĪ, SWĀMĪ SHIVĀNANDA
1969   *Way to God.* Bombay: Jñan Sadan Trust.
SINHA, JADUNATH
1955   *The foundation of Hinduism.* Calcutta: Sinha.
TARKABHUSHAN, PRAMATHNATH
1953   "Pūrva-Mīmāmsā," in *The cultural heritage of India,* volume three. Edited by Haridas Bhattacharya, 151–67. Calcutta: The Ramakrishna Mission Institute of Culture.
TILAK, B. G.
1917   *Gītā rahasya.* Poona: Keśarī Office.
TĪRTHA, SWĀMĪ OMĀNANDA
1967   *Pātañjalayogapradīpa.* Gorakhpur: Gītā Press.
ZAEHNER, R. C.
1962   *Hinduism.* London: Oxford University Press.

A Descriptive Analysis of the Content of Nepalese Buddhist Pūjās as a Medical-Cultural System with References to Tibetan Parallels

WILLIAM STABLEIN

That nature is systematic or thought to be so by man is of crucial importance, but it is even more important that different cultures structure nature according to their own projections. In the case of the Newars and Tibetans of Nepal, whose life-styles have their roots in the *vajrayāna*[1] tantric Buddhist tradition, one cannot help but notice a hierarchically systematic view of the universe which is reflected in the ritual and community processes. When destructive forces plague the community in the form of physical, mental, and social diseases, it is as if a unit of the system is deviating or damaged and needs to be controlled or repaired.

The control center is the ceremonial circle which is a symbolic reality of the *vajrayāna* Buddhist's universe and is believed to have the potential power to correct the ills of mankind.

Like a computer the ceremonial circle is useless without a programmer. The programmer is the *vajrācārya* [hierophant],[2] who feeds the circle with the proper information, i.e. the request of *samkalpa* [intention]

I want to thank Mr. Manavajra, Vajrācārya of Kathmandu, for his expert help in my study of Buddhist tantra. I also appreciate the friendly and scholarly suggestions of Dr. Christopher George and Dr. Alexander, University of Washington.

[1]   In the context of this study, *vajrayāna* tantric Buddhism refers primarily to the traditional Newar Buddhist community of Kathmandu, Nepal. *Vajrayāna* means the way of the *Vajra*. *Vajra* designates an ultimate value that the Newar and Tibetans put on the universe. After a thing is ritually purified to its utmost, it is *Vajra*. Thus the goal of the *vajrayāna* Buddhist is to exist in the state of *Vajra* body, speech, and mind.

[2]   We should understand that the *vajrācārya* is one who presides over the internal *pūjās* (*adhyāmikapūjā*) which are performed in the private *āgama* [chapels] of every Newar monastery (*vihāra* (Newari) *baha*). The chapels are maintained by a social organization called *guthi*.

to repair or control. Actually, the donor of the ceremony (*pūjā*) requests the hierophant to request the divinity's presence. When the donor touches the hierophant's own personal *pūjābandha* [brass pot] at the beginning of the *pūjā*, this triad — donor, hierophant, and divinity — is formed into a bond. The triad represents the basic hierarchical structure, i.e. the projected divinity, the hierophant and the community.

Our first unit then in the medical-cultural system is the symbolic vertical pathway in time and space that leads to the unity between the hierophant and the divinity, which is ideally represented in the Tibetan system by a *tshogs.shin* (Tibetan) [sacred tree], on which dwell the tutelary deities, Buddhas, the sacred community, the projectors, and the sacred books.[3] The neophyte is asked to project into this visual aid all his friends, relatives, and enemies so that all may benefit from the transfer of the *amṛta* (Tibetan) *bdud.rtsi* [curing ambrosia][4] that is believed to be taking place between the divine hierarchy and the sentient beings, via the hierophant. As enemies are also included it is a kind of therapeutic sacred jurisprudence without actual encounter.

The *samkalpa* [intention] of the *pūjā* becomes an *āvāhana* [call] for the projected divinity to descend in the *kalaśa* [flask] (Figure 1.e). The call is symbolized by four *mudrā* [hand gestures] and four syllables: *jaḥ, huṁ, vaṁ, hoḥ*. The *vajrayāna* hierophants, never ones to cling only to the outer projection, have an inner projection as well, which takes the divinity to the lower part of the abdomen which is likened unto a flask. Hence, there was a famous Tibetan lama in Nepal called the *bum.can* (Tibetan) [flasked one].

The essence of the tree is the *bīja* [seed], which has an empty center from which the divinity is imagined to grow. Thus in the Tibetan ceremony the divinity is sung to arise from the inside pith that is empty *stoṅ.par.gyur.pa'i.naṅ.ñid.las.* (Tibetan). The hierophant then must first of all project the *śūnyatā* [emptiness] onto the ceremonial circle from which the divine tree will grow and rain its curing *amṛta* [ambrosia].

Because of the efficacy of the ambrosia, according to the indigenous conception of health, the community emulates and mimics the divine as much as possible. Indeed, the divinity has its own hierarchy, but it is projected on the basis of the community. In the center of the sacred tree there is the supreme *vajradhāra* [*Vajra* bearer], the *iṣṭadevatā*

---

[3] The *tshog.shin* is visually represented by religious paintings. Although they are Tibetan, Newars also use them as reverential objects in *pūjā*. The *tshog.shin* is also mentally visualized. I am using it as an example of the vertical pathway of the sacred. There are other models, such as the *mandala*, in three dimensions, the Nepalese pagoda, the *chaitya*, or even the body itself.

[4] All foreign words are Sanskrit except those marked Tibetan or Newari.

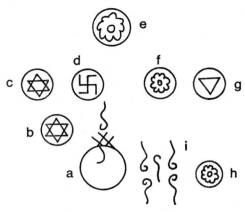

Figure 1.   The Ceremonial Circle of the *Kalaśa* [Flask] *Pūjā*:
a.   *Gurumandala* [of Guru Vajrasattva]
b.   *Samādhibalimandala* [of food offerings for the divinities to produce the during ambrosia]
c.   *Krodhagaṇabalimandala* [of food offerings for the group of wrathful divinities]
d.   *Dadhipatramandala* [of the pot filled with curd]
e.   *Kalaśamandala* [of the main divinity's flask]
f.   *Nāgabandhamandala* [of the divine serpent's flask]
g.   *Dīpamandala* [of the light]
h.   *Pañcagavya* [the five substances of cow]
i.   *Dikpālabali* [food offerings for the protectors in space]

[tutelary deity] sits below, and surrounding the tree at the bottom are the *nātha* [protectors]. These three can be likened unto a seed: the center, the embryo, and the protective layer, respectively. It is believed that the divinities are actually not different from each other in essence, which at least is known and realized by most hierophants. They are like water being poured into water. Water which is in the flask then is a perfect medium in which to project the divinity.

When the hierophant realizes the presence of the divinity, he offers water for its *arghapādya* [feet], for *ācamana* [sipping], and for *prokṣaṇa* [cleaning]. In internal *pūjās* that are conducted secretly, the *mulācārya* [main hierophant], who is dressed in the costume of the divinity, is treated with the same respect. Among the Newars in ancient times and even now among the elders, water offerings are made to guests. The host hopes in turn to receive something from the guest who will feel obligated. Indeed, it is a model subliminal contract that is the foundation of many personal relationships. The water offerings thus reflect the etiquette of the community. Once the divinity is invited, the hierophant can transfer the curing ambrosia to substances, objects, and individuals.

The second unit of the medical-cultural system is the *vajrācārya* [hierophant] himself which includes a projected structural arrangement within the body called *vajradeha* [*Vajra* body]. The hierophant as a member of the social elite is significant. The Newar hierophants are first of all bound by a castelike consciousness which is symbolized by their inner *pūjā* performed in the sacred *āgama* [chapel] which is located in every Newar monastery (*vihāra* [Newari] *baha*). As the participants share boiled rice and other food out of the same pots during the cere- monial proceedings, the *pūjā* must exclude most of the rest of the Newar community. Among the Tibetans, who do not follow the Indian model of caste as the Newars do, the hierophants are nonetheless isolated and educated from birth in order to fulfill their priestly roles. Like the Newar hierophants, their special training provides them with skills for reading the sacred texts, various kinds of contemplation, painting, dancing, medicine, and astrology, as well as the complexities of ritual arrangement and performance. If the elitist quality of the hierophant declined through social or other changes, the medical-cultural system I am suggesting could not exist.

It is important that the hierophant is not considered as separate from the divinity. In the ceremony this is dramatized first of all by the *gurumandala pūjā* (Figure 1.a).[5] The guru is Vajrasattva (whose being is *Vajra*), symbolized by the mythical Mount Meru, in the center of the *mandala* surrounded by the continents of the world. The hierophant imagines the whole world is within this *mandala* which he projects as an offering. As such he imagines his own body as guru Vajrasattva himself, and no matter where he goes he is conceptually in the center of the universe which is symbolized by his self *prādaksina* [circumam- bulation], i.e. he simply turns around with his hands folded.[6]

The education and training of the hierophant may be significant for the existence and maintenance of his *vajradeha* [*Vajra* body] which is the main dynamo of the system. The *Vajra* body is the model system of three nerves (Bharati 1970:175, 292): *lalanā*, *rasanā*, and *avadhūtī*, which are located in the left, right, and middle parts of the body re- spectively (Lessing and Wayman 1968: 327). With these nerves there are five *cakra* [circular arrangements within the head, throat, heart, stomach, and genitals]. The main function of this unit is the sacred procreation, i.e. the creation of the *bodhicitta* [sacred semen].[7] This in

---

[5]   The *gurumandala* is performed at the beginning of every community *pūjā*. The *pūjā* I am offering as a model is the *kalaśapūjā* [flask *pūjā*] illustrated in Figure 1, which in turn is incorporated into larger ceremonies such as the marriage ceremony and so on.
[6]   Spatially, this is probably the smallest distance circumambulated by members of any community.

turn emanates the transferable *amṛta* [ambrosia]. This is the salient feature of the perfect concentration *pūjā* (*samādhi-pūjā*). Symbolic of this *pūjā* is the double triangle in the shape of a six-pointed star (Figure 1.b) that one will find in almost every monastic courtyard, standing for the union of *upāya* [means] and *prajñā* [insight]. On top of the double triangle is offered some rice, on top of which is placed an earthenware pot on a tripod filled with cooked rice, garlic, meat, beans, beer, and a blue and red flag designating the wind and fire *mandalas* that are imagined to cook the contents of the pot. The food is then, through an audiovisual yogic process, projected into the transferable element of ambrosia.

Because the main divinity and his consort are outwardly projected to couple within the food and produce the *bodhicitta* and ensuing ambrosia, the process is referred to as *baliyoga*, i.e. the union within the offerings which generally occurs near the end of the *samādhipūjā*.[8] Before the food is hypostasized into ambrosia, the hierophant must create it within himself. I call this the ambrosia cycle.

Briefly, the ambrosia cycle begins with the creation of the divinities in union with oneself. The whole world is projected as the body, speech, and mind of the divinities which goes through the following audiovisual transformation: the world as body, speech, and mind → (changes to) moon *mandala* → *hum* → the coupling divinities, from whom issues the sound of *suratasabda* [enjoyment]. This changes the above world into a sacred *mandala*, which now is cycled back into the mouth of the divinities and emanates again as *bodhicitta* [sacred semen]. Then the sacred semen → *bījasvarūpa* [seed having its own nature] → *bījāksara* [sound of the seed] which divides into a red and white *hūm* (1) → *hum* (2) → *ham* (3) → *sira* [head] (4) → *ardha-candra* [half moon] (5) → *bindu* [dot] (6)[9] and lastly dissolves to only sound which is first loud, then

[7] Professor Bharati writes that, "Anthropomorphically the *bodhicitta* is the mind of each living Buddha, as of each enlightened person" (Bharati 1970: 293). The rendering "sacred semen" fits the actual function of the unit. The nonhierophants both Newar and Tibetan do not understand *citta* (Tibetan *sems*) as having anything to do with semen; however, the hierophants have no qualms about making the analogy. The *amṛta* [curing ambrosia] is dependent upon the creation of the *bodhicitta* [sacred semen].

[8] Among the Tibetans, the union of the male and female which is pictorially represented in religious paintings is understood as the biological and vegetative procreative energies of the existence, which are projected as sounds inside the *Vajra* body. That it is actually the sexual act itself is taken as a kind of joke. The Newar hierophants who are married, however, feel that it is an intrinsic part of the *sādhana*, but even among them it is not a topic of discursive reasoning.

[9] A similar process is beautifully performed by the *bkaḥ rgyud pa* sect in the invitation (Tibetan *spyan.ḥdren*) of *Mahākāla*. The performance is called *āh hūm*, partly illustrated in the following way (in Tibetan musical notation):

soft, and finally vanishes (7). This is the peak moment of the hierophant's contemplation: He has refined the sacred semen to the quality of sound which can be transferred to objects, substances, and individuals. In this way especially we should understand the efficacy of the *bīja-mantra* [seed syllable]. The *samādhipūjā* then informs us that one of the qualities of perfection that the hierophant must achieve is the perfection or *Vajra* nature of sound. In the *samādhipūjā* all the sounds of the Sanskrit alphabet referred to as *Ali* for vowels and *Kāli* for consonants are projected onto the *Vajra* body, and are then synthesized into the seed syllables *oṁ*, *āh*, *hūṁ*, the matrix of the universe of body, speech, and mind. The seed syllable is cast into the substance which cultivates the sacred tree into a living symbolic reality for those who have *bhakti* [faith], have taken *saṁvāra* [vows] and hence have access to the *samaya-sattva* [pledged beings] on the sacred tree.

The third unit contains the fundamental elements in the community that the projection and flow of the *amṛta* [curing ambrosia] are dependent upon. In fact, without the elements *bhakti* [faith], *saṁvāra* [vow], and *samaya* [pledge], the traditional structure of the *vajrayāna* community, whether Newar or Tibetan, could not exist.

Saṁvāra [vow] presupposes *bhakti* [faith] and is a determinant of the *samaya* [pledge]. The simple model is the *nityapūjā* [continual *pūjā*] where the devotee approaches the image with faith, makes her five ordinary *pancopahāra* [oblation offerings] and then takes in return (usually from the hierophant) some *samayavastu* [substance] which is eaten and produces the cure. The substance is a pledged substance by virtue of having been pledged to the divinity by an individual who has the *saṁvāra* [vow], i.e. the vowed person gives off pure things. The unvowed person or the wicked person emanates impure things.

An example among the Tibetans of how substances take on qualities outside of themselves is the concept of *sdig.zas* (Tibetan) [sin food] as

---

Notice how it goes from heavy lines to light and even lighter (manuscript: *dpal.nag.po. chen.po.yab. yum.hkhor.dan.bcas.par.byed.paḥi.rdo.rjeḥi.glu.dbyan*).

Similarly, notice the numbers 1 to 7 illustrating the gradual dissolution from the bottom upwards to emptiness in the syllable *hum*.

Thus:

opposed to *dsm.zas* (Tibetan) [pledged food]. To dine at the same table with a thief is to take on the qualities of a thief. Sharing food with a respected member of the community leaves one with a feeling of having bettered one's moral being. To share food with a hierophant is tantamount to an actual act of purification, *sbyon, ba* (Tibetan). And to be given *dam.rdzas* (Tibetan) [pledged substance] is to be given *sman* (Tibetan) [medicine]. Occasionally one hears the term *dam.rdzas* (Tibetan) used for gifts exchanged between friends which designates a bond of loyalty far beyond the exchanging itself.

When pledged substance is shared in the course of an initiation ritual where vows are taken, or in the course of any *pūjā*, the participants become *rdo.rje.spun* (Tibetan) [*Vajra* brothers].

As the devotee relies upon the strength of his *samvāra* [vows] to ensure the efficacy of the ambrosia medicine, the hierophant is dependent on his *samādhi, tin.ne.hdzin* (Tibetan) [perfect concentration] to ensure the flow of the ambrosia. The effort of the *vajrayāna* community is to make its daily efforts in the context of the vow. The hierophant protects the *samaya* [pledge] which the community relies upon for health and social stability.

The fourth unit of the medical-cultural system is substances: substances to purify, to offer, and to use as curing remedies. In all *pūjās* above and to the right of the *gurumandala* (Figure 1.i) there are *bali* [food offerings] and *gojā* (Newari) [rice cakes] included which have the function of attracting the protective divinities of *dikpāla* [space]. The hierophant offers the five *pañcagavya* [substances of cow] (Figure 1.h): milk, curd, butter, feces (substituted by honey), and urine (substituted by sugar). The protectors are invited to stand sentinel near the *gurumandala*. Eight flowers are placed around the *mandala* to represent their presence. More eatables are then offered for the ten *daśakrodha* [wrathful deities] on the second six-pointed star (Figure 1.c). It is usually considered that the directional divinities nail the wrathful ones in their places. A pot is filled with *dadhipatra* [curd] and set on a swastika (Figure 1.d) drawn with the *sindūra* [powder of red lead] which stands for the four *caturbrahmavihāra* [holy dwellings], i.e. friendliness, detachment, joy, and compassion. The main flask should not be confused with the divine serpent flask (*nagābandha* [Figure 1.f]).

The *nāga* [divine serpent] must be propitiated in every *pūjā*, for he is though to have power over rain and to be the progenitor of certain diseases such as *pidika* [boils] and *ślipāda* [elephantiasis].

The *dīpa* [lamp] (Figure 1.g) suggests the *raśmi* [rays] of the divinity that disperse the dark clouds of ignorance. Thus when devotees enter temples which always have burnings lamps, they will hold their hands and faces over the fire to receive the *raśmi* [rays] of the divinity. Another light is used (not shown in Figure 1) for a special *nīrājana* [light purification]. A wick is placed in an earthenware dish that contains mustard seeds which are the standard substance for nullifying forces of *bhūta* [disease], flowers and water which clean the *kleśa* [defilements], three balls of rice that designate the dedicating of one's merits to all sentient beings, and the dish itself, symbolizing the removing of the cover of ignorance. The light is waved in front of the flask where the main divinity is thought to dwell.

Añjana [ointments] are well known in *vajrayāna* literature. A surviving remnant of this tradition is the giving of *tika* [dot on the forehead]. Hence the hierophant carries with him a small *tika-bandha* [double-cupped vase] with the powder of yellow pigment in one cup and the *sindūra* [powder of red lead] in the other, these represent the *upāya* [means] of the male principle and the *prajñā* [insight] of the female principle, respectively. Mixed together and pressed first onto a pledged object and then onto the forehead, it signifies the transfer of ambrosia. Ointment in the *Mahākālatantra* is called the *yoga* [joining] of the two principles (*bola* and *kaṃkola*) that produces flavor of oneness. Another form of ointment is *kajjala* [lampblack]. At the beginning of internal *pūjās* a wick doused with oil is placed under a pot where the lampblack is collected. At the end of the ceremony, after the hierophant reads the signs left by the lampblack inside the pot, the participants are given a *tika*. The women take the pledged lampblack and apply it to their eyes. The Indians now produce commercially a special *kajjala* [lampblack] that can be bought in any Nepalese or Indian general store.

Among the Tibetans the most popular pledged substances that are given out for curing are *guṭika, ril.bu* (Tibetan) [pills]. They are made from Ayurvedic substances that become pledged in the process of *pūjā*. The pill, being defined both as the union of body, speech, and mind, and as the sacred semen of the divinity, gives us a practical example of yogic medicine. In fact, the pill is an analog of the whole world in a refined state and is a symbol of what the medical-cultural system of the *vajrayāna* Buddhists is all about.[10]

In summary, the medical-cultural system of the *vajrayāna* com-

---

[10] While making pills out of certain substances with the uttering of seed syllables, "one will be emancipated from disease (*nad.grol*), obtain ordinary magical powers (*mchog.mthun.dṅos.grub.thob*), immortality (*chi.med*) and move in the sky (*mkhaḥ. sbyod.du.ḥgro*) (manuscript: *ñe.bar.mkho.bahi.rdzas.sna.tshogs.kyi.śbyar.thabs.lag.len. ci.rigs.bstan.shel.gyi.ḥphren.ba.gzugs.so*)."

munities in Nepal, which may indeed apply to all those Asian communities that have not undergone a radical modernization, includes the following units: (1) a vertical system such as the sacred tree, with its divinities that function simultaneously in space and in the *Vajra* body of the hierophant, from whom arises a projected field of *amṛta* [ambrosia]; (2) the hierophant who calls the divinity into his *Vajra* body and plants the ambrosia by means of the seed syllables: (3) the community which assembles in *pūjā* to pay respects to the sacred hierarchy, reaffirms their *saṁvāra* [vows], and shares in the sacred feast; and (4) the substances themselves that carry the *amṛta* [ambrosia] to the devotees and the community at large. The *pūjā* system, like any medical system, seeks to control, repair, and prevent suffering.

If correcting the suffering of the community is the main function of medical-cultural systems, and if currently existing *pūjās* reflect the contents of classical tantric texts, then indeed the latter will prove to reflect such a system.

REFERENCES

BHARATI, AGEHANANDA
    1970   *The tantric tradition.* New York: Doubleday.
LESSING, FERDINAND D., ALEX WAYMAN
    1968   *Mkhas Grub Rje's fundamentals of Buddhist tantras.* The Hague: Mouton.
Mahākālatantra
    n.d.   Microfilm copy in the Library of the Institute for Advanced Studies of World Religions, State University of New York, Stony Brook. (Translated copy in personal library.)
ANONYMOUS
    n.d.   *Tib.Dpal.Nag.Po.Chen.Po.Yab.Yum.Hkhor.Daṅ.Bcas.Pa.Mchog.Tu. Dgyes.Pa.Skyed.Par.Byed.Paḥi.Rdo.Rjeḥi.Glu.Dbyaṅs.* [Songs of the *Vajra* concerning the illustrious *Mahākāla* wife and followers which is conducive to supreme happiness.] Tibetan manuscript (personal library).
    n.d.   *Tib.Ñe.Bar.Mkho.Baḥi.Rdzas.Sna.Tshogs.Kyi.Sbyar.Thabs.Lag.Len.Ci Rigs.Bstan.Pa.Shal.Gyi.Hphreṅ.Ba.Bzhugs.So.* [The crystal garland teachings showing whatever methods may be used for the preparation of various necessary substances.] Tibetan manuscript (personal library).

Shamanism and World View: The Case of the Ainu of the Northwest Coast of Southern Sakhalin

EMIKO OHNUKI–TIERNEY

Elsewhere (Ohnuki-Tierney i.p.a) I described in full detail the shamanism of the Sakhalin Ainu of the northwest coast of southern Sakhalin. There I discussed the shamanism with reference to: (1) spirits and deities involved in shamanism; (2) shamans; (3) shamanistic rites; (4) nature of shamanistic power; (5) evil shamans. In the present paper, I shall first briefly restate the points I made in that discussion. However, my primary purpose in this paper is to present my interpretations of the Sakhalin Ainu shamanistic complex in the context of the total culture of the Ainu and especially as it relates to the Ainu world view.

The shamanistic practices and associated cultural phenomena discussed here are those of the Ainu who, during the first half of the twentieth century, inhabited the northwest coast of southern Sakhalin, north of *Rayčiska*[1] (Japanese designation: Raichishika), to the former Russo-Japanese border. It was an isolated area where influence from Japanese, Russian, and other "natives" of Sakhalin penetrated little, least of all in southern Sakhalin (Yamamoto 1943). Together with the rest of the Sakhalin Ainu, they are now, as a consequence of World War II, relocated in Hokkaido.

Regional variations in culture are highly developed among the Ainu.

I wish to thank Professor Jan Vansina of the University of Wisconsin for carefully reading the draft of this paper and offering many valuable suggestions. In particular, he pointed out the symbolism of communication in my marginal symbols, which has given greater depth to my understanding of Ainu shamanism. I am most grateful to the National Science Foundation under whose grant my fieldwork during 1964–1965 was conducted. My particular indebtedness goes to Professor Chester S. Chard of the University of Wisconsin for his generous encouragement during the course of my study.
[1] All the italicized lexemes are in phonemic notation.

In addition to significant differences between the Sakhalin and Hokkaido Ainu cultures as a whole, there are also important cultural differences among the Sakhalin Ainu of the northwest coast, southwest coast, and east coast. Shamanism, in particular, seems to demonstrate marked regional differences. Most scholars who discuss Sakhalin Ainu shamanism point out how it differs from that of the Hokkaido Ainu whose shamanistic complex is less elaborate. These scholars stress influences upon the Sakhalin Ainu beliefs and practices from the shamanism of Siberian peoples (Pilsudski 1961 [1909]: 183; Kindaichi 1925:32; Hanihara et al. 1972:178). This influence is applicable primarily to shamanism on the east coast, to which most of the published data relate (Yamamoto, in a personal communication, confirmed this interpretation). Occasional references are made to the shamanism of the Sakhalin Ainu on the east coast, as described by Pilsudski (1961 [1909]) at the Aihama and other settlements on the east coast; by Kubodera (1960 — fieldwork in 1935) at the Niitoi settlement; and by Chiri and Wada (1943) at the Shirahama settlement. No systematic attempt is made here, however, to include comparative material either from other Sakhalin Ainu groups or the Hokkaido Ainu.

My fieldwork was done during a year (1964–1965) and three months (1969) spent in two communities in Hokkaido, Wakasakunai, and Tokoro, where the Sakhalin Ainu are now resettled. The bulk of the data, however, comes from a Sakhalin Ainu woman, herself a shaman, who proved to be an exceptionally gifted informant. She was born about 1900 near *Esituri* in a winter settlement along the upper stream of the *Masaramamma* River and spent most of her life in settlements on the northwest coast. Ainu was her only language until World War II, during which she learned Japanese. Her idiolect is identified by Hattori as the *Rayčiska* dialect (1964).

BRIEF DESCRIPTION OF THE NORTHWEST COAST
SHAMANISM

The cultural complex described in Ohnuki-Tierney (i.p.a) and interpreted here is what the Ainu themselves call *tusu*. It is an age-old practice of the Ainu and it appears even in their oral tradition in which it is called *kinra* (Kindaichi 1914:36, 109; see also Chiri 1954:143–144).

The sign of the "call" to become a shaman often is an experience in which the person, male or female, is seized by an uncontrollable feeling and engages in behavior which usually involves vigorous physical movements. He gradually gains control over the seizure and transforms his feelings and behavior into those of a shaman. He then should be able to perform a rite only when he consciously chooses.

Shamanistic ability is regarded as an asset. Shamans are considered to have more than average ability to communicate with the deities. Thus they are referred to not only simply as *tusu aynu* (*tusu* [shamanistic rite]; *aynu* [man]), but also as *nupuru aynu* or *nupuru kuru*. The term *nupuru*, as in the last two designations, refers in Ainu to the properties of the deities — most importantly, it is the power which the deities enjoy over the Ainu. The designations for shamans then reflect the Ainu thinking that shamans possess some super-Ainu power which the ordinary Ainu lack. Oral tradition indicates that in the past shamanistic ability perhaps was regarded even more highly than at present. Two brothers, who lived at the *Rayčiska* settlement at the beginning of the world and are regarded by the Ainu as their great ancestors, are said to have been powerful shamans. One of them was married to the Goddess of Sun and Moon and could travel to the sky while performing a shamanistic rite (Ohnuki-Tierney 1968:248–249). In a sacred tale from the east coast, the culture hero during his battle with female demons is saved by a woman whom he subsequently marries. She is depicted as having two characteristics: beauty and shamanistic ability (Kindaichi 1914:103–109). In another story also from the east coast, the culture hero himself is described as being a powerful shaman (Pilsudski 1912:151, Tale 16; reprinted in Japanese in Chiri and Yamamoto 1944).[2] Chiri further generalizes and proposes a hypothesis that the culture hero represents Ainu chiefs who necessarily were shamans in the ancient society of the Ainu (Chiri 1960: iii). In the northwest coast Ainu society, shamanistic ability remained up to the ethnographic present a most desired and desirable quality of a person.[3]

Nevertheless, there seems to be no necessary relationship between

[2]   In this tale the culture hero is referred to as *nupuru* [powerful (as a shaman)]. The content of the story implies that he is expected to excel in miracle performance rather than ordinary cure of illnesses.
[3]   Although the Ainu do not make any necessary connection between the shamans and the *imu: aynu*, when I checked my list of the names of shamans, the majority of the shamans were also *imu: aynu*. An *imu: aynu* is a person who suddenly has spells of compulsory mimicking or nonsensical utterances and has no control over them until they stop on their own. The Ainu do regard the phenomenon of *imu:* to be somewhat abnormal, but amusingly so. Some scholars, however, postulate a relationship between shamanistic dispositions and *imu:* (Chiri 1952:55–58; Wada 1965:264–266), and the latter is regarded as a psychological abnormality which is likely related to *latah*, *saka*, and *pibloktoq* (Barnouw 1963:368–374). Psychological observations on shaman's dispositions are also found in Pilsudski (1961 [1909]:184–185), Wada (1962:149, 151), and Nagano et al. (1966).

either the political or economic position of a person and his status as a shaman. Some amount of economic gain notwithstanding, shamanistic practice alone brings neither fortune nor political power. This is also reported to be the case among the east coast Sakhalin Ainu (Pilsudski 1961 [1909]:188).

Males as well as females can be shamans. In the past the famous shamans often seem to have been males, although there seems to have been an equal number of female practitioners. In the recent past, however shamans have been almost exclusively women. On the east coast, Pilsudski reports, although both males and females can be shamans, female shamans are often regarded as being more powerful (1961 [1909]:186). Among the Hokkaido Ainu, shamanism is almost exclusively the realm of women (Kindaichi 1961:45; Sarashina 1968:188; Segawa 1972:192).

Most of the powerful shamans are older. However, many receive the "call" during their teens and start their careers quite early in life. On the east coast, in the aforementioned sacred tale, the powerful shamaness is referred to as a beautiful "little" (young) woman (Kindaichi 1914:103), and Pilsudski's observation (1961 [1909]) confirms that a shaman's career starts at an early age.

Although the position of a shaman as such is not hereditary, the disposition to be a shaman is considered to run in the family. Among the east coast Ainu, Pilsudski reports that although not hereditary, shamanistic ability is often "inherited" from the father by his children (Pilsudski 1961 [1909]:183, 185–186). On the other hand, in Hokkaido where shamans are almost exclusively females, shamanistic ability is believed to run through the female line (Kubodera 1960:105). A strong tendency for shamans to come from particular families is also reported by Nagano et al., whose informants include both Sakhalin and Hokkaido Ainu (1966:15).

Spirit possession, and not depossession (compare the distinction in Lewis 1971:29–30), characterizes the Ainu shamanism. The Ainu repeatedly stress the passive role of shamans; it is the spirit helpers who decide to possess a shaman without the prior knowledge of the shaman. Due to the paucity of exegetic explanation, despite my repeated attempts, it is hard to pinpoint the identity of either spirit helpers who possess shamans or other deities involved in shamanism. It seems that a shaman becomes possessed by a spirit or spirits, who "fetch" instructions from bona fide deities of the Ainu pantheon and then convey the message through the shaman to his client and the audience. The entire procedure, however, is not possible without the help of the Grandmother Hearth, who is one of the most important deities of the Ainu and who is at all times the intermediary between man and the other deities.

A spirit helper, called *kosimpuh*, may be a grasshopper, crow, raven, crane, or a duck. There are a host of other spirit helpers that are unidentifiable in terms of actual species of animals. For example, there is a demon bird called *kawawe*, a worm called *ruroyaw*, or "*suruku e kamuy*" who is believed to cause a shaman to eat the poisonous root of aconite (*suruku*). Nonetheless, according to the Ainu, these spirit helpers are not *bona fide* deities. The Ainu refer to them as *kamuy* [deities] out of politeness, just as they do even to demons.[4]

The northwest coast Ainu shamanism therefore is characterized by possession of shamans by spirit helpers who are not *bona fide* deities. Thus, the Ainu does not include fox bewitchment in the category of shamanism. The fox is one of the major deities of the Ainu and its bewitchment is depossession of a person's soul. Thus, shamans do not get possessed by a fox and, in contrast, they may perform a shamanistic rite in order to "cure" a person whose soul is "snatched away" by a fox. This contrasts to the situation with the Ainu on the east coast, among whom shamans do get possessed by a fox. According to Sarashina (1968: 188), major deities often become spirit helpers in Hokkaido Ainu shamanism (he does not specify where he gathered this information).

Spirit helpers may be male or female, or sometimes undifferentiated in terms of sex. There is no necessary connection between the sex of the shaman and that of a spirit helper. A permanent relationship is rarely established between a shaman and a particular spirit who haphazardly possesses the shaman, once or repeatedly, according to its own will.

A shamanistic rite may be performed at any time of the year or the month, but must take place after sunset with the embers from the hearth as the only light. A rite must be performed by the hearth, which the Ainu regard as a miniature universe (compare Chiri and Yamamoto 1944: 44) as well as the residence of the Grandmother Hearth. A rite is usually performed at the request of a client, but sometimes at the decision of a shaman when he himself is not feeling well. Drumming is an essential part of the shamanism of the Sakhalin Ainu regardless of the region; the drum is absent in Hokkaido Ainu shamanism, however. The drum, considered sacred, signals the beginning of the rite, chases away evil spirits which try to interfere with the rite, and also helps the shaman reach the state of trance. The shaman's assistant places the following aromatic plants on the embers in order to produce smoke: a branch or two of Yesso spruce or larch; a plant called *nuhča*; and minced dried

---

[4] Perhaps because of this generous use of the term *kamuy* [deity], some scholars state that the Ainu deify all animals, or even everything in nature (e.g. Sternberg 1906:426).

leek.[5] Throughout the rite the shaman frequently drinks a solution considered too salty for ordinary human consumption. The solution consists of: sea water (or river water during winter), a twig of Yesso spruce, the aforementioned *nuhča*, and dried tangle.[6]

After first asking the Grandmother Hearth and other deities for help in general, the shaman presents the specific case for which the rite is being performed. Amidst the smoke from the plants and the sound of drumming, the shaman reaches a state of at least semitrance. His voice changes (perhaps due to the solution) according to the spirit which has entered him. Various unusual sounds from the shaman's mouth and his vigorous physical movements are an integral part of his performance. The climax of the performance is when his spirit helper talks through him, revealing, for example, the cause of the illness of the client.

Shamans do not use special garments for the performance, and thus their paraphernalia include only the following: a special headdress, a headband to which various charms are attached, a necklace, and two ritual sticks with shavings called *inaw*. Of the two ritual sticks, one is considered male and the other female. Both Chiri and Wada (1943) and Kubodera (1960:104) report a more elaborate assortment of paraphernalia used by shamans on the east coast, which seems to be due to the influence from the Orok and Gilyak shamans, as noted earlier.

The majority of rites are performed for a particular category of illnesses which the Ainu call *araka*. These diseases are differentiated from minor discomforts with localized aches and pains, although serious burns, cuts, etc., are included in the *araka* category. Common causes for *araka* are: the wrath of the deities due to improper behavior by the sick person or other humans; bewitchment by a fox deity; and depossession of the client's soul by a troubled soul, i.e. a soul of a dead human or nonhuman that cannot rest in peace in the world of the dead. The curing method, which the spirit helper instructs through the shaman, often consists of repeated performances of shamanistic rites with specified items of offerings or the performance of a particular rite to the offended deity. There is usually no necessary connection between the sick person and the particular cause of the sickness, i.e the person does not deserve his illness.

Rites may also be performed in order to locate missing persons or objects, or to ask deities what the name of a child should be. Although only legendary shamans have performed them, a shaman is believed to

[5]   Yesso spruce: *sunku* in Ainu; *Picea jezoensis* Carr (Chiri 1953: 236). Larch: *kuy* in Ainu; *Larix dahurica* Turcs (Chiri 1953:237). *Nuhča: Ledum palustre* L. var. *dilatatum* Wahlb (Chiri 1953:53). Leek: *kito* in Ainu; *Allium victorialis* var. *platyphyllum* Makino (Chiri 1953:195).
[6]   Tangle: *ruru kina* in Ainu; *Moschus moschiferus* L. (Chiri 1953:173).

be able to perform miracles such as stabbing his own chest without injuring himself, or flying in air, walking on the sea, and the like.

Occasionally there are evil shamans or sorcerers. Sorcery work is proven when the victim, if male, vomits blood in which an arrow tip and ritual shavings are found; if female, the blood should contain a needle and ritual shavings. Evil spirits are believed to disguise themselves as reddish brown birds with long claws and large eyes like those of cats; according to Chiri (1962:202), they look like a kite, *Milvus migrans lineatus* (Gray). The Ainu repeatedly stress that shamans who do sorcery are not to be blamed; they have no control over evil spirits that decide to possess the shamans once in a while. They also emphasize that sorcerers rarely exist among them, and when they do, there is no kinship tie between a sorcerer and his victim. Evil shamans, especially those who always do evil, are found usually among the Ainu of the east coast and among the Gilyaks and Oroks. The northwest coast Ainu are occasionally victimized elsewhere by these evil shamans, who perform their work without having to travel to the northwest coast.

Because it is up to the spirit helper to decide to possess a shaman, there may be a dramatic combat between a good spirit and an evil one, both of which may try to enter the shaman's body simultaneously. It is said that the shaman's behavior indicates that the battle is going on. Then the audience must help the beneficial spirit; men shout and swing their daggers to chase off the evil spirit while women purify the shaman by swinging over his head a branch of fir or a ritual stick made of willow. If all fails, the shaman will fall to the floor.

INTERPRETATIONS

The shamanism of the Ainu of the northwest coast of southern Sakhalin focuses on the diagnosis and cure of a particular category of diseases which are caused primarily by a deity or by a soul of a being of the Ainu universe. An important point of the Ainu concept of their own shamanism is that shamans are at the mercy of the spirits that enter them. Furthermore, their own shamans, according to the Ainu, rarely engage in sorcery work. Only shamans among the Ainu elsewhere or non-Ainu peoples are noted for their sorcery. Ainu shamanism then is a mechanism to provide explanations to the Ainu about causes of human misery, just as in the case of Zande witchcraft (Evans-Pritchard 1937). It does so by simply ascribing causes of human misery to agents that have no personal connection with the sick individual. Also, shamans are not held responsible for spirit possession or absence of it. Therefore, unlike shamanistic and witchcraft-sorcery practices of other peoples (compare Bohannan 1963:340–355; Gluckman 1968 [1965]: Chapter 4; Mair 1969 [1965]: 218–223), Ainu shamanism neither is antisocial in nature, nor does it serve as a means for social control.

Of all the Ainu magico-religious rituals, shamanism is the only cultural institution in which women are allowed to participate. However, men who are "normal" in the Ainu sense and men with high status in the Ainu society likewise can become shamans. Ainu shamanism therefore cannot be considered as an exclusive means of achieving power for those who, in other social contexts, are debarred from advancement in the society — one of the more commonly designated characteristics of spirit mediums and diviners (Mair 1969 [1965]:216). Lewis made an insightful contribution to the study of shamanism by postulating two types of spirit possession: peripheral possession by evil spirits of women and politically impotent men (1971: Chapter 4); and central possession by ancestor spirits or deities of men of power and authority (1971: Chapters 5, 6). Like the Eskimo religion, which Lewis picks as a case in which the distinction between the two types is blurred (1971:173), Ainu shamanism does not conform to Lewis' typology because among the Ainu the shamanistic power is enjoyed both by the powerful and the powerless in the society, and the same shaman may do both evil and good work.

Eliade's monumental work (1964 [1951]) includes the shamanistic practices of many of the Ainu's neighbors, although perhaps due to lack of literature available in Western languages, it does not include shamanism in any of the Ainu groups. His generalizations and interpretations of symbols involved in shamanistic rites are highly valuable, and some of them are applicable to Ainu shamanism. For example, as in the case of the shamanistic practices which Eliade discusses, Ainu shamanism is characterized by an antidemonic theme and defends life, health, and fertility (1964 [1951]:598–509), as I shall discuss later. However, Ainu shamanism departs from Eliade's generalizations in significant ways.

One of the most important of Eliade's theses is that shamanism represents a particular kind of ecstasy, which is characterized by the shaman's ascent to the center of the universe in the sky and descent to the underworld. Thus, in Eliade's view, solar worship is crucial in shamanism. There are two pieces of evidence in Ainu shamanism which may suggest the theme of ascent to the sky. First the smoke from the embers does "go up to the sky" through the skylight constructed in the roof directly above the hearth. Second, as noted earlier, it is said that a long time ago there was a great shaman at *Rayčiska* who used to ascend to the sky in order to see his wife, Goddess of Sun and Moon, and did so while performing shamanistic rites. Aside from the above information, unlike among those peoples discussed in Eliade's work, there is no such theme as the world tree or the world pillar in the Ainu cosmology. Furthermore, I do not see emphasis on verticality in the spatial arrangement of the Ainu universe, as I have discussed elsewhere in detail (Ohnuki-Tierney 1972:442–445). The Ainu universe consists of several layers, like a cake. Each is composed of a layer of ground, a layer of sky, and the space between. The layers of ground are perceived as thin, and the Ainu do not seem to postulate the presence of a world under the ground. Their world of the dead Ainu, for example, is located on the same plane as the present world, and the world of the mountain deities is located in the interior mountains whose major characterization is the distance from the shore rather than height. Therefore, in Ainu shamanism spirits transcend ordinary spatial-temporal boundaries and can visit the world of the deities or that of the dead Ainu, as the shamans in Eliade's work do (1964 [1951]:510). However, Ainu spirits neither ascend nor descend. Furthermore, the supreme deity of the Ainu pantheon is the bear whose importance overshadows that of the Goddess of Sun and Moon.[7]

Another important departure of Ainu shamanism from Eliade's theses is that, while Eliade assigns a minor role to spirits and stresses that shamans have control over spirits (1964 [1951]:6), spirits are an essential part in Ainu shamanism and, moreover, Ainu shamans are at the mercy of the spirits.

This paper, however, is neither a comparative work on shamanism nor a general thesis on shamanism and related subjects. Therefore, the remainder of the paper will be dedicated to a discussion of Ainu shamanism in comparison with the group rituals of the Ainu, and the interpretations of the Ainu cognitive structure as expressed symbolically in the shamanistic rites.

Atypicality of Shamanism as a Ritual

Shamanistic rites depart in a number of significant ways from the group rituals of the Ainu such as the bear ceremony, the fox ceremony, the ash renewal ceremony for the Grandmother Hearth, and the like.

All group ceremonies of the Ainu ritualize the death and subsequent

---

[7] Munro reports that the Sun God used to receive much more worship among the Niputani Ainu of Hokkaido, who consider the sun a male god and the moon his wife (Munro 1963:13–14). The bear is the supreme deity, however, among these Ainu as well.

rebirth of a deity, whether it is a bear during the bear ceremony or the Grandmother Hearth during the ash renewal ceremony (see Ohnuki-Tierney 1968:281–293). In contrast, shamanism aims at the cure of human illness and the saving of a human from potential death. Group rituals are therefore rites of passage, as defined by van Gennep (1909), for the deities, whereas shamanistic rites are those for humans.

Temporal orientations of shamanism also contrast with those of the group rituals. Shamanistic rites are the only magico-religious rituals of the Ainu which are held at night. The Ainu consider the daytime to be the Ainu portion of the day during which humans engage in their activities, whereas the nighttime belongs to both deities and demons (for detailed discussion of temporal categories, see Ohnuki-Tierney 1969a and n.d.). It seems, then, that for the shamanistic rites the Ainu "intrude," as it were, into that portion of the time which they have allocated to the deities and demons. It may be that the Ainu select the time when the deities and demons are awake because direct communication with these beings is achieved during the rites. Furthermore, group rituals have fixed dates in the sense that each ceremony is performed at approximately the same times of the year and the month. Importantly, they must take place during the first half of the month, during which period the Goddess of Sun and Moon is believed to be cheerful. The Goddess serves as a mediator between the Ainu and other deities. When the moon wanes, it means that the Goddess is crying, and hence one's prayer will not reach her. Shamanistic rites, on the other hand, may be performed at any time of the year or the month.

Spatially too the shamanistic rites are the only rituals of the Ainu which are held inside the house, whereas all other rituals are held at the sacred altar located outside but near the house and toward the sacred direction, i.e. the direction toward the mountains. In the Ainu spatial classification, the shore belongs to humans and the house symbolizes this human part of the universe. In contrast, the mountains and the sea belong to the deities. The high mountains in the interior in particular are believed to be the most sacred part of the Ainu universe, and the altar represents the interior mountains (for detailed analysis of the spatial classification, see Ohnuki-Tierney 1972). It seems then that for the shamanistic rites the Ainu are dragging the deities, so to speak, into their realm of the universe.

The contrast between shamanistic rites and group rituals is also seen in the types of supernatural beings involved in the respective rituals. In group rituals the major deities, such as bears, foxes, Grandmother Hearth, and the Sun-Moon Goddess, are the direct recipients of prayers and nonverbal forms of worship on the part of the Ainu. In contrast, during shamanistic rites, those directly involved are spirit helpers; major deities are involved only indirectly as the ultimate source of power. The spirit helpers are, as discussed earlier, not *bona fide* deities.

Another contrast is that in the group rituals women are strictly forbidden to be directly involved. Thus, not only can women never be officiants in group rituals, they cannot be close to the altar where most of the ceremonies take place. During the bear ceremony, by far the most important rituals of the Ainu, women are required to leave the place of ceremony twice (at the time of the shooting of the bear and sacrificial dogs, and then again at the time of the skinning of these animals) and are thus absent during the significant parts of the ceremony. Ainu women are barred, not only during these ceremonies, but at all times from the sacred realms of the Ainu universe. They can traverse neither the aforementioned altar nor the sacred interior mountains. The religious taboo against women comes from the Ainu belief that the smell of menstrual and parturient blood is offensive to the deities and that it does not disappear even after washing; thus women are barred from direct contact with the deities at all times. In contrast, women can even be officiants in shamanistic rites, as long as they are not menstruating at the time. In this respect, shamanism constitutes the sole exception in all religious matters of the Ainu. Thus when a ritual is initiated by the group, directed toward the group, and when the supernatural impact is on the entire group, women are not allowed to officiate, and often even to participate. However, in an individual rite of shamanism, a woman can even officiate, but as an individual. This situation is basically different from such role reversal rituals as those reported by Rigby (1968) which are group rituals in which women figure as men; these rites deal with general welfare of the group.

A distinction between group rituals and shamanistic rites lies in the nature of the communication which takes place during the respective rituals. In the case of group rituals, communication between the deities and the Ainu is only one-way; the Ainu convey their respect and ask for general welfare, such as an abundance of food, from the deities concerned. Offerings are made, but they represent only a long-range prestation; the deities are asked to repay, but only at some unspecified time in the future.

In contrast, during shamanistic rites, communication is two-way and at a close range. A shaman asks an immediate response from the spirits, whether it is information about the cause and cure of an illness or the location of a missing object. Thus offerings demand immediate repayment in the form of specific help from spirit helpers, or ultimately, from the deities. Furthermore, spirit possession represents an intense and intimate contact between a shaman, i.e. a human, and spirit helpers and deities. Even evil spirits are often involved. Thus drumming is believed to aim at, for one thing, the exorcism of evil spirits which often try to intervene in the work of beneficial spirits. Or, as noted earlier, a rite may become a dramatic scene of combat between an evil spirit and a good one, who compete with one another in trying to possess the shaman.

World View and Symbols in the Ainu Shamanism

The above discussion illustrates the uniqueness of shamanism as an Ainu ritual. Yet, paradoxical as it may seem, I see in the shamanism a significant portion of Ainu cognitive structure expressed through various symbols. The symbols may be classified into two groups: those representing the cooking process and the affirmation of life; and those representing the concept of marginality. I shall discuss them in turn.

SYMBOLS OF COOKING AND LIFE   Most abundant in shamanistic rites are symbols of the cooking process. Most importantly, shamanistic rites are held beside the hearth, where the Ainu do all of their cooking. Moreover, the sea water, tangle, and spruce branches in the shaman's drink are all essential ingredients in Ainu cooking. Both tangle and spruce branches are thought to give a good flavor to the cooked food. The Ainu, who do not extract salt, use sea water in all their cooking. When they used to move to their winter settlements further inland at the onset of the cold season,[8] they used river water and dried tangle; there is enough salt on dried tangle. The three plants placed on embers are also closely related to Ainu cooking. Leek is another staple in Ainu cooking, besides the aforementioned spruce; the Ainu spend much time in collecting leek, much of which is dried for winter use. Although not an ingredient in cooking, the plant called *nuhča* is the most commonly used plant for brewing tea (there are two other kinds of plant which the Ainu use for tea when *nuhča* is not available). The embers themselves symbolize the completion of cooking

---

[8]   The custom of using a winter settlement and winter semi-subterranean houses was discontinued due to the introduction of the Russian-style log cabin, which enabled the Ainu to stay in their summer settlements on the shore even during midwinter. For example, on the northwest coast, the winter when my informant, Husko, was born around 1900 was the last winter which her family of orientation spent in the winter settlement. At Naibuchi on the east coast, the Russian-style log cabin replaced both the summer and winter houses around 1901 (Sentoku 1929:20). The change is also noted by Pilsudski (1912:56) and Yamamoto (1943:32).

because wood was the only fuel used by the Ainu until the introduction of coal by the Russians and Japanese. Smoke in this context is also a symbol of cooking.

Cooking has a special meaning for the Ainu who, unlike the neighboring Oroks and Japanese, abhor raw food, especially raw meat. The use of uncooked food is limited to some ritual consumption of blood and brain of the bear during the bear ceremony[9] and to occasional raw fish in brine with leek (the latter, I suspect, is perhaps the result of Japanese influence). The Ainu cook food, and they cook it for a long time.

For the Ainu, then, cooking is the only means to sustain life. Cooked food signifies life, whereas raw nature means death. Seen in this light, these are symbols whose message is not merely the cooking process, but more directly life itself. Spruce is the favorite tree of the Ainu and is often paired with fir.[10] While the latter is used for coffins and other objects relating to human death, spruce is used for ritual sticks and other matters relating to the Ainu deities who are the providers of food and the protectors of the Ainu life. Smoke, too, symbolizes life. When the Ainu travel and find a house, they first determine whether there is smoke coming out of the skylight; human presence, i.e. human life, is ensured by the smoke. This theme appears repeatedly in their folktales (see Ohnuki-Tierney 1969b:34, 132, 133, 153). The plant *nuhča* and leek serve not only as tea and herb for the Ainu, but also as medicine, a means to preserve and restore life. *Nuhča* is used for several kinds of illness including rheumatism, common cold, and stomach ache. The symbolism of leek as a medicine is even more clear; it is used not only against rheumatism but is considered especially powerful when used either after childbirth or for diseases of the sexual organs, i.e. the source of life.[11]

The participation of women in shamanistic rites also symbolizes the process of cooking and the affirmation of human life. In the Ainu culture, cooking is a woman's job. Although the Ainu do not precisely relate menstruation with the reproductive process, they do emphasize the role of woman in reproduction and pay little attention to the male role in it. In this small hunting and gathering society, the survival of a community

---

[9] Even this practice is observed only by the courageous, and thus many do not participate. The bear's tongue, heart, and also often the brain, are cooked and consumed by males. To eat these parts of the bear is taboo for women. Sarashina reports more extensive use of raw food among the Hokkaido Ainu (1968:209–210; no location of the investigation is specified).

[10] Fir: *yayuh* in Ainu, *Abies sachalinensis* Fr. Schm (Chiri 1953:233).

[11] Needless to say, the Ainu categories of diseases differ significantly from the Western classification. Such labels as rheumatism in this passage represent the approximate equivalent.

often depends upon mutual aid and the surest and only guarantee of care in one's old age is through one's children. The Ainu often consider population growth as a sign of prosperity. Elsewhere in Ainu culture, there are abundant indications of the Ainu emphasis on having offspring. For example, twins are greatly valued and are believed to be a special gift from the deities. One of the advantages of polygyny, according to the Ainu, is that a man is guaranteed to have more children than if he had only one wife. If a man is unable to have offspring even with several women, then it is culturally sanctioned that he ask his brother or friend to produce children with his wife (only in this sense is the male role in reproduction recognized). Female participation in shamanism, then, is an affirmation of human reproduction.

The Ainu emphasis on cooking has another dimension. Their preference for cooked food is so strong that, in hating the Oroks, the Ainu choose to point out the "disdainful custom" of their eating raw meat as their reason. On the other hand, the Ainu do not entertain such strong hatred toward the Gilyaks, whose customs, according to the Ainu, are similar to theirs. This phenomenon is of special interest when viewed with the knowledge that both the Oroks and Gilyaks have cruelly exploited the Ainu through what is known as the Santan trade, which involved the Chinese on the northwestern end and Japanese at the southern end, as well as all the "natives" of the Amur and on Sakhalin (Harrison 1954; Hora 1956:59–78; Ohnuki-Tierney i.p.b: Chapter 1; Stephan 1971:24–25; Takakura 1939).

For the Ainu, therefore, cooking means not only the process for producing edible food which sustains human life, but also represents the Ainu way of life as opposed to the way of other peoples (such as Oroks and Japanese). It then gives the Ainu the basis for considering that the Ainu are the only humans in the Ainu universe (see Ohnuki-Tierney 1972:427). Cooking therefore symbolizes the affirmation of Ainu culture, and it is the only culture as far as the Ainu are concerned.

Seen in this light, Ainu cooking represents, on a practical level, the process whereby the raw is turned into the cooked, i.e. human food; and on a metaphysical level, the transformation of nature into culture. The Ainu culture provides an example to support the basic thesis of Lévi-Strauss (1969 [1964]). Following his thesis a little further, Grandmother Hearth, who plays a prominent role in shamanism, may be seen as a symbol of adult women who are in the state of being "cooked." Adult women have gone or are going through the entire process of menstruation, pregnancy, and childbirth. Hence, like cooked food, they signify a complete transformation of nature into culture; they are no longer "raw" like prenuptial girls. An adult woman in Ainu culture therefore is a cook who sustains human life; she is the source of human life by virtue of bearing children, and she is also representative of the state of being cooked.

The drumming of the shaman then best symbolizes the transformation from nature to culture. The drum creates music, which is a patterned regularity. It represents the epitome of man's culture. Shamanistic rites, however, are not merely a singular expression of cooking, life force, and culture. There is another set of symbols, to which I shall now turn.

SYMBOLS OF MARGINALITY There is a host of symbols which represent the concept of "marginal." I use the term "marginal" to designate all that does not fit into the categories of an existing system, or in this case, the Ainu cognitive structure. The "marginal" includes then several kinds of anomaly: those which have properties of more than one category and are hence ambiguous; those which lack identity, including the "formless," literally or symbolically; and those which are out of place, like a pear among apples.[12]

As mentioned previously, the Ainu perform their shamanistic rites in the evening. The Ainu divide the nighttime into the first part of the dark, i.e. between sunset and midnight and the second part, i.e. between midnight and the sunrise. The first part, during which most of the rites are performed, is allocated to demons and the second to deities (for a detailed discussion of the Ainu temporal classification, see Ohnuki-Tierney 1969a, n.d.). Because the most pronounced characteristic of Ainu demons is formlessness, lack of identity, mixing of categories, and the like, I interpret that demons represent a marginal category among the beings of the Ainu universe, which consists of deities, demons, and humans (Ohnuki-Tierney 1972: 450). The portion of the night during which shamanistic rites are performed may thus be interpreted as a temporal symbol of marginality.

Furthermore, during a rite a shaman and his spirit helper transcend ordinary categories of time and space. Thus the shaman or his spirit

---

[12] Douglas' concept of "dirt" is roughly synonymous with my concept of "the marginal"; she defines "dirt" as "a residual category, rejected from our normal scheme of classifications" (1966:36). In her category of "dirt" she does not include formlessness and total lack of identity (1966:160–161). I do not disagree with her statement that there is little meaning to differentiate between the terms anomaly and ambiguity in their practical application (1966:37). I prefer, however, to use the term "anomaly" as an inclusive term for the cognitive category of marginality, and thus make it synonymous with "marginality," and use "ambiguous" as a term describing affective reaction to that which is anomalous.

helper (the distinction is often not clear) can see what has happened at the beginning of the universe or what will take place at the end. Or, he can freely travel to the world of the dead Ainu, or to the world of the deities, to fetch instructions from the deities. Conversely, the shaman's drumming is believed to summon the souls of his ancestors in order to help him.

The transcendence of spatio-temporal boundaries, which represents one type of marginality, is most succinctly symbolized by the white smoke rising at the center of the house. In other cultural activities of the Ainu, white mist or smoke often symbolizes boundaries of domains in the Ainu universe, as each domain is specifically allocated either to deities or to humans. Thus, if a man attempts to climb up an interior mountain without first performing a proper purification ritual, white mist is believed to descend and thereby prevent him from climbing. Some humans are said to have visited a country of mountain deities, and reported to have gone through a thick white fog as they went in and out of the country. When they returned to the world of humans, these visitors were required to be first purified by the white smoke of a shamanistic rite (for further discussion of spatial boundaries, see Ohnuki-Tierney 1972:451–452). In shamanism then the smoke may indicate that the spatial boundary has been moved right into the center of the house, thereby neutralizing, as it were, rules of spatial classification.

Spirit helpers themselves have an ambiguous status; they are neither *bona fide* deities, nor are they ordinary beings of the universe because they have the power to perform, through shamans, extraordinary acts. The particular kind of beings which the Ainu select as spirit helpers most clearly symbolizes their marginality. Grasshoppers are insects and yet have the peculiar behavior of hopping; ducks are birds and yet they swim like fish. Grasshoppers and ducks thus possess behavioral characteristics that do not conform to their kind, i.e. insect and bird, respectively. Crows, ravens, and cranes are all characterized by eating habits that are unusual for birds. Crows and ravens are scavengers for carrion, while cranes on occasion eat frogs and snakes — the two species of animals most abhorred by the Ainu. The particular kind of worm which is believed to become a spirit helper is thought to break into pieces when someone steps on it. It is, in other words, formless. Moreover, the name of the worm, "Dragon of the Sea," further suggests its marginal nature because the dragon typifies a creature having the properties of land, water, and air animals. Last, the demon bird is characterized by a lack of visual identity; the Ainu assign no visual forms to the birds and identify them only by their cries. Their cries are also believed to cause insanity which is an abnormal state of mind. Therefore, all of the spirit helpers represent some kind of marginality.

The water in the shaman's drink is another symbol of marginality because water is formless. Also, because the water is either sea water, or water which is salty from the salt on tangle, it more specifically symbolizes the sea, a vast body of formless water. Although Ainu demons and live spirits do not seem to have a particular location as residence in the universe, the Ainu funeral for the drowned indicates that the Ainu relate the sea with evil spirits. Thus, a funeral rite for a drowned person involves an exorcism rite, which is far more extensive than those in funerals for people who were killed in the mountains or die at home. These are indications that water in the shaman's drink symbolizes formlessness and evil spirits, both standing for marginality.[13]

I discussed in the previous section the idea that women in shamanism symbolize cooking, life, and culture. Female participation, however, may also be interpreted as a ritual sanction of menstrual and parturient blood, which is referred to collectively in Ainu as the "old blood" (as opposed to the "new blood," i.e. ordinary blood in the body). This type of blood is no longer in the body, thus out of place, and furthermore, it has come out of orifices of the body which are themselves marginal body parts (Leach 1964:38; Douglas 1966:121). The potent smell and dark color of the "old blood," often pointed out by the Ainu, may be the affective counterpart of the conceptual marginality which the old blood occupies in the Ainu mind. Likewise, Grandmother Hearth may more specifically symbolize postmenopausal women, who are women and yet not "real women" with the old blood; they belong neither to men nor to women.

In the above I have simply indicated that these symbols stand for conceptual marginality. Further analysis of conceptual marginality and its meaning in shamanism will be attempted in the following section.

SUMMARY AND SPECULATIONS

I will now relate the atypicality of shamanistic rites as rituals, symbols of cooking and life, and symbols of marginality, to one another and attempt to interpret the total complex of shamanism as it relates to the Ainu cognitive structure.

The symbols of cooking and women can now be viewed as expressions of the basic binary oppositions of:

[13]   By not including formlessness in her category of anomaly, Douglas sees creative force in water and totally disintegrated dirt (1966:161). Eliade also interprets formless water as a symbol of the power to purify and regenerate (1958:194).

1. raw . . . .   cooked
2. human death . . . .   human life
3. non-Ainu peoples . . . .   Ainu
4. deities . . . .   humans (=Ainu)
5. human males . . . .   human females
6. sterility . . . .   reproduction
7. new blood . . . .   old blood
8. young girls . . . .   adult women
9. NATURE . . . .   CULTURE

For the Ainu who eat only cooked food, raw material is not even food
(1). While food sustains human lives, lack of food or raw nature means
death to the Ainu (2). They also associate the raw with the non-Ainu
ways of life of "savages" (Oroks and Japanese), in contrast to their own
civilized ways (3). In the traditional Ainu world view, however, the
universe is exclusively occupied by the Ainu and their deities, whose
peaceful coexistence is occasionally threatened by demons (I shall further
discuss demons shortly). Because the Ainu deities are in the main deified
animals, they are equated with the raw and nature (4). Within the human
domain alone, males are conceptually closer to the deities with whom
human males alone can directly deal (5). They are, nevertheless, sterile
without women because the Ainu place little emphasis on the male
reproductive role (6). Females, on the other hand, hold the key to the
Ainu way of life through their cooking ability, and by continuing the
human population (5, 6). It follows then that the "new blood" (ordinary
blood in the body), as important as it may be for the human life, is like
raw nature, while the old blood (menstrual and parturient blood) has the
power to create and maintain the Ainu way of life. When females
alone are being considered, adult women represent "the cooked" —
having gone through all the processes of the Ainu way of life. In contrast,
prenuptial girls are raw material or nature, which is yet to be cooked
(8). The contrast sets (1) to (8) are to be ultimately subsumed under
the most basic opposition of nature versus culture. Culture represents
the Ainu way of life because it is the only culture as far as the Ainu
are concerned. Nature represents anything else, all the nonhuman beings
of the Ainu universe as well as other peoples (when they are recognized).

The dyad presented above represents a classificatory principle, and
does not signify the possession of a specific property or properties (Needham 1960:26). Neither does it represent a dualism of mutually antagonistic forces (Freedman 1968:7). Therefore, it is the particular domain
or context which defines the dualism. Thus, when the domain is the population of the Ainu universe, the humans, both male and female, are con-

trasted with the deities (4). However, when the domain is human alone, then the males, who are included in number (4) and are classified on the right with culture, are associated with nature (5). By the same token, the females, young and adult, are in the right hand column with culture, when contrasted with the males (5); young girls, however, in contrast to adult women, belong to nature (8). Therefore, the dyad represents a set of complementary oppositions, and it does not characterize any property in the dyad in absolute terms.

In addition to the nature/culture dyad, however, we saw a set of symbols which represent marginality. There are several ways to interpret the signification of marginal symbols discussed above. First, because conceptual marginality has the power to threaten an otherwise neatly classified universe, the marginal symbols may be interpreted as constituting a threat to the dyad discussed above. Should we see existentialism in this, as perhaps Douglas would (1966:170), and interpret that the Ainu choose to defy the confinement of their own classificatory structure? Although interesting, this hypothesis is not convincing in the Ainu case.

Another possibility of interpretation is that the marginal symbols represent a threat to human life because a threat of destruction of the Ainu cognitive structure is a metaphysical expression of a threat to human life. Then these symbols would be involved in shamanism in order to dramatize the threat to human life, i.e. illness, relief of which is the most important function of shamanistic rites. We could say further that this is why we see several symbols of demons in shamanism; demons are marginal creatures, as noted earlier, and they are the major cause of human deaths. Sacred stories and folktales abundantly attest to the Ainu fear of demons (Ohnuki-Tierney 1969b: Tales 1–4, 8–12). As noted earlier, however, Ainu shamanism is certainly antidemonic. It demonstrates positivism toward life, health, and the Ainu way of life.

I suggest, then, that the marginal symbols represent mediation — agents that mediate between the binary oppositions in the dyad. In other words, the marginal symbols represent a means of communication between man and the deities.

Before I discuss the more obvious symvols of marginality which stand for mediation, let me first clarify why symbols of demons appear in shamanism and yet do not represent death and destruction. Demons do kill humans — that is their business as far as the Ainu are concerned. However, sacred stories and folktales abound with the theme of human beings killing demons. They do so with the aid of deities. Thus, the aforementioned culture hero[14] receives instructions from his guardian deity to

---

[14]   I might also point out here that the culture hero is another symbol of marginality.

anticipate and attack the demons, and thereby save his people, i.e. the Ainu. Somehow Ainu deities never personally kill demons. It follows then that demons are an important instrument by which the deities convey to the Ainu their favorable inclinations toward them. The Ainu demons, on one hand, stand for death and destruction and, on the other, for agents of communication between man and deities. While the former role of the demons is an exegetic and conscious role, the latter remains unconscious in the Ainu mind. This may explain why we see symbols of demons, such as nighttime and demon birds, in shamanism and yet shamanism is not "demonic" as the English term connotes.

Shamanism abounds with more obvious symbols of communication. Grandmother Hearth, as noted earlier, is the mediator between man and deities at all times. Female participation in shamanism also stands for mediation. In folktales it is an Ainu woman who marries a deity, who in return often provides for her parents in old age, or favors humans in general (e.g. Tales 13 and 19 in Ohnuki-Tierney 1969b). Not only young women but old women become mediators. For example, it has to be an old woman who is officially in charge of a bear cub which is being raised for a bear ceremony. The old blood of women does not seem to symbolize communication, but it, too, has a positive side; the Ainu apply it on a victum of smallpox, which the Ainu believe is caused by demons. The potency of the blood is believed to cure this most dreaded disease of the Ainu.

Another important symbol of communication is birds. Among spirit helpers, there are cranes, crows, ravens, ducks, and demon birds. Birds are by far the most common spirit helpers. Their role as messengers is poetically expressed in a phrase *čikaporo pehka inu: an kohki* [to hear from the birds], which is equivalent to the English phrase "to hear via the grapevine." This phrase is not only presently used but appears frequently in old tales (Ohnuki-Tierney 1969b: Tale 9, 146; Kindaichi 1914:41; Chiri 1962:220, also notes its presence in an old tale from Shiraura on the east coast). In one tale (Ohnuki-Tierney 1969b) a pair of birds, one golden and the other silver in color, appear more specifically as communication agents between man and the deities. In this story, these birds keep a constant eye on the world of the humans in order to report any unusual happenings to the guardian deity of the culture hero. Although not found among the northwest coast Ainu, but among some Ainu both in Sakhalin and Hokkaido, ritual sticks with shavings called

---

He is an orphan, i.e. he does not have kinship identity. Furthermore, he is referred to as *enko kamuy* [half deity], i.e. he is neither man nor deity.

inaw are considered to represent birds. Because the Ainu offer *inaw* to the deities in order to convey their respect to the deities, this information is consistent with the role of birds as communication agents.

Ducks, which become spirit helpers, are particularly said to be messengers to certain bears which cover their bodies with clay. A duck is believed to look for hunters in the mountains and then report to its master, the bear, who later attacks the hunters (Ohnuki-Tierney 1969b: Tale 21). Likewise, a crow is depicted as a messenger of good tidings to an Ainu woman (Ohnuki-Tierney 1969b: Tale 6). A crow is also one of the two birds which revived the culture hero who lost consciousness after his combat with a crane demon (Tale 4); the crane is another bird which becomes a spirit helper. In addition to the association with demons, the demon birds are believed to cause insanity. The Ainu concept of insanity again involves both demons or evil spirits and deities. Thus, the cure for insanity involves both an exorcism rite and shamanistic rites. Furthermore, the Ainu believe that after death some insane people go to the deities for protection.

The symbolism of communication via grasshoppers may be inferred indirectly. The insect is referred to as *pahtaki ahči* [grandmother grasshopper]. The term *ahči* [grandmother] is the same as in *Unči Ahči* — [hearth grandmother], i.e. Grandmother Hearth. *Ahči* means "aged women" in Ainu. Symbols such as water, a worm called "the dragon of the sea," and smoke all serve to mediate between different spatial categories. Water in the rivers links sea and land. The Ainu belief that drowned people ascend in the sky, rather than go to the world of the dead Ainu, may also suggest some linkage between the sea and the sky. The dragon worm symbolizes the linkage of all spatial categories, land, sea, and sky, as the dragon represents creatures in all of these areas. As discussed earlier, smoke symbolizes the boundaries of spatial categories in the Ainu universe when two categories are adjacent, e.g. when humans approach the sacred realm of the universe. The drum, too, serves as an agent for communication because the sound of the drum summons the spirit helpers and expels the evil spirits.

What we see are marginal symbols serving as important agents for communication among different beings of the Ainu universe — deities, demons, human ancestors, and the Ainu. The positive nature of these symbols serving as agents for communication comes from the fact that they are marginal. They are marginal and, therefore, instead of being confined to the limits of one category in the structure, they can traverse different spatial realms and mediate among the different beings of the universe.

This interpretation of marginal symbols then is diametrically opposed to the interpretations of marginal or anomalous symbols by most scholars. Many scholars of symbolic classification have stressed the potent, but negative quality of the power of the marginal, perhaps partly because anthropologists have been concerned with the taboo (Douglas 1966, 1968; Leach 1967 [1958], 1964; Smith 1972 [1889]; Steiner 1967 [1956]). The Ainu case, however, suggests that the marginal can generate a positive power without generating negative qualities such as "dirty," "polluting," etc. This does not mean that these marginal symbols of the Ainu do not generate negative power; they do stand for the negative or destructive power, but not in shamanism.

Shamanism is one of the major means for the Ainu to communicate with the deities and, most importantly, it is accomplished through inter-mediaries, i.e. the spirit helpers. This basic nature of shamanism then is expressed by these marginal symbols.

The above discussion of marginal symbols requires another look at the dyad. The marginal category is too stable to be considered as a residual or temporary category. The question of whether the basic cognitive structure of the Ainu should be regarded as a dyad or a triad, however, seems a matter of semantic preference.

The foregoing analysis of Ainu symbols repeatedly illustrates the multivocality of these symbols. At first glance the situation appears confusing. However, the multivocality of each symbol is precisely the mechanism whereby the highly complex Ainu cognitive structure is so vividly expressed in the rites (compare Beidelman 1964:373–374). Any particular symbol does not stand for a particular idea at all times. It indicates one idea in a particular context and in relation to what it is being contrasted with; in another context it denotes another meaning. In each context a particular symbol is univocal (compare Turner 1969: 1–43).

In interpreting Ainu practices and symbols in the foregoing discussion, I have made little use of exegetic explanations. Instead, my interpretations were in the main based on the operational and positional meanings (for a useful distinction of these three types of symbolic meanings, see Turner 1967: 50–52). Unlike the Ndembu (Turner 1969:15), the Ainu take most of their own practices as age-old customs without offering further ex-planation. Furthermore, in the interpretation of a cognitive structure, which usually lies in the unconscious of a member of the society (Hallo-well 1964:50; Lévi-Strauss 1963:18, 21, 281–282), exegetic explanations are often inappropriate. I do not think that native explanations and conscious models are necessarily inaccurate (Lévi-Strauss 1963:281;

1969 [1964]:295), but they often represent secondary explanations (Boas 1964 [1911]:19–21) and must be closely examined as to their applicability in a particular type of analysis.

This discussion of conscious/unconscious models *vis-à-vis* exegetic/operational-positional meanings of symbols leads to another intriguing facet in the Ainu world view. The Ainu conception of their deities *vis-à-vis* humans stresses that deities are more powerful than humans. The Ainu are extremely humble in their attitude toward their deities. They do not in their consciousness assert themselves over and above their deities who, according to the Ainu, govern Ainu life by rewarding with food and punishing with famine. This conscious exposition then is dramatically contradicted in shamanism, but the thesis remains unconscious. In shamanism the Ainu violate the most sacred rules, such as the performance of religious rites during the first half of the month or the taboo regulation against female participation. The latter is especially daring, when the old blood, symbolized by women, means increase of human population, which in turn means more deaths of deified land mammals. Likewise, we see in shamanism the positive role of demons as mediators between man and deities, which is not revealed in any of the group rituals.

One of the most important distinctions between the individual rite of shamanism and group rituals, therefore, is that the former brings to light the unconscious and deeper structure of the Ainu cognitive world. Thus, the study of shamanism reveals an important dimension of the Ainu world view.

REFERENCES

BARNOUW, VICTOR
  1963   *Culture and personality*. Homewood: Dorsey Press.
BEIDELMAN, T. O.
  1964   Pig (*guluwe*): an essay on Ngulu sexual symbolism and ceremony. *Southwestern Journal of Anthropology* 20:359-391.
BOAS, FRANZ
  1964 [1911]   "Linguistics and ethnology," in *Language in culture and society*. Edited by Dell Hymes, 15–22. New York: Harper and Row.
BOHANNAN, PAUL
  1963   *Social anthropology*. New York: Holt, Rinehart and Winston.
CHIRI, MASHIO
  1952   Jushi to kawauso [Magician and otter]. *Hoppo Bunka Kenkyu Hokoku* 7:47–80.

1953, 1954, 1962   *Bunrui Ainugo jiten* [Classified dictionaries of the Ainu language], three volumes: [Plants, Humans, Animals]. Tokyo: Nihon Jomin Bunka Kenkyujo.

1960   *Kamui yukaru*. [Sacred epics of the Ainu]. Sapporo: Aporo Shoten.

CHIRI, M., B. WADA

1943   Karafuto Aingu-go ni okeru jintai kankei meii [Body terms in Sakhalin Ainu]. *Karafuto Hakubutsukan Hokoku* 5(1). (The entry number 26 on *tusu* [shamanism] is quoted in its entirety in Yamamoto 1949).

CHIRI, M., T. YAMAMOTO

1944   Karafuto Ainu no setsuwa [Folk tales of the Sakhalin Ainu]. *Karafuto Hakubutsukan Iho* 3(1).

DOUGLAS, MARY

1966   *Purity and danger*. London: Routledge and Kegan Paul.

1968   "Pollution," in *International encyclopedia of the social sciences*, 336–342. New York: Crowell, Collier, and Macmillan.

ELIADE, MIRCEA

1964 [1951]   *Shamanism*. Princeton: Princeton University Press.

1958   *Patterns in comparative religion*. New York: World.

EVANS-PRITCHARD, E. E.

1937   *Witchcraft, oracles, and magic among the Azande*. Oxford: Oxford University Press.

FREEDMAN, MAURICE

1968   "Geomancy," in *Proceedings of the Royal Anthropological Institute of Great Britain and Ireland*, 5–15.

GLUCKMAN, MAX

1968 [1965]   *Politics, law, and ritual in tribal society*. New York: New American Library.

HALLOWELL, A. IRVING

1964   "Ojibwa ontology, behavior and world view," in *Primitive views of the world*. Edited by S. Diamond, 49–82. New York: Columbia University Press.

HANIHARA, K., H. FUJIMOTO, T. ASAI, M. YOSHIZAKI, M. KONO, Y. NYUI

1972   *Shinpojumu Ainu* [Symposium on the Ainu]. Sapporo: Hokkaido University Press.

HARRISON, JOHN A.

1954   The Saghlien trade: a contribution to Ainu studies. *Southwestern Journal of Anthropology* 10:278–293.

HATTORI, SHIRO

1964   *Ainugo hogen jiten* [Ainu dialect dictionary]. Tokyo: Iwanami Shoten.

HORA, TOMIO

1956   *Karafutoshi kenkyu* [Research on the history of Sakhalin island]. Tokyo: Shinjusha.

KINDAICHI, KYOSUKE

1914   *Kita ezo koyo ihen* [An old epic of the northern (Sakhalin) Ainu]. Tokyo: Kyodo Kenkyusha.

1925   *Ainu no kenkyu* [Study of the Ainu]. Tokyo: Naigai Shobo.

1961   *Ainu bunkashi* [Culture history of the Ainu]. Tokyo: Sanseido.

KUBODERA, ITSUHIKO

1960   Karafuto Ainu no shamanisumu [Sakhalin Ainu shamanism]. *Nihon*

Jinruigakukai Nihon Minzokugaku Kyokai Rengo Taikai Dai-Jugokai Kiji, 103–106.

LEACH, EDMUND

1967 [1958] "Magical hair," in *Myth and cosmos*. Edited by J. Middleton, 77–108. New York: Natural History Press.

1964 "Anthropological aspects of language: animal categories and verbal abuse," in *New directions in the study of language*. Edited by E. Lenneberg, 23–63. Cambridge: M.I.T. Press.

LÉVI-STRAUSS, C.

1963 *Structural anthropology*. New York: Basic Books.

1969 [1964] *The raw and the cooked*. New York: Harper and Row.

LEWIS, I. M.

1971 *Ecstatic religion*. Harmondsworth: Penguin Books.

MAIR, L.

1969 [1965] *An introduction to social anthropology*. Oxford: Oxford University Press.

MUNRO, NEIL

1963 *Ainu creed and cult*. New York: Columbia University Press.

NAGANO, T., M. ISHIBASHI, S. NAKAGAWA

1966 Hoppo minzoku — Hokkaido Ainu, Karafuto Ainu, Giriyaku, Orokko no shamanizumu ni kansuru hikakuteki kenkyu [Comparative study of the shamanism of the Hokkaido Ainu, Sakhalin Ainu, Gilyak, and Orok]. *Nihon Jinruigakukai Nihon Minzokugaku Kyokai Rengo Taikai Dai-Nijukai Kiji*, 14–17.

NEEDHAM, RODNEY

1960 The left hand of the Mugwe: an analytical note on the structure of Meru symbolism. *Africa* 30:20–33.

OHNUKI-TIERNEY, EMIKO

1968 "A northwest coast Sakhalin Ainu world view." Unpublished doctoral dissertation, University of Wisconsin.

1969a Concepts of time among the Ainu of the northwest coast of Sakhalin. *American Anthropologist* 71:488–492.

1969b *Sakhalin Ainu folklore*. Anthropological Studies 2. Washington, D.C.: American Anthropological Association.

1972 Spatial concepts of the Ainu of the northwest coast of southern Sakhalin. *American Anthropologist* 74:426–455.

i.p.a The shamanism of the Ainu of the northwest coast of southern Sakhalin. *Ethnology*.

i.p.b *The Sakhalin Ainu*. New York: Holt, Rinehart and Winston.

n.d. "Sakhalin Ainu time reckoning."

PILSUDSKI, B.

1961 [1909] Der Schamanismus bei den Ainu-Stämmen von Sachalin. *Globus* 15:261–274, 16:117–132. (Translated by K. Wada and in 1961 published in *Hoppo Bunka Kenkyu Hokoku* 16:179–203.)

1912 *Materials for the study of the Ainu language and folklore*. Cracow: Spolka Wydawnicza Polska.

RIGBY, PETER

1968 "Some Gogo rituals of 'purification': an essay on social and moral categories," in *Dialectic in practical religion*. Edited by E. Leach, 153–178. Cambridge: Cambridge University Press.

SARASHINA, GENZO
1968   *Ainu no shiki* [Four seasons of the Ainu]. Tokyo: Kodansha.

SEGAWA, KIYOKO
1972   *Ainu no konin* [Marriages of the Ainu]. Tokyo: Miraisha.

SENTOKU, TAROJI
1929   *Karafuto Ainu sowa* [The Sakhalin Ainu]. Tokyo: Shikodo.

SMITH, W. ROBERTSON
1972 [1889]   *The religion of the Semites*. New York: Schocken Books.

STEINER, FRANZ
1967 [1956]   *Taboo*. Harmondsworth: Penguin Books.

STEPHAN, J. J.
1971   *Sakhalin: a history*. Oxford: Clarendon Press.

STERNBERG, L.
1906   "The inau cult of the Ainu," in *Boas anniversary volume, anthropological papers*, 425–437. New York: Stechert.

TAKAKURA, SHINICHIRO
1939   Kinsei no okeru Karafuto o chusin to shita Nichi-Man koeki [Trade in the recent past via Sakhalin between Japan and Manchuria]. *Hoppo Bunka Kenkyu Hokoku* 1:163–194.

TURNER, VICTOR
1967   *The forest of symbols*. Ithaca: Cornell University Press.
1969   *The ritual process*. Chicago: Aldine.

VAN GENNEP, ARNOLD
1909   *The rites of passage*. Chicago: University of Chicago Press (Phoenix edition, 1961).

WADA, KAN
1962   Shaman no kyoi kodo [Psychological study of shaman's spirit possession]. *Hoppo Bunka Kenkyu Hokoku* 17:147–163.
1965   Imu ni kansuru jakkan no mondai [Some problems of "imu"]. *Minzokugaku Kenkyu* 29:263–271.

YAMAMOTO, TOSHIO
1943   *Karafuto Ainu no jukyo* [Sakhalin Ainu dwellings]. Tokyo: Aizawa Shobo.
1949   Hokudo no kagura — Minami Karafuto ni okeru Giriyaku Orokko no shaman [Shamanism of the north — Gilyak and Orok shamans in southern Sakhalin]. *Minzokugaku Kenkyu* 14:36–50. (Reprinted 1968, in T. Yamamoto, *Hoppo shizen minzoku minwa shusei* [Folk tales of the northern peoples], 230–286. Tokyo: Sagami Shobo.)

Rituals of Reversal as a Means of Rewiring Social Structure

The frequent occurrence in human societies of rituals of reversal or inversion, in which sexual identity or other behavior patterns are reversed or inverted (e.g. men impersonate animals; ritual actors change their identity by means of masks or special costumes) has long been a topic of inquiry and commentary by anthropologists. What are the symbolic meanings of these rites of reversal? Why have they so universally emerged as key features of ritual systems, and why do they persist?

Field data from the contemporary culture of the Highland Maya community of Zinacantan in southeastern Mexico support the hypothesis that the rituals of reversal that occur at the end of each year serve not only to express the society's concept of calendar time, but to "rewire" the crucial connections in the social structure by providing symbolic statements of traditional social imperatives and basic categories of the Zinacanteco world view.[1]

My field research in Chiapas, Mexico was undertaken in connection with the Harvard Chiapas Project which has been funded by the National Institute of Mental Health (MH–02100) and the National Science Foundation (GS–262, GS–976, GS–1524). The Project was sponsored by the Center for Behavioral Science and the Peabody Museum of American Archaeology and Ethnology at Harvard University and by the Instituto Nacional Indigenista in Mexico. I am grateful to all my younger colleagues and students in Mexico and in the United States who have done field work in Chiapas and have made a significant contribution to my understanding of Tzotzil culture.
[1] Zinacantan is a Tzotzil-speaking *municipio* of some 11,500 Highland Maya Indians located just to the west of San Cristóbal Las Casas in the central Highlands of Chiapas in Mexico. The Zinacantecos live in the Ceremonial Center and in fifteen outlying hamlets. They cultivate maize, beans, and squash which provide the basis for their subsistence; they are patrilineal and patrilocal in social organization. The Ceremonial Center is noted for its religious hierarchy, with four levels arranged in a ladder: Mayordomos on the first level; Alféreces on the second; Regidores on the third; and

END-OF-THE-YEAR AND NEW YEAR RITUALS IN ZINACANTAN

The period extending from December 15 to the last day of the Fiesta of San Sebastián on January 25 is the richest segment of the annual ceremonial calendar of Zinacantan. The complicated rituals that characterize this period dramatize the end of the ceremonial year, and the initiation of a new one. During this time, the religious *cargo* positions of most of the past year's important officials expire and are transferred to the succeeding hierarchies. This crucial transition is characterized by rites of inversion, parody and farce: men impersonate women; Indians impersonate Ladinos; people impersonate animals; and the most solemn ceremonies become the subject of mime and ridicule. It is a liminal period of "betwixt and between" (Turner 1964) when, in Leach's (1961) terms, normal time is "played front to back" as the year ends and the social structure is unwired, then rewired, in a six-week development of ritual activity.

The rites in the first phase (December 15 to January 6) begin with a "flower renewal" by the Mayordomos (the first rung on the ladder of religious hierarchy in Zinacantan), who remove the old pine trees and flowers from their house altars and from the churches and replace them with freshly cut pines and flowers. There follows a period of nine days (December 16 to 24) during which the Mayordomos gather daily in front of the church of San Lorenzo (the patron saint of Zinacantan) to eat sweetened squash in commemoration of the nine months of the Virgin's pregnancy. In this squash-eating ceremony, the symbols of sex and fertility — one of the two most important categories of symbols utilized in the end-of-the-year rites — become prominent for the first time. During the same period, the Mayordomos and sacristans of the church perform the *posada* [inn] ceremony to commemorate Joseph and Mary's search for lodging at various inns before the birth of the Christ Child. Although

---

Alcaldes on the fourth, or top level. These *cargo* positions must be requested in advance and are held for one year each, with rest periods in between the years of service. The officials occupying the positions are referred to as *cargo* holders. The descendants of the Spanish Conquerors, interbred with Indians over the centuries, became the local "Ladinos." They speak Spanish, live mainly in towns and cities, control the economic and political system of Chiapas, are generally strong Catholics, and consider themselves citizens of the Republic of Mexico. The Indians, on the other hand, speak Tzotzil, live mainly in scattered hamlets, are only nominally Catholic, and define themselves primarily in terms of their own tribal groups. Each tribal group lives in a single *municipio*, speaks a unique dialect, and dresses in distinctive clothes. For detailed ethnographic data see Vogt (1969, 1970, n.d.), Cancian (1965), and Bricker (i.p.).

this *posada* ceremony, like the squash-eating rite, is obviously modeled on Catholic rituals performed prior to Christmas, some distinctive Zinacanteco elements are apparent: turtle-shell drums played with corn cobs to produce more maize; and Mary bowing to Joseph. Another striking difference from orthodox Catholicism is the conception of the Virgin Mary as a "loose woman who slept with many different men, but did not have a husband." Because of her bad reputation, no one would provide lodging for her forthcoming child. Only an older brother, Joseph, would consent to give her shelter in his animal stable. Mary bowing to her older brother expressed gratitude for his thoughtfulness and sympathy.

On December 23 the Mayordomos and their assistants construct an enormous and beautiful crèche in the church of San Lorenzo. The corners of the crèche are of large, freshly cut white pine boughs; the walls are of sugar cane, banana leaves, cypress branches, and pine needles; and the roof of bromelias and crab apples. There are additional fertility symbols in the form of lowland squash, resembling the female breast in shape, which are tied on the four white pines. The cribs are placed inside.

On December 24 a reed-mat "bull," which will become the focus of a dance drama, is constructed. The "bull" is carried over the head and shoulders of a man, and it performs with two "married couples" (the males are masked and ride stick horses, while their "spouses" wear women's clothing and are unmasked) impersonated by the Mayordomos. During the next twelve days the drama is repeated over and over: the "bull" attacks the husbands, while their wives lift their skirts to expose their genitalia in an attempt to "tame" the "bull." Finally, the "bull" gores and kills the husbands who are revived when their wives take them to a high official who, in turn, rubs their bodies, especially their genitals, with the rattles they have been using in the dance (Bricker i.p.). The performance is watched by two young boys (older and younger brother) dressed as "angels."

At midnight on Christmas Eve, the birth of the Christ Children (there are two in Zinacanteco belief: one older brother and one younger brother) is reenacted in the church of San Sebastián. The two infants are carried by their godparents — the Alcaldes and Regidores, the highest ranking religious officials and the top civil officials from the town hall — to the church of San Lorenzo where they are placed in the crèche. Zinacantecos come to place seed corn and seed beans beside the cribs for fertility, and pray to the resonant sound of the turtle-shell drums.

On January 6 there occurs the chasing, capture, and killing of the "bull." The boy "angels" (symbolic extensions of the older-younger brother Christ Children) have passively watched the drama up to this point. Now they lasso the "bull" who is then killed by wooden knives plunged into his body. His "blood," (consisting of cane liquor with onions and chili to make it red) is passed around and drunk. Bulls are considered by Zinacantecos to be very "hot," and are always served as ritual meat to high-ranking *cargo* holders. Heat is traditionally associated with sacred power; the sun, being the "hottest" thing in the universe, is, at the same time, the most sacred and most powerful. But an excess of heat, and its related conferment of sacred power, spells danger and destruction: an overly powerful sun can wither the maize crop; an overly powerful shaman, believed to have great sacred insight, can perform witchcraft and bring sickness and death to fellow Zinacantecos. From native exegesis it is clear that the "hot" bull represents an evil power. During the dance drama of the bull, the musicians play "bad" music until the moment of the bull's "death," when they change and begin to play "good" music. Above all, the bull appears to symbolize disorder in the form of uncontrolled power and unruly social behavior; he repeatedly gores the performers who are, at the same time, members of the official religious hierarchy. After each incident, the victims are "cured" by symbolic representatives of social order — the various officials and musicians acting as "shamans." Lasting order is established only when the bull is "killed" and his "blood" drunk.

The second major phase in the ritual sequence is the Fiesta of San Sebastián. (Note that the Christ Children were "born" in the church of San Sebastián before being taken to the church of San Lorenzo.) Now the action returns to the church of San Sebastián whose saint's day in the Catholic calendar is January 20. The rites continue for nine days, from January 17, when the Mayordomos again perform the "flower renewal," until January 25 when the Grand Alcalde (the top official on the religious ladder) transfers the sacred symbols of his authority to his successor. It is, by all odds, the most complex ceremony performed in Zinacantan, and exhibits some unusual features. Perhaps the most remarkable element is that the principal costumed performers are the outgoing *cargo* holders who have "officially" finished their year in service, but who must perform throughout this ceremony in order to fulfill the final responsibilities of their office. The Alcaldes of the previous year become "Spanish Gentlemen" dressed in gold-embroidered red coats and knickers; the two most senior Alféreces become "Spanish Ladies" wearing white-embroidered blouses and carrying combs in small bowls; the Regidores become "White Heads" and other ritual characters; two other Alféreces become "Jaguars"; others become "Spanish Moss Wearers" symbolizing "savages"; still others paint their faces black becoming "Black-men" (Blaffer 1972)

— in all, a most extraordinary collection of ritual performers. Sacred objects are brought into the Ceremonial Center from various hamlets: a *t'ent'en* [small slit drum], carried on a tumpline and played for the dancing of the junior actors; a "jousting target" which symbolizes the heart of San Sebastián; and so on. The sequence of events includes: the running of horses along the path of the sun; the arrival of the Spanish Gentlemen and Ladies on horseback; the "Black-men" dancing with stuffed squirrels with which they engage in comic play, including simulating intercourse between the squirrels; the climbing of a "Jaguar Tree" and the ritual burning of a "Jaguar House"; two enormous ritual meals in which the entire hierarchy of the incoming *cargo* holders sits down to servings of whole chickens; the Jaguars' performance of a mock-curing ceremony with one Jaguar impersonating a shaman and the other playing the role of his patient.

The ceremony finally ends on January 25, when the past year's *cargo* holders escort the outgoing Grand Alcalde with his articles of office to the house of the incoming Grand Alcalde. A solemn and elaborate ritual follows in which he hands over the sacred picture of San Sebastián, two candleholders, a box containing a stamp, a seal, some papers, and the branding iron for Zinacantan.

Even after years of field research (begun in 1957), many of the ritual episodes of this complex Fiesta of San Sebastián are still obscure. A number of strands of considerable symbolic import, however, are beginning to emerge from this rich corpus of data. One interesting and promising line of interpretation suggests that the ritual dramas of San Sebastián recapitulate the cultural history of Zinacantan as interpreted by the Zinacantecos — that the dramas provide a ritual reenactment of historical fact and legend. For example, before the time of the Conquest, Zinacantan was in contact with Aztec traders who especially sought quetzal feathers and amber from Chiapas Highland tribes. The Aztec merchants not only gave a Nahuatl name to the place — Tzinacantlán [Place of the Bats] (Vogt 1969:vii) — but may have also introduced such concepts as the *K'uk'ulcon*, the *Quetzalcoatl* [plumed serpent] who is still impersonated in the Fiesta. It is significant that the "White Head" performers are sometimes referred to as Aztecs.

There are other examples. It is well known that the Indians of the Chiapas Highlands resisted the Spanish Conquest furiously; the period of struggle against the Conquistadores was a long and bitter one in their history. Thus, it becomes highly significant that the saint of this fiesta — San Sebastián — and the original myths related to him were introduced into Zinacantan by the Spaniards. Recall the Spanish Gentlemen and

Spanish Ladies on horseback accompanied by their retinues, and the Spanish Gentleman who assumes the ritual task of "leading off" the "jousting" performance. In addition, some Zinacantecos were forcibly conscripted by the Spanish Conquerors to help fight the "Lacandones" (whether the term refers specifically to antecedents of the present-day Lacandones who live in eastern Chiapas, or, more generally, to various Maya tribes in the lowlands to the north and east who were fighting against the Spanish, is unclear). Two of the ritual actors are frequently referred to as "Lacandones" by Zinacanteco informants.

Elements of a Mayan heritage persist in the ritual of San Sebastián, playing a part at least as important as some celebrated aspects of the Colonial experience. The use of the highly sacred *t'ent'en* drum provides a significant substantiation of this point.

But even if the ritual dramas do portray some version of Zinacanteco cultural history, an even stronger argument for their continued importance in the ritual system of the society is that they serve as crucial symbolic models of the social and natural structures of modern Chiapas. For the members of this *municipio*, the cultural world is still fundamentally divided into Indian and Ladino sectors. The Ladinos, being superior in political and economic power, are impersonated by the Senior Impersonators, while Indian cultural elements are impersonated by the Junior Impersonators, comprised of officials of lesser rank in the *cargo* system. At the same time, the world is distinctly subdivided into Men and Animals of various types, used both as props and impersonated by the Junior Impersonators. The dramas not only restate these social and natural divisions in the universe with ritual force each year, but, more significantly, make Zina-cantecan "judgments" upon them. For example, while the Spanish-speaking Ladinos are "honored" by having their roles filled by high-ranking Senior Actors, their behavior and attitudes are mercilessly ridiculed by the performers. The Spanish Gentlemen are portrayed as licentious old men who wish to marry very young Spanish Ladies who are vain — always looking at themselves in mirrors and combing their hair — and promiscuous. A commentary on the overlap of human and animal realms, and the reprehensible but inescapable "animalism" in all Zinacantecos, is made by the Junior Actors who engage in a wide range of obscene and licentious behavior using their animal props.

What of the *t'ent'en?* Why is this small sacred drum carried on a tump-line, continuously played and carefully tended throughout the Fiesta period?

This type of drum, a *teponaztle*, was called *tunkel* in Yucatan and *tun* in Highland Guatemala (Saville 1925). *Tun* was also the Yucatec Maya word for the 360-day year. As the calendrical deities of the ancient Maya are often depicted carrying the burden of the year on a tumpline on their backs, it seems evident that the *t'ent'en* embodies, above all, the symbol of the arrival of the New Year. In addition, the *t'ent'en* appears in the Ceremonial Center only at this fiesta — the time of the ending of an old year and the beginning of the new, the time of "rising heat."

In the rites of San Sebastián, a significant contrast is created between the miming, mocking, obscene, and licentious behavior of the outgoing *cargo* holders (both Senior and Junior Actors), and the solemn, proper, "correct" ritual behavior of the incoming officials. The outgoing *cargo* holders appear to symbolize "disorder" — the last ritual act in "unwiring" the system — whereas the incoming *cargo* holders symbolize "order" — the first ritual act of the year which "wires up" the system again.

Now, for an overview of the distinctive ritual symbols being utilized in the extraordinary series of events extending from December 16 to January 25. What kind of symbolism can be seen in this ceremonial that occupies so much time and energy and absorbs so many resources of the Zinacantecos?

THE CEREMONIAL SCHEDULE: CHRISTMAS TO SAN SEBASTIÁN

Why is it that the richest ritual segment of the annual ceremonial calendar occurs in December and January? There is an economic factor involved, for this period corresponds to the end of the maize cycle. The maize has been harvested, and, for the first time in months, Zinacantecos have their granaries full and money in their pockets (Cancian 1965, 1972). This explains how the Zinacantecos can afford to pause at this time of the year and put their energy and material resources into intensive ritual activity. Yet, it does not explain why they choose to do so.

All of the Maya cultures with which we are familiar, both past and present, appear to be preoccupied with the passage of time. Witness the extraordinary accomplishments of the ancient Maya in the development of a calendar system. Witness the behavior of contemporary Zinacantecos who are as conscious of time, and the precise planning for and scheduling of events in their lives, as any tribal culture known to anthropologists (Vogt 1969:613). Witness also León-Portilla's conclusion (1968) that "space" in the Maya world view is merely a stage for the conjunction of various cycles of time.

An important aspect of this preoccupation with time is the marking out of the solar year, and, more significantly, emphasis upon the end of one year and the beginning of the next. The period from Christmas to San Sebastián, from the point of view of either the Catholic saints' calendar, or the movements of the sun, is the time of transition from the old to the new year. The events begin just before the winter solstice, when the sun reaches its lowest point, and carry on through what is appropriately called "the rising heat fiesta" as the sun moves higher into the sky again. The danger of frost is passing, and the prospect of a new maize-growing season is taking shape in the minds of Zinacantecos.

The ceremonial schedule is divided into two major phases: (1) Christmas to New Year's to Day of Kings; then, following a lull of equal time, (2) a phase of intense activity during the Fiesta of San Sebastián. The two phases are like the two lines of a couplet in a Zinacanteco prayer: the second part restates and intensifies the ritual symbols and themes found in the first. In the first phase, the low-ranking Mayordomos introduce certain symbolic themes as they eat sweetened squash, perform *posadas*, build the crèche, direct the birth of the Christ Children, and perform the mimes and parodies as the two married couples in the ritual drama of the "bull." In the second phase, many of the same themes are stated in a different form, and their meanings are intensified through the use of many additional, as well as higher-ranking, *cargo* holders in the ritual dramas of San Sebastián.

THE BIPOLARITY OF THE SYMBOLISM

To a greater degree than at any other time of the annual ceremonial round, this Year-End/New Year period utilizes ritual symbolism, which is characterized by two crucial bipolarities:

1. In Victor Turner's terms (1967), there is a marked contrast between the stress on sexual, aggressive, antisocial symbolism, much of it flagrantly physiological (the sensory pole), and the stress upon the norms and values of Zinacanteco society (the ideological pole).

2. There is a marked contrast between formal and solemn ritual behavior ("...formality is increased: men adopt formal uniform, differences in status are precisely demarcated by dress and etiquette, moral rules are rigorously and ostentatiously obeyed" [Leach 1961]) and masquerading and revelry in behavior (inversions and reversals for almost all the *cargo* holders, beginning with the Mayordomos at the Christmas celebrations and adding most of the rest of the hierarchy in San Sebastián).

Why all this bipolarity, especially at this season of the year? What messages are being conveyed? What is the effect on the social system?

UNWIRING AND REWIRING
THE ZINACANTECO SYSTEM OF ORDER

The Zinacantecos may be said to be first unwiring, or unstructuring, the system of order, and then rewiring, or restructuring it, as the *cargo* holders, who have spent a year in "sacred time" in office, are finally and definitively removed from their *cargo*s and returned to normal time and everyday life. This process serves to make them (as representatives of all Zinacantecos) reflect about the essence of their way of life, the contrasts or paired opposites and contradictions: between husbands and wives; between "older brother" and "younger brother" (or "Senior" and "Junior"), in their system of rank order; between men and women as apparent in the patrilineal system and division of labor; between Indians and Ladinos (in their bicultural world); between men and animals (culture versus nature). The ceremonies are essentially a "liminal period," "betwixt and between" (Turner 1964) the old year and the new year, between being in-office and out-of-office in the *cargo* system.

It is in these terms that we are able to understand the astonishing number of inversions in behavior, of role reversals: boys become "angels"; men impersonate women, bulls, and other animals; *cargo* officials and musicians serve as shamans; Indians play Ladinos; and men impersonating Jaguars become shamans who "cure" stuffed squirrels of "soul-loss." Men dance and march backward — the only time this occurs during the entire year. Normal life is being played "front to back" as the ritualists move into a veritable orgy of inversions and reversals.

Edmund Leach (1961) suggests that "formality" and "masquerade" are paired opposites and, as such, modes for moving in and out of "sacred time." He suggests that, "A rite which starts with formality [e.g. a wedding] is likely to end in masquerade; a rite which starts with masquerade [e.g. New Year's Eve; Carnival] is likely to end in formality."

With respect to these Zinacanteco rituals, Leach's hypothesis is applicable in two senses:
1. Taking each of the two phases as a unit, one sees the Mayordomos behaving with rigorous formality in the building of the crèche, the *posada* rites, and the Birth of the Christ Children. Then, they end this ritual phase by masquerading as the married couples in the drama of the "bull." With the outgoing *cargo* holders in San Sebastián, the sequence appears to be reversed: they begin by masquerading (as women, Ladinos, animals, etc.) and end with intense formality on January 25 after the stuffed animals have been burned and as the sacred articles of office are turned over to the new Grand Alcalde.

2. Taking the ceremonial year as a unit, the new *cargo* holders behave with great formality, from the time of the Fiesta of San Sebastián throughout an entire year; they end their year's *cargo* service at the following San Sebastián celebration in ludicrous masquerade and farce.

But there is an additional and interesting process going on WITHIN each phase of this Year-End/New Year ceremony. Here, the two modes of formality and masquerade seem to form a kind of dialogue between, on the one hand, the married couples and their "bull" and the outgoing *cargo* holders representing the masquerade, and, on the other, the incumbent and new *cargo* holders representing the formality mode. It is as if two programs were being played simultaneously on a ritual tape that emits messages about the cultural code — its gaps, contradictions, and attempted resolutions — in this complex interaction of formal, "proper" behavior and reveling, ridiculous, farcical behavior.

Finally, it is evident that the fantastic and skillful miming of social conflicts through various inversions, role reversals, and parodies of solemn ritual — in many cases, utilizing flagrantly physiological symbols of sex — are ways of divesting the powerful drives and emotions associated with human physiology, especially reproduction, of their antisocial quality and of attaching them to the normative order, thereby energizing the latter "with a borrowed vitality" (Turner 1969: 52–53). In the copulating behavior of the stuffed squirrels is presented a sequence that in mime contains prototypical condensed symbolism: *Kol ?Arias'* having sexual intercourse with his wife at the foot of a mango tree instead of attending to his *cargo* duties, is symbolically representing the sexuality, the animality, in ALL *cargo* holders, in ALL Zinacantecos, who are being punished as the squirrel is thrown to the ground and soundly whipped.

By the 25th of January, the bull has been killed; the Mayordomos have relinquished their stick-horses; the stuffed animals have been burned; the Jaguars, Plumed Serpents, and Spanish Moss Wearers have put away their costumes; and the Spanish Gentlemen and Ladies have become normal *cargo* holders again. By the time the transfer of sacred articles of office to the new highest-ranking *cargo* holder has unfolded with great formality, the system of order has been rewired for the year which is being born.

REFERENCES

BLAFFER, SARAH C.
 1972   *The black-man of Zinacantan.* Austin: University of Texas Press.

BRICKER, VICTORIA R.
  i.p. "Ceremonial humor in three Chiapas communities." Austin: University of Texas Press.
CANCIAN, FRANK
  1965 *Economics and prestige in a Maya community: a study of the religious cargo system in Zinacantan, Chiapas, Mexico.* Palo Alto: Stanford University Press.
  1972 *Change and uncertainty in peasant economy: the Maya corn farmers of Zinacantan.* Palo Alto: Stanford University Press.
LEACH, EDMUND R.
  1961 "Two essays concerning the symbolic representation of time," in *Rethinking anthropology*, 124–136. London: Athlone Press.
LEÓN-PORTILLA, MIGUEL
  1968 *Tiempo y realidad en el pensamiento Maya.* Mexico City: Universidad Nacional Autónoma de México.
SAVILLE, MARSHALL H.
  1925 *The wood-carver's art in ancient Mexico.* New York: Museum of the American Indian, Heye Foundation.
TURNER, VICTOR
  1964 "Betwixt and between: the liminal period in rites de passage," in *The Proceedings of the American Ethnological Society, Symposium on New Approaches to the Study of Religion*, 4–20. Seattle: University of Washington Press.
  1967 *The forest of symbols.* Ithaca and London: Cornell University Press.
  1969 *The ritual process.* Chicago: Aldine.
VOGT, EVON Z.
  1969 *Zinacantan: a Maya community in the highlands of Chiapas.* Cambridge: Harvard University Press.
  1970 *The Zinacantecos of Mexico: a modern Maya way of life.* New York: Holt, Rinehart and Winston.
  n.d. "Tortillas for the gods: a symbolic analysis of Zinacanteco ritual." Forthcoming.

The Place of the Cactus Wine Ritual in the Papago Indian Ecosystem

JACK O. WADDELL

Rappaport (1967, 1968) has recently made an important case for the role of ritual in the adjustment of a people's relationship to their environment. The essence of Rappaport's thesis is that local and regional populations maintain a set of shared relations, centering around nutritional needs, with other components of the biotic community. Ritual may serve as a prime mediator between a local community and external entities, both in terms of regulating relations of local and regional groupings, and in reducing complex information into a simpler form for easier cognitive management (Rappaport 1968: 235). The ecosystem is a system of localized trophic exchanges among localized aggregate populations within a region.

As Turner (1969: 7) observes, some students of ritual behavior are critical of those who place too much emphasis on how and what ritual actors think or believe about their ritual behavior, and who do not sufficiently develop external, objective and rational outside judgments about the ritual observed. Turner (1969: 12) recognizes that there is an operational dimension to ritual wherein observers can see and record what ritual actors do, and can try to establish positional relationships in order

I am indebted to the American Philosophical Society, Philadelphia, Pennsylvania for a small grant that facilitated travel to the ceremony July 27–July 30, 1973. While doing research on Papago Indian drinking under NIMH-NIAAA grant RO 1 MH17546, 1969–1970, I was able to attend the ceremony July 25–July 27, 1970. Without the kindness of my very dear friend and teacher, Mr. Joseph Elando, speaker, wine maker and ceremonial coordinator of the Little Tucson feast, I would not have had this informative and emotionally rewarding experience. His family has taken me in and helped me to feel a part of the activities. To the good people of the participating villages which tolerated the presence of my tape recorder, camera, and most of all, me, I will forever be saying thank you.

to ascertain the broader meanings and functions of ritual in a society. On the other hand, the exegetic dimension of ritual, or the explanations and meanings of ritual or symbolic acts as provided by native informants, are extremely important in Turner's mode of analysis (Turner 1969: 11). Rappaport (1968: 237) similarly argues that both the operational and the cognized models of environment and of ritual behavior are significant in ecological interpretations of human actions.

It is possible to apply Rappaport's thesis to another cultural setting. Whereas Rappaport's research population, the Maring-speaking Tsembaga, consisted of about 200 shifting horticulturalists in the highlands of New Guinea, the research population in this study, the Aztec-Tanoan-speaking Papago, consisted of about 500 individuals dependent upon a reservation economy in the Sonoran desert of the southwestern United States. The territorial unit, or local group, in the Tsembaga case was composed of five patrilineal clans, each comprising a residential, subterritorial exogamous group of from fifteen to seventy-eight persons (Rappaport 1968: 17–18). The territorial unit or local group in the Papago case was a village unit, made up of a number of local residential villages ranging in size from thirty to over 200 persons, all ideally exogamous and comprising a total population of about 500 individuals (Kelly 1963: 41–42, 56–57).

Both Tsembaga and Papago territorially bounded units had relations with other localized groups within a larger region. Just as Rappaport was interested in the "operational" and "cognized" role of ritual in regulating a people's relationship to a social ecological environment and in translating complex meanings into more simplified social messages, this study will examine the role of a particular Papago ritual as a similar regulatory and communicational mechanism.

THE SOCIAL SETTING

Space does not allow as complete an ethnographic sketch of Papago ecology, demography and culture as would be desirable in a study of this kind. The most complete data available on these aspects can be found in other works (D. Jones 1962; Joseph, Spicer and Chesky 1949; Kelly 1963; Mark 1960; Underhill 1969a, 1969b). A brief summary does seem necessary in order to appreciate the significance of some of the points made in this analysis.

Papagos have lived in small rancheria kinship communities or villages, scattered over a vast desert area, for many centuries. Irrigation or dry-field farming, supplemented by hunting and gathering of desert fauna and flora, has been the predominant Papago economy since long before the arrival of the Spanish to their area at the end of the seventeenth century. Cattle and European agricultural technology were added to the economic pattern, after which little change occurred in the character of Papago life until the end of the nineteenth century and, more intensively, not until well into the twentieth century. The basic social unit — an exogamous kinship community or village — is made up of a number of virilocal extended families who recognize themselves as related. A number of these villages are more loosely attached to each other through bonds of consanguinity, hence comprising a larger village unit. These villages are also tied together affinally as well as geographically, thus providing further bases of social relationships. There are, therefore, some bonds among village units as well. Tribal district boundaries have, more recently, tended to consolidate political decision making at the expense of earlier village-unit solidarity (D. Jones 1962).

As the most significant Papago social relations take place within the kinship village and among closely aligned villages, which Underhill (1969a: 58) calls a village unit, it is appropriate to concentrate on the relations between these partner villages. The particular village focus in this study is that of Ali Chukson or Little Tucson, with a more or less permanent resident population of 150. This is where the wine-feast ritual reported in this study is annually held. Its relationship to other villages in the larger village unit of Komalik is clearly dramatized in the wine ritual.

The village of Komalik, or Cumaro, is, historically, the most significant village unit. It is the southernmost village unit of the four original village units in the Achi dialect group (along with Kui Tatk, Achi and Ak Chin) (Underhill 1969a: 60). According to Oblasser (n.d.: 6), the ancient fortified pueblo of Komalik and its daughter villages claim the fields scattered all along the valley west of the Baboquivari Mountains from Ali Chukson (Little Tucson) southward to near San Miguel. Many of these field locations became daughter villages, and many, such as Little Tucson, Topawa, Supi Oidak, and Choulic, became permanent villages. Wells were maintained in the foothills of the Baboquivari Range at such locations as Pitoikam and Chutum Vaya.

Another major village unit of Achi, Kui Tatk, or Mesquite Root, was abandoned in the 1850's with many of its descendants settling in such locations as Gu Oidak, Pan Tak, Viopuli, Havan Nakya, Chuapo, and Artesa. A third Achi village unit formed such settlements as Bac, at San Xavier, Sil Nakya, the Achi villages, Covered Wells, Comobabi, and

Ko Vaya. The fourth Achi village unit, Ak Chin, closely allied with the Achi villages, sent some people to Comobabi and Chiawuli Tak. The locations and relationships of these four major village units of Achi, including Komalik, of which Little Tucson is a part, can be seen in Figure 1.

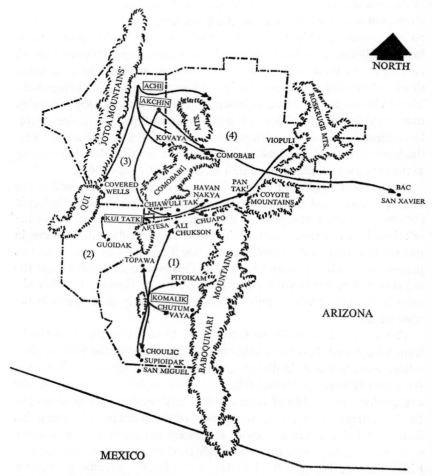

Figure 1.   The four Papago village units of the Achi dialect and their daughter villages showing their historical relationships. Present-day district political boundaries of the Baboquivari (1), Sells (2), Gu Achi (3), and Schuk Toak (4) reservation districts are also indicated (Scale 1 inch = approximately 10 miles)

It is important from the standpoint of this analysis of the wine ritual to see these village relationships precisely because the ritual dramatizes their significance. The whole area is comparable to what Rappaport

(1968: 226) refers to as a regional population, made up of a number of local aggregates sharing regional continuity, dialectic affinity and exchanges of personnel, genetic material, and goods. The Komalik village unit, comprised of its local daughter communities, constitutes an ecosystem in which its local populations also take part in a larger regional ecological system.

The point of departure in this analysis is that of a local community, Ali Chukson or Little Tucson, where the *nawait* [wine-making ritual], in which I have participated, has been observed. Kelly (1963: 56) lists Ali Chukson as having 153 residents. R. Jones (n.d.) obtained an enumeration of about 115 people residing there at the time of his field survey in 1962. Based upon photographs and quick counts during the two occasions when I participated in the wine ritual (1970 and 1972), twenty-five to forty people were involved in the two nights of dancing preceding the *dahiwua k ih'e* [sit-and-drink] ritual, while from seventy-five to 100 people of all ages sat in the circle to drink or circulated outside the drinking circle. People from the villages of the Mesquite Root village unit (Big Fields, Viopuli, Havan Nakya, and Artesa), the Komalik village unit (Topawa, Little Tucson, Komalik, and Supi Oidak), the Achi village unit (Sil Nakya, Bac and Comobabi) and the Ak Chin (Chiawuli Tak) were all disproportionately represented, with the larger number from the Mesquite Root and Komalik units.

THE *NAWAIT* RITUAL

The Papago New Year begins with the *hahshani bak mashad* [Sahuaro Fruit Month], equivalent to the month of June. Four weeks prior to the actual drinking ceremony, the people begin collecting the ripening sahuaro cactus fruit and preparing the pulp into a jam or syrup. The boiled syrup is kept in sealed jars or cans until the person in charge of the wine preparations calls for the syrup to be brought to the *nawait kih* [wine house] (also referred to as *wahkih*). At Little Tucson, the *kih* is located at one side of an adobe house, in which are kept the sacred objects, such as divining crystals, sacred rocks and shells, eagle feathers, divining rods, and other village fetishes. The door is always kept padlocked or is closely guarded in order that only the ritual specialists may enter.

The making of the *nawait* [wine] initiates the *jukiabig mashad* [rainy month], and takes place sometime in the latter part of July. The exact dates on which the wine making and the communal drinking are to occur are determined by the feast leaders, the elders, and the chief wine maker, after consulting with the *siwani mahkai* [chief rain shaman]. For the Little Tucson feast, there were two *mamakai* called upon to direct the activities. The official wine maker, my chief informant and close friend of several years, was from Little Tucson. The chief *mahkai*, a man of widespread reputation, was from Little Tucson, but had moved to Havan Nakya, his wife's village. The other *mahkai* was from Topawa, but had married women from Little Tucson.

When these leaders had determined the date of the sit-and-drink, messengers were sent four days prior to the event to surrounding villages to direct them to bring in their sahuaro syrup to the wine house, at which time the wine would be prepared. The main activities during the *nawait* [wine-making] phase of the ritual centered around the public dancing area outside the *wahkih* [wine house] (see Figure 2).

The dance circle was prepared by stretching the eagle feather trophies of the important men on a line running from west to east and supported by two poles. A small fire was kindled just to the north of the eagle feathers, and the *mamakai* sacred fetishes were displayed on a green canvas close to the fire. Benches were placed before the fire at the west of the dance circle in order that the *mamakai* could look east, the most important direction, as they conducted the dancing ritual and talked to the rain spirits.

Each of the two nights the dancing began with the formal seating of the officials (the two *mamakai* and their two runners or assistants). The official speechmaker, in this case the person in charge of the wine making, addressed the *mamakai*, then made a public address to those assembled for dancing. In his speech he reviewed the origin and purpose of the custom and extended an invitation to the assembly to do its part in helping the rain shaman to divine for rain and to help the wine to ferment so they could have a good feast. All were requested to be cooperative so that rain would come to bless all.

There is, of course, an extensive symbolism involved which is impossible to present in this short discussion. The dancing, led by men who know the appropriate songs of the four directions, continued throughout both nights, in ritual cycles of four, moving in a counterclockwise direction, "just as the clouds do." The dancing continued until the *siwani mahkai* consulted with the other *mahkai* to determine when to cease dancing and return to their homes for sleep. At the end of the second night of dancing, just as day broke in the east, the dancers lined up to drink a bucket of the wine, which had been declared ready. It was served by the chief wine maker as participants stood at the west point of the dance

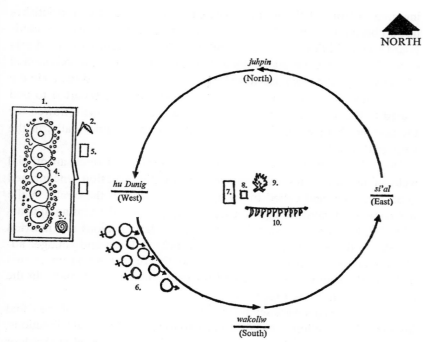

Figure 2. The dancing circle showing the positioning of the officials, the sacred fetishes, and the four cardinal directions in relationship to the *nawait kih* or wine house, where the cactus wine is fermenting during the two nights of dancing

Legend

1. *nawait kih* [wine house]
2. *matcuita'k* [divining plume]
3. serving basket
4. five jars of fermenting wine
5. sentries at door
6. male (♂) and female (♀) song

and dance leaders
7. seating place of *mamakai* and two assistants
8. display of sacred fetishes
9. ceremonial fire
10. line of eagle feathers

circle. The *mamakai* then called all the people around them, and each *mamakai* predicted the exact time rain would come following the sit-and-drink ceremony, scheduled to begin about noon the same day. The chief wine maker then delivered a ritual oration about the origin of the people, their sibs, their settlements of the land, the origin of the rain-making custom and why they hold the feast according to the custom. He then called on all of the people to identify their sibs, then sent them home to await the messenger who would come to invite them to come *dahiwua k ih'e* [sit and drink].

About noon, messengers on horseback were sent to households of participating villages, and people slowly began to assemble at the drinking area in front of the *wahkih*. The eagle feathers and sacred fetishes had all been returned to the *wahkih*. Sheets of canvas and pieces of cardboard were laid down on the ground at each of the four cardinal directions. The chief wine maker then ceremonially seated the ceremonial officials. First, the *mamakai* were brought from the east and seated in the eastern direction. Next, a singer and an assistant were escorted to and seated in the northern direction. The same procedure was followed for the seating of singers and assistants in the southern and, finally, in the western directions.

Once the officials were seated, the wine maker delivered an official welcoming speech, reviewed the reasons for the occasion, encouraged good behavior, and called the people to be seated in the circle. While not completely conforming to a segregated pattern, the seating appeared to fall into a general distribution of: (1) elderly persons and married couples in the east-to-north quadrant arc; (2) children and younger adolescents opposite them in the west-to-south arc; (3) young unmarried males in the south-to-east arc; and (4) young unmarried females in the north-to-west arc (see Figure 3).

Once individuals were seated in the circle, the next phase of the ritual involved the selection of cup-bearers, two for each of the four directions, selected from among the young men. These men assembled at the door of the wine house while two ritual assistants carrying divining rods (*matcuita'k*) with eagle feathers attached emerged from the wine house and proceeded to the east, where they invited the *mamakai* to sing the song of the eastern direction. Once this was done, the assistants walked in the form of a cross, to the north, then south, then west, similarly inviting the singers to lead songs of those directions. They then circled in a counterclockwise direction from east, to north, west, and south, inviting the people at each of these directions to sing simultaneously as the assistants passed each direction. During the ceremonies, a ceremonial buffoon or clown had been "behaving badly," much to the entertainment of the crowd.

After the singing, the *dahiwua k ih'e* proper began. Two cup-bearers brought a large basket and a pail of *nawait* [cactus wine] to the *siwani mahkai* and *mahkai* at the east. Two cup-bearers at each of the other directions carried milk pails full of *nawait* to each of the remaining directions.

The *siwani mahkai* then dipped his right hand into the wine, ran his fingers around the rim of the basket counterclockwise four times, and scattered the wine from his fingers over his shoulder in the direction of the east. He then was offered a coffee can full of wine by the cup-bearers,

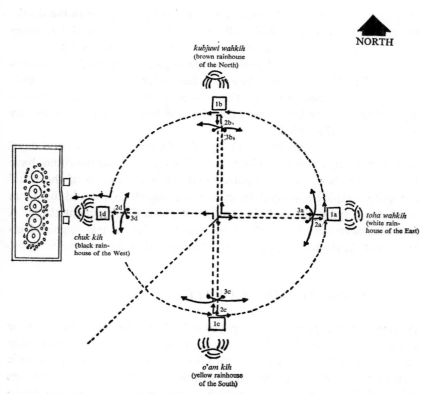

Figure 3. Three phases of the *dahiwua k ih'e* or sit-and-drink ceremony. In phase one (1a-d), the *siwani mahkai* and *mahkai* are seated at the east (1a) and the other singers and their assistants at the north (1b), south (1c), and west (1d), respectively, by the chief wine maker, who then makes an opening speech and invites the people to come sit in the circle. In phase two (2a-d), the assistants to the *mamakai* invite the songs of the east (2a), north (2b), south (2c), and west (2d) in that order. In phase three (3a-d), two cup-bearers at each direction serve those at their respective stations first, then work all the way around the circle in opposite directions until their containers are emptied, then return for refills to repeat the same pattern until the ritual is over

and extended a kinship term to them before he drank it. The *mamakai* then began to sing repetitive cycles of the rain song of the east as the cup-bearers served wine to others in the circle in the same manner. The same ritual was then initiated at the north, south, and west in the same manner, with the singing going on simultaneously as the cup-bearers made their complete courses around the drinking circle, moving in both directions. As the baskets or pails were emptied, the bearers returned to the *wahkih* for more wine, and the singing and drinking continued in the same manner for a couple of hours. By this time the participants were vomiting up quantities of wine, as well as food eaten prior to the drinking ceremony. People occasionally got up and wandered about, going to the bushes to relieve themselves, or, in some cases, to pass out.

Before the wine was all gone, people began getting their containers filled and making their way home. A few older people who were able to stick it out a little longer continued the repetitive song cycles. Drinking continued at the homes until the wine was all gone, and the ceremony was then officially ended.

This has been a very brief and superficial summation of several days' activities. Many details, crucial to a symbolic analysis of the ritual, have been omitted because the cognized and symbolic aspects of the ritual are quite complex and my data are not as complete as I would like them to be for a symbolic analysis. This must await a subsequent study. A few comments can be made about some of the central cognized elements of the ritual as a preparatory step toward an operational analysis.

AN ANALYSIS OF THE *NAWAIT*

As one would expect, when Papagos talk about the wine ceremony, or are asked why they think it important to observe it, they will invariably stress its importance as a means for bringing rain. Much of the semantic structure, as well as the action structure (Turner 1969: 12) expresses this goal. For instance, the eagle feathers stretched across the dance area help "to catch the wind," and draw the rain clouds from the south. The feathers themselves "look like big white clouds." The blackness of the crow, of the horse ridden by the messenger, of the thunderhead clouds, of the sacred *wahkih* in the western sky, all have their references to the coming of rain. The reddish-brown of the hawk, of the water bugs that come out after rain, of the storm-forming clouds, of the cactus wine and vomit, of the sacred *wahkih* in the northern sky, all allude to rain in the songs. The whiteness of the breast-feathers of eagle down, of the mockingbird, of the soft white fluffy clouds, of the sacred *wahkih* in the eastern heavens, all have intimations of pending rain. The yellowness of sandstorm clouds, blowing dust and debris ahead of the pending rain, of corn, of desert flowers that bloom, of the sacred *wahkih* of the south, all foretell rain.

Vomiting is like throwing up clouds, like raining on the earth. A dizzy man, gloriously drunk with wine, is like a dizzy rain cloud ready to shower the earth with moisture. When people dance counterclockwise, they do so because "that is the direction the clouds move, from south to east to north to west." The *mamakai*, during the all-night dancing, depart in the direction of the east "to talk to the ghosts [rain spirits]" to find out when it will rain. They stand waving their divining plumes in the direction of the east as the people dance; they rub the sacred rock and hold it up to the east, asking for rain. If it fails to rain, someone had a wrong thought, drank white man's liquor, or the wine was not made right or was contaminated by a woman. At numerous intervals in the course of the ritual, the origin of the custom is restated, calling the attention of the people to the fact that *I'itoi*, or "Elder Brother," taught them the ceremony in order to have rain.

Rain in a desert environment, as anywhere, is important to the economic maintenance of the community. Without it, cattle will die, crops will fail, the water holes or wells will be hard to locate and man will thirst, and animal and plant life will die or become sparse. Rain, even in today's modern reservation and wage-work economy, is important whether a man has cattle or cultivates a garden. Tribal and family *charcos* or "welsh" need replenishing if cattle are to make it through long dry periods.

As Underhill (1969b: 38) notes, in the desert where material survival is a constant preoccupation, the songs of the Papago are variations on the themes of rain, wind, mountains, desert and food. The symbols, whether word symbols (speeches and songs) or action symbols (dancing, manipulating objects, or drinking wine) are indeed multivocal, having many interpenetrating meanings or significations (Turner 1969: 8). There are also evidences of polarization of reference in Papago ritual symbolism, where physiological objects and ideological or cognitive references are at binary terminals.

I do not want to commit myself to a deep semantic analysis of the cognized dimension, primarily because I am not yet prepared to do so convincingly. I would like, however, to tentatively claim that these semantic poles are identifiable in Papago ritual symbolism and then move on, with this assumption, to analyzing the ritual in terms of another aspect of Turner's hypothesis. Turner argues that cultures that have ritual symbols organized around highly multivocal, polarized symbols of physiological potency, are strongly corporate social systems (Turner 1969: 10). It is the corporate character of social systems, expressed in ritual — and primarily at the operational dimension rather than the cognitive — with which I want to deal in this analysis.

The *nawait* ritual, and the ritual drinking during the *dahiwua k ih'e*, have a number of less explicit functions than the more obvious technological one of bringing rain. They are, nonetheless, every bit as important as the stated goal. In terms of communication theory, it seems that the ritual does translate or reduce complex behavior into more simplified social messages to facilitate cognitive learning of important cultural values. A few such messages seem obvious to me, even when Papago informants do not speak of the wine ritual precisely in these terms.

First, their songs, dances and ritual paraphernalia animate and express many features of their desert homeland — birds, insects and animals; cacti, shrubs and crops; mountains, clouds, winds, etc. A human ecosystem is more than a territorial boundary and a source of subsistence, it is also an emotional space. The wine ritual mobilizes emotional identification with the landscape through powerful multivocal appeals to symbols via a number of expressive media. Something important about man's environment feeds back into Papago awareness through ritual participation.

The ecosystem is also one which is defined in terms of trophic exchanges. Local communities are dependent upon each other for: (1) controlling aggression, (2) providing spouses, and (3) sharing resources. It seems most plausible that the public character of both the dancing and the drinking ritual makes the events of the wine ceremony an epideitic display (Rappaport 1967: 26–27), that is, a way of publicly reminding participants of the size of the circle of relatives or kinsmen from various villages that one can count on for support.

Earlier, I discussed the significant village units and their constituent villages, noting that Ali Chukson, as one of several related villages stemming from the Komalik village unit, served as host village at the annual wine feast. There were social messages communicated in the wine festivity, other than the expression of their common history as descendant villages originating from their fathers' removal from Komalik, Mesquite Root, Achi, or Ak Chin.

There was a division of labor involved in the preparations for, conduct of, and participation in the ritual that fell clearly along sex and age lines. All were encouraged to participate freely, but in quite definitive ways. Woman and children picked the sahuaro fruit, prepared the pulp, and cooked it into syrup. Men delivered it in trucks from collecting areas. The elder men led in all aspects of the ritual sequence and played the major leadership and decision-making roles. Younger men, at the bidding of the elders, carried coals to the fire, sat sentry duty outside the *wahkih*, carried water to the *mamakai*, were conscripted as cup-bearers, or, on occasion, were chosen to lead songs of the directions if they knew them, and there were no elders to lead the singing. Middle-aged men served as right-hand assistants to the *mamakai*, as cane-bearers, or as gourd-rattle musicians and singers leading the dancing. Before each dancing cycle began, the men lined up at the west behind the *mamakai*, and the women fell in behind them. As the dancing circle formed, the male musicians paired off with females, and danced facing the center of the circle, in alternate pairs. Any other persons, young or old, male or female, could then join in as each dancing cycle progressed.

As mentioned earlier, a general pattern emerged in the sit-and-drink circle in which elders at the east faced the young people opposite them, and the young men faced the young women. In the case of the elders, spouses generally sat behind their husbands. In fact, any female, young or old, who sat in the circle where the men were, usually sat behind them. Yet, everyone — young and old, male and female — could and did drink.

I think the phases of the ritual provided many visual reminders of the two significant dimensions of Papago social life — the distinction of sex roles and the respect and privilege due to relative age. Underlying these is the principle that all have a part in the ritual actions subject to these differences. They are important in daily social life and they are vividly dramatized in ritual actions.

In the actual exchange of drinks during the sit-and-drink, kinship terms were always expressed to the giver by the receiver. If no specific term covered the relationship, *nawoj* or "friend" signified a relationship of goodwill. The expectation that one must drink all that was offered also expressed reciprocal goodwill. When the dancers were called together at the end of their second night of dancing for a recitation of their social origins and to identify their *mahm, wahw, apapa, apki,* or *ogol* sib affiliations, they were communicating their social unity to one another despite the fact that they came from several different villages.

I have been studying the available data on villages of origin and where individuals from certain villages obtained their spouses. Without providing quantitative details at this time, it is clear that among those villages participating in the ritual, certain villages consistently provided spouses for other villages. While the marriage exchange patterns have undergone significant changes under contemporary economic conditions, I think that the ritual acts as a visual reminder, not only of consanguinity relations among villages, but also of affinity and prospective affinity relationships.

A basic feature of Papago life is its commitment to egalitarian principles, formally and visually communicated through recurrent sharing of food, labor, clothing, shelter, etc., among kinsmen. The wine feast stressed this in ritual form during the formal ceremony, when each participant was offered a seemingly unending supply of cactus wine by the eight cup-bearers. A participant might, at any time, dip the cup in the wine and extend it to a cup-bearer, who was equally obliged to drink it all, after uttering the appropriate kin term. After the sit-and-drink circle had broken up, the remaining wine was distributed and taken to the homes, where, between intervals of sleep or "passing out," it was passed around until the supply was exhausted. When a household had exhausted its supply of wine, the members ventured to other households, which were obliged to share their stores of wine with them.

There seems to be one last social message communicated in the wine ritual. D. Jones (1962) has noted that until very recently, the Papago village was considered the strong cohesive unit. But with the imposition of a tribal government, the village has become a less cohesive unit, transferring many of its sociopolitical and economic functions to the district tribal organization to develop a pattern of single family households and ranches, that replaced corporate village solidarity. Now that district boundaries have divided historically related villages, political decisions at the district council levels frequently divide peoples who formerly belonged together socially.

This, in my opinion, is an accurate analysis, except that it fails to acknowledge the fact that since the time of the cessation of Apache attacks in the late 1800's, large villages have split into a number of daughter settlements, which have in turn splintered into other local groups. It seems to me, therefore, that the fragmentation and resettlement, begun in the 1870's and continuing until the drilling of permanent wells and the emergence of new tribal district boundaries, was a manifestation of the chronic disruption of the village cohesion that Papagos probably have always had to face. The economic necessity of new settlements and new alignments, as well as the necessity of maintaining old alignments, has always been characteristic of Papago social life. The wine feast, in drawing together individuals from sister villages within the village unit, dramatizes the significance of these past relationships; having the depth of generations, it communicates an identification. Similarly, the feast brings together individuals from villages now within other political districts, dramatizing the significance of contemporary relationships; it communicates an identification that cuts across contemporary political divisions.

SUMMARY AND CONCLUSIONS

What can be said about the significance of the ritual as a means of coping with change in the Papago reservation-community culture? As mentioned earlier, Turner (1969: 10) has hypothesized that ritual symbols organized around highly multivocal, polarized symbols of physiological potency are connected with strongly corporate social systems. The maintenance of the *nawait* and *dahiwua k ih'e* rituals, in the face of numerous disruptive changes, is part of the struggle to communicate basic aspects of the Papago ethos — an ethos primarily concerned with corporate social cohesion of kin-aligned groups.

With economic changes altering many of the Papago's former relationships to their desert homeland, the wine ritual communicates in vivid word and action symbols the character of the desert land, its life, its technology, and how all these things came to be.

As changing economic and social conditions necessitate the breakup of old settlements, and new village communities and new political arrangements are established, the ritual communicates temporal as well as geographical relatedness to other important social groups.

With changing sex roles and with the threat of greater gaps between the generations, the ritual communicates the valued status system wherein men and women are reminded of distinctive but important roles, and elders are listened to and respected.

As people move away for jobs, or as children go to distant schools, new patterns for finding mates are increasingly possible. The ritual communicates the importance of the participating villages to each other in terms of affinal connections and as sources of prospective spouses.

With the assumption of nuclear family economics and social life at the expense of extended family and kinship obligations, and with the increasingly unequal access to wealth promoted by the relative adoption of job-oriented, capitalistic, economic behavior, the ritual communicates the significance of egalitarianism, of sharing, of meeting reciprocal obligations, and of curbing aggressive behavior toward one's kinsmen that new forms of behavior evoke.

Yet the Papago still depend on rain, and it is for this explicit reason that they meet annually at Ali Chukson and that they attend the feasts of other Achi villages. Sacred paraphernalia are religiously guarded and maintained. The *mamakai* are called to invoke the rain spirits and to lead the rain dance. There is obligatory behavior and tabooed behavior related to the solemnity of the events; and the Papago believe that this behavior has a direct bearing on whether or not it will rain.

While I was impressed with the "sacredness" of the ritual, and convinced that its few participants engaged in it solemnly and intensely, I was also aware of the larger number who never make it to any aspect of the feast. Also, a number of young people, while they seemed eager to take part, did not know the wine songs, and there was a serious problem of recruitment for future officialdom. Large numbers were present at the sit-and-drink, but remained marginal to the activities, they were more curious onlookers than active participants.

As long as there are ritual specialists, as long as there are persons who know the songs and ritual language, as long as there is consciousness of past social realities, and as long as the commitments to social cohesion, reciprocal exchange, and egalitarian values remain, the ritual symbols can be expected to be activitated before a few loyal participants at the annual ritual. If some of its importance is rediscovered by a new generation of Papagos, it may be a meaningful form of identification, but it may never again communicate the same social message. It may, instead, embody new social realities.

REFERENCES

JONES, D. J.
   1962   "Human ecology of the Papago Indians." Unpublished master's thesis, University of Arizona, Tucson.

JONES, R. D.
   n.d.   "Demographic data for Ali Chukson." Unpublished field notes, Bureau of Ethnic Research, University of Arizona, Tucson.

JOSEPH, A., R. SPICER, J. CHESKY
   1949   *The desert people*. Chicago: University of Chicago Press.

KELLY, W. H.
   1963   *The Papago Indians of Arizona: a population and economic study*. Tucson: Bureau of Ethnic Research, Department of Anthropology, University of Arizona.

MARK, A. K.
   1960   "Description of and variables relating to ecological change in the history of the Papago Indian population." Unpublished master's thesis, University of Arizona, Tucson.

OBLASSER, FR. B.
   n.d.   "Papagueria, domain of the Papagos." Manuscript on file, Arizona Pioneer Historical Society, Tucson.

RAPPAPORT, R. A.
   1967   Ritual regulation of environmental relations among a New Guinea people. *Ethnology* 6:17–30.
   1968   *Pigs for the ancestors: ritual in the ecology of a New Guinea people*. New Haven: Yale University Press.

TURNER, V.
   1969   "Forms of symbolic action: introduction," in *Proceedings of the 1969 Annual Spring Meeting, American Ethnological Society*. Edited by R. F. Spencer, 3–25. Seattle: University of Washington Press.

UNDERHILL, R.
   1969a *Social organization of the Papago Indians*. New York: AMS Press.
   1969b *Papago Indian religion*. New York: AMS Press.

SECTION THREE

The Violation of Taboo and Magical Power

LAURA MAKARIUS

Sympathetic magic, as a concept developed by Frazer, has shed considerable light on a fundamental aspect of magical thought and practice in tribal society. And yet, in spite of the mass of information that has accumulated from the time *The golden bough* was written, theory has hardly marked any progress in this field. The examples of magic and sorcery that still persist in developing countries, as attested by the relatively recent cases brought before the courts in Rhodesia (Crawford 1967), cannot be said to have been adequately interpreted.

This shortcoming is partly to be explained by the fact, among other things, that sympathetic magic, far from accounting for all reported cases of magic, is flatly contradicted by some, and to that extent its validity is open to question.

Frazer used the not too happy term, "sympathetic magic," to describe the action of like on like, of the part on the whole, of the contiguous on the contiguous, and of the symbol on what it symbolizes. Pain, supposedly inflicted on the image, causes pain to the person it represents. The treatment of a lock of hair will harm or benefit its owner. In one case, the image, in the other, the lock of hair evokes a mental picture that assumes the dimensions of reality. Whether based on analogy or some symbolical manifestation, it has causal power.

Sympathetic magic thus accounts for a large number of magical phenomena, but signally fails to explain, for instance, why rainmakers sometimes pour blood instead of water, when it is rainwater that they desire; why medicine men dabble with substances associated with death, not health, when proceeding with their cures to drive away sickness; and why the so-called "divine" kings commit incestuous acts that will remain without issue, when intent on promoting the fertility of nature, instead of resorting to ordinary intercourse that will prove fruitful. Such examples may be multiplied indefinitely. They run counter to the implications of sympathetic magic, based on analogy and imitativeness, and are in contradiction with its underlying principle. This is the basic contradiction that has to be overcome before the problem of magic and sorcery can be solved.

All those practices, which are contrary to the magic based on the principle of analogy and which ignore and defy it, may be described as "transgressive magic," because they involve the violation of taboo. Field observation shows that while taboos are usually strictly respected, they nevertheless are sometimes deliberately violated to obtain positive benefits from their transgression. The belief underlying such behavior relates to the taboos concerned, and these have to be analyzed.

Taboos are so many measures destined to protect the individual and the group against dangers of all kinds, real or imaginary, which manifest themselves in various ways, but which, we think, ultimately spring from a common source, the danger inherent in blood (Durkheim 1897: 47ff.; Makarius and Makarius 1961: 50–59). Blood, of course, is not always considered dangerous. It is employed for different purposes, ritually and nonritually. It is spilled in cases of "redemption by blood" as a substitute for uncontrollable loss of blood, when such blood-flow is deemed imminent (Durkheim 1897:49–50).

When, however, blood is not endowed with qualities which neutralize the danger it contains, it is regarded as the most dangerous of all substances (Durkheim 1897:41ff.; Makarius and Makarius 1961:50ff.).[1] Blood connected with women's sexual functions — menstrual blood, blood due to defloration and delivery — arouses particular fear. This fear extends to all fetal matters (placentas, umbilical cords, membranes, etc.),

---

[1]   That blood, while placed under taboo, should sometimes be freely utilized, that while the object of great fear, it should nevertheless sometimes be viewed without any kind of fear, becomes intelligible in the light of Hubert's and Mauss's remarks on the phenomenon of "exclusive attention," or "wilful intent," showing that magical thinking casts a veil over those aspects of a phenomenon which are at cross-purposes with those on which attention is concentrated to obtain a given result (1902–1903:69). When blood is utilized to create bonds of brotherhood, or absorbed to acquire the qualities of its owner, or spilled deliberately in acts of "redemption," its dangerous character is completely thrust aside. Its real nature, however, reasserts itself fully in transgressive magic, of which it is the principal condition. "Redemption by blood," moreover, bears witness to the recognized dangerous nature of blood, as it is ultimately motivated by the desire to avert a flow of blood, at the cost of material losses and physical pain (Makarius 1969:19–20, Note 2).

to the newborn, polluted by lochial blood, to all complications attending delivery — abnormal births, twins, miscarriage, abortions — and, lastly, to cadaverous substances. All these substances are under taboo because of the danger they represent to the group.

The dangerous and dreaded power, which imagination ascribes to blood, becomes reassuring and beneficial when turned against hostile elements and influences, such as enemy forces or physical agents of disease, or against any cause of danger and harm that has to be repelled or destroyed. Various authors have pointed out the magical efficaciousness of the use of blood, as in the case of menstruating women running naked through the fields in order to destroy pests, or of the menstrual cloths fastened around the neck of weak infants in order to protect them against illness (Briffault 1952: II 410; Caillois 1963:38–39, 52ff.).

From this conception of the negative power of blood, which may be summed up in the phrase "blood drives away all evil," one passes by imperceptible gradations to the belief in its positive power: "blood will procure all that is good." However, while the first formula is, as it were, "rational," the second arises from the "overdetermination" of the power of blood, through an extension of its range of action from that of repelling evil to that of fulfilling all wishes and procuring all that is desired. Henceforth, blood will ensure not only security and health — "negative" goods, since they represent the absence of danger and ill health — but also those "positive" goods which are luck, power, riches, prosperity and success, as well as knowledge, wisdom, etc. Seeing that such a development of the concept of blood is abusive — because it implies neglect of the fact that its power owes its beneficent character simply to its aptitude to drive away evil — and does not consist of a conscious process, blood will produce its good effects in a way that will remain mysterious. It will produce them MAGICALLY (Makarius 1969:19–22).

To master such power for magical purposes, it is necessary to violate the taboo on contact with blood. This act of transgression, supposed to unleash the power inherent in blood, will therefore consist in the handling of blood and other forbidden substances in order to make "medicines," amulets, or simply smearing objects with blood. It will also consist in committing incest.

The relation between sorcery and incest is familiar — sometimes the same word applies to both (Beidelman 1963 — even if it has not yet been explained. The explanation is to be found in the fear and prohibition attached to sexual relations with consanguines. The notion of organic interdependence leads to the belief that loss of blood by an individual places all his, or her consanguines in a state of danger. Consequently, loss of blood on the part of women — at defloration, delivery or during menstruation — will constitute a greater danger if they are consanguines, and sexual relations with them will be avoided (Makarius 1969:64 ff.). The incest prohibition is a special case of the more general taboo on blood. To transgress this taboo is tantamount to coming into contact with the most dangerous of all blood, and therefore the most efficacious in magic. For the same reason, when murder, as a deliberate act of transgression, is committed, the victim will be preferentially chosen among one's consanguines.

Magical power emanates from the deliberate breach of a taboo on blood, and owes to it its characteristics. It is "overdetermined" and viewed as possessing an efficaciousness that allows it to procure all that is good, except immortality (Makarius 1969:28–29). This "overdetermination," by adding a beneficent quality to the maleficent character of blood, renders magical power at once maleficent and beneficent, that is, ambivalent. Blood being the most dangerous of all substances, this power will always be associated with danger. Furthermore, since blood is a substance endowed with the active quality of a force, magical power will manifest both the properties of a force and those of a material substance. In short, it will manifest the contradictory properties and qualities of *mana*. There is nothing surprising in this, for the magical power of blood constitutes *mana*.

The magical transgression of taboos is therefore an instrumental act to gain the overdetermined power of blood in order to satisfy certain wants and fulfill certain wishes: victory in war, luck in hunting, fishing or gambling, success in some undertaking, happiness in love, the gift of healing or of bringing rain and, in a more general way, the attainment of wealth, prosperity and all personal endowments.[2]

If the blood taboo, as the fundamental taboo of primitive society — since all other taboos may be viewed as its derivatives — serves the function of upholder and guardian of the social order, transgressive magic must be regarded as subversive and antisocial. It must therefore remain secret, clandestine. Furthermore, since the act of transgression draws its magical force from the danger inherent in blood and the taboo on blood,

---

[2]   The separating line between beneficent, or "white" magic, and maleficent, or "black" magic, which anthropologists have vainly attempted to draw, is in no way determined by the nature of the results to be obtained. For one of the inherent contradictions of transgressive magic is that it is precisely the most innocent and desirable results sought, such as plants overladen with fruit, or hunting nets filled with game etc., that call for the performance of acts, dangerous not only to the individual, but to the group. Whatever the results aimed at, transgressive magic is "black" magic, fearful and sinister.

this taboo must be maintained and violated only exceptionally and individually. Otherwise, if constantly transgressed, and by many, it would lose its force and vanish, and the transgression would become meaningless.

I shall not discuss here such questions as the violation of taboo for the benefit not of the individual but of the group; or the relation between transgressive magic and impurity; or between transgressive and sympathetic magic. Let us note, however, that transgressive magic is rooted in sympathetic magic, and that the relation between the two, though contradictory, is necessary. And, lastly, that whereas sympathetic magic springs from thought processes, transgressive magic is the result of a cultural process.

REFERENCES

BEIDELMAN, O. T.
1963   "Witchcraft and sorcery in Ukaguru," in *Witchcraft and sorcery in East Africa*. Edited by J. Middleton and E. H. Winter, 57–98. London: Routledge and Kegan Paul.
BRIFFAULT, R.
1952   *The mothers*, three volumes (second edition). London: George Allen and Unwin.
CAILLOIS, R.
1963   *L'homme et le sacré* (third edition). Paris: Gallimard.
CRAWFORD, J. R.
1967   *Witchcraft and sorcery in Rhodesia*. London: Oxford University Press, International African Institute.
DURKHEIM, E.
1897   La prohibition de l'inceste et ses origines. *L'Année Sociologique* 1:1–70.
FRAZER, J. G.
1911–1915   *The golden bough*. London: Macmillan.
HUBERT, H., M. MAUSS
1902–1903   Esquisse d'une théorie générale de la magie. *L'Année Sociologique* 7:1–146.
MAKARIUS, L.
1969   Le mythe du *trickster*. *Revue de l'Histoire des Religions* 175:17–46.
MAKARIUS, R., L. MAKARIUS
1961   *L'origine de l'exogamie et du totémisme*. Paris: Gallimard.

A Rjonga Curing Ritual: A Causal and Motivational Analysis

MARTHA B. MORRIS

THEORETICAL BACKGROUND

Until fairly recently, studies of religion were most often concerned with two problems. The first concerned definitions: should religion include such things as magic and sorcery? The second concerned the problem of whether religion, however defined, was most usefully analyzed as functional for the individual or for the society. That is, should the analyses be primarily sociological or psychological? One outcome of this sociological-psychological controversy is an exaggerated concern with what is essentially a false dichotomy. The differences in interpretations reflect, in part, the kinds of studies that were being made in the prewar decades, and, in part, a difficulty with definitions. Almost every study of religion begins with the problem of defining it and of indicating the relevant data. However, the question of how and why religious symbols, beliefs, and rites acquire efficacy continues to be a little-studied one.

Clifford Geertz concerns himself with this problem after writing a rather pessimistic analysis of the current status of anthropological studies of religion. Reviewing the kinds of analyses that have been made showing the complex interrelationships of ritual with politics, kinship, economics, etc., he concludes that "anthropologists are, like theologians, firmly dedicated to proving the indubitable" (1966: 2). He then suggests, as have others, that the source of power of religious symbolism remains obscure:

The notion that religion tunes human actions to an envisaged cosmic order and projects images of cosmic order onto the plane of human experience is hardly

The research on which this paper is based was made possible by a National Institute of Mental Health Research and Training Grant, 1968–1971.

novel. But it is hardly investigated either, so that we have very little idea of how, in empirical terms, this particular miracle is accomplished. We just know that it is done, annually, weekly, daily, for some people almost hourly; and we have an enormous ethnographic literature to demonstrate it (Geertz 1966:2).

The major problem areas in the study of religion, then, are: (1) to define it in such a way that social structure, equilibrium, tension, or any specific acts do not become definitional attributes; (2) to investigate how beliefs are learned and acquire an aura of unassailable truth; and (3) to determine what the motivational bases for religious behavior are.

Spiro (1966: 94) gives a definition of religion that makes very few *a priori* assumptions and thus enlarges the universe of facts which the anthropologist studies:

I would argue that the belief in superhuman beings and in their power to assist or to harm man approaches universal distributions, and this belief...is the core variable which ought to be designated by any definition of religion.

In addressing the problem of how beliefs are learned, how they acquire potency, and why they motivate behavior it is important to remember that the concern is with the persistence of religious beliefs and practices from generation to generation, not with the origins of religion. If we can learn how these beliefs are learned anew by each generation, then we are also equipped to understand how they change, or why they do not change.

There is no adequate integrated theory of religion, and I take a series of ideas, methods, and approaches from Hallowell (1955); Parsons and Shils (1951); Turner (1966); and, especially, Spiro (1953, 1961, 1966) and present them more as a collection of ideas pertinent to the study of religion than as a single theory. The major concepts, from all of these sources, can be summarized as four statements:

1. A social order is a moral order, and the function of the cultural system is to legitimize the social system.

2. Culture, society, and personality are analytically distinct concepts, role being the principle construct which permits analysis of the intersection of the personality and social systems.

3. Role performance must be motivated, and motives (consisting of drives, goal-gaining techniques, and goals) must be learned.

4. Equilibrium is not assumed to be a natural condition of society; to understand behavior it is more fruitful to study events and processes. This necessitates concern with psychological as well as structural and cultural variables.

Hallowell's argument emphasizes that the emergence of a concept of "self," and of the moral order, constitutes a cultural product. Values, concepts, symbols, motives must be learned anew by every child, and these ideas are learned as a part of the process of becoming aware of the self, and they constitute a large part of the child's behavioral environment.

Much behavior, therefore, is held to be meaningfully related to concepts of good and evil, the nature of the universe, society and man, to ideas on ultimate meanings, and the problems of suffering. If the cultural system is defined as a system of values, beliefs, and symbols, it follows that it is to this realm that we must look for an explanation and understanding of behavior. However, the problem is not that simple. Culture, in and of itself, does not satisfactorily explain all behavior. A society is defined as a patterned system of interpersonal relationships which are a product of cultural dicta, environmental exigencies, and personal idiosyncracies. Similarly, a personality is a patterned system of motivation which is also a social and cultural product, as well as an idiosyncratic one. In short, as Parsons and Spiro both put it, in order to understand behavior it is necessary to keep these three levels analytically distinct. None is reducible to another.

Spiro (1961) conceives role to be the central, integrating concept which permits an ordered analysis at all three levels. His greatest contribution in discussing roles lies in his analysis of motivation; he deals primarily with the question of why roles are performed. Social sanctions cannot compel people to conform; they can only motivate them, and he states that we must look to socialization practices to discover which motives are learned, how and why.

Since my analysis of a Rjonga curing ritual follows Spiro, I will very briefly summarize some of the salient points he makes in his article "Religion: problems of definition and explanation" (1966: 85–126). He treats religion as a cultural institution which is instrumental for the satisfaction of needs, and the components of this institution "are acquired by means of the same enculturation processes as the other variables of a cultural heritage are acquired" (1966: 97). A causal analysis of religion makes reference to the antecedent conditions, and a functional analysis refers to the consequent conditions (1966: 100). Therefore, an analysis of religious beliefs and practices addresses itself to the questions "on what grounds are religious propositions believed to be true?" and/or "what is the explanation for the practice of religion?" (1966: 101). Stated another way, the questions to be answered are: why are beliefs held to be true, and what are the motivational bases for the acquisition of taught beliefs? Spiro answers the first question:

Most theorists seem to agree that religious statements are believed to be true because religious actors have had social experiences which, corresponding to these beliefs, provide them with face validity (1966:102).

These social experiences, initially, have reference to the child's interaction with his parents or surrogates, "powerful beings, both benevolent and malevolent, who — by various means which are learned in the socialization process — can sometimes be induced to accede to his [child's] desires" (1966: 103). Following Freud and Kardiner, Spiro states that "the independent, sociological variable may be said to "cause" the dependent, religious variable by means of a set of intervening, psychological variables" (1966: 104). The TRUTH of religious beliefs, then, is acquired by children because of the correspondence between the beliefs and certain experiences they have within the family. The PRACTICE of religion must be explained by reference to learned needs:

Institutional behavior, including religious behavior, consists in the practice of repeated instances of culturally constituted behavior patterns — or customs. Like other behavior patterns they persist as long as they are practiced; and they are practiced because they satisfy, or are believed to satisfy, their instigating needs. If this is so, an explanation for the practice of religion must be sought in the set of needs whose expected satisfaction motivates religious belief and the performance of religious ritual (1966:106–107).

The question then becomes: what desires or needs are satisfied by religion? As Spiro states, this is a question which must be answered by empirical research, although he postulates three general sets of desires: cognitive, which deal with problems of meaning and suffering; substantive, which have to do with the specific goals desired, such as rain or health; and expressive, which have to do with painful drives and motives which seek reduction (1966: 109). With reference to the substantive needs, he states:

Everywhere man's mammalian desires...must be satisfied, and IN THE ABSENCE OF COMPETING TECHNOLOGIES WHICH CONFER REASONABLE CONFIDENCE, religious techniques are believed to satisfy these desires. Almost everywhere, moreover, the human awareness of the cessation of existence and/or of the unsatisfactory character of existence, produces anxiety concerning the persistence of existence ...AND IN THE ABSENCE OF COMPETING GOALS FOR THE REDUCTION OF ANXIETY, belief that one is successfully pursuing these religious goals...serves to reduce this anxiety (1966:112).

The expressive needs have to do with culturally forbidden motives such as aggression, dependency, sexuality. Spiro suggests that dependency needs "inevitably seek satisfaction in religious behavior, in that the religious actor depends on superhuman beings for the gratification of his desires" (1966: 115). Also,

...since all religions of which I am aware postulate the existence of malevolent, as well as benevolent, superhuman beings, repressed hostility motives can be displaced and/or projected in beliefs in, and rituals designed for protection against, these malevolent beings (1966:116).

It is postulated that religious drives are learned by children early in life so that "the family...once again is the nuclear structural variable" (1966: 116). Finally:

Indeed, because these motivational variables are acquired within specified structural contexts...differences in the kinds and/or intensity of desires which constitute the motivational basis for religious behavior should vary systematically with differences in family systems (including socialization systems), AS WELL AS WITH THE ALTERNATIVE, NON-RELIGIOUS MEANS FOR THEIR SATISFACTION. ...In short, a motivational explanation of religious behavior can, in principle, explain variability and, hence, can be tested empirically (1966:116–117).

To summarize, the persistence of religious beliefs and practices should be explained in terms of the causes of religious beliefs (expectation of satisfying desires), and the functions of religious behavior (satisfaction of desires). In this instance, religion becomes the dependent variable and motivation the independent one (1966: 117–118).

Applying this model to the Rjonga of Mozambique, specifically to the *xipoko* or *mulhiwa* curing ritual, we must first examine some of the Rjonga beliefs about illness and its causes. We then examine some psychological characteristics common to the Rjonga in the context of some structural variables of their society. This makes it possible to identify some common goals, the sources of anxiety, and, finally, some of their religious needs. Space does not permit an analysis of how the truth of the belief system is learned by children; rather, the analysis focuses on the motivational bases for participating in certain rituals.

The Rjonga are an agricultural, Bantu-speaking people in southern Mozambique. They are currently undergoing change at a fairly rapid rate, but ideally they have patrilineal lineages and clans, and practice patrilocal residence and village exogamy. The tribe, better known in the literature by the misnomer "Thonga," is divided into eleven politically autonomous kingdoms, but constitutes a single cultural entity.

SOME RJONGA BELIEFS AND VALUES

Rjonga beliefs relating to the supernatural are many and complex, and they are related to beliefs about the nature of man, in general. These latter beliefs include the concepts for *moya* [soul], *hika* [breath], and *ntchuti* [shadow], and how these combine to form the personality. These ideas will become relevant in discussing some of the beliefs, attitudes and values which relate to interpersonal relations; therefore, I will take them up briefly at the end of this section. They are necessary to an understanding of some common psychological characteristics of the Rjonga.

The Rjonga may well be characterized as disease ridden; infant mortality, as shown by the census data, is high, but there are many diseases which attack young adults and mature adults as well. Coughs, swollen stomachs, diarrhea, and vomiting are the symptoms most often given as resulting in infants' deaths; in addition, there are the not inconsiderable dangers from scorpions, tarantulas, cobras, mambas, vipers, and a particularly venomous spider, the wolf-spider. I can attest from personal experience the obtrusive presence and quantity of all of these uncharming creatures, and well remember the horror of a mother returning from church one night to find a cobra curled up asleep between her two young children on their sleeping mat. For young children and young adults, there are the dangers of hepatitis, tuberculosis, leprosy, tick fever, bilharzia, various forms of malaria, and a particularly virulent and fatal disease acquired from diseased peanuts, one of the staple foods of the Rjonga. This latter disease especially affects young adults and, according to information given me by doctors in the capital city, is the biggest killer of young adults. Tuberculosis is apparently most frequently contracted in the mines where most Rjonga men spend at least one tour of eighteen months, often many more. In addition to these, and other illnesses, syphilis (*buba*) and gonorrhea (*xikandjameti*) are endemic and are believed to be one of the greatest causes of barrenness in women, although many native doctors (*nanga;* plural, *tinanga*) specialize in treating these diseases. The entire body of diseases which the Rjonga believe to be caused by illicit sexual relations is called *tingati*, literally "bloods". These include a disease called *mulhwa;* I have no specific explanation for this other than it is a sexually linked illness, but I assume it to be related to *mulhiwa*, the "evil spirit" believed to cause many illnesses. This word is not in Nogueira's excellent Rjonga-Portuguese dictionary (1960) but the prefix *mu-* designates a personal agent, and I believe the root to come from the verb *ku-lwa* meaning "to fight". The *-iwa* suffix denotes the passive voice, so that the entire word might be translated as "he who was fought over", and this translation makes sense in view of native beliefs about some of the primary agents of illness.

Before pursuing the meanings of *mulhiwa* as a disease agent, it is necessary to explain the different beliefs about the causes of disease. This entails a very brief description of the Rjonga categories of supernatural agents. It also entails understanding that the Rjonga believe disease to be the sanction for almost all infringements of social, especially sexual, norms, and the punishment may fall on a relative, including newborn babies, rather than the transgressor.

There are three major categories of gods: *xikwembu;* plural, *bsikwembu,* the "ancestor gods" proper; the Nguni gods; and the Ndjao gods. The ancestors come back (*ku-pfuka:* literally "wake up") only because they want a "service"; that is, they feel neglected, or they feel the members of the household are not behaving properly. The Rjonga say this is not true *mupfukwa* [one who wakes up], because the ancestor, "wants to live in his own house. He sends illness, only; not death. Our things aren't heavy, they are light... that person wants to arrange well the things of his household." On the other hand:

The spirits of other races [the Nguni and Ndjao] are very fierce; they take medicines from birth so if they are killed, they photograph the face of the killer and come back to possess all the relatives of those who killed them. ...Their children have to eat of the *mupfukwa* tree, and you cut them in their flesh and rub in the medicine of the tree — then if they are killed, they come back for revenge and the killer swells up and rots, like a potato which has been boiled to the point of disintegration. Only the Ndjao and those of Gaza [the Nguni] have that tree. When it is morning, the leaves fall from that tree. When the sun sets you find it with leaves, the same tree.... When one of these is killed, the spirit comes back and kills in your house, and you have to pay what your fathers and grandfathers killed (text from an interview with the elders).

There are two kinds of killing gods, then: the Nguni and the Ndjao. The Rjonga have been defeated in battle by both of these tribes in the past. These are the only gods that can possess a Rjonga, forcing him or her to become an apprentice in an established diviner's household until he or she becomes a diviner; failing to do this can result in the death of the one possessed.

When there are many deaths or illnesses at home, you go to the diviner. He tells you that your fathers killed such a person who wants a house (*ndumba*). The diviner will come nail down the spirit so he can't ruin the village. ...You can't build a house without being told to. Then you get a boy and a girl, and the spirit chooses one of them to work with, to cure the people, and the one chosen gets sent to play music for the gods (*ku-tchayeliwa*).

The *ndumba* is a house built for the spirit who demands it, and it always faces the west, unlike the people's houses which face east. The west or "part of the setting sun" is the side of the dead; corpses are laid out with their heads pointing westward and are carried out of the *muti* [household] through the western path, a path which only members of the household may use. This area of the household is fraught with mystical dangers and associations which I cannot elaborate on here. The diviners hold their rituals inside these *tindumba*, and they are built only when a spirit has returned and demanded "a place to work."

Before continuing with this exegesis, I should point out the ambivalence and contradictions in these beliefs. An *ndumba* is also built for the ancestor gods by the head of a household because one of the ancestors demanded it. Here the head of the household will *ku-pahla* [pray] and make offerings to the ancestor on behalf of the lineage. There need be no consulting of bones or spirits or any form of divination associated with the rites of an ancestor's *ndumba*. A *nanga* [doctor] who has learned how to cure certain diseases (most *tinanga* specialize in one or two diseases) will pray to his fathers in the *ndumba* before going out to collect the roots for medicines, or before treating a patient. This is so because most men become *nangas* by virtue of having been taught the healing art by a close relative who was also a healer.

When these doctors are consulted, the patient must be careful to describe his symptoms exactly so as "not to confuse the doctor." These practitioners are viewed by the Rjonga exactly as we view our own doctors, with the exception of the hereditary element. Not all sons of a *nanga* become *nangas*, however, and the doctor may choose anyone of his extended family, including his sister's son who is not of his lineage, to teach his art to. It is to the *tinanga* that new mothers go to get the *milombyana* [medicine] without which they believe their infants could not survive, and which is administered until the age of weaning. The *tinanga* are, in the Rjonga view, empirical healers and are resorted to for illnesses like the venereal diseases, and other diseases which do not seem to linger, and which respond to treatment. The *ndumba* in this case is associated with the healing arts of the fathers whose skills have been taught to the sons; or, in other cases, simply with an ancestor who wants to be remembered and visits a slight illness on his family to call attention to his desire. There is no possession involved in either case.

The Nguni and Ndjao gods, on the other hand, possess a person who will die if he or she does not learn to become a diviner. These spirits bring severe illness and death to a household, and these illnesses cannot be treated by a *nanga*. After going through the apprenticeship and passing the tests, the person possessed (or an acceptable surrogate) builds an *ndumba* in his household where the divining rites take place. Thus the *ndumba* is associated with the ancestors, with "empirical" healing practices, with possession and divination, and with killing spirits. The *ndumba* is both a place to seek relief, and a place of fear. Furthermore, note that the Nguni and Ndjao "come back" seeking revenge, and the person possessed is "paying what his fathers and grandfathers killed" — literally, the sins of fathers are visited on the children.

There are two categories of diviners: the *nyamusoro*, most often women who deal with Ndjao spirits by a form of divining called *ku-femba* [to smell out]; and the *mungoma*, most often men, who consult the bones to "find hidden things," and with whom the Nguni spirits are associated. (I may note here that the color symbolizing the Rjonga ancestor gods is white; that for the Ndjao, red; and of the Nguni, black.) In practice, one person (male or female) has both kinds of spirits: Nguni and Ndjao, the former spirit, male, the latter, female. Formerly, the *nyamusoro* never treated illnesses, simply divined (smelled out) their cause; today, they can also heal. The *mungoma* [one of the drum] never practices the "smelling out," but works by consulting the bones and/or his spirit; he was and is a healer, as well, although sometimes he can send a patient to a particular *nanga*. His skill, *par excellence*, however, is still "finding hidden things." The *nanga*, in contrast, never "smells out," nor finds hidden things, nor consults the bones — he only uses medicines.

Although the possessing spirits are believed to be seekers of revenge for having been killed, they always establish some sort of kinship link with their host — often a difficult and tortuous task as they belong to foreign tribes. Once established in a household, however, they are inherited by other members of the family. When a spirit host dies, the spirit will seek out another member of the same family, usually a person of the same name as the deceased host. Because children are most often named after their paternal grandparents and father's sisters and father's brothers, then their maternal grandparents and mother's sisters and brothers, finding a new host of the same name is not difficult. One woman was pursued by the spirit of her recently deceased father's sister, whose name she had, but because she belonged to the Methodist church she was protected ("he [the spirit] found her praying there"), and the spirit went off and possessed her brother's daughter, whom she had named after herself. These foreign spirits, then, are believed to travel; that is, they visit illness on the daughters of a family who are living patrilocally with their husbands. A wife never acquires her husband's spirits, nor can she pray to or be prayed for to the husband's family ancestor gods. She always "remains in the hands" of her own family's ancestor gods and other spirits. If her family has a foreign spirit, that spirit can come and "ruin" her husband's household rather than wreak ruin on the host's family household. The word for another family's spirit that travels bringing illness and death is *mulhiwa* or *mukwasana*. That is, one family's god is another family's evil spirit. The host family will refer to this entity as *xikwembu* [god], whereas the visited family will call the same entity a *mulhiwa* or [evil spirit].

It is important to make clear that illnesses and death can be caused either by a spirit who is initially seeking a host and will cause a member of the distressed family to become a diviner; OR they are caused by a wife's visiting spirit in her husband's household. The latter explanation is the one most often given for a woman's barrenness, spontaneous abortions, stillbirths, and high infant mortality within one household. Such events are almost always attributed to a woman's having a *mulhiwa* or *xipoko* "put on her" by someone in her natal home. The belief is that when these calamities befall a household, the *mulhiwa* spirit was deliberately sent by a member of the wife's family, or was deliberately brought by the woman herself.

There are several other kinds of spirits which can also cause illness: the *matlharji* spirits, also called *mukwasana;* the *nhoba* spirits; and *xibiti* spirits; they are all closely associated with possession and/or witchcraft and sorcery.

In addition to the beliefs about the various kinds of gods, the Rjonga also believe in (and distinguish between) witchcraft and sorcery. A *noyi* [witch] (*buloyi* [witchcraft]) does not use medicines; the Rjonga believe that witchcraft is inherited from either parents or grandparents, and can also be taught by husbands to wives, and vice versa. Witchcraft involves eating people because Rjonga witches, like the Nyakyusa, lust after meat. Sorcery does not always cause illness; it is associated with the use of medicines to steal, frighten, or to kill out of envy. The powers of sorcery are called *usalamusi* and the medicines *masalamusi:*

To do sorcery, you have to cut yourself with medicines. When a person has *masalamusi* it is medicine. When he is threatened by so-and-so who is used to eating meat all the time, and he goes to hunt rabbits and comes to make a meat sauce for breakfast, and I don't find anything — I have to kill him, he dies, so that people of my family can live suffering like me, because I don't know how to kill the rabbits.

These medicines can be bought. The most potent ones, apparently, are available in South Africa, acquired by the men when they go to work in the mines. There are also medicines for stealing what another person has; pickpockets, for example, are known, and it is believed they have a medicine which enables them to practice this particular skill. This is sorcery. Killing by putting a *milumbu* in someone's beer is also sorcery. In general, although many of the effects and practices of witchcraft and sorcery are similar, the distinction the Rjonga make is between the use of medicines and the inherited and inherent power of witches.

The case of witchcraft comes from envy. When people dislike you, you can be a witch. People are called witches because they have lots of food, or livestock.

The people say a chief has to be a witch. But only the old can be witches.

If the children die young, just when I have begun to say I have found riches, luck, pleasure [in having healthy children], then I think of witchcraft. The wife may have an *ngole* in her body which bites the child at the moment of birth. He may appear healthy, but he won't live long. This is called *wumba*. The *nanga* cuts it out. Only women know the secret; this work is of the women. That is a very big secret; it is very profound.

These texts demonstrate that there are two distinct beliefs about witchcraft. The first text illustrates that accusations ("cases") of witchcraft are recognized to be related to envy, particularly in matters relating to food and conspicuous success in the raising of crops and/or livestock in a harsh and barren environment. Only adults, who have had the time and acquired the experience to be successful, are accused of witchcraft for these motives. The second set of beliefs deals with the witchcraft which women bring into their husbands' households, and this is related to the disease *wumba* caused by the *ngole*, a rat which burrows underground and "bites" the infant at the moment of birth. Having an *ngole* is inherent in being a witch; it is not volitional and may have been inherited by the woman from other witches in her family.

The Rjonga also believe that most witches are women, and the effects of their witchcraft are always to cause the death of children in the household. Note then that diseases and deaths attacking infants and young children are most often attributed either to inherent witchcraft ("the witch has a spoiling in her") or to the deliberate imposition of *mulhiwa* by the woman herself, or by members of her natal household, which is related to the possessing gods. *Wumba* (associated with witchcraft) and *mulhiwa* (associated with possessing spirits) both relate to the woman's family and are the two causes most frequently cited for the illness and death of infants and young children. They are also the most frequent causes of divorce, at worst, or of seeking a diviner and the curing ritual at the woman's home, at best. In either case, the couple must return to the wife's family to have the ritual performed there; only her father or father's brother (also called "father"), or own brothers can have the ritual performed which will cure her.

I have at least a dozen cases, collected over two years, relating to women going home to their parents to be cured of either *wumba* or of having *mulhiwa*, some of these resulting in divorce. Accusations of witchcraft, within a family, are most often leveled between husbands and wives, co-wives, father's sisters and brother's sons, and fathers and sons. One woman's husband's sister screamed at her sister-in-law:

Do you think thus as you killed your children, now you want to kill my children? The thing with which you kill your children, you went to borrow from your sister. Because every year she usually cries, saying that her children die when she knows where they are going. She who doesn't want children, and who when she gives birth eats them.... Leave her, she who is a witch, to kill her daughters.

Very young children know about witches and their lust for meat, although they do not seem to have learned the more complex beliefs relating to sorcery and the possessing spirits. A very young boy, approximately five or six years old, fell asleep in a room with his fellows and dreamed that his mother came for him and they went to visit a household where they were given meat to eat. Upon awakening, he told his companions about the dream, but was convinced that he had really gone. The children said he was a witch, but it was not strange since his mother was also a witch, as they all knew. They said they knew how the witches say: "Kill him, kill him. We are very hungry." Another boy, about ten years old, told me that children learn about witchcraft from hearing stories from their playmates at night, in the bush.

The children play together in the bush at night. The young children learn from the older ones, who learn from their parents. Witches only eat the shadow (*ntchuti*) of a person.... Owls are witches.... I know a boy who is a witch because his grandfather is, but only the grandparents can eat big meat [that is, only old people can "eat" adults]. A person leaves his shadow at home when he goes out as a witch. He takes the shape of an owl, or a snake. He can also ride the back of the hippopotamus.

These beliefs, and many others not discussed, are obviously very complex and could entail a very lengthy analysis for which I have no space at this time. It is important here to note the ambivalent attitudes concerned with these beliefs. The curing performed by the *tinanga* involves the use of medicines, so does that performed by the other two kinds of specialists, the *nyamusoro* and the *mungoma*, and thus the people say "curing is also sorcery." Powerful diviners are feared because they might use their arts "to kill the village." It is believed that a person can be rid of a possessing spirit (of the *matlharji*, *nhoba*, or *xibiti* types) by the diviner transferring the spirit to an object such as a note of money, or a cloth, which is then dropped on a path. A person seeing it and picking it up will then be possessed by the spirit. This is called making a *milumbu*. This is a difficult concept to translate. The word comes from *ku-lumbela* which literally means "to invent, lie, defame for or against," and is the verb used to refer to practicing sorcery. A sorcerer wanting to terrify an enemy can turn a matchstick into a snake — that is, he makes the matchstick into a *milumbu* which only the intended victim will then perceive as a snake on the path. The word *milumbu* is also used to refer to the medicine a sorcerer puts in his intended victim's beer in order to make him very ill or to kill him. The *milumbu* concept is intimately associated with the *xipoko* concept:

Milumbu and *xipoko* are the same thing because they begin in the same way. You can't make a *milumbu* without having a *xipoko*. If you don't have *xipoko*, you can't make *milumbu*.

Before examining the *xipoko* concept in more detail, I call attention to the word for the medicines given to infants by their *tinanga* — "*milombyana.*" The word is obviously related to *milumbu* with the suffix -*yana* added which denotes the diminutive form of a word. Given the intimate association of *milumbu* with sorcery, the ambivalence towards the *tinanga* [healers] and their medicines is apparent. If *milumbu* can be translated as "the object which induces fear and causes harm," then the term for the medicinal course given infants in the first two years of life translates as "a little object which induces fear or causes harm," although the explicit meaning of the term is quite the contrary. Seeking a *nanga* to treat infants with *milombyana* in the first two years is as common a practice among the Rjonga (even Christians) as is ours of acquiring a pediatrician for our babies' care.

The *xipoko* concept is a fascinating one. In his dictionary, Nogueira says the following about the term:

...a certain exorcism rite. — Junod, *Moeurs*, II, 441, says: "Exorcism by beating the drum is the classic method of removing spirits. In the last few years, since 1910, another method called *ku-femba*, was invented and, a strange thing, it is related to a new word taken from European animism, the word *xipoko* which became current in Thonga terminology. *Xi-poko* comes from the Boer *spook* which means a soul from another world *revenant*. According to native belief, the witches have the power of dominating the souls of the other world as slaves and make them work during the night in their own fields, (1960:580, my translation from Portuguese).

The assimilation of the word "spook" to the *xi/psi* class in Xi-Rjonga is informative. Again to cite Junod in Nogueira's dictionary:

Junod, *Gramm.*, #99, says: "It's the true neutral class. It also contains some nouns referring to HUMAN BEINGS, but only of people whose personality is reduced to its minimum... Ex.: *xi-lema*, a cripple;...*xi-rjombe*, an orphan... (1960:544).

Of particular interest is the association of the *xipoko* with the *ku-femba* ritual "smelling out" which, in turn, is associated with the rites performed by the *nyamusoro* who works with a spirit, it will be recalled. The term itself seems to refer to a person "of reduced personality"; the word is used by the Rjonga in such a way that it obviously refers to a person or being. The diviner refers to his spirit as a *xikwembu* [god], but it is believed that this spirit can be sent as a *xipoko* to cause harm in other households. Thus, *mulhiwa* and *xipoko* are virtually the same thing. It is believed that if a person talks to a *xipoko* as a lay person he will go crazy or die. Only the diviners can handle these beings, and a diviner should never talk to another's *xipoko:*

The law of the gods is if you catch someone's spirit or *xipoko*, you shouldn't ask anything. Just send him away. The god is caught and sent away. ...The *mulhiwa* may not talk; *xipoko* isn't permitted to talk, because it will provoke cases. (Text from a court trial when one diviner was counseling another).

A woman who cannot conceive, or whose children are stillborn, or who aborts often, is believed to have a *xipoko* or *mulhiwa* for which she must be treated in her parents' home. A very common expression by women and members of their natal families is: "We don't have *mulhiwa*, we have children."

To conclude this section on beliefs, very briefly, it is necessary to deal with the Rjonga concept of personality, and the values relating to a good person. Every individual has a *moya* [soul], *hika* [breath], and a *ntchuti* [shadow]. The shadow is the personality of an individual: "If you don't have a good shadow, people won't notice you and will ask who you are when you come to sit down in a group of people. Then they will laugh and say 'oh, give him a place to sit'. " A person can develop his shadow through his own behavior:

The shadow of a person is to be a good person. To like everyone. He will have a good shadow so that all the people will like him. The little ones and the big ones. Because he gives himself to the people and doesn't judge himself to be an adult. They won't speak ill of you. Even if you are a king, they will speak good things of you.

However, a person who feels he is unnoticed or deprecated can buy a shadow. "Then people will respect you. You will have the medicine so that they will respect you in a bad way. They will say you are a lion." The word for "fear" and for "respect" is the same; a person who earns a good reputation is "respected," the one who buys medicine to gain a reputation is "feared" — that is, respected in a bad way. When you want to compliment someone you say that the person "has a shadow."

Hika is breath and you cannot have *hika* without having *moya* [soul]. However, if you do not have a good *hika* you cannot have good thoughts. The concept of soul (*moya* also means 'wind') is closely related in that you can have a good or bad soul. If you have an ugly *moya* "you don't think good things. If it is good, you won't deprecate people younger than you. If it is an adult person, you will find a good life because you want a good *moya*." Finally:

Then a good *moya*, a good *hika*, the being of a person and the *ntchuti* of a person — all these things is when a person takes himself close to other people.... These are brothers [the concepts]; the difference is of their actions, but they are brothers. The person spoils his *moya*, *hika*, *ntchuti* by going to a *nanga*. His personality is spoiled.

I should note here that it is the *moya* [soul] that returns as a spirit or god.

The most important thing to note about these concepts relating to personality is the great concern with respect from others, and the fact that the Rjonga believe an individual is responsible for his thoughts and behavior, and that he can control these. A person acquires respect through his own good actions which involve "coming close to other people," and is feared in a bad way if he fails to earn his reputation and must buy it from the doctors. The value of being a good person by "coming close to others" is closely associated with the attitude of "not deprecating those younger than you" — that is, people who have not yet earned a reputation, who are not yet adults. The relationship between thoughts and actions is recognized in these three concepts; of paramount interest is another Rjonga belief which states that you can never know what a person is thinking or intending. It is forbidden to try to infer a person's thoughts or motives from his behavior; a person attempting to do so in court, in order to excuse his own behavior, will be shouted down by the others present, and be fined if he persists.

Finally, it is necessary to know that the Rjonga believe a person "becomes a person" or "is an adult" only when he or she has had several children and has managed to raise them successfully. That this is true becomes abundantly clear from many different kinds of data I collected, but most notably in the responses to the Stewart Emotional Response Test.[1] Both men and women recalled the day they married and the day their first child was born as among their happiest: "Because now I, too, am a person" or "an adult." I received this response without fail from all of the respondents to whom I administered this projective test. I will elaborate on this further when discussing some of the most common Rjonga goals.

It should be quite clear at this point that at the level of cultural beliefs there is an intimate association of the following: diseases; ancestor gods who heal; foreign possessing gods who kill as well as cure; the three major

---

[1] In administering this projective test I asked the informant to tell me the three times in his life when he was most happy, why and what happened; the three times in his life when he was saddest, why and what happened; and the three times in his life when he was the angriest, why and what happened.

kinds of specialists; witchcraft and sorcery; the role of women in witch-craft and children's diseases; concern with a reputation and the associa-tion of having children with being "a person" or "an adult."

SOME PSYCHOLOGICAL CHARACTERISTICS

The data on which this analysis is based are of five kinds: (1) the responses to the Stewart Emotional Response Test (SERT) administered to twenty men and five women (women showed considerable resistence to respond-ing); (2) five extensive life histories, including a child's; (3) transcripts of trials which often run well over fifty typewritten pages, and are one of the richest sources of data; (4) an extensive interview of six men in the village who were either elders or noted doctors and from whose interviews I accumulated a one-hundred-page transcript on witchcraft and sorcery (already cited extensively in this paper), as well as on beliefs and customs relating to kinship and marriage, the roles of men and women; and (5) long interviews and informal conversations with the Rjonga over two years. I have not submitted the projective tests for a "blind analysis" as yet, but think the characteristics to be discussed are fairly obvious. These will be seen to be important in understanding motives for participating in religious rites, especially the curing rituals.

The three characteristics are dependence, hostility, and concern with prestige.

Dependence

The Rjonga live in a very harsh environment in which they are subsistence farmers. The yield from their fields has steadily decreased over the years because they do not practice any system of crop rotation, fallowing, or fertilization. The concern with food is constant, and the fear of starvation real and everpresent. Rjonga farmers can no longer cultivate new fields in areas of uncleared bush as freely as they once did because they are hemmed in by other villages and by Portuguese or other foreign farmers. Concern with food and the symbolism connected with eating indicates the great concern the Rjonga have with eating. Children are still fed the scraps left by adults, and it used to be that the adults would eat holding their bowls high in the air so that children could not reach them. When the adult males were well fed they would give the bowls with the scraps to the women and children.

In addition to concerns over food and health, the Rjonga have a new concern; acquiring sufficient cash to pay the annual tax to the Portuguese, and to *lobolo* a wife.

Ideally a man is totally dependent on his father or father's brothers, or his own older brothers, for the necessities of life, including cash. The ideal is an extended family household: father and father's brothers with wives and children; brothers with their wives and children. The head of this minimal lineage controls all of the resources: crops, livestock, and cash, and is supposed to share them as needed by the members of his household. *Lobolo* money is supposed to be collected for a young man by his father, father's brothers, and own brothers, and this cash is shared according to seniority, older brothers marrying before younger ones. Thus, the junior members of a household are dependent on the goodwill of the seniors to meet their needs. The Rjonga resemble the Nyoro in their concepts of superordination and subordination; everyone has a senior to whom he owes respect and must defer, as well as a junior for whom he is responsible. The head of the household is the absolute authority and, before the advent of the Portuguese, had the power of life and death over the members.

Concern over being properly cared for is expressed in various ways. Rjonga can be heard to lament the death of a father or older brother in terms of: "Who will care for me now?" or "To whom can I talk when I am in trouble?" One man, responding to the SERT, said:

The first time I was very sad was when my father died. And since my father liked me a lot, I missed him very much knowing I would never see him again. And I also thought I wouldn't be respected by anyone, knowing we wouldn't have a place to complain about whatever lack we might feel at home, physical or spiritual, and it was a loss of advice, of being supported, etc.

This example could be multiplied by numerous others drawn from the projective tests, as well as from trial transcripts wherein brothers or fathers and sons are counseled by the court on proper behavior. The recurrent theme was, "If you quarrel at home, where will you turn in need?" The ethic of the corporate lineage is still quite strong among the Rjonga, despite the breakdown of the large, extended family households. Fathers, fathers' brothers, and own brothers should help in time of need, be that at a court trial, collecting *lobolo*, harvesting a field, building a corral, etc. As will be seen, uncertainty and anxiety about whether that help will be forthcoming accounts for much of the hostility the Rjonga also feel.

Another form of dependence is spiritual in that only the head of the household and/or lineage can pray to the ancestors on behalf of the junior members. If a young man's children become ill, he must go to his own father or the head of his minimal lineage to have the necessary rituals performed. Women are always dependent on their own fathers or brothers for necessary prayers or rituals; they can never be cared for by their husband's ancestor gods. In general, women are totally dependent on either their husbands (their "owners") or their fathers and brothers because they have virtually no legal rights. A woman may not visit her own family without her husband's permission; she may engage in no business transactions on her own; and she is long considered a "stranger" in her husband's household, where she must act as a servant for the members of his family. She has no authority in the raising of her children.

That the Rjonga have fears about unmet dependency needs is amply attested by their verbal concern over who will care for them. They constantly seek the advice of others; and numerous court cases arise because their dependency needs have not, in fact, been met — that is, the obligations of seniors to juniors have been ignored. There is a paradox in that the structure of Rjonga society enforces dependence of juniors on their seniors. Their values, however, contradict this by holding that men should work to better themselves and to earn a name, and they should not rely on fathers and brothers to help them. Considerable resentment over demands made on one by others is often expressed.

Attempts to insure that help will be available when needed include being helpful to others, and complying with the obligations of juniors toward seniors. A good person is he "who takes himself close to other people and helps everyone." A very common method of attempting to gain security for the future, as well as a good reputation, is role reversal. I often observed, and have several cases relating to, younger members of a family taking on the responsibilities and obligations of senior members. That at least one of the goals of this behavior is to insure help for the junior when he needs it is demonstrated by the bitterness of the juniors who fail to receive that help from those seniors whose responsibilities they had assumed. This, of course, reinforces fears of unmet dependency needs and leads to hostility. Also productive of fears about unmet dependency needs and consequent hostility, is the seniors' resentment of sons' and younger brothers' dependence, as already suggested. "Why doesn't the son of a father work to support himself?" summarizes this attitude. Resentment over having to support others compounds feelings of anger and helplessness at not being supported oneself. This, too, was a near universal response to the projective test.

Hostility

There is a built-in "structural strain" among the Rjonga which accounts, in part, for the hostility they feel towards those who are supposed to care for them. Although sons of a father are supposed to inherit the father's fields, livestock, and cash, it is the elder surviving father's brother who acquires authority and control over the resources. If a man's sons are still fairly young when he dies, they will be raised by his brothers. When the sons grow up and try to claim their inheritance in order to *lobolo* a wife, for example, they are often told by their father's brother or own older brother that the inheritance was "eaten" in raising them. This, understandably, leads to considerable anger and bitterness and the splitting up of an extended household.

Today, these young men have resources in that they go work in the mines in South Africa and acquire enough cash to enable them to move out of the lineage household and set up their own. They have enough money to *lobolo* a wife without being dependent on the goodwill and charity of their seniors. Even though younger men may feel justified in moving out, there is obviously considerable ambivalence involved, because they are still dependent on their senior kin for help in such matters as quarrels with nonkin, prayers and/or ancestor, rituals, and any other unexpected matters (the Rjonga express much concern over "the unexpected"). Furthermore, a man who has left his lineage homestead has not complied with the expectations of a good person who "takes himself close to others and helps everyone" so that this behavior, in turn, reinforces fears about unmet dependency needs.

There does not seem to be so much concern with suppressing the expression of hostility, as with containing it within the household so that other villagers will not be aware of it. There are several prohibitions related to this: one forbids meddling in others' family affairs; and another enjoins women not to spoil their husbands' reputations by gossiping about them. Sinners must never be directly confronted with their sins except by the aggrieved party who should face the person who has injured him and ask, "Why have you done this to me?" The affair should be settled then by the parties involved, and failing that, by the respective heads of households. Nonexpression of grievances (that is, avoidance) seems to be the most common method of handling hostility, but it not infrequently erupts in fights when men drink together.

There are two other times when expression of anger seems to be institutionalized. One is in court trials, and the Rjonga are extraordinarily litigious. There always comes a point near the end of a trial when everyone yells at everyone else, and there is general pandemonium. The chief does not interfere in this immediately; he allows the expression of anger for at least a few minutes — an unusual circumstance given the rules governing behavior in court. Concomitantly, however, there is strong emphasis on a case "ending the affair." After a trial, when the participants have eaten and drunk together, "The case should die," and if a grudge is still expressed, the person is severely reprimanded. There seems to be a close connection between values relating to the expression of hostility, cases "dying," and the Rjonga belief that no man can infer another's thoughts from his behavior. This could be interpreted as an institutionalized mechanism for ignoring or not recognizing hostility. Imputations of hostility to another are forbidden.

Finally, hostility and anger are supposed to be expressed at all rituals to the ancestors or any other supernatural being. At one ritual gathering of a lineage to pray to a recently deceased member, one of the living expressed his anger at not receiving a shirt from a brother whom he had helped a lot and who had given a shirt to another member of the family. The lineage elder said, "Yah. That is right; get it all out now so that we may live in peace."

Prestige

Concern over prestige or a good reputation is closely linked to dependency and hostility, and evidence about this characteristic has already been given. Sadness over the death of seniors because the junior would no longer be "respected" is frequently expressed. A man's concern with his status and reputation is abundantly clear in the consistent responses to the SERT which indicate that by being married and having children he (or she) is now "a person." Brothers explaining why their younger brothers left the lineage household to build their own would say, "He, too, wanted to be an adult, to give orders." One of the most frequently expressed concerns to me, as an anthropologist, by various Rjonga was: "What will the Americans think of us when you go home and tell them about the Rjonga?"

Having a good shadow, or reputation, as has been discussed, is dependent on a man's behavior — on his taking himself close to others, helping everyone, not deprecating those younger than he. Fears about unmet dependency needs which can lead to hostile behavior or behavior which, at least, does not comply with the norms of a good person, compound the fear over not being respected. This is especially true because respect is most often accorded a man who has, as head of a large household, demonstrated that he has virtue, wisdom, and fairness. The large household, it will be remembered, can be acquired in two ways: first, by having many children, and, second, by being able to keep one's own brothers and their children. It takes all the characteristics of a good person to be able to keep all these various members happy. Notably, it also takes the cooperation of the wives to build a man's reputation by making guests feel welcome and always being ready to provide them with good food and drink. "A man builds a *muti* in order to receive guests," and the visitor confers honor on the household visited.

A man's reputation is dependent on his wives in two other, very important ways: she must provide him with healthy children, and she must never discuss her grievances or unhappiness outside the household. "Gossip kills the *muti*," the Rjonga say, and women are believed to be the prime gossipers and capable of ruining their husbands by discussing their faults. In addition, fathers remain forever responsible for their daughters' behavior and their reputation is, to that extent, dependent on the daughters being good wives and mothers in their husbands' households. Several times I have heard grown women, as well as young ones, being told, "Be quiet, if you are the daughter of a well-bred person."

These characteristics, common to the Rjonga, highlight some important, common goals as well.

SOME RELIGIOUS NEEDS

Accepting the definition that a motive consists of a drive, means for achieving a goal, and the goal itself, and that a "need" refers to a drive and its goal (Spiro 1961), it is possible to consider some of the Rjonga's religious needs. First, however, I will address myself to some of the most important goals of a Rjonga.

The previous discussion indicates that security and respect are two very important goals for the Rjonga. Security involves food and health, and respect is closely associated with having good wives and many healthy children; that these two goals are related is clear, but they are not identical. There are limited means for attaining these goals among the Rjonga, and the number of roles available to an individual for gaining the goals is limited as well. Especially in regard to the goals of health and respect, the corresponding drives can best, and sometimes only, be expressed by resorting to rituals, notably the curing rituals. Anxiety over food, health, and prestige is learned early, and some of the alternative means for reducing this drive have already been touched on. It is in the area of health that a man is most helpless, given the incredible numbers of diseases and the absence of adequate medical care (that is, European medical care). Furthermore, given the belief that a woman brings witch-craft and/or spirits from her home which can result in the death of children, or barrenness, a man has NO OTHER MEANS available for reducing the anxieties related to health and, indirectly, to prestige, than participating in rituals that will restore his wife to good health and enable her to have healthy children. Again to cite Spiro (1966: 112):

Everywhere man's mammalian desires...must be satisfied and IN THE ABSENCE OF COMPETING TECHNOLOGIES WHICH CONFER REASONABLE CONFIDENCE, re-ligious techniques are believed to satisfy these desires...anxiety concerning the persistence of existence... AND IN THE ABSENCE OF COMPETING GOALS FOR THE REDUCTION OF ANXIETY, belief that one is successfully pursuing these religious goals...serves to reduce this anxiety.

Participating in the curing rituals related to women and their failure to give birth or have healthy children also satisfies hostility and dependency needs. A man has no control over his wife's state of health or being; it is the one area of a woman's life over which the husband cannot exercise control. In this he is totally dependent on the goodwill of her family in that they not "put on" his wife a *mulhiwa* which will prevent his family from growing. Alternatively, if she should have the *wumba* disease, he is also dependent on her family having the necessary ritual performed so that she may be cured and have children. Husbands' hostility toward barren wives or wives whose children always die is openly expressed in trials for divorce. In this way, a woman can directly threaten a man's attempts to achieve security and prestige. (Having enough food requires several children and/or wives who can work in the fields.) Hostility toward her family is also expressed, as it is they who are responsible for her condition. If the matter has not reached the stage of a man's seeking a divorce, however, he is dependent on these "strangers" for restoring him to a good condition through their treatment of his wife.

It should also be remembered that rituals are occasions for the sanc-tioned expression of ill will and hostility, and that the recovery of the patient is said to be dependent on all ill feelings being expressed. The conscious drive which results in participation in the curing ritual is un-doubtedly anxiety over health; a good case for the operation of uncon-scious hostility and dependency, however, can also be made. Beliefs in a *xipoko* or *mulhiwa* enable a man to displace the hostility he feels towards the wife and her family who are preventing him from attaining security and status. As one man said in court: "It isn't you [wife] that we dislike. It is the *xipoko* that is disliked." Similarly, unmet dependency needs can be satisfied by relying on supernatural agents who are ALWAYS RELATED BY KINSHIP TIES either to the man or to his wife.

In this latter regard, it will be remembered that the Rjonga project hostility by saying that it is the foreign gods, Nguni and Ndajo, who bring severe illness and death to a family, whereas their own ancestor gods visit mild illnesses as a rebuke, or to call attention to themselves because they have not been properly respected and recognized. By analogy, it can be seen that a wife's gods are always foreign to her husband who cannot control them. The foreign, possessing gods always establish a kinship link with the host family, moreover, so that they become hereditary. The ambivalence (dependence and fear of punishment) associated with all healing, whether through the agency of the possessing gods, the ancestor gods, or the *tinanga* [doctors] is also relevant. A man expects succor from his ancestor gods or his doctors, just as he expects it from his living seniors, but experience teaches that this expectation is not always met.

CONCLUSION

The persistence of many beliefs relating to supernatural agents is well attested by Rjonga statements, trials concerning witchcraft and/or sorcery, and many other kinds of data. However, according to natives' statements to me and to Junod's monograph (1927), many of the rituals are seldom or never practiced. Included among these are daily offerings to the ancestors in individual households; services to the ancestors by the entire lineage; cleansing ceremonies for widows and/or widowers; and several others. Almost all the rituals which the Rjonga still participate in are curing rituals and, prevalent among these is the ritual for curing a woman of having a *mulhiwa* or the *wumba* disease.

I have been unable to discuss the ways and the reasons for children learning about their parents' beliefs, and how these beliefs are reinforced by the children's experience, but it is these experiences which are changing and which account, in large part, for a different set of needs being learned (new goals, in particular). Children still learn about witchcraft, however, as has been shown, and the belief that witches are most often women is still widely taught. And there is still an insufficient technology to ensure an adequate food supply or good health. New means are available to the Rjonga today for satisfying some of their security and prestige goals but children are still considered "the African's greatest riches" and the primary means of achieving both security and prestige. Alternative goals have been learned which can account for the marked decrease in the rituals of the lineage, etc., but, as yet, there are no alternatives to the religious goals concerned with curing rituals, and the consequent satisfaction of the desires concerned with good health and many children.

REFERENCES

GEERTZ, CLIFFORD
  1966   "Religion as a cultural system," in *Anthropological approaches to the study of religion*. Edited by Michael Banton. A.S.A. Monograph 3. Edinburgh: Tavistock.
HALLOWELL, IRVING
  1955   *Culture and experience*. Philadelphia: University of Pennsylvania Press.
JUNOD, HENRI
  1927   *The life of a South African tribe*, two volumes (revised). New Hyde Park: University Books.
NOGUEIRA, RODRIGO DE SA
  1960   *Dicionario Ronga-Portugues*. Lisboa: Junta de Investigacoes do Ultramar, Centro de Estudos Politicos e Sociais.
PARSONS, TALCOTT, E. SHILS
  1951   *Toward a general theory of action*. Cambridge, Massachusetts: Harvard University Press.
SPIRO, MELFORD
  1953   Ghosts: an anthropological inquiry into learning and perception. *Journal of Abnormal and Social Psychology* 48.
  1961   "Social systems, personality, and functional analysis," in *Studying personality crossculturally*. Edited by B. Kaplan. Evanston, Illinois: Row, Peterson.
  1966   "Religion: problems of definitions and explanations," in *Anthropological approaches to the study of religion*. Edited by Michael Banton. A.S.A. Monograph 3. Edinburgh: Tavistock.
TURNER, VICTOR
  1966   "Colour classification in Ndembu ritual," in *Anthropological approaches to the study of religion*. Edited by Michael Banton. A.S.A. Monograph 3. Edinburgh: Tavistock.

Synoptic Comments on Religion, Ethos, and Science in American Culture

GEORGE J. JENNINGS

The implicit problem considered in this essay is simply this: Can mankind, characterized by cultural pluralism, achieve through science an utopian state wherein contentment is common to all individuals? Since American culture appears to adhere to the view that science is the most likely means of attaining such a state, it seems reasonable to analyze its features in order to assess its prospects for giving birth to a desirable Utopia. I incline towards pessimism when I evaluate ethnological evidence and the conclusions of some scholars. My opinion rests upon considerable doubt that man, American or otherwise, will be able to resolve problems which threaten existing cultural systems and tend towards chaos. It seems to me that Sorokin's prophecy (1941) that our sensate culture is doomed remains valid after a lapse of over three decades. My brief investigation first attends to religion because Christianity undoubtedly has influenced Western culture, including the American version.

The contemporary definitions of religion seem to minimize its supernatural essence as held in traditional views. For example, a popular definition offered by Clifford Geertz is that religion is:

(1) a system of symbols which acts to (2) establish powerful, pervasive and long-lasting moods and motivations in men by (3) formulating conceptions of a general order of existence and (4) clothing these conceptions with such an aura of factuality that (5) the moods and motivations seem uniquely realistic (Lessa and Vogt 1965: 206).

This statement is remarkably comprehensive, but it suffers from a serious weakness. It neglects the essence of religion, that is, the supernatural. The supernatural concept correlates with man's feeling of dependence upon forces beyond the natural realm. It is in relation to the supernatural that man seeks aid to compensate for his ultimate limitations in life. Wallace correctly identifies this critical feature in religion when he asserts that "It is the premise of every religion – and this premise is religion's defining characteristic – that souls, supernatural beings, and supernatural forces exist" (1966:52). Therefore to understand one of my basic assumptions in this essay assessing contemporary American culture, we must view religion as man's beliefs and behaviors in relation to the supernatural. The beliefs and behaviors provide compensation for his dependent state and inability to cope with life's personal and cultural circumstances.

The second concept necessary to this abbreviated scrutiny of American culture is ethos, which I envisage as an integrating force in every cultural system. Bateson employed ethos over thirty years ago in his New Guinea studies. He concluded that it was an appropriate term to emphasize the emotional quality or character that fuses cultural behavior (1937: 119). Kroeber later held that the concept is enmeshed in a culture's value system (1948:294). A contemporary definition regards ethos as "The predominant ideas, values, and ideals of a culture or subculture which give it distinctive character" (Theodorson and Theodorson 1969:93). In applying the notion to American culture, I suggest that it refers to the emotional quality attending cultural values, postulates, and ideals which induce socially patterned behavior within the American cultural scheme.

Third, while viewing religion as the mystical support for man, and ethos as the emotional "ought" in a culture, I am confronted with the American culture which seems to be dominated by secularism and technology. Hoebel, within an ethnological context, sums up this dominance in what he proposes to be "The American world view" (1972:554-557). He sees a Judaeo-Christian-Hellenistic complex (each phase steeped in supernaturalism) transformed into secularism and technology by influences from the Renaissance, the Reformation, and the Industrial Revolution. Science began with a dedication to knowing the truth, but science in America became subject to technology with its materialistic ends. Hoebel puts it in these words: "Because they view the universe as a mechanism, Americans implicitly believe that man can manipulate it. He need not accept it as it is; he may work on it, and as he gains in knowledge and IMPROVES HIS TECHNIQUES, he may even redesign it so that it will be more to his liking" (1972: 555; emphasis added). Few cultures exceed America's emphasis upon secularism and technological products in a frantic quest for satisfaction or contentment (which is defined largely in terms of physical convenience and ease).

Fourth, Hsu observes that Americans are characterized by self-reliance, fear of dependency, and insecurity. Having the advantage of a Chinese background coupled with ethnological investigations in several contemporary civilizations, Hsu believes that:

Individuals may have differing degrees of needs for their fellow human beings, but no one can truly say that he needs no one. It seems that the basic American value orientation of self-reliance, by its denial of the importance of other human beings in one's life, creates contradictions and therefore serious problems, the most iniquitous of which is insecurity (Hsu 1961: 219).

Hsu finds the source of aid for the individual in society, but it is my opinion that ultimately even a society has limitations since it is comprised of limited individual members. In fact a sociocultural system may pose problems rather than resolve them. In America, an ethos of self-reliance, with its accompanying fear of dependency, militates against the basic assumption in my view of supernaturalism, that is, the sense of dependency. Americans undoubtedly experience much insecurity because they are given to individualism and independence. This insecurity is aggravated by a rejection of supernaturalism which, in some form, has been the traditional belief by the majority in all known cultures.

Fifth, in a secularistic and self-reliant culture marked by insecurity, permissiveness and leniency have emerged in America's enculturation process. Every enculturational system rests upon sanctionary disciplines. Ethnologists are quite aware that "traditional" societies have effective enculturational systems to instill in their maturing members the values and ideals of the culture. In these "simple" and relatively stable societies, this conditioning process enables most individuals to move easily within the limits of accepted behavior set by the culture. But in contrast, the complex American way of life, committed to accelerated change, complicates and vitiates the learning process by offering heterogeneous features which frequently include incompatible alternatives.

Keniston, among others, notes that in America biological motherhood and childhood care are often accompanied by a minimization of the father's responsibility for both emotional life and child training due to his occupational absence (1965: 171). An American mother's task is unusually critical and difficult, for, with minimal aid, she must prepare her children for a society changing at an unprecedented rate toward ever greater fragmentation, specialization, and impersonality. Not only does the relationship that causes intense dependence of the child upon the mother exist, but also the permissiveness and leniency that characterize American parents have emerged. These features, which fail to give the child respect for his parents, are aggravated by the common practice whereby withdrawal of love is the major disciplinary sanction used to gain compliance.

Ethnologists have noted that various methods are available and practiced for inducing children to behave. Physical punishment, isolation, punitive work, ostracism, and social shaming as employed in varying combinations by other cultures seem to be less traumatic than the withdrawal of love. Such threats have special implications in religiously oriented homes where the parents attempt to enculturate the child with statements about "God is love," and "God is our Heavenly Father." Ambiguity and ambivalence emerge in the individual's thinking and he either resents or rejects the supernatural being who is portrayed as the source of mystical and condemnatory sanctions. At the same time, the maturing individual, in facing the reality of overwhelming problems, must recognize his limitations and resort to dependency (at least, covertly) upon this same supernatural being which might be envisaged as hostile and formidable.

Sixth, ethnologists frequently point out that American society is characterized by considerable fragmentation, insecurity, and indecision in comparison with many traditional societies. Perhaps an adequate demonstration of this cultural phenomenon is to be found by examining the polarities of competition and cooperation in American life. Competition has dominated many American behavior patterns to an obsessive degree. Its dominance is manifested in the efforts, the crucial choices, and the verbal affirmations of those representing approved behavior. Competition is essentially a process whereby individuals or groups strive to surpass others in quest of a limited goal or good. To emerge victorious in a struggle for what is limited means that one does so only at the expense of the others.

Potter's analysis of the American character or "social personality" outlines the competitive theme as found in various studies (1954). He cites Mead's ethnological approach, Riesman's sociological approach, and Horney's psychoanalytic approach, all three in agreement about competition and its impact on American culture. Potter suggests that Mead's interpretation places an emphasis upon success, social and economic mobility, conformity, and a tendency to push children into precocity. The result is that the attainment of the competitive goal is more consequential in the individual's life than the attainment of personal satisfaction. Conformity requires individuals to accept this competition system not only by embracing its goals but also by accepting the behavior codes which one associates with these goals (Mead 1965).

Horney, who incorporates ethnological emphasis in her psychoana-lytic views, cites the competitive nature of American life as a pervasive cause for inner conflicts and anxiety. In her analysis, she sees rivalry as the stimulation for an aggressiveness which the tradition of Christian ideals requires the competitors to curb. According to Horney, competi-tion gives Americans a false assurance of a freedom which is never to be realized (1937). We are brought back again to anxiety in American culture.

The origin of anxiety in America has other factors at play. In the struc-tural-functional school outlined by Durkheim and his successors in eth-nology, dependency is a critical feature of the individual's life. The human infant is the example *par excellence* of dependency. But with en-culturation, the American child is encouraged to become self-reliant, individualistic, and independent. With such behavior, the American com-monly finds himself in competition with those upon whom he is more or less dependent for his needs. The competition-versus-dependency situa-tion introduces the individual to ambivalence and tensions. He seeks to resolve these by compartmentalization, but usually with insecurity and uncertainty as a result.

If competition and self-reliance are hallmarks of the American ethos, what about cooperation and conformity? Many observers have noted that Americans tend to conform, especially youth in response to peer influences. Americans with competitive and self-reliant values find it necessary to identify with status-giving individuals or groups. To be suc-cessfully competitive and self-reliant, the individual submits overtly to institutional dominance by conformance. In other words, he shares the behavior patterns as a means to status and rank. The person is thus caught in a dilemma; he must compete and conform. Such conformance tends to be overt or superficial cooperation — a matter of expediency. Pa-thetic neurotic consequences commonly attend the dilemma.

Riesman's analysis of American character implies the unhappy state of the "other-directed" person who, equipped with a radarlike sensitiv-ity to his fellows, is really an individual in the throes of conflict. With his highly competitive disposition, the individual acquires an orientation towards situational rather than internalized goals. His sensitivity to the opinions of others is accompanied by an acute need for approval from those who are his competitors. In fine, the individual reluctantly yields to conformity, or overt cooperation, as a means of attaining competitive success (Riesman et al. 1956:34–38). Anxiety so favored could hardly find a more favorable source.

Seventh, one may select from innumerable statements the conclusion that science dominates the Western world in general and American culture in particular. Kluckhohn offers this observation:

Mysticism and supernaturalism have been very minor themes in American life. Our glorification of science and our faith in what can be accomplished through education are two striking aspects of our generalized conviction that secular, humanistic effort will improve the world in a series of changes, all or mainly for the better (1957: 178).

Science in American culture has opened a cornucopia of productivity and profits. As Max Lerner comments, "America became the Enormous Laboratory" because science "whipped technology on because every discovery of new techniques and processes meant the cutting of costs, the opening of new areas of investment, the reaching of new heights of productivity" (1957:216). Out of this "laboratory" have poured whole new industries with a vast array of products.

America's scientific emphasis depends upon two imperatives: the mutation outcroppings of scientific genius, and the pervasiveness of the scientific outlook. Assuming a fair share of the first, there must be a favorable climate in which the insights demanded by the modern scientific revolution can flower. The young Einstein, pondering the question of the speed of light and the errant behavior of the planet Mercury, could not have reached his solution by empiricism alone. He reached it by undercutting the assumptions of classical physics, seeing the universe as a series of observations by a scientist who was himself part of the frame.

It is commonplace to observe that the application of science and related secular rational approaches have transformed the external conditions of American culture. Applied science is highly esteemed as a tool for controlling nature. Significant here is the interest in order, control, and calculability – the passion of America's engineering culture. This interest is linked to the fundamental assumption of an ordered universe in which rational human beings can continually improve their situation and themselves.

But the prime quality of "science" is not in its application but in its basic method of approaching problems — a way of thought and a set of procedures for interpreting experience. I need only mention the long history of the "warfare of science and religion" in order to suggest the conflicts of belief and value that have accompanied the rise of science. However, it may be well to remember that the antievolution trials occurred only a few years ago, and that popular attitudes toward science still contain strong ambivalences. Gillin has this in mind when he writes that "Science is appreciated so long as it is applied in such a way as to 'make things work better'. Pure science or curiosity for its own sake is each regarded as dubious in the general culture" (1955:108).

Science, therefore, has become a fetish when linked with technology and the two are usually inseparable in the minds of most Americans. As such, science and technology are media *par excellence* for self-reliance and fear of dependency (on others, not on machines). In accepting a technological emphasis with its insistence on continuous change, Americans have adopted a theme which robs them of an essential sense of historical connection. This is the "cult of the present" which prevails in much contemporary thought. The specific themes of science and technology include specialization, organization, efficiency, raising role requirements, and innovation – all of which serve as the rationale for fragmentation of social roles and the shattering of security usually provided in traditional communities.

Furthermore, with the dominance of science geared to technology, former goals that were designed to provide balanced cultural satisfaction have been rejected. Now the maximization of instrumental values seeks to produce men and women of cognitive and emotionless constitution with what might be called a "mechanical personality." Rather than the ego serving as an organizing, synthesizing, and coordinating component of the personality, the ego has become a dictator performing such functions as problem solving, cognitive control, measurement, rationality, and analysis. These new functions have been at the expense of such traditional functions as playfulness, fantasy, relaxation, creativity, and feeling. The American has made the cult of science a tribal symbol, just as he had made the cult of success a personal symbol!

Eighth and finally, despite the dedication and aspirations of scientists to contribute to personal, social, and cultural equanimity, I am quite skeptical that science can provide these in and of itself. Various reasons for my skepticism have been suggested by different scholars. Cohen singles out one reason when he notes the tentativeness of science with its unending quest in these words:

Like religion, science extends or expands the world of sensory experience — but where religion extends and expands our world view to include the supernatural, science extends it to include the data and theories it continually creates. Unlike religion, at least until quite recently, science is by its very nature "open." That is to say, it is in constant tension because of the social organization of scientists and the lack of finality built into its intellectual materials and norms (1970: 31).

It seems likely that science guards against dogmatism only as the evidence appealed to is genuinely objective. This limitation upon scientific objectivity does not negate the claim of its proponents that it is the best method for achieving reliable knowledge yet devised. It suggests, how-- ever, the reason why science has had its greatest successes in the realm of the physical sciences rather than in the realm of social sciences. To deal with a problem scientifically means to deal with it objectively, dis- interestedly, impartially. The greater the personal distance between the scientist and his objects, the greater the objectivity. To deal with persons objectively, either legalistically or scientifically, is to be guilty of inhu- manity. Men are not mere "objects." Scientific study of men can be not merely false but degrading. One can study human behavior — culture — scientifically, analyzing and interpreting, but the center of man's being is never discovered by this kind of observation of the surface. To deal with our fellows exclusively in a scientific way is to depersonalize them into mere animate objects.

Critical questions have emerged in relation to ethnological efforts: is man required by the nature of things to rely always on some blind faith? Can we give meaning to life only by some uncritically accepted ideology? Are various forms of intellectual bigotry the only way to avoid confusion and meaninglessness? The brevity of this essay allows me to cite the opinions of only two or three scholars who have probed such questions.

Lundberg attacked and attempted to resolve these human issues in his work, *Can science save us?* (1961). He sought to provide us with an ap- proach to human problems that does not lean on emotional surrender to an established ideology; nor does it force us to respond with a hopeless shrug of the shoulders as we retreat into a modern cult of despair. Quite simply, Lundberg suggested that we acquire faith in a form of reasoning which is itself constantly skeptical of faith. We can be confident only of the method we use; we can never be confident of our conclusions. This is the paradox of the position taken by the modern social scientist, in- cluding ethnologists.

Lundberg begins by suggesting that of all the ways of coming to grips with nature man has tried so far, the most successful has been science. Science, after a rough and often bitterly vituperative struggle for survival among ideas, has won out over religion, magic, and tradition as a means of bringing nature under man's control. It has not yet, however, won out over these less effective thoughtways when it comes to an understanding of man. In social and cultural concerns, preference is still given to cus- tomary forms of thought, to religion, and even to reliance upon magic.

Lundberg does not equivocate in his defense of the social sciences as sciences. In his estimation they are legitimate sciences in every respect. The ideal social scientist is an objective observer and writer whose own values and emotions do not intrude into his quest for decisive facts —

facts which will either lend further support to a theory or weaken it to the point where it is no longer tenable. The scientist Lundberg offers us is a detached, dispassionate, and thoroughly rational intellectual. He offers no panaceas. He does not plead for some reform or cultural change. He can tell you with equal effectiveness how to stimulate a race riot or build a dam. His duty is not to tell you where to go; only how to get there.

The characterization of the social scientist which Lundberg draws for us is not especially attractive. If we are to avoid situations in which the masses of men become dedicated to inhuman values, we cannot do it by giving the scientist moral power. We can do it only by giving greater freedom to men whose task it is to concern themselves with human values — writers, theologians, philosophers, artists, poets, and politicians. The scientist, says Lundberg, does not dare step into the moral arena; the moment he does so his scientific character becomes blemished. His facts become suspect. His arguments and his writings are directed not toward scientific truths but toward what he believes ought to be, or what he would like to think, is man's condition.

When reading Lundberg, it is difficult to avoid the feeling that he, in defense of science, is using a number of nonscientific devices to achieve the effect he is seeking. We may note the fact that Lundberg is behaving like the spokesman of any faith — that is, he is relying on authority, rhetoric, tradition, and, perhaps, an essentially personal hope to generate the argument that science is the way we SHOULD develop an understanding of ourselves.

It is difficult to examine Lundberg's writing or that of other social scientists, ethnologists like Tylor, Boas, Kroeber, and White, who explicitly plead for the acceptance of a new faith. Any human activity must be grounded, in the final instance, in beliefs which are not, in themselves, subject to any form of test. These beliefs we take at face value, endorse them, and act upon them without critical examination. Often the elements of faith become so thoroughly a part of our intellectual and emotional baggage that we come to believe they are instinctive features of men in general — they are simply human nature. We may take on faith the idea that polygyny is immoral. Faith may lead us to believe that work is a test of an individual's worth. We may, through faith, become followers of men who range in thinking from the fundamental evangelism of Billy Graham to the racial vituperations of George Lincoln Rockwell. It is a matter of faith.

The French scholar Ellul, whose *Technological society* (1964) is being widely read, argues convincingly that science has become the bond slave of technology. In his brief work, *The presence of the kingdom,* he has this rather telling observation:

This process [that of exchanging "means" for the "end"] can be seen every-where. Another example comes from science and technology. At first men felt it important to know the Truth; after the philosophers came the scientists. They elaborated their theories, while others applied them; these have been used first of all to prove the truth of these theories, and then for the use of man; from that moment science was lost. Gradually technical means became more important than the search for Truth. Science has become more and more effective for technical purposes, and now science is only significant in terms of technology. Its whole direction is towards applied science. It is at the service of means. It has become a means for the creation of more perfect means; and the abstraction called "science," to which homage is always paid, has replaced the search for Truth. This development is particularly evident in the United States of America and in the Soviet Union, but inevitably it is gradually penetrating the rest of the world (1967: 64–65).

To draw this essay to its proper conclusion, I wish to refer to Robert Lowie's conclusions when he compared religion and science. He observed that science, even in its ideal form, can never provide for the masses of men the security that is to be found only in religion. Lowie cannot be accused of religious bias, for he acknowledges no religious commitment in his numerous writings. He did claim to be an informed ethnologist in religious study after analyzing cultural phenomena in many cultures. His conclusion is best summarized in his own words:

What an average man wants above everything else is security. But does science supply this? The answer is "No." That complete world-view that science explicitly renounces is precisely what the layman craves. In this perilous universe he is forever beset with dangers beyond his control. He wants at all odds to survive, and here science leaves him in the lurch — not everywhere and always, but often enough to make him keenly sensible of its imperfections. If he is dying of an incurable disease, it cheers him little to be told that medical science has made great strides in the past decades and that a remedy will almost certainly be found a hundred years hence, and probably sooner . . . . Science has achieved remarkable results, both practical and theoretical, but it has not made man a superman; so long as the enormous chasm yawns between man's rational control of nature and his biologico-psychological drives, there will still be room for belief in a Providence that grants not mere comfort, but security — not mere probability, but certainty (1963: 542).

Personally, I do not wish to hold the view that it must be either science or religion to resolve personal, social, or cultural problems. To me it is the recognition that both science and religion are essential to ultimate contentment now and in the future. I wish to dedicate my intellectual energies to science with all that it can provide to the solutions in what

Sorokin calls "The crisis of our age," but, in the awareness of the limitations of science, I feel the need to rely on the supernatural. Hence, I am strongly attracted to the position of the apostle Paul, who was a religious and charismatic fanatic in early Christianity, when he concluded with boldness:

For this gospel I was appointed a preacher and apostle and teacher, and therefore I suffer as I do. But I am not ashamed, for I know whom I have believed, and I am sure that He is able to guard until that Day what has been entrusted to me. Follow the pattern of the sound words which you have heard from me, in the faith and love which are in Christ Jesus; guard the truth that has been entrusted to you by the Holy Spirit who dwells within us (2 Timothy 1:11–14).

REFERENCES

BATESON, GREGORY
   1937   *Naven*. Stanford: Stanford University Press.
COHEN, RONALD
   1970   "Generalizations in ethnology," in *A handbook of method in cultural anthropology*. Edited by Raoul Naroll and Ronald Cohen, 31–50. Garden City: Natural History Press.
ELLUL, JACQUES
   1964   *The technological society*. New York: Vintage Books.
   1967   *The presence of the kingdom*. New York: Seabury Press.
GILLIN, JOHN
   1955   National and regional cultural values in the United States. *Social Forces* 34:107–113.
HOEBEL, E. ADAMSON
   1972   *Anthropology: the study of man*. New York: McGraw-Hill.
HORNEY, KAREN
   1937   *The neurotic personality of our time*. New York: W. W. Norton.
HSU, FRANCIS L. K.
   1961   *Psychological anthropology*. Homewood: The Dorsey Press.
KENISTON, KENNETH
   1965   *The uncommitted*. New York: Dell.
KLUCKHOHN, CLYDE
   1957   *Mirror for man*. New York: Fawcett World Library.
KROEBER, A. L.
   1948   *Anthropology*. New York: Harcourt, Brace, and Company.
LERNER, MAX
   1957   *America as a civilization*. New York: Simon and Schuster.
LESSA, WILLIAM A., EVON Z. VOGT
   1965   *Reader in comparative religion* (second edition). New York: Harper and Row.
LOWIE, ROBERT H.
   1963   Religion in human life. *American Anthropologist* 65:532–542.

LUNDBERG, GEORGE A.
  1961   *Can science save us?* New York: David McKay.
MEAD, MARGARET
  1965   *And keep your powder dry* (second edition). New York: William Morrow.
POTTER, DAVID M.
  1954   *People of plenty.* Chicago: University of Chicago Press.
RIESMAN, DAVID, NATHAN GLAZER, REUEL DENNEY
  1956   *The lonely crowd.* Garden City: Doubleday.
SOROKIN, PITIRIM A.
  1941   *The crisis of our age.* New York: E. P. Dutton.
THEODORSON, GEORGE A., ACHILLES G. THEODORSON
  1969   *A modern dictionary of sociology.* New York: Thomas Y. Crowell.
WALLACE, ANTHONY F. C.
  1966   *Religion: an anthropological view.* New York: Random House.

In Search of the Miraculous at Zuni

DENNIS TEDLOCK

The most accessible Zuni rituals are the masked dances of the *kotikanne* Kachina Society, in which ancestral gods are impersonated. The character of this society is revealed by the story of its origin, in which the Zunis ask themselves, "How shall we enjoy ourselves? ... It is not clear with what pleasures we shall pass our time" (Bunzel 1932b: 605). Most kachina dances are not considered to be *tehya* [valuable, precious] or *?attanni* [sacred, dangerous]; instead, they are *co?ya* [beautiful, novel]. In the Zuni view this beauty and novelty is contained largely in the songs and song lyrics rather than in the costumes and dance steps. What remains for the outsider, given that the fine points of the songs are inaccessible to him, gives an impression that helps account for Ruth Benedict's characterization of Zuni ritual in *Patterns of culture* as "a monotonous compulsion of natural forces by reiteration" in which experiences "outside of ordinary sensory routine" are avoided (1934: 84, 87). As for the priestly use of jimson weed, she went so far as to say that "all connections with the physical properties of the drug are lost sight of" (1934: 81). This picture of Zuni religion went unchallenged in the debate which developed around her description of Zuni personality (Li 1937; Goldfrank 1945; Bennett 1946), and it has been echoed many times over the years.

The Zunis do have rituals which they consider to be valuable and dangerous rather than merely beautiful, and which are, moreover, *pikʷayina* [passed through to the other side] or *?ayyu?či?anna* [amazing, miraculous], but these are not in the keeping of the Kachina Society. They belong, instead, to fourteen medicine societies and to the *?uwanam ?a·šiwani* [rain priesthoods]. Some of these rituals, once performed in public, have been withdrawn during the present century because of the increasing presence of non-Indian observers; others have been hidden always, even from the Zuni public. Nevertheless something of their nature may be pieced together from three sources: past ethnographic accounts, primarily those of Matilda Coxe Stevenson, who gained access to many performances during the nineteenth century; passages in traditional Zuni narratives; and descriptions offered by present-day Zuni eyewitnesses.

Most of the medicine societies are composed of people who once came close to death, temporarily escaped it through a society cure, and finally received a new heart and a new name in a society initiation (Bunzel 1932a: 541). Eight of these societies may be grouped in pairs, the oldest pair consisting of the *šiwana•kʷe* [Priestly People] and their "younger brothers" the *newe•kʷe* [Clowns]. Like most of the other societies, these two are divided into orders, each with its particular capabilities for performing remarkable acts. Both societies have orders of *ʔicepčo•kʷe* [Magicians] and *ʔona•ya•naka ʔa•šiwani* [Priests of the Completed Path], of whom the latter are also called *wema• ʔa•šiwani* [Beast Priests]. In addition the Priestly People have an order of *makkʔe•kʷe* [Fire People] and the Clowns have one of *kokko łana•kʷe* [Big Kachina People], the latter having masks separate from those of the Kachina Society proper (Stevenson 1904: 428–429). The Clowns, sometimes augmented by Priestly People, present public parodies of traditional and contemporary life, but they have private ceremonies of a more sober nature.

Another pair of societies consists of the *łewe•kʷe* [Sword Swallowers], sometimes thought of as Ice People (a play on words), and the *makkʔe łana•kʷe* [Big Fire People]. The Sword Swallowers have two orders, the Sword Swallowers proper and the *kłacilo•kʷe* [Fir Tree Swallowers]; the Big Fire People have an order of Fire People proper — with suborders of Sword Swallowers, Fir Tree Swallowers, and Arrow Swallowers — and orders of Big Kachina People and Beast Priests (Stevenson 1904: 447, 485–515). Formerly these two societies joined for an annual swallowing exhibition.

A third pair of societies comprises the *ʔuhuhu•kʷe* [Uhuhu People], probably named after a cry they use during their initiation (cf. Stevenson 1904: 524–525), and the *čikkʔali•kʷe* [Snake Medicine People], who came into being through a schism within the Uhuhu group. The Uhuhu People have an order of Magicians and the Snake Medicine People do not, but otherwise the composition of these two societies is identical, each of them having Fire People, *halo•kʷe* [Red Ant People], and Beast

Priests (Stevenson 1904: 521; Parsons 1933: 19).

The fourth pair of societies, consisting of the *makk?e c?ana•kʷe* [Little Fire People] and the *pešacilo•kʷe* [Bedbug People], is also the result of a schism. There are orders of Fire People, Magicians, Beast Priests, and *payatamu* [Youth] (a Keresan word), this last devoted to a god of song (Stevenson 1904 : 549). Formerly these two societies alternated in performing a quadrennial fire-walking exhibition.

Of the remaining medicine societies the only one which closely resembles those already named is the *?ačiya•kʷe* [Knife People], with orders of Magicians, Red Ant People, Beast Priests, and Knife People proper, this last order consisting of warriors (Stevenson 1904 : 528). Another society, the *šuma•kʷe* [Spiral People], has an order of Fire People, like some of the societies already mentioned, but its curing order is the *šume• kuli*, named after the Kachina masks it possesses, and it has no Beast Priests (Stevenson 1904: 530). The *saniyaka•kʷe* or *suski•kʷe* [Coyote People] also have an order of Fire People; their other order, the *lata•kʷe* [Hunters] is unique to them (Stevenson 1904: 438).

The remaining societies are all associated with warfare: the *koši•kʷe* [Cactus People], the *?a•pi?la ?a•šiwani ?a•wan tikanne* [Society of Bow Priests] (Stevenson 1904: 413), and the *c?u?lana•kʷe* [Big Shell People] (Parsons 1933: 80n.), none of them divided into orders. Among all the medicine societies, only these three, together with the Coyote People, the Knife order of the Knife People, the Arrow order of the Big Fire People, and the Youth orders of the Little Fire and Bedbug People, exclude women.

Among the war societies, the most miraculous was Big Shell. Their approach to warfare was that of priests rather than that of warriors: during a siege, they remained in a *kiva* and caused the enemies to fall dead by blowing on their conch shell trumpet (Benedict 1935 : II, 206-7; Tedlock and Tedlock 1971: Tape D). Today, with only a handful of members still living, Big Shell no longer functions as a society.

The Cactus People, whose feats in war were those of warriors (only men who had killed in combat could join), put on a dance in which they whipped one another with cactus and willow switches and passed cactus through their mouths (Stevenson 1904 : 575; Tedlock and Tedlock 1971: Tape E). A man who had witnessed this dance expressed its miraculous aspect as follows: "They're having a GOOD TIME with this cactus BECAUSE they whip each other with it. They KNOW HOW, that's their way." (Tedlock and Tedlock 1971: Tape E; emphasis mine). Their curing specialty was puncture wounds, from arrow, bullet, or bite (Stevenson 1904 : 570), and in this dance they were displaying their mastery over punctures, even taking pleasure in them. Today the few remaining members no longer meet as a society.

The orders of Fire People, present in eight of the medicine societies, take pleasure in mastery over fire. During the Big Fire initiation, that society's Fire order puts on a display during which dancers, with "beastlike" motions, stick burning bundles of cornhusks or juniper splinters in their mouths; they take coals from the fireplace and hold them in their mouths for as long as a full minute, and these coals "scintillate with every breath" (Stevenson 1904 : 503, 506). Among the Spiral People, the night before they put on a large public dance in the plaza, the following takes place in a house:

A number of dancers now congregate on the floor. . . . Another and another light great bunches of the husks until the room is ablaze, women and children vying with one another. . . . Cedar brands succeed the husks and a grand mêlée ensues. A warrior runs up the ladder and descending with an armfull of husks ignites them and runs about among the people with them blazing in his arms. The excitement grows greater and greater as the male and female members run around pell-mell, showering one another with sparks. Clubs are thrown upward, and much dodging is necessary to avoid being struck. Another and another join in the excitement until only the drummer and two companions remain in the choir; but the cries and yells of the dancers drown all other sounds. . . . They are too crazed with excitement to be conscious of physical pain (Stevenson 1904: 541–542).

The Fire orders of the Little Fire and Bedbug People formerly prepared a bed of coals in a round pit in the plaza and danced on them (Stevenson 1904 : 566; Tedlock and Tedlock 1971: Tape E). One of the dancers, the head of the society, would take a handful of cornmeal and run his arm deep into the coals, causing the meal to blaze up (Tape E). If someone got burns they told him, " 'You froze yourself' — they talked opposite" (Tape E).

The society of Sword Swallowers (or Ice People) displayed, as part of the physical regimen which kept them fit for swallowing, a mastery over cold. They bathed in the river during the winter, even if they had to break the ice, and when they got back to the house they kept away from the fire, using "their own natural heat" to warm up (Tape E). Their "swords" were blade-shaped but made of wood and measured from the tip of the middle finger to the elbow (Stevenson 1904: 451n.). In their public dance in January the performers paused from time to time to do the swallowing, not in unison but separately; some members were able to swallow even "during the most violent motions of the dance," but they saved this particular display for initiation ceremonies and did not do it in public (Stevenson 1904 : 466-78). Their Bow Priest swallowed a sword cut to a zig-zag lightning pattern, and their Society Chief swallowed whole stacks of swords (laid flat side to flat side) at a time (Tedlock and Tedlock 1971: Tape E). When the Sword Swallowers Society proper had finished with its dance, the Sword Swallowers suborder of the Big Fire People came into the plaza and performed similar feats.

The Fir Tree Swallowers marked Douglas firs with eyes and mouths and carved the butt ends to the same shape as the swords (Stevenson 1904 : 485, 515-20). The swallowing, in February, was first done in a house, with the top of the tree sticking out through a hatchway and the trunk guided by two assistants (Tedlock and Tedlock 1971: Tape E), but later in the same day it was done in the plaza, where it was more dangerous. A man who has seen this remarked: "I don't know how they do it. But suppose you were in that society. I wonder what it could be? I wonder how you would feel? But it's the medicine and it's their religious way. They used to do that" (Tape E). The practice of tree swallowing lapsed forty years ago or so after two fatalities.

The Arrow Swallowers, a suborder of the Big Fire People, ran arrows with stone points down their throats, some of them giving the arrow vigorous shoves while it was down; the idea was to run the arrow down to the heart (Stevenson 1904 : 511–13). Here we have a clue to the meaning of swallowing in general, aside from the fact that it displays a mastery over the dangers of choking or internal injury. The swallowed object is probably a sculptural representation of what has been called, in Zuni (and other) pictorial art, a "life line" or "breath line," when an animal in profile is shown with a line running from its mouth to its heart. The mountain lion, bear, badger, and wolf, the principal patrons of most of the Zuni medicine societies, are always pictured with such a line; in fact, they are so represented on the wooden boxes which the Sword Swallowers use during their public dance (Stevenson 1904: Plate CX). The pictured lines are always red and they have a gentle curve similar to that of the swords, which are also red. The swords, in addition to being painted, are rubbed with grease from a mountain lion or a bear (Stevenson 1904: 451n.). Both the pictured lines and the sculptured ones (the swords) may represent the new life which is conferred upon a society initiate by the human representatives of the patron animals.

In the societies of Priestly, Big Fire, Uhuhu, Snake Medicine, Little Fire, and Bedbug People, membership in the Fire order (including, in Big Fire, the swallowing suborders) is a prerequisite for becoming either a Magician or a Beast Priest, except that a person in extreme danger might be initiated directly into the Beast Priests (Stevenson 1904 : 416) to the extent of altering or reversing the natural order. A magician may, for example, violate gravity, as when he lifts a large stone figurine from an altar with the tip ends of a pair of eagle feathers (Stevenson 1904 : 429, 522). Or he may hang a blanket on the wall and then set the personal corn-ear fetish of some society member there as if the blanket were a horizontal surface; if that member has *ce?ma k?okši* [good thoughts] "all on one side," the fetish will stay there (Tedlock and Tedlock 1971: Tape E).

Power over the qualities of liquids and solids is shown in weather control ceremonies. A magician may hold water in a willow basket without any seepage and then cause it to drain out with the touch of his eagle feathers; this act, though performed by a medicine society member, represents the summer retreats of the Rain Priests, who attempt, as it were, to bring water to Zuni and then release it (Tape E). Uhuhu magicians turn balls of soft blue corn mush into rocks, while prayers are said for snow, and then turn them back again (Stevenson 1904: 526–27), an act which seems to deal with the paradox that snows can mean good crops. Where the lower orders give a person the power to withstand such assaults on the body as burning, freezing and choking, that of the Magicians gives him the power to actively manipulate the external world.

One of the most frequent acts of society magicians is the reversal of incineration. A man may burn a pair of eagle feathers, pass the remains all over his naked chest and shoulders, and have the feathers come out new again (Stevenson 1904: 20–71). In an initiation, a prayerstick may be burnt and then passed all over the body of the novice, and "if you're really interested it comes out a new one" (Tedlock and Tedlock 1971: Tape E). On a more public occasion a magician may burn *telna•we* [very powerful prayersticks] and restore them; "It means there'll be a long life for the whole public. That's what it means, to come out new" (Tape E).

Related to the reversal of incineration is the reversal of digestion. In the plaza an Uhuhu magician used to line up two of the *koyemši* [clown or idiot Kachinas] and feed a downy white eagle feather through both of them, mouth to anus and mouth to anus again. Taking it from the anus of the second one: "He shook it. It was new. That's the life of the people and the life of the Sun Priest. When we do that and you see it with your own eyes, I bet you'll think about that" (Tape E).

Sometimes the life — or rather, the defeat of death — represented by these reversals is shown more directly. Two Uhuhu magicians put an initiate to a test in which they hold opposite ends of a rough yucca rope and cut through the middle of his body, from front to back; at the end he is unharmed (Stevenson 1904 : 526). It is said that there were once magicians who would even hack off a man's limbs and throw them into the fire; when they dropped the body into a *kiva* the man stood up new again inside. A person who had been through this experience would never "die," but would instead "fall asleep" in his old age and wake up among the dead at Kachina Village (Stevenson 1904: 567). The Zunis say that the Hopis once performed not only this wonder but that of "throwing one another off the cliff" as well (Tedlock 1972 : 62).

Excessive displays of power by magicians caused public alarm. The Uhuhu society once put on a spectacle at Zuni in which a magician, pointing a feathered stick, started fires on mountaintops in the four directions, one after another. The people said that this was evil and so it was not done again (Tedlock and Tedlock 1971: Tape E).

More dangerous (for the initiate) than the Fire, Sword Swallowing, and Magician orders is that of the Priests of the Completed Path or Beast Priests, which exists in eight of the societies. The members of this order go beyond the dangers of fire, ice, and sword when they allow the bear, mountain lion, and other carnivores, "the most dangerous and violent gods in the Zuni pantheon" (Bunzel 1932a : 528), to enter and possess their bodies and minds. At the same time they practice the most important form of magicianship, that of drawing illness from the bodies of patients. To do this they must have a third skill which is without parallel in the other orders:

Suppose you're really a medicine man. Why, there's a glass [crystal] like this [holds up a six-sided bottle] and I see you like this [looks through it]. When I see you I see if you've got some different kind of mind, or you might think in another direction, or probably you don't believe in me. That's the kind of thing you'll find out for yourself [with that glass]. And with that special root too. If you've got that one, you'll SEE (Tedlock and Tedlock 1971: Tape E).

The power to SEE includes the power to locate the foreign objects which those who "think in another direction" shoot into the bodies of their victims to make them ill. The "special root" is that of *tenacali,* an unidentified plant whose flowers (in six colors) and roots are used by nearly all the medicine societies (Stevenson 1904: 569n.).

In a curing ceremony, the Beast Priests begin by dancing before the society altar with twisting and bending motions which are "exquisitely graceful" (Stevenson 1904 : 496). As they become possessed, one after another, some of them may put bear paws on the left or both hands; they begin to dance in a bent-over or squatting position or "dash about wildly," growling and uttering "wild cries," wrangling with one another and pawing the singers and patients, the women acting even wilder than the men (Stevenson 1904 : 495-501, 525, 563).

It is not clear at what point the *tenacali* is used, or whether it is sometimes omitted, but in any case the possessed Beast Priest is able to SEE. The crystal is taken in the left hand and held before the patient or touched to his body, or else cornmeal is sprinkled on the body and its patterns of adherence observed; with or without such devices, the Beast Priest "opens the windows of the body" (Stevenson 1904 : 394, 415, 501). Having located the sickness he draws it near the surface with an eagle feather or by sucking, finally "catching" it in his mouth or with his hand; in an initiation the heart itself is sucked, the male Beast Priests doing this for the male novices and the females for the females (Stevenson 1904 : 415, 494, 501). The objects removed, which are thrown in the fire or collected in a bowl, include dust, stones, cactus spines, feathers, charred fragments of goat horn, fur, animal entrails, bits of cloth, and yards of yarn (Stevenson 1904 : 396, 500-1; Bunzel 1932a: 532; Benedict 1935: I, 67).

Three of the societies with Beast Priests also have a curing order of Red Ant People, who specialize in sore throats and skin troubles caused by ants. With the help of the ants, these people are able to see bits of gravel in the body, bring them to the surface in huge numbers, and brush them off with broom straws (Stevenson 1904 : 529).

The Rain Priests, unlike Fire People, Sword Swallowers, and Magicians, perform no public miracles; unlike the Beast Priests and the Red Ant People, they perform no cures. Their powers are concentrated in seeing or in *tuna• ?ehkʷi* [seeing ahead] not into people's bodies but in the six directions, all over and under and above the world, and they can help their clients to see. In addition to *tenacali,* they use the roots, leaves, and flowers of *?aneklaka;* the flowers of this plant, like those of *tenacali,* are said to come in different colors, though the plant is sometimes called *?uteya• k?ohanna* [white flowers] and has been identified as *Datura inoxia (D. meteloides),* jimson weed (Stevenson 1915 : 46).

When a man wishes to find a lost or stolen object, a Rain Priest can help him have a vision in which he is guided to the object and learns the identity of the thief; many other things may be revealed in the course of the search, and I know of one man whose visionary experience on such an occasion was the cause of his reconversion to the Zuni religion. Stevenson says that the Rain Priests administer *?aneklaka*

to these clients (1904 : 386–87, 1915 : 89–91); *tenacali* is also given.
During the summer the Rain Priests "go outside" at night to meet
with the birds of the six directions, putting powdered jimson root in
their eyes, ears, and mouths so that "the birds may not be afraid and
will listen to them when they pray to the birds to sing for the rains";
they also use jimson in asking the dead for rain (Stevenson 1904: 386;
1915 : 89).

The greatest divinatory feats of the Rain Priests are recounted in
the *čimik?ana?kowa* [origin story]. It was they who discovered, with the
help of the *?ahayu•ta* [twin war gods] and the water strider (an insect),
the location of the Middle of the World, the spot where Zuni now
stands (Tedlock 1972: 277–280, for example), and it was their responsibility to divine the hiding place of the Corn Mothers during a famine.
A member of a Rain Priest's family, in telling the story of this famine,
describes four different kinds of divination in some detail (Benedict
1935: I, 24–43). The priests, in their first attempts to find the Corn
Mothers, met in an empty room. "The Tenatsali Youths [twins] came
into the back of the room. They were like shadows" (1935: I, 35). The
priests asked them to look for the Corn Mothers; the twins searched
on four successive nights, going all the way to the oceans, to the sky,
and to the underworld, without success. Next the priests tried Jimson
Weed (*?aneklaka*), who never searches for more than one night. He
told them, "Sit straight. Do not sleep. Do not let your minds wander.
Do not speak" (1935: I, 36). When he had searched all over and failed,
his leaves were given to the son of one of the priests. The boy "slept,"
and when the priests questioned him later he said:

I have gone to the plains, the lakes, the tall trees and the high mountains.
Jimson Weed went with me. Sometimes we travelled high up and sometimes
low down. I looked into the eagles' nests on the cliffs but there was nothing
but their eggs. I looked into the hawks' nests in the high trees but there was
nothing there but their young. I looked into the springs to the north but
there was nothing there but water reeds. I looked into the springs to the
east but there was nothing there but water reeds. I looked into the springs
to the south but there was nothing there but water reeds. I looked in the
springs to the west but there was nothing there but water reeds. This is all
I have to say (Benedict 1935: I, 38).

Next the priests asked the *?ahayu•ta* [twins]; the discipline was the same
as for Jimson Weed. Then, as a last resort, they called upon the patron
deity of the Clowns, the ducklike *picici* or *nepayatamu* [Clown Youth],
who wears his hair knot on his forehead and sometimes says the opposite of what he means (see Tedlock 1972 : 118, 289). This time the
discipline is the severest of all: for four whole days the priests must

refrain from all drink, food, speech, idle thoughts, and sleep (Benedict 1935: I, 40–41). The Corn Mothers are found, and the event is still commemorated by a milder fasting on the part of the entire community (Tedlock 1972: 296–298).

Neither *tenacali* nor *?aneklaka* is mentioned in connection with the searches by the *?ahayu•ta* [twins] and Clown Youth, but it is the *?ahayu•ta* who originally turned the people called *?aneklaka* into a plant (Stevenson 1915: 46), and *tenacali* originated from the spilt blood of Clown Youth (Tedlock 1972 : 110). Moreover, both the *?ahayu•ta* and Clown Youth, and therefore both *?aneklaka* and *tenacali*, are associated with the ability to travel on the Milky Way (Benedict 1935: I, 38; Tedlock 1972 : 129–32). As has already been mentioned, *tenacali* and *?aneklaka* are alike in other ways: both are described as having flowers of different colors, and in both cases not only the flowers but the roots are used. The difference is in the sites where they are gathered: *tenacali* and *?aneklaka* come from separate shrines which bear their respective names (Benedict 1935: II, 140; I, 36). The shrines, or better, the respective plants, BELONG to the Rain Priesthoods and the medicine societies, *tenacali* to all of them (except Bow, Cactus, and Big Shell) and *?aneklaka* only to the Rain Priesthoods and to the heads of the Little Fire and Bedbug People (Stevenson 1904: 386, 569n.). It may be that we are dealing with a single species, whose Zuni name is probably the aforementioned *?uteya• k?ohanna* [white flowers], and that the differences between *tenacali* and *?aneklaka* are purely a matter of ritual practice. But it is also possible that *tenacali* and *?aneklaka* are separate cultivars of *Datura inoxia* and have OBJECTIVELY different effects (see Schultes 1972 : 49 for a similar situation in highland Colombia).

From all of these fragments and glimpses it should now be apparent that Zuni religion has a great deal to offer besides colorful Kachina dances. One need not appeal to Puebloan personality to account for the fact that Zuni, along with all the other Pueblos except Taos, has shown no interest in the peyote cult. The priesthoods and societies of Zuni have a considerable knowledge of physical disciplines, magicianship, and psychopharmacology, and this knowledge allows the initiate, and sometimes the spectator, to "pass through to the other side" and enter the world of the sacred, the dangerous, and the miraculous.

REFERENCES

BENEDICT, RUTH
1934   *Patterns of culture.* New York: Mentor Books.
1935   *Zuni mythology.* Columbia University Contributions to Anthropology 21.
BENNETT, JOHN W.
1946   The interpretation of Pueblo culture: a question of values. *Southwest Journal of Anthropology* 2:361–374.
BUNZEL, RUTH L.
1932a   Introduction to Zuni ceremonialism. *Annual Report of the Bureau of American Ethnology* 47:467–544.
1932b   Zuni origin myths. *Annual Report of the Bureau of American Ethnology* 47:545–616.
GOLDFRANK, ESTHER S.
1945   Socialization, personality, and the structure of Pueblo society. *American Anthropologist* 47:516–539.
LI AN CHE
1937   Zuni: some observations and queries. *American Anthropologist* 39:62–76.
PARSONS, ELSIE CLEWS
1933   *Hopi and Zuni ceremonialism.* Memoirs of the American Anthropological Association 39.
SCHULTES, RICHARD EVANS
1972   "An overview of hallucinogens in the Western Hemisphere," in *Flesh of the gods: the ritual use of hallucinogens.* Edited by Peter T. Furst, 3–54. New York: Praeger.
STEVENSON, MATILDA COXE
1904   The Zuni Indians. *Annual Report of the Bureau of American Ethnology* 23.
1915   The ethnobotany of the Zuni Indians. *Annual Report of the Bureau of American Ethnology* 30: 31–102.
TEDLOCK, DENNIS
1972   *Finding the center: narrative poetry of the Zuni Indians.* New York: Dial.
TEDLOCK, DENNIS, BARBARA TEDLOCK
1971   Tape recordings from the field, in their possession.

SECTION FOUR

Signs and Symbols in Israeli Electioneering

SHLOMO DESHEN

Noteworthy in Israeli election campaigns is the fusion that sometimes occurs between traditional religious activities and the practices of modern electioneering. In an earlier study (Deshen 1970a), I discussed this fusion in terms of the study of religious change. There I focused on a particular election campaign incident, analyzed the kinds of change that a certain religious symbol underwent on that occasion, and developed a series of analytical terms that can conceptualize changes of religious symbols generally.

In this paper the focus shifts to the political aspect of symbolic activities that take place during election campaigns. Here I seek to understand the nature of some of the symbols that appear in the course of electioneering and shall argue that in certain sectors of the electorate there operates a process whereby political signs are transformed into symbols charged with religious content. A large proportion of the Israeli electorate consists of first-generation immigrants who come from traditional communities which were situated in the lesser-developed regions of Muslim countries. To many of them, traditional Jewish symbols are highly resonant. At election time their vote is greatly sought after by the political parties, and in their competition for the popular vote the politicians exert themselves in a variety of strategies: one general line of electioneering is their manipulation of religious symbols in order to obtain the immigrant vote.

The parties are divided over a great variety of issues: economic, foreign, social, and religious. In the present context the religious issues are noteworthy. There are recurring controversies in Israel as to the extent to which Judaism, as currently interpreted by religious authorities, should be accorded legal status. This problem has many practical ramifications that reach down to the individual citizen. The most debated of these are such questions as: should public transport run on the Sabbath? Should commercial amusement places be open on these days and on religious holidays? Should personal law be formulated according to canon or civil law? The problem of personal law has been particularly acute. At present personal law is enacted and executed by rabbinical authorities. In practice this means that, among other things, all marriage and divorce contracts are religious acts, and certain categories of marital unions are not legal because they are prohibited by religious law. This has been the cause of suffering and tragedy for a number of people. The attitudes of the various sectors of the population and their political organs toward this setup run the gamut of opinion — from radical secularism, through liberal forms of traditionalism, to fundamentalism and extreme orthodoxy. At the latter end of the continuum operate several religious parties whose major election plank consists of assuring legal standing to various requirements of canon law as currently interpreted by rabbinical authorities. The major political parties in the country generally support the Orthodox position, while a group of small, radical parties is consistently pitted against it. In general, however, the present setup seems to enjoy a great deal of support that is rooted in Jewish folk sentiment.

The political parties, as stated above, operate among an electorate consisting largely of people who are recent arrivals from countries where free elections are not held. On the average, these people have only a very limited education and their civic experience has been minimal. People who have grown up in such places as rural North Africa do not differentiate very clearly between the variegated motivations and aims of the different parties. To them all parties and politicians are novel and foreign. Though they are personally attuned to the policies and aims of the religious parties, they find the concrete organizational phenomenon of these parties profoundly baffling. This paradox is rooted in complex sociohistorical factors, into which we can here go only very cursorily. In North Africa, particularly among Moroccan Jewry, religious authority was generally invested either in charismatic individuals who were more or less self-appointed or in the scions of aristocratic families that traditionally provided religious leaders. In either case, religious authority did not stem from a broad base of communal decision. Among European Jewry, on the other hand, religious authority was, to a considerable extent, a function of communal decision. Oligarchic community leaders had much say in the "making" and "unmaking" of rabbis. In traditional European Jewry, since late medieval times, lay religious leaders played a role distinct from that of the clericals whom they appointed. In the modern context of

Israeli democracy, this lay role has readily been translated into the role of lay religious politicians. Among North African Jewry (and this is also largely true of Jews of other Muslim countries), clerical leadership was not clearly differentiated from other types of communal leadership. Religious leaders therefore did not have a clearly defined standing *vis-à-vis* other local personalities who wielded power, and they were certainly not subjugated to them as was very often the case among European Jewry. A North African rabbi, to a large extent, filled the role of general community leader, simply because the communities had no figures comparable to the oligarchs of the European communities who appointed their own rabbis and sometimes terminated their contracts.

This background is relevant to Israeli politics. Immigrants from such countries as Morocco are baffled by the phenomenon of laymen propagating religious policies, as they are struck by the novelty that persons who wield authority have to seek popular support. From their experience in Jewish communities abroad, these immigrants expect religious policies to be promoted exclusively by aristocratic, venerable, and saintly rabbis. They expect the propagators of religious policies to exhibit the qualities of patriarchal behavior associated with the aristocratic rabbinical leadership of old, such as generosity, charity, and dignity. Instead the immigrants are confronted by small politicians pettily seeking bits of power. The fact that the politicians of religious parties promise, by and large most sincerely, to use their powers for religious purposes does not make them a less novel and strange phenomenon than all the other politicians. Politicians competing for power in a democratic system are for these immigrants a novelty, and religious politicians are even more so; the latter are not only baffling to them but deeply disappointing. One man of Ayara (the town in which I carried out most of my fieldwork), a Moroccan immigrant and father of nine, characteristically remarked to me during the 1969 election campaign:

I dislike the Religious National Front. They ought to go around asking people what is bothering them. There are large families in need who are ashamed to ask for assistance. True, none of the parties do this, but the religious party ought to help because that is its raison d'être (*ha'ikar bishvilam*). It would then not need to spend much money on campaigning because people would vote for it anyway. Now only people of deep piety (*sheyesh lahem yire'a va'fahad*), who understand the need for religious schools and the other things that the Religious National Front aims for, vote for them.

The man expressed his bitterness at religious politicians who do not live up to the noble patriarchal role that he envisages for religious leaders. In his opinion the religious party is now popular only among persons who dissociate the attractive aims of the party from its unattractive organizational and personal features, but not among ordinary folk.

Religious symbols figure not only in the electioneering of religious parties whose explicit *raison d'être* is the advancement of religious legislation and which naturally seek support among the traditional and pious, but in the political campaign of parties which are indifferent to religion. They appear mainly in two converse ways: in the charging of political signs with symbolic content of a religious nature or in their manipulation in such a way as to charge religious activities with political content. It is with the latter that I was concerned in my earlier work (Deshen 1970b, 1972), where I described religious feasts, Torah scroll presentations, and the reading of religious texts, and showed how these were used as vehicles to project political messages. In this paper I turn to the study of political signs: how are they manipulated and transformed in Israeli electioneering? The thrust of my argument is that we do not have here two distinct processes, but two facets of one phenomenon. The charging of religious symbols with political content implies its reverse: the charging of political signs with religious content. Only in an analytical context can the changes in religious and political symbolism be separated; in actuality they constitute a single phenomenon.

Let us now turn to the data. At the polls the Israeli voter is confronted with the choice of voting for different lists of candidates, not for individual candidates. The lists represent the various political parties. Because most of the parties have long and rambling names, each party, as a matter of convenience, presents itself to the electorate with an alphabetic sign. These signs are decided upon by the Central Elections Committee. Usually the particular alphabetical letter under which a party campaigns figures prominently in the actual name of the party (and indeed the campaigners like this to be so). Often, however, the choice is arbitrary, and the sign is devoid of any partisan content. In the 1969 election campaign, which I observed in a town I name Ayara, the main contestants were the Labor Alignment (the Israel Labor Party, the United Workers Party, and nonpartisans) and the Religious National Front (the Mizrachi, the Hapoel-Hamizrachi, and nonpartisans). The Alignment presented itself with the letters "AMT" and the Religious National Front with the letter "B." To these designations I apply the term "sign" as now commonly used in anthropological writing (see for instance Comstock, et al. 1971: 56–59; Turner 1967: 19–47). The term is generally used when referring to a designation that has a simple, direct meaning known to the actor. On the other hand, the term "symbol" refers to designations that have a variety of meanings.

The complexity of symbols renders them opaque to the actor. Even when the meanings are explicated, they are likely to be problematic and ambiguous. The designation of political parties by letters is clearly an act of signifying, and the letters are political signs. I shall argue that in Ayara, with its predominantly North African electorate, and I suspect in many similar localities, the purely technical signs of "B," "AMT," etc., underwent transformation and became powerful and effective symbols.

In electioneering the alphabetical signs were often exhibited on placards, the size of posters, with the full names of the parties appearing in small print. In oral campaigning the signs also figured very prominently in the slogans of the campaigners. People, especially those not conversant with the techniques of political campaigns and electioneering, were puzzled by the political signs. In the case of the religious parties, however, the source of unease lay much deeper. Inasmuch as many of the electorate were frustrated by the phenomenon of lay politicians propagating religious policies, they were even more perplexed by the phenomenon of these policies being expressed through the vehicle of religiously neutral, technical signs. People therefore repeatedly sought in the political signs deeper inherent meanings, that went beyond the obvious simple messages. Often after attending a lengthy political harangue, at which partisan ideology and policy had been aired and the name and sign of the party repeatedly and emphatically mentioned, I would observe the blank, uncomprehending faces of people in the audience. Sometimes they would express their feelings and ask, "But what does "B" mean?" While the haranguing politicians had elucidated the practical political meaning of "B," this had failed to register in these people's minds, probably because of the overall strangeness of the phenomenon of a religious party. What they missed and sought was elucidation of the political sign at a deeper symbolic level; they wanted an interpretation in true religious terms.

Not all campaigning politicians were equally insensitive in this matter. Those politicians who came to Ayara as emissaries from the party centers in the large cities, such as Tel Aviv, to address mass meetings and rallies, and who were often of an ethnic and cultural background very different from that of the local electorate, were usually the most insensitive. Most of the smaller campaign gatherings, however, were addressed by comparatively minor local politicians whose social background was identical with or similar to that of the electorate. These politicians were much more attuned to the mood of their audiences and they offered symbolic meanings to the signs, thus obviating questions and misunderstandings. Religious National Front campaigners commonly interpreted their sign homiletically to bring it within the range of comprehension and familiarity of the electorate. I quote from my 1965 observations of a small election meeting in an Ayara home:

Towards the end of the meeting only one practical issue was raised. Since nearly all the women were illiterate, one lady asked how would they remember and recognize the "B" symbol of the party? Aharon reacted to the question as to a challenge. He perceived it as being more than a mere demand for information, but also as implicit disagreement and rejection of the arguments he had presented. He countered by presenting emotional slogans, i.e., a string of homiletic associations of the Hebrew character "B." The women would remember the symbol by bearing in mind that it figures in such hopeful phrases as "in the beginning the Lord created ..." [*bereishit bara*], the opening verse of the Bible. "B" also stands for *beriut* [health], and for *berakha* [blessing]. As against this, Aharon warned in conclusion, let no one by mischance vote *Ma'arakh*, whose alphabetic sign was AT. The AT sign is ominously symbolic: it stands for *ayn Tora* — no *Tora:* Each woman was advised to tuck a scrap of paper marked with a "B" in her bosom before entering the polling booth, and in the booth to choose the election slip according to the model. Upon this the meeting was closed and all went home (Deshen 1970b:168).

From the context, it is clear that this particular group of voters was not solely moved by the practical problem of illiteracy. The politician evidently considered these women literate enough to be able at least to compare the letters in the ballot booth with the sample letter they were advised to bring with them. The homiletical interpretations were in any case irrelevant to that practical problem. However, the politician had perceived the woman's question in much more profound terms, "What is the inherent meaning of the party's sign?"

In this reply he transformed the strictly technical political sign into a veritable religious symbol by associating "B" to some of the major themes in popular Judaism: the fundamental creation myth related in the Torah (by stressing the opening verse in particular), the universal quest for welfare, and diffuse blessing. Yearnings and feelings, traditionally articulated in theological or liturgical terms, were here expressed in a form that suits modern political action — namely through the sign "B." The politician sought to associate with the "B" sign such profound religious feelings as the deep sentiments evoked at the ritual reading of the opening Torah verses, to which traditionally is attributed the joy at being part of the nation that studies the Holy Writ and practices its precepts, as well as the steadfast resolution to be forthright in continuing to study and practice also traditionally called forth by the reading. By investing the election sign with these meanings, the politician and the audience through their acquiescence have transformed it into a religious symbol: the sign attains a variety of meanings, some of them referring to very deep layers of Jewish religious sentiment, which the actors are able to articulate only with great difficulty, if at all. Moreover, the religious message attains form and shape in terms of concrete political action and is now somewhat akin to this: by selecting the "B" slip in the voting booth, I express joy and satisfaction at being one of those who trust in the Creator of the world, who treasure the Holy Writ and exemplify it personally, and I act to assure that the Holy Writ will also be treasured by society at large. For this good deed the Lord will grant health and blessings. The politician in fact creates a new religious symbol that is attuned to the election procedure.

Not only are religious symbols created in the process of electioneering, but derogative content of a religious nature is attributed to the signs of rival parties. The 1965 "AT" sign of the Labor Alignment, the rival party of the Religious National Front, was interpreted by the religious politician as having the substantive content of *ayn Tora*. By making the voter aware of this particular interpretation, the politician sought to caution him against voting the "AT" slip, for he would thereby express repudiation of Torah, the holy teaching. In 1969, when the Labor Alignment sign was "AMT," I encountered variations on this theme at gatherings of the Religious Party. One was *ayn emuna* ["no faith"]. This was a somewhat clumsy play on the letter "M" in the party's sign, but the interpretive effect was similar to the one previously mentioned. Another "anti-AMT" slogan is remarkable because the interpretation is not in religious symbolic terms but in political terms. Because in Hebrew most of the vowels are eliminated in writing, the letters *AMT* (the Hebrew "A" is a dipthong) can technically be read as *A Met*. During an election address, a campaigner of the Religious National Front interpreted the "AMT" sign as meaning *Aleph Met!* ("A is dead!"). The letter "A" had for many years been the election sign of Mapai, the senior partner of the Labor Alignment that was formed in the 1960's. Mapai had in the past attracted the votes of many observant people, to the sorrow of the religious parties. But during the 1960's Mapai merged with other Labor groups whose position on religious issues was much more inimical to religionists than that of the old Mapai. Therefore, one of the arguments of the religious parties in 1969, expressed both orally and in leaflets, was that the old Mapai no longer existed and that the new Labor Alignment was inimical toward religious policies. The Religious National Front thus attempted to wean some of the traditional support among religious voters away from the Labor Alignment. The *Aleph Met* slogan of the Religious National Front transformed the "AMT" sign not into a religious symbol but into a political symbol, through which the voter expressed a view of developments within the party in recent years.

The other Ayara parties also engaged in the practice of symbolic innovation. In 1969 the new sign of the Labor Alignment — "AMT" — lent
itself very neatly to homiletic manipulations. It is in fact reasonable to
assume that the party leaders exerted themselves at the Central Elections
Committee to be assigned this particular combination of letters. The consonants *a*, *m*, and *t*, read as a single word, form the word *emet* (the con-
sonant *a* receiving the vowel *e*) meaning "truth." Alignment campaigners
sometimes exploited this fact gleefully.

Alignment campaigners developed the pun very imaginatively and systematically. Buses in Israel carried paid advertisements. During the 1969
campaign, throughout the country, buses were plastered along their entire
lengths with the slogans *Emet Ve'Emuna* [True and Trustworthy] and
Emet Ve'Yatziv [True and Firm]. These phrases, which figure prominently
in Jewish liturgy, appear immediately after the recital of the verses beginning "Hear, O Israel" (Deuteronomy 6:4), which form the credo of
Judaism and the climax of religious services. The phrases *Emet Ve'Emuna*
and *Emet Ve'Yatziv* convey the worshiper's acquiescence to the credo, and
in their liturgical context are vehicles that express acquiescence in a mood
of unconditional trust and ecstasy.

One of the most pervasive of the campaign arguments of the Alignment
was rooted in the fact that since the creation of the state it had been the
mainstay in the formation of all governments. Alignment campaigners
argued that the party should be returned because it had proved itself in
the past, its leaders were experienced in statecraft, whereas the opposition
politicians had never wielded power and were inexperienced. The latter
should therefore not be entrusted with forming a government and should
not be supported at the polls. In their campaign, Alignment politicians
transformed the bare "AMT" sign into the resonant word *emet* and
associated it with powerful liturgical phrases that express sentiments of
rock-firm trust, belief, and constancy: feelings that suited the party's
political slate admirably. Alignment's *Emet* did not become as sweeping
and imaginative a religious symbol as the Religious National Front's
"B," but it has become infused with very potent and intense feelings rooted in Jewish liturgy.

One of the most dramatic instances of symbolic creation that I observed
occurred during the 1965 Ayara election campaign. The party involved
was Poalei Agudat Israel (generally known by its initials, PAI), a small
religious party, whose election sign was "D." The sign as such was devoid
of any substantive significance and it is one of the many letters that compose the party's full Hebrew name. Elsewhere (Deshen 1970a), I have
described and discussed the incident at length. Here I shall recall only

those details that pertain to the present analysis. The occasion is that of a Torah scroll presentation by the party to a synagogue congregation of immigrants from southern Morocco.

The procession finally came to the synagogue and, to the sound of excited and devotional chanting, the scroll was placed into the Ark. The assembled then sat down and listened to speeches. The tone of the speeches was emotional: PAI helps people to maintain their religion; here in Ayara a scroll is brought to the synagogue for the enhancement of tradition; the same is done in other towns and villages; everywhere PAI helps people to remain religious *vis-à-vis* rampant secularism and the efforts of secular parties. The last speaker brought the speeches to a climax. He closed the harangue with the dramatic call "Hear O Israel, the Lord is our God, the Lord is One *(Ehad)* ! This is the D, the great D, the D of PAI! Vote D! The assembled then proceeded to the regular evening service (Deshen 1970a).

    Two symbols figure in this incident: a religious text ("Hear O Israel ...") and a political sign (the letter "D") that signifies the PAI party in election procedures. I devoted my previous analysis of this incident to a discussion of the types of changes that the religious symbol underwent. Here I develop the analysis by focusing on the concomitant of the changes in religious symbolism, namely, the changes in signifying.

    Throughout Jewish history, the most intense religious emotions have been focused on the ancient monotheistic call that constitutes the credo "Hear O Israel ..." These emotions erupted particularly at periods of crisis and ultimate sacrifice, and generations of Jewish martyrs died with this verse on their lips. There is a traditional form in which the credo is written, and preserved, in the script of Torah scrolls. The last letters of the first and last words of the verse are written in characters larger than the rest, and this form is copied in all prayer books. The politician linked this verse, richly charged with associations, to the election sign of his party, which quite coincidentally happened to be the Hebrew character made prominent in the credo. Thus the colorless and bare election sign has been invested with a halo of religious associations; it has become a religious symbol. The politician, in the context of the highly charged Torah presentation ceremony, is suggesting to the electorate that by selecting the "D" slip they are in fact expressing the credo, and all that is traditionally associated with its liturgical expression. The associative content of the verse is of such theological and existential profundity that virtually a whole literature of rabbinical homiletics has developed around this single verse. To believers over the centuries, the verse has been fascinating, but has remained unamenable to a clear interpretation, hence the unabated attempts of commentators to articulate what they feel to be its true meaning. All this is now linked to the "D" of PAI in the context of the selection of slips in the ballot booth.

I suggest that the infusion of religious content into the otherwise quite colorless signs of political mechanics should be seen in conjunction with the whole electoral atmosphere outlined above: an electorate to many of whom the workings of elections and democratic politics generally are novel and strange and to whom the phenomenon of religious policies propagated by laymen is foreign. This feeling of novelty and strangeness is intensified by the fact that at the crucial stage of ballot selection, religious policies are expressed through the medium of neutral and unaffective political signs. Those involved, religious politicians and members of the electorate, attempt to resolve these problems by transforming the political signs into religious symbols, causing the mechanics of elections to fall into the grooves of activities more familiar to the electorate, namely, activities pertinent to religious symbols. As a consequence, the electoral procedure as a whole becomes more understandable and the various parties project their messages more effectively. Those parties that do not explicitly champion religious policies and identify in explicit religious terms, such as the Labor Alignment, do not face the complex problems of their religious rivals when approaching the electorate. On the other hand, the Labor Alignment, by far the most vigorous of the parties, cannot stand by idly while the religious parties develop such powerful campaign techniques as the creation of religious symbols. All the more so because Labor traditionally gains much of its support from first-generation immigrants from Muslim countries. Curiously then, we also find the Labor Alignment, in effect the Israel socialist party, basing some of its appeal on the resonance of religious symbols.

I was treated to a graphic and convincing illustration of the transformation of political signs at a discussion on the elections among a group of Ayara men originating from Morocco. One, a staunch supporter of the Religious National Front who was enthusiastically expounding his views to his more sober companions, stated emphatically: "When I go to vote I take the B slip in my hand. I kiss it. I say the *Lesheim yihud kudsha.* And I drop it into the ballot box!" This is a typical description of routine behavior associated with acts of ritual devotion. The *Lesheim yihud* prayer is a mystical text of the late Kabbala that according to certain variants of Jewish rite (including those of North Africa) prefaces a great variety of ritual actions. The text is in Aramaic, the content highly esoteric; it is virtually untranslatable without engaging in a preliminary discourse on its complex theosophical terminology. The ordinary worshiper does not usually have a full understanding of the text. What he does understand, the meaning he attributes to the text, is the relevant point for present purposes. By reciting the *Lesheim yihud*, the worshiper expresses his hope that the ritual act he is about to perform be carried out in pure devotion without any extraneous, secular attributes or intentions. The worshiper prays that the act may have certain profound mystical effects, one of which is to hasten the ultimate redemption and the coming of the Messiah. The *Lesheim yihud* prefaces standard ritual actions such as daily prayers, putting on phylacteries, eating unleavened bread on Passover. Frequently when the ritual hinges on an artifact, one kisses the object prior to performance of the act.

The act of voting just described has thus become not a medium to effect political aims, or even to effect religious policies, but a ritual action gaining the appropriate attributes customary in Judeo-Moroccan tradition. Remarkably, this instance of symbolization was the work of neither a propagandist nor an outsider but of an unsophisticated local who expressed what he felt. Here it can be seen that the process of symbolization of political signs, far from stemming only from the machination of advertisers, has roots in the culture of many of the electorate, who were unfamiliar with the phenomena of differentiation, both social and symbolic, operating in democratic electoral procedures. It is the reactions of these people that drove the politicians to try to adapt their approach. In the matter of social differentiation the politicians could be conformable only to a very limited extent — the politicians, after all, were no saintly rabbis, and the roles of an Israeli politician and of a rabbi, as conceived by traditionalists from North Africa, are not easily bridged. As to symbolic differentiation — of political aims articulated by political signs and not by religious symbols — the politicians were more pliable and acquiesced in the fashion that we have followed.

A final point is relevant to the sociological study of migration and directed change. All too often one comes across studies that discuss the changes experienced by people subjected to directed change or by migrant groups such as the Israeli electorate of North African origin only in terms that are strictly limited to the people who are presumably changing. Thus there are many studies on the changing economy, political organization, culture, or what-have-you of this or that migrant group, remote tribe, or colonially subjugated people, which focus strictly on the group undergoing change. These studies ignore, because of their limited focus, any changes that the dominant society and its institutions might concomitantly be undergoing. Therefore although they may illuminate their delimited fields, such studies create distorted perspective because their silence on the wider field of the absorbing or colonial society (or whatever may be the case) implies that no concomitant changes take place elsewhere in that society. Weingrod (1962) forcefully argued that studies of directed change or migration should not be rigidly focused on the delimited population that is presumed to be changing. In a study of the economic practices of new farmers in Israel, Weingrod demonstrated that changes flowed in at least two directions. The administrators of the new farming projects indeed caused profound occupational and economic changes among the immigrants, but the latter also provoked very considerable modifications of the economic institutions to which they were supposed to adapt. Weingrod applied the term "reciprocal change" to this dual process. His insight has hitherto not drawn the attention it merits, for discussing social change in terms of a variety of levels of change, or at least in terms of "reciprocal change," affords a more sophisticated view of reality than that which one gains from the more traditional approaches in studies of social change. The process of "reciprocal change," I argue, also operates in Israeli election procedures as analyzed here. The new voters adapt to democratic practices, as Weingrod's farmers adapted to new economic practices. However, just as the latter cause the economic institutional arrangements to change, so do the new voters cause certain aspects of electioneering practices to be modified quite profoundly.

REFERENCES

BENAYAHU, M.
1953   *Marbitz Tora.* Jerusalem: Harav Kook Institute.
BEN-SASSON, H. H.
1959   *Hagut Ve'hanhaga.* Jerusalem: Bialik Institute.
COMSTOCK, R. W., et al.
1971   *Religion and man: an introduction.* New York: Harper and Row.
DESHEN, S.
1970a On religious change: the situational analysis of symbolic action. *Comparative Studies in Society and History* 12:260–274.
1970b *Immigrant voters in Israel: parties and congregations in a local election campaign.* Manchester: Manchester University Press.
1972   " 'The business of ethnicity is finished!'?: the ethnic factor in a local election campaign," in *The elections in Israel, 1969.* Edited by A. Arian, 278–304. Jerusalem: Academic Press.
ELKIN, F.
1969   Advertising themes and quiet revolutions: dilemmas in French Canada. *American Journal of Sociology* 75:112–122.

KATZ, J.

1961 *Tradition and crisis: Jewish society at the end of the Middle Ages.* Glencoe, Illinois: Free Press.

SHOKEID, M.

1971 *The dual heritage: immigrants from the Atlas Mountains in an Israeli village.* Manchester: Manchester University Press.

TURNER, V. W.

1967 *The forest of symbols.* Ithaca: Cornell University Press.

WEINGROD, A

1962 Reciprocal change: a case study of a Moroccan village in Israel. *American Anthropologist* 64.

Inward-Looking and Outward-Looking Symbols

GRACE HARRIS

What kind and degree of order should we expect to find in symbolic systems? The question emerges sharply in Peter Worsley's essay on Groote Eylandt Totemism (Worsley 1967), with its criticisms of Lévi-Strauss. Strauss purports to solve the problems of Australian and other totemisms by elucidating their conceptual nature (Lévi-Strauss 1963). Worsley replies that the thought underlying Australian totemism is not conceptual at all. While Australians, he says, exhibit the capacity for conceptual thought in their ethnobotanical and ethnozoological classifications (1967: 153), the bodies of totemic elements have only the properties of "heaps" or "congeries," not of ordered series. The totemic mode of thought is devoid of logic and abstraction (p. 150–151).

Worsley's view of the relationship between totemic elements and social units also differs radically from that of Lévi-Strauss. He comments on Lévi-Strauss saying that because totemic elements do not form a series, they can be ordered only by an extrinsic principle, by the association between totem on the one hand and clan or moiety on the other. In so arguing, Worsley rejects the Lévi-Straussian notion that totemism represents and expresses the structure of the mind. To him, Lévi-Strauss (like others) falls before the temptation to oversystematize Australian totemism. Further, Worsley holds that Lévi-Strauss has failed to attend properly to the use by Australians of a number of distinct classifications, each serving its own purpose and not related to the others by the supposed master principle of binary opposition (p. 153–157).

To the initial question, then, Lévi-Strauss answers that we should expect a very high degree of order, of logical coherence in symbolic

systems, as demonstrated in his treatment of totemism. Worsley holds
that at least some bodies of symbolic elements are not systems at all —
they have no intrinsic order or logical coherence. The system of social
units possesses autonomy and imposes order upon the body of symbolic
elements associated with it.

An assessment of the positions of Lévi-Strauss and Worsley, and a
follow-up of some aspects of the initial question, requires a view of the
nature of symbolic elements and their relationship to social units. In
order to present an outline of such a view, I will use elements drawn
from the symbolic systems of Judaism and Christianity, returning now
and again to Australian totemism. Doing so requires a vast cultural and
geographic leap. But I take comfort from Evans-Pritchard's suggestion
that early comparativists might have done well to study the "higher"
religions, "proceeding from the better known to the less known" (1965:
16). Although today we know much more about "primitive" religions
than did the speculators of the nineteenth century, we can find it profitable to make use of knowledge about all members of the genus
religion.[1]

Within any body of religious symbols we find series or clusters of
symbolic elements which I call DISPLAYING symbols. In belief, ritual,
and often in artistic representation, any particular item from a given
series or cluster appears only in specifiable contexts. The presence of
one item from the series or cluster may entail the presence of another
item from the same grouping, or it may require the absence of all other
members of the set. Whatever the rules dictate (and these must be discovered by investigation), no symbolic element or symbol has a meaning in isolation from the others of its series or cluster. The totality of
meanings-in-context is what is "displayed" by the symbols and by any
one symbol.

To illustrate: liturgical colors comprise a cluster of symbols occurring
in Roman Catholic, Orthodox, Anglican, Lutheran, and some other
Christian rites. The use of one liturgical color according to the ritual
rules precludes or allows the use of certain other colors.[2] But no color
has a meaning apart from the others. The totality of meanings-in-

---

[1] The scope of the paper does not allow for sorting out the similarities and differences between religious and nonreligious symbolism. Suffice it to say that I do
not hold that all symbolism is religious.

[2] Only one color can be "the color of the day"; of course complete "matching,"
e.g. of altar cloth and vestments, does not always occur, A full description and
analysis would have to take into account differences between churches and also
the complexity of the rules of equivalence and nonequivalence of colors. Then,
for example, the use of yellow, gold, and blue vestments in the Orthodox Church
could be dealt with.

context, displayed by the liturgical colors, presents an aspect of the world as structured by Christianity. It presents the existence of ritually significant states of purity, penance, mourning, and martyrdom. The various states connect with other aspects of the Christian world having to do with the nature of man in relation to God, the stages of life and the meaning of death, salvation, history, and so on.

I purposely avoid saying that the symbolic colors "refer to" ritually significant states or that the use of the colors is "explained by" concepts or beliefs. We have to give up the notion that symbols stand for a reality that exists somewhere else or somehow else. For symbols are pre-sentative, revealing, DISPLAYING the reality that religion creates and sustains.

Where a grouping of symbolic elements apparently forms a congeries, this may itself display important aspects of the world. The world may be revealed or displayed as one thing made up of many things clustered together. In such a world one might find as much or more emphasis on a principle of simple discriminability as on a principle of categorizing. Even a congeries or a "heap" is made up of discriminable items; otherwise we would speak of a "mass" or a "lump"! And the world of Australian totemism does indeed appear to be a world of discriminable "items": of species, individuals, sexes, body parts, artifacts, processes, events.

Therefore, on the matter of ordering, Lévi-Strauss and Worsley each has hold of a partial truth which he has exaggerated. Worsley does offer a corrective to Lévi-Strauss's exaggerated systematizing. However Worsley fails to recognize the conceptual importance of the "itemizing" character of totemic congeries.

In making this suggestion I must recognize its intuitive and tentative character. The meanings-in-context of displaying symbols must be sought out, first, by way of rituals. The proper analysis of ritual in turn depends on giving up the notion that symbols "stand for" something. Hence, analysis of ritual must meet the requirement of proper identification of the constituents of symbol sets or clusters.[3] Second, analysis requires investigation of the concepts which coordinate the elements of a symbol set. We have, unfortunately, no magical key with which to unlock meanings. To return for a moment to the liturgical colors: the total set includes the red-black-white triad elucidated by Turner (1966b). Though Turner's treatment helps to grasp some major features of the liturgical color set, it cannot alone account for certain characteristics of the WHOLE set (which includes violet). The relevant

[3] A topic I intend to publish on elsewhere.

concepts must be sought out.

Finally, and this I state here only as an article of faith, the concepts which coordinate the elements of a symbolic set are those of which the users are aware. No doubt unconscious processes contribute to the creation and effectiveness of symbolic elements, but for understanding meanings-in-context, we must look to consciously shared concepts.

Now I turn to the relationship between symbols and social units. Symbolic elements have a MARKING function when their association with a social unit (group or category) provides one of the features marking out that unit AS A UNIT. But symbolic elements with this function do not by any means always serve as diacritics marking out each unit FROM other like ones. This being the case, I suggest that we find at least two kinds of marking symbols: (a) symbols performing diacritical functions, which I call DISTINGUISHING MARKERS; and (b) symbols by means of which members of a unit recognize their unity, which I call RALLYING MARKERS. Worsley notes that among Groote Eylandt aborigines ". . . the totems do NOT neatly discriminate one clan from another" (1967: 149). May we then suppose Groote Eylandt totems to be rallying markers? This question receives brief attention later.

Of the symbols I call displaying elements, I have said that they do not "represent" but rather "present" an aspect of the religiously created and sustained world. When we come to marking elements the notion of "representation" seems more justifiable. Marking elements in fact lie on the borderline between symbol and sign, just as their social uses lie on the borderline between the religious and the political domains. Distinguishing markers are visible as such to members of all the relevant social units. For any given social unit, then, the associated distinguishing marker or markers can and do come to stand for, or represent, the unit. But "representativeness" is not intrinsic to rallying markers. Another way of labeling the two kinds of marking symbols calls attention to this difference in their relationship to the social order. Distinguishing markers are OUTWARD-LOOKING SYMBOLS. Their representativeness comes into play in the contraposing of social units in thought and action. Rallying markers are INWARD-LOOKING SYMBOLS, involved in the recognition of unity.[4]

It must be pointed out that the same symbolic word, gesture, act, attribute, artifact, etc., can occur as a displaying symbol in one or many sets and as either or both kinds of marking symbol within the same symbolic system. In Christianity, the Cross is one of a group of

---

[4] The distinction was suggested to me originally by Godfrey Lienhardt's treatment of Dinka clan divinities (1961).

displaying symbols which present and reveal basic features of the Christian world. It also functions as a rallying marker, being the symbol *par excellence* in relation to which Christians define their (ideal) unity. But also, in the wider social world the Cross is a distinguishing marker, "standing for," or "representing," Christians in contraposition, especially to the adherents of the other two related monotheistic faiths. Like other symbols of multiple occurrence, the various meanings and functions of the Cross affect each other and provide material for a continual elaboration of associational meanings.[5]

For the remainder of this discussion I refer to marking elements simply as inward-looking and outward-looking symbols, and turn to a last pair of examples. They are taken from Judaism and are the Star (or Shield) of David — the Magen David — and the Menorah — the seven-branched candelabrum. The information comes primarily from the work of the eminent Judaic scholar Gershom Scholem. He not only provides an examination of the Magen David's history and significance, but offers the point of view of a highly sophisticated native exegete.

Symbols arise, says Scholem in writing of religion

... when a man's world possesses spiritual meaning for him, when all of his relations to the world are conditioned by the living content of this meaning ... (1971:257).
The community lays hold of some detail of its world, apprehends the totality in it, and derives from it and through it that totality and its content .... The more such a detail contains ... the more suited it is in the eyes of the community to become a symbol (p. 257). [Symbols] crystallize and encompass a world-view (p. 258).

Since religious symbols, for Scholem, "both crystallize and reveal" the religious world, what is one to think of elements which arouse great emotion and yet are known to be religiously "empty"? Even to use the word symbol for such elements seems a contradiction in terms. The problem arises with the Star of David as it appears on the flag of the modern State of Israel. Is it a symbol, he asks, "... of the religious content and intellectual world of monotheism ..." or is it only "... a symbol of Jewish 'statehood' or 'sovereignty' ..."? He rejects as idle fancies the attempts to read into the Magen David all manner of esoteric meanings "which correspond to nothing in the Jewish tradition" (1971: 259).

Elucidating the history of the Magen David, Scholem distinguishes

[5] The Cross is, of course, what Turner would call a "dominant symbol" (1966a: 30–31). However, I contend that dominant symbols can be described and analyzed in a much more systematic way than Turner appears to believe.

between the hexagram made up of two interlocking triangles and its history as the Shield or Star of David. He says:

The hexagram is not a Jewish symbol, much less "the symbol of Judaism." None of the marks of a true symbol nor its manner of origin . . . apply to it. It expresses no "idea," it awakens no primeval associations which have become entwined with the roots of experience, and it does not spontaneously comprise any spiritual reality. IT CALLS TO MIND NOTHING OF BIBLICAL OR RABBINICAL JUDAISM, it arouses no hopes" (1971:259, emphasis added).

How shocking a statement this is for those who, like myself, are accustomed to seeing the Magen David occupy some of the same positions on and in synagogues as the Cross occupies on and in Christian churches; who have seen Jews wearing the Magen David on a neckchain as Christians wear the Cross; who have received greeting cards expressing ecumenical sentiments and decorated with the Magen David, the Cross and the Crescent; who are sent, as advertisements for books, brochures decorated with the symbols of Judaism, Christianity, and Islam.

In the Hellenistic age the hexagram and pentagram were associated, and both appeared among Jews and Christians. In later times, Scholem discerns two lines of development as the hexagram gathered meanings, and became known as the Shield of Solomon, the Shield of David, and the Star of David. Of the two lines, one magical and the other decorative, the latter claims our attention here.

Some Christian churches of the Middle Ages displayed the hexagram as a decorative motif: the sign could hardly, then, have been a symbol of Judaism. Among Jews, it occurred on the official seals of various communities, and also as a printer's mark. But the official use of the hexagram as the insignia of a Jewish community Scholem traces to Prague. "When in 1527 Emperor Ferdinand I entered Prague, the municipal authorities ordained that the Jews were to march out toward him 'with their flag' " (1971: 275), a flag that displayed the Magen David. From there the "official" use spread to other communities, east and west.

Crucial evidence comes from the old cemetery of Vienna where the year 1656 produced what Scholem calls "the first instance of a clear juxtaposition of the Cross and the Shield of David as signs of the two religions." For the boundary stone between the Jewish and Christian sections of the cemetery showed the Magen David and the Cross chiselled into the stone in equal size (1971: 277–278).

The final development of the Magen David as a "symbol of Judaism" Scholem sees in the nineteenth century.

The Jews of the emancipation period were looking for a "symbol" of

Judaism to match the symbol of Christianity which they saw everywhere before them. If Judaism was nothing more than an "Israelite persuasion," it seemed only proper that, LIKE OTHER RELIGIONS AND CONFESSIONS, IT SHOULD HAVE a visible distinguishing sign (1971: 279, emphasis added).

At this time the star of David could not truly, in his view, be a JEWISH symbol. It had became a symbol OF Judaism derived from what he calls "the drive to imitate" (Scholem 1971: 279). A gulf lies between the Magen David with its distinguishing function and the Menorah, a truly Jewish symbol. The seven-branched candelabrum was one of the major sacra of the Temple. In representations it occurs early in juxtaposition with the two lions holding onto the Tree of Life or the Ark of the Torah. Says Scholem, "These emblems possess a living relationship to the spontaneously apprehensible contents of the Jewish imagination" (p. 261). The Menorah is filled with biblical and rabbinical associations.

Yet the Magen David does appear on the flag of Israel. What, then, is its present significance? At last Scholem is ready to grant that the Star of David has a wealth of meaning. For the yellow "Jewish star" was forced upon Jews by Nazis as a sign of exclusion and annihilation. "Under this sign they were murdered; under this sign they came to Israel" (p. 281). The historical association of the Magen David with the martyrdom of the Jewish people has associated that ancient figure with symbols revealing the Jewish world.

I conclude with an effort to put my inadequate summary of Scholem's study into the context of this discussion. Taking first the contrast between the Menorah and the Magen David: the Menorah occurs primarily within a group of displaying symbols. To properly understand its meaning requires an exposition of its ritual uses in conjunction or contrast with other related Temple sacra and other lamps (such as the eight-branched Hanukah lamp). It also requires exploration of the relevant Judaic concepts of LIGHT in relation to God's nature, the *Shekhinah* or Divine Presence, the interaction of man and God, the results of sin and virtue and so on.[6] It is not surprising that our native exegete reserves for such a displaying element the assertion that it has "towering symbolic significance" (p. 261).

During the assimilation period, when the Magen David functioned largely as a distinguishing marker, it served a purpose which must seem wholly at odds with biblical and rabbinical Judaism. It merely marked off the Jews as one group among many. Now, having absorbed the experience of the Holocaust as the experience of the People of Israel, the

---

[6]   The *Encyclopaedia Judaica* (1971) contains some important figures and photographs as well as useful bibliographies appended to the relevant articles.

Magen David is also a rallying marker. It has been transformed from an outward-looking symbol into one that is both outward- and inward-looking. In the process it has become more akin to the displaying elements. Meanwhile the Menorah, by virtue of appearing on the emblem of Israel has acquired a marking function almost new to it.[7]

The history of the two symbolic elements, then, finds them changing their significance relative to each other, relative to other symbolic elements, and relative to social units. One conclusion is inescapable. Markers that rally are more likely to acquire connections with displaying symbols than are distinguishing markers. What, then, shall we expect concerning the logical coherence of groups of marking symbols? I suggest that distinguishing markers, outward-looking symbols, have a tendency to form coherent sets. Rallying markers, being inward-looking, need not be brought into line with the rallying markers of other social units.

During the period when the Magen David was no more than a distinguishing marker, it contributed to the formation of a simple, coherent set of symbolic elements. The adherents of the three related monotheistic religions became marked off from one another by the use of three simple figures, associated with David, Jesus Christ, and Muhammad. Later, through its profound associations with group experience, the Magen David became a rallying marker. Having acquired further associations with the displaying symbols of biblical and rabbinical Judaism, the Magen David has too many meanings for it to be crammed into any simple logical scheme. Its old logical ties with the Cross and the Crescent have diminished in relative importance within its total body of meanings. At the same time, I would assert, the Magen David has become more like the Cross, with which it shares meanings and functions it formerly lacked.[8]

Finally, I return to Australian totemism. The absence of logical co-

[7]   The Magen David has in fact been in the process of acquiring multiple occurrences and multiple meanings which parallel those of the Cross. However, where the Magen David has become an inward-looking symbol after it functioned as an outward-looking symbol, the symbolic development of the Cross took place the other way around. Christians and Jews alike must regret that the Cross ever became an outward-looking symbol.

[8]   I regret that space limitations do not allow mention in the text of Franz Rosenzweig's curious work of what might be called "ecumenical mysticism" (1970). After using the hexagram in his construction of a mystical schema, Rosenzweig compares Judaism and Christianity. For the former the Star "blazes inward," for the latter the Star "blazes outward." Most assuredly, my formulation of "inward-looking" and "outward-looking" symbols does not come from Rosenzweig. However, his use of the hexagram as well as its use by adherents of the heretical Jewish sect of Sabbatians could be fitted into a discussion of wider scope.

herence which Worsley notes may be connected with the operation of totemic elements as rallying markers as well as displaying symbols. It may be that precisely BECAUSE totemic elements do not neatly discriminate one social unit from another they can accumulate and exchange meanings. To know whether that is true requires a kind of analysis not yet fully carried out.

REFERENCES

Encyclopaedia Judaica
  1971   Articles on "Menorah," "Shekhinah," "Temple." Jerusalem: Macmillan.
EVANS-PRITCHARD, E.
  1965   *Theories of primitive religion.* Oxford: Oxford University Press.
LÉVI-STRAUSS, C.
  1963   *Totemism.* Translated by R. Needham. Boston: Beacon Press.
LIENHARDT, G.
  1961   *Divinity and experience.* Oxford: Oxford University Press.
ROSENZWEIG, F.
  1970   *The star of redemption.* Translated by W. Hallo. New York: Holt, Rinehart and Winston.
SCHOLEM, G.
  1971   "The Star of David: history of a symbol," in *The messianic idea in Judaism.* Edited by G. Scholem, 257–281. New York: Schocken Books.
TURNER, V.
  1966a   "Symbols in Ndembu ritual," in *The forest of symbols.* Edited by V. Turner 19–47. Ithaca and London: Cornell University Press.
  1966b   "Color classification in Ndembu ritual: a problem in primitive classification," in *The forest of symbols.* Edited by V. Turner, 59–92. Ithaca and London: Cornell University Press.
WORSLEY, P.
  1967   "Groote Eylandt totemism and *Le Totemisme aujourd'hui*," in *The structural study of myth and totemism.* Edited by E. Leach, 141–159. A.S.A. Monographs 5. London: Tavistock.

Crosses and Souls

ALICJA IWAŃSKA

In the concepts of "functional" and "dysfunctional" anthropologists have overemphasized gratifications derived by the individual from a smoothly functioning, integrated society; they forget about individual happiness and self-realization and that people are sometimes harmed rather than helped by such an ideal entity.

Inspired by the concerns with individual happiness and self-realization of such nonprofessional social scientists as Freud and Bertrand Russell,[1] I would like to explore those unfashionable but always desirable "human conditions" in two Mazahua communities of central Mexico which have the same cultural past, similar sociopolitical structure, and strongly contrasting magico-religious cults.

I studied one of those communities, El Nopal, in the early 1960's (Iwańska 1971); another one, San Simon de La Laguna, was studied from 1967 till 1969 by the Mexican anthropologist Efrain C. Cortés Ruíz and is described in detail in his conscientious and intelligent book (1972).

The term "happiness" may be defined for the purpose of this article as (a) an objectively assessed minimum of somatic well-being (sufficient food, safety, shelter, etc.) and (b) a subjective sense of well-being (lack of anxiety, suspicion, some *joie de vivre*).

The term "self-realization" (and, maybe one should speak only about possibility of self-realization) will be understood here as the possibility of living according to one's goals and values. If, for instance, a typical person from a given community believes that in order to be a self-respecting human being one should hold (i.e. subsidize) at least some public offices

---

[1] I have in mind Sigmund Freud's book *Civilization and its discontents* and Bertrand Russell's *Conquest of happiness*.

during his lifetime, and he cannot afford it because of lack of means, such an individual is deprived of the opportunity for self-realization. Societies which force women into choice between marriage and career obviously deprive them of an opportunity for self-realization.

In this article I will try to analyze the relationship between beliefs (religious and magical) and the chances for happiness and self-realization of a typical Mazahua villager in the two communities in central Mexico.

Both villages (San Simon with 1275 inhabitants in 1969 [Cortés Ruíz 1972: 35], and El Nopal with around 1120 inhabitants in the early 1960's) are well-integrated, corporate communities, governed by traditional politico-religious Indian governments. San Simon, however, is much more isolated geographically and more traditional. This isolation and traditionalism are strengthened by the lack of a school, by the type of land tenure (private *minifundias* of about five hectares per family) and an almost below-subsistence farming which does not force villagers into contacts with the larger world and does not make them open to innovations.

El Nopal is much less isolated. There is a Pan-American highway less than one mile from the village. The population since early 1930 has been organized into an *ejido* [an organization of the recipients of land distributed in consequence of Agrarian Reform] with the local *mestizo* population from the county seat, Las Animas, situated about two miles from El Nopal. Since 1962 El Nopal has had its own school as well. The contacts of these villagers with the larger world (with local *mestizos* and even with Mexico City) are much more frequent than those of the villagers from San Simon.

In both San Simon and El Nopal three administrative systems operate: (1) the national administrative network represented at the community level by so-called *delegados* [representatives of the county elected from among the villagers]; (2) a Catholic Church organization which at least in El Nopal is only occasionally served by a parish priest; and (3) traditional Indian government.

Those last two administrative systems, though formally separate, are in both communities (as in many other Mexican Indian villages) represented by one and the same group called sometimes *autoridades* [authorities], sometimes *gobierno*, as in El Nopal or sometimes *junta* as the villagers from San Simon call it.[2]

Efrain C. Cortés Ruíz (1972: 58–60) documents conscientiously and analyzes very well indeed the complicated processes which have resulted in this still changing strange politico-religious structure known as "traditional Indian government." This government actually governs in

[2]   It seems that in San Simon the network of national authorities is integrated into the *junta*, the village government (see Cortés Ruíz 1972: 69–77).

both villages in question. The other two administrative systems (that of the Catholic Church and the network of national delegates) though backed by powerful national and international institutions respectively appear rather pale, powerless, or even nonexistent in comparison with the village government. In San Simon for instance the network of national *delegados* (quite strong numerically because it is composed of as many as nineteen persons) (Cortés Ruíz 1972: 69), seems to be almost absorbed by the traditional Indian government. In El Nopal on the other hand a very small network of national delegates is truly nominal and its existence is explained by the villagers as a necessary compromise with local *mestizos*.

Because the church at least in El Nopal (but probably in San Simon as well) is used mainly for Catholic-pagan services performed by Indians themselves (in El Nopal for instance every night the headman of the village (*cabezilla del pueblo*) has to ring the church bells and every second afternoon or so he has to conduct the rosary) it would be easy to conclude that the Catholic administration simply does not function in such villages. Such a conclusion would have to be promptly rejected however, at least for El Nopal where the complex Mazahua marriage ceremony is not only dependent upon but even strongly controlled by the Catholic administration. Because the Mazahuas from El Nopal believe that their Mazahua weddings should be preceded by a religious Catholic ceremony, they are forced to do it "properly," i.e. to confess and take communion (which they usually do not do) and to rent Western clothes for the church wedding.

Most of the important and enjoyable social roles performed by the villagers of both communities and contributing greatly to their prestige, happiness, well-being, and self-realization are connected with the functioning of the traditional Indian government in which they have their *cargos* [offices] held jointly by married men and their wives.

In spite of the common precolonial culture, the identical cycles of their Catholic-pagan festivities, and the very similar structure of their contemporary Indian governments, the content of the religious beliefs and rituals is very different in the two villages.

Mazahuas from San Simon have singled out as main objects of their cult dangerous crosses located in their small and carefully locked family chapels (*oratorios*), and they spend a great deal of their energies appeasing those malevolent deities.

Among Mazahuas from El Nopal the ritual of appeasement of a malevolent cross (placed in an open chapel at the entrance to the village and decorated every Wednesday with fresh flowers) has played only a minor role.

While in San Simon all people fear the blackmail and vengeance of their crosses, the cross from El Nopal is dangerous to little boys only. ("It makes them sick if it is not well attended, or when the boys approach it, or for no reason whatsoever.") Even this belief, however, so mild in comparison to beliefs in the malevolent powers of the crosses in San Simon, has been disappearing from El Nopal.

While the malevolent cross seems to be the main cultural symbol in San Simon, the main cultural symbol in El Nopal is the full-of-flames-but-also-full-of-hope purgatory where the souls of Mazahua ancestors and all other souls of deceased villagers reside (only the souls of little children, *angelitos*, go directly to heaven according to the villagers from El Nopal). Life is seen as very difficult by those villagers but full of hope; it is very much like their purgatory through which everybody has to pass but from which everybody will be rescued eventually. This outlook on life perhaps could be called "optimistic fatalism" because nobody, even the worst human being, according to those Mazahuas from El Nopal, is condemned to hell; everybody (without special prayers or favors from the saints) who serves his term in purgatory eventually will reach heaven.

Mazahuas from San Simon live in constant anxiety as they try to appease their malevolent and irrational crosses, and they are never sure whether their frantic appeasement rituals will really help, because the crosses are malicious, whimsical, and hard to understand.

Mazahuas from El Nopal are free of such anxieties. Their beliefs do not terrorize them into costly and uncertain rituals. In fact their anxieties are largely secular (mainly related to health, communal identification, and economic problems). Their religious beliefs (though expressed in rituals costly in time and money as are all Indian rituals) give them a great deal of moral support in the difficult realization of their communal goals such as preservation of their Mazahua identity and introduction of such selected elements of *el progreso* [progress] as education, electricity, and running water.

There are two identical seats of religious cult in San Simon and El Nopal. There is a communal church inhabited by various Catholic saints and attended by *cargueros* [office-holders in the traditional Indian government]. The Christ on the cross (which is not malevolent like the crosses of family chapels) is found in the communal church of both villages, and in in El Nopal (I do not have information for San Simon) there is also a picture of *Las animas*, representing the souls of Mazahua ancestors in purgatory, usually nude, with fair complexion, and often with blue eyes — a physical type contrasting with that of Mazahua Indians — placed together with various other images at the main altar.

The second seat of the religious cult common to both villages is the household altar. On these altars — little wooden structures attached to the walls — villagers accumulate various saints and often (as in El Nopal) other sacred objects, e.g. such cherished and "sanctified" things as alarm clocks, little Mexican flags, pictures of metal biscuit cans from newspaper clippings, etc. The picture of *Las animas* [souls in purgatory] usually occupies the central place on such a home altar in El Nopal. I observed that during the two-day All Souls' Celebration, the image of the ancestral couple is taken out of the home altar and placed on the floor in a corner of the room where it is appropriately illuminated and attended.

In San Simon in addition to the two seats of religious cult described above, there is a third seat of religious cult, family chapels (*oratorios*), miniature windowless houses, carefully locked and opened on occasion of the cult only. Efrain C. Cortés Ruíz describes in detail the cult of the crosses (the only ritual objects located in the *oratorios*) and through the description of the rituals of appeasement of those crosses he shows us the whole complex family, kinship, and lineage structure of this isolated and traditional Mazahua village.

Otomi and Mazahua *oratorios* were, so far as I know, described first by Jacques Soustelle (n.d.); these, however, are not inhabited by malevolent crosses. Rather, like El Nopal home altars, they house various saints and cherished objects and probably the images of the ancestral couple as well. I did see personally such images in two of the visited *oratorios* in a village studied by Soustelle, San Bartolomé del Llano. The images of *Las animas* in San Bartolomé del Llano were very similar to those in El Nopal and the villages in both communities claimed that they were painted by Mazahua painters in the old days; the explanation is highly improbable because of the non-Mazahua physical type of the ancestral couple and because of the availability of such images at various antique markets in Mexico City. It is quite possible, however, that the old Catholic cult of All Souls' Days got fused at some point with the Mazahua cult of their ancestral couple — *Padre Viejo* [Old Father] and *Madre Vieja* [Old Mother] (Carrasco Pizana 1950: 133–134) venerated probably throughout the whole Mazahua (García Payón 1942).

On the second visit in San Bartolomé del Llano I invited a few of my Mazahua friends from El Nopal in order to show them those family *oratorios*. Only then did I learn that El Nopal used to have similar family chapels which were abandoned only a generation ago. On the basis of this information I hypothesized (Iwańska 1967) that the images of an ancestral couple "emigrated" (along with other saints and objects) from their family chapels to home altars, and their cult diminished, giving way to a more "modern" (and less ritualized) belief emphasizing the dwelling place of the ancestral couple, the full-of-flames-but-also-full-of-hope purgatory. It is possible that this shift coincided with the increased secularization of communal life in El Nopal, stimulated by the land reform occurring at that time and the incorporation of the Mazahuas from this village into a completely new, future-oriented secular organization of *ejido*.

So far as I know there were never any malevolent, dangerous crosses inside the *oratorios* of El Nopal, as they did not exist and do not exist in the area of Ixtlahuaca investigated by Jacques Soustelle. But there were other malevolent crosses in El Nopal and there still is one such cross, as I already pointed out, which is, however, becoming less and less dangerous. This is what the people from El Nopal have to say about their crosses:

Years ago everybody had a cross in his house made of wood or stone. According to our grandfathers, if the cross was not paid attention to, if it was not brought its branch of flowers, and candles were not lit for it, the cross became angry and seized boys who would become sick with fear (Iwańska 1967: 204).

The same dangerous characteristics are still being attributed to the cross placed at the entrance to El Nopal, this cross being definitely a close relative of malevolent crosses from San Simon.

The relationship between the increasing modernization of the people from El Nopal and the diminishing of their belief in malevolent crosses is well illustrated by the following account of the villagers from El Nopal:

But now we know that this is not so, the cross cannot do anything and that only God can punish a child. If the child is sick the best thing to do is to take him to the doctor because it is certain that it is sickness which is bothering him and that this has nothing to do with the cross (Iwańska 1967: 207).

Efrain C. Cortés Ruíz had argued very convincingly that the crosses have probably acquired their malevolent, dangerous characteristics in Mazahua Catholic-pagan cults because they became associated with the Conquest. It was the cross which was first imposed upon the conquered Indians and only later were such deities as *Virgen María* and other saints introduced. The crosses were placed on the flags of Spanish ships, they were immediately erected in places of destroyed Indian idols (Cortés Ruíz 1972: 93–94), and one should add that the monks who did convert Indians carried on them their large crosses and sometimes they preached with a large crucifix in hand.

There are numerous examples from contemporary life which help us to understand such "guilt by association" acquired by objects. Since injections were used in Nazi concentration camps to kill prisoners (Iwańska 1957) and later less powerful evipan injections were used by Soviet

Russians during political investigations, it is no wonder that there was some reluctance among those who remembered those times to the use of evipan as anesthetic during operations. It is possible that the Japanese of Hiroshima would have reacted at first with a similar reluctance if atomic energy had been presented to them for peaceful uses shortly after the atomic bomb had destroyed their city.

In both San Simon and El Nopal there are, however, good, benevolent crosses side by side with the malevolent ones. There are such good crosses in the church of San Simon (Cortés Ruíz 1972: 96) and there is such a cross on the top of the mountain in the area of El Nopal, the cross venerated by the people from the whole region every May 3.

Because the symbol of the cross was known in pre-Hispanic America, we need much more prehistorical research to find out whether it was known by the Mazahuas as well. Much more research also should be done on the details of the cult of ancestral couples throughout the Mazahua area. This belief, as I hypothesized, was fused through Christianization with the Catholic cult of All Souls' Days, a hypothesis which should be checked through even further inquiry into the processes of Christianization. Christianization apparently was conducted in the Mazahua region by the Franciscan Order (Cortés Ruíz 1972: 96).

It is possible, however, even without such further research to return to the question of happiness and self-realization of a typical Mazahua in the two villages.

If we consider the Declaration of Human Rights as a document formulating the minimum conditions for human happiness and self-realization, the people of San Simon and El Nopal (like those of similar rural communities of the underdeveloped areas) do not have most of those minimum conditions (adequate diet, shelter, medical help, education, etc.) though Agrarian Reform implemented in this particular area in the early 1930's greatly helped in rescuing some of those rural people from the worst misery. It seems that people from El Nopal have profited much more from Agrarian Reform than people from San Simon. Both communities have integrated corporate social structures and because their inhabitants are all poor (no great economic differences exist even in El Nopal where a few of the "wealthiest" families have mules and painted houses) they all have more or less equal access to the system of traditional Indian government offices (*cargos*) so essential to their self-realization. The sense of usefulness and the amount of social participation are, maybe, even stronger in San Simon than in El Nopal due to the frequency of frantic magico-religious rituals performed in family *oratorios* whenever the malevolent crosses begin to "behave strangely." Word about such "strange behavior" spreads quickly among the members of the extended family, throughout kinship groups and often increases to the level of communal paranoia.

Unlike the other communal festivities which have their exact dates, the cult of *oratorios* depends on a variety of signals given by the crosses (such as cracking, sickness in the family, or a message given in dreams) and maintains the people of San Simon in a constant alert. Whenever they think that the cross is dissatisfied with something they mobilize all their energies and resources to appease it. They buy expensive food, candles, and fireworks for the fiesta given to the cross ; sometimes an exigent cross even demands a godfather from a neigboring village, and once it "gets used" to him the godfather has to be begged to continue forever his attentions to the capricious cross.

In El Nopal all religious and magical rituals not only produce social solidarity but also help to maintain high morale among the villagers.

In San Simon some of such rituals (those related to the functioning of traditional Indian government) are morale maintaining, while others (related to the cult of *oratorios*) though no doubt maintaining the kinship and communal solidarities, are at the same time so morale destroying and energy draining that they impede or even prevent villagers' sense of well-being.

Though, apparently, most of the villagers in San Simon believe in malevolence of their crosses and live in constant anxiety and terror, some individuals have already abandoned this belief and "nothing has happened to them whatsoever." About a person who is not afraid of his family cross and does not pay attention to it any more, one says in San Simon: "That man does not want to cooperate [in the cult of *oratorio*] since if something happens to him he can go to cure himself elsewhere" (Cortés Ruíz 1972: 110).

In El Nopal, too, the belief in the capacity of the village cross to make little boys sick has disappeared with the availability of medical help in a nearby county seat.

This type of substitution of scientific for magical beliefs is rarely sufficient, however, in such Indian communities as San Simon and El Nopal. If the belief in malevolent crosses had disappeared suddenly from San Simon, through the establishment of a village clinic for in-stance, some painful social vacuum probably would have taken the place of kinship solidarities maintained by frantic and anxious cults. And such a social vacuum with its lack of norms and confusion could turn out to be even more damaging to San Simon villagers than their strong but specific anxieties and terror.

I strongly suspect that it was not only the availability of the doctor in the neighboring village which helped almost completely eliminate the belief in the dangerous village cross in El Nopal, but also the basic restructuring of the village which occurred with introduction of *ejido* (Iwańska 1965) and later with the inauguration of the school (Iwańska 1963).

Participation in *ejido* probably distracted the energies of adult Mazahuas from the maintenance of the extended family solidarities, made them abandon family *oratorios*, and replaced their kinship solidarities with a new communal *esprit de corps* so indispensable to their survival in that period of change.

What the *ejido* did for Mazahua adults, inauguration of the school did for Mazahua boys. Involved in their demanding and interesting school activities and boys' club organized by the social worker they forgot about dangers coming from the village cross, and their parents did not remind them about those dangers either.

In spite of the loud assertions of the villagers in El Nopal that the cross cannot harm anybody, and the increased awareness of modern medicine, the cross has been decorated nevertheless with fresh flowers every Wednesday. It is quite possible that when with time the belief in the dangers of this cross disappears completely those decorations will remain anyway, acquiring a different meaning. Because the cross is located at the entrance to the village, maybe the villagers will start believing that it protects rather than harms them, thus allowing Christianity to enter their village this time without sword and fire. Or, maybe the cross decorated with fresh flowers will become a symbol of hospitality greeting the guests to an increasingly open and modern Mazahua village of El Nopal.

REFERENCES

CARRASCO PIZANA, PEDRO
  1950   *Los otomies*. Mexico City: UNAM Instituto de Historia, with the collaboration of the Instituto Nacional de Anthropología y Historia.
CORTÉS RUÍZ, EFRAIN C.
  1972   *San Simon de La Laguna*. Mexico City: Instituto Nacional Indigenista.
GARCÍA PAYÓN, JOSÉ
  1942   *Matlacincas y pirindas*. Ediciones Encuadernables. Mexico City: El Nacional.
IWAŃSKA, ALICJA
  1957   "Values in a crisis situation." New York: Columbia University. On microfilm.

1963 New knowledge. *Sociologus* 13(2).
1965 The impact of agricultural reform on a Mexican Indian village. *Sociologus* 15(1).
1967 Mazahua purgatory: symbol of permanent hope. *America Indigena* 27(1).
1971 *Purgatory and utopia.* Cambridge, Massachusetts: Schenkman.

SOUSTELLE, JACQUES
n.d. Le culte des oratoires chez les Otomies et les Mazahuas de la région d'Ixlahuaca. *Mexico Antiguo* 3(58).

Dreams as Charismatic Significants: Their Bearing on the Rise of New Religious Movements

VITTORIO LANTERNARI

Dreams may be scientifically analyzed from physiological, psychological, sociological, or anthropological viewpoints. Those of us who take an anthropological outlook must face a fundamental problem: that of the cultural value of dreams. Such a problem needs a preliminary explanation. The cultural value of dreams may have two different interpretations, which are interrelated, depending on which of two possible criteria is used to measure the dream-culture relationship. On the one hand, the culture/tradition has a deterministic influence on the dreams, or on the thematic contents of the individual dream. On the other hand, the individual dream has a deterministic influence on the preservation or the creation of that culture, i.e. in maintaining traditions and introducing innovations. A closer look reveals that the two aspects of this relationship are closely connected. For if a dream can contribute to keeping alive or strengthening tradition with respect to individual behavior and decisions (in some cases the dream itself inspires such decisions), then the dream is a "product" of the culture/tradition and, at the same time, one of its determining factors — i.e. it is both cause and effect. It is better, however, to distinguish between the two aspects of the above relationship: first, we have "culture versus dream," i.e. the cultural determinants of the dream; second, "dream versus culture," i.e. the determining influence of dream on culture.

The dream accounts of Nzema religious leaders were gathered by the author during field work in Ghana in 1971. Information on Kapo's movement in Jamaica and the account of Kapo's dream were collected bij film producer A. Pandolfi in 1972 (on the basis of some indications provided by the author) and were kindly put at the author's disposal.

As far as the first aspect is concerned, the determining influence of the cultural background, of traditions, ways of life, and beliefs, on the configuration of individual dream experience may be taken for granted. A comparative analysis of the dream contents of the average representatives of different cultures and societies would be enough to prove the determining influence of culture on the dream themes, once we have excluded individual psychological factors. Therefore, we will take a closer look at the second aspect of the relationship and consider the ways in which individual dream experience acts as a determining factor in the preservation and creation of cultural patterns.

At this point an important distinction must be made between what is officially known as modern society, i.e. urban and industrial, and traditional societies, i.e. preindustrial, underdeveloped or developing. Rural and marginal groups and classes in modern society should also be associated with the latter because they have many substantial similarities in experience, cultural attitudes, and value systems. This distinction directly concerns the cultural value of dreams in the two types of society or social group. There is an increasing tendency in "modern" society to consider dreams as indicators of certain unconscious or latent contents of the individual psyche, to be used as scientific and therapeutic tools in psychological, psychiatrical, or psychoanalytical diagnosis and treatment. Thus, a dream is regarded as a symbolic document which, once in possession of a psychologist or a psychoanalyst, becomes a basic tool for identifying individual psychic traumas and for the choice of a liberating therapy. This, then, is its real cultural value in "modern" society which is entirely different from that ascribed to dreams in traditional societies.

In traditional societies, and partly also among certain marginal and subordinate groups in "modern" society, dreams have the generally accepted function of "setting the foundations" for an individual's fate through the very symbols they express. The dream establishes a direct relationship between the dreamer and certain supernatural forces and beings belonging to the local cultural tradition, which the group recognizes as having an independent existence, a typically creative potentiality, and an authority which is capable of conditioning human behavior. As I have already pointed out in another article (Lanternari 1966), when, through the dream experience, the dreamer comes into contact with these typically creative, sacred forces and beings, he, in turn, acquires a creative, sacred power. Thus, from his dream the individual draws the certainty of a favorable fate, a reason for self-confidence, inspiration for his decisions and actions and, therefore, his self-identification. Thus, in traditional societies, the individual enters the "sacred sphere" through his dreams. These dreams become an extremely significant, charismatic type of experience, and they act as a guarantee of an individual's fate within the limits of certain traditional value orientations. There is a close psychological and cultural link between dream and myth. Both appear as models and paradigms of cultural elements — dream in relation to the individual, and myth in relation to the society as a whole. If a dream is the archetype of the individual's fate, a myth, then, is the archetype of the entire culture. In certain cases the two are identified together, both linguistically and in psychological experience; this is revealed by the famous example of the Australian natives who use the word *alchera* to indicate both the time of mythical origin and the period of time in which a dream occurs, with the relative events.

In my essay I identified certain categories of recurring dreams and/ or visions in traditional societies: the prophetic dream, the magical-shamanic dream, the initiation dream, and the mystical dream. But if by "mystical dream" we mean that in which the dreamer believes he has captured the original source of an exceptional, let us say charismatic, power, then it becomes a general category, within which the other types of dreams and/or visions, referred to above, form specific subcategories related to the different circumstances and personal roles. Naturally, in traditional societies and in certain subordinate groups of modern society, a dream and/or vision has an important function as a periodical confirmation of the relationships existing between individual and cosmos, between present reality and mythical origins, and between the sacred and the profane. The dream finds its position within the dialectical relationships of man and world, history and myth, the living and their ancestors which permeate the existence of people belonging to such groups and/or societies.

But the function of a dream is also important in relation to cultural change. In fact, the mystical dreams of founders of new religions contain elements of a symbolic system which differs from the traditional one. Such dreams in themselves reflect strongly charismatic personalities; sociologically speaking, this implies an exceptionally creative capacity. As has already been pointed out by Kluckhohn (1942), it is in cases like these that individual dreams become the source of a "private ritual" which, in turn, will be elevated to the role of a new "group ritual," having been socialized through the dreamer's individual influence on his group. But we believe that it also becomes a "group myth," in relation to the charismatic dreamer's personal prestige. In other words, the founder's dream becomes the starting point of a process of "cultural creation." It can give rise to a new type of culture and to a renewal of the world view and of tradition through the foundation of new socioreligious movements.

In those cases with which we are better acquainted, the innovative dreams are stimulated by the dreamer's personal contact with Christian culture. We are not taking into account the very many "dreamers" or "dreaming prophets" who were responsible for movements such as the Ghost Dance, the Sionist Churches of South Africa, the Cargo Cults of Melanesia, the messianic war movements of Polynesia, etc. (Lanternari 1960, 1966). We will simply refer to certain dreams of religious founders of the Nzema people in Ghana. These dreams contain both traditional themes and elements derived from models of Western culture, particularly from the Bible and from Christianity in general. The following examples illustrate how an individual dream can act as a decisive factor in the process of cultural change.

The cases reported here refer to dreams which reflect a crisis within a traditional society and give rise to socioreligious movements. I will begin by describing a series of dreams personally narrated to me by the founder of the Action Church among the Nzema of southwest Ghana, Mr. Moses Armah. The Action Church is a new spiritual church founded in 1948, and is now widespread throughout Nzemaland of Ghana. Its rise is tied to a series of dreams experienced by its founder, a former Methodist imbued with a number of religious influences from the Bible, from the Hindu prophet Paramahansa Yogananda, and from the English theosophical writings of H. T. Hamblin. Mr. Armah was induced by these dreams to found the new Christian cult, which differs from both traditional religion and from the syncretic cults, namely Water Carriers or Twelve Apostles' Church, which sprouted from the prophet William Harris's movement in the Ivory Coast and are now diffused among the Nzema people. Mr. Armah was born in 1908.

It was in 1941. One night I dreamt and saw Jesus personally. He was walking on something like a bridge. A big house was nearby. I had the house in front of myself, and the bridge on my side. I was standing there. I saw Jesus personally and he was walking like a person. He was a person, and he was clothed with a blue cloth. The wind was blowing; he was walking and his hair were all on his back. I was looking at him, and he was turning slowly. At a moment he gazed at me and I fell down. I put up and saw that he had gone. "This is Christ, he is going." Now Jesus returned again. He looked at me: as soon as my eyes met his, I fell down: three times. After this I could not see him again, and I came out of the dream. At that time

I had not yet thought of founding a new Church. This is the first dream I had.

Then Mr. Armah had a second dream.

The second dream was that I dreamt that from my hair was growing a bunch of banana. It grew and became mature. Then I saw somebody cut it down. That banana was "longhands" [there are two kinds of banana]. I saw on the way come to get them plucking them to eat. But the person came and said: "Don't eat!" Then he brought me another kind of banana, the short one, which I ate. He told me: "Don't eat the long one, but eat this." Then I came out from the dream. I was puzzled. From that day I dreamt that long banana, each time I smell it I vomit. I don't touch it at all. At first I did not understand the meaning of the bunch of banana. But now I understand it. Should I found this church. The banana bunch was the symbol of the new church. Eat the short one means found the new church.

After a period spent in reading the Bible and other experiences, Mr. Armah had a third dream.

It was a light. I was sleeping; then I saw a light. Then I began to read the Bible. After that my heart started to shake, and I began to sing. After the dream was over, I was singing . . . . Then I came out and I go to sing and go from place to place, always singing. I turned on the back of my house. I felt that I was singing and that I should sing all the time. In the morning I could not chop [eat], but sing. My wife began to worry. She made me to chop, but I said no. I was singing. My heart was very joyful as I was singing. Then my wife went to say: "You are reading books, books, books, you are crazy." I left eating, always singing. While I was singing, my wife thought: "Something happened to my husband." My wife thought that I was getting crazy. But it was joy, that: joy, joy. I could not sleep, too. Then I went on singing again and again for three days. Then I began to cool. From that day I had a change of my mind. "The church I was belonging to does not fill my heart. The church does not give me the things that are now good. I shall found a church. I shall found a new Church."

The themes of the three dreams act as private myths for the foundation of a new religion. As far as the individual is concerned, we can speak in terms of "conversion," but the myths will then pass from private experience to group ritual experience. Jesus, appearing as a new figure in the first dream, will become the central figure of the new church. The refusal of the first kind of banana and the choice of the second kind corresponds to the abandoning of the old religion and the birth of the new one; the prophet's untiring song and the Bible become the central elements of the group ritual which, in fact, calls for a great number of choral songs inspired, as in the dream, by joy, exultation, and Bible reading. Private myth passes into group ritual in another sense, too; after his dream, Armah officially became a healer, curing the sick through prayer, and this becomes an essential feature of the new cult.

Something similar also happened to the cofounder of the Action Church, Mr. Andoh. Already a Catholic, Andoh practiced the sacrifices and rituals belonging to the traditional religion, worshiping the *awosonle* spirits. But having received certain religious scripts from Armah, the very same which had stimulated the latter's revelation, one night he had a vision. "A street full of light" appeared to him, and he heard "a voice telling me, 'This is the way'." After this experience, Andoh ceased to follow traditional rituals, now bitterly refused and condemned by the Action Church, and he too obtained the power of curing the sick through prayer. Once more, the dream's charisma, symbolized by the "light," reappears as a foundation myth. Ritual activity of the Action Church is centered on reading of the Bible, sermons, dances, and songs inspired by joyous feelings. The notion of a divine spirit which inspires man is fundamental in it. This spirit is manifested through the enthusiastic behavior and sentiments of followers, and by no means through possession, glossolalia, and shaking, as happens among Nzema Pentecostals.

Nevertheless, the Action Church and Pentecostal Churches have something in common. All of them emphasize the presence of a divine spirit inside the follower's soul; in all of them a drastic demarcation is felt between the "obscure" time before conversion and the "luminous" time after conversion, between a false "heathenism" and the "true religion of Christ." The demarcation line is made, for every individual follower, by a dream experience, and/or sometimes, by a healing experience. The latter happens every time a person, possessed by evil spirits and/or a bad illness, is healed by other people's prayer and faith. In all spiritual churches like the Action Church and Pentecostals, prayer-healing or faith-healing, as much as dreams and visions, operate as charismatic significants. Common followers as well as leaders can share both kinds of gifts. But the dreaming activity of charismatic leaders is more widespread and intensive.

Another example of a new religion founded as a result of a prophetic dream among social groups living in precarious conditions has recently occurred in a poor Negro neighborhood in Kingston, Jamaica. It is the Afro-Christian religious movement created by the prophet Kapo. The following dream account was directly recorded by the ethnographic film producer A. Pandolfi, to whom I had given certain indications regarding aspects of the local religion. Having had a somewhat superficial Christian education during childhood, Kapo still felt deep down the influence of African religiousness. This was probably due to the Jamaican environment, in which the Rastafarian back-to-Africa movement flourished side by side with a Garveyan-inspired "autonomous Copt Church" and other Afro-Christian cults, such as Pocomania and Revival Zion Cult, which were largely based on possession, trance, ecstatic dances, and healing practices. All these cults are a syncretic and tendentially escapist expression of the reaction of the poorest Negro classes (who have been living in a state of social emargination since colonial times) to the privileged conditions of the whites and of the black bourgeoisie. In some cases, as in Kapo's movement, there is a genuine rediscovery, or rather recovery, of the messianic and millenarian value of original Christianity, such as was being spontaneously relived by the prophet and his followers.

Through his dream Kapo knew he had a mission to accomplish: that of teaching his people a new religion. In the first dream Jesus appears to him and orders him, after having "annointed" him, to act as his representative on earth. This is his story:

When I was twelve years of age, I was put on to this way of Christianity, and develop afterwards into art. When I was twelve years of age I dreamt one night that I saw a man. He was not a white man, and he was not a very dark man. But he came and he took me from my father's home, down a glade, underneath a white coco tree. Reaching the white coco tree, he asked me the question if I know who he was. I told him "no." He asked me a second time, and then a third time, and I remember that I said to him "If I know who you was, I would have told you." He said, "My name is the Lord Jesus Christ," and he took a bottle from his pocket, about the length of my hand, and he anoint me from my head down to my foot. And then he said I was to go and tell the Nations, my mother and also my father, that he, Jesus, was in need of them . . .

A second dream soon follows the first.

The following night I dreamt that I saw a garden; the garden was a half-moon shape, wider than this yard here. Seventy-two angels were sitting around the edges of that half-moon garden, and seventy-two chairs were set by the edges around, and there were seventy-two little tables, there were seventy-two trumpets, and I was led into the middle of the garden and put on a chair to sit, by the Head, one of the angels. Then they began to play on their trumpets a very wonderful song. I couldn't retain or remember anything about the melody of that song. Before waking in the morning, I was told by the angels that I was to go and tell my mother and my father, my sisters and my brothers and the people around, that Jesus was in need of them. I got up and I did this in the morning and my father and my mother began to feel now that something was wrong with me. But nothing was wrong. But all this comes up about after visiting a revival meeting about three nights before the time when the vision came unto me. And it keep going on like that until I was commissioned to go out and preach the gospel. I preached for about twenty-five years before I became an artist. And while I became an artist I prayed. . . . I never liked the idea of seeing some of the ministers just sit down in those days and they never work, and then they have a fair salary. So I believed to myself that if I put my shoulder to the wheel I could be happy more than burdening the people's shoulders. Well, what came up out of that prayer, I found myself scraping on a stone. On that stone a face came out and then I cut eyes and nose and mouth.

As we can see, for Kapo, art accompanies and completes the activity of a religious preacher and founder. It, too, is a sign of the charisma, to the same degree as that of the mystical dream he had received. "I believe," says Kapo, "that there are many ties between spiritual life — i.e. the Church — and art. I think that art does much for the spiritual Church." Thus, the movement founded by Kapo has the same connotation of "spiritual church" which is typical of Ghanaian and many other African churches. The prophet's dreams betray the influence of the "revelation:" the "twelve years of age" of the first dream, and the "seventy-two angels with trumpets" of the second one. In the actual cult the faithful pray and sing in expectation of universal renewal, which they feel is at hand; this will be followed by the resurrection of the dead, peace and unity in the world, and mystical enlightenment. Under the prophet's guidance the faithful reach a state of mystical exaltation, during which they call out to the spirit to come, and finally fall into a trance. The strong rhythm, the rocking of the body, the flowing arm movements, the continuous summoning of the spirit, the choral songs, and the dances are all ecstatic techniques which help bring on the final, collective trance. In this way, the cult helps its followers overcome the feeling of existential precariousness that results from the conditions of underdevelopment, misery, and social subordination in which they live. Here again we have another case of "Africanized Christianity," like that of the Ghanaian Action Church mentioned above. In such cases, the old African possession cult was tied to a series of beliefs involving divine figures of an ambivalent nature, i.e. possessing both good and evil powers, but, in fact, provoking a condition of suffering during possession.

Today, the cult is fused together with, and at the same time substituted by, a cult of the Spirit, which is experienced as a source of uniquely joyous and exalting redemption. Particular importance seems to be attached to the role of Jesus, who appears in the founder-leader's visions as a bringer of "light"; this symbolizes a psychologically liberating experience which can be easily recognized in the mystical, enthusiastic, and choral character of the ritual activity. Jesus, the light, the burning fire, and the joyous song are all recurring themes in a great number of foundation or "conversion" dreams. They are the symbolic expression of, and are tightly linked with, the expectation of a forth-coming deliverance from impending evil, in other words, from the frustrating conditions of misery, isolation, and social emargination which become all the more explosive when compared to the conditions of other, privileged groups. In this sense, the founder's dream activity acts as an explosive outlet for all the frustrating experiences accumulated by the individual himself and by the group of which he is the exponent and interpreter.

The pattern of the burning fire (symbolizing the light and the Spirit) also comes from the Bible. This is clearly illustrated by the dream of a young Puerto Rican Pentecostal minister, recorded by me in 1965 in one of the storefront churches of Harlem, New York City. Ten years before, he had had a dream which determined his fate. Here is his story:

I was at home one night, sleeping next to my wife; it was almost sunrise when all of a sudden I was woken up by a bright flame burning in front of me in the room. Frightened by this sight, I called out to my wife to get up because a fire was burning the house. But my wife, having woken up, could see nothing: neither fire nor light. At a certain point a voice spoke to me from the depths of the flame, saying: "Go to Minister XY; he will explain everything to you and tell you what to do." The next day, frightened and shocked by this vision, I did as I had been told. The Pentecostal minister whom I visited calmed me and explained that the fire was that of the Holy Spirit, and that I should rejoice, for God had touched me.

Since then this man, who had an unfortunate family situation (he was the father of two paralytic boys) and who, together with his group of Puerto Rican fellow immigrants, had always sought in vain the mean-ing of life and an impossible social self-identification in the immense city of New York, was able to take over a socially recognized role as minister of a cult. He found his self-identification within the group of Puerto Rican Pentecostal followers, whose ritual gatherings express an intense community feeling. "Before that time," he said, "I was a non-entity. Now it's all over."

In these different individual experiences the patterns of the dream and/or visionary themes are clearly taken directly from the visions of Moses, in which the angel of God appears to the prophet inside a tongue of fire (Exodus 3, 1–8); or from the "Transfiguration," in which Christ Himself appears to the Apostles transfigured and shining brightly like the sun (Matthew 17, 1–3); or from the conversion of Saul of Tar-sus, with the apparition of a great celestial light (Acts 9, 3–8); or, finally, from John's "Revelation," with the apparition of the golden candlesticks and the sound of the trumpet (Revelation 1, 10–12).

Another example of an enlightening, revelation-type dream appears in the following story of a Pentecostal minister from a small town in the "Subappennino Irpino," an underdeveloped area of southern Italy. (The data were collected during field research by a student of the University of Bari). Euplio Aucello, a Pentecostal minister from Anzano, passed from Catholic indifference to active participation in the Pentecostal movement through a series of dreams which, together with an assiduous Bible-reading, dominated his life from adolescence onwards. At the age of eighteen, during a fit of depression in his search for the truth, he was praying to God when he had his first vision. "The room I was in was suddenly filled with light and the bust of a smiling man appeared in the balcony opening, gently calling me. My heart was filled with joy." This was the beginning; having met a community of Pentecostals, he joined it enthusiastically and suffered the Fascist persecutions of Italian evangelists which were later continued by the postwar Christian-Democratic governments. He was put in prison for having refused to give up the cult, and there he had a new vision: "The whole room was filled with light and the words 'you will be released' appeared in golden writing on the wall in front." In fact, he was almost immediately released from prison.

On different occasions other visions followed, accompanying the minister's passionate proselytism and prayers. At one time, Jesus' two hands appeared to him, bigger than life-size, each respectively overhanging the crowds of male and female faithful ("brothers" and "sisters"); at another time, he saw the number "10," the mysterious meaning of which was revealed exactly ten months later, when at the very same hour he received the "gift of the Spirit" — that is, he began to "speak tongues." At yet another time, after a doctrinal discussion with one of his followers, at the end of which neither had succeeded in convincing the other nor in convincing himself of being in the wrong, the minister was depressed and grieved; during the following cult he had a vision in which he saw bicycle whose wheels, tied together with an iron chain, seemed to be striving to turn in vain. According to Aucello's interpretation, the wheels were the two arguers and the chain was Satan, binding them. Thus, he prayed to God to free his "brother" first and then himself; and as a matter of fact, he saw first one wheel, then the other being released and beginning to turn.

These dreams and/or visions, including all those received by the prophets mentioned above, together with shamanic and initiation dreams and others in general, all show how the unconscious-irrational and conscious-rational elements are strongly linked together. Moreover, it is only after it has been interpreted that each individual dream of this kind becomes of particular importance for the dreamer and, therefore, for the group to which it is communicated; it is thus that the dreamer becomes aware of its symbolic value. The dream's interpretation, either by the dreamer or by others, is based on rational and partly conscious, sociologically significant criteria, while the dream material is of an irrational and completely unconscious nature.

Among the Nzema, for example, when Armah says to himself and to others: "The banana tree meant that I had to found a new church and abandon the old one," he is acting under a rational, sociologically significant stimulus. This stimulus helps him solve an individual crisis and at the same time solve a social crisis of the group that he feels he is representing; as a matter of fact, he opens up new possibilities for the traditional culture, and he discovers a new path for his own social ascent, contributing toward the creation of a new elite. The same can be said about Euplio Aucello's visions of Christ's hands or of the bicycle, etc. It is not through their raw, "neutral," oneiric material that we come to know about these visions, but only after they have acquired a cultural significance through the dreamer's interpretation. For the latter and his followers, such visions help explain the dreamer's charismatic role and his new status as interpreter-minister of the cult. The sociological significance of this fact is that it gives the dreamer an exceptional social prestige. The same holds true for the mystical/prophetic dreams and/or visions of all religious founders and for the traditional shamanic or initiation dreams. In each case, the dream and/or vision indicates a polyvalent function. It is a source of self-confidence as well as a means toward a special kind of prestige and consequently, toward a leadership position of one kind or another. It is a source of self-identification both on a psychological and social level.

This helps explain the structural continuity and the original close relationship existing between innovative dreams and traditional dreams of a prophetic and/or shamanic nature. This can be seen, for example, in a number of traditional dreams recorded among the Nzema. The following examples show how an individual becomes aware that he is being "called" to become a *komenle* [fetish-priest or priestess] through dreams. It is the case of *komenle* Hannah Kofi and of *komenle* Komili Akye Mokoah.

Here is the story told by Hannah Kofi, wife of the *ninsili* [native doctor] Kofi, in the village of Qpokazo, when she was asked what had made her decide to become a *komenle*.

I was born in Enchi, I was a Methodist but now I am a *komenle*, that is, an interpreter of the *awosonle* [traditional divinities]. When I was in Enchi I fell sick with an illness which lasted five years: I was sick in my whole body, even in my heart. Thus a woman of that place, who was also ill, went to a man who was a healer and this was Kofi (now my husband) and he had come from the village of Qpokazo to heal the sick. I was therefore introduced to Kofi and he said he would try to cure me. My whole body was trembling. My mother had taken me to other *ninsili* more than once, but it was Kofi who discovered the real cause of my illness. He is also a fetish-priest. He carried out *adunyi* [a divination ritual]. What was the cause of my illness? Kofi said that I would have to become a *komenle*. This is what had happened: when I was a child, my father had a "cottage" near the Duwasua river, roughly three miles from Enchi. I normally went down to the river to fetch water. I knew nothing. At that time I used to go to church, I was a Methodist and I did not like these things. Later, when I was pregnant with my first child, I was in bed one night when I had a vision. A woman came towards me and said: "I like you very much, Hannah. If you won't do what I tell you, I will make you die. You must interpret my words and my will. You shall be my *komenle*." She told me her name: she was the river *bosonle* [singular of *awosonle*] whom I had gone to fetch water from as a child. Since that time, the *bosonle* had noticed me and loved me. That is what Kofi the *komenle* understood, and he told me that if I wanted to be cured I should "pacify" the *bosonle*. Thus I married Kofi and together with my husband I went to pacify the *bosonle* by pouring libation and making sacrifice of a sheep and some chicken. It was the *bosonle*'s love that caused my illness, until I became her *komenle*.

Another similar example is that of *komenle* Akye Mokoah from Aiyinasi. The first part of the story was told by her mother.

When my daughter was a child of seven I placed her in the care of her grandmother (my mother) who lived in a village on a side road branching off from the Atuabo-Aiyinasi road and who had a groundnut plantation. The girl was in the plantation when someone told her to fetch water from the nearby river. She went with three friends. As soon as she reached the river, being a little behind her friends, she heard a voice from the river calling her name. She turned round and saw a woman sitting on a stool [the stool is a symbol of power], just like the *bosonle* in the small statue [the *komenle* is holding the small statue]. The woman held in her hands some pounded herbs [used as medicines by the *ninsili* and *komenle*] and two small coins — a one-shilling piece and a threepence piece [the smallest coins used by the Nzemas]. The woman said: "Take these things and go cure people!" But the girl was frightened and ran away. Then the woman threw the herbs and coins at her from a distance. The girl fell down in a faint. Frightened, her friends left her there and ran to warn the village that their friend had fallen and was "dead." People ran to the place and carried her home. A *ninsili* and a *komenle* were asked to visit her; they cured her and she was better. But they said that once she would be grown up she would become a *komenle* of that very *bosonle* who had possessed her on that occasion. For a long time nobody thought about what had happened on that occasion. Being a Catholic Christian, I did not give it much thought either. Things changed when my daughter got married.

At this point the *komenle* herself picks up the story.

After I got married I gave birth to six children, all of whom died one after the other. I had to discover the cause of all those deaths. I went to the *komenle*. The *komenle* said that unless I made up my mind to become the *komenle* of the *bosonle* Azira (for that was her name), I would continue to lose every one of my children. Thus I began to practice as this *bosonle*'s Azira's *komenle*. And in fact, after that, I had another three children, and they are all alive. Thus I began to heal people who come to me to be cured from their illnesses.

The girl's dream and/or vision contains the symbols of power (stool) and of social ascent (medicinal herbs and money).

The above examples show the dream and/or vision as a decisive factor in the personal fate of an individual, according to the traditional Nzema religious system and custom. Illness and death may produce an individual crisis from which the priestly "calling" and, therefore, salvation may be determined through the dream and/or vision. In fact, being a *komenle* means repeating the archetype experience of the individual's first vision and possession, at every public ritual performance, thus repeatedly renewing ties with the original source of charismatic power and social prestige. Dreams and/or visions form, as we have seen, constant "patterns" both in traditional and modern Nzema religious systems, of which the Action Church is an example.

If we are considering mystical dreams and/or visions (i.e. those in which the dreamer is convinced he has gained control of the source of some extraordinary charismatic power) in relation to the process of cultural dynamics, then it is possible to distinguish two different patterns of mystical dreams and/or visions: (1) a traditional pattern, and (2) an innovative one. The themes of the first type of dream and/or vision stem from a heritage of ancestral beliefs, myths, and mythical figures, i.e. traditional values, practices, and world view, the importance of which is thus confirmed. In relation to the process of cultural dynamics, they therefore assume a conservative function. A number of themes in the dreams and/or visions of the second type, however, belong to a different culture with which the dreamer has come into contact. Figures, beliefs, and myths, which have nothing to do with the dreamer's cultural heritage, are reshaped and reinterpreted in an original way. These processes are the result of unconscious psychic operations made by particularly sensitive individuals after the shocking experience of cultural clash; they occur particularly when the individuals are faced with new cultural models and new, fascinating existential perspectives, however disintegrating they may be.

From the analysis of founder-leaders' dreams and from the study of the sociocultural role of the dreams themselves we learn that the acculturation process has important roots in the activity of the unconscious. The syncretic tendency, too, largely stems from the activity of the unconscious; the contents of the dream and/or vision are its initial expression.

If it is true, then, that culture reflects the creative quality in man as a rational member of a given society, we must not forget that a considerable amount of this creative activity is deeply rooted in the irrational unconscious. The product of such irrationality, however, is immediately, consciously re-elaborated by the individual who selects, interprets, and uses it, both personally and on a group level. In fact, the dream which the dreamer "reveals" to his people is sooner or later consciously selected, interpreted, and adapted by the dreamer himself. It is, therefore, halfway between rationality and irrationality, the unconscious and consciousness, subjectivity and objectivity, and becomes a means through which the individual may achieve active social participation as interpreter and exponent of his own group, while the latter will find its frustrations, needs, and expectations symbolically expressed in the "prophet's" dreams or in the ensuing myths and rituals.

REFERENCES

BURRIDGE, K.
  1969 New heaven, new earth: a study of millenarian activities. Oxford: Blackwell.
CLEMHOUT, S.
  1966 The psycho-sociological naure of nativistic movements and the emergence of cultural growth. Anthropos 61(1–2):33–48.
FABIAN, J.
  1966 Dream and charisma: "theory of dreams" in the Jamaa movement (Congo). Anthropos 61(3, 6):544–560.
FRIEDLAND, W. H.
  1964 For a sociological concept of charisma. Social Forces 43(1):18–24.
KLUCKHOHN, C.
  1942 Myth and ritual: a general theory. Harvard Theological Review. 35:45–79.

LANTERNARI, V.

1960 *Movimenti religiosi di libertà e di salvezza dei populi oppressi.* Milano: Felrinelli. (English translation 1963: *The religions of the oppressed.* London: McGibbon and Kee, and New York: Knopf.)

1966 "Il sogno e il suo valore culturale dalle società arcaiche alla società industriale," in *Il sogno e le civiltà umane.* Bari: Laterza.

LEWIS, I. M.

1971 *Ecstatic Religion.* Harmondworth: Penguin Books.

OOMMEN, T. K.

1967 Charisma, social structure and social change. *Comparative Studies in Society and History* 10(1):85–99.

PEEL, J. D. Y.

1968 Syncretism and religious change. *Comparative Studies in Society and History* 10(2):121–141.

SCHIAVONE, S.

1969 "I Pentecostali di Accadia e del Subappennino Irpino." Unpublished Ph.D. thesis, Bari.

SECTION FIVE

Moon and Reincarnation: Anthropogenesis as Imagined by the Surára and Pakidái Indians of Northwestern Brazil

HANS BECHER

The following is the myth of creation of the Surára and Pakidái Indians, two tribes of the Yanomamö in northwestern Brazil, as told to me by the Surára chief Hewemão in 1955, during my first nine-month stay with him (Becher 1960:113–114).

The earth already existed but was still without people. One day the first man, Uruhí, came from the leg of the Xiapó, a little bird with black and yellow feathers, similar to the Japím. Shortly thereafter the bird's leg bore a second man, then a third, a fourth, and finally a woman, Petá. These four men and the woman lived together in complete harmony. Petá was the wife of Uruhí, the first born, but the other three brothers were allowed to have sexual relations with her.[1]

The Yanomamö Indians are an independent linguistic and cultural group, whose habitat is in the Brazilian state of Amazonas as well as part of Venezuela, and is located between the Rio Uraricuera in the north, the middle Rio Negro in the south, the Rio Branco in the east, and the Serra Parima in the west. They probably belong to the oldest stratum of population in South America. Systematic investigation of the Yanomamö began only in the early 1950's. Among the pioneers are Meinhard Schuster, Johannes Wilbert, Otto Zerries, and the author.

The Rio Padauarí, a left tributary of the middle Rio Negro, divides the Yanomamö into an eastern and a western half. The eastern half is ruled by the Xiriána and their numerous satellite tribes. The west is ruled by the Waiká, along with those allies who pay them tribute and war services. Both groups have been enemies for centuries, especially because of their fear of incest, which leads to the reciprocal stealing of women.

In 1966–1967 and 1970 I was able to extend and deepen my investigations of 1955–1956 of the eastern Yanomamö tribes, the Surára and Pakidái. I also gained additional knowledge of the Ironasitéri, members of the western Yanomamö group.

[1] In the Surára and Pakidái tribes the younger, unmarried brothers have the right to sexual relations with the wives of their older brothers. In addition, the members of both tribes believe that a woman can only bear strong children if she has frequent relations with other men during her pregnancy.

After one year Petá gave birth to a strong and healthy boy, who grew quickly and called all four men "Father."[2] The boy's greatest pleasure was shooting at little birds with his bow. But one night just for fun he aimed at the moon and shot an arrow. Immediately there was an eclipse of the moon and blood dripped down and flooded the entire earth.[3] From this blood originated all the Yanomamö: the Surára, Pakidái, Xiriána, Pusehewetéri, Ironasitéri, Aramamestéri, Karauatéri, Waiká, etc.

In 1970, during my third visit with them, Chief Hewemão and his younger brother Kurikayawö of the Surára tribe, as well as Chief Xomirawö of the Pakidái tribe, gave me additional informative details on this subject. These were confirmed by several older men of both tribes.

The little bird was then sent to earth by Poré, the lord of the moon,[4] in order to settle the first Yanomamö there. The bird was identical with Petá, but in reality it was Perimbó (the feminine principle of the moon), who carried within her those four souls of the men. After their births and her own, she lived as an earthly woman, but was equipped with godly attributes. This was also true of her little son, whose arrow had caused the blood of the moon to flow down, which, in turn, had caused all the rest of the Yanomamö to originate.

As the Surára and Pakidái Indians imagine it, the moon consists of two half moons,[5] which are held together by a river of blood flowing in a north-south direction, called the Parauke iniíke. This same river of blood flows through three large lakes of blood: Oxokora iniíke mahón, Oxokora iniíke porokabö, and Oxokora iniíke prukatabö.

In the middle lake (Oxokora iniíke porokabö) lives the lord of the moon, Poré, in the form of a *Cobra Grande* [great snake]. However, he can change himself at any time into a human (man or woman), a mammal, a fish, a bird, or a plant.

According to my informants, this middle lake of blood is a huge vagina. The *Cobra Grande* living in it is perceived as a penis. From this it is clear that the moon, Perimbó, embodies the feminine and Poré the masculine principle.

From the middle lake of blood Poré/Perimbó rules the two halves of

---

[2]   The Surára and Pakidái children also call the unmarried brothers of their father "Father" rather than "Uncle."

[3]   For this reason Surára and Pakidái children are still forbidden to shoot an arrow in the direction of the moon.

[4]   The moon, consisting of the feminine principle Perimbó and the closely connected masculine principle Poré, lord of the moon, is the Supreme Being of the Yanomamö. It is believed to be bisexual. The moon is the paradise of the dead and the soul reservoir of the Yanomamö, who believe in reincarnation.

[5]   The Surára and Pakidái believe that this explains why people sometimes see only one moon crescent, sometimes decreasing, sometimes increasing.

Plate 1.   Chief Hewemão of the Surára tribe with red painted body. This symbolizes the middle blood lake on the moon, Perimbó (female principle), and the upward-tied penis of the master of the moon, Poré (male principle), who lives there in the shape of a snake

Plate 2. Kurikayawö, the younger brother of the chief of the
Surára tribe with his wife

Plate 3. Woman of the Pakidái tribe with characteristic dotted
tattoo above the upper lip

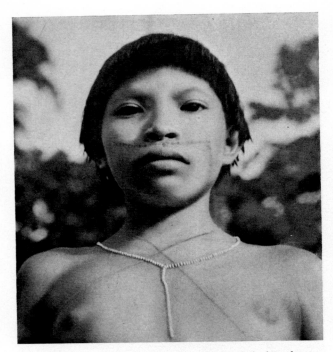

Plate 4.   Girl of the Surára tribe with characteristic dotted tattoo above the upper lip

Plate 5.   Pakidái warrior with tonsure (here: the embracing
fight done in a sitting position)

Plate 6. Family of the Surára tribe with child. The woman is
a member of the Pusehewetéri tribe

Plate 7.   Boy of the Surára tribe with his penis tied upward

Plate 8.   Women of
the Pakidái tribe
with child

Plate 9.   Cachoeira dos Indios at upper Rio Aracá

the moon (the bright eastern half and the dark western half), heaven, and the earth, which they created and which lies directly beneath the moon.[6]

Temporarily dwelling on the two halves of the moon are the souls of the tribe's dead members, who reached the paradise of dead souls via the smoke that rose from their combination tree and fire funeral. Here they begin a remarkable process of rejuvenation.

Both the Surára and the Pakidái tribes agree in their belief that every person has an *Uwexík* [a physical soul], which is located in the bones. The *Uwexík auá* [soul of boys and men] is bright, while the *Uwexík miritíti* [the soul of girls and women] is dark.[7]

In addition to the physical soul, these Indians believe that every individual after completing the third year of life, is also surrounded by two external souls sent by Poré/Perimbó: *Petaxíbe* [the free soul] and *Petanuahi* [the shadow soul].[8] These two souls are closely connected with the physical soul, but at the same time they must also fulfill important functions of their own, which can influence life in a positive sense (free soul) as well as in a negative sense (shadow soul).

As I discovered during my first expedition, the physical soul (*Uwexík* — identical with cloud, smoke), which is located in the bones and never leaves the body during life, can only reach paradise via the smoke that rises during the cremation of a dead member of the tribe (Becher 1960: 91). It rises together with the two external souls. During later expeditions I discovered that after their arrival on the moon, the souls of men, which

---

[6]   Thus the picture, which the Yanomamö have of the moon's surface, corresponds to the round form of the *maloka*, which is located in the middle of a settlement and is surrounded by woods, mountains, and rivers. It also corresponds to their view of the world, with its center being the living and wandering area of the Yanomamö. Here, too, there is an eastern half and a western half and a border river, the Rio Paduarí, which they associate with the blood river of the moon.

The religious view of life of the Ironasitéri differs somewhat from the above. Here I discovered a horizontal and vertical structure in the form of two heavens. The lower heaven represents conjointly the paradise of the souls of dead Ironasitéri, the earth, and the underworld. Napoleon Chagnon gives similar details in this regard (Chagnon 1968:44–45).

Very far to the west and east, respectively, there are two high island mountains supporting the heavens. Behind each mountain is a hole, dug by an armadillo, through which one enters the tunnel connecting heaven and the underworld. This tunnel is regularly traversed by the moon and the sun.

But the Ironasitéri also believe that the two heavens, as well as the earth and the underworld, are ruled by Poré/Perimbó.

[7]   The dark color is evoked by the blood of the female sex. It is also believed that women have more blood than men, and that this blood is equipped with magical powers.

[8]   Both names, Petaxíbe and Petanuahi, contain the name of Petá, that first woman from the myth of creation.

are bright, populate the eastern half-moon and the dark souls of the women populate the western half.

On both half-moons there is an abundance of game animals, quadrupeds, birds, and fish, as well as edible plants of all kinds, so that no soul needs to suffer hunger. No wars are fought on the moon, because the deity Poré/Perimbó wants it to be peaceful there. Any soul who violates this is thrown into the lower course of the river of blood by the *Hekurá* [gigantic animal and plant spirits] that act as intermediaries between humans and the moon[9] and maintain peace and order. It is then washed away so quickly that it lands in the blood lake of heaven and drowns there. There is also no sexual intercourse on the moon because the souls lack the necessary bodies for this.

Usually a physical soul stays on a half-moon for two dry seasons — two years. After that it is transformed into a little water snake by Poré/Perimbó and it spends the same amount of time in one of the large blood lakes. Here the souls are rejuvenated and prepared for their new existence on earth, which will be entirely different from the previous one. Whoever was a man in the first life on earth will be a woman in the next and vice versa. In this way the balance of the sexes will remain constant. All the male and female Indians questioned explained to me that they often had the feeling that they had lived as a woman as well as a man.

Picturing the souls of men as bright and those of women as dark distinguishes them for Poré/Perimbó and prevents that deity from confusing them during their stay on the moon. If a soul, which had been in a man, were to live again immediately in a male body, it would not be capable of life. This is also true for the soul of a woman. If a child dies during or shortly after birth, it is because its soul was mistakenly located again in a body of the same sex.

During the regeneration of the physical souls in the lakes of blood, they change color; the bright souls then gather in the lake that lies in the upper course of the river and the dark ones gather in the lake in the lower course. In both lakes the souls are so reduced in size by Poré/Perimbó that they fit into a drop of blood.

The double deity then sends blood from these lakes to the earth by shaking the blood-trees (or rain-trees). This blood changes to rain when it strikes the clouds. Many of the drops contain such tiny souls, and in this way they reach a man's penis, which is tied upward. The primary

[9]   They can only be invoked during the snuff intoxication, at which time the men identify with the gigantic animal and plant spirits. In their intoxication they become personified *Hekurá*. The nervous activity of the men is excited by *Epen* [the alkaloids in the snuff]. Associations develop within them between the moon and the earth.

reason why all Yanomamö men tie up their penises with waist strings is because the foreskins then work as sucking funnels. During intercourse the soul enters a woman's body, in which an infant then develops. Without a soul, I was told by Chief Hewemão, who knows nothing of cell division, no new body can originate. (See Plates 1 and 2.) Souls which are not caught by the foreskin of a man return to the moon with the mist that rises every morning from the Amazonian rain forests. This rising mist is especially prevalent over rivers and brooks; this is one reason why the Yanomamö tribes always live near the shore.

Thus all life on earth really comes from the moon, and the Surára and Pakidái, as true descendants of the moon, firmly believe that their blood is identical with the liquid of the moon lakes and the moon river, as described in the myth of creation.

The rejuvenated soul still needs several more years in order to develop again completely. This process is not yet completed even at birth. For this reason in the first three years of life the infant still belongs to the flesh, blood, and soul of its mother. It does not even have its own name until the beginning of its fourth year of life; then its name is always taken from the plant or animal kingdom. From then on the child has its own soul, one which has once again fully developed after the stage of rejuvenation.

A child that is born with physical disabilities is killed immediately after birth and thrown into a river, because these disabilities are proof that the soul is sick and is no longer capable of developing into a healthy child. It must therefore be drowned.

The souls of members of the tribe who were not cremated, whether during a war or as punishment for committing incest, are eliminated from the cycle of reincarnation. From that time on they must wander about as shadow souls between the moon and the earth. These souls will soon die of starvation and thirst, but before this happens they try to harm the other members of the tribe as much as possible because their continual hunger and thirst make them malicious.[10]

It is believed that a close connection exists between the moon and women, especially during their menstrual periods, since the vagina symbolizes a moon lake and the bleeding suggests the myth of creation of the early Yanomamö. It is thought that every magical act, in a good and a bad sense, can be carried out with menstrual blood. It is possible to heal the sick with it or to make the healthy ill. Therefore the men are very afraid of it. They fear that the women, in anger, might mix this blood

---

[10]   After these members of the tribe die, the ceremonial endocannibalistic drinking of the bone ashes mixed with banana soup is also omitted.

with a drink. This would give the women complete power over the men. The men tried to protect themselves against such magic by demanding a rite of initiation for the girls when they began to menstruate. This custom still exists today. During this rite the girl is isolated from the rest of the tribe and sits in the menstruation hut. Her mother rubs her with the blood. If that is insufficient, she rubs her with *Urucu (Bixa orellana)* [a red vegetable dye] as a substitute. At the same time her mother makes a dotted tattoo over the girl's upper lip with a palm quill to represent the crescent moon. The material used for the tattooing is *Genipapo* [a blue vegetable dye.] (See Plates 3 and 4.)

The men believe that this tattooing removes every danger that threatens them from the menstrual blood. But the women know better; the blood still has the same power and the tattooed crescent moon over their upper lips only strengthens this power because now they are externally marked as moon women.

There is a second sign, which both sexes carry from the fourth year of life on. This is the tonsure, which represents the face of the moon. The tonsure is shaved and often painted red (Becher 1959:162–167).

Furthermore, men, women, and children paint themselves for religious celebrations and during hunting and war parties with crosses, dots, and snakelike lines. Many tools and ornaments are also decorated with these attributes. (See Plates 5–9.)

The crosses represent the moon, the dots its allies the stars,[11] and the snakelike line represents a snake and at the same time the tied-up penis, a connective symbol between the moon and the earth.

On the basis of the above facts it can be concluded that a religious belief in the moon is probably a very old concept of the Yanomamö Indian culture.[12]

---

[11]   There are no special names for the individual stars and constellations. One speaks only generally of *Purim* [stars] and *Purim breu* [big stars].

[12]   When I stayed again with the Surára and Pakidái in 1966, we sometimes saw satellites slowly flying by in the tropical night sky. I explained to the Indians that these were sent into the sky by the Americans and Russians to carry out tests so that one day people could go to the moon. I added that this would be a great and sensational achievement.

But my friend, Hewemão, shook his head thoughtfully. One really couldn't speak of an achievement, he said, because he himself, or rather his soul and those of all the other Yanomamö, had often been on the moon. Life there was much more pleasant, he went on, than that on the earth, but Poré had ruled that they always had to return here.

During a new visit in 1970 I was able to inform my Indian friends that American astronauts were on the moon, but that they hadn't met the souls of dead Indians there. This was completely understandable, answered the Surára chief quickly and with conviction, because souls were invisible to mortals!

REFERENCES

BECHER, HANS
1955   *Cintos e cordões de cintura dos indios sul-americanos (não andinos)*. Revista do Museu Paulista n.s. 9. São Paulo.
1959   *Xelekuhahé. Das Stockduell der Surára und Pakidái-Indianer*. (*Ein Beitrag zum Problem der "Nilotenstellung" und der Tonsur in Südamerika*). Mitteilungen aus dem Museum für Völkerkunde Hamburg 25. Hamburg: Kommissionsverlag Ludwig Appel.
1960   *Die Surára und Pakidái. Zwei Yanonámi-Stämme in Nordwestbrasilien*. Mitteilungen aus dem Museum für Völkerkunde Hamburg 26. Hamburg: Kommissionsverlag Cram, de Gruyter. Walter de Gruyter & Co.

BIOCCA, ETTORE
1965–1966   *Viaggi tra gli Indi. Alto Rio Negro-Alto Orinoco* 4. Rome: Consiglio Nazionale delle Ricerche.

CHAGNON, NAPOLEON A.
1968   "Yanomamö: the fierce people," in *Case studies in cultural anthropology*. Edited by George and Louise Spindler. New York: Holt, Rinehart and Winston.

FUCHS, HELMUT
1959   Die Völkerverhältnisse am Oberlauf des Rio Ventuari. T.F.A. Venezuela. *Wiener Völkerkundliche Mitteilungen* 7, n.s. 2 (1–4): 45–62.

POLYKRATES, GOTTFRIED
1969   *Wawanauteri und Pukimapueteri. Zwei Yanonámi-Stämme Nordwestbrasiliens*. Publications of the National Museum, Ethnographical Series 9. Copenhagen: The National Museum of Denmark.

SCHUSTER, MEINHARD
1958   "Die Soziologie der Waiká," in *Proceedings of the Thirty-second International Congress of Americanists* (xxxx). Copenhagen.

WILBERT, JOHANNES
1963   *Indios de la Region Orinoco-Ventuari*, Monografia 8. Caracas: Fundacion la Salle de Ciencias Naturales.

ZERRIES, OTTO
1964   *Waiká. Die kulturgeschichtliche Stellung der Waiká-Indianer des Oberen Orinoco im Rahmen der Völkerkunde Südamerikas*. Munich: Klaus Renner Verlag.

Creative Process in Ritual Art: Piaroa Indians, Venezuela

LAJOS BOGLÁR

In 1967–1968, while doing ethnographical fieldwork among the Piaroa Indians in the forests of southern Venezuela, I was able to observe some phenomena at a seasonal rite that may throw light upon certain features of the creative process. The present paper is an attempt to sum up the problems of analysis on this subject.

For the examination of the creative process appearing under ritual conditions it was also necessary to ascertain secular relationships among creators, interpreters, and participants.

In their economic formation, the Indians under examination hardly differ from the other tropical-forest tribes. Besides their horticultural activity other ways of obtaining food — hunting and gathering — also play important roles. As to the social aspect of obtaining food we can establish above all that a clear and consistent division of labor prevails according to sex. The cultivation of plants, and some of the gathering and the preparation of food belong to the women's scope of duties, while the men are chiefly engaged in hunting (Boglár 1971). The economic basis of existence is secured by the integration of the cultivation of plants and the hunting activity — neither branch can be neglected. At the same time, primarily male dominance is typical in their life. A male bias arises from the fact that certain very important ritual functions can be performed only by men.

The fieldwork was sponsored by the Wenner-Gren Foundation for Anthropological Research, the Ethnographical Museum (Budapest), and the Hungarian Academy of Sciences. István Halmos, ethnomusicologist, also participated.

RELIGIOUS SPECIALISTS AND THE PERMANENT RITE

The head of the local group is the religious specialist whose duty it is to perform a series of ritual functions. His most important activity is a partly preventive, partly curative "struggle" against illnesses, but he is also responsible for organizing the ritual ceremonies, such as initiation and masked dance. He is the one best acquainted with mythical traditions and his duty is to prevent their sinking into oblivion. Finally, he is the master of preparation and use of the ritual objects.

According to observations he is also highly respected in everyday life if he fulfills his duties "without fault." This refers particularly to the magical chants concerning mythical animal relations which are performed almost every day. Searching for the sources of the prestige of the *menyerua* [man of the songs],[1] we have to observe, above all, the field which is in the center of his activity, namely, hunting or to be more exact, THE ANIMAL WHICH IS HUNTED. As the animal also carries magical powers, its meat has to be sung "pure" before eating it in the evening, in order that it may not bring "danger" (illness) to those who eat of its flesh. The epic content of the *menye* [magical chants] deals with the killed animal referring abundantly to the myths.[2]

Clearing up the relations of myths and rites is of utmost importance first of all because of social resonance. It is the questions concerning first of all, the language, that occur in connection with the magical chants and mythical narratives. I would refer to the fact that besides the everyday language there also exists an esoteric one: the mythical narratives are usually only understood by the initiated, and sometimes only by "the narrators." (The fact that the men hiding behind the masks sing in a changed voice during the dances is also relevant here.)

The role of the prohibition of language is remarkable in other cases, too: the names of certain objects and representations are identical to

[1]   One of the guarantees of the religious specialist's prestige is a good memory: this particularly pertains to the magic songs performed almost every day. We know an example when the group expelled its *menyerua* because he did not sing the magical chants correctly. This man was a narcotics addict, so his mind became disturbed and because of lapses of memory he could not recite the ritual texts correctly.
   A way of learning for the *menyerua* is that he meets highly respected and skilled religious specialists, and he repeatedly listens to their narratives. Even mythology refers ot the importance of remembering Wahari, the culture hero. To avoid being forgotten by people he created illnesses, which are carried by animals, so the meat-eating Indian is bound to "remember" the creator day by day.
[2]   The central figure of the mythology, Wahari, appears during the creation in the form ("mask") of several animals. After his death his soul went into the tapir, which is under taboo.

the denomination of the raw materials. The real or ritual denomination remains hidden. The ritual "instrumental language" is a further step in hiding: by means of a certain instrument it is possible to contact the women who are excluded and cannot see the men playing the music.[3]

Concerning the ideology, it is important to clear up the relation of idea and act. It is the religious chief and some chosen who possess the idea (with all its important details). The mythical texts mentioned several times are mostly incomprehensible to the members of the community, but they can hear them and they know that the religious chief "fulfills" his duty. He performs traditionally maintained rites; this is most important for the audience, which reacts with a real social resonance.[4]

According to an informant the chants sung in the hut in the evenings belong together, like "pearls on a necklace." He could hardly have pointed out more correctly and poetically the complexity of the phenomena. Describing the connection of a magical chant (pearl) and the chain of the magical chants (necklace) is not only an example for dialectical thinking but it also allows one to suppose the social need for totality. It casts a light on the problem if we draw our attention to the all-embracing rite of the Piaroa culture: the rite connected with the seasons.

RITUAL "SCHOOL": THE CEREMONIAL CONDITIONS OF CREATIVITY

The *warime* rite is the grandest event of the Piaroa Indians. During the masked rite many concepts of mythology are revealed as well as ritual painting, sculpturing, music, and dance as a chain of manifestations of expressive culture. During the ceremony the mask bearers represent animal spirits or, more exactly, the "lords" of certain animals. These are the peccary, the monkey, and the wild bee. According to the idea of the Piaroa, spiritual identification with the animal makes their relationship with the animal more intimate, and at the same time it induces them to multiply.

---

[3] The *muotsa* [leaf-whistle] made of palm-tree wood is a ritual instrument, an accessory of the masked ceremony. Indians playing this instrument can ask different questions, also related to everyday life. They can play the Piaroa name of palm nuts and fruits favored by birds on another instrument, the *dyaho* flute, which bears the name of the toucan bird.

[4] The situation with nonritual narratives (tales, "true" stories, etc.) is different, as described in an earlier paper of mine (Boglár 1970).

During the preparation of the masked rite the members of the local group (summoned from several settlements) under the direction of religious leaders and under ritual circumstances prepare the ritual accessories (masks, musical instruments) while they are initiated into the knowledge of mythology, religious ideas, and activities. Women and girls are forbidden to see the preparations; they do not know the identity of the mask bearers, nor can they see who play the instruments. The organization of the rite is an important task of the religious leader. He has his assistants who are to a certain degree acquainted with the ritual "crafts," yet all the responsibilities of organization are his. The masks and the musical instruments are made under his supervision, and he directs the course of the ceremony. In the view of the Piaroa Indians, however, it is not simply a matter of organization and staging; it is another proof that the religious leader is capable of controlling the powers of nature. The oldest religious chief I have met owes his distinguished authority to the fact that in his lifetime he has organized several *warime*s, or masked rites. During the rites and its preparations the harmony of individual and collective actions also defined from the point of view of relationship is clearly expressed. This dialectic chain of relations can be summed up as follows: the rite results from social needs; the making of ritual accessories is directed by an individual; securing the raw materials is the duty of specialists; the basic operations are done by specialists; the painting is the operation of individuals; although the rite is communal it enhances the prestige of the individual.

IDEOLOGICAL BASES

The basic concept, which is expressed in myths, religious ideas, and acts, is the humanization of nature. In the following I would like to mention identification as an important means of humanization. While examining the world concept of tribal societies it is repeatedly stated that man identifies himself with certain natural phenomena. Several factors — environment, cultural *milieu,* mentality, etc. — can determine the group of phenomena preferred by a community. It is evident, that animals are particularly suitable for such purposes. What factors can play a role in establishing the man-animal relationship with the Piaroa Indians?

This relation is the most striking in the *warime* rite, where the animals are represented by forms, voices, and movements. Representation of the mythical "lords" of animal spirits is not only a formal act, but contextually they are also an animation and direction "from within." (Representation and identification are well conditioned by an intense situation established by the common presence of rhythmical sound and motion.) The figure of the peccary, which is to be found in several myths and magical chants, rises out of the threefold unity of animal spirits, and it is determined by the incestuous relation of Wahari (the culture hero, the Creator) with his sister from which the peccary was born. The myth also explains the origin of the *warime* rite, and makes the community conscious of the "relation" of man and animals which has existed since ancient times.

It is important from the point of view of the identification examined that according to the myth the peccary was born from the sexual act of "humans." Why does the peccary play the role of the "most human" animal? What are the common traits of the peccary, monkey, and wild bee that helped them to play a distinguished role in the masked ceremonies?

Assorting these animals on the basis of their way of life we can establish, that:

1. all three animals live in the woods — not on savannahs or clearings;
2. they live in communities — rather than alone, like the jaguar, tapir, etc.;
3. they are plant-eating animals, not beasts of prey.

Since obvious questions pertaining to food acquisition are raised, the basic one for the Piaroa naturally is whether the animal (or plant) is edible or not. It is obvious that the hunting of communal animals is more desirable in the woods (where the Indian hunter feels more at home). It must be mentioned that the animals examined provide the raw materials for some ritual instruments too (tooth, bone, bristle, etc.), and the importance of the wild bee is emphasized by the fact that it supplies honey and wax (honey is not simply food but also medicine in the hands of the religious specialist and a symbolic material for the cohesion of the community; wax is used for several works of the religious specialist, e.g. for making masks, sculptures).

Besides the above facts — which can be verified biologically — the Piaroa also establish some secondary marks which indicate the continuity of identification and which make the relation of man and animal more profound. (The silver lip pendant is like the white beard on the peccary; the tongue of the Piaroa men is pierced at the initiation to make it similar to the tongue of the peccary, which has two natural grooves in it.)

Summing up we can establish that identification with the spirit of the animal not only confirms the continuity of the mythic state, but it also promotes the rebirth "from inside" as the creature being represented and finally helps its multiplication.

THE CREATIVE PROCESS

Studying tribal culture (generally the expressive culture) the investigator has to analyze ready forms and objects. The relation of myths and rites and the idea of identification call our attention to the fact that the forms and objects are the result of a continuous transformation, and their value can be revealed by examining specific cultural surroundings.[5] Now let us sum up some thoughts on the subject, mainly to indicate the process of cognition which leads to representation. In the process of preparing the ritual masks we can observe a line of transformation:
1.   For realizing an abstract idea (animal spirit, whose "owner" is the religious specialist),
2.   they need a concrete model (peccary, monkey, wild bee) and several materials.
3.   Under the direction of the chief certain specialists transform and compose the materials so that the representation shall be identical with the model (and to make identification easier for the interpreter during the performance).
4.   The identified representation finally gets the attributes from the religious specialists to raise the world of the spiritual beings to a more abstract sphere.

The transforming process of creation can be well observed in the preparation of the *redyo* [wild bee] mask. The *redyo* is a frequent figure of the narratives, a manifold being which can be benevolent as well as malevolent. As to its representation, the Indian sculptor takes a concrete living picture from nature which represents the abstract spirit, namely the wild bee, and its nest on the jungle tree. During the shaping process the sculpture gradually withdraws from the living picture by means of putting different covers (bark, wax, and paint) on top of one another. Meanwhile the elements of the image of nest and wild bee absorbed in

---

[5]   We must agree with d'Azevedo (1958: 703), that in anthropological literature, "The processes of art are obscured by an emphasis upon its formal products and their value as a source of information about other things." The paper of Goodale and Koss (1971: 190) represents a similar view: "Descriptions of art objects frequently fail to consider the ways in which initial values associated with or achieved in the construction process influence terminal values associated with the finished product."

each other return from time to time. At the end the white earth-paint used by the Indian sculptor "to alienate" emphasizes that there is a spiritual being present.

Besides the creative process it is very important that the community should see finished forms. It is only the creators, the initiated, the participants of the ritual "school" who can feel and know, that in a mask there is a line, a process registered, and its further life is full of motion and dance, which takes place before the others' eyes. The interpreters remain hidden like Wahari, the culture hero, who has appeared in front of the Indians in an everchanging form. Not only the hiding is interesting in this case, but also the fact that, similarly to Wahari, the Piaroa Indian also strives to humanize nature. This is a basic tendency of the man who lives within nature and I believe that this is the essence of "the art of the forests."

REFERENCES

D'AZEVEDO, WARREN L.
    1958   A structural approach to esthetics: toward a definition of art in anthropology. *American Anthropologist* 60:702–714.
BOGLÁR, LAJOS
    1970   Aspects of story-telling among the Piaroa Indians. *Acta Ethnographica* 19:38–52.
    1971   "Besuch bei den Piaroa-Indianern: T.F. Amazonas, Venezuela" in *Verhandlungen des 38ten Internationalen Amerikanistenkongresses* 3:23–27. Munich: Renner.
GOODALE, J. C., J. D. KOSS
    1971   "The cultural context of creativity among Tiwi," in *Anthropology and art*. Edited by C. M. Otten, 182–200. New York: Natural History Press.

Ritual Poetry: Ceremonial Songs in Eastern Europe

TEKLA DÖMÖTÖR

When I refer to ritual poetry in Eastern Europe, I am thinking of oral poetry which has no apparent connection with any church or state ritual (even though it may contain motifs which can be traced back to some earlier literary source), but as a whole belongs to those folk customs which mark some important, transitory period of human life or of the seasons. Genuine ritual poetry can still be found at weddings, funerals, and is further connected with midwinter and midsummer customs and with customs performed at the beginning of spring.

The importance of this ritual poetry has long been stressed by ethnomusicologists. Bartók wrote about Hungarian folk songs: the melodies fall into well-differentiated groups: (1) several groups of ceremonial songs: wedding songs, laments, the so-called *regös* songs; (2) tunes for dancing; (3) lyrical or narrative songs which do not belong to any ceremony or occasion (Bartók 1966: 77). According to Lord:

The nonnarrative types of oral poetry include: a) the incantation or charm; b) the love song; c) the lament; d) the wedding ritual song; e) other ritual songs for special festivities. Indeed all these types, including the love song are ritual in origin and in ultimate purpose (Lord 1965).

Of course with the rapid changes in peasant life today, these poetic creations also drop into oblivion and disappear. The new songs, expressing festive joy, cosmogonic views or great emotions of peasants become the same as those we find among town people as well. They are created nowadays by professional poets and composers and come to the peasants through the customary routes of the mass media (printed works, radio, television, etc.). These are not dealt with here, although they certainly deserve our attention as they reflect the present taste for poetry of the peasants and correspond to the needs of common people.

The chief forms for ritual poetry are dialogues and ceremonial songs. As I have already dealt with the dialogues (Dömötör 1964, 1972), I am going to discuss here only the second category.

Ceremonial songs are generally connected with folk customs, which consist of three chief components: (a) ritual action, (b) the "spoken rites," i.e. ritual poetry, and (c) etiological explanations which might or might not be recited during the ceremony.

Ceremonial songs in Eastern and Central Europe contain Christian religious elements, nonreligious motifs and "non-Christian" mythical and magic motifs, the relics of antique cults, and the tangles of autochthonous pagan beliefs and pseudoreligious elements. Very often, the people who recite the songs have no explanation at all for the songs or their motifs. Their tenacious survival can be explained by different factors: (a) peasants still believe that ceremonial texts must be repeated word by word, because any change may hinder their effectiveness; (b) the formerly mythical or religious themes keep their aesthetic value long after the symbols have lost their meaning. In this way, old mythic motifs become aesthetic factors in oral poetry.

I have been also concerned with the question of how long certain mythical symbols may keep their functional role, transplanted into different cultural and philosophical systems. Some of the old symbols have been taken over and reinterpreted by the Christian churches, but in other cases, Christianity could not accept them and forbade their use often without any result.

I presumed further, that these symbols are not mere creations of human fantasy, but, like myths, obey some inward logic and endeavor to offer vital information about the world, mankind, the supernatural, the forces of life, and the fate of man. Thus, the symbols used in ceremonial songs differ from those used in other types of narrative or lyrical poetry.

In the center of my investigation are Hungarian ceremonial songs, but I also quote some parallels from the ceremonial songs of our neighbors, especially Romanian ceremonial songs.

The first group consists of dirges and laments. At present, the situation in Hungary is rather complicated because, at a burial, very different kinds of songs can be heard: (1) Church songs; (2) religious songs folklorized to such an extent, that they may be called at present "folk songs" (Lajtha 1956); (3) farewells spoken in the name of the deceased by a member of the community in first person singular; (4) nonreligious dirges sung by choirs; (5) laments in a kind of speech-song, sung according to the rules of Hungarian diction "in which 'speech elements' are represented first by the rhythm, and second by an irregular pattern of periods" (Bartók et al. 1966: 1065). The last group is generally performed by the members of the family, or by some other local person who has a special talent for lamenting. These free laments sometimes come close to the stanza form too.

Let me mention here the extraordinary Romanian songs for the dead which have been analyzed by Romanian folklorists, especially the "Song of the Dawn," and the "Song of the Pine"; the latter might be a survival of ancient cults, e.g. the Attis cult.

The laments in "speech-song" and their melodies belong to the oldest layer of Hungarian poetry and music and very similar laments can still be found among other people speaking Uralic-Altaic languages too.

These laments, composed partly of formulas, further relate actual facts from the life of the deceased or of the family. Among the formulas we find the theme of "looking for the dead." The lamenting person looks to the north, east, south and west, but does not find the deceased. Other formulas call the deceased person a flower, a crown fallen from the head, a pretty bird, etc. I could trace some of the formulas back to the seventeenth century, but some might be in fact much older. There are of course, recent formulas, too; for instance, the rather trivial one of the "black train" carrying away the deceased.

Alas my dear father, my dearest heart! Where shall we look for you, where is the place to watch for you? ...
In vain do I look for you, I shall not meet you anywhere. ...
Alas, where shall I turn my eyes? Shall I turn to east or west or north? Alas, wherever I turn, I see none of my own dear ones. ...

The real events recalled may name the hospital where the deceased had been treated, the doctors, or the surviving members of the family, or recall other events from the life of the family.

We might also consider "traditional" the farewell said in the name of the dead person, as already, in medieval Latin chronicles, mention is made of this custom (Dömötör 1964, passim).

Most Hungarian wedding songs are love songs, which can be sung on other occasions too. There are however some categories which belong strictly to weddings. Such is the bride's farewell, similar in form to the above laments for the dead (and sometimes recited by the best man). Other songs describe the various stages of the long wedding ceremony, e.g. the transportation of the bride's bed linen, the "donning of the cap," etc.

Endless verses describe the preparation of the dishes during the wedding feast. Many of these texts were also printed in chapbooks and it is difficult to say which are older, the printed texts, or the oral versions.

Another category of the calendrical rituals consists of the songs sung at the end of the old year and at the beginning of the new year.

These songs are performed on different days, in the period from December 13 till January 6. Apart from religious songs and general well-wishing songs, I found the following mythic symbols in this group:

1. A demonic being is evoked on December 13 (St. Lucy's Eve or Day). This custom has been analyzed by Kretzenbacher in a very erudite monograph (Kretzenbacher 1959). I consider this demonic being called *Luca* to be a survival of the cult of Juno Lucina (the Greek Eileithyia). Young boys go from house to house with luck-wishing songs, which refer to the fertility of poultry, other animals, and to human fertility as well (Dömötör 1970). This demonic being is called by the same name as Lucia of Syracuse, the Catholic saint, but her cult is quite different from that of the woman saint.

2. Prominent in the ceremonial songs is the figure of a miraculous stag. In Hungary, Romania, and Bulgaria religious legends are connected with this motif. The stag as a symbol of the winter sky occurs however in Asia too and even among Cora Indians (Preuss 1906). Hungarian folklorists have written several monographs about this question, as the Hungarian ceremonial *regös* songs kept a very poetic version of this mythic motif.

Yonder where the stream appears,
My sheep are grazing,
Wonder stag!
Antler with a thousand branches,
On each branch a thousand candles
Blaze in splendour,
Flicker and die ...

3. A miraculous tree plays an important role in the Christmas and New Year luck-wishing songs both in Hungary and among other European people. This tree appears in various combinations. In its allegorical form it is a genealogical representation, Jesse's tree, from which according to Isaiah, Christ descended. The tree motif is correlated with the tree growing in Paradise and the legend of the Holy Cross. The same tree figures in faith-healing charms and in name-day greetings. Often, the tree is an apple tree and Christ himself a "golden apple." The tree also might be connected with the winter solstice according to astrological speculations: this can be deduced from incantations and the "wakening of trees," a custom known from England to Japan (Dömötör 1971).

The tree in a name-day song:

So we are come, good evening
To greet Stephen ...
In the court, in the court of St. Stephen
There is a beautiful apple-tree.
Its root has brought the tree,
Its tree has brought its branches,
Its branch has brought its blossom,
Its blossom has brought its apple ...

The same motif in faith-healing charms:

A green tree issues branches on an island of the sea,
The branches bore the leaves,
The leaves their flowers,
The flowers bore St. Anna,
St. Anna bore Mary,
Mary bore her Saint Son, etc.

4. A very curious motif, known only in Transylvania, is the "infant sun-god born from the rock" (Mithras motif). In the Romanian version Christ is imprisoned in a stone and can only soar to heaven after his mother has swept the rim of heaven with a broom.

The Mother of the Son
Sits on a rock,
She stares and cries,
She weeps.
And her tears are as big as apples,
And as light as feathers.
And the Son in the rock says:
I cannot fly away from this stone
As long as you do not buy
A golden broom,
And you sweep
The face of earth,
And the rim of heaven,
And you strike the stone three times ...

In the Hungarian Christmas song, the young god is situated in the "stone-garden of Paradise." In his left hand he holds an apple, in the right a twig; he swishes his twig, or plays with the apple and the whole world is in uproar. This corresponds to the legend of Mithras' birth, as shown on the various reliefs still to be found in Transylvania and other old Roman provinces. To quote Campbell:

The head and torso of a naked male youth emerges from a rough rock formation. The god usually holds a dagger in his right hand and a torch in his left (or a sphere for the torch). A globe held in the hand by a god indicates with fair certainty that the holder is a kosmokrater. ... Such a ball is held by Mithras Invictus or Sol Invictus (Campbell 1968:272–279).

In the stone garden of Paradise,
A golden carpet is spread.
On it, there is a golden cradle,
In which Jesus is lying.
Golden apple in his left hand,
Golden twig in his right hand,
He swishes the twig,
Sound the forests, ring the fields.

Spring ceremonial songs may be divided into the songs of early spring and late spring (May songs, Whitsun songs). Most of these songs have lost their original role and appear today as songs accompanying children's games. There are however a few clear features: quite a few of the symbols used allude to the search for a future spouse. The singers must undertake a long trip to find the girls "sitting in a tower." I think it is possible to call some of these games "labyrinth-games," according to the choreography of the game; and the texts make allusions to long journeys undertaken.

In the songs which are sung for the Whitsun queen, we hear of a mysterious being who was born on a rose bush. Many of these spring songs make allusions to flowers, but the exact meaning of the texts is hard to understand, although the general atmosphere corresponds to the season.

Hungarian Midsummer Night's songs are connected with lighting a bonfire, and girls jumping over the fire. The Hungarian songs recited on this occasion contain several parts. Some stanzas are evidently love songs. Others describe the lighting of the bonfire and the behavior of the villagers around the fire. One song is a "certamen," i.e. altercation of the flowers, a well-known genre since the Middle Ages. There is also a rather curious stanza about the Virgin Mary asleep in the shortest night of the year. The deacons are warned not to wake her from her dream. It also seems that the Virgin is responsible for the course of the sun and the moon; she is begged to call down the sun and send up the moon to the sky.

Young deacons, be quiet when you ring the bell!
Let Mary sleep, until the sun rises!
Golden haired Mary, call down the sun
Bring forth the moon, where the sun sets,
Sets in Mary. ...

This stanza is related to another group of ceremonial songs, which were hitherto not analyzed: the nonclerical prayers, which often are sung and not recited. Catholics and Protestants may know these prayers, which are, however, at present forbidden by Catholic and Protestant Churches. In the eighteenth and nineteenth centuries, many of these prayers were written down or even printed by the clergy, but in the last century they have been transmitted as oral poetry. Several hundred prayers were collected in recent years by Hungarian folklorists. These lay prayers may also contain the mythic motifs mentioned above; for instance, we often find as a typical introduction the sleeping Virgin Mary, then the cock crows, and someone wakes her. In some evening prayers, mention is made again of the Virgin as the guardian of the period from midnight to the dawn; while before midnight and after the dawn, several other saints, or God himself is responsible for the sleeping person.

Protect me, angel, till midnight,
The Holy Virgin till the dawn,
Jesus Christ forever.

Here I have to mention the fact that these symbols do not occur in other genres of folk poetry, or in living folk beliefs. They do not occur in the several thousand texts of legends which give a good insight into the world view of Hungarian peasants and their attitude towards the supernatural world. They occur only in ceremonial songs and are considered "beautiful," even if they are not understood. This enables them to live some time after the disappearance of the customs to which they were attached.

As for the function of the ceremonial songs, it is somewhat similar to that of incantations or charms, or even to that of the recital of myths in those cultures where myths still have a real function. They are often considered as having magic power (e.g. the well-wishing songs).

Others describe festive activities (the bulk of wedding songs), or are sung because the living relatives either feel the urge or are forced by the tradition to take leave in this way from the departed and express their feelings of loss. It is notable, that in the laments people speak more often about their own grief than about the dead: what they really complain about is their own hopeless situation and bereavement. Ceremonial songs often consist of two chief parts: an epic introduction (describing events that happened long ago, at the beginning of the world, or at the time when Christ lived among men) and well-wishing formulas. In this respect, they also resemble myths and healing charms. Their function is of course mainly psychological: the repetition of the songs gives hope to the community and also cements the solidarity of the group.

I have in several cases alluded to the fact that ceremonial festive songs and healing charms may contain similar motifs. Still, as the latter have a very special function they have to be considered as a special genre, even if we are aware of the similar traits of these categories (see Cs. Pócs 1968).

In an earlier book I tried to describe the general philosophical trend of ceremonial songs. As quite a lot of them have a magical function, they can be called optimistic and people hope to ensure with their help fertility, good luck for the community and for individuals, plenty of rain, etc.

Laments and dirges of course, are different; they very seldom promise the Christian "life after death" but generally express utter hopelessness.

I have stressed that I always start my analysis with Hungarian ceremonial songs. Similar genres are to be found among other Eastern European peoples too, and we find an even richer variety of mythical motifs among Romanians, Bulgarians, Russians, etc.

Let me emphasize that it was not my intention to look for direct correlation or migration of motifs, the less so, since the mythical symbols mentioned have long been known in Eastern Europe; they represent a common property from which ceremonial songs were free to draw. Since cults like that of Juno Lucina (the divine midwife), of Mithras and Attis were oppressed by Christianity long ago (or their elements and iconography were embedded in Christian tradition) it is astonishing to find that in ceremonial songs they may still be found in recognizable form.

I must further state that I have not expatiated at all upon symbols we can regard as typically "Hungarian." It is not so much the motifs but rather the melody and the prosody which may display typically Hungarian features. The cosmogony and beliefs of Hungarians (who came from the East and settled in the Carpathian Basin among people speaking Indo-European languages) certainly contained some elements which formed connecting links with the old European myths. They certainly also expressed a belief in the existence of a sort of "divine midwife," helper of mothers, in a tree connecting earth and sky (and still very well known in shamanistic types of religions). Their legend of origin comprised the motif of a miraculous stag (or hind) and they probably knew a goddess in command of sun and moon. These motifs survived in the ceremonial songs, stripped of their old contexts, and were embedded in the common Eastern European tradition.

REFERENCES

BARTÓK, BÉLA
  1966   Összegyüjtött irásai, volume one. Budapest: Zenemükiadó.
  1968   Melodien der rumänischen Colinde. Budapest: Editio Musica.
BARTÓK, BÉLA et al., editors
  1966   Siratók [Laments]. Corpus Musicae Popularis Hungaricae V. Budapest: Akadémiai Kiadó.
CAMPBELL, L. A.
  1968   Mithraic iconography and ideology. Leiden: Brill.

CS. POCS, ÉVA
1968   "A magyar ráolvasások müfaji és rendszerezési problémái," in *Népi kultura-népi társadalom.* Edited by Gy. Ortutay, 253–280. Budapest: Akadémiai Kiadó.

DÖMÖTÖR, TEKLA
1964   *Naptári ünnepek — népu szinjátszás.* Budapest: Akadémiai Kiadó.
1970   "Mythical Elements in Hungarian Midwinter quete songs," in *Acta Ethnographica.* Edited by Gy. Ortutay, 309–408. Budapest: Akadémiai Kiadó.
1971   "Riten zur Förderung der Fruchtbarkeit von Obstbäumen," in *Studia Ethnographica et Folkloristika in Honorem Béla Gunda.* Debrecen: Kossuth L. Tudományegyetem.
1972   *Hungarian folk customs.* Budapest: Corvina.

KRETZENBACHER, LEOPOLD
1959   *Santa Lucia und die Lutzelfrau.* München: Oldenburg.

LAJTHA, LASZLÓ
1956   *Sokron megyei virrasztó énekek.* Budapest: Zenemükiadó.

LORD, ALBERT B.
1965   "Oral poetry," in *Encyclopedia of poetry and poetics.* Edited by A. Preminger. Princeton: Princeton University Press.

PREUSS, I. TH.
1906   "Reisebericht aus San Isidro, Mexiko," in *Zeitschrift für Ethnologie,* volume thirty-eight. Braunschweig: Behrend Verlag.

Krou Popular Traditions in the Ivory Coast

B. HOLAS

THE PROBLEM

As it stands, the bibliography on the traditional civilizations of the Krou complex is impressive enough in volume and diversity of the aspects covered; however, the subject is still one of the least known of western Africa. This is especially true of the Krou cultural sector proper, namely, the coastal populations of the area around Tabou, an extensive study of the traditions of which could provide a great deal of new material for the sociologist-ethnologist and for the specialist in oral literature.

What is the picture, seen panoramically, and with what figures of the imagination is it animated?

HUMAN FRAMEWORK

First of all, the peoples established on both sides of the lower Cavally, which acts as a natural frontier for Liberia and the Ivory Coast, the various fractions of the Krou entity, while speaking a common language of the Kwa type, present great variations in their respective cultural expressions.

Nevertheless, as can be observed on first approaching the environment, in spite of the considerable progress made not long ago in their material existence, which used to be known for seasonal emigrations of volunteers on board the merchant vessels serving the west coast of Africa, the Krou villagers in the privacy of their homes continue their daily routine according to barely changed customary rules.

On the surface of course the changes are striking, in particular in those areas where industrial plantations, mainly coffee plantations, are gradually encouraging a new system of community association, apparently in conflict with the former social structures.

These structures undeniably present archaic features, modeled after the example of the very first human society, as depicted by the myth of man's origins.

THE CURRENTS OF MYTH MAKING

Thus, both theoretically and by its practical applications in the social routine, the tale considered by its very definition to be a moral heritage of a sacred nature, of the beginning of the world and of the foundation of the first human community, is the starting point of all other intellectual steps.

The myth's value as an example obviously has no absolute or compulsory characteristic: nevertheless, the principle entails, as stated above, a number of important actual consequences. Thus, if we want to deal with the life of the Krou as an individual and a member of a community, we must, above all, ask ourselves by which paths and to what extent the mythical models interfere in the community's thoughts.

THE SEARCH FOR A *RAISON D'ÊTRE*

Oral tradition, in the absence of writing, conveys and preserves the basic ideas of existence, either using a direct and clear language or the prevailing collection of everyday symbols. It comprises, in fact, the constitutional, empirical elements, fixed by use, of a philosophy offering the framework for the conception of all things forming a part of the universe perceptible by the senses, and serves as a stage for the individual careers and thereby for the material life of the community.

But really, the concepts thus described also play a part in metaphysics, eschatology and, in a word, in everything connected with the great problems of survival and, in general, of the beyond.

Once this has been accepted, we have to follow the winding paths of the system.

Faced with the "why" of existence, the Krou tries to conquer his confusion by doing extrapolations and tackling, in the absence of a capacity for objective analysis, any questions he is asked one by one. He does this in the only possible way, by assimilating transcendent phenomena with notions of experience on one hand, and by creating appropriate images on the other.

With the latter method of interpretation we are already entering the field of the irrational which we would rather in the long run, qualify as NONRATIONAL.

Here, the observed fact withdraws, to a great extent, behind the creations of the mind.

The intellectual manipulation that is implied here is not in any way new: to give forms to the subjects of his imagination, the bases of the mythical network and landmarks of his myth making, the Krou proceeds in the same way as all other peoples in this cultural stage — the creators of a more or less articulated concept of the world. On one hand he elaborates independent, purely fictional images, and on the other hand he attempts to find in his natural environment objects and animals whose typical or even unusual aspect, or whose specific psychic nature, pre-destines them to act as emblems. And he sometimes makes them act as real condensators of spiritual energy.

These THINGS-and-IDEAS relationships then become, in the speculative language, real axioms of truth (if we dare to say it), conventional references which finally end up in the common vocabulary. At the highest level, and this goes without saying, there are a number of logical equations, of a noetic nature, which are only for the initiates. But this is, in the case of the Krou, a heritage that has been broken into extensively.

THE INTERPRETATION OF NATURAL PHENOMENA

At this stage of mental and economic development, nature, whether nearby or distant, constantly nourishes man's thoughts. Certain atmo-spheric phenomena can thus be connected with a specific human pre-occupation and may influence the destiny of individuals or of the whole society.

The Krou often compares the succession of the seasons or, to be precise, the alternating rainy periods and dry intervals, with the fluctuations of life. Humidity is usually more favorable to important undertakings than drought, which is however preferred for the organization of the great ceremonies of union, such as the celebration of marriages, and of the separation rites, mainly funerals.

In the Krou's mind, the mists and fog which may lie for a long time over the forest and the seashore, with the obscured sun as a corollary, are associated with nature asleep. This state encourages man to rest, to cease his activities, but also to undergo sudden changes of mood, to commit suicide, and even murder.

As in most Western countries, the appearance of a rainbow acts as a favorable premonitory sign, although the assimilation with the notion of the heavenly serpent, which is, incidentally, frequently found in the Gulf of Guinea civilizations, does not seem to be clearly certified here.

In Krou country, the storms which are current during the interseason period covering the first months of the year, always produce a striking psychological effect in addition to the material damage they cause to villages and fields. It would be incorrect, however, to think that such an attitude, an essentially affective reaction, could paralyze man's reflected actions in any way at all. The two behaviors coexist without any mutual hindrance.

It is, however, the emotional behavior that we are trying to understand for the time being. Now, it is not surprising, under the circumstances, that lightning, its flashes and its rumbling, creates the illusion in the human mind of a terrifying unknown power. Some villagers associate the rumbling of thunder and the accompanying gusty storms with the acts of a Nieswa, an acting supreme divinity, in a temper; thus, the next day the chief worshiper will willingly recommend the offering of appeasement sacrifices.

In some cases, it is found necessary to look for the person who has caused the anger of the supernatural beings; the "guilty" person is then forced to carry out, at his own expense, a forgiveness rite followed by an act of purification.

Local altars often contain, apart from a few stones of exceptional shape acting as ex-votos, so-called lightning stones, or neolithic type axes, sometimes imported from the northern regions by traveling marabouts of Mande-Dioula origin.

The Krous, who do not consider this point to be an exception to the common rule, take ancient polished stone tools to be messengers of the great uranian power, whose features they are incidentally not too keen to define any further: as far as they are concerned, this power is a primary force, distant, diffuse and inoperative, but nevertheless always to be feared because of its sudden outbursts of temper. The Nieswa, who is nearer and a jack of all trades, always offers to be his plenipotentiary representative on earth and consequently receives the appropriate ritual offerings on his behalf and instead of him.

This Nieswa divinity, although actually occupying the summit of the pantheon, is probably only a late-comer who, belonging to a great family of divinities reigning over the vast forest area of the western Ivory Coast, has had among the Krous a destiny full of risks and readjustments.

Generally speaking, the symbolic meaning of the stone seems to be fairly explicitly established in the traditional Krou philosophy; it is especially associated with the dynamic energies of life whose cyclic permanency it recalls by a logical detour. Thus, sometimes, on the advice of the soothsayer, the *doyo* [sterile women], after carrying out the suitable propitiatory rite, wear a number of little pebbles representing future newborn babies.

But the stone takes on truly metaphysical aspects in the popular tales: the stone, suspended in mid-air, can also act as a receptacle for the occult forces destined to play a part in the myth or in the tales justifying a specific cult.

The concept, however, often has other uses and is transferred to the field of practical liturgy; this often happens to erratic isolated blocks and to some submerged rocks which, in effect, are excellently suited to be sacred places. The lower reaches of the Cavally offer a number of examples of this.

FACING THE COSMIC SPACES

Among the cosmic subjects, the moon very clearly dominates the horizons, with a few other stars and constellations way behind. The sun, belonging to the realities of the day, does not seem to be favored with cultual honors among the Krous, and — considered more as a mere phenomenon — does not have, to our knowledge at least, any specific function in the fragments of what was probably a real cosmogonic system.

The moon, on the other hand, has a decisive and multiple influence on the daily routine and calls for more or less precise attitudes from the individual and the community.

The selenian symbolism, to tell the truth, can be summed up as nothing very much; based, as can be expected, on the notion of periodicity, it automatically implies the image of the mother-woman, associated with the earth as a provider of means of subsistence. The events of the land year — together with the whole of the social calendar — are consequently regulated according to the phases of the moon. The same division of time is in fact observed by the cult rituals.

In the popular imagination, moonlight offers a particularly suitable backcloth for the apparition of all kinds of specters. Creating a mysterious, if not frightening, atmosphere, the moonlit night is definitely preferable to the dark night; the latter is more representative of emptiness, nothingness, than of a field of bad deeds. All evil spirits, the malicious creatures of the forest, and especially the wandering souls of the unusually deceased, the ghosts, who like to prowl very close to the limits of the village, nearly always choose a palely moonlit night to appear to the living.

It should be noted, however, perhaps quite fairly, that a starry night provides folklore with a rich material for the creation of narrative themes. The most usual example of these is the allegorical association of an exceptionally bright star or a striking constellation with a mythical personage or hero.

In the Krou mentality, the need for the miraculous flourishes and therefore feeds itself best, and to a considerable extent, under the wan and ambiguous light of the moon. The stars, in this psychological system, finally only act as confederates.

From the point of view of empirical experiences, the situation is slightly different, obviously. But there is no lack of a few well-established preconceptions, in other words "superstitions." Generally speaking, astronomical observations are confined to the notion of the coincidence existing between the presence and the movements of certain constellations that are easily identifiable, and the rotation of the seasons relative to farming, fishing, or hunting.

FAUNA, IN REALITY AND IN FABLES

Taking into account the given orographic and hydrological conditions, all the Krou vital space presents itself as a compound consisting of innumerable places likely to shelter immaterial forces. These places can be either various natural prominences of the land, from a cathedral-size termites' nest to a mountain, or some natural cavity, or else water points such as a pond or a river, or sometimes just a section of a pond or a river, specially designated. In the latter case, which is very frequent in Krou country, full observance of the place is generally noted, including in particular the fish, which are acknowledged as sacred animals.

Snakes, bats, and small rodents such as porcupines, atheruruses, and aulacodes, are sometimes compared with a farmyard of the spirit living in the cavern concerned. On another occasion, a big python usually found in a given place can be taken for an authentic emanation of the invisible deity.

Most of the Krou family groupings, the *tougba*, thus know about haunted grottoes at whose entrance their elders periodically leave offerings of no great value, simply as a gesture of good relations. Apart from a few fragments of pottery which have survived from better times, places of this kind are hardly identifiable today as the cult is fated to be abandoned.

Whereas according to the norms of the old symbolic system, grottoes, the image of the vulva, are the subject of cultual solicitations from the men, water, containing fish which are suggestive by their slender bodies of the idea of the male copulatory organ, is obviously associated with the women. Thus, on the banks of rivers and ponds, traces are sometimes found of sacrificial libations — broken calabashes or pots, or fragments of fishing nets, etc. — which were left there by the devout women of the village, mainly with the intention of thereby guaranteeing the prosperity of the lineage, with the help of the fertilizing energies. During the irregularly spaced community ceremonies, the population feeds the fish of the sacred waters, taken to be the visible representatives of the tutelary aquatic powers; to the latter, the sacrificing priest sends up chants and prayers on behalf of the group.

The specific position of the snake in Africa seems sometimes to have been misunderstood by certain observers who have been too inclined to see in them what the depositaries of the tradition themselves did not see.

This is perfectly applicable to the Krou we are studying here, because, in fact, without of course disregarding the phallic nature of the snake, their traditional symbolism hardly mentions it.

The snake, in the ontological order, is associated with both land and water and also retains the characteristics of the fertilizing male. Its propitiatory image is often found among the subjects of wall paintings where it is easily confused with other reptilian monsters of no precise vocation.

It is a favorite subject for the village storytellers, and it is also the subject of tales justifying family totemic interdicts, known as *kpade*.

The snake, in fact, performs functions of a polyvalent model as will be understood later on, when we will deal with its multiple derivatives or amplifications of the *mami wata* type; the snake, it is a well-known fact, has a constant tendency to turn into a dragon or another snakelike fabulous monster.

Acting as a counterpart to the heavily masculine snake, the tortoise, by the shape of its rounded and curved shell, suggests the idea of the receptive and reproductive nature of the woman and is automatically ranked as one of her main emblems.

The ideal comparison with the female sex organ in fact goes so far that the head of the tortoise is seen as a reminder of the clitoris; in the far northern part of the Krou country, where excision rites are performed, the surgical operation of the first of the novices is thus preceded by the ablation of the head of a tortoise.

The figures of Krou imagination rarely enjoy conceptual independence but are usually grouped in a more or less established class of everyday images.

How does all this affect practical thinking, in fact, and what is the topical framework surrounding each of the above allegorical representatives?

ALLEGORICAL ANIMALS

All the symbol animals are generally associated with a few natural landmarks, a cavern, a shelter under the rocks, or preferably a tree with a hollow trunk.

But what is also important, and perhaps especially so, is the typical behavior of a specific confederate involved in the game.

There is no doubt that the animal world offers man nearly inexhaustible inspirations for the invention of parables.

To do this, the architect-man of this universe of the para-real, uses "technical" processes of his own invention; and their results are often not only real masterpieces of distortion but, as soon as they take shape and begin to act, definitely differ from the model. Others are so different that they are lost on the way to "reality."

The collection of models is in fact relatively small, and approximates the range of the local fauna. We mention below the most representative species for the Krou cultural sector.

At the top of the list we have a leading mythological actor: the *gbaina*, the dwarf cephalopholus, is associated with sly intelligence and is involved, more or less explicitly, in the destinies of the primary human society. This rather suspicious but on the whole pleasant character is the center pin of a number of adventure stories which form the richer folklore cycle. We will be dealing with the latter in greater detail in a vast survey of the Krou traditions.

The elephant naturally represents power, physical force, and the notions of headship and command, while the leopard, symbolically associated with political leadership, is mainly symbolic of craftiness and cruelty — the warrior's main characteristics. In a great many of the popular tales based on the image of the military hero, like the famous *tabio*, the Hodio Niepaplo war chieftain, the latter comparison is found to be very meaningful, and the fact is, in a certain sense, one of the principal characteristics of this type of civilization.

Unlike the dominant role taken, for example, in the Akan mythologies, by the crocodile, this hydrosaur does not have any noteworthy function in the Krou's mythical and philosophical speculations, in spite of its abundance in the Krou country. It is of course the subject of food bans and of numerous superstitions; at the same time it has an episodic role in hunters' fables and stories.

Most of the great ungulates such as the buffalo, the bongo and other forest antelopes, receive relatively little attention in Krou metaphysical thoughts. They easily make up for this lack of attention in another field, that of the totem tales and of the food bans which are extensions of these with ritual applications. The crocodile, in any case, has a leading place among the ally-animals of the family groups which the Krou, as we know, refer to as *tougba*.

Some popular beliefs are especially associated with the chameleon and the porcupine: the former is considered as a suspect, if not dangerous being — a mediating agent of the supernatural powers whose messages, usually unpleasant, he brings to humans; the latter is suspected, if someone decides to anger him, of hurling the evil spell far away with his spikes.

MAN'S FOLKLORE CYCLE

Several legends also mention the chimpanzee, supposed to be a survivor of a prehuman race and an ally of little red men of Pygmoid origin, called *ngame* by the Krou storytellers. In the whole area of the great western forests, the theme of a prehuman species, held to be the race of the first occupants of the land, is still prevalent; and there are still places where the present users of the arable land, before actually making use of it, deposit there a number of compensating offerings to show acknowledgement of the land rights.

The conventional symbol of the evil witch doctor, the owl is part of a group of announcers of bad news: if he perches on the roof of a house at night, this is a sign of a forthcoming sickness or death among the village inhabitants.

Even insects, such as the praying mantis, the myriapod, or the phasma, and sometimes even large arachnidae, such as the mygale, can, if necessary, provide man with divining material.

UNTAMED NATURE AND VILLAGE MICROCOSM

It is quite obvious that free nature (as compared with "conquered nature") is an additional area of exploitation (offering practically unlimited and consequently highly exciting possibilities) and forms a suitable environment for stimulating the creative imagination even more than the village universe.

Nevertheless, the village, with its public square, its meeting places around the center tree, known by the Krou as the *tougbakayou*, and with all its periphery which contains a few vegetable "gardens," ablution arrangements, and the household garbage dumps, offers vital space to a whole range of domestic animals, starting with the inevitable chickens and ending with the skinny cow of the Ivory Coast forests.

Now, although they are easier to observe in their daily contacts with man, with some exceptions these domestic animals do not seem to stimulate the Krou storytelling imagination. Nevertheless, they occupy a few good places in the symbolic imagery. The sheep, — lacking the solar symbolism it has, for example, among the Akan peoples — the ox, the he-goat, the duck, and the cock have inspired ritual disguises, in particular within the choreographic framework of the feminine initiations.

The dog's position, on the other hand, is fairly exceptional in that the dog not only appears in the role of mythical carrier of the first fire but also in the extremely frequent role of totemic ally of the founding ancestor (who first trained the dog to help him when hunting), and can replace, if necessary, a human victim in certain major sacrifices. All domestic animals, of any given species, are in fact frequently the subject of a totemic ban.

As for the plant kingdom, it contributes little to any mythical arrangements in the true sense of the term. However, nearly all the healing plants included in large numbers in the empirical pharmacopoeia have been given, and quite rightly, supernatural properties.

Among the cultivated plants, the plantain banana, the yam, the manioc, the taro, and sometimes even mere condiments such as the gumbo represent the simple examples of the food ban prescribed and explained by the family myth, or to be more precise, the family totemic tale. In the language of the initiates, the yam tubercle is sometimes compared with the human embryo waiting, in a state of latent existence peculiar to the reincarnatable ancestral substances, to arrive in the world.

ON THE PATHS OF FREE CREATION

We must now pass from the field of inspiration to the field of pure and free invention.

We must first realize one thing, after summing up the experiences acquired up till now; the resources afforded by the physical environment to the repertoire of the oral tradition are no more fertile than those which arise straight from fiction.

In tackling this vast field of mythical creation, we will not include the witch doctor in the discussion; his function, which is both psychological and social, would easily exceed the limited framework of our subject. The witch doctor figure (generally called *gwenion* by the Krou) is at the center of very ample myth making, sometimes reaching the limits of the fantasmagorical, and is very distinctly detached from the figure of the *doyo*, a perfectly licit specialist, responsible, in the name of threatened society, for tracking down and eliminating occult criminals.

Apart from the witch doctor and his equals, the Krou folklore operates with so great a range of fabulous creatures that we will have to simplify the situation substantially in order to outline the system.

The organization then appears to be very simple. It has tiny beings on the first step of the ladder and giants at the top of the ladder. Between the two there are monsters of all shapes and sizes whose morphology varies according to the circumstances.

The narrations, with as their theme the generation of dwarfs with a reddish complexion, long hair and ingrown feet, are maintained with extraordinary persistence in the Krou country, and the image of these little spirits is always more or less intermingled with that of the *ngame* mentioned above. On tackling the problem again here, we can wonder whether, really, we should recognize a distant memory of some kind attached to the first probably very primitive occupants of the land which was then occupied by the contemporary Krou, as was claimed by certain observers of the start of the century, relying only on the data of oral tradition. For the moment, no valid answer can be given to the question, although several finds have been made in the region, including the remnants of an old and very rudimentary civilization which has no connection with the present Krou civilization.

Whether they are related to the mainland or to the waters, including estuaries and the sea, all the creatures of this world have one thing in common, a changing, if not irascible or frankly violent temper, and their reactions are always unforeseeable. Consequently every meeting with such beings entails happy results or serious disappointments for the person concerned, depending on the circumstances.

This is where popular imagination goes haywire: the people of the Tabou region say that there are huge wild men, great jokers, who force isolated hunters, lost in the forest, to eat their own excrement and who then attack them or throw them into the water.

The red dwarfs also like practical jokes, but theirs are more innocent at least, and they are quite capable of being generous; they will, in particular, help hunters to track the game they are after, to find a track they have lost, to avoid snake-bites, attacks from elephants, buffalos, etc. They sometimes come into the villages to remind the inhabitants to leave the expected offering on a crossroad near the village; the offering usually consists of an egg, a cluster of dates, scraps from yesterday's meal, and a receptacle full of palm wine.

Apparitions of this class are all related to a specific place in the area; and they choose their homes preferably in a hollow or the top of a tree, in a termite ants' nest, in a cavern, or simply in the solitude of a dark forest.

The great forest in fact shelters many other unusual creatures whose descriptions generally give the teller's imagination a free run: hairy, claw-footed, horned, cyclopean, one-legged, tailed, bat-winged, etc. All these strange beings are constantly mingled with the village tales meant for the younger and elder public who always listen to them eagerly.

But in the Krou country, there is not only the forest, there are also stretches of water — the Cavally and the Tabou, the Hana river, in particular — and the sea, with its beaches, its coves, and its rocks, not forgetting the evil barrier reef, the obsession of the mariners. This environment also gives rise to its legends.

Occupying a privileged position in the aquatic folklore, the huge *mami wata* overlaps, with its renown, the strict extent of the Krou country; it is in fact more or less known by all the populations bordering the Gulf of Guinea.

The manatee, a large sirenian which visits the West African estuaries, is said to be the origin of this belief. What does this monster, with its many misadventures, really look like?

It is well known that the female manatee, provided with projecting mammae, suckles its only child. This may explain why the *mami wata* has taken on, in the mazes of popular imagination, the aspects of a young and beautiful woman. Gifted with a long body resembling the body of a huge snake, the creature has a human head with flowing hair, several arms and one or two pairs of legs. Wall paintings often show the *mami wata* provided with surprisingly modern attributes — for example, earrings, stockings, high-heeled shoes — no doubt to emphasize its femininity, by definition temperamental and even dangerous. In fact, the storytellers like to say that the *mami wata*, after dressing up as a pretty girl, generally enters the houses of bachelors by night and acts the part of a loving wife, preparing meals for its partner and only leaving him after dawn has broken, after giving him a pile of gifts and wealth. Unfortunately, its appearance can also lead to an incurable madness and sometimes to suicide.

The monster's habits are thus known accurately enough: all the Krou are quite convinced that the creature, without disliking the sea beaches, prefers fresh water and travels far up the current of the rivers, depending on the seasons. In the lower and middle sectors of the Cavally, and this is a fact, the fishermen from time to time mention the presence of the manatee.

From the liturgical point of view, however, the presence of the prodigy among the Ivory Coast Krou does not entail any consequences and apparently does not give rise to any regular cult. This may be due, of course, to its too exclusively fabulous nature.

Compared with the *mami wata*, all the other aquatic spirits of the Krou country apparently are only moderately important, unless one mentions family or tribal divinities of great importance, often purely conceptual, such as the *ble niepa*, which are associated with the liquid element, without in any way losing their basically earthly nature.

In fact, every village located near the water has its own sacred place, inhabited by one or another tutelar entity, in connection with the respect for certain animals or inanimate objects which, materially accessible, act as supports for a cult. Whirlpools, waterfalls, and waterbeds are favorite places, chosen by these little divinities; the latter are known by name but rarely defined as to their exact morphology and their modes of action.

They lend themselves all the more to the storyteller's imagination.

Religious Practices of a Mysore Village

N. K. KADETOTAD

The religious practices in Mysore villages are numerous. Here only the gods and goddesses that they worship are taken into account. It can also be seen how the villagers worship the deities in order to cure their diseases. Sometimes they make pilgrimages to their home gods and other holy places for many reasons. These religious practices of villagers give us a picture of their supernatural beliefs and practices. However, the rituals and magical practices are not taken into account fully.

The most popular deity in the village I want to talk about is Yallamma. The deities in order of popularity are: Yallamma, Kalmeshwar, Demavva, Hanuman, Basavanna, Veerabhadra, Mailarlinga, and Durgavva.

In all, twenty-six male deities and seventeen female deities were listed as worshiped by the villagers.

Yallamma is worshiped at home. If the idol is brought to the village or to the family by devotees of Yallamma, it is also worshiped by offering grains to the priests of Yallamma known as *Yallammana Hottavaru*. Sometimes the pilgrimage is made to the Yallamma temple near Savadatti, about twenty-five miles away from the village in the Belgaum district. Villagers go to that temple in groups, riding in carts or on foot to offer their worship.

The Kalmeshwar temple is popular in the village. It is the center of frequent community worship in the village. The deity is worshiped on all festival days and, by some people, every day.

Demavva is a deity in a village known as Grama Devata. All worship pertaining to the village takes place here. Traditional offerings and worship are made to the goddess Demavva by villagers irrespective of caste.

The temple of Hanuman is seen in this village as well as in other parts of the country. Hanuman is also worshiped by all castes of people in the village. The offerings are generally made on Saturdays, as this is supposed to be the day of Hanuman.

Basavanna is the bull god, worshiped by farmers and others dependent on agriculture. Basavanna is worshiped at home, outside the home in the village, and also in their fields. The bulls and cows are also worshiped as the bull god, and the cow as the mother of the bull god.

Veerabhadra is the home god of many people. Most of the Saivaits have this male deity as their home god. The people who have this deity as home god are supposed to be very clean in their daily habits. Otherwise the wrath of Veerabhadra gives them various troubles. The people who have got Veerabhadra as home god practice a special ritual connected with it known as *Guggala.*

Mailarlinga is the home god of many people. This male deity is also worshiped irrespective of caste. The deity is worshiped at home and pilgrimages are also made to Mailarlinga near Ranibennur. The people who worship Mailarlinga cry out *elu koti, elu koti* [Seven crores, seven crores]. Many tales are told about this deity as a heroic person connected with the great god Shiva of the Hindus.

Durgavva is a female deity situated among the untouchables of this village. Sometimes this deity is also worshiped by people of other Hindu castes along with untouchables. Demavva and Durgavva are supposed to be sister deities, of which the former belongs to the village as a whole and particularly to touchables and the latter to the untouchables.

Other male deities worshiped by the villagers are: (1) Jinna Devaru, (2) Padeshidda, (3) Allama Prabhu, (4) Timmayya, (5) Rudraswamy, (6) Bhimarai, (7) Shiva, (8) Dariya Devaru, (9) Ganapati, (10) Revanasiddha, (11) Trikuteshwar, (12) Alla Devaru, (13) Bira Devaru, (14) Yamanur Devaru, (15) Hirekumbi Devaru, and (16) Vithoba.

Though there is only one Muslim family in the village, the Muslim gods such as Yamanur and Alla are worshiped by six families. Mostly the untouchables and Walmikis are included in the worship of these deities.

Lingayats are mostly attracted by Saiva gods such as Veerabhadra, Shiva, Allama Prabhu, Revanasiddha and Trikuteshwar. They also worship the saints of the Veerashaiva monasteries and religion. They sometimes visit the religious functions and fairs of the Veerashaiva monasteries. Vithoba is worshiped by the Bovis, who are Vaisnavaits.

Bira Devaru is the male deity of the Kurubas, or shepherd caste. They especially worship this deity at home and outside the home.

On the basis of worship there are four broad categories: (1) Lingayat deities, (2) Hindu deities, (3) Muslim deities, and (4) Jaina deities. Jina is specially worshiped by Jains.

Other important female deities to be mentioned are: Kariyavva, Banashankari, Mayavva, Kallamma, Honnavva, Padmavati, Huligevva, Laxmi, Parvati, Tulasa Bhavani, Udachavva, Kunniyavva, and Bikatima.

Padmavati is worshiped by Jains, and Parvati and Banashankari are especially worshiped by Lingayats. Kallamma is worshiped by Panchals, Udachavva and Kunniyavva by untouchables, Bikatima by Muslims and Mayavva by Walmikis. Thus most of the deities can be broadly classified on the basis of caste. However, every caste gives secondary importance to all deities including those of Harijans and Muslims.

It was expressed by the villagers that since ten years ago the goddess Honnavva is worshiped on every Friday so that the cattle are protected from diseases in the village.

The female deities of nearby villages are also worshiped in order to get favor in their various undertakings.

THE WORSHIP OF NONANTHROPOMORPHIC DEITIES

Besides the worship of anthropomorphic deities, most villagers worship trees, plants, animals, stones and other objects. Among 175 respondents, it was found that 141 worship such objects, that is, 80 percent of the villagers worship trees, plants, animals, stones, etc.

Worship of Trees

Among the trees worshiped it was found that the goddess Kariyavva is supposed to be living in the trees on farms. So one of the trees on the farm is worshiped as goddess Kariyavva. Such trees are worshiped mostly by farmers.

The most sacred tree for villagers is the Banni tree. This tree is mentioned in villagers' mythology. It is said that the Pandavas at the time of their wandering in the forest hid their weapons in a Banni tree. That is why it is worshiped as the goddess Banni Mahankali. Leaves of the Banni tree are also exchanged between persons, with salutations, at the time of the Dasara festival.

Another important goddess tree is the Tulashi. This is a basil plant worshiped by most of the castes. The wife of the god Vishnu is supposed to be residing in this plant. The leaves of this tree are also used as medicine for many diseases. Many times at the time of worship of this deity the marriage of god Vishnu is observed with this plant, since the wife of Vishnu is supposed to be residing in it.

Other trees described as worshiped are Belva Patri, Ari, Ala and Mula Muttala. Belva Patri is sacred to Shiva. The leaves of Belva Patri are used to make offerings to god Shiva as Linga. These leaves are very important in the worship for Shaivas. The other trees are known for their economic significance.

Worship of Animals

Among animals worshiped only cows and bulls were mentioned by the villagers. As many as 67 percent of the villagers said that they worship cows and bulls. Cows are sacred to every Hindu. The bull god is the favorite god of Shaivas.

Many villagers who have cows and bulls in their houses worship them daily at home. The image of the bull god is also worshiped by them at home, outside the home in the village and sometimes on their farms. Usually the bull god is the image of a bull carved in fine stone.

Stone Worship

Small stones called Pandavas are worshiped in the fields. Five small stones are kept in the field in the names of the five Pandavas. At certain times, such as at sowing and harvest, the stones become the center of worship in the fields.

Another stone to be worshiped is called Dharama Deva. This is the deity of Brahma, the great god of the Hindus. This stone is found at almost every village street corner. The villagers often pour oil on this stone as a part of worship. The stones are therefore covered with oil-soaked earth.

Most of the low caste people in the villages worship a stone erected in the streets such as the Bharama Deva. It is called Kariyavva, a female deity. This deity is worshiped with cinabar and flowers.

Villagers frequently find ball-shaped stones in the fields while cultivating. These are kept at one side of the village and are worshiped.

Other strangely shaped stones are placed near Belva Patri and Banni trees and are also worshiped, mostly as female deities. These stones are kept on platforms beneath the trees.

If anyone finds stones having the shape of a bull god or Lingam, these stones become objects of worship.

Other Objects Worshiped

Implements of agriculture are also worshiped. The entrance of the house, pillars within the house and similar objects also become objects of worship.

It was stated by villagers that if an image of the god is not available, a stone can be taken as the image.

Belva Patri and Banni trees are especially worshiped when a person is suffering from a disease caused by being attacked by a spirit known as Gali.

Certain deities have much importance in particular festivals and particular days of the week. The cow and bull and the Belva tree are mostly worshiped on Mondays and in festivals connected with the god Shiva. Female deities are worshiped on full-moon days. Farm implements are worshiped before they are used. The Banni tree is worshiped in Manavami, a festival connected with the mythical story of Pandavas. Kariyavva is worshiped in the festival of Hatti, which is connected with cattle.

WITCHES

There is a strong belief in the village that witches can do both harm and good to the people by magical rituals that they know. Somehow not everyone believes in witchcraft.

Generally, black magic is described by the villagers as *mata*. This kind of witchcraft is done to buffalos to stop them from giving milk. It is also said that by doing harmful black magic to others they are benefited or they experience goodness on their part. It is also believed that due to black magic, buffalos begin to give blood or bad-smelling milk which nobody buys. Thus the income of a person is cut off.

Witchcraft is done to younger people so that they may not obey their elders. Many people in the village get headaches, leg pains, and other such ailments due to *mata* performed on them. Some people explained that by observing countermagic, the witchcraft can be remedied. Often villagers are killed when given herbs thought to be medicines, but actually this is taken as black magic by them. This is explained by them as *Gida Hakuvadu*.

It is believed that some people do black magic so that in-laws may quarrel among themselves. Thus, divisions within joint families are believed to be due to the witchcraft. The effect of black magic is so strong that some people even commit suicide and some become insane.

Commonly it is the women who believe more in magical rituals and in witchcraft. If an epidemic cattle disease starts in a village, then it is believed that the neighboring villagers have performed black magic on the animals. Many magical rituals in the village are observed by the community as a whole, therefore, to act as countermagic.

Generally, a *mantra* [spell], a *yantra* [magical figure], or a *tantra* [magical ritual] are the common elements of magic use by a witch.

One of our respondents told us that her elder sister loved her parents too much, but after marriage she did not even talk to them. This, it was believed, was due to some black magic done on her by someone in the family of her husband.

The prevalence of the evil eye is a very strong belief among the villagers. Even the buffalos stop giving milk if they are seen by the persons who have the sight of an evil eye. For such afflictions, magical spells are used to remove the bad effect of an evil eye. A buffalo which suffers from the evil eye is tied with an iron chain upon which a spell has been cast, or the buffalo may be given some cotton seeds to eat bearing such a spell. Witchcraft is also practiced on farmers' fields so that they may stop yielding good crops.

It is believed that people who engage in performing black magic will, sooner or later, be destroyed by themselves. So the black magic is always considered to be bad for the villagers, and only a few people are engaged in such activities. White magic is practiced to remove diseases and for the good of the family, their fields and their cattle by means of spells and rituals and by attaching talismans and magical figures on copper and tin plates. The people who do not believe in witchcraft say that if a cow does not give milk properly it is the fault of the owner who has not fed it well. If the crop does not yield well, the farmer lacks the proper knowledge of cultivation.

MAGICAL CARE FOR ILLNESS

In Kelgeri 90 percent of the families have visited a doctor in the nearby city of Dharwar at least once. In most cases of illness, however, village families rely on the local priest and on village medicine. The latter is mostly herbal medicine known by the people or prescribed by the priest. However, very few of them (about four or five families in the whole village) had never taken any kind of medicine. They relied on one of the gods for their ailment to be cured.

It is also observed that many of them consulted oracles before going to a dispensary. If the oracle says that there is any trouble given by a particular deity, they do not go to a doctor. If the oracle checks his books and learns that the person is being troubled by a particular deity, he prescribes the particular worship that is required. It is held by the villagers that many times a disease was not cured in the hospital, but when a priest was approached they were advised to offer the proper worship to a particular deity and they got their disease cured.

The goddess Yallamma is worshiped for many diseases. Promises, known as *Harake*, are made to particular deities specifying that if the desired objective is fulfilled, particular worship, payments or articles would be given to the deity. The magical cures are mostly spells, figures and rituals for various diseases known by the people or prescribed by the village shaman.

It is observed that villagers go to doctors only when the illness is serious. Of the respondents, 20 percent said that they had had the experience of hospitalizing members of their families. The other 80 percent had had no experience whatever with hospitalizing their family members.

There is a German charitable hospital very near to Kelgeri on the way to Dharwar, but villagers have not made full use of this hospital. Among the villagers who were hospitalized more than 50 percent were hospitalized in Dharwar at the civil hospital or municipal hospital, or in Karnatak Medical College hospital at Hubli, twelve miles away from Dharwar.

PILGRIMAGES

We mentioned in the beginning that the villagers worship their gods and goddesses in distant holy places by making pilgrimages. These pilgrimages of the villagers are very interesting, as they sometimes travel in groups, riding in carts pulled by specially decorated bullocks. The carts, also, are covered to protect the passengers against the sun and bad weather.

Pilgrimages may be made to the family deities in times of crisis. They may also be undertaken at the time of important life rituals such as a marriage or a child's haircutting ceremony. The most prevalent pilgrimage made among villagers of Kelgeri is the pilgrimage to Yallamma mountain near Savadatti, about twenty-five miles away from the village.

A second important pilgrimage by the villagers takes them to Ulavi in

Karwar District. It is the holy place of Lingayats where there is the tomb of Chanabasaveshwar, a Lingayat religious reformer and a saint. As 45 percent of the families in the village belong to the Lingayats and political, social, and economic dominance is held by them, this pilgrimage is of importance to all sections of the village. As buses to the holy place Ulavi are now available, many villagers take the opportunity of riding in comfort.

There is a saying in Kannada that in general "those who visit Ulavi should visit Gokarna," a nearby holy place of Shaivas. Generally half of the pilgrims who have visited Ulavi have also visited Gokarna.

Among the twenty-seven holy places mentioned by the villagers are: Phandarapur in Maharashtra, Shirahatti in the Dharwar district, Kudala Sangam in the Bijapur district, Hampi in the Bellari district, Shrishaila in Andhra Pradesh, Shravana Belgola in the Hasan district, and Mantralaya in the Raichur district.

The question was put to villagers as to whether or not they have visited any important cities in the country. Of course, most of them know only the nearby cities such as Hubli, Kharwar, Belgaum and Gadag. But a few of them have traveled widely. A total of forty-seven cities were mentioned by villagers as having been visited by them. Among the important cities they have visited and the number of persons who mentioned going to them were: Bangalore (10), Bombay (6), Panjim (2), Hyderabad (2), and Madras (2). Among district towns: Karwar (8), Hasan (1), Poona (5), Mysore (9), Kolhapur (2), Mangalore (1), Sangli (1), Bijapur 2), Anantpur (1), and Raichur (1). Some people visited such cities as Mahabaleshwar in Maharashtra (1), Jog (1), Bhadravati (1), Udipi (1), Hospet (1), and a few others.

From this it is clear that most of the villagers still lead an isolated life. But the contact with the outer world is kept through some persons in the village. It is chiefly the religious and social factors that are important for these ties of the villagers with the outside world.

REFERENCES

DUBE, S. C.
  1967   *India's changing villages*. Bombay: Allied Publishers.
HALPERN, J. M.
  1958   *A Serbian village*. New York: Columbia University.
HOGBIN, HERBERT IAN
  1950   *Transformation scene*. London: Routledge and Kegan Paul.

HUGHES, CHARLES CAMPBELL
   1960   *An Eskimo village in the modern world.* Ithaca, N.Y.: Cornell University.
ISHWARAN, K.
   1966   *Tradition and economy in village India.* Bombay: Allied Publishers.
LEWIS, OSCAR
   1951   *Life in a Mexican village.* Urbana: University of Illinois Press.
   1958   *Village life in northern India.* Urbana: University of Illinois Press.
REDFIELD, ROBERT
   1959   *A village that chose progress.* Chicago: The University of Chicago Press.
   1968   *A Mexican village.* Chicago: The University of Chicago Press.
SAYE, MURA
   1946   *A Japanese village.* London: Kegan Paul, Trench Trubner and Co.
YOUNG, J. E.
   1963   *Village life in modern Thailand.* Berkeley: University of California Press.
WILLIAMS, W. M.
   1956   *The sociology of an English village.* London: Routledge and Kegan Paul.

A Multiple Burial Custom of Korea: Ch'obun

DU-HYUN LEE

Ch'obun refers to a bone-washing burial custom or a multiple burial custom on the southwest coast of Korea. More specifically, the word Ch'obun itself means "a grass-roofed tomb," or "a temporary grave" in Korean. The custom had been widespread over the country until fifty years ago. Nowadays, however, it can be found only in the southwestern parts of Korea.

A review of the literature revealed that this custom had been practiced as early as the first century B.C. The chapter on the Okjo Tribe in Wei-Chih, a history of the Wei Dynasty (220–265 A.D.), dealt with the custom of the Okjo Tribe, an offshoot of the early Koguryŏ group. It said:

When a man died, his body was placed in a temporary grave and left there until the flesh had completely disappeared. Then the bones were dug up and buried in a wooden box which also contained the bones of other members of the family (Chen).

The chapter on Koguryŏ (37 B.C.–668 A.D.) in Sui-Shu, a history of the Sui Dynasty (581–618 A.D.), also mentioned the burial custom: "they placed the dead in a cabin in the house for three years, then inhumed the bones on a good day selected by a shaman" (Wei).

Archaeological data concerning dolmen, however, indicate that the origin of the Ch'obun could go back to the seventh century B.C. Dolmen seem to have been used as the places of the disposal of the bones, rather than the body itself, because the length of the stone chambers of most dolmen is less than one meter. This fact suggested that Koreans had a multiple burial system, i.e. Ch'obun, in ancient days (Kim and Youn 1967: 8–9). Urn-coffins also provided evidence that Koreans used a multiple burial system. A tomb of the early period of the Paekje Dynasty (18 B.C.–660 A.D.), discovered recently in central Korea, had an urn-coffin. The size of the coffin and that of the mound itself were too small to contain the whole body. This seemed to indicate that the urn was used only as a container of the bones of the dead (Kim 1972: 180). The stone epitaph of the tomb of King Munyŏng (501–522 A.D.) and his queen also provide supporting evidence for the existence of the burial custom in the sixth century of Paekje. The epitaph clearly indicated that the king died in 523 A.D. and the queen in 526 A.D. But it also said that the king was buried in the tomb in 525 A.D. and the queen in 529 A.D. (Kim and Lee 1972). The two years' gap between the year of death and the year of burial as well as the three years' gap for the queen could be interpreted as an indication of having *Ch'obun* for two and three years, respectively. This suggested that Koreans must have had a multiple burial system or a bone-washing burial custom in the early period of the Paekje Dynasty.

Ethnographical materials also suggested that the bone-washing burial custom had been widespread over the country. According to a survey of folk cultures in South Chŏlla Province conducted in 1968, *Ch'obun* is still practiced in 20 counties out of the total of 22 counties (Lee 1969a: 143). Fifty years ago, it was reported, 538 villages had *Ch'obun*; thirty years ago, there were 295 villages in which *Ch'obun* was practiced. Even nowadays, 126 villages still have the custom. North Chŏlla Province also showed almost the same statistics as those of South Province. A total of 1,693 villages practiced *Ch'obun* fifty years ago; 935 villages thirty years ago; 502 villages even nowadays. The survey clearly indicated that the burial custom was widespread all over the provinces until fifty years ago. Nowadays, however, the custom is retained mostly in the islands and coastal villages of the southwestern parts of Korea.

The burial custom is not uniform; it varies somewhat according to the modes of disposition of the dead. The data gathered from fieldwork by the present writer and his colleagues revealed that there have been several methods of *Ch'obun*, the temporary disposal of the dead until the removal of flesh before a final inhumation. These modes may be used as the criteria for a classification of *Ch'obun*.

a. Surface Burial: The corpse was wrapped with hemp cloth and then placed on the surface covered with rice straw.

b. Stone Platform Burial: A platform was made of stones. A bamboo or a straw mattress was spread and a coffin was placed on the platform. Then the coffin was roofed with grass.

c.   Scaffold Burial: The corpse was placed on a wooden bed, wrapped with rice straws. The bed itself was sometimes roofed with grass.

d.   Y-Shaped Scaffold Burial: Two Y-shaped logs were erected high in the air, and the coffin was placed across the two logs.

e.   Tree Burial: The corpse wrapped with straws was placed in a tree. It was sometimes stood upright against the trunk of a tree and tied up.

f.   Sand Burial: The corpse or coffin was buried in sand until the flesh was removed.

g.   Beneath the Floor Burial: There was a burial beneath the floor of the room where the deceased had lived.

The above are general methods of *Ch'obun*, a temporary disposal of the deceased until the removal of flesh before the final inhumation of washed bones. It was usually one, two, or three years between the temporary disposal and the final burial of the body. During this period, the mourners took good care of the *Ch'obun* and had ceremonies on the memorial day and the holidays such as New Year's Day and August Moon Festival Day. On the last day of every year, the grass on the roof of the *Ch'obun* was renewed.

Ch'obun was carried out only when old persons died, who were supposed to have lived out their life spans. If persons, even if they were old enough, were killed by accidents or died away from their homes, they did not deserve to have *Ch'obun*. They were buried directly without any process of *Ch'obun*. Children did not deserve to have *Ch'obun* either. In the areas where the bone-washing burial custom is practiced even nowadays, dead children are put in sacks or wrapped with rugs, and then put in urns. The urns are set upright in holes in the ground and buried under a heap of stones. The urn burial custom of children seems to be a remnant of the urn burial custom of adults in ancient days.

As mentioned above, the funeral ceremony for the final burial was delayed for one, two or three years until the flesh was removed from the bones. In the final ceremony, a favorable day was selected by a *Chikwan* [geomancer]. On the day chosen, a man known for his clean life took out the bones with bamboo or willow sticks under the supervision of the mourners. He took out the bones from the upper part of a body down to the leg, and cleaned them with a straw-brush or with white liquor or water of Chinese juniper. The washed bones were then placed on a white paper in order of skull, neck, arm, body, leg, and foot bones. The bones were then wrapped with white papers tied up with cloth and put in a coffin. The coffin was carried on a catafalque to a grave site. In some areas, instead of using a coffin, the bones were placed on a wooden board, named *Ch'ilsŏng-pan*, tied up with silk or cloth, and buried without a coffin. Interestingly enough, in Wido Island in Chŏlla Province, the bones were steamed and then washed. When the bones were steaming, a shaman conducted a religious ceremony with a cock or rooster whose feet were tied. If the cock crowed, the shaman stopped the ceremony and the bones were taken out of the steaming pot. The crow of the cock meant that the spirit of the deceased had returned to his bones. In the final funeral ceremony, services were conducted for the spirit of the mountain and for the spirit of the earth, too.

A survey revealed that there had been several somewhat different reasons for having *Ch'obun*. One of the most frequent answers people gave to the question as to why they had *Ch'obun* was that *Ch'obun* was an indication of their filial piety to their deceased parents. Most of the informants thought it was very inhuman to forget the deceased parents by burying them immediately after their deaths. They believed, therefore, the longer they had *Ch'obun*, the more dutiful they became to their deceased parents. It was quite understandable that the children of a deceased person did not want to be parted from their beloved fathers or mothers even after their death. In later days, Confucianism backed up having *Ch'obun* by teaching filial piety. In the Yi Dynasty, it became a sort of ethical duty that children had to have *Ch'obun* of their deceased parents if they could afford to.

The second reason for having *Ch'obun* was a little bit more religious. They said that it was forbidden to dig in the ground in January and February. If they dug in the ground for burial in January, they believed that the very act would make the spirits of mountain and earth angry. If they dug in the ground in February, the goddess of wind would be angry because a service is held for her in this month. And thus, the spirits would bring misfortunes such as other deaths in the village. When epidemic diseases prevailed, it was also strictly forbidden to dig in the ground. If people dug in the ground for burial of the dead, they believed that there would be more deaths from the disease in the village.

Another reason given was that *Ch'obun* or a temporary burial was necessary so that families of fishermen could postpone the actual burial until the fishermen came back home from their fishing trips in the open sea. In this way, the entire family could attend the funeral ceremony. Last, it was also said that they had *Ch'obun* to get time to find a good grave site for burial in the Yi Dynasty when *feng-shui* was extensively practiced.

No one seems to know, however, the actual reason for having

Ch'obun. Most of the informants said they merely followed the custom without knowing the exact reason. What would be then the actual reason for having *Ch'obun*? In old days, persons believed that a death meant a parting of the soul from the body. Immediately after death, therefore, there always came a religious ceremony begging the soul of the deceased to return to the body. In the ceremony, one of the friendly neighbors brought the garment of the dead outside of the house and cried aloud the full name and the address of the deceased. For the same reason, it is assumed that they had *Ch'obun*; instead of burying directly, they hoped that the soul of the deceased would come back to his body. Korean folklore is full of stories about how the dead returned to life from *Ch'obun.*

When the flesh of the dead was removed completely from the bones, they washed the bones and finally buried them. By burying the washed bones in a good place, they completed the funeral ceremony to repose the spirits of the dead. Reposing spirits was thought to be very important because they believed a wandering spirit, who did not repose at a certain place, would bother the living members of the family. By having *Ch'obun* and washing the bones, they provided good abodes for spirits to rest. The reposed spirits would protect their descendants and bring prosperity to them. The bones from *Ch'obun* are yellow or pink in color and remain unrotted for a long time. But the bones from a direct burial are black and not to be preserved to make a good abode for the spirits of the dead.

Closely related to the multiple burial custom, Koreans as well as Chinese and Formosans liked to rebury the deceased in a better grave site selected by a geomancer whenever they had misfortunes in their families such as diseases or accidents. In the areas where *Ch'obun* is practiced, one may still find a shamanistic ceremony named *ssikim-kut* [washing ceremony] to repose the spirits. There are two types of *ssikim-kut*, the wet-washing ceremony and the dry-washing ceremony. The wet-washing ceremony is conducted just after the dead person is put into a coffin while the dry-washing ceremony is performed usually three years after the death of the deceased. In the ceremony, a shaman washes the abode with clean water, water of Chinese juniper or mugwort water. This reposing washing ceremony is clearly related to the bone-washing burial custom.

In the southwestern coastal areas where *Ch'obun* has been practiced, another interesting burial custom is also practiced. The body is buried, but not in a family graveyard, when a person has passed away. Three years after the death, however, the bones are dug up, washed, and reburied in a family graveyard. This burial custom seems to be changed form of *Ch'obun*, and has a close connection to the two-tomb system of Japan.

Ling once attempted to compare the bone-washing burial customs in Southeast Asia and the circum-Pacific areas (Ling 1955: 25–44). He suggested that the custom originated in Lake Tung-Ting of the Middle Yangtze River in China. Unfortunately, however, Ling failed to mention the Korean burial custom, *Ch'obun*, and left Korea unmarked in his map of the distribution of the bone-washing burial custom.

The multiple burial custom in Korea, especially the bone-washing custom, is an element of the prehistoric cultural complex with megaliths, e.g. dolmen, and sacred poles. The origin and development of the custom in Korea could be clarified by a thorough investigation of archaelogical and ethnological data in Korea. Also, in order to clarify the problem, an ethnological study is suggested in which comparisons would be made of the bone-washing burial customs among the rice-cultivating peoples in the countries of Southeast Asia and the Far East.

REFERENCES

HAN, S. B., K. S. JUN
　　1969   The double burial custom and human mentality. *The Journal of the Korean Association of Cultural Anthropology* 2:74–86.
INOGUCHI, S.
　　1965   *Nihon no sōsiki* [Japanese funeral rites]. Tokyo: Hayakawa Shobō.
KIM, C. H., U. C. LEE
　　1972   "The tomb of King Munyŏng of Paekje Dynasty," in *Kangoku no kōkogaku* [Korean archeology]. Edited by C. H. Kim, 273–279. Tokyo: Kawade-Shobō Shinsha.
KIM, C. W., M. B. YOUN
　　1967   *Hanguk chisok-myo yonku* [Studies of dolmens in Korea]. Seoul: National Museum.
KIM, K. U.
　　1972   "The changing of old tombs," in *Kangoku no kōkogaku* [Korean archeology]. Edited by C. H. Kim, 168–203. Tokyo: Kawade-Shobō Shinsha.
KUBO, T.
　　n.d.   Kodai zenki ni okeru nijyū-sōsei ni tsuite [Multiple burial system in ancient Japan]. *Sikan* 75:13–28.
KUNO, A.
　　1969   *Sōso no rinri* [Ethics of funeral rites]. Tokyo: Kinokuniya.
LEE, K. K.
　　1969a   "The rites of passage," in *Hanguk minsok chonghab chosa pokoso* [A report of a general survey of Korean folk culture]. Edited by

The Ministry of Culture and Information, 117–144. Seoul: Ministry of Culture and Information.
1969b Remarks concerning the grass-tomb system on a southern island (Tschodo) in Korea. *Korean Classics Studies* 3:67–95.
LING, S. S.
1955 The bone-washing burial custom in Southeast Asia and its circum-Pacific distribution. *Bulletin of the Ethnological Society of China* 1:25–44.
MURAYAMA, C. J.
1931 *Chosen no hūsui* [Korean *feng-shui*]. Seoul: Chōsen Sōtokufu.
OBAYASHI, T.
1965 *Sōsei no kigen* [The origin of the funeral system]. Tokyo: Kadokawa Shoten.

Permanence of Traditional Rites in the Tunisian Marriage Ceremony Today: An Interpretational Approach

A. LOUIS

When attending marriage festivities in Tunisia[1] today, whether in the country or in towns, one is struck by the retention of ceremonies and rites which seem odd today, even superfluous; they are considered by the participants and guests to be "practices which must be submitted to" but about which it is difficult to obtain any clear explanation. The practice has been retained, often in a distorted manner, but its meaning has been lost.

In some places, for example, during the nights before the wedding night, one sees the presentation of girls to a public that already knows them, or, before the assembly of women, to a parade of men whom they meet nearly every day. In other places, even when the young wife has crossed the threshold of her future bridal room twenty or thirty times in order to arrange it with her betrothed, it is nonetheless usual to carry her over the threshold when she comes officially into this room on the wedding night, or at least to perform beneficent stepping-over rites.

There are also, for instance, almost no young wives, even among those who claim to be relatively free of tradition, who do not accept the ritual of putting henna on their hands and feet. And everywhere the married woman is brought to the new couple's home with a great deal of display. She may be taken for a ride in the village paths or through the streets of the town in a "bridal-cage," placed on a camel or a horse, or made comfortable in a luxurious car.

---

[1] The description of marriage and customs has tempted many travelers and geographers who came to Tunisia. A survey of their works is published in our *Bibliographie ethnologique de la Tunisie* (Louis 1969–1971: s.v. Mariage).

When the family, the neighbors, and the people of the quarter or the tribe have learned through the press or by a woman-messenger that a specific marriage is to take place, the young woman is obliged to a long and tiring presentation to the public, in a hieratic pose. In many places, the announcement of the happy consummation of the marriage, the man finding his wife with her "good share of girl" (quota of virginity), is still done, with more or less discretion.

These are only a few examples, but it is easy to see why, struck by the permanence of these rites, we have attempted, while observing them, to explain them with reference to the life patterns of the past and the economic system of self-subsistence in which traditional Tunisian society was immersed.

BEFORE MARRIAGE

Thanks to primary school coeducation and pastimes common to the "Youth Clubs," there are hardly any boys or girls today who have not met each other before thinking of founding a home and who have not talked to each other long before thinking of marriage. This was not the case in the past: choices were made without taking into account the preferences of the young; the girl, most of the time without being consulted, was given by her parents in marriage to the boy whom they had chosen; as for the boy, his parents chose a specific girl for him.[2]

Even if it is usual in making these choices for men to give their daughters to cousins, and in particular to their brother's son (i.e. a "parallel" cousin), or else to members of the part of the tribe to which they belong, it can happen that they look elsewhere among the young men of the adjacent villages or the other neighborhoods of the town. But then how can they let it be known that a specific girl is nubile? And, even if the immediate circle knows it, how could one tell a neighboring group, with whom the premium exchange (marriage) is foreseen, that a specific girl is able to be the object of this exchange? As to the boys, how could the women know them, so that a mother could choose the one who would suit her daughter? This is where the numerous rites of presentation of nubile girls to society and of introduction of boys to girls come in.

---

[2]   About arranged marriages, see Louis (1961–1963: II, 122–124, and the notes); for the south, Louis (1972: 104, n. 2); for Tunis, see also de Montety (1941: 32).

Public Proclamation that a Girl is Nubile

In an environment as closed as the Jerba Ibadite environment, we have seen "nubility processions":

When the girl reaches puberty, her kinswomen and neighbors who have a male child, and only these, get together on a date determined according to the moon's phases. They form a procession, each of them holding an olive branch, and head for one of the rare gum trees of the locality. This procession has to take place after sunset. Thus, to illuminate herself, the girl carries a lighted earthenware lamp (*majemra*) on her head. The lamp has a spout and seven cups and is only used for this purpose.

During this procession, the participants sing verses in the Berber language "which the men do not understand." Near the gum tree, a cock is slaughtered; in the lamp, the women burn some gum, glue-thistle, and other grains, together with sweet-smelling plants and hold libations to protect the girl from evil influences (Combès and Louis 1968: 280).

This is a rite that is precise and full of symbolism, but rarely found. In most cases the girl simply "parades" in front of the boys at the marriage festivities. For example, in Douiret, a Berber village in the far south of Tunisia:

The marriageable girls are brought by their mothers or by a relative. They present themselves entirely covered in a large cotton or colored silk veil, bordered with a golden fringe. This veil is arranged so that none of the girls can be seen, but so that they have a thin and narrow opening in front of the face, at eye level. They pull this veil to the side with their left arm and make sure that the part of the veil which is held above the head and in front of the body is arranged at eye level, up to the elbow of the arm holding the veil (Louis 1972: 107).

From time to time, the boys dance in front of them to the rhythm of the music while a paid praiser praises their generosity.

In another village, Tamezredt of the Matmata region, the nubile girls are arranged in three sides of a square on benches consisting of palm-tree trunks. Their heads are covered with two white sheets: one sheet, in front, shows only the bottom of the legs with the silver ankle rings and the moccasins; the other sheet is thrown over the head and falls behind the head, showing only the eyes. The boys parade in front of the girls, friends of the same district joining each other.

The difficulty is for the boys to recognize behind these long white sheets the chosen girl of their heart or the girl the parents have chosen. We will see later on the trick played by the girls. But here already, the girls can have a good look at the boys parading in front of them.

A more direct way of showing who one is is the hair dance. Kneeling behind a stone, the nubile girls remove their *bakhnoug* and loosen their hair. To the rhythm of the drum and the *gha'yta*, they throw their hair in frantic jerks from left to right, moving their head in every direction as if possessed by a devil ordering them to make these mad gestures. And the object is to see which girl can go on for the longest with these whirling hair movements, admired by the boys and their mothers who are there in front of them (Boris 1951: 138–141; Louis 1969–1971: "Danses").

Several of these rites have disappeared today. Some of them have retained their form, but with no object: it is the same girl, met the day before on the village paths or near the well, who parades and is "divined" by the boys. And the boy, as soon as he has seen the eyes of his future wife (or as soon as she has made sure he will see them), will not have to guess what beauty is hidden behind those veils. The boys and girls have known each other for a long time: they often meet on the village path or when staying in Tunis, or else in the classes at college. Nevertheless, the girls still show themselves veiled, as they did in the past. And, as a Douiri said to us, "if the girls did not parade, the marriage would not be complete."

Presentation of the Boys to the Girls

We used to see, in the past, real "courts of love." The boys would enter the marriage enclosure one by one, dressed like sultans; they would make their offering to the dancing musicians. A paid praiser would announce, as follows:

Utter *youyous*, ladies, in honor of such and such, son of so and so, so that God does not take him away from us nor remove his property. Why do you not ask from whom I have received this gift? Why do you not ask, o you with the languishing gaze? . . . I have it from the lord of lords, from the most generous among the generous, from such and such, son of so and so, slender one, dainty one, little silver stick, little gold stick, lover of the beauties who pass to and fro. He has said: I have made a gift only in honor of the marriage, of those who have come and who have been generous for it. . . . I have made this gift (without daring to name her) only for this Particular girl, a child of noble family and of great beauty. So bright is the brightness of her cheeks, blushing and radiant, that you could pick up a coin in its radiance . . . A trill, O ladies, in honor [of the marriage] and of my master (Boris 1951: 137–138).[3]

[3]   The announcement declaimed by the village crier is practically stereotyped. Only the verses which end it can vary. In fact, they are dictated to the praiser by the boy, whose spokesman he is.

Youyous are heard from all sides; the boys come forward to fire a salvo, and the boy concerned withdraws, glad that this ceremony has made him better known and has revealed his intentions in covert words.

Today, the "court of love" enjoys the same popularity as in the past, even if the young men already know the girls and are known by them; but the girls, happy at being together, chatter and they do not seem to listen much to the paid praiser. And he no longer utters such fine verses and only tries to get the best possible offering for himself and the musicians from the purse of the boy entering the enclosure.

We have also attended, in the Tataouine region, what is known as the *mah'fel* [bridal procession]. In twos, the boys — clothed in fine white "*houlis*," over which they have thrown a spotless *burnous*, and carrying guns — stand in front of the group of women. They pay their share to the dancing musicians, while the "paid praiser" praises them. The women stress this by uttering vibrating *youyous*. The power speaks. ... And already some mother has identified among the boys the one she would like her daughter to marry.

This same parade is held nowadays. The boys no longer stand in twos: instead, adult men and marriageable boys come into the marriage enclosure in a long line. They pay their share to the musicians and all they have to do is to be the most generous one, so as to be praised in front of the assembly and to have it shown to all that, bachelor or not, they are worthy to be called men (cf. Louis 1975).

In Tamezredt, the boys parade in front of the girls, who sit in the square formation we have described earlier, only showing the line of their eyes. Very richly dressed, they pretend to look (or do look) along the line of eyes they have in front of them, searching for the eyes of the girl they have chosen. They are allowed to leave the place they were in to get closer to her, and while the musicians play their instruments and the praiser makes the announcement, they stay standing there, facing the chosen one of their heart or the girl they think they have recognized as such. The girls do not move, but from time to time a belt falling outside the sheet hiding them, or an anklet flashing, or even the clinking of jewels, is enough to show the girl's acceptance (Louis and Sironval 1972: 99).

This court of love has, in fact, a very artificial nature, because many of the boys have been able to meet the girls directly, or at least their parents, and find out the feelings of the latter towards them. But this standing in front of the beloved and the thousand and one tricks the girl has to reply to it have as their special purpose, as a young man told us, "to compromise the parents in the eyes of the people of the quarter or the village," as everything is seen by the mothers who stand behind the nubile girls, and the fathers who are in front, among the marriage guests.

In these courts of love, the meaning of which is often lost, one element has remained very much alive: the feeling of prodigality, the search for prestige, even the attempt to show that one is better than the rest of the clan that is giving or receiving — to such an extent that the boys borrow money or make arrangements with the head of the dancing musicians so that of a ten dinar bill which has been given to them at least nine dinar are returned.[4]

Sometimes, however, only the rite remains: a chance to take part in the festivities and no more. The boys and men give because it is the accepted thing to give, but the amounts given are smaller and more in proportion with the status of the giver. The serenade lasts many hours, until the dancing musicians are satisfied with the gifts. No one leaves the place; everyone stays because "it is the tradition."

MARRIAGE

In the traditional marriage, various rites stretch out over several days and contribute to showing three aspects of this great moment of life: the PASSING of the bride from the state of a virgin girl to that of a married woman, the OFFICIAL PROCLAMATION of this passage, showing the group which family the girl has been welcomed into, and CON-FIRMATION that the passage from the virginal state to the married state has taken place and that honor is safe. Without mentioning all the marriage ceremonies here, we will describe one or two rites, each linked with one of the above aspects.

Passing from the Virgin State to the Married State

The girl has to leave her father's house where she was particularly protected and, since her puberty, entirely under guardianship if not

---

[4] This type of prodigality, for the musicians' gifts, is also fashionable for the "refundable gifts" made for a marriage or a circumcision. These are made in cash, with everyone's knowledge and, as everyone knows, they give the subscriber the right to obtain a gift of the same value or higher when one of his children marries or is circumcised (cf. Maunier 1927: 56; Louis 1973). It used to be a matter of honor and an important way of asserting oneself in terms of generosity. But today there are other means of "asserting oneself," so the prodigality can be purely fictitious.

cloistered. And it is not without fear that she leaves the warm atmosphere of her father's home. In marriage, the (young) girl is "born to a new world." Protection rites and beneficent rites have grown up to surround this passage.

Certain regions have the rite of the "farewell to the father's house" (as in the Kerkena Islands). When night falls, the girls surround the betrothed, each carrying an oil lamp. They stand up, put their hands on her shoulders and, to the sound of a tambourine and preceded by the mistress of ceremonies, walk with her around the courtyard of her father's house seven times singing:

Her father says: No, I did not give her to him, he did not pay me anything . . .
So many tears when I am seized by nostalgia for my daughter
(Louis 1961–1963: II, 149–151).

Another example is:

Ah, my house, my dear house . . .
Where are your walls, so high?
Where are you, welcoming home?
Why did I not take your keys in my hands? (de Montety 1941: 49).

In other regions there is the "farewell to the fatherly olive tree," the ritual of which is meant to keep the new bride from losing her share of the "blessing" which she enjoyed until then by her presence in her father's home.

Before sunrise, the women of her family take her to an olive tree close to the house. The marriage dresser-woman carries a special lamp and the girl's sister carries a scent-burner. During the procession, the female group hides under a long red veil woven with a silk woof and silver thread. When she gets close to the olive tree, she walks around it seven times.

After executing this rite, the girl faces Mecca. Then, with an olive branch she has just picked, she strikes three young men who are brought to her (and who, thanks to this, will get married within the year).

Her sister has brought along an egg and a red string: her legs are tied together and then the bond between the two legs is cut; she also has to break the egg with a movement of her heel (Combès and Louis 1968: 279, 281).

Without losing ourselves in the symbolism of this rite, which is quite clear enough, we would like to note to what extent it is related to gestures meant to ensure the facility of marriage relations and fertility.

Several fertility rites, meant to facilitate the girl's passage to her new state, take place when she reaches the husband's house.

The first thing is the breaking of an egg on the top lintel of the

bridal chamber before entering it, the egg being the perfect symbol of
fertility (cf. Boris 1951: 148; Louis 1961–1963: II, 158; Louis and
Sironval 1972: 103; Louis 1972: 114, Note 4).

This also includes the rite of stepping over the threshold. Here the
girl takes off her left slipper and dips her foot in water, so as to
remove anything which might stick to her that is bad, which would be
liable to render her infertile. Then she does a series of seven little jumps
over beneficent and fertilizing objects: fish, for example (Narbeshueber
1907: 14).

Stepping over the threshold is a rite symbolizing the ease of the
marriage relations which are to come and is also full of dangers for
the fertility of the woman: evil spirits can attack her sex when she
steps over the threshold; hence the fertilizing rites we have described
(Graf de la Salle 1946; Marçais and Guiga 1925: 370).

There is also, among nomads, a rite in which the young woman
entering her husband's tent has to plant a peg where the sleeping mat
is to be spread: this symbolizes both the attachment to this tent which
is henceforth hers and the extent to which it is hoped that this woman,
now the wife, will be productive (see Duhamel 1924: 166).

Less realistic in terms of symbolism, one also meets here and there
a rite of preperforation. A jug is brought to the house of the bridegroom, its neck covered with taut white paper. When the girl arrives,
a relative holds the jug over her head. In order to ensure that she
has easy pregnancies, her father-in-law, by a gesture of sympathetic
magic, puts his finger through the sheet of paper covering the jug and
pours oil into it (Combès and Louis 1968: 283).

Official Proclamation

It is officially proclaimed that the girl is to be the wife of a particular
boy by taking her around the village or the quarter, when she goes to
her husband's home, and thereby stating in a legitimate way into which
family she is to be welcomed.

There is a simulated kidnaping, as if the tribe (in fact, the family
to which the girl is given) were seizing the girl.

It is, actually, in a kind of bridal-cage chair, the *jah'fa* (already
described in the sixteenth century by Léon l'Africain), sent by the
husband's house, that the girl will be brought to the couple's home.[5]

[5] Boris 1951: 129. See also Louis 1961–1963: II, 153–154. Today the palanquin
is usually replaced by a luxurious car. This does not exclude, however, in the

A procession is formed with musicians and dancers; the procession stops near the mausoleums of the village saints. Even if the girl lives in a house next to her husband's the procession goes all the way through the village to return to the starting point, because the news must be known by all the villagers.

Attempting to reenact what used to happen formerly, armed groups pretend to stop the procession and seize the girl and take her back home.[6] They talk and allow her to go on if she consents to show her foot. And the aggressors, as a penalty, pay their share to the dancing musicians. The powder speaks and all set off again happily.

She was then made to enter a palanquin which was decorated according to custom by means of a red shawl and red carpets, surrounded by a white *haik*. Then bags were brought containing the trousseau and the provisions of the bride and they were loaded onto the camel, which was made to rise. A little boy called Ali was also placed next to the bride. The Negro, with the rein in his hands, advanced a little and then stopped. The little girls, vying with each other in speed, ran to catch up with him; they caught hold of the fringes of the carpet on each side of the mount and, on its traces, opened the concert of their twittering:

"Made of sumac wood, o supple palanquin,
A strong camel carries you on his shoulders,
Your master, with his great renown, is clothed with fine cloth"

(or this other verse)

"They have lifted her to the palanquin,
Girl precious as a jewel . . .
You seem beautiful in your sheet!" (Louis 1961–1963: II, 155).

The riders came up in a gallop of fantasy! The palanquin was pushed forward and the crowd went on behind it noisily. It was still near the bride's home when the young people tried to "confiscate" it: they formed two clans and gunshots broke out on either side: they rivalled each other in ardor, because the party that fired the most shots would win. This was followed by close fighting between them and a rush to seize the bride. The older people intervened to bring about peace. They came between the fighters and the palanquin was then released. But its passage in front of

---

country, the presence of a camel with the palanquin in the bridal procession to the couple's home. If the palanquin is also used, either the married woman's sister or a "maid of honor" rides there.

The long circuit around the village or the town quarter makes the passage from the father's house to the couple's home official and the honking of the horn at the same time expresses the happiness and advertises that a marriage is taking place.
[6] In the past the cousin's rights (the son of the bride's father's brother) towards his cousin were such that he could stop the procession which brought her to another's home and make her get down from the palanquin (cf. Marçais and Guiga 1958–1961: 568).

the mosque was the occasion for another "confiscation." From there it headed for the south of the cemetery and went toward the Little Spring, where it halted. The bride had to show her hand on three occasions ... (Boris 1951: 147).

It is a very important thing for one's honor thus to announce throughout the village that so-and-so is passing from one family to another, that she is leaving the state of a young girl to become a bride. Thus, many stops are made on such a journey. They stop at such and such a little square, in front of the house of a noteworthy personality, at the tomb of a saint. As this marriage is carried out "with the best and most honorable intentions," should not this gift of the daughter to another family be sanctioned by the blessing of the protective saints (*baraka*) of the tribe or of the quarter?

Confirmation of the Change of State

It is observed that the passage from the state of a girl to the state of a wife has taken place properly and that to all intents and purposes, honor is safe.

There is first of all the official confirmation of defloration. This is a very intimate ceremony where the mother of the bridegroom and her close relatives come to make sure of the fact that the marriage has been consummated with a virgin girl. The rites vary but the object is to make sure there is hymenal blood on the new bride's linen.

These rites, which are as important for the honor of the families as for the honor of the tribe, are related to traditions hundreds, if not thousands, of years old. Thus, among the Hebrews (Deut. 22: 15–21), we see the importance of the signs of virginity and the unfolding of the linenware carrying these signs (verse 17) in front of the Ancients, to prove the innocence of a young bride falsely accused of not being a virgin when the marriage took place.[7]

In certain regions of the extreme Maghreb, the "ceremony of the *serouel*" had great importance. Placed on a tray and covered with a green silk fabric, the *serouel* was carried to the women's patio, where they greeted it with many *youyous*. Every person placed a silver coin on top of it, saying:

---

[7] This care for the woman's physical integrity at the moment of marriage is a prevailing rule of a traditional society and is a mark of "agnatism." See the relevant reflections of Bassagna and Sayad (1974: 119–120), with quotes from "*Le monde des femmes et son entrée dans la cité*," pages 8–9.

Ah, Lella, she is the daughter of a noble woman,
The daughter of the men who watched over her.
Her beauty had a belt,
Her *serouel* came out spotted with red! (de Lens 1917–1918: 48–49).

The fact is so important that sometimes a bride who has not been found untouched by her husband is sent back at once and sometimes in a shameful way (infamous masquerade). This does not date back only to yesterday; already in the sixteenth century, Léon l'Africain noted this fact in his *Description de l'Afrique*.

We will point out here that

... certain women of the family, doubting the integrity of the young woman they are giving away in marriage, after an accident or an illness, used to take a spot of the blood from the sacrifice of a young kid which was made on the entry of the girl into the husband's home. They filled a small bottle with the blood which they discretely gave to the girl. The latter could thus, if need be, use this blood to spot her linen, and thus avoid the punishments she was likely to incur if she were not found to be untouched by her husband (Louis 1972: 115, Note 6).

Once the deflowering has been made official, on the day after the consummation of the marriage, there is a parade meant to publicize the new state of the young bride. The dresser-woman uncovers her face three times, lifting and lowering the scarf: the girl is thus presented face to face with the women, with the palms of her hands at shoulder-height, and turned towards the public. During this official presentation of the young bride as a woman, people come to congratulate her and offer her gifts, happy to show their satisfaction or to see her enter "suitably" into her new state.[8]

As a way of making the marriage official, the entry of a girl in a specific home and her new condition as a bride, the bridal chair, the *jah'fa*, in which she was deflowered, is lifted onto the roof (or one of the walls) of the house. In Douiret, it stays there throughout the festivities. In the Kerkena Islands, it is placed on the terrace and it stays there until the first child is born. The uprights of the chair are then used to light a fire meant for the preparation of the herbal tea which is given to the mother-to-be; and it is the girl's mother who is responsible

---

[8] Cf., for Tunis, de Montety (1941: 50); for the country, Louis (1961–1963: II, 159–160; 1972: 115). De Montety noted, thirty years ago, that already in the town this presentation often had lost its ritual character, but nevertheless the practice was maintained.

for this office (Louis 1961–1963: II, 168). Thus, among the numerous rites which mark the three (or seven) days taken up by the marriage festivities, there are many which stress the new state into which the girl passes and which serve to signify officially that so and so has become a bride and under the best possible conditions. But also, on the girl's side as well as on the husband's, this important period is related to numerous fertility rites which must be mentioned here as several of them are found even in the marriages which claim to be the most modern.

RITES FOR THE PROTECTION OF THE COUPLE

Of the two partners, the woman is said to be the more delicate because of her physical constitution and is also the most likely to be attacked by evil spirits. She will necessarily, then, be the subject of more precautions than her future husband, although the husband, at such an important time as marriage, also runs a lot of risks.

The Protection of the Wife

RITES OF PURE PROTECTION   We will mention, among others, the ferrule (*tesfîh'a*) which is used to "close" the girl's female sex organ, as she could run risks in her integrity and thus would be protected from any attempt made by a man against her. In one place, we see the symbolical fixing of a padlock to a little string that the girl has passed round her waist. Elsewhere, the girl is made to pass through the slack chain of a weaving loom, from the outside towards the inside (next to the wall, where the weaver girls sit), and to let the chain close on her (Marçais and Guiga 1925: 395; see also Louis 1972: 113, n. 33).

This ferrule then has to be opened just before the girl is transferred to the couple's new home.

BENEFICENT RITES   These include:
a.   Laying on of henna. A paste made with leaves of henna (*lausonia inermis*) is put on the girl's hands and feet. The henna is thought to bring blessings (*baraka*) and to be an element of purification.
b.   Breaking of an egg on the top lintel of the home.
c.   Dipping of the right foot in a tub of water while passing the threshold, for "in water is a guarantee of security (*fel-mâ amân*)."

RITES OF SYMPATHETIC MAGIC   Here are a few:

a.   Hanging of belts in her house, before the girl is brought to the couple's home. This is a way of saying that she is no longer wearing anything which might hinder her in the function of a wife which she will soon be called upon to fulfill and, generally speaking, that she is breaking with a past which forbade her the act of love.[9]

b.   Repeated jumps over beneficent objects. These jumps are connected with a stepping-over rite which has a clear symbolism (to facilitate fertility of the woman), as the evil spirits of the threshold could attack her sex; thus, the stepping-over is done over beneficent objects. In Sfax, for example, the seven jumps are made over a dish of fish.

c.   Preperforation rite. A vase with a taut sheet of paper over the neck is held over the head of the girl. The husband's father perforates it with his extended finger and pours oil into the vase (see above).

d.   Loosening of the hair. At the time of the consummation of the marriage, the hair must be free, because no KNOTTED element may be allowed to hinder the accomplishment of the act of love (Dornier and Louis 1954–1955: 119–121).

e.   Opening of the "ferrule." The girl passes through the slack chain of the loom, once again, but this time going outwards.

The Protection of the Husband

RITES OF PURE PROTECTION   These are protections against the eye of the envious man who could affect the husband's potency.

Three or four persons are able to make the husband impotent by their evil doings (writing of a sacred text and gesture of ligature while saying the name of the person): they are therefore conciliated at the time of the marriage (Louis 1961–1963: II, 163, n. 96; 1972: 113, n. 23).

BENEFICENT RITES   Rites of a purely beneficent character include the laying on of henna, while the husband's sister holds a candle above the husband's head, and the dipping of the right foot in a tub of water, containing a silver ornament: the water and the silver foretell the peace and abundance which will reign in the new home. (Note that the ornament is meant for the wife.)

---

[9]   See Louis 1972: 111. Westermarck (1921) specifies that the young wife must not wear a belt during the henna ceremony (129–131), during the couple's act (208–213), or during the week after the marriage (229–231, 290).

RITES OF SYMPATHETIC MAGIC   Some of these rites are:

a.   The extended index finger is dipped either in a mixture of flour and very sour oil (preparatory preperforation rite), or, in other places, in a dish of *açida* which is offered by the husband's mother (for the sweetness of the relations).

b.   In the Berberophone environment, we have come across the curious ceremony of the *hanna achbuk*. Powdered henna is given to the husband, together with an egg. He eats half of the egg and crushes the remainder, which he then mixes with the henna in the hairnet of his future wife. The man adds a sum of money to the paste held in the hairnet, and it is sent to the young woman. The girl uses some of this paste to cover her right foot, and some to make a line on her head (or even on her vulva?).

This transfer from the fiancé to his future wife has the value of a contract. The hairnet exchanged between the two future spouses, thanks to its squared mesh, acts as a shield for the eyes of the envious.

The henna and the egg which form the paste mean fertility; the henna adds the idea of blessing. The fact of crushing the egg is said to prefigure the rupture of the hymen. The paste, mixed by the young man and accepted by the girl, seals their union and protects them against possible separation. The egg fluid which penetrates into the henna is said to be the seminal fluid, and the whole mixture is held in the hairnet which is said to represent the woman's genital system.

As for the money which the husband offers his future wife, it is considered to be *premium virginitatis* [the price of virginity] (Louis 1972: 108–109).

CONCLUSION

There are numerous examples of rites to which people are loyal even though their meaning has faded or is no longer perceived. We limited our subject here to the more important moments of marriage and therefore concentrated on rites of passage. Yet we should have distinguished between city-dweller society, village society, and country society (nomadic society) in a more accurate way, and even between the different social strata within these societies. Within the society of the city, for example, it is clear that the same rites (the presentation of the married woman to the public or the passage of the girl from her father's home to the couple's house) are not perceived in the same way by the city dwellers who have been long exposed to the patterns of the Occident and by the migrants from the inner country who are still in the process of acculturation to the realities of the city.

Our aim here has only been to collect representative facts; to attempt an interpretation; and to furnish specialists of the field with material which will permit them, when examining the effects of rapid social change on the rites related to marriage, to distinguish what endures from what is transitory, i.e. to discriminate between what must be maintained in the name of tradition and what can be changed or even lost as a society becomes open to new values.

REFERENCES

BASSAGNA, R., ALI SAYAD
1974 *Habitat traditionnel et structures familiales en Kabylie.* Mémoires du Centre de Recherches Anthropologiques, Préhistoriques et Ethnographiques 23. Alger: S.N.E.D.

BORIS, G.
1951 *Documents linguistiques et ethnographiques sur une région du Sud tunisien (Nefzaoua).* Paris: Imprimerie Nationale.

COMBÈS, J. L., A. LOUIS
1968 *Les potiers de Jerba.* Publications du Centre des Arts et Traditions Populaires, Tunis, 1.

DE LENS, A. R.
1917–1918 Un mariage à Meknès dans la petite bourgeoisie. *Revue du Monde Musulman* 35:31–55. Paris.

DE MONTETY, H.
1941 *Le mariage musulman en Tunisie* (with illustrations by Roubitzoff, Aly Ben Salem, and R. de Souza). Tunis: Ed. SAPI.

DORNIER, P., A. LOUIS
1954–1955 Le mariage dans le bled (Région de Thibar). *IBLA* 17:251–268; 18:93–126.

DUHAMEL, G.
1924 *Le Prince Jaffar.* Paris: Mercure de France.

GRAF DE LA SALLE, MADELEINE
1946 Contribution à l'étude du folklore tunisien. Croyances et coutumes relatives à la maison chez les Musulmans de Tunis. *Revue Africaine* 90:99–111.

LOUIS, A.
1961–1963 *Les Iles Kerkena (Tunisie),* volume one: *Les "Travaux";* volume two: *Les "Jours";* volume three: *Index.* Etudes d'ethnographie tunisienne et de géographie humaine, Tunis.
1969–1971 Orientation bibliographique: ethnographie tunisienne. *Cahiers des Arts et Traditions Populaires* 3:135–172 (A-J); 4:131–192 (K-Z). Tunis.
1972 Le mariage traditionnel en milieu berbère dans le Sud de la Tunisie. *Revue de l'Occident Musulman et de la Méditerranée,* 2° sem.: 93–122. Aix-en-Provence. (Section on A Douiret, 24 km. southwest of Tataouine, pages 105–122.)

1973   Les prestations réciproques en milieu berbère du Sud tunisien. *Anthropos* 68: 456–472.

1975   *La Tunisie du Sud: Ksars et villages de crêtes.* Paris: Editions du C.N.R.S.

LOUIS, A., MARIE MARTHE SIRONVAL

1972   Le mariage traditionnel en milieu berbère dans le Sud de la Tunisie. *Revue de l'Occident Musulman et de la Méditerranée,* 2° sem.: 93–122. Aix-en-Provence. (Section on A Tamezredt, 14 km. southwest of Matmata, pages 96–104.

MARÇAIS, W., A. GUIGA

1925   *Textes arabes de Takrouna,* volume one: *Textes.* Paris: Leroux.

1958–1961   *Textes arabes de Takrouna,* volume two: *Glossaire.* Paris: Imprimerie Nationale.

MAUNIER, R.

1927   (1924–1925) Recherches sur les échanges rituels en Afrique du Nord. *L'Année Sociologique* 2:12–97. Paris.

NARBESHUEBER, K.

1907   *Aus dem Leben der arabischen Bevölkerung im Sfax* (Regentschaft Tunis). Leipzig.

SECRÉTARIAT SOCIAL D'ALGER

1967   *Le monde des femmes et son entrée dans la cité.* Secrétariat social d'Alger, series 5, numbers 8, 9, and 10.

WESTERMARCK, E.

1921   *Les cérémonies du mariage au Maroc.* Translated by Jeanne Arin. Public. de l'Ecole Sup. de Langue arabe et de dialecte berbère de Rabat 7. Paris: Leroux.

Aquatic Rites in the Danube Straits at the Iron Gates

IOANA IONESCU-MILCU

The Danube Straits at the Iron Gates, one of the most picturesque areas through which this great river flows, have been inhabited, as recent archaeological investigations have shown (see Nicolăescu-Plopşor, et al. 1968), since prehistoric times. Being in an area that belonged to the nucleus of King Decebal's Dacian state, they were the point of passage of the Roman armies on their way to the capital of Dacia and, after the conquest, the area was part of Roman Dacia until the final retreat south of the Danube of Emperor Aurelius' legions and administration.

Traces are frequently found in this area of the occupation, during the subsequent centuries, of proto-Romanians and Romanians unaltered by either the temporary passing or by the settling down during various historical periods of populations having different ethnic origins.

These brief comments about the past explain the present ethnic configuration of this area, namely the existence, in addition to the Romanian majority, of a number of villages of other populations: Serbian (Sviniţa, Liubcova), Turkish (the Ada-Kaleh island, submerged by the waters of the hydroelectric power station), and Czech (Bigăr, Gîrnic, Ravensca, etc., colonized by Czechs during the period when this region belonged to the Austrian Empire). South of the Danube, in the Iron Gates area of the Negotin region in Yugoslavia, the population includes Serbians and others of Romanian origin called, locally, Vlachs (Draškić 1968–1969: 11–64).

Although the coexistence of these populations is of long standing (in the case of Romanians and Serbians about a thousand years) and although the relationship between them has always been a very good one, they lived, until recently, as relatively closed ethnocultural units, each having kept its language and customs. This is consistent with the fact that the

Iron Gates area is nowadays one of the few enclaves of traditional folk culture with archaic features found in both Romania and Yugoslavia.[1] Thus, the Romanian and Yugoslavian ethnologists who have carried out intensive investigation in this area for the last eight years could obtain data both for the cultural history of their own people and of a comparative nature, important for the whole of southeast Europe. (This work was done with a sense of urgency, because construction of the hydroelectric power station at the Iron Gates meant displacement of the population and the disappearance of some places.)

Obviously, different aspects of this more archaic folk life are represented with varying degrees of completeness and are more apparent in beliefs and customs than in material culture, differing according to the distance from the nearest urban center. This difference appears also between the Serbian population in the villages in Romania and the Serbians in Yugoslavia, while the Vlachs in Yugoslavia have more archaic linguistic and cultural features than the Romanians in general.

The marked tendency of each population to keep its traditional cultural elements is not inconsistent with the existence of natural cultural contacts in the course of such a long coexistence. It is precisely this joining of the marked tendencies towards keeping one's own traditional values with the still extant contacts between populations of different ethnic origin inhabiting the Danube Straits which makes up the fundamental characteristic of this area and which must be taken into account in any ethnological investigation carried out here.

Within the system of beliefs and customs studied, the author picked out, as being characteristic, those connected with water. For the inhabitants of this area, the Danube was the river with which their whole life as well as all their material fortune was connected. It was the driving force of the part of the Straits called *Cazane* [the Kettles] where their boats sank and where people were sucked in by the whirlpools, where the onrush of waters in the periods of floods carried away dwellings, cattle and people. Since earliest times the Danube has worn, like all the elements of nature, the garments of the sacred in the meaning pointed out by Mircea Eliade: "In manifesting the sacred, any object becomes SOMETHING ELSE, without ceasing to be ITSELF, because it continues to be part of the cosmic milieu surrounding it" (Eliade 1965: 16). Generally, "…waters symbolize the whole of that which can be effected; they are, at base and in origin,

---

[1]   In the French abstract of his study published in Serbian, Professor Slobodan Zečević clearly says: "Les régions de la Serbie de nord-est sont certainement celles où la mythologie est le plus richement développée" [The regions of northeast Serbia are certainly those where mythology is most richly developed] (Zečević 1968–1969:361).

the matrix of all the possibilities of existence" (Eliade 1953: 168). Thus, more and more aquatic symbolism gained multiple meanings and survived more strongly in the sea and river areas, where the "profane," the concrete, had continuously been supporting the persistence of old myths and rites.[2]

The Iron Gates area is not an exception to this rule. Moreover, the historical and ethnocultural considerations mentioned above led to the maintenance — in spite of intense modernization during the last decades — of many of the sacred and ritual aspects connected with the Danube.

The dangerous portion of the cataracts has enhanced the apparently contradictory and antagonistic significance that is often assumed by the sacred. Indeed, in this area too water has simultaneously beneficent (purifying, regenerating, fertilizing, healing) as well as maleficent meanings, for demons[3] dwell in it that lure people into the depths (Milcu and Simionescu 1969). This dual significance of the water symbolism is conspicuous in rites, for in addition to the ritual bathings at birth, marriage, and death, and its use in almost all spells and in the preparation of the majority of empirical remedies, water is also often used in magic and charms with maleficent aims, precisely through invoking the forces of evil that dwell in the depths. However, the general tone of the aquatic symbolism in this area is the beneficent one that grants healing, fortune, and fecundity to people and cattle. Thus, among the Romanians and Serbians of almost the entire area the custom exists of milking the sheep on the morning of St. George's Day (April 23) through a large, pierced, fancy bread put on the milking bucket. There is a garland of flowers over it that is subsequently put into the Danube, in the belief that "milk should flow the same as water" (Ionescu-Milcu 1972).

Another custom of the Romanians of the village of Pojejena is of particular interest: at daybreak on Epiphany the householder brings some "holy water" from the river in a bowl. On coming home he stops on the threshold. Members of the household ask him from within: "What good hast thou brought us?" He answers: "Health and prosperity." The water is kept all the year long and is drunk in case of illness. The para-religious character of this ritual is quite obvious, for, as far as we are

---

[2] From the rather sporadic information given by the ancient authors (Herodotus, Strabo, etc.) in connection with Dacian myths and rites, we can infer the deification of the Danube. Note, for example, the "eucharist" with water from the Danube before going to battle and other rites.
[3] This belief is found among the Romanian and Serbian population, among the latter with additional mythological details (Zečević 1968–1969:330–33).

informed, in the rest of the country there exists only the custom of taking home water hallowed in church on Epiphany.

Within the framework of the customs connected with the life cycle, we find the ritual bathing of the newborn immediately after birth, of the bridal couple on the morning of the wedding, or of the deceased; the obligatory glass of "holy water" on the "table of the fate fairies" (who are expected to come on the third night after a birth); water given during a forty-day mourning period after death, as well as many other customs. These give us a picture of an area abounding in multiple meanings of rites connected with water. In connection with the virtues of water related to fecundity, we shall mention here the wedding ritual of the Turkish population of the Ada-Kaleh island. While the bridegroom and the men are attending the divine service in one of the rooms, in another room the bride sits with her feet in a basin of water from the Danube listening to Quran verses read by an old woman. Our informants were aware of the meaning of this rite, stressing that thus the young bride "will have numerous and healthy children."

Particularly significant is the custom called "setting free water for a dead person," which is widespread in different areas of Romania, and is part of our fund of very old funeral rites. Here, on the Danube, it is not only frequently practiced but also enriched by an almost pompous ceremonial as well as by the magnificence of the surrounding site. The ceremony takes place on the fortieth day after death. In the morning, people go to a river or to the Danube itself and there must be included among the participants a girl of eight to thirteen years who, on each of the previous forty mornings, has brought a bucket of water as a gift for the soul of the dead. Nine hollowed-out pumpkin halves in the shape of boats are arrayed on the bank. Each of these contains a fancy cake of a special symbolic form called Sun, Moon, Archangels, God, Holy Virgin, customs-house officer, etc., as well as a lighted candle. The little girl takes water three times from the river with the bucket and throws it back over her shoulder, repeating each time the formula: "I set free the water for [name of deceased]." The gifts are then put into the water one after the other for their destinations: "for the Sun," "for the Moon," "for the Archangels," the next to the last "for the customs-house officer," and the ninth "for the dead [name]." These small "boats" with their lighted candles drift downstream. If one of them gets to the bank, he who finds it takes the cake and carries the candle to the church. On the one hand, this ritual is connected with the ancient belief in the river that separates us from the underworld (this significance is also enhanced by the cake called "the customs-house officer," which is given to the mythical boatman who carried the souls over the Styx in his boat). On the other hand it marks the end of the forty-day period when the dead person's thirst must be quenched by means of gifts from the living, as the deceased person's soul is still present around the place where he lived.

We shall limit ourselves to one more ritual represented in some villages along the Romanian shore of the Danube (Ieşelniţa, Berzeasca, Sicheviţa) as well as among the Vlachs along the Yugoslav shore (the villages of Sîrbovlaş, Tekija, and Dealu Gol). I found this custom only among the Romanians of the area and, sporadically, during other investigations, I traced it also in several localities in Romania (e.g. in the village of Piscani, district Arges, or Lupşa in the western Carpathians). If the first child or the first children die (in popular language "they have no luck with their children") then, at the occasion of a new birth, after the christening in the church, the child is carried to the river and christened a second time by the midwife or, in her absence, by any "forgiven" woman (an old woman who for a long time has had no husband). The child is thrice immersed into the water of the river (the Danube), the old woman repeating each time the formula: "Henceforth your name will no longer be Ion. Your name will be Niculae. Amen." Thus the name given by the godfather in the church is changed to a new one. Subsequently, during his entire life nobody from the family or from the village will call the "rechristened" child by anything but his new name, though, evidently, the original name remains in his papers. The ritual has, of course, more complex motivations, being connected with the belief in the magic power of the word, in the magic religious relationship between the object and the name it bears. Nevertheless, the purifying and regenerating function of water remains predominant in the essence of this rite. I could not explain better the essence of this extremely old paraecclesiastical christening of a child born after the death of several preceding brothers, than by quoting the passage in which Mircea Eliade so convincingly synthesized, over twenty years ago, the profound significance of rites of this kind:

L'immersion dans l'eau symbolise la régréssion dans le préformel, la régénération totale, la nouvelle naissance, car une immersion équivaut à une dissolution des formes, à une réintégration dans le mode indifférencié de la préexistence; et la sortie des eaux répète le geste cosmogonique de la manifestation formelle. Le contact avec l'eau implique toujours la régénération; d'une part, parce que la dissolution est suivie d'une "nouvelle naissance," d'autre part parce que l'immersion fertilise et augmente le potential de vie et de création (Eliade 1953: 169).[4]

[4] [Immersion in water symbolizes a throwback to the preformal, total regeneration, a rebirth, because immersion is equivalent to a dissolution of forms, to a reintegration with the undifferentiated state of preexistence; and emergence from the water echoes

REFERENCES

DRAŠKIĆ, MIROSLAV
1968–1969   L'origine de la population et les procès ethniques dans les villages de la commune de Negotin. *Glasnik Ethnografskog Muzeja* (31–32): 11–64.

ELIADE, MIRCEA
1953   *Traité d'histoire des religions* (second edition). Paris: Payot.
1965   *Le sacré et le profane* (second edition). Paris: Gallimard.

IONESCU-MILCU, IOANA
1972   "*Apa în obiceiuri: cartogramă și comentariu*" [Water in customs: cartogram and comment], in *The iron gates microzone atlas*. Edited by Roumanian Academie. Bucharest: Academie Press.

MILCU, IOANA, PAUL SIMIONESCU
1969   *Aspecte etnosociologice ale vieții spirituale î zona Porților de Fier* [Ethnosociological aspects of the spiritual life in the Iron Gates zone]. Preprint. Craiova.

NICOLĂESCU-PLOPȘOR, C. S., et al.
1968   *Recherches archéologiques dans la zone des Portes de Fer*. Preprint. Craiova.

ZEČEVIĆ, SLOBODAN
1968–1969   Les êtres mythologiques dans la croyance populaire de la Serbie du nord-est. *Glasnik Ethnografskog Muzeja* (31-32): 327–362.

---

the achievement of the formation of the universe in a formal manifestation. The contact with the water always implies regeneration; on the one hand because the dissolution is followed by a "new birth," on the other because immersion fertilizes and augments the potentiality of life and of creation.]

Folk Medicine in a Settlement of the Székely People in the Southern Banat Region of Yugoslavia

OLGA PENAVIN

Székelykeve-Skorenovac, a village in the lower region of the Danube valley in the Banat, is inhabited by a mixture of peoples. This mixture is made up of the Székely people who settled there from the Bukovina, the Palots (Cumanians), the Bulgarians, and families who arrived later. The inhabitants belong to two or three different communities, if the Palots can be viewed as a separate community. Their common language is Hungarian; however, it does show evidence of distinctive characteristics in the dialects of the communities. This variety of backgrounds, together with a wider range of traditions than those at the disposal of the Székely people, leaves its marks on their realm of belief as well as on their communication scheme. (A superior opportunity for the examination of interethnic relations!) Another definitive trait of the inhabitants of Székelykeve-Skorenovac is that they belong to the peasant class, with only a few exceptions. The farmer in Székely, a laborer, lives his entire life with certain norms that he more or less respects. The rural surroundings determine the norms of behavior, traditional and proper behavior, opportunities for communication, content of communication, the world image, the groups taking part in the communication, the associations of communication, the imprintation of individuals in the different groups, the length of the association with each group, and even the actualization of the communication types.

The peasant and his wife who own little land are the most devoted preservers of the traditions. These are mainly people who are over forty years old. The inhabitants of Székelykeve have never had much money and only seldom were there farmers who were wealthy. For this reason, the people are, on the average, great preservers of tradition. Naturally, not only women, but also men have kept these customs, which, through the people's work and other activities, are closely connected to the harvest, stockbreeding, and production. Along these same lines, the women are skilled in the practices of healing, magic, protection from evil spirits, superstition, and customary rituals — partly because of their low cultural standard, but also for other reasons.

THE HEALING OF DISEASES CAUSED BY WITCHES, "BEAUTIFUL WOMEN," AND OTHER PERSONS SAID TO POSSESS MAGIC POWERS

Not only real people, but also unreal instigators, evil and bad-tempered people, "beautiful women," and others have an influence on the vital energies of men and animals, so that these often lead to the edge of the grave, or even to death. Above all, those people with magic powers at their disposal should be identified.

The witches, "beautiful women," bewitch people and animals; they take milk away from the cows. These are women who engage in witchcraft; little is known about men who do the same. Women tend to engage in this activity more frequently when they are old. According to the opinion of the peasants, these women are usually either small of stature or very thin. Their eyebrows are connected or have grown together, which is the most striking characteristic of their type. Their eyes are like those of the devil — deceptive. Their noses are bent. One of their legs is either a horse's hoof or a hen's foot. Of course, some people are witches who lack these characteristics.

"Beautiful women" arrive at their knowledge through learning; they are not born with it. It is difficult for one of them to die when no one holds her hand who can thereby take over her knowledge. If there is no one to hold her hand, she is given a broom to hold. This way she takes her abilities with her. When such women die and are buried, a strong wind or storm arises. The "beautiful women" perform their bad and harmful deeds at night between 11:30 and 12:00. They fly on divining rods or run, fly through the air without the aid of anything, or they ride horses. In one night, it is possible for them to visit the boundaries of two fields. After such a ride, the horses they have used are exhausted and ruined and will not let themselves be harnessed on the following day. The "beautiful women" hold their meetings on the mountain Szent Gellér. They advise each other as to whom they could carry away. They have a big celebration with dancing where men are also included.

One should protect oneself from the "beautiful women." The best means for this purpose is garlic. A wreath of garlic is hung in the stable so that the witches will not go into the stable with the cattle. A horse's skull can protect the livestock if it is hung above the horse railing, and then the "beautiful women" cannot leave their brooms and go into the house, nor can they do any damage to things living or nonliving.

Aside from the "beautiful women," those people with deceptive eyes, that is, those whose eyebrows have grown together, cause mischief of a lesser magnitude. This occurs when they see something, be it an animal or a child, that they take pleasure in and care for greatly. When someone loves something in this way, he says, "My God, how beautiful!" and the child or the animal is already bewitched by his eyes. The spell can be broken by the pouring of water or the apportionment of beans. Forty-four beans are counted and apportioned according to the latter cure, so that the person who cast the spell is revealed.

Stories about fairies and the fairies' ways can be heard on occasion, but no one seems to know anything about their outward appearance.

There are other people who are able to perform magic, for instance, wizards. A wizard has a fleshy growth, a little wing as it is called, under his arm. Some people are of the opinion that such persons are born with only one tooth, can walk immediately after birth and generally go around everywhere. A wizard cannot speak, so that he cannot give away any of the knowledge he possesses. Even his mother is secretive about this.

Old people tell about even more mythical creatures, about a chicken that crawled out of the smallest egg. In the opinion of some people, this chicken is like a blue-colored "flying star." It is fiery, fire accompanies it and follows after it. According to others, "This chicken is a ghost that visits houses; it is a spirit coming into a house." The householder is supposed to warm the egg under his arm for three weeks and then the chicken will creep out and fulfill every wish of the householder. This chicken is instrumental in the service of man; it helps him with its magic deeds.

In general, those people who have been taken away from the mother's breast too soon are the ones vulnerable to witchcraft. The people with connected eyebrows can cast spells. When a child has been bewitched by these eyes, it is laid on a table and the window is positioned in a reversed manner. The mother is supposed to walk around the table three times completely naked and the effect of the spell disappears. Someone who is bewitched with the eyes is supposed to wash with cold water. To prevent a small child from becoming bewitched with the eyes, his forehead should be smeared with soot.

An animal bewitched with the eyes can be healed by a process called water pouring, whereas humans must be healed by people who are also able to cast spells and who are experts at witchcraft. Such people are called "learned." A learned woman prepares a fire, breaks twigs from an old broom, throws them into the fire and prays. As the twigs turn into coals, she crosses herself, and after cutting the coals with a knife, she takes out a small amount on the tip of the knife. She makes the sign of the cross on a small pot of water on the hearth, and throws nine pieces of the glowing coals into the water. With every piece of coal thrown, the people think about something or someone that could have bewitched the child. Whenever the ember drops down suddenly to the bottom of the pot, it means that the child has been bewitched. The number of embers that sink to the bottom of the pot indicates the number of people who have bewitched the child. The woman then makes the sign of the cross three more times on the water and prays while she gives the water to a woman, who in turn gives it to the child to drink. If the water pouring is done for a very small child, the glowing coals can be thrown into milk. Whether water or milk is used, much more remains after the drinking than before, and that shows that the cure will be successful. The remains are poured onto the threshold and the child's face and head are washed with water. The Lord's Prayer is said three times along with three "Hail Mary's" which conclude with the following: "My God, take this disease away from the child!" Some other people have healed bewitched small children by having the oldest member of the family fetch a bucket of fresh water, so-called untouched water, from a well (the one appointed to do this is not allowed to speak to anyone). A little of the water is poured onto a plate where a spoon is already lying. The people pray while the forehead of the child is stroked with the spoon. The water is licked three times and spit out, and the water from the plate is thrown onto a pillow. The empty plate and the spoon are put by the doorpost, where no one is allowed to touch them all day. If someone does touch the plate, the spell is broken. Mud taken from a shoe sole and soot are used to make signs on the forehead of the child to counteract bewitching with the eyes.

Animals are also healed with the water throwing process. Either the sick animal is moistened with water, or the person doing the healing takes water in his mouth, spits it into the palms of his hands and washes the face of the sick animal. His hands are then dried with the wrong side of a skirt hem. The disease disappears for sure.

An old medallion with a picture of Saint Anthony is hung around the neck of one of the wise women on a red string. That way, when the woman throws water, that is, when she throws the embers into the water, she dips the medallion hanging from her neck into the water as well. This water is then given to small sick geese that are healed by it.

People who are bewitched with the eyes have headaches. In order to relieve the headache, "one blows it away," or spits on the head of the afflicted. The person directing this cure stands behind the chair of the person who has the headache. She repeats the following three times out loud:

The eyes have seen it
The heart felt it
Holy God
Blessed Mary
Heal me!

Others maintain that the saying is as follows:

The eye has seen it
The heart is fond of it
A thousand angels should comfort this child
(or: little Pista, little Erzsika, or whatever the child is called).

Third version:

The eye has seen it
The blue eye, the green eye
Yellow eye, take the pain
of the one who
is bewitched.

After this has been said three times, one "spits on his head." "Pui, pui, pui! Take this sickness away from the little one!" Then, the woman doing this makes the sign of the cross on the left and right

sides of the child's face and licks its forehead with her tongue. She
then continues, "When Jesus was on earth, the mountains were growing, the valleys were being filled. After Jesus went to heaven, everything was converted. The sickness in the child's head and stomach
should be converted." Again she spits over the child's head, "Pui, pui,
pui!" In this way, the afflicted is freed from his headache. The others
spit on the child's head and say:

The eye bewitched
The heart loved
A thousand angels
Comfort little Erzsika
(or little Jani, Bela).

Then they say the prayer, "I believe in one God," and then the following:

You have come out from under the hat
Go under the hat!
You have come out from under the bonnet
Go under the bonnet!
You have come out from under the scarf
Go under the scarf!
The heart bewitched
A thousand angels should comfort it!

The woman says this three times, and then she prays: "I believe in
one God" and spits on the child's head.

If someone is frightened, the fright can be remedied by means of a
process called lead pouring. According to one well-informed woman,
this occurs in the following manner:

At the new moon, I fetch water, and while doing this, I don't speak to
anyone. (One is not allowed to speak to anyone, not even if asked a question.) I build a fire. I pray. Into an iron spoon, I put some lead and a little
bit of fat. I put everything over the fire. Next to me are the crying child and
its mother. I cover their heads with a red cloth until I have prepared everything. Next to them is a large bowl which is half-filled with water. When
the lead in the spoon melts, I hold it over the water. I cross the water twice
and pour in the lead. It separates. A figure develops, that is, the lead shows
the figure of whatever frightened the child. I take this figure out of the
water, put it in a handkerchief, and give it to the mother to put under the
child's head while it is sleeping. I wash the child with the water. With a

small pot, I dip out some of the water, which is given to the child to drink at home. In this way, it is freed from the fright.

According to other people, the lead pouring occurs as follows: someone takes a piece of lead, puts it in a spoon, and holds it in the fire. When it begins to melt, he says the Lord's Prayer and crosses it. In the meantime, the water has been prepared in a little bowl along with a pointed knife. When someone has said the Lord's Prayer, he pours some water on the child's head, on its right and left hands, and in the same manner on its right and left legs. Then the spoon is taken from the fire, the lead is poured, and it is put back. During this time nine Lord's Prayers are said. Likewise, the prayer, "I believe in one God" is said nine times. The lead should be poured nine times and thereafter homage should be paid to the Holy Trinity, to the comforting Holy Ghost, and to Saint Elisabeth. Different forms result from this lead-pouring process. Sometimes it is a goose, sometimes a man, a heart and so on. After the lead-pouring process is completed, the afflicted child feels better. This improvement can already be ascertained with the third pouring, when the amount of lead diminishes and loses its gleam.

THE HEALING OF CHILDREN'S DISEASES

When a child is suffering from a fever and is very thin, it can be healed by baking it in the oven. At least two women are needed to carry out this method of healing — one to heat the oven, and the other to be in it. Before she begins the healing process, the child's mother is supposed to run around the house naked. If more women — nine — are present, they say the following: "Give good health back to the child, for if you don't, I'll put it in the oven and throw you in, too!" The child is then laid on the shovel used for baking bread and pushed into the lukewarm oven.

In the meantime, the women ask, "What are you baking, woman?" "I am baking a thin and sickly child." She repeats this three times, or according to other people, nine times. They cut a hole in the oven, and two women dig the child out. They then bathe it. If, after application of this method, the sick child is not yet healed, they go to the butcher and buy the belly of a large cow. They stand the child up to its neck in the belly, so that only its head is visible. The belly is then bound at the child's throat, and a hole is dug in a dungheap, where both the child and the belly are placed for three days, or in the opinion of others, for only one day. The child is "cooked" in the dung. Its mother protects it so that the dogs are unable to do it any harm. This generally cures the sick child. Afterwards, the child is given another name so that the illness will not find it again, because it is said to have been reborn in the belly of the cow.

As a remedy against diarrhea or intestinal colds, the "German woman's tent" (a plant similar to a peony, having small, white, spider-like flowers and growing along country roads) should be cooked for an hour in a large pot. Four kinds of dirt are taken from the church-yard (black, yellowish, white and true yellow), and salt is mixed with them. These should be put into the corner of a trough. The dirt should be formed like a cross and while this is taking place, the Lord's Prayer should be said once. "I believe in one God" should be prayed over the bath water. This bath water should be as deep as the child can stand it, as no water may be added later. The child feels better after having taken this bath. To cure the mange, some people are of the opinion that one should smear it with black beans that have been mashed in a copper mortar. Some people recommend a solution of lapis lazuli in sour cream. Others consider the best remedy to be iodine painted on the mange.

As a cure for stomach ache, lard should be mixed with egg yolks and smeared onto the stomach of the child. The child should then be covered up well and prayers should be said.

If the child fails to have a bowel movement, it should eat plum jam mixed with garlic.

THE HEALING OF ADULTS WITH MEDICATIONS OF PLANT AND ANIMAL ORIGIN

The natural healing of adults is done with medications made from wild plants or those grown in gardens. Adults are subject to many illnesses. For most of these, water and lead pouring and spitting on the head are not beneficial; therefore, natural plants should be used. Almost every illness has its natural remedy or its natural medication.

In order to keep from becoming ill, we should roll around in the first snow. If we contract an illness in spite of this, it should be cured with a plant or by some miraculous means, or we should employ the services of the women who perform witchcraft so that they can help us. We should take care to protect ourselves from certain threatening circumstances if we want to avoid sickness at the outset. For example, one should not look into a death chamber, because one will contract jaundice. If one steps into the soapy water that has been poured out into the yard, one's feet will be wounded.

If someone has broken his leg, he should pour spirits (schnapps) on the broom. If a callus forms on someone's hand, he should smear the area with a dead frog, and then it will disappear. If someone washes his hands in a trough, he will be wounded.

Against rheumatism grated horse chestnuts soaked for eight days in turpentine, denatured alcohol, or spirits are a special cure. The rheumatic area should be treated with compresses soaked in elderberry roots and nut tree tea. Garden balsamine is another good remedy for rheumatism. The afflicted person should bathe in water in which elderberry and tomato stems have been boiled. The painful area is besmeared, and then a horseradish is pared, put into a piece of cloth and laid on the rheumatic spot. The leaves of the plague root (*Pestwurz*) can be pulverized, put on a larger leaf, moistened with grapeskin liquor and applied with a compress to the afflicted area. During the cholera epidemic, birthworts were boiled in a pot and this water was used for bathwater.

Pulmonary diseases are healed with boiled stinging nettles and sugar water. Tea made from bryony, wheat blossoms, linden blossoms, and mercury helps greatly.

A mixture of rabbit fat, soap water, tomatoes, and baked onions is put into a rag and applied to the affected spot to heal a festering boil. In some cases, resin, egg yolks, and fat are put into a rag and then applied to the wound. "The egg yolk flowed out." Egg yolks, honey and fat, or soap water, fat, and wheat flour can be applied to boils. Tomatoes and baked onions help, too. According to the custom of the Bukovina, if a person has pains in his stomach or in the small of his back, he is healed by sacrification. This takes place in the following manner: heated cloth, glasses, or pouches are laid on the painful area. These draw the pain out. Bloodletting is used, too, for the relief of pain and is performed by a barber. He cuts the painful spot with a razor and applies a hot knife to it.

Against nasal colds, egg white mixed with a pinch of salt should be applied to the head of the patient, who is then put to bed with a bonnet on. Meanwhile, prayers should be said.

Against sore throats, it is beneficial to catch a lizard and strangle it. The fingers used to strangle the lizard should then be used to massage the throat of the sick person.

A helpful cure against the shivers is a bath in which linden leaves, thyme, "battle grass" (*Kampfgras*), and mousetails have been boiled.

If someone is nauseated or upsets his stomach, he should lie down on a hot stove.

Heart disease should be remedied by drinking a tea made of red poppy stems and basil leaves. The use of young red poppy buds helps those afflicted with heart disease greatly.

THE HEALING OF ANIMALS

Animals are considered to be treasures, and all possible remedies are used to heal them. The animals have a patron saint named Wenceslaus. On Saint Wenceslaus' Day the animals are protected; whoever violates this practice will do harm to the livestock.

A red ribbon should be bound around the necks and the tails of the animals to protect them from witchcraft.

Small geese should be spit upon, so that they are not subject to visual witchcraft.

If cattle, horses, or swine are bewitched with the eyes, they are healed with water throwing. The animals should never be beaten with brooms, because then they can be saddled and ridden by the witches.

A shiny coin is hung around the necks of dogs in order to ward off the powers of the witches.

One night, a shepherd heard someone relate the following:

There were once women who took away the yield from the cattle. Whenever the householders would cut through the milk with a sickle, those people who had taken the yield came to the door to prevent this activity, because they themselves were being cut.

It is said that Mrs. Erzsébet even milks the gatepost.

One evening my mother saw that Mrs Erzsébet was going to the farm. Once there, she gathered more and more wood splinters. She became very happy. Whenever she went into someone's home, this Mrs. Erzsébet generally went directly into the stable to look at the livestock. She was especially interested in the cattle. When a cow noticed her, it climbed up into the manger because it was so afraid of her. It felt her presence. This old woman had eyes like the devil.

There is a method for finding out who has taken the milk from the cow. At night, the stove should be heated and a little bit of milk should be poured in. The person who has taken the milk appears and asks, "Why have you heated the stove?" This person can no longer take the milk away, because he has been revealed.

Illnesses occurring in horses due to the cold can be healed with pressed roots. The horse's skin is pierced at its breast with an awl and the narrow root threads are drawn into it. The roots draw out the abscess.

Old rags that have been burned are held in front of the horse's nose as a cure for colds.

Stamping horses are quieted with oatstraw that has been smoked in the excrement of hens. Occasionally they can be given a mixture of shredded radishes and clover.

Diseases of the mouth are best treated with rags soaked in a solution of vinegar, lapis lazuli, and crushed garlic. One of the rags is fastened to the end of a staff and put into the animal's mouth.

Urinary stoppage can be healed by those people whose index and ring fingers are the same length, and who can pick up a straw with these fingers.

If the wound of an animal is covered with the discharge of flies, prayers should be said at dusk. The wound is washed with tea made from basil weed. Ribwort is also beneficial.

SUMMARY

Those customs which were still alive, active, and readily collected in the second half of the twentieth century bear witness to the veneration of superstition, magic, certain original powers, and natural powers. In the year 1972 one encounters the veneration of water, fire, mother earth, wind, etc. The belief in wondrous, unexplainable, protected, consecrated, and purged powers leads people even in our time to make use of water throwing, lead pouring, and smoking activities.

These ruinous elements (fire, water, wind, storms) can work against certain patterns of activity, and even FOR human life through ceremonies in which these elements are blessed and consecrated. This ability is, however, not afforded to everyone; only certain people are the "wise ones," who never demand for their services, and who at most let the "commissioner" know that their pantries are empty, or that one thing or another is lacking. A gift is made to compensate for this ability.

Belief and Cult in Human Prehistory

FRANCISZEK M. ROSIŃSKI

Specialists hold very different, even extreme, views concerning the origin and age of conceptions of religious belief. Many scientists (for example Nikolskij 1949, Noss 1953, Weckler 1954, Boriskovskij 1957, Tokarev 1964, Leroi-Gourhan 1964, Suxov 1967, and Anisimow 1971) believe there to have been a long nonreligious period in human prehistory. They point primarily to the absence of any material traces of religious objects and practices (particularly in the early and middle Old Stone Age), and also to the extremely primitive cultural level and the inferior intelligence of hominids of that time, whom they have credited with only a very limited practical thinking capacity, which led to impulsive actions in compliance with the surroundings and the situation. "The social existence of these prehistoric men was so primitive that their consciousness was totally bound to practice and was incapable of producing any religious abstractions" (Tokarev 1968: 21).

Unfortunately, too little attention has been given to these arguments, and they should not be dismissed with the remark that we are dealing here with an "evolutionary apriorism" which, "it is true, likes to clothe itself in the garment of 'lack of prejudice,' but which, in its origin and also in its later background, is by no means free of ideological tendencies" (Narr 1965: 52).

In trying to reconstruct through material cultural findings the psychic capabilities and spiritual activities (especially possible faith content and cult practices) of the people of the Old Stone Age, one should recognize above all that out of the whole cultural inventory, only very resistant objects remain intact, whereas the majority of the objects used, as among many present-day aboriginal tribes, were probably made of impermanent materials.

It is also unlikely that one can speak of a universally valid rule that faith content and cult practices must be represented materially, particularly in stone. This assumption, among others, was the reason that at one time various tribes were characterized as religionless — an assumption later decisively refuted by other researchers, sometimes after weeks of field observation (Vroklage 1948–1949). Koppers (1951) determined, in addition, that "among the ethnologically ancient or prehistoric peoples, such as Tierra del Fuego Indians, Pygmy tribes, etc., not only was the main God not represented — let alone in durable material — but the same is also true of the spirits and higher beings in which they also believe." Among the Jews, there was even a strict prohibition against production of such images. Among some hunting tribes, Schebesta (1961) ascertained the existence of a highly developed religious life, despite the absence of cult objects; in some cases the lack of an external cult was compensated for by an intensive inner religiosity.

One can really only make conjectures — to be sure, of a rather positive sort — concerning the social organization of *Homo erectus* and *Homo sapiens neanderthalensis*. Old Stone Age man was very familiar with the hunt for big game. Among the game animals there were quick, dangerous, and shy species, which made individual hunting, especially of the cave bear, out of the question (Lubin 1969).

In the production of stone tools, prehistoric men paid attention increasingly not only to their usefulness but also to their geometric, harmonious form. In some artifacts one can distinguish an amazingly precise execution, which not only necessitated a considerable additional expenditure of time and energy, but which also reflected an aesthetic sense, tradition, perhaps even a set order of steps in production and its scrupulous execution. According to Coon (1965), on the basis of the large temporal and spatial spread of the stone implement one can even deduce the existence of linguistic communication, rigorous forms of schooling, and intensive human contacts, for which a human society is a prerequisite.

The discovery, production, and utilization of fire, especially in caves, which, in Choukoutien, for example, was already being burned on a specially arranged stone base (Weinert 1951), testify to the inventiveness of the society. A hunting society's continuous upkeep of a fire presupposes a minimal number of regulated social structures, and in addition, according to Gehlen (1966: 125), represents an "achievement of abstraction . . . not possible without a language."

These and other reasons seem to suggest that Old Stone Age man was no longer completely dependent upon the surroundings and did not devote his time and energy exclusively to a circle of immediate bio-logical necessities, but was also capable of enlarging his scope of con-sciousness and experience, of giving expression to "aesthetic feelings," and of searching for new causal connections between various events.

Old Stone Age man was forced, also, to deal with the problem of death and his relationship to the dead, especially because he was familiar with the practice of killing for the purpose of food and defense. He was also already capable of planning and foresight. After all, even on a subhuman level the death of another member of the species is noted, and one cannot exclude the possibility that the australopithecines al-ready manifested a certain interest in their dead. Their bone remains were found at the wall of the cave to the side of a large pile of animal bones (Young 1971). However, this circumstance could be attributed to other causes, because as is known, sick and injured monkeys crawl into cracks in rocks and dark spaces in caves to seek coolness, water, and safety from pursuers. Water sometimes drips down from just such cracks and occasionally collects in a depression (Schultz 1961; Zapfe 1957).

Researchers who assume the existence of at least a "minimal religion" (von Eickstedt 1963: 2218) in the *Homo erectus* stage, point primarily to a certain selectivity and intentional damage to the discovered human bone fragments, which brings to mind recent cult practices among various primitive tribes. One notes the peculiar fact that in sites from the Early and Middle Paleolithic it is almost exclusively the skull or parts of it that are found, but seldom postcranial bones, although frequently entire animal skeletons have been hidden at these sites — for example, in Choukoutien, where, despite a careful search, no neck vertebrae could be brought to light (Weidenreich 1943; Breuil and Lantier 1959). We find similar circumstances also in Ngandong (Wei-denreich 1951).

The question has been asked, to be sure, whether such a selection could not have come about naturally (Leroi-Gourhan 1964). For ex-ample, Washburn (1957) has pointed out that especially the brown hyena carried into its lair various bones of minimal nutritional value, particularly skulls and loose jaws. However, in many cases one can eliminate this possibility — for example, in the case of the *Sinanthropus* skulls. No tooth marks could be found on them (Bergounioux 1961) and, in addition, they were found in layers containing cultural materials.

Also, on the *Homo erectus* and *Homo sapiens neanderthalensis* skulls one can nearly always distinguish injuries caused by blows from weapons. Often, too, the skull base has been broken open in the vicinity of the *foramen magnum*; thus, judging on the basis of the known material, a violent death was nearly always the rule at that time (Courville 1951).

Researchers usually express the opinion that the selection and destruction of hominid skulls and long bones must be attributed to the humans of that time, and that, therefore, cannibalistic practices must be responsible, but they do not agree whether there was already ritual cannibalism in the Early and Middle Paleolithic. Stęślicka, for example (1964: 18), holds the view that

... most scholars are of the opinion that cannibalism first appeared only in times of pronounced food deficiency and was, to some extent, an act of desperation in view of the inevitable death due to starvation. Only later, with a growing capacity for abstract thought, did cannibalism begin to turn into a rite of mystic significance.

It seems, however, that one does not do justice to the facts in assuming that cannibalism was due to nutritional problems. For the origin as well as the continuation of this practice, hunger is inadequate as an explanation. In the animal world, with very few exceptions, even when there is an extreme scarcity of food, animals of the same species do not consider each other as food objects. Nor are there any reports of cannibalism among other primates, although some classes of monkeys occasionally catch and devour animals of other species, including even the brain; it is said that there have even been attacks on children (Dart 1963; van Lawick-Goodall 1968; DeVore and Washburn 1964; Hofer 1972).

Also, if one takes into account the great wealth of game animals that were available to men at that time, and that were in fact hunted (von Koenigswald 1955; Movius 1950; Lubin 1969), one finds it difficult to relate anthropophagy to a food shortage. The immense areas were sparsely settled, and there were, of course, also small animals and plants, especially in areas with lush vegetation. Besides, as Garn and Block (1970) have calculated, a small group of hominids would cease to exist in a relatively short period of time if it systematically practiced anthropophagy. There are more recent reports that slain enemies, and even members of the same tribe who had died a natural death, were devoured (Tischner 1939), but it is difficult to cite a single example of any society which has allowed a systematic killing of its members for food purposes (Walens and Wagner 1971). According to Narr (1965: 45), "the assumption of a purely nutritional cannibalism ... can be supported by virtually no analogies." Nutritional cannibalism seems to be only a debased form of ritual anthropophagy, which occurs among tribes with a relatively well-developed culture, ordinarily on a higher level than that of their neighbors who do not practice cannibalism (Behm-Blanke 1962; Muschalek 1963).

If one were to assume "culinary cannibalism," it is difficult to solve the problem of bone selection. If we assume that such a meal took place in a cave (in Choukoutien, for example), one would expect to find there a much greater number of postcranial bones, especially from the spine or pelvis (which are surely somewhat more resistant than the bones of children's skulls), especially since frequently entire skeletons of other animals were found.

If, in the interior of caves, people had contented themselves with severed heads, one would have expected to find at least the missing fragments of the base of the skulls and the highest attached neck vertebrae; this, however, has not been the case. On the other hand, if the meal took place outside the cave and the people then brought the skulls inside with missing facial parts, this could hardly have been done for "culinary" reasons, for their nutritional value was by then already very slight because of the damage to the skullcap. They were poorly suited to serve even as drinking bowls; the base of the skullcap was, in any case, not suited for drinking purposes.

Therefore, many researchers (including Kraft 1942, Weidenreich 1951, Koppers 1951, Gieseler 1959, von Koenigswald 1960, Varagnac 1960, Grigoriev 1969, and Hofer 1972), reject the notion of a purely nutritional cannibalism. With certain reservations, they explain the peculiar selection and intentional damage to the bone material as a ritual cannibalism, sometimes in connection with headhunting, or as a special burial ritual or skull cult. In this connection, they frequently bring in for comparison analogous facts and actions among various primitive tribes. For example, Schmidt (1932) has pointed out that a relationship to the dead similar to that of Peking Man exists also among the Andamanese and Kurnai, who carefully preserve the skulls of the dead, but seldom their long bones. Researchers adduce similar facts concerning the headhunting and cannibal Dayaks on Borneo, the Bataks on Sumatra, and various tribes in Indonesia and Micronesia (Wernert 1936; Körner 1939; Nevermann 1939, 1941). Some natives in Africa also preserve gorilla skulls with broken bases, but even here one could assume certain religious beliefs. Women are forbidden to eat the brains of these animals, for fear that this would prove fatal to them (Blanc 1961).

Recent headhunting, which is usually bound up with anthropophagy, is rooted in a magical-religious world of ideas, and rests on the belief that "the spiritual strength and knowledge of a person are concentrated in his head or, more accurately, in his brain . . . and after the death of the prey, one can own his spirit through the possession of his head and acquire his strength and knowledge through the savoring of his brain." Among the Asmat and Marind-anim, for example, head-hunting and cannibalism are brought into the closest association with the cult of ancestors and cosmogonical conceptions (Nevermann 1941; Zegwaard 1959).

But these interpretations, too, seem inadequate, even aside from the large temporal and cultural differences which separate the Paleolithic from the present day. One is struck by the great number of children's skulls in some Paleolithic discovery sites — for example, in Choukoutien, where fifteen out of twenty-two individuals had not yet reached the fourteenth year of life (Vallois 1961). This is precisely contrary to the custom among recent headhunters, which is understandable, as children do not yet possess the physical and psychic qualities which a cannibal wishes to incorporate; besides, a child's skull has no great value as a hunting trophy.

Nor did a rigorous selection of the bones occur — for example, in Choukoutien, beyond the skull- and hollowbones, a collarbone and *os lunatum* were found. One may presume that the human bones were not handled reverently, because they were found mixed with animal bones — unless they were subsequently pushed aside by intruding cave animals. The hollow bones had been broken open, probably to extract the bone marrow (Weidenreich 1943; Courville 1951; Gieseler 1959). Also, one must not forget that "Cannibalism, like head-hunting, is known to exist today only among peoples with an agrarian form of economy" (Narr 1965: 44), who are, thus, already on a decidedly higher level of economy than the hunters and gatherers.

Some researchers (such as Schmidt 1932, Breuil 1932, Wernert 1948, Maringer 1958, Bergounioux 1960, and Schebesta 1961), interpret the Paleolithic human finds as remnants of a two-stage burial rite, as it is practiced among a number of primitive tribes today. The corpses are not devoured, but ritually interred or displayed. Later, after the decaying process, the skulls are brought home, preserved with honor as family mementos, sometimes even worn — as is done, for example, among the Andamanese, Negritos, Tasmanians, Digul tribes, and Australians (Körner 1939; Nevermann 1941; Narr 1966a).

With this hypothesis, it is true, one could explain the occurrence of skulls and loose lower jaws even of children — because the mortality rate was surely high among children — as well as the absence of the uppermost neck vertebra; but hardly the damage, especially to the back of the head, the breaking open of skull and long bones, the traces on them of fire action, and the mixing of them with animal bones.

Definite burials of the dead are known only from the last stage of Neanderthal man — among others, in Mugharet et-Tabun, Mugharet es-Skhūl, Teshik-Tash, Kiik Koba, Monte Circeo, La Ferrassie, and La Chapelle aux Saints. There are known, in addition, numerous deposits of the bones of game animals in the vicinity of the burial sites. For example, in La Ferrassie a small family cemetery was discovered. The grave of a five- to six-year-old child was covered by a stone on the surface of which were small indentations, presumably artificial. At or near the grave there had burned a fire. Tools and animal bones were in the vicinity of the dead. There were, in addition, nine small hills arranged in three rows, of which the outer rows ran parallel to each other; the middle row was displaced by half a length with respect to the others. These rows contained no bones, and it is uncertain what their purpose had been (Bergounioux 1960; Narr 1966a). Also revealing is the special position or direction in which the dead were buried, that is, the squatting position: probably the extremities were bound with thongs to the head, perhaps out of fear of their return to the society of the living (Clark 1967). So, on the one hand, people were aware that they had a corpse in front of them; on the other hand, apparently they already believed in the independent existence of a soul or spirit.

In some cases, for example in the cave system near Monte Circeo, which is very difficult of access, a special burial space appears to have been sought out for the dead. Here, in the middle of a wreath of stone, was found a Neanderthal skull with broken-out base and broken temporal-orbital region. Blanc (1961) is of the opinion that we are dealing here with a ritual murder committed 55,000 years ago.

Here, and in similar cases, to all appearances cannibalism was practiced. However, a ritual burial at least of the skull took place, which one could evaluate as an intermediate form of ritual burial without anthropophagy, a practice which was making increasing headway. It can be seen, however, that in some places this intermediate form existed for a long time, e.g. in Ofnet, where thirty-three skulls were buried. Some cervical vertebrae found with the skulls bearing traces of a violent decapitation, which renders improbable a two-stage burial (Mollison 1936; Jullien 1965). Possibly this tradition was preserved into modern times, although in time it was probably given new motivations and interpretations as a result of cultural and economic changes.

In some cases a pit, usually flat, was dug out for the dead, even in rock ground, as in Kiik Koba (Tokarev 1964). However, inasmuch as this did not always offer sufficient protection against carrion eaters, sometimes the burial site was secured additionally by one or more stones. Included with the corpses we find food, ochre, tools, and even objects of jewelry (Bergounioux 1960; Carrington 1963; Mauser 1972).

Also from the end phase of the Neanderthal period are dated the first burials of entire corpses. However, Goździewski (1959) would like to attribute this to the influence of an early stage of *Homo sapiens fossilis.* This seems to be indicated by the accompanying cultural inventory, as in La Chapelle aux Saints.

In addition, animal burials are known from the Middle and Late Paleolithic. Like the human graves, they were protected in some cases by heavy plates of stone. According to all appearances, these proce-dures were rooted in certain religious conceptions linked to the dangers of the bear hunt, and in time developed into a richly ceremonial bear cult, which is found among various tribes in northern Europe, Asia, and America; it usually possesses a magical-totemistic content (Krickeberg 1939; Varagnac 1960; Narr 1966b; Grigoriev 1969).

It is possible that the strict adherence to a set method of producing certain artifacts (e.g. Paleolithic flints) was also based on a magical conviction as to their effectiveness, which one wished under no circum-stances to endanger. In view of the large dimensions of some of these stone implements (as much as 30-40 centimeters), some of them prob-ably had no secular use at all, unless they were used by a race of giants (Mauser 1972). Probably they were "ceremonial instruments ... to be compared to the large stone implements of New Guinea, which were not intended for use" (von Koenigswald 1968: 163; Coon 1965).

Thus, on the basis of Paleolithic materials which have been found, one can consider the existence of certain religious conceptions prob-able; a long nonreligious period, on the other hand, is hardly likely. This does not contradict the assumption of a development of intel-lectual capabilities in man, but is, on the contrary, in harmony with it. However, a more precise reconstruction of the content of Paleolithic belief and cult seems hardly possible. It is hardly probable that a tra-dition several hundred thousand years old would have remained sub-stantially unchanged despite cultural and social shifts, especially in view of the fact that the available material cannot be explained ade-quately by any recent forms of cult and belief.

We can probably assume that, like material and mental culture, belief and cult, too, have their prehistory, and that the initially very primitive elements of belief (i.e. those related to the death of other members of the species or to the hunt) in time were enriched by new realizations and experiences to form new, more complex structures in which certain original elements of faith could be "bracketed out," superimposed, or mixed with new ones. As to their content, one can make at the most only vague assumptions.

REFERENCES

ANISIMOW, A. F.
1971   *Istoričeskie osobennosti pervobytnogo myšlenia.* Leningrad: Nauka.
BEHM-BLANCKE, G.
1962   *Höhlen, Heiligtümer, Kannibalen.* Leipzig: Brockhaus.
BERGOUNIOUX, F. M.
1960   "Mentalité religieuse en préhistoire," in *Cahiers d'études biologiques.* Edited by P. Lethielleux, 75–87. Paris: Lethielleux.
1961   "Notes on the mentality of primitive man," in *Social life of early man.* Edited by S. L. Washburn, 106–118. Chicago: Aldine.
BLANC, A. C.
1961   "Some evidence for the ideologies of early man," in *Social life of early man.* Edited by S. L. Washburn, 119–136. Chicago: Aldine.
BORISKOVSKIJ, P. J.
1957   *Drevnejšee prošloe čelovečestva* Moscow: Akademija Nauk SSSR.
BREUIL, H.
1932   Le gisement de *Sinanthropus* à Choukoutien (Chine) et ses vestiges de feu et d'industrie. *Anthropos* 27:1–10.
BREUIL, H., R. LANTIER
1959   *Les hommes de la pierre ancienne.* Paris: Pavot.
CARRINGTON, R.
1963   *A million years of man.* Cleveland: World.
CLARK, G.
1967   *The stone age hunters.* London: Thames and Hudson.
COON, C.
1965   *The story of man.* New York: Alfred A. Knopf.
COURVILLE, C. B.
1951   "Cranial injuries in prehistoric man with particular references to the Neanderthals," in *Yearbook of physical anthropology.* Edited by G. W. Lasker and J. L. Angel, 185–205. New York.
DART, R. A.
1963   "The carnivorous propensity of baboons," in *Symposia of the Zoological Society of London.* Edited by J. Napier and N. A. Barnicot, 49–56. London.
DE VORE, I., S. L. WASHBURN
1964   "Baboon ecology and human evolution," in *African ecology and human evolution.* Edited by F. C. Howell and F. Bourlière, 335–367. London: Methuen.

GARN, S. M., W. D. BLOCK
1970   The limited nutritional value of cannibalism. *American Anthropologist* 72:106.

GEHLEN, A.
1966   *Der Mensch.* Frankfurt-am-Main: Athenäum.

GIESELER, W.
1959   "Die Fossilgeschichte des Menschen," in *Die Evolution der Organismen.* Edited by G. Heberer, 951–1109. Stuttgart: G. Fischer.

GOŹDZIEWSKI, S.
1959   Rasy paleolitu starszego. *Przegląd Antropologiczny* 25:235–246.

GRIGORIEV, G. P.
1969   "Pervobytnoe obščestvo i ego kul'tura v must'e i načale pozdnego paleolita," in *Priroda i raswitie pervobytnogo obščestva na teritorii evropejskoj časti SSSR,* 196–215. Moscow: Nauka.

HOFER, H.
1972   "Prolegomena primatologiae," in *Die Sonderstellung des Menschen.* Edited by H. Hofer and G. Altner, 1—146. Stuttgart: G. Fischer.

JULLIEN R.
1965   *Les hommes fossiles de la pierre taillée.* Paris: N. Boubée.

KOPPERS, W.
1951   "Der historische Gedanke in Ethnologie und Religionswissenschaft," in *Christus und die Religionen der Erde.* Edited by F. König, 75–109. Vienna: Herder.

KÖRNER, T.
1939   "Indonesien," in *Die grosse Völkerkunde,* volume two. Edited by H. A. Bernatzik, 251–294. Leipzig: Bibliogr. Institut AG.

KRAFT, G.
1942   *Der Urmensch als Schöpfer.* Berlin: E. Ebering.

KRICKEBERG, W.
1939   "Amerika," in *Die grosse Völkerkunde,* volume three. Edited by H. A. Bernatzik, 18–258. Leipzig: Bibliogr. Institut AG.

LEROI-GOURHAN, A.
1964   *Les religions de la préhistoire (Paléolithique).* Paris: Presses Universitaires de France.

LUBIN, W. P.
1969   "Rannij paleoli Kavkaza," in *Priroda i raswitie pervobytnogo obščestva na teritorii evropejskoj časti SSSR,* 154–168. Moscow: Nauka.

MARINGER, J.
1958   *L'homme préhistorique et ses dieux.* Arthaud.

MAUSER, P. F.
1972   Die eiszeitliche Technik als Ausdruck der unterschiedlichen Bewusstseinsstruktur von Urmensch und *Homo sapiens. Homo* 23: 129–144.

MOLLISON, T.
1936   Zeichen gewaltsamer Verletzungen an den Ofnet-Schädeln. *Anthropologischer Anzeiger* 13:79–88.

MOVIUS, H. H., JR.
1950 Zur Archäologie des unteren Paläolithikums in Südasien und im Fernen Osten. *Mitteilungen der Anthropologischen Gesellschaft in Wien* 80:101–139

MUSCHALEK, H.
1963 *Urmensch — Adam*. Berlin: Morus.

NARR, K. J.
1965 "Ursprung und Frühkulturen," in *Saeculum Weltgeschichte*. Edited by H. Francke, et al., 1:21–235. Freiburg: Herder.
1966a "Geistiges Leben in der frühen und mittleren Altsteinzeit," in *Handbuch der Urgeschichte*, volume one. Edited by K. J. Narr, 158–168. Bern: Francke.
1966b "Religion und Magie in der jüngeren Altsteinzeit," in *Handbuch der Urgeschichte*, volume one. Edited by K. J. Narr, 298–320. Bern: Francke.

NEVERMANN, H.
1939 "Südsee," in *Die grosse Völkerkunde*, volume two. Edited by H. A. Bernatzik, 295–364. Leipzig: Bibliogr. Inst. AG.
1941 *Ein Besuch bei Steinzeitmenschen*. Stuttgart: Kosmos.

NIKOLSKIJ, V. K.
1949 *Proisxoždenie religii*. Moscow: Goskul'tprosvet.

NOSS, J. B.
1953 *Man's religions*. New York: Macmillan.

SCHEBESTA, P.
1961 *Ursprung der Religion*. Berlin: Morus.

SCHMIDT, P. G.
1932 Remarques sur le fait qu'on n'a trouvé que les crânes et des mandibules du *Sinanthropus. Anthropos* 27:9–10.

SCHULTZ, A. H.
1961 "Some factors influencing the social life of primates in general and of early man in particular," in *Social life of early man*. Edited by S. L. Washburn, 58–90. Chicago: Aldine.

STĘŚLICKA, W.
1953 Środowisko i domniemany tryb życia Australopithecinae na podstawie towarzyszącej fauny. *Przegląd antropologiczny* 19:351–369.

SUXOV, A. D.
1967 *Filosofskie problemy proisxoždenia religii*. Moscow: Mysl.

TISCHNER, H.
1939 "Australien," in *Die grosse Völkerkunde*, volume three. Edited by H. A. Bernatzik, 1–17. Leipzig: Bibliogr. Inst. AG.

TOKAREV, S. A.
1964 *Rannie formy religii i ix raswitie*. Moscow: Nauka.
1968 *Die Religion in der Geschichte der Völker*. Berlin: Dietz.

VALLOIS, H. V.
1961 "The social life of early man: the evidence of skeletons," in *Social life of early man*. Edited by S. L. Washburn, 214–235. Chicago: Aldine

VAN LAWICK-GOODALL, J.
1968   The behaviour of free-living chimpanzees in the Gombe Stream Reserve. *Animal Behaviour Monographs* 1(3).

VARAGNAC, A.
1960   "Das Mittel- und Jungpaläolithikum," in *Epochen der Menschheit*. Edited by L. Febvre and F. Braudel, 71–94. Düsseldorf: E. Diederich.

VON EICKSTEDT, E. V.
1963   *Ursprung und Entfaltung der Seele*. Stuttgart: Ferdinand Enke.

VON KOENIGSWALD, G. H. R.
1955   *Begegnungen mit dem Vormenschen*. Düsseldorf: E. Diederich.
1960   *Die Geschichte des Menschen*. Berlin: Springer.
1968   "Probleme der ältesten menschlichen Kulturen," in *Handgebrauch und Verständigung bei Affen und Frühmenschen*. Edited by B. Rensch, 149–171. Bern: H. Huber.

VROKLAGE, B.
1948–1949   Die angebliche Religionslosigkeit der Ridan-Kubu von Sumatra. *Anthropos* 41–44:41–48.

WALENS, S., R. WAGNER
1971   Pigs, proteins, and people-eaters. *American Anthropologist* 73: 269–270.

WASHBURN, S. L.
1957   Australopithecines: the hunters or the hunted. *American Anthropologist* 59:612–614.

WECKLER, J. E.
1954   The relationships between Neanderthal Man and *Homo sapiens*. *American Anthropologist* 56:1003–1025.

WEIDENREICH, F.
1943   The skull of *Sinanthropus pekinensis*. *Palaeontologia Sinica* 10: 1–486.
1951   Morphology of Solo Man. *Anthropological Papers of the American Museum of Natural History* 43:203–290.

WEINERT, H.
1951   *Der geistige Aufstieg der Menschheit*. Stuttgart: Enke.

WERNERT, P.
1936   L'anthropophagie rituelle et la chasse aux têtes aux époques actuelles et paléolithiques. *L'Anthropologie* 46:33–43.
1948   "Le culte des crânes à l'époque paléolithique," in *Histoire générale des Religions*. Edited by M. Gorce and R. Mortier, 53–72. Paris: A. Quillet.

YOUNG, J. Z.
1971   *An introduction to the study of man*. Oxford: Clarendon Press.

ZAPFE, H.
1957   Die Entstehung fossilreicher knochenführender Ablagerungen in Höhlen und Karstspalten. *Mitteilungen der Anthropologischen Gesellschaft in Wien* 87:98–101.

ZEGWAARD, G. A.
1959   Headhunting practices of the Asmat of Netherlands New Guinea. *American Anthropologist* 61:1020–1041.

Animal Sacrifices in the Balkans

ANCA STAHL

In the Balkan peninsula, the peasant to this day still practices a large number of blood sacrifices. The occasions which call for them are diverse: the festival of St. George, Christmas, Easter, funerary rites, the construction of a house, etc. All of these sacrifices have several common elements among the different peoples of this region.

The ritual which accompanies the killing of the victim sometimes seems debased; many of the gestures and actions appear to be devoid of meaning, but it is supposed that at one time they did have meaning. The peasants continue to sacrifice from fear: "in order to avoid misfortune," or from tradition: "the ancients performed it thus," to receive rain or abundant harvest.

In all of these sacrifices, the victims are domestic animals and are chosen in accordance with the beliefs which are attached to this or that festival. Thus, sheep are sacrificed to St. George, a pig at Christmas, and a bull (in Greece) to St. Helen. A goat is never sacrificed for the soul of a dead person nor is a pig at Easter. The peasants furthermore make a very clear-cut distinction between the "pure" and "impure" animals, distinctions to which we shall return later.

We are going to limit our discussion to two examples: the sacrifice for construction and the sacrifice for the souls of the dead.

1. We have deliberately chosen the sacrifice for construction for two reasons: it is not connected to any religious festival and it is still widely practiced in Bulgaria, Greece, Romania, and Yugoslavia.

It must be made clear from the outset that animal sacrifices are made for the erection of houses and rarely for larger constructions (churches, monasteries, bridges, etc.).[1] The succession of actions which constitute the sacrifice are always and everywhere the same: consecration, immolation, ritual meal.

The sacrifice must take place on the site of construction. Because the life of a traditional society lends itself to the observance of propitious moments for different kinds of activities, it is natural that the work of construction can only begin at certain times. Each day of the week has its particular value; each is considered a sacred being who can help or punish people in their actions. Monday and Thursday are deemed auspicious days for the commencement of all labor.

The time of the day is equally significant: thus, the sacrifice is performed early in the morning, and all of the ceremony is completed before noon, because all of the rites and prayers of morning aim at exorcising misfortune and attracting the forces of prosperity and wealth, in order to attach them firmly to the land chosen for building.

THE CONSECRATION   Before the slaughter of the victim, the village priest reads a prayer (*sfeştanie*) in the presence of the whole family, the neighbors, the relatives, and the masons. While reciting the prayer, the priest walks about the building site and sprinkles it with consecrated water in order to purify it, "to drive out the evil spirits and the devil." During the religious service, the priest and all of the domestic group look toward the east, toward the rising sun. If the priest is absent, it is the sacrificer (the head of the family or mason) who replaces him and sprinkles the ground with consecrated water brought from the church.

The animal destined for sacrifice, brought at the beginning of the religious service, is purified by the prayer of the priest, who, in certain villages, sprinkles the animal with holy water instead of with incense. In the case of the sacrifice of a ram, the priest or sacrificer places lighted wax candles on the horns of the ram before the religious service.

THE IMMOLATION   No particular attention is devoted to the color of the sacrificed animals, as is done in the sacrifice for the souls of the dead or for a cure, when the animal must be black, However, in certain cases, when the peasant intends the victim for the earth spirit, a black animal is chosen. The animal's sex is of no importance: a cock can be sacrificed as well as a hen, a ewe as well as a ram.

The sacrificer is almost always the head of the domestic group which is to reside in the house. Sometimes it is the master mason who performs the

---

[1]   We shall analyze only animal sacrifices and not discuss the stories referred to as "the flight of the shadow" and the legends and ballads which describe human sacrifices.

sacrifice, especially if the head of the family is absent. Women never have the right to slaughter an animal, and they attend the ceremony without playing any particular role.

The animal to be sacrificed is oriented toward the sun, and its head is cut off with a metal knife; when it is slaughtered, the blood gushes and sprinkles the earth. In certain villages, the sacrificer drags the decapitated, bloody cadaver around the site, while following the outline of the future foundations, moving from left to right. He thus imitates the sun's path through the sky.

The victim's head is buried in the southeast corner of the site. After having finished the prayer, the priest begins to dig up the ground there with three thrusts of the spade. It is not an accident that the sacrificed animal's head is buried in the east, because it is there that the peasants place their icons and beneficent plants, as well as all the objects intended to protect them and assure the prosperity of the domestic group; in the specialized literature, this corner is designated "the sacred corner of the house."

THE MEAL   Immediately after the ceremony, the women prepare the body of the animal, which will be consumed during a feast at which all the participants must consume the flesh of the victim. The meal is a moment during the ceremony which has a social significance that transcends the familial frame. Furthermore, every sacrifice is accompanied by a meal, which is a festive occasion.

TO WHOM IS THE ANIMAL SACRIFICED?   The explanations given by the peasants are multiple, and sometimes different responses are obtained within a single village.

One example explanation is that the sacrifice is intended for the earth spirit (*omul pamîntuli*). The earth is conceived of as a sacred being: while it is being dug up, the earth is blessed; it also must be compensated, and the evil that has been done to it must be redeemed. The villagers believe that they are committing a grave sin in breaking up the earth with sharp tools. "It is a grave sin to thrust stakes into the earth when there is no reason. Those who do it will have to uproot the stakes in the world beyond by pushing them with their eyes" (Niculiţa Voronca 1903: 563).[2]

Often the sacrifice is accompanied by the deposit of gold and silver

[2]   This idea of "compensation" due to the earth spirit is encountered again during funerals: "At the moment when the deceased is lowered into the grave, the husband or the wife, the mother or the sister, or one of the members of the family, throws into the grave some silver coins, with which the dead will be able to pay the earth, where he is going to live" (Marian 1892: 325).

coins in the four corners of the foundation that correspond to the four cardinal points of the compass. "When a man puts in gold coins, he places them with the intention of paying in order to avoid a death in the family" is the explanation with which we were regularly provided. If the earth spirit does not receive offerings, he seeks vengeance and the lives of the people or the livestock are in danger.

Another explanation is more widespread: any construction (no matter which) requires "a man's head" or "a soul" in order to be completed and to insure that it lasts. In this case, the peasants say they are consecrating the victim to God. At the moment of the immolation, the soul of the victim leaves its body and becomes "the guardian spirit, protector of the building (*stafia*)." If the sacrifice does not take place, the construction cannot be completed, and much later, the misfortunes which occur in the family (illnesses, death of livestock) are attributed to the absence of the sacrifice.

The process of the construction sacrifice is the same in Greece, in Bulgaria, and in Yugoslavia, all with the same sacrificial animals: cock, sheep, or ram. Here, for example, is the description of the sacrifice during the construction of a house in Yugoslavia:

When the building of a house is begun, the proprietor is obliged to slaughter an animal in order that the foundation be stable. The animal is sacrificed in the east corner in front of the first stone's location. Generally, a lamb or a chicken is slaughtered. The flesh of the sacrificial animal is consumed immediately after the sacrifice by the proprietor, his family, and the masons; only the head is buried (Filipović 1939: 494).

In an investigation carried out in Yugoslavia between 1963 and 1968, in twenty villages of the Timočka Krajina region (of which ten were Romanian and ten Serbo-Croatian), the sacrificed animals for construction of a new house were: for the Serbo-Croatians, lambs 48 percent, suckling pigs 5 percent and chickens 47 percent; for the Romanians, lambs 20 percent, suckling pigs 12 percent, and chickens 65 percent.

Hubert and Mauss, in their study on sacrifice, call an "objective sacrifice" that which is performed during construction: "The characteristic trait of objective sacrifice is that the principal end of the ritual affects by definition an object other than the victim; the things which are meant to be modified are outside the victim" (Hubert and Mauss 1898: 103). One observation can readily be made: above all, the sacrifice must prevent a danger. By the killing of the victim, the sacrificer avoids the death of a member of the domestic group, the danger having been transferred to the victim.

2. The second example that we have chosen is the sacrifice for the soul of the dead person (*comândare*). It is part of the funereal ritual which is comprised of two sacrifices: the first takes place at the moment of the lowering of the corpse into the tomb and is related to the burial; it thus consecrates the tomb. The second takes place during the ritual meal which follows the interment. This latter sacrifice, which we are going to analyze, is related to the raising of interdicts which weigh upon the family of the deceased.

A solemn reunion takes place after the funeral, from three to forty days after the death.[3] The interpretations of this festive meal are quite varied, but it is certain that it is related in some manner to the soul of the deceased. The ceremony necessitates laborious preparations and expense which often reduce the family of the deceased to poverty; a number of animals are sacrificed, and invitations are extended to all inhabitants of the village for this occasion.[4] The ceremony can be repeated at three-, six- and nine-month intervals, just as are certain periodical festivals, and it is celebrated in common for all those who have died in the interval. Once more, we see the appearance of the collective meal, which this time is entrusted with purification rites.

The killing of the animals which are eaten during the meal is done in a ritual fashion. The sequence is the same as for the construction sacrifice: consecration, immolation, and ritual meal. But the purification rites, which Hubert and Mauss call "the rites of entry and departure," are in this case obligatory. Thus, it is necessary to wash the animal's feet and turn it around while burning incense before the immolation. Similarly, all the participants in the festival wash their hands before and after the meal.

The sacrifice takes place at the house of the deceased, in the yard. It is performed late in the evening, after sunset, "when the stars are in the sky" (Marian 1892: 362). Another aspect to consider is the orientation of the victims. In the construction sacrifice, the victim is oriented toward the east, toward the rising sun, while in the sacrifice for the soul of the deceased, the victim is oriented toward the west. This orientation is related to the peasant belief according to which the souls direct themselves toward the west in order to join the world of the dead. The sacrificed animals

---

[3] After the separation from the body, the soul stays on the earth for an interval of forty days to a year (the delay varies according to the region), a period which corresponds to the decomposition of the cadaver. Before arriving at its final destination, the soul must complete a "stage," during which it stays on the earth in the vicinity of the cadaver, wandering in the forests or in the places which it inhabited while living. It is only at the end of this interval that the soul enters the land of the dead.

[4] Mary Durkham (1929) emphasizes the importance of the funereal meal in Montenegro and in Albania.

— sheep, rams, calves, and cattle — must be black. Before the immola-tion, the priest reads a prayer and places lighted candles on the animal's horns. The victims' throats are cut on the edge of a pit which is dug beforehand, and the participants in the ceremony take care not to be splattered by the blood.

For the meal, the place of the priest is designated in advance and the skin of the victim is deposited there. A place is also reserved for the deceased. At the end of the meal the family of the latter offers the priest a live cock and hen "for the soul of the dead."

In the two sacrifices that we have described, as in a good many others, the animal's throat is cut. In order to understand why the killing of the animal is accomplished by cutting the throat, we believe it is useful for us to refer to a story concerning death:

When a man is ready to die, the spirit of death, the Archangel, arrives with a scythe. He wrestles with the man in order to cut off his head; it is only thus that he manages to separate the soul from the body. All the walls of the room in which the man died are supposed to be splattered with blood three days after his death, and after his burial, the house is whitewashed to efface the bloodstains (Marian 1892: 368; see also Niculița Voronca 1903: 377).

The souls of those who die hanged, smothered, or drowned cannot leave the body and are transformed into demonic beings (*stryges*) who harm the living. Because of this, the greatest concern of the people is to help the dead leave the world of the living. The souls of the dead who are trans-formed into demonic beings can meddle with the living and provoke numerous misfortunes.

One of the means of freeing the soul and separating it from the body is to exhume the corpse suspected of having been transformed into a demon and cut off its head with a scythe or a sickle, as if this were being done to the spirit of death.

Dead animals which have been smothered accidentally or as the result of an illness are considered impure and it is absolutely forbidden to eat their meat.

We always encounter in these sacrifices the same domestic animals: cocks, hens, sheep, rams, calves, lambs, etc. Popular representations, as we have seen, distinguish between two categories of animals: pure and impure. The animals enumerated above are considered to be of divine essence and the offering of them, in consequence, will be received by God. On the other hand, cats, dogs, goats, and horses are considered impure, and everything they touch is tainted. The devil or other malevolent spirits (for example, the spirits of the dead transformed into *stryges*) can disguise themselves as dogs, cats, or goats. Among the winged creatures, the cock and hen play a particularly important role. The souls of the dead during their sojourn on earth are reputed to inhabit the body of a hen, sheep, or calf in order to purify themselves (Marian 1892: 492).

If the sacrifice is intended to cure a sick person who is near death, or to exorcise an epidemic, the sacrificial victim must be black. For certain diseases, such as epilepsy, impure animals (cats or dogs) of black color are sacrificed, but their throats are not cut; they are buried alive.

The two sacrifices that we have analyzed are intended to prevent a danger: the death of a member of the domestic group (or a mason in the case of a construction sacrifice) or the loss of its livestock. The life of the animal is offered in exchange for a human life. What is important is not what the man sacrifices, but the intention with which he offers it. If someone is poor, he can sacrifice a cock or a hen in place of a ram or a sheep.

The idea of "contract," of "redemption," which Hubert and Mauss have emphasized in their study on sacrifice, is evident.[5] The idea of contract is evidenced by the relationship of the peasants with the guardian spirit of the house (*stafia*) or with the spirits of the dead. A spirit that is cared for and nourished is no longer dangerous; on the contrary, he can serve men and protect them in their actions.

There is a permanent opposition between the world of the living and that of the dead. All the spirits of the dead live in the wild world: in nature, the forests, the deserted terrains, the mountains. The souls of the deceased must effect a passage from the world of the living into the world of the dead. The sacrificed animals help the deceased to make the passage and to arrive in the world beyond. Thus, the equilibrium between the dead and the living is restored.

REFERENCES

ARNAUDOFF, M.
1920 Vagradena nevesta. *Sbornik za narodni umotvornija i narodopis* 34: 245–512.
1921 Jertva per gradej. *Bulletin du musée ethnographie de Sofia* 3–4: 181–193.
BURDICK, L. D.
1901 *Foundation rites with some kindred ceremonies. A contribution to the study of beliefs, customs and legends connected with buildings.* London: Abbey Press.
CIAUSIANU, G.
1914 *Superstitiile poporului român în asemănare cu ále altor popoare vechi si nouă.* Bucharest: Academia Română.

---

[5] Hubert and Mauss (1898) state: "There is no sacrifice in which the idea of 're-demption' does not intervene."

COCCHIARA, G.
1950   *Il ponte di Arta e i sacrifici di construzione*. *Annali del Museo Pitré* 1: 38–81.

DURKHAM, M.
1929   "Birth, marriage and death," in *Some tribal origins, laws and customs of the Balkans*, 187–229. New York: Macmillan.

ELIADE, M.
1943   *Comentarii la legenda Meşterului Manole*. Bucharest: Publicom.
1970   "Maître Manole et le Monastère d'Arges," in *De Zalmoxis à Gengis Khan*, 162–185. Paris: Payot.

FILIPOVIČ, M. S.
1939   Običaji i verovanja u Skopskoj Kotlini. *Sprski Etnografski Sbornik* 56.

FRAZER, J. G.
1927   *Le cycle du rameau d'or*, volume three: *Tabou et les périls de l'âme*. Paris: P. Geuthner.

GUNDA, B.
1962   Die Raumaufteilung der Ungarischen Bauernstube, ihre gesellschaftliche Funktion und kultische Bedeutung. *Deutsches Jahrbuch für Volkskunde* 8(2): 368–391.

HERTZ, R.
1970   "Etude sur la représentation de la mort," in *Sociologie religieuse et folklore*, 1–83: Paris: Presses Universitaires de France.

HUBERT, M., M. MAUSS
1898   Essai sur la fonction et la nature du sacrifice. *Année sociologique* 2.

LAWSON, O.
1964   *Greek folklore and ancient Greek religion: a study in survivals*. New York: University Book.

MARIAN, S.
1892   *Inmormântarea la români*. Bucharest: Academia Română.

MEGAS, G.
1971   *To tragoudi tou gefiriou tis Artas*. Eug Kritiki meleti. Anatypon ek tis "Laografias," tom. KZ' 27. Athens.

MILOSFVIČ, M.
        Prinosanje žrtve pri zidanju stambenih zgrada u selima Timočke krajine. *Razvitak* 4–5.

MUŞLEA, I., O. BIRLEA
1970   *Tipologia folclorului după răspunsurile la chestionarul lui Hasdeu*. Bucharest: Minerva.

NICULITA VORONCA, E.
1903   *Datinele si credintele poporului român*. Cernăuţi.

PAMFILE, I.
1916   *Mitologie românească*, volume one: *Duşmani şi prietani ai omului*. Bucharest: Academia Română.

POLITIS, N.
1902   *Grand recueil des traditions*. Athens.

RÄNK, G.
1949   Die heilige Hinterecke im Hauskult der Völker nordosteuropas und nordasiens. Helsinki: *F.F. Communications* 138.

RICAUT
1696 *Histoire de l'état présent de l'église grecque et de l'église arménienne.* Amsterdam.

ROMAIOS, C. A.
1949 *Cultes populaires de la Thrace.* Athens.

ŞAINEANU, L.
1902 Les rites de construction d'après le poésie populaire de l'Europe orientale. *Revue de l'histoire des religions* 45: 359–396.

SARTORI, P.
1898 Über das Bauopfer. *Zeitschrift für Ethnologie* 30: 1–54.

STAHL, A.
1968 Stidiul riturilor de construcţie româneşti *Revista de etnografie şi folclor* 13(4):309–316.

TALOS, I.
1968 Riturile de construcţie le români. *Folclor literar* 2:222–262.

TRAJANOVIC, S.
1911 Sprski zvitveni običaji. *Sprski Etnografski Zbornik* 17.

TYLOR, E.
1924 *Primitive culture.* New York: Brentano.

VACARELSKI, C.
1969 *Bulgarische Volkskunde.* Berlin: Walter de Gruyter.

The Mystery Play and the Carnival

G. G. STRATANOVICH

As a theme, the mystery play and the carnival may be considered both new and old — new, because the concepts are not found in combination in the literature and because the events are experiencing a revival; old, because innumerable works have been devoted to them and because their origins lie in an epoch that preceded written language in the history of the culture of mankind.

A variety of definitions have been offered. The most common in regard to the mystery play is the concept traceable to an esoteric dramatized action (comprehensible to the initiated alone) built up around a mythological theme or a dramatized version of incidents from the Scriptures, or scenes from the "Lives of the Saints." In Russia, examples were the Christmastide "Fiery Furnace" play, the "Washing of the Disciples' Feet" on the Thursday before Easter, the "Entry into Jerusalem of Christ Riding an Ass" on Palm Sunday, and, in European countries, the "Passion Play" (Chudnovtsev 1970:4–5). The accepted idea of a carnival is of a riotously gay popular holiday with mummers and jesters in fantastic costumes. The general carnival program includes a procession, singing, and even a comic vocal contest, dances (for the most part grotesque), and parody scenes in which gestures, poses, and expressions familiar in a certain sphere of society are conveyed in traditional mimicry, easily recognizable by spectators whether they are accustomed to this kind of entertainment or educated to some degree. The farcical theme is always in the foreground. It is a satire, either as a whole or in the unfolding of its parts. Sometimes it might be satirical, whatever the nature of what is formally regarded as the principal part (Bakhtin 1965:57). Such, for example, are the Russian Shrovetide and the typical Italian carnivals.

The mystery drama, especially in Southeast Asian countries, is often merged with the carnival. In fact, it is sometimes hard to distinguish between them. Perhaps for this reason, it is often asserted that the carnival scenes are ennobled in the mystery play. More often, it is correctly argued that simultaneously with the mystery play, a "travesty" parodying it both in theme and language, a comic version of the carnival type, emerges. Examples of this are found in the *Batrakhomiomakhia* and the various forms of *Antihomeria* (supposed, with reason, to have been created by Homer himself) and in the Vietnam tragicomedies of the "how-the-mice-buried-the-cat" type. Occasionally the travestied scene is an unintentional parody, a topsy-turvy affair resulting from a reverse perception of the essentials of some event. As an instance, we may take the travestied scene of "The Theft of the Sun" by crows (in which skeletons hinder the theft, whereas in the original the sun is stolen from the crows) found in a Tibetan mystery play in numerous acts (Tsam-cakma) but also in the ritualistic dances (on Tsam, see Shastina 1935: 92–113).

The answer to the implied question of which is the more ancient — the mystery play or the carnival — is by no means easy to find. Let us trace the path of development of each.

In the West as in the East, the source of the mystery play lies in the *litia*, the esoteric rite of prayers pronounced while accompanying the corpse of some prominent member of the community from the temple to the burying-ground (or the dramatized farewell gathering for a dead god). Research scholars, both atheists and theologians, seem to have ignored this ritual.

Considerably more attention has been devoted to the exoteric *officia*, or services for the public. These were services of worship held in Christian churches at Christmastide, New Year, and Eastertide. They might take place within the sacred building or on the hallowed ground in front of it. In the East, not only the theatrical scenes enacted before the temple (for example, on the *noumshan* [the space in front of the temple or the home of the leader and governor], the *Duva*, of the Kachins of Burma), but also the ritualistic scenes enacted under the sacred tree in the marketplace, represent religious services. The transfer of ritualistic scenes from the confines of the temple to the streets heralded the appearance of two different types of theatrical performances.

The first of these, the mystery play, based on themes from religious classical canons, aimed at drawing the attention of the masses to the clerical dogmatists, increasing the number of believers by means of a more vivid presentation of the canons or ecclesiastical laws, more firmly establishing these canons as divinely inspired truths of God himself, and ensuring approbation of them.

The second medium of emotional influence, less important for the church at first but far more impressive and effective as a means of convincing "vacillating" believers, was the medieval "miracle" (from the Latin *miraculum*). Most frequently, this was a play in many acts or consecutive parts, showing the miracles worked by the deity and the saints. As these shows gained in popularity, they supplanted the mystery. Consequently, when the word "mystery" was used, it signified, more often than not, scenes of the "miracle" vairety.

In the East, the boundaries of these two groups of ritualized theatrical action were not so clearly marked. Just as, in the Buddhist Jatakas, episodes from the life of Buddha were interwoven with folklore in a form resembling novellas based on etiological myths, in the mystery plays episodes of a biographical nature were closely bound up with typical miracle scenes. For instance, the Lamaist and Mahayana performances show scenes of the struggle between Mara, the Ruler of the "Dark Kingdom," and the most sacred Buddha; in the same way, the triumph of Buddhism and the conversion of untold thousands of Mara's adversaries into legions of the defenders of the new faith were depicted. Other scenes were based on myths of the birth of the country and the people and on legends of heroes or ancestors, animal and other.

In both West and East, subjects reflecting the mythology and beliefs of olden times were presented in liturgical performances. A brief interpretation, with mimicry, of the etiological myth at first had no immediate relation to religion. Gradually, it was interspersed in a series of scenes of the "appearance-of-the-deity-to-the-people" type, thus creating an impression of "implication," of the actual presence of the deity in the personification witnessed at public celebrations such as "thanksgiving" or "repulsion-of-evil" as well as public supplications for blessings. In the course of its development, the mystery play underwent transformation into an intricate complex of liturgical action, processions, and prayers. The basic element in this complex frequently bore a resemblance to the religious processions involving sacred objects — gonfalons or sacred banners, icons, conventionalized effigies of the deity or a statue of the Virgin Mary (as at anniversary celebrations in Brittany or in Central America). In some instances, as in Greek *phallofores* processions (and later in those of the Latin peoples) and in certain Asian countries until comparatively recent times, phallic symbols and the "tree of life" were carried. Processions of this kind closely resemble the carnival. The distinction lies in the substance of these demonstrations.

Undoubtedly, the carnival is the more ancient in origin, dating back to the period of transition from isolated individual synthetized experience, which opened the way for that essential element of the production process most aptly termed "training" and led to religious performances or displays. The carnival proceeds through definite stages from crude enactment of production processes through a period of generalization of experience in which attempts are made to depict in scenes or acts some important social event (that is, important for the society at the prevailing level of production development).

In the West, the sources of the carnival are only dimly discernible, while in the East some of its earlier features have survived almost to our own day. For example, the Chinese *yange* of antiquity is widespread in East and Southeast Asia as the rice-planting ritual, the song-and-dance culmination of the labor process of transplanting the seedlings (Komarovskiĭ and Stratanovich 1966; Utida 1966). A role of immense importance in this ritual is played by biorhythmics, preserving the work rhythms but accelerating their cohesive effect. The rite symbolizing the idea of training remained nonreligious for a very long period. A similar instance is found in ritual assemblies of warriors and huntsmen among the Chinese of antiquity (or, to be exact, their ancestors). This was discovered in one of the complex early sources, *Shan-hai Ching*; it is said of the Po Mountains:

The first mountain is a demon to which offerings are made of glutinous rice, a black sacrificial animal, and vessels for the ritual of the Great Invocation. Liquor is brewed from the juice of intoxicating roots and drunk. The thousand participants in the ritual dance and beat the drums in their excitement (*Shan-hai Ching* 1936).

At celebrations in honor of the Bear Mountain:

A dance with weapons is performed to ensure the harvest. A headdress made of tinkling precious stones (the Tsiu stones) is donned, and they dance to the sound of the stones (*Shan-hai Ching* 1936:84).

Here we have plain evidence of the biorhythmic collective dance to ritualistic music of a military or hunting type (drum rhythms), which undoubtedly produces a cohesive effect.

The recorder of this ancient rite, making notes from its oral transmission (perhaps a thousand years after the actual event), endows it with the character of a magical effect,[1] deepened by intoxication. In fact,

---

[1]   The term "magic" is often used in referring to these rites and similar activities. But as Tokarev (1959:73), the eminent Soviet ethnographer and student of religions, has said: The connection between activity of a magical kind and corresponding forms of reasoned human activity is so close that at times it is impossible to determine the

however, we are dealing here with a celebration of the culmination of a massed military or hunting exploit familiar to us from studies of the Naga and Wa of Burma.

According to our own information dating from 1957 and accounts by learned Burmese research scholars (U Min Naing 1960, 1962), the Naga people live in such scattered groups that linguistic unity has been lost. Each clan occupies its own territory, which is often a mountain gorge. Among the Khemi Naga alone (one of the three tribes of the San Naga, the second of the four main subgroups of Naga), there are forty-nine of these clans. The social role of the tribal spring and autumn assemblies is of exceptional importance. It takes the place of military-and-hunting training for the men, occasions contact with the rest of the groups, and is a kind of holiday for all clansmen capable of taking part in the assembly, the carnival procession, and the ritual feast. Similar training assemblies, concluding with festivities of the carnival type, are observed among the mountain people of Laos and North Vietnam.

The meaning of the carnival performances associated with early cultivation of the land is less easily grasped. These take place near or in the fields during the transplanting of rice seedlings and the harvest and in the village later. Like the *yange*, these occur among many nationalities in Southeast Asia and in Japan; they take the form of stages in the production process — clearing and burning the land, turning the soil, setting the seed in holes made with sticks, protecting the rice from the ravages of wild pigs and monkeys, threshing the grain (this process is omitted by all but a few nationalities, among them the Tkhai of Northwest Vietnam), and finally the "harvest-home" of the "Mistress of the Rice" (or the "Soul of the Rice") that we encounter occasionally in the literature. It is to be regretted that these, like many other training performances, have attracted scarcely any attention from research scholars (see Utida 1966; Komarovskiĭ and Stratanovich 1966). Far more attention is devoted to scenes we would group under the heading of fertility stimulation ritual.

In a developed, slave-owning, feudal society and in capitalist societies carnal relations ceased to be regarded as one of the two principal forms of production; but in early society reproduction of the human collective

---

borderline between them. It is especially difficult to establish this boundary in elementary, embryonic forms of magic.... The borderline is at first purely subjective. One or another approach ... rational in its basis, is gradually realized by the individual himself [by the society] as witchcraft, that is — action based upon supernatural association of phenomena. The determinant here is the idea of the supernatural, the same that is characteristic of any religious phenomenon. A large proportion of all that has been recorded in the arsenal of magic, and lays claim to infallibility, is wholly unsubstantiated.

retained its aureole of noble purpose. In developed clan society, the social purpose of the process maintained its ascendancy over the biological. Even stock breeders, who understood clearly the cause-and-effect linking the act of uniting the sexes and appearance of progeny, readily accepted the idea of the return of the ancestor to the world of the descendants by penetration in the form of an embryo into the bosom of the future mother through the mouth or the skin of the hollow between the breasts while she stood close to the totem-center (hence the age-old idea of "immaculate conception"). True comprehension of the act of conception without human intervention was found in nature alone, and it was considered that the ritualistic union of couples in the fields (followed by the collective act of sexual union) had the power to stimulate fertility of the soil, of rice, vegetables, animals, and birds. The direct transition from this was worship of the generative organs, the stimulators of fertility, the making of ritual vessels and tools in their form, their depiction upon banners, etc., the poles crowned with branches of the tree of life and hung with molded or sculptured generative organs, separate or merged — in short, all that had been typical of the phallic processions in ancient Greece and Rome and, in epochs nearer to our own times, in the processions of suppliants to Nammon in Thailand, the *noniung* in Vietnam, etc. (Rajadhon 1960: 39–40).

An instance of direct stimulation of fertility has survived almost to our own day in Thailand (and also in Burma and Laos, among other places) in the carnival-type procession to the fields on the eve of the rainy season. The culmination of this activity is the preparation of *pan-mek*, [effigies of embracing couples]. These sculptures, which are sometimes life-size, have totally supplanted the living couples in the ritual. Various poses from olden times are repeated. The effigies are made from a finely ground clay mixture, easily eroded by the rains. The belief persists that the sooner the rain washes them away, the more abundant will be the harvest and the greater the fecundity of the cattle (if the effigies should remain intact until the field is flooded, this means misfortune) (Rajadhon 1960:39–40).

In the mountainous regions of North Vietnam, after a series of preliminary scenes (after the harvest) within the village, a procession advanced, singing and dancing, to the fields, and the demonstration reached its culmination at the community water source, a stream or a drainage canal. On the banks of this watercourse women were given a chance to shake the ritual pole, the "tree of life," and catch in their raised, widespread skirts the clay models of generative organs that fell from it. It was believed that whoever caught one would soon produce a son or daughter (according to the sex of the organ). Songs, jokes, and comic dialogues were full of direct or allegorical allusions. In the text of these, a tail (or the lotus) symbolized the male organ, a bosom (or the tortoise) symbolized the female organ. Good wishes were expressed for the birth of many sons and for the health of the future offspring and the parents. But even when the plainest terms were used in the songs or the comic dialogues of sham quarrels, they were always perfectly natural expressions of moral purity, while the lustful, the greedy, and the mercenary were ridiculed (Nikulin, 1969:203–230). Perhaps it is for this reason that in the feudal societies of Southeast Asia and in Japan (which in certain features resembles them) the industry of sexual voluptuousness never gained a footing; the molded or painted symbols which had no direct connection with any phallic cult were invariably grotesque, in keeping with the carnival spirit (van Gulik n.d.: 85–95).

In class society, the carnival becomes a demonstration in which "ambivalence of laughter" is no longer adequate. Mordant satire is all-pervasive. It is the inevitable outcome of three circumstances: (1) class oppression, leading to the "supercharging of the existing situation to the point of explosion"; (2) the emergence of towns and trading settlements, parallel to the dismemberment of the population by the antagonistic social class structure — the ruling upper stratum and the lower ranks (proletarianized artisans, transport workers, and men in other public "services"; *déclassé* elements of different origin); and (3) the realization by the municipal governing body (and, in the capital, the ruler and administrative officials) that at times it was simply necessary to "let off steam" and that the mockery allowed at the carnival was a harmless safety valve for popular indignation. The participants from the rank-and-file realized that they were not yet prepared for revolt. The time for mock rebellions came when those who took part in them could obtain — depending upon the circumstances — not only a taste of freedom, but also a temporary grasp of administrative powers. Carnival days were a time of toleration. It was understood that the powers would not venture to hinder public ridicule of the most ferocious oppressors or even the most formidable measures.

In the southeastern coastal region of China, official sources designate the fifteen-day carnival period in the first moon of the New Year as a time of total anarchy. In Southeast Asia, where towns were not such many-faceted organizations, there is no record of periods of anarchy such as these. Even among the Chinese population, New Year processions with mummers were comparatively widespread. We saw the carnival performance of "The Dragon's Attempt to Swallow the Sun" enacted in

1957 in Mitchina (Burma). At each house good wishes were expressed in honor of the year, the master of the house, his family, and China. They were accompanied, however, by comparatively rowdy escapades, by a group of "turbulent youths" permitted — through the connivance or the aloofness of the local government — to do whatever they liked. Research scholars in Thailand, Laos, Burma, and North Vietnam have remarked upon the same thing. New Year celebrations among the people of Burma, Thailand, and Laos closely resemble in type those described here. In the literature on the subject, they are considered as imitative-magical ceremonies connected with the evocation of rain. Even if the possibility of postponing monsoons and rainy seasons were to be admitted, imitative-magical evocation of rain, or prayer for rain, appears pointless for all Southeast Asian groups. We can only suppose that this ritual originated among the ancestors of many Southeast Asian peoples, who may have come from northern regions where droughts were prevalent.

The survival of the "water-madness," when the ban on rowdiness was lifted and, though it was customary to respect old people, even small children could douse the aged grandmother with cold water — or, again, "patriotic" youth could turn the hose on an "ex-colonialist," European or American — shows that wild carnival gaiety afforded an outlet for protest against overstrict religious and social norms.

Occasionally, one encounters in the Burmese holidays and Thai *songran* features reminiscent of the north Indian *holi* [dousing with water stained with red lead, soot, or dirt]. The thesis is that rain and the rice crop depend upon the good-humored reaction of the victims of these jokes. Any expression of displeasure or offense may result in failure of the crop, cattle disease, and the spread of disease among people.

With the passage of time, the increasing participation of peasants in the struggle for their liberty and rights, the growth of class consciousness, and influence of the results of two series of peasant wars (in the mid-nineteenth century and in the 1930's) led to change in the carnival and the mystery play. In the latter, Messianic ideas, hopes of some miraculous liberation, or expectation of benefits from an external source make their appearance. Carnivals show increasing popularity of the tendency to ridicule colonial oppressors and of appeals to the masses to unite in their own country and with the masses in other countries whose destiny resembles their own; the theme of liberation assumes an increasingly important place and ultimately becomes the leading, and even the sole, theme.

The liberation of the peoples of Asia and Africa from the colonial yoke, the people's victory over their exploiters in the course of democratic and socialist revolutions, mark the turning point at which the carnival and, to some extent, the mystery play acquire new life, a new meaning, and a new form. The first example of the new type of carnival was the fairy-play that appeared in Soviet Russia immediately after the victory of the great October Socialist Revolution. O. Tsekhnovitser, an observer of insight and author of research on the new culture of the broadest masses of toilers in our country, stressed the fact that the revolutionary fairy-play justified this term in every respect. It was "a performance with lavish decor, on a magic theme, a magical fairy-like display" in which the place of the fairy was taken by the Revolution itself. I had the good fortune to see these performances at the very outset of the 1920's. These were difficult years for the Soviet Republic, and consequently carnivals and shows had to be of a somewhat restrained character, but even so, they made a lifelong impression. The principal mass demonstrations were timed for the May Day holidays and the anniversaries of the October Revolution. As an eyewitness I could not simultaneously be in the thick of things and observe different parts of the carnival composition that unfolded against the background of the whole city of Petrograd (as it was then called). The decor of the portion within my field of vision was the "arrow" of Vasilievsky Island, and the main action took place on the steps of the "acropolis" of what was once the Stock Exchange (now the Army and Navy Museum) and that section of the Lesser Neva reaching as far as Tuchkov Bridge, with the brilliantly illuminated keelwater line of ships. The central theme and the course of the dramatic action were merely sketched in outline. This offered the widest scope for the fairy display, especially as all the spectators inevitably became participants. This was the case, for instance, with a relatively large unit of revolutionary troops whose line of march lay across the scene of the demonstration and with the seamen allowed ashore at the time. As the action unfolded, its boundaries extended to include the crowd of spectators. The musical composition of the display was also impromptu; besides the prearranged band of wind instruments, the drummers of the military and the chorus of spectators could be included, as occasion arose, with suitable revolutionary songs and marches.

In later times, as new tasks confronted our country, carnival themes became concrete, topical, politically purposeful, less general and more particular. The display itself acquired a more distinct scenic character. But the purely carnival forms persist in the decor and design of holiday demonstrations.

The history of the development of the carnival in the countries where communism triumphed, in those with a people's democracy, and in those that have won independence passes through approximately the same phases. More often than not, the underlying meaning of the vast scale of the popular holidays reproduces the struggle for national liberation and its triumphant culmination. Purely carnival effects persist in processions of people in national costumes on holidays (such as Burma's Union Day, February 12) and at displays of singing and dancing.

REFERENCES

BAKHTIN, M. M.
1965   *Tvorchestvo Fransua Rable* [The work of François Rabelais]. Moscow.
CHAKRAVARTI, C.
1963   *Sex life in ancient India.* Calcutta.
CHUDNOVTSEV, M. I.
1970   *Tserkov' i teatr* [Church and theater]. Moscow.
DANG NGIEM VAN
1972   An outline of the Thai of Viet-Nam. *Vietnamese Studies* 1 (32).
KOMAROVSKIĬ, G. E., G. G. STRATANOVICH
1966   Risovodcheskaia abriâdnost' i eë mesto v kul'te Privody u narodov Vostochnoĭ i IUgo-Vostochnoĭ Azii [The rice-planting ritual and its place in the cult of nature among the peoples of eastern and southeastern Asia]. *Sovetskaiâ etnografiiâ* 2.
NGUYEN TU CHI
1972   A Muong sketch. *Vietnamese Studies* 1 (32).
NIKULIN, N. I.
1969   "O poezii Kho Suan Khyong [On the poetry of Ho Suan Hyong]," in *Teoreticheskie problemy vostochnykh literatur.* Moscow.
RAJADHON, PYA ANNUMAN
1960   Fertility rites in Thailand. *Journal of the Siam Society* 48 (2). Bangkok.
Shan-hai Ching
1936   (Svod Goram i moriam) [Arch to the mountains and seas] (in Chinese). Shanghai.
SHASTINA, N. P.
1935   Religioznaiâ misteriiâ "Tsam" v monastyre Dzun-khure [The religious mystery *Tsam* in the Dzun-hure monastery]. *Sovremennaiâ Mongoliiâ* 1 (8).
TOKAREV, S. A.
1959   Sushchnost' i proiskhozhdenie magii [The essence and origin of magic]. *Trudy I.E. A.N. S.S.S.R.* n.s. 51.
U MIN NAING
1960   *Rases of Burma* (in Burmese). Rangoon.
1962   *Palaungs of Burma* (in Burmese). Rangoon.
n.d.   *Manao* (in Burmese).
UTIDA, RURIKO
1966   Tauè saĭ. *Sovetskaiâ etnografiiâ* 2.
VAN GULIK, W. R.
n.d.   De Tengu: een merkwaardige Langneus [Demon in Japan]. *Verre naasten naderbij* 3.

Mythic Elements of Petroglyph Sites in the Upper Ohio Valley

JAMES L. SWAUGER

Carnegie Museum researchers define the Upper Ohio Valley as ". . . all territory draining into the Ohio River Basin upstream from New Martinsville, W.Va." (Mayer-Oakes 1955: 36). At its greatest extent north to south, the Upper Ohio Valley is about 250 miles long; at its greatest extent east to west, it is about 125 miles wide. In area it covers about 23,000 square miles in fifty-six counties of the five states of Maryland, New York, Ohio, Pennsylvania, and West Virginia (Plate 1a).

Twenty-nine petroglyph sites have been investigated in the region. Twenty-one are believed to be American Indian. Discrete site descriptions of fifteen of them have been published (see Swauger references), and one has been submitted for publication to the *Ohio Archaeologist*. A full report on the complete petroglyph complex is in preparation (Swauger i.p.), and this article contains the gist of the conclusions of that report.

The first step to understanding archaeological phenomena is to place them in an acceptable chronological and cultural framework. Logic requires that Upper Ohio Valley petroglyphs be placed in the following order:

8000 – 3000 B.C.: Paleo-Indian
3000 – 1000 B.C.: Archaic
1000 – 100 B.C.: Early Woodland (locally, particularly the Adena)
100 B.C. – A.D. 900: Middle Woodland (locally, particularly the Hopewell)
A.D. 900 – 1600: Late Prehistoric

A.D. 1600 – present: Historic (Mayer-Oakes 1955: 8).

The rate of deterioration of outlines of figures, as exemplified by those on the Indian God Rock on the Allegheny River near Franklin, Pennsylvania, is rapid. When discovered by a French expedition in 1749, the figures on the God Rock were evidently very clear (Lambing 1885–1886; Marshall 1878; de Bonnécamps 1750). By the 1930's the figures were difficult to see (Lewis 1950–1960, personal communications). In 1958 Edwin L. Peterson, a keen and competent observer, described them as very dim (Peterson 1958: 127). Dates carved on this and other sites less than a hundred years ago are already faint.

While I do not find figures on the God Rock as difficult to discern as did Lewis and Peterson, I cannot find some figures shown on Captain Seth Eastman's portrayal of the site for Henry R. Schoolcraft in the middle of the nineteenth century (Schoolcraft 1853–1856: IV, Plate 18). It is certain that the petroglyphs have become noticeably dimmer within the last two centuries. This being so, I do not believe they could have been packed and rubbed during the distant Paleo-Indian or the more recent Archaic periods.

The succeeding Early and Middle Woodland periods cover the years from about 1000 B.C. to about A.D. 900. Conceivably they are in chronological range even though the rate of deterioration of the petroglyphs would seem to rule against their having been produced as much as a thousand years ago. Another factor also rules against their having been created by Early and Middle Woodland peoples. The Adena and the Hopewell, who represent some of the strongest local manifestations of these periods, were accomplished artisans. It is unlikely that they would not put special effort into religious figures, and produce much finer results than those of our Upper Ohio Valley sites where the best work was done with naturalistic figures.

Only the Late Prehistoric and Historic periods remain. With respect to the latter, on our sites there are no designs indicating European contact. In those instances where houses, horses, guns, flags, or men with hats occur, they are palpably recent and were carved with metal tools. I am confident no American Indian carved a site in the Upper Ohio Valley in which motifs from both Indian and white settler sources were mingled.

By elimination, then, I believe our petroglyphs were carved sometime between A.D. 900 and 1750, for European penetration into the Upper Ohio Valley was not significant until about 1750. This is the time of the Late Prehistoric period. The rate of deterioration indicates that the sites were not created earlier than A.D. 1200.

The most important Late Prehistoric group in our area is archaeologically known as Monongahela Man, a local designation for the bearers of Monongahela Woodland Culture (Butler 1939: 9; see also Dragoo 1970, for a discussion of variation and complexity among the groups labeled Monongahela Man). Characteristic Monongahela Man settlements were being established sometime between A.D. 1200 and 1400 during which time some of our petroglyph sites probably were carved. Distribution of petroglyph sites and Monongahela Man villages is in some respects similar, but I have been unable to associate a particular petroglyph site with a particular village site and cannot say Monongahela Man site distribution proves association between Monongahela Man and the petroglyphs. It is likely, however, that Upper Ohio Valley petroglyphs were carved between A.D. 1200 and 1750 by people of the group known as Monongahela Man.

Understanding of petroglyph sites is achieved primarily by interpretation of petroglyph designs. Nearly ninety years ago Garrick Mallery detailed the difficulties of interpreting pictographic and petroglyphic symbolism even for living tribes (Mallery 1886: 16; 1893: 45, 46). Interpreting such symbolism for people known only archaeologically is infinitely more difficult, and the process is in its infancy in regard to Upper Ohio Valley petroglyph sites.

Nevertheless, efforts to achieve understanding by studying petroglyph figures resulted in a hypothesis concerning cultural identity between Monongahela Man and another historically known tribe. A large number of figures on petroglyph sites in the Upper Ohio Valley are of the same genre as figures on birchbark scrolls used as memory aids in Ojibwa *Midéwiwin* or Grand Medicine Society rites, as reported and illustrated particularly by Henry R. Schoolcraft (1853–1856) and W. J. Hoffman (1888, 1891) (see Plate 1, b through i). Long ago Mallery pointed to this fact (Mallery 1893: 680).

The similarities between figures on our sites and those on *midé* scrolls is too evident to be coincidental. The conclusion is inescapable that those who carved our petroglyphs were somehow associated with Ojibwa.

From archaeological evidence, Ojibwa folk history, and eighteenth-century written records, it is evident that there have never been significant numbers of Ojibwa in the Upper Ohio Valley. It is not plausible that there were ever enough of them in the region to have created the petroglyph sites.

I prefer the hypothesis that association between those who carved our petroglyphs and the Ojibwa was more remote in time and space. It is possible that the artists of the Upper Ohio Valley petroglyph sites did not share the *midé* concept with Ojibwa but did share an older set of spiritual concepts and a set of symbols to express them with the Ojibwa and other historic tribes that had the *midé* concept, such as the Fox, Pottawatomie, Sauk, Menominee, and Winnebago (Trowbridge 1939: 36).

These are all Eastern Woodland tribes and, except for the Winnebago, they speak an Algonquian tongue. Since mythic concepts and the symbolism to express them usually travel along linguistic lines, it is likely that the petroglyphs of the Upper Ohio Valley were carved between A.D. 1200 and 1750 by Late Prehistoric Monongahela Man and that Monongahela Man spoke an Algonquian language.

Of the historic groups speaking an Algonquian tongue, the one most likely to have had ancestors inhabiting the Upper Ohio Valley during the Late Prehistoric Period was the Shawnee; therefore, I suggest that archaeological Monongahela Man was prehistoric Shawnee.

This suggestion is not entirely original with me, nor is this the first time I have advanced it publicly (Swauger 1963a, 1966a, 1968a, 1972a). The hypothesis is buttressed by the work of a number of other investigators from the disciplines of archaeology, physical anthropology, ethnology, and history.

In 1947, Mary Butler, who defined Monongahela Woodland Culture, posed the question: "Were the Shawnee the bearers of Monongahela Woodland Culture?" (Butler 1947: 121, 122). In 1952, James B. Griffin suggested equating historic Shawnee with some of the groups indentified archaeologically as Fort Ancient (Griffin 1952: 364). In 1954, Glenn A. Black and George K. Neumann found Griffin's idea acceptable on physical, archaeological, ethnological, and historical grounds (Black 1954: 333; Neumann 1954: 360). In 1955, William J. Mayer-Oakes emphasized relations between the Clover Complex of Fort Ancient and Monongahela Man (Mayer-Oakes 1955: 12, 122, 123, 164, 171, 220, 228). Space dispersion and variation in many aspects of material culture among Monongahela Man and Fort Ancient groups is consistent with the documented tendency of historic Shawnee and culturally related peoples to split into small groups and wander away from each other (Voegelin 1954: 57, 93).

The gaps between historic Shawnee and the Algonquian-speaking, Eastern Woodland Ojibwa are not bridged by producing evidence that they used the same symbols in a shared cult. Indeed, Erminie Voegelin points out that the Grand Medicine Society which existed among the Ojibwa did not exist among the Shawnee (Voegelin in Trowbridge 1939: 36).

However, I suggest that, as the Algonquian tribal groups dispersed from an ancestral center somewhere in the northeastern United States and/or southeastern Canada and began moving west and south, most, if not all, retained the symbols, but that some groups such as Monongahela Man forgot, discarded, or more likely did not develop the *Midéwiwin* ritual. The Grand Medicine Society may not be ancient. It was in existence prior to the coming of Europeans to the Great Lakes region (Kinietz 1940: 215–217), but it was possibly not very old at that time and did not become a recognizable formal ceremony until "about the turn of the 18th century" (Hickerson 1962: 6). It includes in such elements as the physical arrangement of its lodge similarities to European models such as Masonic lodges (Olafson 1971, personal communication).

If so, the application of an ancient symbolism as part of a developing *Midéwiwin* ritual was taking place during the period immediately prior to the advent of Europeans into the Upper Ohio Valley precisely during the years when Monongahela Man was living in the region and symbols like those of *midé* bark scrolls were being carved on our petroglyph sites. Further, the full development of the *Midéwiwin* ritual was taking place when there was little contact between the Algonquian-speaking peoples of the Great Lakes region and the Algonquian-speaking Monongahela Man.

Although there is no incontestable physical evidence in support of the hypothesis, I am gratified that intensive study of the petroglyphs of the Upper Ohio Valley yields the foundation for an acceptable theory.

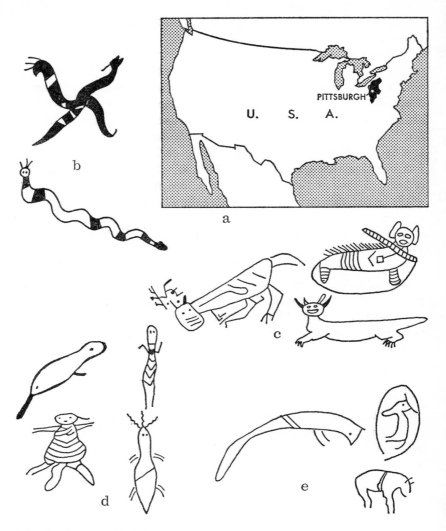

Plate 1.   Some mythic figures on petroglyph sites in the Upper Ohio Valley:
a.   Location of the Upper Ohio Valley.
b.   Upper figure: Schoolcraft (1853: I, 411, Plate 59).
       Lower figure: Dam Number 8 Site, Columbiana County, Ohio.
c.   Left figure: Parkers Landing Site, Clarion County, Pennsylvania.
       Right upper figure: Schoolcraft (1853: I, 385, Plate 53).
       Right lower figure: Schoolcraft (1853: I, 407, Plate 57).
d.   Left upper figure: Smith's Ferry Site, Beaver County, Pennsylvania.
       Left lower figure: Francis Farm Site, Fayette County, Pennsylvania.
       Right upper figure; Indian God Rock, Venango County, Pennsylvania.
       Right lower figure: Hoffman (1891: 253).
e.   Left figure: Parkers Landing Site, Clarion County, Pennsylvania.
       Right upper figure: Hoffman (1891: 292).

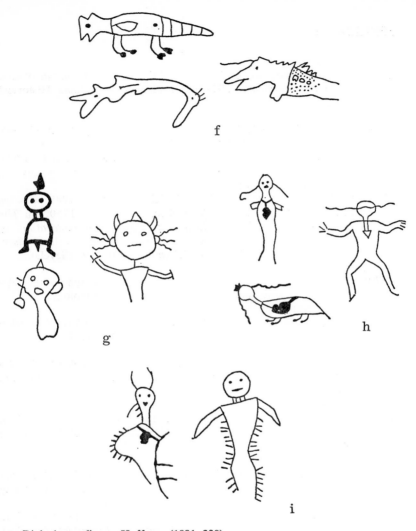

Right lower figure: Hoffman (1891: 230).
f.   Left upper figure: Brown's Island Site, Hancock County, West Virginia.
     Left lower figure: Brown's Island Site, Hancock County, West Virginia.
     Right figure: Schoolcraft (1853: I, 387, Plate 54).
g.   Upper left figure: Smith's Ferry Site, Beaver County, Pennsylvania.
     Lower left figure: Dam Number 8 Site, Columbiana County, Ohio.
     Right figure: Schoolcraft (1853: I, 385, Plate 53).
h.   Upper left figure: Dam Number 8 Site, Columbiana County, Ohio.
     Lower left figure: Babb's Island Site, Columbiana County, Ohio.
     Right figure: Hoffman (1891: 196).
i.   Left figure: Babb's Island Site, Columbiana County, Ohio.
     Right figure: Hoffman (1891: 272).
Note: Where no source is given, the figures are from the author's field records.

REFERENCES

BLACK, GLENN A.
1954   "An archaeological consideration of the Walam Olum," in *Walam Olum or Red Score,* 292–348. Indianapolis: Indiana Historical Society.

BUTLER, MARY
1939   *Three archaeological sites in Somerset County, Pennsylvania.* Pennsylvania Historical Commission, Bulletin 753. Harrisburg.
1947   Pottery types in Pennsylvania. *Pennsylvania Archaeologist* 17(1): 117–122. Harrisburg: Society for Pennsylvania Archaeology.

DE BONNÉCAMPS, JOSEPH PIERRE
1750   "Relation du voyage de la Belle Rivière fait en 1749 sous les ordres de M. de Céleron. A Québec, October 17, 1750," in *The Jesuit relations and allied documents, travels and explorations of the Jesuit missionaries in New France, 1610–1791,* volume sixty-nine. Edited by Reuben Gold Thwaites, 150–199. Cleveland.

DRAGOO, DON W.
1970   *Remarks on Monongahela Man.* Monongahela Symposium. Allegheny Chapter, Society for Pennsylvania Archaeology.

GRIFFIN, JAMES BENNETT
1943   *The Fort Ancient aspect: its cultural and chronological position in Mississippi Valley Archaeology.* Ann Arbor: University of Michigan Press.
1952   "Culture periods in eastern United States archeology," in *Archeology of eastern United States.* Edited by James B. Griffin. Chicago.

HICKERSON, HAROLD
1962   *The Southwestern Chippewa: an ethno-historical study.* American Anthropological Association, Memoir 92. *American Anthropologist* 64(3):Part 2.

HOFFMAN, W. J.
1888   Pictography and shamanistic rites of the Ojibwa. *The American Anthropologist* 1:209–229. Washington: Anthropological Society of Washington.
1891   "The *Midéwiwin* or 'Grand Medicine Society' of the Ojibwa," in *Seventh Annual Report of the Bureau of Ethnology* 143–300. Washington.

KINIETZ, W. VERNON
1940   *The Indians of the western Great Lakes, 1615–1760.* Museum of Anthropology of the University of Michigan, Occasional Contributions 10. Ann Arbor: University of Michigan Press.

LAMBING, A. A., *translator*
1885–1886   Translation of the journal of Céloron de Blainville. *Catholic Historical Researches* 2–3:61–76, 103–117, 132–146. Pittsburgh.

MALLERY, GARRICK
1886   "Pictographs of the North American Indians, a preliminary paper," in *Fourth Annual Report of the Bureau of Ethnology* 5–256. Washington.

1893 "Picture writing of the American Indians," in *Tenth Annual Report of the Bureau of Ethnology* 5–822. Washington.
MARSHALL, JOHN
1878 De Céloron's expedition to the Ohio. *Magazine of American History* 2–3:129–150.
MAYER-OAKES, WILLIAM J.
1955 *Prehistory of the Upper Ohio Valley: an introductory archeological study*. Annals of the Carnegie Museum 34. Pittsburgh.
NEUMANN, GEORGE K.
1954 "The Walam Olum in light of physical anthropological data on the Lenape," in *Walam Olum or Red Score*, 349–365. Indianapolis: Indiana Historical Society.
PETERSON, EDWIN L.
1958 *Penn's woods west*. Pittsburgh: University of Pittsburgh Press.
SCHOOLCRAFT, HENRY R.
1853–1856 *Information respecting the history, condition and prospect of the Indian tribes of the United States*, five volumes. Philadelphia: Lippincott, Grambo.
SWAUGER, JAMES L.
1963a Address at the 28th annual meeting, Society for American Archaeology, May 1963. Boulder, Colorado.
1963b Petroglyphs at the Hamilton Farm Site, Monongahela County, West Virginia. *West Virginia Archaeologist* 15:1–6.
1963c The Table Rock petroglyphs site, 46-Oh-68. *West Virginia Archaeologist* 16:5–11.
1964a The Timmons Farm petroglyphs site, 46-Oh-64. *West Virginia Archaeologist* 17:1–8.
1964b The Francis Farm petroglyphs site, 36 Fa 35. *Pennsylvania Archaeologist* 34(2)53–61.
1964c The New Geneva petroglyphs site, 36 Fa 37. *Pennsylvania Archaeologist* 34(2):62–68.
1965 The Sugar Grove petroglyphs site, 36 Gr 5. *Pennsylvania Archaeologist* 35(1):50–56.
1966a Address at the sixty-fifth annual meeting, American Anthropological Association, November 1966. Pittsburgh, Pennsylvania.
1966b The Parkers Landing petroglyphs site, 36 Cl 1. *Pennsylvania Archaeologist* 36(1-2):1–11.
1968a The Dam Number 8 petroglyphs site, 33 Co 2. *Ohio Archaeologist* 18(1):4–11.
1968b The Midland petroglyphs site, 36 Bv 89. *Pennsylvania Archaeologist* 34(3–4):7, 8.
1968c The Circle Rock petroglyphs site, 36 Bv 13. *Pennsylvania Archaeologist* 34(3–4):8, 53, 54.
1969 Petroglyphs opposite Millsboro, 36 Fa 36. *Pennsylvania Archaeologist* 41(3):67–69
1970 The Brown's Island petroglyphs site, 46 Hk 8. *West Virginia Archaeologist* 21:5–19.
1971a The Dunn petroglyphs site (36-Fa-54). *Pennsylvania Archaeologist* 41(3):61–66.

1971b   The Cooksburg Bridge petroglyphs site (36-Cl-23). *Pennsylvania Archaeologist* 41(3):67–69.

1972a   Address at the Valcamonica 1972 symposium on pre- and proto-historic religions.

1972b   The Rainbow Rocks petroglyphs site, 36 Ve 20. *Pennsylvania Archaeologist* 42(3):37–42.

i.p.   *Rock Art of the Upper Ohio Valley.* Graz, Austria: Akademische Druck- und Verlagsanstalt.

n.d.   The Babb's Island petroglyphs site, 33 Co 3. Submitted to the *Ohio Archaeologist.*

TROWBRIDGE, C. C.

1939   *Shawnee traditions.* Edited by Erminie W. Voegelin and W. Vernon Kinietz. Museum of Anthropology of the University of Michigan, Occasional Contributions 9. Ann Arbor: University of Michigan Press.

VOEGELIN, ERMINIE W.

1954   "Ethnological observations," in *Walam Olum or Red Score*, 3–215. Indianapolis: Indiana Historical Society.

Family Religion in Japan: the Ie and Its Religious Faith

CHOSHU TAKEDA

The life of the Japanese family has been based religiously and socially upon ancestor worship. This is so because of the unique characteristics of the family system and of the form of ancestor worship that has existed in Japan. The family system, which is generally called *ie*, is the basic unit of Japanese society, and ancestor worship as a traditional and socioreligious institution has developed in close connection with the *ie* system.

Ie is a social system based upon one idea of a family. The word *ie* has three meanings: (1) a house or dwelling place, (2) family or home, and (3) lineal kinship or lineage originating from an ancestor and maintained generation after generation by a succession of patriarchs. These three meanings are in fact closely related as shown by the fact that a family — or ANY family — is supposed to have a genealogy of its own and also by the fact that a family LIVES in a house.

A conjugal family normally consists of a husband and a wife and their children. In Figure 1, (ab[cd]), (gh) and (cdef) are three families: they are independent or "nuclear." However, in Japan a family is inconceivable without or apart from some lineage. A family is usually considered as a "dependent" member of a larger entity called an *ie*.

Ie may be then best understood as a vertical lineage consisting of member families, living and dead, which are all related by blood, lineally and collaterally. Moreover, it is generally believed that the *ie* as such exists above and beyond all the members of a family of each generation. One instance of an *ie* lineage is (abcdefgh) in Figure 1. According to the Japanese concept the members together as a whole con-

stitute a certain lineage. They may or may not be living in the same household, but it is possible theoretically for any number of persons or families of the same *ie* lineage to live together. For example, there has been
found a case of as many as five generations of a family living in the same
household (Figure 2).

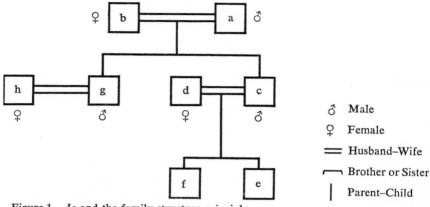

Figure 1. *Ie* and the family structure principle

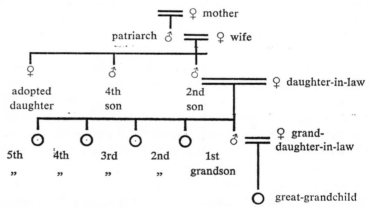

Figure 2. Example of family structure with many generations (taken from Toda
1937: 478)

The rule of descent that prevails in the *ie* lineage is patrilineal. But
exceptions to this rule have been admitted, supposedly to maintain gen-
erational continuity and ensure the succession of the *ie* without a break.
This will show that the Japanese *ie* is a matter of lineage itself rather
than of blood connection and that the social consideration is always
given priority over the biological in maintaining the *ie* lineage.

One example of such exceptions is the custom of bringing in a person who is a total stranger biologically but who will as an heir assume the senior position so that the lineage may not become extinct. In another case, a widow or sometimes a widower who has no children is allowed to assume this position, although she (or he) does not constitute a family by herself (or by himself).

In still another case, that is, when all the adult members die and there is no one living to succeed at the time, an infant orphan will be placed temporarily under the care of a different *ie* household. The rationale behind such an arrangement is that this infant orphan will someday, upon reaching the age of maturity, revive his native *ie*.

In a fourth instance, when there is no direct descendant surviving, the possession of the *ie* title, properties, ceremonial tools and the family tomb will be placed under the custody of some trustworthy person who is expected to find a suitable heir in the manner described above.

As the life of a Japanese is inconceivable apart from and without an *ie* — he can prove his place in society only by identifying himself with a certain *ie* lineage — the eternal continuity or eternity of the *ie* is a rule or norm for Japanese in general. Once established, an *ie* is supposed to last forever and never to become extinct. It exists even as an immanent entity as the last two examples cited above show.

Lastly, the ancestor is the genesis of this vertical *ie* lineage and the notion of an ancestor worship which is uniquely Japanese has emerged out of this presupposition. It is often pointed out by scholars that it is really the *ie* which is the basis of the ancestor cult in Japan. We shall next turn to the question of ancestor worship in Japan.

In every *ie* there is supposed to be an ancestor or one who founded the lineage. The implication of such a concept of the ancestor for each member family of the *ie* and each person is twofold: ethical and religious. Ethically, everyone of an *ie* is obliged to act in a way worthy of a distinguished lineage. In other words he is never to bring disgrace to the great names of his ancestors. Religiously, it is required of everyone in the *ie* to pay tribute to and show his respect for the ancestor. It is important to respect and worship the ancestor not only because he is the founder but also because he is ever concerned about the happiness and welfare of his descendants and has already given them enough protection and security.

Thus the concept of the ancestor as the genesis of the vertical *ie* lineage has existed in the general mentality of the Japanese as a postulate rather than as a fact. There are two other things to be said about ancestor worship in connection with the institution of the *ie*. First, it is not a matter of the individual's choice to accept or reject it. As a member of an *ie* he is bound by the obligations to worship his ancestor. Second, ancestor worship is a matter that concerns a family as a whole; that is, it is a family matter to hold the rites for the ancestors and observe various ceremonies dedicated to them. The concept of the ancestor serves as a postulate for the family as well as the individual.

This is perhaps a good place to discuss the nature of ancestor worship in Japan with a special emphasis on the religious meanings of the Japanese concept of the ancestor.

1.   The ancestor is a spiritual being or exists in spirit. Therefore it is not thought important that he should have human qualities or appear in a human form.

2.   The ancestor is a conglomerate being or a spiritual whole. In other words, it is supposed there is not one ancestor but many ancestors whose spirits merge into one or conglomerate indistinguishably to form a spiritual whole.

3.   The ancestor exists as a postulate or his existence is presupposed. It is not deemed necessary to have biological data for all the forebears now dead including the one who is supposed to have founded the *ie*. In fact, except in a few cases like the Imperial Family or families of some especially aristocratic lineages, the identity of the founder is not usually known. But this is not considered a serious defect. The important thing is to conceptualize the existence of some being who may be regarded as the founder.

4.   The ancestor is a sacred being. However, as a nameless being, he should be distinguished from the various deities who appear in classical Japanese mythology. The ancestor is nevertheless to be revered; otherwise divine retribution is sure to follow.

There are two more important observations to be made. The first is that the ancestor was often identified with the guardian god of a village or a province, the Rice Spirit, or some other agricultural deity. The reason is not difficult to find. As rice was the staple crop in Japan and the Japanese were devoted agriculturalists, the best thing that the Japanese could expect was a good harvest — of rice in particular. A rich harvest was the sign that the *ie* was in a happy and prosperous state, and it was widely believed that the hand of the benevolent and affectionate ancestor was at work here.

The second observation is that Buddhism, a foreign religion, had greatly influenced the form of ancestor worship. However, this is not so much the influence of Buddhism on the Japanese ancestor worship as the metamorphosis of Buddhism in the course of its interaction with the

Plate 1. Family tomb dedicated to the ancestral spirits of the *Ie* of the Yagis

Plate 2. *Kamidana*, [Shintoist divine shelf]

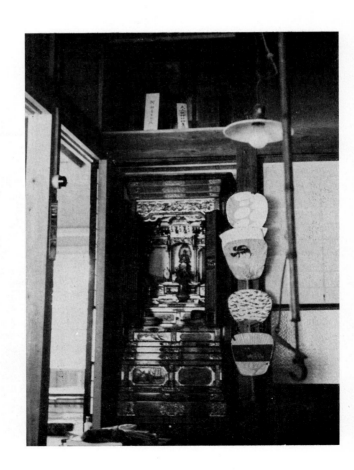

Plate 3. *Butsudan*, [Buddhist altar]

Plate 4. *Irori*: in the living-kitchen-dining room

Plate 5. *Kamado* [furnace]: the roof of the *kamado* at the extreme left serves as the seat of the *Kojin* [Fire Deity] (scale: 1 to 25)

Plate 6. Wooden *stupa*s erected beside the *sekitọ* [stone tower] (scale: 1 to 33)

Plate 7. Deformed *stupa* for a
fiftieth anniversary (scale: 1 to 20)

Plate 8. *Butsudan* without image of Lord Buddha and with only monumental wooden tablets (scale: 1 to 8)

Plate 9. New Year's ancestral ritual: holy pine tree dedicated to the Rice Spirit (scale: 1 to 15)

indigenous folk faith. What really happened was the transformation of Buddhist deities into the ancestors of Japanese families.

Such a transformation was made possible by two factors: the Japanese concept of the ancestor as a sacred being and the latitudinarian nature of Buddhist doctrines. In the course of centuries more and more Buddhist deities were provided with ancestral significance and became a substitute for the ancestors. But this was not the transformation of Buddhism alone. It may be safe to assume that the form of ancestor worship we see today is very different from what it was in ancient times. With so much interaction having taken place between Buddhism and ancestor worship, one cannot conceive the transformation of one without thinking of that of the other.

One instance of the influence of Buddhism is that the ancestor is today constantly referred to as *hotoke*, or Buddha. In the most strict sense of the word *hotoke* means the person who has attained the spiritual awakening (*Nirvana*), but as a general term it means anyone who is dead and his or her spirit. It was natural that the Japanese ancestor, a sacred and spiritual being, was in the course of time identified as an *hotoke*. He was now regarded as the spirit of the dead or an ancestral spirit.

Another instance is the *Bon* (also *Obon*) Festival or the Festival of Lanterns for the Dead. Recent studies have shown that in olden times, before the introduction into Japan of Buddhism and the Chinese calendar, it was a widely held belief that the spirits of the ancestors would return to the family twice a year, once at the night of the full moon at the beginning of spring and the second time at the night of the full moon at the beginning of the fall. Each time special rites were held for the visiting ancestors. It has been pointed out by several scholars that the fall rites have survived in the form of the *Bon* Festival, originally a Buddhist ritual for the souls of the dead; and that the spring rites have survived in the form of the New Year's Festival.

The religious life of the Japanese family is manifest even in the structure of its dwelling place. In other words the Japanese house is built to be best suited for the purposes of observing the rites for the ancestors.

There are five places which are designated as holy and have a special meaning for the members of an *ie* religiously: (1) the family tomb (Plate 1); (2) the *kamidana* [Shintoist divine shelf] (Plate 2); (3) the *butsudan* [Buddhist altar] (Plate 3); (4) the *irori* [hearth] (Plate 4); and the *kamado* [stove] (Plate 5). The family tomb is built outdoors; the rest are inside the house. (See Figure 3.)

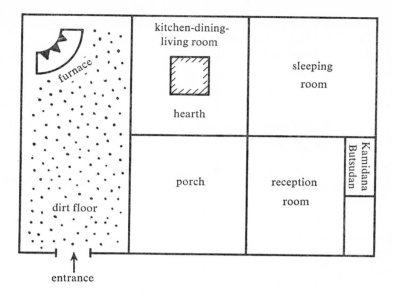

Figure 3.   Sacred places in the Japanese house: a model plan (scale: 1 to 90)

THE FAMILY TOMB

This is the symbol of the *ie* and marks the eternal presence of the spirits of the ancestors. It is not customary to erect a new tomb whenever someone dies. In most cases there is just one tomb, a family tomb, in which the souls of all the dead members of the family are deified and under which their bodies or cremated bones are buried. In some cases, however, a special tomb will be erected to commemorate the founder or some prominent forebears of the family.

The custom of erecting a family tomb did not become popular until the period 1600 to 1800. Before that time the custom had been either to use the clan or village temple, or to designate some natural object — a rock or tree — as the symbol of ancestral spirits. The material used is stone; hence the name *sekito* [stone tower] given to a typical Japanese family tomb. The *sekito* is another instance of the Buddhist influence. It has been modeled after the Indian mound or tower *(stupa)* artificially constructed of earth, brick, or stone and containing the sacred relics.

It is interesting to note that on the occasion of the rites for the ancestor a wooden *stupa* is made and placed beside the stone tower (Plate 6). The wooden *stupa* also marks the presence of the spirits of the ancestors, but unlike other objects of ancestors worship it symbolizes the body of Buddha. However, the use of wood is considered typically Japanese and the indigenous form of ancestor worship is still maintained in this way. On some memorable occasion such as a thirty-third or fiftieth anniversary of the death of a person a deformed wooden *stupa* may be erected (Plate 7). This is interpreted as an even clearer manifestation of the form of ancestor worship as it had existed before the introduction of Buddhism into Japan.

THE *KAMIDANA* [SHINTOIST DIVINE SHELF]

Such a divine shelf is found in almost every house in Japan. But it differs according to which deity each family chooses to worship. The most popular one, however, is the guardian god of a village or province.

THE *BUTSUDAN* [BUDDHIST ALTAR]

The fact that there is such a Buddhist altar in the house does not necessarily mean that the family are adherents of the Buddhist faith. Nor is it customary to build a new altar whenever someone of the family is converted to Buddhism. A Buddhist altar is built sometimes when someone of the family dies, but it is not absolutely necessary to do so every time.

The *butsudan* is essentially an altar dedicated to the ancestors and as such is symbolic of ancestor worship. Therefore it is quite acceptable to build one without a Buddhist image. But a wooden tablet with the name of the dead member of the family written on it is indispensable (Plate 8).

It has been suggested by some scholars that *kamidana* and *butsudan* may be regarded as a miniature shrine and temple respectively. For, although the general practice might have been for several families who were of the same *ie* lineage to hold jointly and as a group the rites for the ancestors — either at a village (clan) shrine or temple — it became no longer possible to do so once the member families were scattered and the clan dissolved. After a time, the custom gradually developed by which each family held the rites for the ancestors separately; and in the meantime a copy was made of the village shrine or temple, which had been the place of worship in old times, in the form of a *kamidana* or *butsudan*. They are both the symbols of ancestral spirits in this sense as well.

THE *IRORI* [HEARTH] AND *KAMADO* [FURNACE]

According to recent scholarship they were one and the same thing for a long time; that is, before the forms, the positions and functions of the two became differentiated. It is generally assumed that the *kamado* [stove] which is now mainly used to cook meals grew out of the *irori* [hearth], which not only has the function of heating the house but also is the place for eating and visiting.

Both *irori* and *kamado* are the symbol of the *ie*. For one, the seats around the hearth are specifically as signed to the patriarch, his wife and the rest of the family, and it is imperative that they observe the order. For another, the word *kamado* is used synonymously with *ie* in some areas of Japan. For example, in the Tohoku (northeastern) area, to "split a *kamado*" means to set up a separate family.

The *irori* and *kamado* are not without religious significance. First, at both of these places the Fire Deity (*Kojin*) is enshrined. It is this deity that is supposed to protect the house from fire and other catastrophes. Second, it is customary at New Year to place pine trees, which are considered holy, near these places on top of a straw bag or tub containing newly harvested crops (Plate 9). It has been pointed out that this custom is the remnant of the old ritual of calling into the house the spirits of the ancestors who were identified with the Rice Spirit and various agricultural deities.

From the foregoing discussions it may be concluded that one cannot understand fully the meaning of ancestor worship in Japan, which is the family religion there, without referring to the social and religious significance of the *ie* lineage concept. The *ie* was the soical basis of ancestor worship for two reasons: in the first place, it was the basic unit of Japanese society and as such required the existence of the ancestor as a postulate if not as a fact; in the second place, the ancestor of the *ie* was traditionally identified with agricultural deities in general and the Rice Spirit in particular — hence the notion of the ancestor as a spiritual, sacred being.

The influence of foreign religions such as Buddhism is discernible, but in reality these did not alter substantially the unique form of ancestor worship in Japan. It is probable that it underwent some change but, more important still, the foreign religions had to undergo more notable changes when introduced into Japan. Such metamorphosis or transformation was necessary in order for them to be assimilated to Japanese culture. The case of Buddhism will serve as a good example.

The institution of the *ie* was so deeply established and ancestor worship was such an integral part of the religious life of the Japanese that when the work of modernizing the country was commenced in the latter half of the nineteenth century, it was deemed wise — and socially more desirable — to keep them intact. Both the *ie* and ancestor worship were recognized as social institutions of long standing and various folk customs regarding them were made into law. For example, Article 987 of the Civil Code under the Old Imperial Constitution of 1889 recognized the succession of the patriarchal status and defined the supervision of genealogy, ceremonial tools and the family tomb as a right attached to such status.

The institution of the *ie* is not legalized under the present Civil Code, which was enacted after the Second World War, nor is ancestor worship enforced. But the facts of the *ie* lineage are admitted as shown by the following excerpt from the present Civil Code:

The possession of genealogy, ceremonial tools and the family tomb shall be inherited by the person who, ACCORDING TO THE CUSTOMS OF SOCIETY, will assume the responsibility of SUPERVISING THE RITES FOR THE ANCESTORS. (Article 897; emphasis added.)

REFERENCES

ARIGA, K.
1943 *Nihon Kazōku seido to kosakuseido* [The family system and tenancy system in Japan]. Tokyo: Kawade.
1972 *Nihon no ie* [The family in Japan]. Tokyo: Shibundo.
FUKUSHIMA, M.
1967 *Nihon shihonshugi to ie seido* [Japanese capitalism and the *ie* system]. Tokyo: University of Tokyo Press.
FUKUSHIMA, M., *editor*
1959 *Koseki seido to ie seido* [Census registration and the *ie* system]. Tokyo: University of Tokyo Press.
FUKUSHIMA, M., *compiler*
1959–1967 *Ie seido no kenkyu* [Study of the *ie* system]. Tokyo: University of Tokyo Press.
HORI, I.
1968 *Folk religion in Japan, continuity and change.* Tokyo: University of Tokyo Press.
HOZUMI, N.
1938 *Ancestor worship and Japanese law.* Tokyo: Hokuseido.
KAWASHIMA, T.
1957 *Ideologi toshiteno kazoku seido* [Family system as an ideology]. Tokyo: Iwanami.

KITANO, S., K. OKADA, editors
1959 Ie, so no kōzō-bunseki [An analysis of the ie structure]. Tokyo: Sobunsha.

ŌKAWACHI, K., et al.
1968 Ie. Tokyo: University of Tokyo Press.

TAKEDA, A.
1970 Ie o meguru minzoku kenkyu [Study of folk customs of ie]. Tokyo: Kobundo.

TAKEDA, C.
1957 Sosen-sūhai, minzoku to rekishi [Ancestor-worship in Japanese folklore and history]. Kyoto: Heirakuji Shoten.
1971 Minzoku-Bukkyo to Sosen-shinko [Folk-Buddhism and ancestor-belief in Japan]. Tokyo: University of Tokyo Press.

TAKEDA, C., M. TAKATORI
1957 Nihonjin no shinkō [Japanese folk faith]. Osaka: Sogensha.

TAKEUCHI, T.
1969 Kazoku seido to ie seido [Family customs and ie system]. Tokyo: Koseisha.

TODA, T.
1937 Kazoku kosei [The structure of the family]. Tokyo: Kobundo.

TSURUMI, S., H. ADACHI
1972 Ie no kami [Deities of ie]. Kyoto: Tankosha.

YANAGITA, K.
1946a Senzo no hanashi [About our ancestors]. Tokyo: Chikuma Shobo.
1946b Ie kandan [Lectures on ie]. Tokyo: Kamakura.

Relics of Paganism among the Baltic Peoples after the Introduction of Christianity

J. M. JURGINIS

It is formally assumed that the date of baptism of a people is the year when the supreme authority and the ruling class adopt Christianity and declare it to be a binding religion for all the citizens of the given country or state.

In this sense, the Baltic peoples were baptized at a relatively late period: the Prussians and Letts were baptized in the thirteenth century, one section of the Lithuanians, the Aukshtaitians, in 1387, and the other, the Zhemaitians, in 1413. The difference in these dates is due to the fact that the Prussians and Letts, who are related to the Lithuanians, and the Estonians, who are of Ugro-Finnish origin, were forcibly baptized following their conquest by the Livonian Order, while the Lithuanians had by that time built their own state, the Grand Dukedom of Lithuania, and for more than a century and a half defended their pre-Christian religion.

The introduction of Christianity exerted only minor influence upon the outlook and customs of the peoples under review. This is indicated, among other things, by the fact that Jesuit missionaries who traveled all over Lithuania in the seventeenth and eighteenth centuries mention in accounts of their journeys (*Liber Spiritualium Collegii Academici Vilnensis Societatis Jesu* n.d.) a number of beliefs and cult rituals which they recognized as heathen. The Jesuits did not explain why the Catholic Church was unable, in the 250 years after its establishment, to strike deep roots in the mass of the people. It should also be borne in mind that the Prussians fought for some 100 years, and the Lithuanians for almost 200 years, against the Livonian Order which used the banner of Christianity as a disguise for its conquests. At that time, paganism contributed, to some extent, to the national resistance movement.

The introduction of Christianity in Lithuania was an act of more political than religious significance which promoted the interests of princes and boyars. By laws passed in connection with this event, the peasantry were deprived of all political rights and of the right to own land. From the very outset, Christianity in this country was an instrument for perpetuating serfdom and feudal relations. In turn, paganism was a specific religious expression of the peasants' resistance. Beginning with the end of the sixteenth century, in the course of the Reformation and Counter Reformation, peasants were forced to go to church and perform religious rituals. Relics of paganism had their national and social roots which are worthy of researchers' attention.

Literature on pagan beliefs of the Baltic peoples in the sixteenth century is quite extensive. The most prominent authors in this field are Hennenberger (1584, 1595), Hennig (1589: 293–330), Stryjkowski (1582: 152–163), Lasickis (1969: 39–45) and Maletius (1742: 198–207). Their information is interesting, at times with a touch of the exotic, and also quite inaccurate. These authors cannot provide answers to a number of questions brought forward by today's scholars, as in their descriptions of relics of paganism in the sixteenth century they often used information contained in the works of the German chronicler of the fourteenth century P. de Dusburg (1861: 21–254) and the Polish historian of the fifteenth century J. Dlugos (Dlugosii 1877: 159–162).

They made long lists of gods and idols of the Prussians, Lithuanians, and Letts without trying to answer the question as to when these gods were worshiped by the Balts and when, under the influence of the Christian outlook, they disappeared or lost their divine features. Besides, these authors only recorded what they had heard from others, not what they had seen with their own eyes. The most trustworthy data on different beliefs of the Lithuanians are contained in the works of Johan Lasickis, but even this author only recorded what he had heard from Jacob Laskowsky, a land surveyor who worked among the Zhemaitians at the time of the agrarian reform in the mid-sixteenth century.

Most sixteenth-century authors who wrote about the Balts' paganism did not know the language of the local population and for that reason did not understand much of what they were told. For example, they would use the term "god" instead of "ritual" and often took pre-Christian rituals for Christian. Besides, they were prone to describe rare or isolated phenomena as typical; thus, unusual or exotic phenomena were passed for characteristic and decisive regularities.

The sixteenth-century authors did not leave any description of the

Balts' pantheon, nor any information on their priesthood. They were unable to follow the evolution of pagan rituals, because paganism in Lithuania, to say nothing of Prussia and Livonia, was at the beginning of the sixteenth century strongly influenced by the dominating Christian religion. Economic and sociopolitical transformations were followed by transformations in the pagan pantheon: each individual deity in this pantheon acquired several new features.

These transformations of local gods disguised by the veil of Christianity were noted by authors of the sixteenth century, both by supporters of the Reformation and advocates of the Counter Reformation. Their works, as well as archaeological and folklore sources allow us to regard relics of paganism as a product of a changed outlook of the peasants who were gradually being turned into serfs.

Let us now deal with those aspects of social and family life which the Catholic Church regarded as pagan and subject to persecution. Chronicles and other sources of the thirteenth century contain much contradictory information about the family of the Prussians and Lithuanians. A letter of 1217 by the Pope (Philippi and Wölky 1882: 9–10) and the Christburg Treaty concluded in 1249 between the Livonian Order and newly baptized Prussian rebels (Wölky and Saage 1860) both insist that each of the latter had several wives who were bought and sold. The same information is contained in the chronicle by Petri de Dusburg (1861 53–55). This gave rise to the belief that the pagan Balts in the thirteenth century and at later periods were polygamous.

Yet sources that deal with concrete events testify against this. The chronicle of Dusburg and other German accounts often describe raids of German knights on Lithuanian princes, boyars and peasants, and provide detailed lists of the loot, mentioning the number of children and menials taken prisoner; sometimes the name of a boyar's or prince's wife is mentioned. It is significant that no mention is ever made of more than one wife of a boyar or prince, to say nothing of peasants. We know the names of wives of the grand princes of Lithuania prior to the introduction of Christianity; however, no mention has ever been made of a pagan prince having two or three wives.

Authors of chronicles and other written sources took for polygamy nothing other than the fact that the social order allowed divorces. Divorces were practiced by both pagans and Christians, the only difference being that with the former a divorce was a legal procedure, while the later regarded it as illegal, for marriage was indissoluble for the whole of one's lifetime. Following the introduction of Christianity in Lithuania, both townspeople and countryfolk married and divorced for a long time in compliance with pagan laws, without resorting to the church procedure. Testifying to this is the code of laws of the Lithuanian state, including the Lithuanian statutes and judicial statements.

On February 10, 1509, the grand duke sent a letter to all city authorities of the Lithuanian state to the effect that a great number of townsmen lived with unwed wives, i.e. they were not married in church, that they did not christen their children and, on the whole, their family life was un-Christian. The Lithuanian statute declared such families illegal (*Akty otnosiäshchiesia k istorii Zapadnoj Rossii* 1848). The Statute of 1529 (3[12]) says, in part:

And here is the way to prove that a child was born out of wedlock: if his own father repudiates him and says he is not his son or writes so in his will, thereby disowning him, or had him by an unwed wife, then such a child is to be considered illegitimate without any additional proof.

Corresponding paragraphs of the Statutes of 1566 and 1588 apply to unwed wives.

Judicial statements (Bardach 1963) indicate that men did exercise their right to a divorce according to customary law, although this could not be an arbitrary and socially uncontrolled action. The Lithuanian Statute of 1588 (14[30]) envisages a death penalty for adultery. It is hard to explain such severity which at the time was unknown in Christian legislation of other countries. Apparently, in this case a heathen custom was raised to the level of a law to perpetuate the Christian pattern of the family. Property relations were another obstacle to a divorce. In contracting marriage, a man pledged to be faithful to his wife and guaranteed her dowry by one third of his property.

When speaking about the selling and buying of wives practiced by the Baltic peoples, Christian chroniclers referred to the traditional bride money which was initially paid to a bride's father and later on, when the peasants were turned into serfs, to the landowner. This tradition survived in Lithuania until the mid-eighteenth century. Gradually it became a symbolic element of the wedding ceremony.

The Christburg Treaty stipulated that the Prussians were no longer to burn their dead or bury them with their horses, weapons, and treasures. The Prussians pledged to bury their dead in the Christian manner. The burning of the dead became common with some Baltic tribes in the sixth to eighth centuries. As to the Zhemaitians and some of the Letts (the Zemgalians and Latgalians), they never burned their dead.

The Aukshtaitians and Prussians put into a grave weapons and tools of the deceased; in the ninth to fourteenth centuries, when burying a prince or a very rich boyar, they also buried his horses with him. In the thirteenth to fourteenth centuries, cremation was replaced by interment. It is hard to say whether that was due to an impact of Christianity, although most scholars are inclined to think so.

Yet, despite all their promises, the Prussians and Lithuanians did not observe all the prescribed Christian rituals during a funeral ceremony. They no longer burned their dead, or did so in isolated cases, but they continued to put into graves weapons, tools and all kinds of household articles. Researchers have found a great number of burial grounds of the Christian period in Lithuania with a variety of such items.

A burial ground of the fourteenth to sixteenth centuries was discovered in 1961 in Rumshishkes; there were five cases of cremation and 255 of interment. An excavation revealed charred axes, knives, steels, awls, buckles, fibulae and other finds pointing to a greater number of cases of cremation; evidently, many graves had been robbed or destroyed. In cases of interment, the deceased was put into a grave in a wooden coffin, head to the west. Things found in graves of the latter type are identical with those found in graves of the former type. The dates of interment were established with the aid of coins found in the graves. These date back to the period from the late fourteenth to the sixteenth centuries and point to the fact that the burial ground appeared after the introduction of Christianity.

A number of graves contain vessels with charcoal. These could be symbols of cremation or were meant to warm up the deceased in case he was buried in winter. There was money in almost all the graves, for the most part small coins that were in circulation in Lithuania at that time. In most cases, the sum was equal to the price of a hen, although in some instances it was enough to buy a sheep (Urbonavičius 1970).

The Lithuanians' pagan concept of the next world survived till the mid-nineteenth century. They buried their dead with their caps on. In winter, it was a fur cap and in summer, a light summer cap. They also put into a dead person's coffin his favorite things or tools he had used in his lifetime: a smoking pipe, playing cards, tobacco, wine, a shepherd's whip, etc. (Reitelaitis 1914: 422).

Traces of paganism persisted for a long time in monuments placed at the feet of a deceased. The Lithuanian word for these monuments is *krikshtai*. They were also widespread among the Prussians and the West Lithuanians. *Krikshtai* were made of planks. Until the seventeenth century, monuments on men's graves carried an image of a horse's head; women's monuments were decorated with an image of a bird, in most cases, a cuckoo. Late in the seventeenth century, men's monuments began to be decorated with bird and plant motifs and women's with hearts.

The church anathematized the *krikshtai* and insisted that they be replaced with crosses. But even these displayed traces of heathen influences, especially when they were forged by a smith.

The favorite element of the Lithuanian decorative pattern is a ray. The upper part of a cross was richly ornamented with a ray pattern so that the cross looked like an image of the sun, moon, or a star. Also common are the motifs of the lily and the grass snake, which are much favored in folk songs and fairy tales (Basanavičius 1912).

It was the primary duty of every Christian to baptize his children. Yet in many cases, secular and religious authorities complained that peasants did not attend to that duty. In 1562, the land surveyor J. Laskowsky ordered that village welders see to it that peasants worshiped the Christian God, forgot about their idols, learned prayers and christened their children *(Akty, izdavaemye Vilenskoiu kommisseiu. . . 1898: 92).* When baptized, children were supposed to be given Christian names which for a long time was neglected not only by peasants, but also by boyars. Juridical and economic documents of the time often feature pagan names. Christian names did not become common with the mass of the people until the sixteenth century.

In the same century, as a result of the Reformation movement, landowners started to use force to make their peasants go to church. Those who did not fulfill the orders were subject to corporal punishment and fines, and their corvée was increased. This practice continued till the late eighteenth century.

That, however, did not always help. Accounts by Jesuit missionaries contain information about stones that were believed to be sacred and were worshiped by countryfolk. The number of such findings grew, especially in the eighteenth century. These stones were distinguished by their great size and often had imprints like dish-shaped hollows, footprints, and other symbolic signs. To ensure happiness and health for themselves, worshipers made sacrificial offerings to those stones. Missionaries destroyed sacred stones by drowning or breaking them, accompanying such actions with sermons. It has to be noted that sacred groves and trees mentioned by missionaries in the fourteenth to sixteenth centuries were on the way out in the eighteenth century; in any case, they were not mentioned by Jesuits in that century. Sacred trees had been replaced with sacred stones.

Missionaries left rather detailed descriptions of sacrificial rituals performed on different occasions. Their information disproves the theory which originated in the nineteenth century and was repeatedly reflected in works of art, that stated that sacrificial animals had been burned.

According to a 1604 story, a sacrifical offering to the god of one's home was made as follows: after killing and boiling a rooster, its meat was eaten and the bones were thrown in the hearth. According to 1605 information, harvesting was followed by a feast. A priest took a place of honor. He killed a rooster and put its legs in the fire; by the way they burned he foretold the prospects for the next year's harvest. After that the rooster was boiled and eaten. Some gods were made offerings of goats, pigs and sheep. As a matter of fact, gods took only the blood of the slain animals which was poured into a river; the meat was taken by worshipers.

Similar offerings were made to ancestors and dead relatives. The places were reserved for them at a table during a feast; food was thrown under the table for them or carried to the cemetery and left by their graves. The first cup of wine or other beverage was spilt over the floor for the dead. Customs of sacrificial offerings were described on many occasions and in great detail in documents dating back to 1718–1728; however, these documents do not list a single case when a sacrifice had been made without any use for those who made it. In fact, sacrificial offerings of the Lithuanians in the seventeenth and eighteenth centuries were nothing other than ritual feasts. Stories of animals burned in a campfire or on stone altars are only fanciful fables by nineteenth-century romanticists. Relics of paganism were interpreted in different ways to corroborate all kinds of theories about the origin of the Lithuanians.

The spread of the Renaissance in the fifteenth and sixteenth centuries gave rise to a theory according to which the Balts, including the Prussians and Latvians, had originated from the ancient Romans. This theory was substantiated by the fact that the Latin and Lithuanian languages are close to each other and that Lithuanian heathen gods are in many respects similar to those of antiquity. This theory played a very important role in historiography till the end of the eighteenth century.

The nineteenth century saw the beginning of a mass national movement in Lithuania which was headed by intellectuals of the peasant stock. The latter brought forward and propagated a theory to the effect that the Lithuanian language was the basis of all the Indo-European languages and that the Golden Age in the history of the Lithuanian nation had been prior to the introduction of Christianity whose influence had been disastrous for the Lithuanians' ancient advanced culture. These views meant the idealization of the remote past typical of romanticism, but at the same time they were a realistic assessment of the fact that the church had contributed to the colonization of Lithuania, as the introduction of Christianity had been a result of a political union with Poland and a sub-

stantial section of the clergy had been made up of Poles.
Lithuanian ancient mythology was very popular with those who participated in the national revival movement. Everybody considered it his duty to discover relics of pagan culture in folklore and monuments of material culture. There were even attempts to revive paganism as the national religion of the Lithuanians.

Thus, relics of paganism of the Baltic peoples must not only be regarded as a manifestation of cultural backwardness. Some of these have been used as ideological and political instruments of the class and national movement.

REFERENCES

Akty izdavaemye Vilenskoiu komisseiu dlja razbora drevnikh aktov
1898   [Acts published by the Vilnius commission for the analysis of ancient acts] 25. Vilnius.
Akty otnosiashchiesia k istorii Zapadnoj Rossii
1848   [Acts pertaining to the history of Western Russia] 2(51):1506–1544. St. Petersburg.
BARDACH, JULIUSZ
1963   Swiecki charakter zwyczajowego prowa malzenskiego ludnosci ruskiej w Wielkim Księstwie Litewskim (15–17 wiek). *Czasopismo prawno-historyczne* 15(1).
BASANAVIČIUS, JONAS
1912   Lietuvių kryžiai archaialogijos šviesoje. *Lietuvos Kryžiai*. Vilnius.
DE DUSBURG, PETRI
1861   Chronicon terrae Prussiae. Edited by M. Toeppen. *Scriptores Rerum Prussicarum*, B. 1. Leipzig.
DLUGOSII, JOANNIS
1877   *Historiae Polonicae.* Edited by A. Przezdiecki, libri 12. Cracoviae.
HENNENBERGER, CASPAR
1584   *Kurtze und wahrhaftige Beschreibung des Landes zu Preussen.* Königsberg (Kaliningrad).
1596   *Erklärung der preussichen grösseren Landtafeln oder Mappen.* Königsberg (Kaliningrad).
HENNIG, SALOMON
1589   Wahrhaftiger und beständiger Bericht, wie es bisher und zu heutiger Stunde in Religionsachen im Fürstenthume Churland und Semigalen in Lieffland ist gehalten worden, Rostock, 1589. *Scriptores Rerum Livonicarum*, B. 2 (1848).
LASICKIS, JOHAN
1615   *De Diis samagitarum caeterorumque sermatarum et falsorum christianorum.* Basileae.
1969   *Apie žemaičiu, kitų sarmatų bei netikrų krikščionių dievus.* Reprinted edition. Vilnius.

Liber Spiritualium Collegii Academici Vilnensis Societatis Jesu
n.d.   Vilnius Universiteto Biblioteka, Rankraščiu Skyrius 3(2318, 10627, 2504). Annuae Litterae Societatis Jesu; C.D.5.

MALETIUS, HIERONYMUS
1742   Wahrhaftige Beschreibung der Sudawen auf Samland, sammt ihrem Bockheiligen und Zeremonien, Königsberg. *Erläutertes Preussen*, Bd. 5.

PHILIPPI, R., K. P. WÖLKY, *editors*
1882   *Preussisches Urkundenbuch*, volume 1, part 1, number 13. Königsberg (Kaliningrad).

REITELAITIS, JONAS
1914   Gudelių parapijos monografija. *Lietuvių tauta*, kn. 2, dalis 3. Vilnius.

STRYJKOWSKI, MACIEJ
1582   Która przedtem nigdy swiatła niet widziała, Kronika polska, litewska, źmodzka i swzystkiej Rusi, Królewiec. Księgi czwarte.

URBONAVIČIUS, VYTAUTAS
1970   Rumšiškenai XIV-XVI amžiais. *Acta Historica Lituania* 6. Vilnius.

WÖLKY, K. P., J. K. SAAGE
1860   *Codex Diplomaticus Warmiensis, oder Register und Urkunden zur Geschichte Ermands.* Diplomata 19. Mainz.

Epilogue

SAMARENDRA SARAF

The papers submitted in the present volume are as numerous as they are wide in their ethnographic coverage. They are focused in their emphases and delineations and diverse in their orientations and themes — thereby displaying wide-ranging academic explorations within the field of religious beliefs and rituals.

Neither the descriptive nor the analytical sides of many of these papers show any imbalance. Furnishing maximal details within the space at their disposal, the descriptive sections have added a rich crop to our ethnographic granary. Redefining old and familiar concepts with precision and rigor, while also introducing some newer concepts and definitions, the analytical sections have returned their humble, though appreciable, dividends.

The diversity in the disciplinary orientations of the researchers is, again, as apparent as their lack of commitment to any classical grand-design theories of the last century. An interdisciplinary perspective, thus, appears to be redeeming the present-day scholarship from the narrow and parochial demands of an intradisciplinary loyalty.

In the pages that follow, a thematic or topical recapitulation is attempted, restricting the discussion to the following: eschatological rituals, myths, symbols, and dreams.

Perception of death as an epilogue to the biophysical phenomenon has universally generated many sets of beliefs relating to the world beyond the grave as well as to the modes of disposal of the dead — these rituals vary from simple rites to complex and highly formalized ancestor worship. Many papers in the present volume spell out these beliefs and practices.

The new interest in "dissociational states" has generated many other studies. Bourguignon worked a societal typology, through a cross-cultural survey, into polar opposites where the parameter of differentiation is the presence or absence of institutionalization of altered states of consciousness. She has further sharply delineated the institutionalized and the uninstitutionalized complexes of dissociational states in their societal extensions by indexing and coding their societal variables, the *Ethnographic atlas* providing her the raw material.

Exploring the effects of transhumance on a pastoral ecology, Cramer outlines the secular rationale of the Irish pastoralists as well as "the symbolic significance of the two kinds of animals [and] the ecological, ritual, judicial, and political ramifications of this long-term adaptive process." Differential manipulation of the two kinds of livestock is due to such factors as typecasting the animals on the basis of folk belief generated by emotions. Formal and ceremonial modes of transfer by sale and ideational values ascribed to cattle and the sheep have the effect of a complex ceremonial formalism overriding rational, economic considerations.

Canfield examines the diagnostic-*cum*-curative role of the shaman specialist against the backdrop of the Islamic world view of the rural folk in central Afghanistan. The village people direct their religious quest toward the explanation of suffering. Since suffering inevitably generates a state of psychic discordance, a concordance is sought to be worked out through the shaman specialist and his good offices. It is for the cathectic and cathartic value of his rituals, Canfield argues, that the shaman specialist is sought out and well paid.

In contrast with Stablein who sees Nepalese Buddhist ritual worship (*pūjā*) as "a medical-cultural system [or] a serious intention to alleviate the suffering caused by physical, mental, and social illness," I chose the Hindu ritualistic idiom, as evinced in its textual sources, in an attempt to trace its underlying orientation. A triple process characterizes the cosmic perspective entailed in this idiom: i.e. from the gross to the subtle, from the material to the immaterial, from the factual to the symbolic, or, summarily, from the finite to the infinite. I tried to exhibit the formal steps which effect this triple process in the Hindu idiom, steps the scriptures spell out in great detail, and then attempted to read the implied cosmic design and orientation from the formalized injunctions of the texts.

Treating shamanism as an expression of cognitive structure, Ohnuki-Tierney examines an atypical ritual of the Ainus of the northwest coast of southern Sakhalin. Tabulating the Ainus' "basic cognitive categories," the symbolic interplay of binary or polar opposite categories, and the symbolic mediation by another set of cognitive categories, this researcher discusses the indispensable mediational role of the shamans in the larger context of the Ainu world view.

In his interesting paper Waddell discusses the role of the *Nawait* [Cactus Wine Ritual] in the Papago Indians' ecosystem, highlighting the wine feast ritual as a "regulatory and communicational mechanism." Following Rappaport's thesis and Turner's model of analysis (a model which Turner [1969] tried out on Verrier Elwin's field data) Waddell analyzes: the rain symbolism and its floral-faunal parameter, the word symbols and the action symbols as expressive of the corporate character of the social systems, the division of labor, the egalitarian ethos, the historical unity of the indigenous ethnic populations, and the perpetuation of the Papago lore in the present-day changing context. Waddell demonstrates how a complex ritual like the *Nawait* can and does have far-reaching social, cultural, political, and economic implications in the ecosocial system of a people.

Taboos as ritual sanctions have their functional relevance: on the cognitive level, they ascribe definitive meanings and values to objects, persons, and situations; on the operational level, they control and channel desired behavior. Makarius cites the large number of blood-related taboos, which she sees as the fundamental taboo of primitive society and as the matrix for all other taboos. She illustrates the destructive and the benevolent potentials that inhere to it. To quote her:

The dangerous and dreaded power, which imagination ascribes to blood, becomes reassuring and beneficial when turned against hostile elements and influences, such as enemy forces or physical agents of disease, or against any cause of danger and harm that has to be repelled or destroyed.

As dangerous, blood must be avoided and averted; as beneficent, its force must be harnessed and tamed. The violation of a taboo as an extraordinary method of acquisition of magical power may be resorted to "only exceptionally and individually" with a view to ensuring mastery over the inherent force; but, otherwise, "the taboo must be maintained." Hence transgressive magic ". . . must be regarded as subversive and antisocial. It must therefore remain secret, clandestine." Having described the violation of a taboo as an expression of transgressive magic or a variant of Frazer's SYMPATHETIC MAGIC, Makarius concludes:

Whereas sympathetic magic springs from thought processes, transgressive magic is the result of a cultural process.

Makarius thus suggests an explanation for another Frazerian armchair nomenclature.

Looking at the Zuni Indians' quest for the miraculous, Tedlock checks into a number of Zuni rituals — those directed to ancestral gods, to medicine, and to warfare, which in turn penetrated the fraternities of the *kotikanne* Kachina Society, the fourteen Medicine Societies, and the many War Societies of the Zuni. There are, thus, two kinds of rituals: those which are treated as *tehya* [valuable, precious], and *?attanni* [sacred, dangerous]; and those which are treated as *co?ya* [beautiful, novel]. Because of their sensuous quality, aesthetic exuberance, lyrical and rhythmic content, dance, and dramatization used to impersonate the ancestral gods, Kachina Society rituals seem to emphasize the aesthetic rather than the miraculous. However, in the rituals of the Medicine and War Societies the miraculous overshadows the aesthetic. Tedlock's portrayal of these rituals, designating them as *tehya* and *tattani*, thus emphasizes their magical as well as their more commonly emphasized aesthetic qualities.

Harris raises the same old issue which has vexed many anthropologists: why do sets of symbols not exhibit complete logical coherence? In her attempt to answer the question, Harris has drawn on the data from the symbolic systems of Judaism and Christianity, with some references to Australian totemism. Starting off with the dichotomy of symbols — the "displaying" symbols as "presentative, revealing, displaying of the reality that religion creates and sustains" and the "marking" symbols "when their association with a social unit (group or category) provides one of the features marking out that unit AS A UNIT" — the author has suggested the further subdivision of the latter kind into two types — the "inward-looking" or "rallying" symbols "by means of which members of a unit recognize their unity" and the "outward-looking" or "distinguishing" symbols as "performing diacritical functions." The author also points to the possibility where "the SAME symbolic word, gesture, act, attribute, artifact, etc. can occur as a displaying symbol within the same symbolic system"; the Christian cross being one example.

Iwańska uses the context of change to examine the decline of the indigenous cult of *oratorio* (or the extended family chapel) among the Mazahua Indians of central Mexico. Comparing and contrasting the *oratorio* cult as practiced in two villages — one representing the traditional rural setting relatively untouched by extraneous institutions, the other exemplifying the transitional type with educational, agrarian, and political institutions — Iwańska sees the cause of decline of the cult in what Lerner (1965) has characterized as the emerging LIFE-WAYS and THOUGHT-WAYS.

Lanternari suggests that dreams are "both cause and effect [i.e. in the cultural context] — that is, the cultural determination of the dream [and] the determining influence of dream on culture." He points to the "close psychological and cultural link between dream and myth," arguing that "both appear as models and paradigms of cultural elements — dream, in relation to the individual, and myth, in relation to the group as a whole . . . dream [as] the archetype of the individual's fate, myth [as] the archetype of the entire culture." Proceeding on Weberian lines (without, however, saying so), Lanternari relates the charismatic property of dreams to religious movements as the unusual, the spontaneous, and the creative quality, or as Weber (1947) had put it:

. . . a certain quality of an individual personality by virtue of which he is set apart from ordinary men and treated as endowed with supernatural, super-human, or at least specifically exceptional powers or qualities . . . not accessible to the ordinary person, but [is] regarded as of divine origin or as exemplary . . . .

Lanternari concludes that man's creative faculty expresses itself through dreams either in a CONVENTIONAL PATTERN with content deriving from a heritage of ancestral beliefs, myths, and mythical configurations or else in an INNOVATIVE PATTERN with themes belonging to a different culture with which the dreamer has come into contact. In the one case conservative and revitalizing elements are released, in the other case, change is generated.

While addressing himself to an archaeological and ethnographic survey of the *Ch'obun* (a bone-washing burial or a multiple burial custom that is still prevailing in the islands and coastal villages in southwestern parts of Korea), Lee has spelled out the functional significance of the Korean burial: an expression of the moral obligation rooted in the natural filial bond with the deceased parents; the fear of offending the spirits of mountain and earth and the goddess of wind, which forbid the digging of ground in the months of January and February; the preservation of the dead body as a provisional procedure pending the seafaring survivors' homecoming, in consultation with whom a suitable grave site is then chosen; and the folk beliefs relating to the expected return of the soul to his body, a belief often vocally dramatized in Korean folktales. Although Lee treats the *Ch'obun* burial as a complex of folk beliefs about existence after death and about the rewards and punishments visited upon their descendants by departed souls, he does not discuss the notions of ritual purity and removal of danger which underlie the ritual of bone washing, nor does he discuss the role of the *Chikwan* [geomancer] who determines the auspicious time for the ritual.

Swauger gathered data from the petroglyphic sites in the Upper Ohio Valley, and he invokes the ethnography of the area as an aid to arriving at an "acceptable chronological and cultural association" between the archaeological Monongahela Man, the prehistoric Shawnees, and the historic Ojibwa. He projects his conclusions on the basis of striking similarities between the entire "genre of figures on birchbark scrolls used as memory aids in the Ojibwa *Midéwiwin* or Grand Medicine Society rites" and those in the petroglyph sites of the valley. And he not only suggests a tentative succession of layers of cultural growth from the paleohistoric to the historic times but also shows awareness of such frustrating factors and forces as decadence through dispersal and through migration which tend to frustrate the archaeologist's efforts.

Takeda's paper looks at ancestor worship "not as a religion but a matter of national ethics" in the context of the folk belief that the structural unit of the *ie* [a house, a house line, a dwelling place, a family or home, or kinship] originates from the ancestors who have "the utmost concern for the family's well-being [and] are its greatest protection and security." Takeda shows how processes of sacralization, apotheosization, and identification raise the dead ancestors to the status of "suprahuman beings." Their gravestones are called *sekito* (*seki* = stone; *to* = abbreviation for *sotoba*, the Japanese version of Sanskrit *stupa*, the ancestors being identified with the Buddhas).

Changing emphases, the pooling of cross-disciplinary orientations and resources, and the partial rejection of the heritage of Durkheim, Weber, Freud, or Malinowski signal a phase where practitioners of our craft share a feeling that "no theoretical advances of major importance" have been made, and that they have been "living off the conceptual capital of [their] ancestors, adding very little, save a certain empirical enrichment, to it" (Geertz 1966) since the Second World War. This may be a counsel of discomfort or a goad to action: either way, *nil desperari*, the contributors to these two volumes did not seem to think that they have reached an impasse; hopefully we can survive without new theories until the next congress.

REFERENCES

BENEDICT, RUTH F.
  1934 *Patterns of culture.* Boston: Houghton Mifflin.
GEERTZ, CLIFFORD
  1966 "Religion as a cultural system," in *Anthropological approaches to the study of religion.* Edited by Michel Banton. London: Tavistock.
LERNER, DANIEL
  1965 *The passing of traditional society.* New York: The Free Press.
OTTO, RUDOLF
  1952 *The idea of the holy.* Translated by John W. Harvey. London: Oxford University Press.
TURNER, VICTOR W.
  1969 "Some aspects of Saora ritual and shamanism: an approach to the data of ritual," in *The craft of social anthropology.* Edited by A. L. Epstein. London: Tavistock.
WEBER, MAX
  1947 *The theory of social and economic organization.* Edited by Talcott Parsons. New York: Oxford University Press.

Biographical Notes

HANS BECHER (1918–   ) was born in Berlin. He studied Americanistics, Ethnology, and Folklore at the Universities of Hamburg, Valencia, and São Paulo. He received his Ph.D. in Hamburg (1952) with a dissertation on "Belts and waist strings of the South American Indians." In 1955–1956, 1966–1967, and 1970 he did fieldwork in the Amazon region and investigated the Yanomamö Indians. Since October 1961 he has been Director of the Department of Ethnology in the State Museum of Lower Saxony Hannover, West Germany. His numerous publications include, above all, works of South American Indians. He is Editor of the *Völkerkundliche Abhandlungen* [Ethnological Essays]. In 1967 he founded the Ethnological Society of Hannover.

AGEHANANDA BHARATI (1923–   ), born in Vienna, has been a U.S. citizen since 1968. He studied ethnology and indology at Vienna University and moved to India in 1947 where he was ordained a Hindu monk. He obtained the Acharya (Ph.D.) degree at the Samnyasi Mahavidyalaya in Varanasi, India, in 1951. He was Reader in Philosophy (1951–1953) at Benares Hindu University, India, Visiting Professor at the Royal Buddhist Academy in Bangkok, 1956, at the Universities of Tokyo and Kyoto in 1957, Research Associate in the Far Eastern Institute at the University of Washington, Seattle, 1957-1961 and joined the Department of Anthropology at Syracuse University in 1961, where he is now Chairman and Professor of Anthropology. His special fields are South Asian languages and cultures, religious behavior, and cognitive systems. He is a Fellow of the American Anthropological Association, a Fellow of the Royal Anthropological Institute of Great Britain and Ireland, a Fellow of the Society for Applied Anthropology, and a Member of the

Association for Asian Studies. The following books are among his numerous publications: *The ochre robe* (1970, New York: Doubleday); *The tantric tradition* (1969, London: Rider); *A functional analysis of Indian thought and its social margins* (1964, Benares); *The Asians in East Africa: Jayhind and Uhuru* (1972, Chicago).

LAJOS BOGLÁR (1929–   ) was born in São Paulo. He studied ethnology and archaeology at the Budapest University (1949–1953). He received the degree of Candidate of Historical Sciences and his Ph.D. in 1969. Since 1953 he has been Curator at the Ethnographical Museum, Budapest, and since 1969 Head of the Department of Ethnology. His fieldwork has been in South America and Brazil (1969), and in Venezuela (1967–1968, 1974).

ERIKA BOURGUIGNON (1924–   ) was born in Vienna. She received her Ph.D. in Anthropology from Northwestern University. She is currently Chairman of the Department of Anthropology at the Ohio State University, where she has taught since 1949. During 1963–1968 she directed the Cross-Cultural Study of Dissociational States at Ohio State. She edited and co-authored *Religion, altered states of consciousness, and social change* (1973) and is co-author, with L. Greenbaum, of *Diversity and homogeneity in world societies* (1973). Her special interests include religious and psychological dimensions of culture and, in particular, the cultural patterning of altered states of consciousness.

ROBERT L. CANFIELD (1930–   ) is Associate Professor of Anthropology at Washington University, St. Louis. He received the B.A. degree in Clinical Psychology from the University of Tulsa and the M.A. in Linguistics, and the Ph.D. in Anthropology from the University of Michigan. He also studied at the School of Oriental Studies, University of London. He is author of *Faction and conversion: religious alignments in the Hindu Kush*. He is presently doing research on the structure of leadership in traditional societies of the Muslim world.

ALOIS CLOSS (1893–   ), born in Neumarkt in Styria, Austria, has studied Ancient History, Orientalistics, Indoiranistics, and Natural History (Ph.D.) at the University of Graz and Germanistics and Anthropology (physical, cultural, and prehistorical) at the University of Vienna. Habilitation: History of Religion, Graz, 1936; changed to Historical Ethnology with reference to Science of Religion in 1949. He retired in 1968 with the title of Univ. Prof. Phil. Fac. Graz, Decor, 1 cl. of Science and Art. His many publications in scientific periodicals and collected editions include: *Steinbücher* (Mineral Mitteilungsblatt des Joanneums, Graz, 1958); *Die Religion des Semnonenstammes* (Wiener Beiträge für Kulturgeschichte und Linguistik IV, 1936); *Ethnologische Bestimmung des Altgermanentums* (Austria Wenner-Gren Symposium II, 1939); "Aufriß und Abgrenzung einer speziellen historischen Ethnologie" (*Zeitschrift für Ethnologie*, 1956); *Kulturhistorie und Evolution* (Mitt. Anthropol. Ges., Vienna, 1956); "Schamanismus bei den Indoeuropäern" (*Mem. W. Brandenstein*, 1968); "Asia, Central and North," in *History of religion* (Leiden II, 1971).

EUGENIA S. CRAMER. No biographical data available.

SHLOMO DESHEN (1935–   ), Senior Lecturer in Social Anthropology at Tel Aviv University, has studied at the Hebrew University in Jerusalem (B.A., 1960) and at Manchester University (Ph.D., 1968), specializing in the history, culture, and sociology of various Jewish subethnic groups. He has done fieldwork among immigrants from Tunisia and other Muslim countries in Israel, focusing on questions of religious and political sociology. Deshen has published *Immigrant voters in Israel: parties and congregations in a local election campaign* (1970) and, jointly with Moshe Shokeid, *The predicament of homecoming: cultural and social life of North African immigrants in Israel* (1974).

TEKLA DÖMÖTÖR (1914–   ) is Professor of Folklore at the Budapest University, Hungary. She received her Ph.D. in Hungary and continued her studies in Paris till the outbreak of the war in 1939. After the war, she received two higher academic degrees in Budapest. Her special interests include Hungarian and European folklore, folk religion, customs, legends, and medieval and seventeeth-century drama. She published twelve books in Hungarian and a handbook on Hungarian peasant customs in English, German, and French. Her numerous essays have been published in Europe and the United States.

GRACE HARRIS (1926–   ) studied anthropology at the University of Chicago (M.A., 1949), Oxford University, and the University of Cambridge (Ph.D., 1955). She is Associate Professor of Anthropology and of Religious Studies at the University of Rochester, having previously taught at Brandeis University, the University of Massachusetts at Amherst, and Boston University. Her primary field research was among the Taita of southern Kenya. Major interests include comparative social structure and the anthropology of religion, with particular emphasis on the speech forms of ritual and the interpretation of ritual action.

Théophile B. Holas (1909–) received his Docteur ès lettres from the University of Paris. As an ethnologist he has specialized since 1945 in the study of African civilizations, particularly in that of the Ivory Coast. He is author of several works on African ethnology and has led several scientific expeditions in Africa, Asia, South America, and Oceania. He is Director of the Human Science Center and Administrator of the National Museum at Abidjan.

Åke Hultkrantz (1920–) received his Ph.D. in Stockholm in 1953 and has been Professor of Comparative Religion and Ethnology of Religion at the University of Stockholm since 1958. His special field is North American Indian and circumpolar cultures and religions. His primary interests are the perspective of the ecology of religion and morphology and ethnohistory of tribal religions. His latest publications include a methodology of comparative religion (1973), a survey of Plains and Prairie Indian iconography (1973), and a study of Hare Indian religion (1974).

Ioana Ionescu-Milcu (1938–) studied philology at Bucharest University and is Senior Researcher at the Institute for Ethnological and Dialectological Studies in Bucharest. She has been Member of the Commission for Anthropology and Ethnology of the Romanian Academy of Sciences since 1971. Between 1968 and 1972 she participated in the projects of the study group "Iron Gates" (Danube Strait). She has carried out and published theoretical studies on symbolic thinking, on the problem of the isolates, and on folk beliefs, customs, and medicine, both in Romania and northern Yugoslavia. Her major interest is in research on customs connected with the cycle of life: birth, marriage, and death.

Alicja Iwańska (1918–) was born in Poland. She received her M.A. in Philosophy from the University of Warsaw in 1946 and her Ph.D. in Sociology from Columbia University in 1957. She has been Professor of Sociology and Anthropology since 1965 at the State University of New York, Albany, and has done fieldwork in Mexico, Chile, and the United States. Her recent publications include: *Purgatory and Utopia: a Mazahua Indian village* (1971); "Without art" (1970); "Emigrants or commuters: Mazahua Indians in Mexico City" (1973); and "Indianscy Intelektualiści" (1974).

GEORGE JENNINGS.   No biographical data available.

JUOZAS JURGINIS (1909–   ) is a Professor of Lithuanian History at the State University of Vilnius and Research Fellow of the Institute of History of the Academy of Sciences of the Lithuanian S.S.R. In 1948 he received his Ph.D. with a dissertation on the history of Vilnius in the Middle Ages. In 1963 he took his habilitation with a research work on the agrarian history of Lithuania between the fourteenth and sixteenth centuries. His publications include works on the agrarian and cultural history of Eastern Europe.

N. K. KADETOTAD (1933–   ) received his M.A. from Karnatak University, Dharwar, India, in 1958 and his Sahity Ratna from Hindi University, Prayag, India, in 1967. He was Research Scholar at Karnatak University in the Anthropology Department from 1960–1963 on the subject of religion and magic among the Untouchables and has been Researcher in that Department since 1963. He has published three books on religion and the Untouchables. He has attended numerous national and international conferences and has published and presented papers on various subjects of anthropology.

ALICE B. KEHOE (1934–   ), born in New York, studied at Barnard College (B.A., 1956) and Harvard University (Ph.D., 1964). She has pursued both archaeological and ethnographic research in the Northern Plains (Blackfoot, Plains Cree, and Saskatchewan Dakota) since 1956, writing her dissertation on a comparison between the Ghost Dance religion of Saskatchewan Dakota and traditional Plains Cree religious beliefs and practices. Since 1968 she has been Associate Professor of Anthropology at Marquette University, Milwaukee, Wisconsin; previously she taught at the University of Nebraska (1965–1968) and at the University of Saskatchewan, Regina Campus (1964–1965). Her publications include *The roads of life: Dakota and Cree adaptations to twentieth-century Saskatchewan* (1975) and papers on theoretical, archaeological, and ethnological topics in books and journals.

VITTORIO LANTERNARI (1918–   ) has been Full Professor of Ethnology at the University of Rome since 1972. From 1959 to 1972 he was Professor of Ethnology and of History of Religion at the University of Bari. Strongly influenced by the views of the late Professor Raffaele Pettazzoni, he has been concerned since the beginning of his studies with comparative religion and the religion of traditional societies and is concerned primarily with the study of traditional religions, culture contact, and socioreligious movements among non-Western societies. His field-work in Ghana, in 1971 and 1974, emphasized the study of spiritual churches. His major publications are: *La grande festa: storia del Capo-danno nelle civiltà primitive* (1959); *Movementi religiosi di libertà e di salvezza dei popoli oppressi* (1960), which has been translated into English, French, Spanish, German, and Hungarian, and which recently appeared in a new edition (1974); *Occidente e Terzo Mondo* (1967), which was translated into Spanish in 1974; and *Antropologia e imperi-alismo, e altri saggi* (1974).

DU-HYUN LEE (1924–   ) received his Ph.D. from Seoul National Uni-versity in 1968. He has been Professor of Korean Drama and Folklore at Seoul National University since 1962, Director of the Research Institute of Korean Mask-dance Drama since 1968, and President of the Korean Society for Cultural Anthropology since 1972. His present interest is in Korean folk culture, especially folk drama and folk religion including shamanism. His recent publications are: *Modern history of Korean drama* (1966), *Korean mask-dance drama* (1969), *A history of Korean folk-life* (1973), *A history of Korean theatre* (1973), and *Introducing Korean folklore* (1974).

ANDRÉ LOUIS (1912–   ) born in Champagne, received his Master of Research at C.N.R.S. in Paris and is Director of the C.N.R.S. Bureau in Tunisia. In 1969 he received his Docteur ès lettres from the Sorbonne, presenting his thesis on the Islands of Kerkena (Tunisia) on ethnology and linguistics (Araba dialect). He has been Advisor to the Centre of Arts and Popular Traditions in Tunisia for seven years and gives courses on Rural Sociology at the University of Tunis. He has published the following ethnographical works: *Artisans saxiens* (1945); *Potiers de Na-beul* (1956); *Illes Kerkena* (1961–1963); *Potiers de Jerba* (1967). He has collected documents for publication on ethnography and linguistics, with commentary (Sahel, 1949; Kerkena, 1962; Sud). His present re-search is on the populations of southern Tunisia: their material culture, the problems and difficulties presented by technical progress, and the change brought about by their sedentarization. His recent publications are *Ksars et villages de crête* and *Bibliographie ethnosociologique de Tunisie*.

LAURA MAKARIUS.   No biographical data available.

JACQUES MAQUET (1919–   ) has been Professor of Anthropology at the University of California, Los Angeles, since 1971. He holds the degrees of Docteur en droit (Louvain, 1946), Docteur en philosophie (Louvain, 1948), Ph.D. in Anthropology (London, 1952), and Docteur ès lettres (Paris, 1973). He was field anthropologist and Head of the Scientific Research Center of Rwanda-Burundi (1949–1957); he taught anthropology at the State University of the Congo (1957–1960), at the Ecole pratique des Hautes Etudes of the University of Paris (1961–1968), and at Case Western Reserve University, Cleveland (1968–1970). He is the author of seven books on such diverse topics as: sociology of knowledge, inequality in traditional Rwanda, power in the African societal networks, and civilizations and cultural unity of Black Africa. His current research interests are in the anthropological approach to aesthetic and symbolic phenomena, and to monastic and other intentional communities in South Asia.

MARTHA BINFORD MORRIS (1939–   ), born in Washington, D.C., received her education in Latin America and the United States. She attended Radcliffe College, received her B.A. from Portland State University in Anthropology and Literature in 1965, and her Ph.D. in Anthropology from Michigan State University in 1971. Her dissertation on value change was based on two years of fieldwork as an N.I.M.H. Fellow among the Rjonga of Mozambique. She was Assistant Professor of Anthropology at Wayne State University from 1971 to 1974 and is currently Assistant Professor of Anthropology at the University of Michigan, Dearborn.

EMIKO OHNUKI-TIERNEY (1934–   ) was born in Japan. She received her B.A. from Tsuda College, Tokyo, in 1957, an M.S. and a Ph.D. in Anthropology from the University of Wisconsin. She has done fieldwork with the Detroit Chinese and with the Sakhalin Ainu now resettled in Hokkaido, Japan. Her major interest lies in the subjects related to symbolic classification and perception in general. Her publications include two books and a number of articles on the Ainu. She has taught at the University of Wisconsin and Marquette University and is presently Assistant Professor at Beloit College.

OLGA PENAVIN.   No biographical data available.

FRANCISZEK M. ROSIŃSKI (1932–   ) studied philosophy in Lublin and Warsaw, receiving his Ph.M. in 1966. He then studied Natural Sciences in Wrocław and received his Sc.D. in 1974. He taught cosmology and anthropology at the High Seminary in Kłodzko and at the Academy of the Theologie Catholic in Warsaw. He is continuing his anthropological research by order of the University of Wrocław and of the Polish Academy of Sciences. His publications include works on the prehistory of religion, anthropogenesis, clinical anthropology, and dermatoglyphics.

SAMARENDRA SARAF (1931–   ) received his education at the University of Saugar (Madhya Pradesh, India), where he graduated in Anthropology (M.A., 1959) and Law (LL.B., 1957), receiving his Ph.D. (1971) on "Hindu caste system and the ritual idiom." He is presently working as Reader in Anthropology at the University. In 1965 he participated in the International Development Seminar at the East-West Center, Hawaii. His publications include research papers on the Hindu ritual idiom, the sociology of religion, and communication; those awaiting publication include his doctoral thesis, an anthology of published and unpublished research papers entitled "Hindu ritual idiom: perspectives and orientations," and a collection of essays, memoirs, and satires.

ELAINE SCIOG.   No biographical data available.

WILLIAM STABLEIN (1933–   ) is Associate in the University Seminar on Oriental Thought and Religion at Columbia University, New York. After completing his B.A. at the University of Washington in Seattle, he studied Indic Languages and Culture at Columbia University, where he also taught in the Oriental Humanities Program. In 1967 he was granted a Fullbright-Hayes Fellowship to study Tantric Buddhism in Kathmandu, Nepal. There his interest in ethnography and medicine led to the establishment of the Karma Clinic. After completing fieldwork for his doctoral dissertation, in 1971 he made a survey of Buddhist-Sanskrit manuscripts in India and Nepal for the Institute for Advanced Studies of World Religions. His present research is the elucidation of Nepalese and Tibetan Buddhist rituals as a medical-cultural system and an investigation of how this system can serve as a cross-cultural model for health delivery.

ANCA STAHL (1942–   ), born in Romania, graduated in History from the University of Bucarest and received her Ph.D. in Ethnology from the University of Paris. She is presently Member of the Laboratory of Ethnology and Comparative Sociology at the University of Paris X. fieldwork in Romania and in Nepal has specialized in rituals. *Les rites de construction des paysans roumains* is her main publication.

GRIGOTY STRATANOVICH (1912–) graduated from Leningrad State University in Ethnology, specializing in the regions of east and south-eastern Asia and in Sinology and Philology, and in 1947 received his Ph.D. in History. He is the Senior Researcher at the Institute of Ethnography, U.S.S.R. Academy of Sciences and is one of the contributors of the Soviet dunganology (a series of works, the last of which is *The history of the Soviet dungans*, 1967). His main fields of interest are the history of spiritual culture and ethnic processes in southeastern Asia, and he has written the chapters "Burma" and "Laps" in *Ethnic processes in the sea* (1974) concerning these interests.

JAMES L. SWAUGER (1913–) received his B.S. from the University of Pittsburgh in 1941, his M.Litt. in 1947, and his D.Sc. from Waynesburg in 1957. He was Assistant Secretary of Archaeology and Ethnology at the Carnegie Museum in 1935, Curator in 1949, Assistant Director in 1955, and has been Associate Director since 1964. Since 1971 he has been Professor of Anthropology and Educational Communications at the University of Pittsburgh. He has done fieldwork locally, in the High Plains, and in Jordon, Israel, and Yemen.

CHOSHU TAKEDA. No biographical data available.

DENNIS TEDLOCK. No biographical data available.

EVON Z. VOGT (1918–) was born in Gallup, New Mexico, and educated at the University of Chicago where he received his B.A. in 1941 and Ph.D. in 1948. He is currently Professor of Anthropology, Director of the Harvard Chiapas Project, and Master of Kirkland House at Harvard University. His recent publications include *Zinacantan: a Maya community in the highlands of Chiapas* (1969) and *Aerial photography in anthropological field research* (1974).

JACK O. WADDELL (1933–) received his Ph.D. in Cultural Anthropology from the University of Arizona in 1956. He is presently Associate Professor of Anthropology and Chairman of the Anthropology Section at Purdue University's Department of Sociology and Anthropology. His special research interests are in the areas of the cultural use of alcohol, ritual as an adaptive mechanism, contemporary social and economic adaptations of native peoples, and the development of culturally based life-styles in contemporary societies. He has done field-work among the Papago Indians intermittently since 1963. His publications include: *The American Indian in urban society, Papago Indians at work, American Indian urbanization,* and a number of journal articles dealing with aspects of contemporary Papago culture.

Index of Names

Index of Subjects